Aberdeen

The European E

1966-96

DESERT ISLAND FOOTBALL HISTORIES

Aberdeen

The European Era
1966-96

Clive Leatherdale

DESERT ISLAND BOOKS

First hardback edition published in 1997
First paperback edition published in 2007
by
DESERT ISLAND BOOKS LIMITED
7 Clarence Road, Southend-on-Sea, Essex SS1 1AN
United Kingdom
www.desertislandbooks.com

British Library Cataloguing-in-Publication Data
A catalogue record for this book is available from the British Library

IBSN 978-1-905328-32-1

Printed in Great Britain
by
4edge Ltd, Hockley. www.4edge.co.uk

Note: This book covers the Dons from the 1966-67 season, in which they first
qualified for Europe, until their elimination from the UEFA Cup in October
1996. League details for the 1996-97 season also terminate at that time.

CONTENTS

MACLEOD & MCNEILL 1975-78

THE YOUNGER FERGIE 1978-82

THE ELDER FERGIE 1982-86

THE HANGOVER 1986-91

CAPTAINS COURAGEOUS

SEASONAL SUMMARIES 164

Author's Note

In March 1986 I was invited to write a history of Aberdeen FC since 1945. The publishers wanted statistics and nothing else, except for brief summaries of key games. There was not much written about the Dons at that time and all the research had to be done from scratch. Twelve weeks after being asked to write it, the manuscript of *The Aberdeen Football Companion* was delivered to the publishers. It was not in the form they had requested. Two thousand matches, teams, goalscorers, etc, was to my mind as dry as dust. I had added snippets and summaries, not just to big matches, but to each and every one. This meant the book could be read from start to finish, not just picked up as a source of reference.

Now, ten years on, I offer readers another book on Aberdeen FC. It is, I hope, far more than just a sequel. The format has been changed, dividing the book into two halves. The first half tells the story of the Dons' European era in words, the second tells it match by match. The new format gives scope for far greater detail than was possible in *The Aberdeen Football Companion*. It also provides a belated opportunity to correct the inevitable errors that crept into the first book, a consequence of the speed with which it had to be written.

There is no place in this volume for short-lived tournaments – the Drybrough Cup, the Anglo-Scottish Cup, and the Texaco Cup – nor any friendlies Aberdeen have played these past thirty years. As for the matches of the season, some are obvious, others are not. Every cup final Aberdeen have contested since 1966 is included, along with whatever other games took my fancy. The book leans towards, without being dominated by, matches in Europe.

I hope readers will excuse a non-Aberdonian, indeed, a non-Scot, writing this history. The years I spent in the Granite City – 1977-89 – were as happy as I have ever known. When abroad, I rely on the BBC World Service to keep me abreast of the Dons' fortunes. I happened to be in Transylvania at the time of the Dunfermline play-offs, tuning in at some god-forsaken hour when my companions were tucked up in bed. I like to think my whoop of joy on hearing the score made passing vampires take to their heels.

I am grateful to Kevin Stirling, David Innes and Donal Cullen for going through these pages with a fine-tooth comb and drawing my attention to errors and oversights. Kevin Stirling also put much of his vast archive on the Dons at my disposal. My thanks, too, to Ian Taggart and Teddy Scott at Aberdeen FC.

CLIVE LEATHERDALE

Preface

The perception of Scottish football, outside the country itself at least, seems to be that it consists of two teams – Rangers and Celtic – and nothing much else really. That perception is, of course, quite incorrect, as this volume illustrates perfectly.

When you actually see what Aberdeen have achieved in Europe through the years, it makes very impressive reading and puts many supposed top clubs' performances quite literally to shame.

No foreword to a history of The Dons' record in Europe would be complete without mentioning that wet night in Gothenburg on the 11th May 1983. The night when the Granite City's finest joined that elite, small band who have achieved what almost amounts to immortality by lifting a European trophy, namely the Cup-Winners' Cup.

However, the triumphs of the game against Real Madrid should not be allowed to overshadow what else the Pittodrie club has achieved through the years on its quest for glory at European level. Whilst the name of Aberdeen is synonymous with the oil industry, it would not be untrue to add that, for many, The Dons are right up there – 'Oh yes, Aberdeen, the oil capital of Europe; their football team's not half bad either!'

Looking through this work, which has been painstakingly compiled, makes me realise just what hard acts I have to follow. This season's campaign in Europe has been my first as a manager and I have thoroughly enjoyed it. Being involved in Europe is very addictive – the more you experience, the more you want. And believe me I want much more!

So, watch out for the sequel to this excellent publication – Aberdeen's record in Europe has been first class to date. But as far as I am concerned, the following is only Part One . . .

Roy Aitken

Introduction

Timing is as important in football as it is in everything else. By no stretch of the imagination could Aberdeen FC claim to have a distinguished history. Although founded in 1903, the club did not win anything until after World War II, and the League Cup they won at Hampden in 1946, when organised football was barely back on its feet, does not feature in official records.

The one Scottish Championship won by the Dons in the pre-Ferguson era – in 1954-55 – was equally badly timed. It coincided with the birth of the European Cup, to be contested by the best clubs across the continent. Perfect timing, one might think. But in this, its inaugural year, entry to the European Cup was by invitation, not qualification. The SFA nominated Hibernian, who had finished fifth, to be Scottish football's first standard bearers. Instead of competing against the likes of Real Madrid from the start, Aberdeen's European bid was put on hold for twelve years, until they qualified again. Ironically, in 1966-67 they did not strictly qualify at all, having been beaten at Hampden in the Scottish Cup Final. The Dons entered the Cup-Winners' Cup by default, on account of Celtic's league and cup double. That was, perhaps, small consolation for the lost opportunities of 1955.

To look back at Aberdeen in 1966 is to see a very different club to what one finds today. Thirty years ago the Dons were a provincial outfit in every sense, overawed by the Glasgow giants, and beaten by them on almost every occasion when it mattered. Few Dons' supporters in those days genuinely expected league titles and cup finals each season. How different it is today. Though Aberdeen FC passed through bitter waters in the wake of the Ferguson era, it remains a power in Scottish football. Three cups have been lifted since Fergie left, and but for Rangers' extraordinary dominance, five more league championships would have been claimed too.

We pick up the story in 1966. England have just won the World Cup, substitutes have just been introduced, and under Jock Stein Celtic are building up a head of steam. Aberdeen haven't won anything for years, and Eddie Turnbull, their manager since March 1965, finds himself at the helm of a middling team heading nowhere. But all that is about to change. Bit by bit, the Dons grow in strength. Sometimes it's a case of two steps forward, one step back, but by the mid-1980s the Granite City could boast a team voted the best in Europe.

Older supporters, who lived through the Dons' lean years of the 1950s and 60s must have rubbed their eyes in disbelief.

1

EDDIE TURNBULL 1966-1971

SCOTTISH LEAGUE DIVISION 1   1966-67

Division 1   Fourth
League Cup   Semi-Final
Scottish Cup   Runners-Up

The scent of league titles was a long forgotten sensation for most Aberdeen supporters by the mid-1960s. Not for a decade had the team nudged into the top five, and for most of that time was more likely to find itself scrapping against relegation than knocking on the door of Europe.

The appointment of Eddie Turnbull as manager in March 1965, replacing Tommy Pearson, looked to betoken better times. Insofar as he was a Hibs man, a mainstay of their Famous Five, Turnbull's had been a surprising appointment. When Jock Stein quit Easter Road to take charge at Celtic, Turnbull – then at Queen's Park – had been favourite to succeed him. Instead, Hibernian plumped for Dundee's Bob Shankly, leaving Turnbull free to take the Aberdeen job.

Turnbull was a no-nonsense sort who liked his football played in a no-nonsense manner. In this respect he was a man of his time. The mid-1960s are widely remembered without affection as an age of sterility and defensive-minded tactics, encouraged by Helenio Herrera's *catennaccio* in Italy and Alf Ramsey's wingless wonders in England.

Taken aback by what he inherited, Turnbull slapped free-transfer notices on seventeen players. He enjoyed the best possible baptism – beating Rangers 2-0 at Pittodrie in his first match in charge – but come the end of the season the Dons could finish the season no higher than twelfth.

DID YOU KNOW?

It was Eddie Turnbull who introduced Aberdeen's all red strip, which they retained until reverting to white shorts in 1996-97.

At the end of Turnbull's first full season the team had climbed to eighth. The players, though, seemed inhibited by Pittodrie, where they won rarely and unconvincingly. The highlight was reaching the Scottish Cup semi-final, losing to Rangers after a replay.

The legacy of 1965-66 was less a matter of games won or lost than of players signed. Jim Smith was a silky midfielder who would be taken to supporters' hearts. Goalkeeper Bobby Clark had played for Turnbull at Queen's Park. On coming north, it was not long before he displaced John Ogston.

With the 1966-67 season just days away local lad Dave Smith defected to Ibrox. Smith was the latest in a conveyor belt of talent draining away from Pittodrie, and his loss convinced many that the coming season would be spent treading water, at best. Just 5,000 turned up the first League Cup match, against St Johnstone.

The draw for Section 1 was inviting. No Glasgow or Edinburgh giant stood between Aberdeen and the quarter-finals. Brushing aside both Dundee clubs the Dons cruised into the last eight. There they met Morton. Trailing 1-3 from the first leg, Aberdeen were still in arrears with five minutes of the second leg remaining. But goals from Jim Smith and sweeper Jens Petersen saw Aberdeen through to a Hampden semi against Rangers. Aberdeen earned extra-time and a replay, but in those days it was necessary to beat the Old Firm at the first time of asking. Few teams got the better of them second time round, and the Dons did not buck the trend.

That Hampden replay provoked accusations of unsportsmanship. Substitutes – one per team – had been sanctioned in the close season. But they were to be used strictly in the case of injury. They were not permitted as a tactical instrument. Besides, managers had no experience of using them as such. More often than not the sub started the match on the bench and stayed there. Turnbull would call upon just half a dozen all season. But once the semi-final dragged into extra-time both managers plumped for fresh legs. For this they were roundly rebuked.

DID YOU KNOW?

Aberdeen's first official substitute was Pat Wilson, who replaced Billy Little in extra-time in the League Cup semi-final with Rangers on 19 October 1966. The Dons' first scoring substitute was Ernie Winchester v Hibs ten days later.

> **DID YOU KNOW?**
>
> During their 8-game winning run in 1966 the Dons kept not one clean sheet.

It was now late October, and the Dons embarked on an eight-game winning run. By New Year they were second behind Celtic.

The second half of 1966-67 heralded a return to the Dons' baffling inconsistency. At times they were electric, scoring seven against Airdrie, six against Stirling and Falkirk, five against Dundee and Ayr. But often enough the attack spluttered and failed to fire at all. Not least of these inexplicable results was a 0-1 defeat at lowly St Johnstone, fodder for the Dons' marksmen on four other occasions.

Celtic and Rangers were engaged in their own private championship duel, leaving the rest to battle for Fairs Cup places and a sniff at the Scottish Cup.

Aberdeen had a tilt at both. In a barnstorming cup run they went nap against Dundee and St Johnstone before Jim Smith hit a late equaliser at Hibs in the quarter-final. Ernie Winchester's 'double' in the replay was seen by Pittodrie's record crowd for a midweek fixture. In the semi Dundee United's Tommy Millar put through his own goal to send the Dons to their first Scottish Cup Final in eight years, seeking their first win in twenty years. Celtic awaited.

For Aberdeen the dream of European football was tantalisingly close. They would contest the Cup-Winners' Cup automatically if they lifted the Cup. But the league season still had a lap to go, and neither the championship nor Aberdeen's entry-ticket to the Fairs Cup was settled. Circumstances could conspire to leave Aberdeen out in the cold once again.

> **DID YOU KNOW?**
>
> In order to play in the Scottish Cup replay with Hibs, Bobby Clark had to sit an examination at Jordanhill College earlier than all other students.
> He had to promise to keep the questions to himself.

Match of the Season

Celtic 2   Aberdeen 0

Scottish Cup Final, 29 April 1967

With hindsight, Aberdeen were pitched against the finest team in Europe, never mind Scotland. Stein's players were going for an unprecedented haul of trophies. They had already claimed the League Cup and Glasgow Cup, but the three top prizes were still up for grabs. Celtic had squeezed past Dukla Prague in midweek to reach the European Cup Final. Viewed dispassionately, the Scottish Cup was the least precious of the three trophies still open to them.

With Rangers shortly contesting the Cup-Winners' Cup Final, the Old Firm's European feats took the gloss from the domestic cup final, for which Aberdeen were quoted at 4-1 against.

Aberdeen prepared at Gleneagles with quiet confidence. Gone were the memories of recent thrashings, 8-0 and 7-1, at Parkhead. This season they had forced two league draws, the second at Parkhead just ten days prior to the final.

But plans were thrown into confusion when Turnbull was taken ill overnight. The players' bus delayed as long as it dared, in the hope that he might recover, and when he did not was involved in an unseemly dash to the stadium,. allowing barely enough time for the players to change.

At least they were unburdened by injuries. Nine of the team played in every round, and two others – Jim Smith and recent signing Jim Storrie – missed just the odd tie. Two of the team had seen it all before. Skipper Harry Melrose was a veteran of two finals with Dunfermline, winning in 1961, losing in 1965, the same year Storrie's Leeds lost to Liverpool at Wembley in the FA Cup.

Sadly, Aberdeen fell short of the standards demanded of themselves. Melrose and Jim Smith played deep, hoping to stifle Celtic in midfield, the consequence of which was to cut the supply line to their own forwards. The Dons created little and lost to two Willie Wallace goals, Lennox setting up the first, before the break, and Jimmy Johnstone the second, just after. Tuning in from his sickbed, Turnbull was helpless to prevent Aberdeen's third Scottish Cup Final defeat by Celtic.

Two days later Aberdeen were back on league business, hoping to secure their Fairs Cup place at Kilmarnock. The 1-1 draw was good enough, but when Celtic clinched the league title they vacated their berth in the Cup-Winners' Cup. Twelve years after Aberdeen should have competed in the European Cup the new generation of Dons could dust down their passports.

SCOTTISH LEAGUE DIVISION 1   1967-68

Division 1	Fifth
League Cup	Bottom of section
Scottish Cup	Second Round
European Cup-Winners' Cup	Second Round

It was perhaps a consequence of raised expectations that 1967-68 went down like a lead balloon. Much was expected of a team that had finished fourth and reached a cup final. If much was expected, little was delivered.

Section 2 of the League Cup was the stuff of fantasy. Or nightmares. Aberdeen were pooled with Celtic, Rangers and Dundee United. Such a grouping in the 1980s, pitching the Old and New Firm together, would have produced an explosion or two. In the 60s, the east coast teams lacked the punch they would later acquire, but the group was still sure to entice huge crowds.

The 36,000 that crammed Pittodrie to greet Rangers would not be bettered all season. Storrie's equaliser flattered to deceive, for next came a 0-5 mauling at Tannadice. All told, the six ties cost nineteen goals. The defence – Clark, Whyte, Shewan, McMillan, Petersen – were unchanged throughout, making it harder to make sense of it all.

The season's first tournament had turned sour. But there was no time to dwell. Four days after Aberdeen were sunk 1-5 by Celtic, humbler opponents – KR Reykjavik – came by.

Soccer in Iceland is a summer sport. The season ends in September, too late to qualify for the new Euro season. Entry is therefore deferred a year. KR Reykjavik were big fish in a small pond, winners of the Icelandic championship a record nineteen times, and winners of the domestic cup every year but one since it was introduced in 1960. Icelandic teams had an abject record in Europe, but none fared worse than KR did now, losing ten goals at Pittodrie in the first leg.

The Dons bagged four more in the return. If this was typical of European soccer, the more the better. But Standard Liege in Round 2 painted a more accurate picture of what to expect.

DID YOU KNOW?

During their 1967 summer tour of USA the Dons took the field as the 'Washington Whips', in honour of the American city they represented. They lost to Wolves in the final of the American President's Cup.

Cigarette card from 1910 and postcard from 1929

The main problem was easy to see. Hearts, on 10 February, became only the third Scottish team not to score at least once at Pittodrie. A porous defence, coupled with an inability to win on their travels, caused Aberdeen to languish in mid-table. The forwards did their best – Dundee United and Raith were hit for six – but they too often failed to fire at all, and in any case could not compensate for the failings behind them.

Dunfermline did much to ruin Aberdeen's season. Four goals past Clark in the league left the Dons peering over their shoulders. In the Scottish Cup Aberdeen were six minutes from a Pittodrie replay when Edwards bagged the Pars' winner.

The Dons were so low they lost their next three games. Turnbull, never one to shilly-shally, kicked out half the team. Francis Munro was sold to Wolves. Jim Storrie, a misfit from the start, returned to Yorkshire, to Rotherham. Jimmy Wilson, who had missed hardly a game for two seasons, went to Motherwell, and Dave Millar and Pat Wilson signed for Raith.

DID YOU KNOW?

**Aberdeen's biggest ever European win came in their very first game.
Aberdeen 10 KR Reykjavik 0.**

Turnbull's rebuilding was already under way. Jim Hermiston, Ian Taylor, and – initially in midfield – Martin Buchan had been introduced back in October 1966. George Murray and Tommy Craig had since joined them, and this quintet looked set to form the nucleus of the side over the next few years.

1967-68 appeared to be meandering to a close. The only glimmer of light was the hope that, with so many teams bunched in mid-table, a winning run might yet earn a Fairs Cup place. Nothing was certain, for the number of entries varied from year to year. No one knew in advance what league position was necessary.

Right on cue Aberdeen started winning. In fact they won their last four, popped in ten goals, and finished a flattering fifth. They left their most improbable result till last.

Match of the Season (1)

Aberdeen 2   Standard Liege 0
Cup-Winners' Cup, 2nd Round, 2nd Leg, 6 December 1967

Standard Liege looked a tough nut. Though the Belgian national team of the period carried little weight, the best club sides held their own. Standard were twice Belgian champions in the early 60s, and had won the Belgian Cup in 1966 and 67.

They had also left their mark in Europe. In the 1961-62 European Cup they had put Rangers out before falling to Real Madrid in the semis. In 1966-67 they reached the same stage of the Cup-Winners' Cup, where they lost to the eventual winners, Bayern Munich.

It is easily overlooked that two-leg soccer in the 60s was a novelty for most British clubs, unused to the cat and mouse tactics required in foreign lands. All too often British teams approached the away leg as they approached the home. They would learn, of course – and increased opportunity helped Celtic and Rangers learn quickly – but for most the process took time.

It was corner-kicks that proved the Dons' undoing in the Sclessin Stadium; they produced two home goals inside eleven minutes. A third goal came just after the hour, and from that point the Dons were chasing a lost cause. The attendance for the second-leg was smaller than that to see KR Reykjavik. An early evening snowstorm kept thousands more indoors. Munro's volley gave hope at the halfway stage, whereupon Melrose added another. Jim Whyte had the best chance to force extra-time, but he snatched at his shot.

Standard's pedigree was evident in the next round, when they forced two drawn games with AC Milan before going down in a third match. Milan went on to claim the Cup-Winners' Cup.

Match of the Season (2)

Rangers 2   Aberdeen 3

Division 1, 27 April 1968

Aberdeen's season began and ended with Rangers. They started with a 1-1 draw in the League Cup and finished with a sensation.

The Gers were smarting at Celtic's ongoing superiority. They had been runners-up by a whisker for the past two seasons and the championship was going to the wire once again. Rangers were unbeaten, yet trailed on goal-average to Celtic, whose final match – against a Dunfermline side otherwise engaged in the Scottish Cup Final – was held over.

Aberdeen had not won at Ibrox since 1961. 40,000 packed the stadium anticipating the formality of another win. All seemed to be going to plan when Dave Smith, an Aberdeen player not so long ago, put the Gers in front. Though Dave Johnston levelled, Alex Ferguson – Rangers' elbowy centre-forward – restored the lead. This time Rangers' advantage lasted barely two minutes. Johnston was again the party pooper. With Rangers straining at the leash to recapture the lead, the Dons broke away seconds from time and substitute Ian Taylor silenced the vast throngs with the winner.

Celtic needed to lose to Dunfermline by an astronomical margin to relinquish the title. In fact, they won 2-1. Aberdeen had denied Rangers a potential Trivial Pursuit question: 'Which team went a whole season unbeaten yet finished second?'

SCOTTISH LEAGUE DIVISION 1   1968-69

Division 1	Fifteenth
League Cup	Third in section
Scottish Cup	Semi-Final
Fairs Cup	Second Round

Despite the astute signing from Preston of that prolific ex-Ranger, Jim Forrest, 1968-69 was mostly a season of torment. The first match in August, at Clyde in the League Cup, set the tone. Without the guile of the suspended Jim Smith, the Dons were overrun 1-4, despite the stimulus of scoring first.

The league began with a splash – eight goals shared with Dundee – but as September flowed into October defeats began piling up. Five in a row, all by the odd goal – and three of them at home – left the Dons hovering two places off the bottom. The sequence was arrested by a second successive win at Ibrox, by the same score, 3-2, and supporters anticipated a steady rise up the table.

But it didn't happen. When Dunfermline – then at the peak of their powers – thrashed Aberdeen 1-5 in late November, Turnbull indulged in another bout of hay making. Out went Jim Hermiston, Tommy Rae, and Dave Johnston. The outcome? – a 2-6 demolition by Hibs in front of the Pittodrie faithful.

This time Turnbull's scythe cut down even more players – Ian Taylor, George Murray, Billy Little. Even Bobby Clark, who had won two Scottish caps, lost his place. He would remain in the wilderness for a whole year. Ernie McGarr took his place but results remained dismal.

Turnbull just couldn't get it right. As the months rolled by it was clear this season was about survival, to live another day, to avoid the dreaded drop.

Excursions in the cups proved welcome distractions from the tensions of the league. In the Fairs Cup Aberdeen were drawn to play the Bulgarians of Slavia Sofia. On 22 August, five days before the first leg, Soviet tanks invaded Czechoslovakia. With the Cold War turning icy it was uncertain whether teams required to cross the Iron Curtain would be granted the necessary visas. UEFA hastily scrapped the original pairings and remade the draw, this time in two geopolitical blocks. At least, that was the solution for the European and Cup-Winners' Cups. The Fairs Cup, for some reason, UEFA left alone. Aberdeen's first official trip behind the Iron Curtain went ahead. Hours of hassle over visas and paperwork awaited them in the Bulgarian capital.

Bulgarian club football was dominated by Slavia's rivals, CSKA. Slavia had not won the national championship since World War II, though they had claimed the Bulgarian Cup three times in the 1960s. In the 1966-67 Cup-Winners' campaign they slaughtered Swansea in the first round, edged out Strasbourg in the second, beat Servette Geneva home and away in the quarter-final to find themselves paired with Rangers in the semi. Rangers won both legs 1-0.

Turnbull plumped for a defensive 5-3-2 line-up in Sofia. In doing so he made an important positional switch. Young Martin Buchan had been in and out of the team for two years. In Sofia he wore No 11 but played as a stopper alongside Tommy McMillan. In searing heat Aberdeen preferred to sit back, and Slavia lacked the nous to break through. When they did so they came upon Buchan at his imperious best. A star was born.

The second leg provided one of those great Euro nights that Pittodrie-goers would come to treasure. A packed stadium, Aberdeen piling forward, great goals. Two were enough to see off the Bulgarians. Round 2 saw more thrills, but Real Zaragoza proved too strong.

The Scottish Cup would extract Aberdeen's best and worst results of the season. Dunfermline were defending Cup-holders, they were through to the semis of the Cup-Winners' Cup, and were chasing hard in the league. Aberdeen had home advantage over the Pars in Round 4, and might have scraped through there and then but for Renton's late leveller. In the replay two Dave Robb goals earned a home tie with Kilmarnock, another side going strongly. Once again home advantage was squandered before Aberdeen triumphed in the replay.

Now only Rangers stood between the Dons and the final. A semi-final in a season of gloom was something to be thankful for. Rangers approached the tie – at Parkhead – with trepidation, the Dons having won on two previous trips to Ibrox.

The occasion proved humiliating for Aberdeen. The Dons got stage fright and were hit for six. Jim Forrest's goal on the stroke of half-time pulled the score back to 1-2 and might have inspired a revival. Instead the second period belonged to Willie Johnston, who recorded a famous hat-trick. With the final whistle went Aberdeen's last hopes of playing in Europe next season.

DID YOU KNOW?

Aberdeen's three consecutive league defeats at Pittodrie – in September and October 1968 – has never been repeated.

Firemen tackle the blaze at Pittodrie in February 1971

Success in Europe was small beer compared to staying up in Division 1. Losing 2-3 at fellow strugglers Raith Rovers three days before that apocalyptic semi-final, plunged the Dons deeper into the mire. Aberdeen shrugged off these double blows to take seven points from five unbeaten games, among them a 6-3 thrashing of Morton. By the end the safety margin was eight points, but the figures made grim inspection. Aberdeen had posted their lowest points total (26) and fewest league wins (9) for twenty years, and their lowest goals tally (50) for almost as long. They mustered just three points out of eight from Arbroath and Falkirk, the two relegated teams.

The season offered one final kick in the teeth. Two of the team's young jewels, Jim Smith and Tommy Craig, were sold for English gold. The prospects for 1969-70 looked bleak.

DID YOU KNOW?

Aberdeen's 1-6 thrashing by Rangers in the Scottish Cup in 1969 is the last time the Dons have conceded six goals in any competitive fixture.

Match of the Season

Aberdeen 2   Real Zaragoza 1

Fairs Cup, 2nd Round, 1st Leg, 23 October 1968

By the time Round 2 of the Fairs Cup came around the Dons were reeling from five defeats off the cuff. This should have handed the psychological advantage to their opponents, but Real Zaragoza were propping up the Spanish League and had enough problems of their own.

This sorry state proved to be temporary. In any case, Zaragoza were proven masters in Europe. This was remarkable, considering they had never won the Spanish championship, and prior to 1964 had never won anything else. But in the mid and late 1960s they were a power to be reckoned with. Their *forté* was demolishing British opponents.

1963-64 was Zaragoza's wonder year, claiming both the Spanish Cup and Fairs Cup. Their victims in the Cup-Winners' Cup the following season included Dundee and Cardiff, before West Ham disposed of them in the semi-final.

In the 1965-66 Fairs Cup campaign, Zaragoza left a trail of British and Irish havoc – Shamrock Rovers, Hearts, Dunfermline, Leeds United – but were denied the ultimate prize by losing to Barcelona in the all-Spanish final.

In 1966 Zaragoza won the Spanish Cup for a second time, and duly packed off Everton in the subsequent Cup-Winners' campaign before Rangers 'won' on the spin of a coin. In short, no other continental team had visited comparable devastation on British football. Only West Ham had proved superior, leaving Zaragoza with seven British scalps. Aberdeen would be the eighth.

When the Dons led 2-0 at Pittodrie all seemed ripe for an upset. Tommy McMillan's own-goal changed all that, and in the return leg the Spanish team won as they pleased. They would fall at the next hurdle, to Newcastle United on the away-goals rule. Newcastle, like West Ham before them, would win the Cup. For British clubs the lesson was clear: beat Real Zaragoza and the trophy was there for the taking.

SCOTTISH LEAGUE DIVISION 1   1969-70

Division 1	Eighth
League Cup	Quarter-Final
Scottish Cup	Winners

Though Turnbull's new broom swept out many players it had failed to sweep away the spectre of defeat. Events in the close season clouded Aberdeen's prospects. Losing Craig and Smith to Sheffield Wednesday and Newcastle was good for the bank balance but bad for the team. Left-back Ally Shewan had hung up his boots and Martin Buchan broken an ankle in a car crash. Right-back Jim Whyte ruptured an Achilles tendon in the League Cup curtain-raiser and missed nearly the whole season. Alec Willoughby, signed from Rangers to stiffen the midfield, must have wondered what manner of misfits he had joined.

In the circumstances it was an achievement to survive the League Cup section, which Aberdeen managed despite winning just two games. By holding off Hibs they lined up a two-leg quarter-final with Celtic. Aberdeen's record against Jock Stein's multi-championship side could not be worse. Against the odds they look the lead, but a combination of Celtic genius and ill-conceived offside tactics cost the Dons dear.

Disappointment in the League Cup coincided with two new signings. Turnbull had liked the look of Morton's winger-cum-striker Joe Harper for some time, and £40,000 was enough to bring the wee man to Pittodrie. Harper's introduction – three goals in thirteen matches, two of them penalties – was not the stuff of headlines. Come the New Year Turnbull was even playing Harper out wide. A hat-trick against Raith failed to ignite the expected spark, and in March Harper was dropped.

The other signing cost nothing. Derek McKay hailed from Macduff. He had begun his footballing life at Deveronvale, but landed at Pittodrie on a free from Dundee. Unlike Harper, he had never faced Aberdeen on the pitch. Little was expected of McKay, and after a couple of substitute appearances he was despatched to the reserves.

Aberdeen's league form was indifferent. This was at best a middling team, winning and losing as though each was the natural consequence of the other. While Harper was finding his goalscoring touch, Jim Forrest and Dave Robb banged in enough goals to keep Aberdeen's head above water. The rebuilt defence was meaner than before, and kept the number of defeats in check.

DID YOU KNOW?

Dropped keeper Bobby Clark played as an outfield substitute at Rangers. On 20 September 1969 he played the whole match in defence at St Johnstone.

Aberdeen suddenly found themselves with two international goalkeepers on the books. Since taking over from Clark, Ernie McGarr excelled to such an extent that he earned a couple of caps. The second of these, against Austria in Vienna on Guy Fawkes' night, 1969, coincided with Aberdeen's fixture at St Mirren. As McGarr couldn't be in two places at once this meant a recall for Clark, who otherwise might never have returned to the side – other than in the outfield, which he did from time to time.

It was Airdrie's Drew Jarvie who put the skids under McGarr's tenancy, scoring the winner at Pittodrie. McGarr's Scottish career was over, barring one more game his Aberdeen career too, and he was soon on his way to Dunfermline.

McGarr therefore missed out on the Dons' cup heroics. Aberdeen had managed three semis in four years under Turnbull, and were looking to go one better. Clyde were the first victims, battered at Pittodrie for the third time in a matter of months.

Clydebank from Division 2 put up more of a show but earned only sympathy. Pittodrie at one stage even booed its own team. It was in the quarter-final at Falkirk that Derek McKay started to make a name for himself. A flu epidemic that struck down several players earned him his first starting place in the side, and he popped in the goal that yet again took the Dons into the last four. The three other survivors were Kilmarnock, Dundee, and – clearly the one to avoid – Celtic.

Kilmarnock's name was drawn, the tie to be played at the odd choice of Perth's Muirton Park. Aberdeen had overcome the same opponents the previous season, and having recently won 2-0 at Rugby Park in the league were quietly confident. The semi-final would be marred by crowd trouble, but was settled by another goal from McKay.

Celtic awaited in the final. The Dons had two league fixtures outstanding but were too low in the table to be summoned to the Fairs Cup. But with Celtic already champions, defeat at Hampden would see Aberdeen enter the Cup-Winners' Cup, as in 1966-67.

DID YOU KNOW?

Aberdeen were the only Scottish opponents to score three goals against Celtic in any competition in 1969-70.

Match of the Season

Celtic 1   Aberdeen 3

Scottish Cup Final, 11 April 1970

The psychological skirmishing that enlivens cup-final build-ups shifted in Aberdeen's favour shortly before the big day. The Dons had gone twelve games without a win over Celtic before the fixture at Parkhead, with Celtic requiring two points to cement their fifth successive title. The story goes that the sight of crates of champagne being ferried into the stadium got up Aberdeen noses, so to speak, and the indignity of being considered fodder to the chopping block spurred the Dons to a shock 2-1 win.

The Monday before the final saw the Dons on league business against Kilmarnock. No one wanted to be injured now, of all times, but that was the fate of Alec Willoughby. Jim Whyte made his long-awaited return in that match, but was clearly in no condition to face Celtic. Joe Harper was also recalled, and kept his fingers crossed.

Aberdeen's £50,000 record signing, Steve Murray from Dundee, was cup-tied. But a fairy tale place awaited 17-year-old Arthur Graham, who played his first full ninety minutes in the win at Parkhead, scoring the winner to boot. Bobby Clark and centre-half Tommy McMillan were the only Dons survivors of the 1967 final. Now was their chance for revenge.

In the minds of bookies Aberdeen hadn't a prayer. This was their seventh Scottish Cup Final, and they had lost all but one. Celtic were on a high, following their 1-0 win at Leeds in their European Cup semi-final first leg. They hoped to complete the job four days after playing Aberdeen.

Yet the Dons achieved the near impossible, inflicting on Celtic a third defeat in 26 Hampden appearances under Jock Stein. This time Turnbull was there in person, this time his team would play positively. Midway through the first half McKay drove the ball against Bobby Murdoch's arm at close quarters. To this day every Celtic supporter and most neutrals agree the ball struck the arm, not *vice versa*. Aberdeen appeals were half-hearted but referee R H Davidson gave the balance of any doubt to the Dons. Tommy Gemmell was so outraged he flung the ball at the official and was booked. In today's climate Gemmell would have been off.

DID YOU KNOW?

Martin Buchan, at 21, was the youngest player ever to captain a winning team in the Scottish Cup Final.

DID YOU KNOW?

Free-transfer Derek McKay scored four vital goals as Aberdeen won the 1970
Scottish Cup. He also played in 13 league games, but failed to score at all.

Joe Harper, nerveless when taking penalties, put Aberdeen
ahead. Over an hour remained. In fact Aberdeen were in front just
two minutes when Lennox robbed Clark to 'score' as the keeper
tried to clear. Mr Davidson blew for a Celtic infringement that not
many had seen. Two potentially match-winning decisions had gone
Aberdeen's way in as many minutes. A third was not long in coming. Martin Buchan's trip on Lennox looked a penalty. Mr Davidson
thought otherwise, and booked Jimmy Johnstone for his ungentle-
manly protests.

The second half passed agonisingly slowly. Seven minutes from
time Forrest shot, Evan Williams parried, McKay pounced from a
tight angle. The Cup looked safe. But it wasn't. Lennox scored with
barely a minute left, whereupon Harper capitalised on an under-
populated Celtic defence to free his room-mate 'Cup-tie' McKay for
a sweeping third goal. Skipper Martin Buchan, just 21 years old,
held aloft the Scottish Cup. A crowd of 50,000 welcomed the team
back to Aberdeen: it was Eddie Turnbull's 47th birthday.

Celtic had to be content with the championship. Having lost the
Scottish Cup, they then lost the European Cup Final to Feyenoord.

DID YOU KNOW?

Aberdeen's substitute in the 1970 Scottish Cup Final was Martin Buchan's
brother, George. Had he come on it would have been the first time brothers
had played in the same final since Celtic's O'Donnell brothers in the 1930s.

SCOTTISH LEAGUE DIVISION 1   1970-71

Division 1	Runners-Up
League Cup	Second in section
Scottish Cup	Quarter-Final
European Cup-Winners' Cup	First Round

Aberdeen had won the first trophy of the 1970s. The triumph over Celtic was just the spur they needed to take them on in the league.

The comings and goings during the close season were muted. McGarr went and Willie Young came, though the red giant would play second fiddle to Tommy McMillan for much of the coming campaign. For Chalky Whyte everything had suddenly turned sour. Out for almost all the cup-winning season, he lasted just one game in 1970-71 and headed off to Kilmarnock.

Aberdeen's tub-thumping seemed ill-judged when they threw away qualification in the League Cup in a flurry of suicidal defending against Airdrie and Hibs. The first league matches were none too heart-warming either, as first Airdrie, then St Johnstone, departed from Pittodrie with precious points.

The Cup-Winners' Cup was viewed with a particular sense of expectation. This time Aberdeen were competing as of right, not through default, but the Hungarians of Honved ensured they did not overstay their welcome.

The players flew back from Budapest in low spirits, and appeared to be still on a downer when losing at Morton. Then something remarkable happened. Aberdeen won their next fifteen games, the last twelve without conceding a goal. Never before or since have the club come close to repeating those statistics. By mid-January 1971 the championship seemed tantalisingly within reach. The only team within striking distance was Celtic, naturally, but if the Dons held their nerve the title was theirs. Then came defeat at Easter Road, scene of Aberdeen's earlier exit from the League Cup.

Joe Baker's winning goal for the Hibees was the first of several crippling blows to be endured in the first weeks of 1971. In the early hours of Saturday, 6 February, the main stand at Pittodrie went up in flames. The players were due to play at Dunfermline and heard the news by telephone. Part of the stand was gutted, records and irreplaceable memorabilia destroyed. Makeshift changing rooms had to be found elsewhere, the players conveyed to the ground already kitted out. That Pittodrie's capacity was not unduly diminished was clear from the first home game after the fire, when 36,000 were admitted for the visit of Rangers.

DID YOU KNOW?

Goalkeeper Bobby Clark was unbeaten in 19 hours 15 minutes of play between 14 October 1970 and 16 January 1971.

But this is to anticipate. The team needed to win at Dunfermline. In retrospect, the result transformed the season for both clubs. Had Aberdeen won they would have been champions and Dunfermline relegated. Instead, the Dons were denied by Robertson's first-half goal, which ultimately ensured the Pars another season in Division 1. Not the least of the ironies was that the home goal was protected by Ernie McGarr, an Aberdeen player till the summer. Regrettably, on this occasion, he did his job well.

The Dons still hoped for a league and cup double when Rangers stripped them of the Scottish Cup in a frenzied quarter-final at Ibrox, settled by a goal from Gers' Aberdonian centre-half Colin Jackson. League points also went astray. All told, of eight matches between 16 January and 6 March the Dons won just two. The finishing line looked awfully far off.

Many expected Aberdeen to crack in the face of a challenge by battle-hardened Celtic. To their credit, the Dons found their second wind, dropping just one point from twelve, setting up a Pittodrie showdown with Jock Stein's five-times champions.

It was not to be. Amid the post-season search for explanations, one statistical oddity stood out. Joe Harper had bulged the net at a rate of more than one a game during the first half of the season. Then he dried up like a puddle in the desert.

DID YOU KNOW?

Joe Harper scored 19 league goals up to Boxing Day 1970-71.
After Boxing Day he did not score any.

Match of the Season (1)

Aberdeen 3   Honved 1
Cup-Winners' Cup, 1st Round, 1st Leg, 16 September 1970

Younger readers surveying the contenders for Euro 96 may have little idea of the aura attending Hungarian soccer in former times. Hungary was to European football what Brazil was to the world as a whole. The Hungarian national team had captured hearts as recently as 1966 during the England World Cup. A year later Florian Albert was crowned European Footballer of the Year.

Honved's heyday was the 1950s, when the three-times national champions were invited here, there and everywhere, just for the prestige of playing them. Recent years have seen them upstaged by Ferencvaros and Ujpest Dozsa: indeed in 1970-71 Honved were only eligible for the Cup-Winners' Cup by default, when Ujpest claimed both league and cup.

The first leg at Pittodrie was a mini-epic. Honved played in all-white – evocative of Real Madrid. The Dons clawed their way back from losing the first goal to go ahead by half-time, though Harper's effort, possibly offside, sparked angry protests. Seven minutes from time Steve Murray fended off two Hungarian challenges to make it 3-1.

On a night of fluctuating fortunes in Budapest the Dons had the chalice snatched from their lips. Kocsis halved the deficit, the referee ignoring a linesman's raised flag. After the interval Kocsis scored again, a neat chip. As things stood Honved were through on the away-goals rule, introduced in 1965. Kosma then beat Clark for number three, whereupon Steve Murray took a pot shot and saw the ball fly in off a defender. 4-4 on aggregate, with one away goal apiece.

Hitherto, matches that finished all-square on away goals were settled by the toss of a disc. This flagrant unjustice was now abolished, to be replaced by a piece of gladiatorial theatre that remains with us today – the penalty shoot-out. Honved v Aberdeen would be Europe's first competitive match to be settled in this fashion. One imagines it took an age for Italian referee Lo Bello to orchestrate names and kicking sequences and to corral non-participating players in the centre-circle.

In those days – other than regular takers – players might have no experience of penalty-taking. The idea of asking five or more, many of whom had never taken a competitive spot-kick in their lives, to put their heads on the block was a nerve-jangling innovation, both for participants and supporters.

Aberdeen won the toss to go first. It was 2-2 when Forrest stepped up for Aberdeen's third. Though a keen goalscorer, Forrest was new to the art of penalty taking, which at Aberdeen was the responsibility of Joe Harper or – in his absence – Jim Hermiston. Forrest's effort hit the bar. Honved's fifth and winning kick was taken by their goalkeeper, Bicskei.

DID YOU KNOW?

Like Aberdeen, Honved were national champions in 1954-55.
Like Aberdeen, Honved were unable to compete in the first European Cup.

Honved lost to Manchester City in Round 2. Aberdeen had to wait another twenty years before winning a penalty shoot-out.

DID YOU KNOW?

Falkirk's team that played Aberdeen on 19 December 1970 contained two future Scotland managers – Alex Ferguson and Andy Roxburgh.

Match of the Season (2)

Aberdeen 1   Celtic 1

Division 1, 17 April 1971

In this lively season the April fixture with Celtic had the mark of destiny stamped upon it.

Aberdeen could not have wished for a better opportunity to claim their first title in sixteen seasons. This was their penultimate match. They led Celtic by three points but had played two games more. Victory would secure the crown, defeat would surely lose it, while a draw would make the punters smile on Celtic.

In fact, Celtic were close to winning nothing in 1970-71. They were out of the European Cup, had lost the League Cup for the first time under Jock Stein, and would be taken to a replay by Rangers in the Scottish Cup Final. Defeat at Pittodrie might have spelled curtains for Stein's remarkable run.

First blood to Celtic. Jimmy Johnstone swung over a corner and Scotland's leading marksman, Harry Hood, hooked the ball past Clark. Aberdeen replied after 38 minutes through Alec Willoughby, also from a corner. The moment that would haunt Dons' fans came when Arthur Graham took the ball round keeper Evan Williams, only to find Billy McNeill sprinting back to clear off the goal-line.

The match ended 1-1. Celtic were further assisted by Aberdeen's unexpected loss at Falkirk, which left Celtic needing just three points from three games. For two Dons, however – Clark and Robb – the disappointment was eased by being picked for Scotland against Portugal. It was Robb's first cap. More would follow in the summer, and for Jim Forrest too. Against the Soviet Union in Moscow, all three would be selected. Aberdeen's star was rising.

ABERDEEN HONOURS UNDER EDDIE TURNBULL

1. Scottish Cup-winners 1969-70.
Runners-up in Scottish Cup 1966-67 and Scottish Championship 1970-71.

2

JIMMY BONTHRONE
1971-1975

SCOTTISH LEAGUE DIVISION 1   1971-72

Division 1   Runners-Up
League Cup   Third in section
Scottish Cup   Quarter-Final
UEFA Cup   First Round

The first six months of 1971 had been as eventful as any in the club's history – the fire, the duel with Celtic, the caps awarded. The season had ended on an up-beat note. Then in July, Turnbull quit.

Eddie Turnbull would never claim to be the most likeable of men. He had a sour-puss reputation, but his players respected him and were responding to him. Despite his indifferent health Turnbull was said to have been offered, and declined, the top job at Rangers. He had been passed over by Hibs back in 1965, but when a fresh offer was made he quickly accepted. One could understand his decision, except that Hibs were in turmoil and had finished 24 points behind Aberdeen. If it was trophies he sought, Turnbull would surely have stayed at Pittodrie. To that extent his decision was baffling. Good managers go up in the world, not down.

The Aberdeen board duly promoted Jimmy Bonthrone from his post as Turnbull's assistant. The new order would be more convivial and less confrontational than the old.

Bonthrone could not have wished for a better introduction, victory over Celtic in a new pre-season tournament, the Drybrough Cup, in a packed and renovated Pittodrie. The next objective was to progress in the League Cup. Aberdeen should not have stumbled in a modest section, but needing a draw at Brockville to force a mouth-watering quarter-final tie with Turnbull's Hibs they were struck down by two goals from Alex Ferguson.

Joe Harper celebrates scoring v Airdrie, 18 September 1971 (Aberdeen played in blue)

The Dons set a blistering pace in the league. Reinforced by the arrival of Bertie Miller – who took one wing while Arthur Graham took the other – the team saw off all challenges well into November. The highlights of those first months were a 7-2 thrashing of Partick (in the wake of Thistle's 4-1 League Cup Final win over Celtic), a backs-to-the-wall draw at Parkhead, and the staging of the first full international at Pittodrie. Belgium were the opponents, and caps awarded to Martin Buchan and Steve Murray raised Aberdeen's international brigade to five. A week later the Italian giants Juventus came visiting in the UEFA Cup. These were heady days for all associated with Aberdeen Football Club.

Elimination by Juventus was cause for sorrow, not anger, and the Dons held their heads high. The next home game, with Hearts, had darker ramifications. Pittodrie had become a fortress, no visiting side having won since Hearts themselves twenty months previously. Hearts now scored through Donald Ford. Aberdeen hit back with goals from Harper and Robb, the second of which saw Hearts' Townsend sent off for bad-mouthing the referee. 2-1 up against ten men, four minutes to play. Game, set, and match one would think, except that Ford somehow squeezed two headers past Clark to reduce Pittodrie to apoplexy. This was not the way of champions. Celtic thumbed their noses by leap-frogging the Dons to go top.

Bobby Clark is injured in the 3-0 win at Kilmarnock, 9 October 1971

DID YOU KNOW?

Prior to Donald Ford in November 1971, the last player to score a league hat-trick at Pittodrie was Hibs' Peter Cormack in December 1968.

Aberdeen held their nerve. It would be another two months before they lost again, most of their intervening opponents being buried under an avalanche of goals.

But February again proved the cruellest of months. It was hard to know which was worse, the fire that struck Pittodrie in February 1971 or the numbing departure of Martin Buchan a year later. Many considered Buchan to be the richest talent the club had ever known. He was barely into his twenties, was the established captain of the side, and brought a calm, cultured authority to his defending that alerted clubs the length and breadth of Britain.

Even so, the announcement that he had signed for Frank O'Farrell's Manchester United came as a bolt from the blue. A pall hung over Pittodrie for months, exacerbated when Turnbull's Hibs booted a Buchan-less Aberdeen out of the Scottish Cup. Of the nine league games outstanding after Buchan's departure, Aberdeen won just three, finishing ten points behind Celtic. Once again the season stretched too long. The Dons harvested thirty points from their first seventeen games, only twenty from the last seventeen, which was little better than mid-table form. By the turn of the year Aberdeen had lost the knack of scoring away from home.

Yet one diamond shone throughout Aberdeen's frustrating season. Joe Harper's 33 league goals were a post-war record for the club. English hawks were poised to swoop for him, too.

Match of the Season

Aberdeen 1   Juventus 1
UEFA Cup, 2nd Round, 2nd Leg, 17 November 1971

The Fairs Cup, with its foolish aims and foolish name, had become the UEFA Cup. Aberdeen's reward for overcoming Celta Vigo in Round 1 was a plum tie with Juventus, the biggest name ever paired with the Dons. Juventus had won the Italian championship six times since 1945, most recently in 1967.

Furino was the only current Juventus player to have helped Italy to the 1970 World Cup Final, though the blond German, Helmut Haller, had played and scored against England in the 1966 final. Defender Salvadore had faced Scotland twice in 1966 qualifiers. It was, however, their emerging stars which made Jueventus such a force. Pietro Anastasi was the world's most expensive footballer. Striker Roberto Bettega and winger Franco Causio would put England to the sword in the 1974 qualifiers.

Juventus had lost the final of the last, 1970-71, Fairs Cup to Leeds United on the away-goals rule, and were almost unchanged to face the Dons. Keeper Carmignani was new, and Causio was banned from the first leg, having been sent off against Marsa of Malta in Round 1.

Aberdeen's hopes were dashed within five minutes in Turin, when Anastasi finished a coruscating run with a mighty shot. A deflected free-kick in the second half added to Aberdeen's woes and left them chasing the improbable at Pittodrie. This did little to deter 30,000 supporters – Aberdeen's biggest gate for a European tie – from turning up. It was only seven days since Pittodrie hosted its first international, and midweek European nights were acquiring the special atmosphere that would become such a feature of the 1980s.

DID YOU KNOW?

Heart's Donald Ford scored 10 league goals against Aberdeen between October 1967 and November 1973.

Harper challenges Celtic's Evan Williams and Jim Brogan, 11 March 1972

The Dons hoped to have recruited a secret weapon in the early winter snow that sprinkled the pitch. Half-time arrived with the contest goalless, but five minutes after the change-round Anastasi wrong-footed Buchan to shoot inside Clark's near post. The contest was over – Aberdeen needed to score four – though Harper salvaged some pride with a late header. Juventus thereby became the first European opponents to escape defeat at Pittodrie.

Juventus tumbled in a semi-final against Wolves, who in turn lost an all-English final to Tottenham.

SCOTTISH LEAGUE DIVISION 1   1972-73

Division 1	Fourth
League Cup	Semi-Final
Scottish Cup	Quarter-Final
UEFA Cup	First Round

Behind the scenes everything was falling apart. Turnbull had gone, Buchan too. The dressing room was full of airy talk of fancy money to be earned in England and severe turbulence lay ahead. The disharmony overshadowed the arrival of Drew Jarvie from Airdrie. Jarvie had earned three Scottish caps, each as substitute.

The League Cup went soft, allowing two teams through from each section. Aberdeen crushed both 'Queens' to accompany Hibs through to a newly constituted Round 2. Falkirk and East Fife put up little resistance to the Dons' march to the semis, by which time they had logged an improbable 36 goals.

The semi-final with Celtic was Harper's penultimate match before leaving. He had become the latest Don to rise to international ranks, winning two caps against Denmark. Now he shattered Aberdeen's transfer record by signing for Everton for £185,000. The lure of industrial Lancashire had claimed Aberdeen's star defender and star forward. It seemed that Bobby Clark was on the move too, but a proposed deal with Stoke City – who had lost Gordon Banks to an eye injury – fell through. Even so, the despair hanging over Pittodrie was palpable. Many lifelong supporters vowed never again to set foot inside the stadium. Their threats were happily short-lived, but perhaps only because of a will-o'-the-wisp Hungarian footballer by the name of Zoltan Varga, who paraded his talent from October 1972 to April 1973. Varga arrived from Hertha Berlin under a cloud – later disclosed to be a bribery scandal – and when he left Scotland eventually found his way to Ajax, who needed to fill the chasm left by Johan Cruyff's departure to Barcelona. Varga's six months at Pittodrie were enough to convince many fans that they were witnessing the most extravagantly gifted player ever to pull on an Aberdeen shirt.

But not even Varga could help overturn Celtic. Aberdeen's biggest problem was inconsistency. They scored an 8, 7, 6, 5 (twice) and 4 (five times); yet also failed to score on twelve occasions.

DID YOU KNOW?

Aberdeen scored 8 second-half goals v Falkirk in the 1972-73 League Cup.

DID YOU KNOW?

Drew Jarvie scored in each of his first four League Cup matches for Aberdeen.

Celtic saw off the Dons' challenge in all three competitions. They added to their League Cup scalp by winning a Pittodrie replay in the Scottish Cup – courtesy of Billy McNeill's late header. They had already completed the league double. Four wins in one season over Aberdeen had turned the clock back years.

The Dons finished fourth, a distant fourteen points behind Jock Stein's eight-times champions, but high enough to secure a place in next season's UEFA Cup.

The season offered a little cameo as postscript. Half an hour from the end of the final game – at Cappielow – Jimmy Bonthrone threw on a young substitute. His name was Willie Miller. For those brief, fleeting minutes the future Aberdeen captain humbly shared the stage with arguably to the most magical Don of all – Zoltan Varga.

Match of the Season (1)

Aberdeen 2   Borussia Moenchengladbach 3
UEFA Cup, 1st Round, 1st Leg, 13 September 1972

Borussia Moenchengladbach are not considered among the natural aristocrats of the Bundesliga. Bayern Munich, Eintracht Frankfurt, Cologne, Hamburg, Werder Bremen and Borussia Dortmund rank higher in the German soccer hierarchy. Borussia's home is a small town in the Rheinland, not far from the Dutch border. In the early 1970s the club burst into life and for a few years its fame marched hand in hand with that of the German national team.

Borrusia claimed the German championship for the first time in 1970 and retained it in 1971. Early excursions in Europe were ended by Everton, on penalties, and Inter Milan. In April 1972 a German team containing Borussia's Netzer, Vogts, Heynckes and Bonhof had made a mockery of England at Wembley. Netzer was one of the most charismatic midfielders of his day, and Vogts a redoubtable full-back later to mastermind Germany in Euro 96.

The tie lived up to its billing. Netzer took centre stage at Pittodrie, fair hair streaming over his shoulders, spraying passes with geometric precision. One pass carved a goal for Heynckes, which put the Germans two up. A thigh strain prevented Netzer's reappearance for the second half. Harper quickly pulled a goal back. Jarvie headed a second, and the din from Pittodrie could be heard in Stonehaven. It was silenced by a breakaway goal which restored the Germans' advantage and sealed Aberdeen's first home defeat in Europe. With three away goals to Borussia's credit, Aberdeen would have to win 2-0 or 3-1 in Germany to go through.

Owing to a UEFA ban, imposed on Borussia for crowd trouble, the return leg was played in Nuremburg. Netzer was still out. At half-time Aberdeen led 3-2, it was 5-5 overall, and they stood on the threshold of a sensational triumph. Alas, four German goals in the final twenty minutes burst the bubble. One moment the Dons were dreaming of making headlines, the next they were nursing their heaviest aggregate defeat.

No opponents got within five goals of Borussia until they faced Liverpool in the final. Liverpool won 3-2 on aggregate.

Match of the Season (2)

Celtic 3   Aberdeen 2

League Cup, Semi-Final, 27 November 1972

Aberdeen's six-game unbeaten run against Celtic ended 2-3 at Pittodrie in October 1972. A month later, on a filthy wet Monday evening, the teams lined up at Hampden for a League Cup semi-final. While Celtic were racing away with the championship, Aberdeen seemed less potent than of late.

Jock Stein needed a large pool of players to wage war on many fronts. Regulars McNeill, Murdoch, and Macari were missing, but there was room for Dalglish and Deans, who between them accounted for half Celtic's goals this season.

The Dons' side was settled. This was one of the few times Varga and Harper played together. Varga had scored both Dons' goals in that recent defeat by Celtic.

Those supporters deterred from travelling by the weather missed a thriller. Few teams enjoyed the luxury of leading Celtic once, never mind twice. Hood's penalty had cancelled out Harper's opener, but with sixteen minutes to play Robb headed in Varga's corner to make it 2-1. A place in the final beckoned.

The explosion of joy lasted less than a minute. Jimmy Johnstone beat Clark from close range, with Dons defenders raising their arms in a mute plea to the linesman. There was no stopping Celtic now, and five minutes later Callaghan volleyed their third goal. The best Aberdeen could hope for was extra-time, but that was denied them by Evan Williams' block from Ian Taylor.

It was Jimmy Bonthone's first and last Hampden semi-final. He would never again come so close to winning a trophy for the Dons. Eddie Turnbull's Hibs beat Celtic in the final.

Manchester United's Martin Buchan exchanges pennants with Steve Murray, in a match played as part of Buchan's transfer

Manchester City's Denis Law shakes hands with Willie Young before this friendly

SCOTTISH LEAGUE DIVISION 1   1973-74

Division 1	Fourth
League Cup	Quarter-Final
Scottish Cup	Third Round
UEFA Cup	Second Round

1973-74 was the season two substitutes were introduced into Scottish football and when Aberdeen became universally popular in the world of Pools punters. They took on the role of the nation's draw specialists, having more matches squared than in any other season since World War II.

For a side accustomed to winning, this new trait was hardly endearing to supporters. Nor was the loss of yet more players. The midfield had been stripped of Varga and skipper Steve Murray, who had added insult by signing for Celtic. Jim Forrest had also played his last match and was off to South Africa. Bonthrone felt increasingly beleaguered, partly because he had been unable to prevent the exodus, partly because he had been unable to recruit decent replacements, and partly because of what Turnbull was achieving down at Easter Road. Hibs were a shambles when Turnbull arrived. Within two seasons they had won the League Cup and finished higher than Aberdeen; this time they would push Celtic hard for the championship. One sensed the likeable Bonthrone needed to pluck rabbits from hats to survive much longer.

Performances were predictable. The Dons' engine room lacked elbow grease and polish. Up front, the supply of goals without Joe Harper to score them dried up alarmingly. It was necessary to go back 25 years to find an Aberdeen team more goal-shy than this one. Fortunately, a robust defence marshalled by Willie Young and Willie Miller ensured a tight rein on the goals-against column. No fewer than twelve Aberdeen fixtures ended 0-0.

Drew Jarvie had arrived when the team was shedding its brightest and best. He could play with equal aplomb in midfield or attack, and banged in the goals no matter where he played. He had topped the Dons' scorers in his first season and would do so again now, in his second, by which time his tally would exceed fifty.

DID YOU KNOW?

Against Celtic in the League Cup on 21 November 1973 Aberdeen fielded three Millers – Willie, Jimmy, and substitute Bertie.

Aberdeen 1973-74. *Left to right. Back row:* Jim Hermiston, Billy Williamson, Joe Smith, Bobby Clark, Henning Boel, Andy Geoghegan, Eddie Thomson, Barrie Mitchell, Arthur Graham; *Front row:* Bertie Miller, Ian Purdie, Drew Jarvie, Willie Young, Ian Taylor, Alex Willoughby, Zoltan Varga.
Copyright Aberdeen F.C.

Aberdeen squad 1973-74

Despite the luxury of two teams qualifying from each League Cup section, the Dons required goal-difference to pip Dundee United for second spot. Stirling Albion had little chance to deny Aberdeen a place in the two-legged quarter-finals, where they were paired yet again with Celtic.

It was galling to see Steve Murray lining up for the opposition. The one consolation of losing Buchan and Harper was that they had gone south and would not rub salt into wounds by taking the field in Old Firm colours.

The first leg was at Parkhead on the last day of October, by which time the Dons were undefeated away from home in all competitions. Drew Jarvie did his bit, scoring twice, the first after just four minutes, but George McCluskey netted a third goal for the Celts, seconds after Jarvie's equaliser, to leave Aberdeen facing a one-goal deficit in the return leg. Owing to the power restrictions caused by the 'three-day week', this was played on a Wednesday afternoon. The game produced 47 free-kicks but no goals. Aberdeen were out.

The fixture list dictates that October and November is crunch time for clubs of Aberdeen's stature. That is when the later knock-out stages of the League Cup take place, interspersed with the second phase of European matches, when opponents are unlikely to be pushovers. Two games a week is the order of the day. A blank midweek as the nights draw in can only mean Aberdeen have fallen early.

It happens often that defeat in one tournament ushers in defeat in another. In 1973-74 this fate befell Aberdeen, who in the space of eight days lost three times in three competitions. It mattered little that they would not lose again till January. They had been dumped from two cups and barring a Celtic collapse had no realistic hope in the league.

Further back-to-back defeats in early January finally killed off Aberdeen's season and, looking back, put Bonthrone on borrowed time as a manager. What was particularly frustrating was that both defeats were at home, to Dundee in the first hurdle of the Scottish Cup, and to lowly St Johnstone in the league, in which Walker McCall made his debut. Giant defender Henning Boel quit the club soon afterwards. The season had almost four months to run, leaving Aberdeen nothing to play for. Attendances plummeted to a low of 3,945 against Ayr in April.

Even by finishing fourth Aberdeen failed to qualify for the UEFA Cup.

Match of the Season

Aberdeen 1   Tottenham Hotspur 1

UEFA Cup, 2nd Round, 1st Leg, 24 October 1973

Tottenham Hotspur were Aberdeen's first English opponents in official competition. The tie attracted an audience of 30,000, Pittodrie's biggest gate of the season.

In those days Spurs were as big a name as any in English football. Manchester United were headed for relegation, the Revie dynasty was ending at Leeds, and Liverpool had just won their first championship under Bill Shankly.

Spurs were old hands in Europe and had won the Cup-Winners' Cup in 1962-63 and the first UEFA Cup. Defending the latter in 1972-73 they reached the last four, where they lost on away goals to Liverpool, the eventual winners.

Not for some seasons had Spurs been a force in the English First Division. Indeed, they were down to fifteenth when they journeyed north for the first leg. Bill Nicholson was trying to rebuild, though in a couple of years Spurs would be relegated. The backbone of the side was familiar enough – Mike England and Joe Kinnear in defence; Martin Peters and Steve Perryman in midfield; Ralph Coates and super-Scot Alan Gilzean in attack. Goalkeeper Pat Jennings was missing for the first leg.

For their part Aberdeen were unbeaten in the league and through to the last eight of the League Cup. The season's disappointments all lay ahead. But other than through Jarvie, it was hard to see from what other source Aberdeen might score.

Spurs took an early lead. Willie Miller tackled Chris McGrath, the ball ran to Ralph Coates, and he stuck it past Clark from ten yards. Nicholson's favoured European tactics were to shut up shop to protect an away lead. Some suggested that as Aberdeen lacked firepower, Nicholson might have been better advised urging his players forward. Be that as it may, the score was unchanged until the closing minutes, at which point Ray Evans tripped Bertie Miller and Hermiston beat Barry Daines from the penalty spot.

The away goal meant a goalless draw at White Hart Lane would suffice for Spurs, for whom Jennings returned. Other than replacing Ian Taylor with Willoughby, Aberdeen were unchanged. The turning point came after sixteen minutes. Peters had moments earlier punished Miller's poor clearance to put Spurs ahead, when Jarvie had his legs whipped from under him. West German referee Tschenscher awarded a penalty, but irate Spurs players all but dragged him to consult a linesman, who convinced him otherwise.

Goals by Jimmy Neighbour and Jarvie made the aggregate score 3-2, with Aberdeen needing one more to triumph on away goals. Instead, Spurs scored twice in the final ten minutes.

Spurs marched on to the two-leg final, losing to Feyenoord.

SCOTTISH LEAGUE DIVISION 1   1974-75

Division 1	Fifth
League Cup	Third in section
Scottish Cup	Quarter-Final

After years of talk the complete restructuring of the Scottish League was upon us. Celtic's long monopoly was part of the problem. Cut off the dead-wood, it was argued, and let the big boys play each other four times a season. Tougher opposition would sharpen Scottish football and yield tougher champions. The smaller clubs in Division 1 did not like the sound of it. Gone would be the cash and kudos of playing Celtic and Rangers every year. Initially it was proposed to have a new top division of twelve clubs, playing 44 matches. This was later trimmed down to ten, playing 36, which was considered more conducive to long-term success in Europe. The new league would constitute an elite, with half its members qualifying for one European tournament or another.

To bring about this change, which would take effect from 1975-76, the existing Division 1 would be split in two, the top ten being founder members of the Premier League, the bottom eight joining with the top six from Division 2 to form a new Division 1. In effect, relegation was extended from two clubs to eight. The dog-fight would take place in mid-table, normally the habitat of turgid end-of-season fixtures. Those at the very bottom, who would ordinarily be struggling for their lives, would have long since known their fate. These would be the teams with nothing to play for, and these changed realities would affect the complexion of many a match.

Not since 1970 had Aberdeen finished outside the top four, and all things considered should have little difficulty in making the Premier League. But all concerned with the club sensed it was on a downward slide. Supporters were uneasy, too, with no European fixtures to look forward to, and no major signings to whet the appetite. One stalwart, Alec Willoughby, had gone and another – Dave Robb – would miss all but the final few games.

The experiment with the League Cup was abandoned; now it was back to one team qualifying. By losing their last match at Hearts the Dons failed to go through. No Europe, out of the League Cup, and the league too began badly. First visitors to Pittodrie were Hibs, who had a new face in their ranks. Joey Harper had failed to move mountains at Everton. Having scored twelve goals from forty league starts he sought to re-boot his career is Scotland, where his worth was appreciated. He harboured hopes of a return to Pittodrie, but ended up not with his former club but his former manager. The sight of Harper in Hibs' green merely emphasised the sterility of Aberdeen's own attack.

Harper did not leave pleasant memories. His late free-kick made it 2-2, and in injury-time his blocked effort fell to Cropley to score Hibs' winner. Not for fourteen years had Aberdeen lost a Pittodrie curtain-raiser. It was early days, but storm clouds were gathering.

Those much-loved midweek evenings under floodlights seemed like a distant memory. With only the league to focus upon, Aberdeen strung together five wins that by the end of October lifted them to third. Celtic promptly dumped them on their backsides and the Dons did not win again for nine matches. This run of defeats – which if unchecked might have threatened Aberdeen's position in the top ten – ended in the most unexpected of places, at Easter Road, in a match where mutual antipathies boiled over. One player apiece was sent off, Bobby Clark saved a penalty, and Willie Young kicked Joe Harper black and blue. More to the point, Billy Pirie's goal gave Aberdeen a 1-0 win.

In the Scottish Cup, the pairing with champions Rangers in Round 3 boosted the bank balance while dampening prospects for advancement. Aberdeen were three minutes from elimination when Miller chipped Kennedy to force a replay at Ibrox, the result of which would prove to be the highlight of the season.

In Round 4 Aberdeen travelled to Tannadice, to a ground where they had recently collapsed to a 0-4 defeat. Jim McLean's Dundee United were already beginning to make their presence felt, with Hamish McAlpine in goal and rumbustious young Andy Gray in attack. United's Frank Kopel would remember this cup-tie for all the wrong reasons. It was his back-pass that presented Aberdeen with a goal, and his miscue from the penalty spot after Miller handled five minutes from time that denied United a replay.

Perhaps this would be Aberdeen's year after all. Motherwell, who came out of the hat in the quarter-finals, were one of those dog-eat-dog mid-table teams preoccupied with securing a place in the Premier League. In any other season Motherwell would have had only the Scottish Cup to play for, and presented added dangers on that account. Now they would probably have washed their hands of the wretched pot in exchange for half a dozen league points.

The bad news was that Motherwell had hit form. Willie Pettigrew had sat on the bench for half a season and never scored when brought on. Since being restored in December he had gone berserk, bagging fifteen goals in thirteen games. He would end the season with 22. Here was a one-man band if ever there was one.

Perhaps Messrs Miller and Young were too preoccupied with him. Pettigrew played no part in Motherwell's goal, scored by Bobby Graham just before half-time, and try as they might the Dons could find no way back. Their season was over.

Aberdeen's fortunes in the mid-1970s were duplicating those of the late 1950s. Having won the championship in 1954-55 their points total dropped five seasons in a row. Similarly, following second place in 1970-71, Aberdeen's tally had also diminished, gradually but relentlessly, year by year. Next season – with two clubs to go down (a casualty rate of twenty per cent) – might see Aberdeen embroiled in the throes of relegation.

Match of the Season

Rangers 1   Aberdeen 2
Scottish Cup, 3rd Round replay, 10 February 1975

Jock Wallace's Rangers had ended Celtic's nine-year monopoly of the Scottish championship and were on schedule for retaining their crown. Spearheaded by Derek Parlane, Rangers failed to dispose of Aberdeen at the first attempt but were confident of doing so at the second. History was on their side: Aberdeen had never won a Scottish Cup-tie at Ibrox.

Aberdeen were unchanged for the replay; Rangers, playing in all white, switched McKean for McDougall. Inside two minutes Arthur Graham side-stepped Forsyth to put the Dons ahead. McKean's header restored parity before half-time. Under the watchful eye of referee Davidson, who had overseen Aberdeen's 1971 Scottish Cup win, the Dons held their own as the ninety minutes expired.

It was in the second period of extra-time that Aberdeen's two substitutes sprung the trap. Joe Smith may not have possessed the silky skills of brother Jim, but he was a neat enough player to carve a niche for himself in midfield. Now he met Arthur Graham's cross with a header that flew back of the post for Duncan Davidson to grab the winner.

This was Aberdeen's finest hour of 1974-75: there weren't many.

DID YOU KNOW?

In season 1971-72 Aberdeen had 5 current Scottish internationals.
Bobby Clark earned his last cap in the 0-5 defeat by England in February 1973.
No other Don was capped for two and a half years. Clark remained Aberdeen's
most-capped player until overtaken by Willie Miller.

3

THE TWO MACS
1975-1978

SCOTTISH PREMIER DIVISION   1975-76

Premier Division   Seventh
League Cup   Third in section
Scottish Cup   Fourth Round

For some years Aberdeen had been becalmed, with every indication that storms lay ahead. But few could have anticipated the waves which rolled over Pittodrie in the autumn of 1975.

When the players reassembled it was to welcome a third internationalist alongside Clark and Robb. Willie Miller, wearing number 8, had been capped in the 1-1 draw in Romania, the first Don to represent Scotland since Clark in February 1973.

Aberdeen had said goodbye to one player and hello to another. Jim Hermiston's retirement had been announced in advance. Jocky Scott, the newcomer, added bite in attack and began a relationship with the club that would endure, on and off, for sixteen years.

Excitement hung in the air at the prospect of so many big games. No more matches with the likes of Arbroath and Clyde. Instead a minimum of four against Rangers and Celtic – six against Celtic when the League Cup sections were announced. Attendances were certain to soar – in the Premier League if not the lower divisions – and for the moment few gave much thought to the problems of over-familiarity and the hatreds they would nourish.

The Dons were awful in the League Cup, suffering double defeats by Celtic and Hearts, and made an apologetic start to the league. In the first match, at Dens, Aberdeen led 2-1 but succumbed to two late goals. The match would be savoured by statisticians as the last occasion Dundee beat the Dons at home for many years, falling victim to one of the great jinxes of modern soccer.

Referee Gordon gives Dave Robb a finger-wagging v Rangers, 14 February 1976

Two goals by Motherwell's Willie Pettigrew denied Aberdeen a win in the first game at Pittodrie. The next visitors were Dundee United. Trailing at half-time, Aberdeen had Joe Smith sent off after a bust-up with Paul Hegarty. When the Dons fell further behind Bonthrone pulled off skipper Willie Young and sent on Billy Pirie. Young was incensed. Never in his career had he been substituted. Manager and player conducted an unseemly touchline row. Young flung his shirt at Bonthrone and stormed out.

Young already had a bad boy reputation. On a Scotland trip to Copenhagen he, and others, got into a scrape. Punishment would take the form of an international ban. Despite Young's talent and his raw courage, he would never win a full cap.

As for Aberdeen, it was hard to know which was the more damaging – the defeat which left them bottom of the league or the repercussions of Young's substitution. Bonthrone's authority had been publicly undermined. Young had to go, and within days he had signed for Tottenham Hotspur for £100,000.

The manager survived one more month. Form had not improved, and following back-to-back defeats by the Old Firm Bonthrone knew the time had come. The season was barely into October but Celtic had already beaten Aberdeen three times. Bonthrone became the first high-profile victim of the Premier League and its pressures.

It took almost a month to agree upon Bonthrone's replacement. As always in these situations, the question for the club is whether to recruit from within or without. Bonthrone had come from within. Coach George Murray hoped he would get his chance too, but was passed over in favour of Ally MacLeod, manager of Ayr United for the past nine years. Not the least of MacLeod's achievements was earning his part-timers a place in the new Premier League. But nine years is a long time for a managerial apprenticeship, and MacLeod's name was not usually short-listed when big jobs came around. Aberdeen were prepared to gamble where others were not.

MacLeod's most obvious quality was his rampant enthusiasm, which some interpreted as mindless bluster. He was not a man to stay quietly on the sidelines, or to use one word when ten would do. For a club grown used to Bonthrone's introspection, Aberdeen welcomed MacLeod as a breath of fresh air – though perhaps tornado might be a more fitting description.

He arrived in time for a 0-3 defeat at Motherwell and was left in no doubt as to the gravity of the Dons' plight. Ally's response was typical of what was to come. He urged sceptics to come to the Hearts game 'to see the rejuvenated Dons.' Some joke. The match was dreadful. His old team, Ayr, then beat his new one.

The barrage of quips and homespun wisdom never slackened, but games with Rangers and Celtic loomed and the league position was desperate. MacLeod had had the sense to appoint Willie Miller captain, and suddenly the storm clouds parted. Rangers were beaten at Pittodrie, Celtic at Parkhead. Nine unbeaten games, five wins, four draws, the Dons were in the top half and chasing a place in Europe.

MacLeod was succeeding where Bonthrone had failed with the same squad. The only changes were Andy Geoghegan's run in goal and a debut at centre-half for Willie Garner. MacLeod believed management was esentially about motivation.

His team, like the man, blew hot and cold. The Old Firm had started the winning run; now they started a losing one. On successive Saturdays Rangers won in league and Scottish Cup. The following week Celtic clocked their fourth win over the Dons, and this time the pit appeared to have no bottom. Fate played its part in Aberdeen's slide. March brought five defeats on the trot, four by the odd goal, three with the referee about to blow for time.

ABERDEEN HONOURS UNDER JIMMY BONTHRONE

None (except the Drybrough Cup).
Runners-up in Scottish Championship 1971-72. League-Cup semi-finalists 1972-73.

The league table was a mirage. As the season neared its climax the Dons were still fifth, but apart from St Johnstone, who had given up the ghost, half the division was slogging it out to avoid the dreaded ninth place. Safety beckoned with the penultimate match at St Johnstone, who hadn't won for 28 games and who had not kept a clean sheet since the first day of the season. Amazingly, incredibly, Aberdeen lost 0-2. They now had one foot and one heel over the precipice. The final match was against Turnbull's Hibs.

Match of the Season

Aberdeen 3   Hibernian 0

Premier Division, 24 April 1976

Supporters who lived through the agonies of 1994-95 may have forgotten that the crisis facing Ally MacLeod's team was even more acute. Survival under Roy Aitken could be guaranteed by wins over Dundee United and Dunfermline. In 1975-76, not even victory over Hibs could ensure safety, for results elsewhere could conspire to send Aberdeen down. This was the situation at kick-off time:

		P	W	D	L	F	A	(GD)	Pts
5	ABERDEEN	35	10	10	15	46	50	(-4)	30
6	Hearts	33	11	8	14	37	44	(-7)	30
7	Dundee Utd	33	11	7	15	44	47	(-3)	29
8	Ayr	33	12	5	16	39	52	(-13)	29
9	Dundee	34	10	9	15	47	61	(-14)	29
10	St Johnstone	34	3	4	27	29	78	(-49)	11

Outstanding fixtures: HEARTS – St Johnstone (h & a), Celtic (h); DUNDEE UTD – Rangers (h & a), Hibs (h); AYR – Celtic (a & h), Motherwell (h); DUNDEE – Motherwell (a & h).

With the exception of Dundee, who had one, each of Aberdeen's lowly rivals had two games in hand. Hearts, with two fixtures against St Johnstone, looked safe. Dundee United and Ayr, on the other hand, both had to face one or other of the Old Firm twice. Whatever else, Aberdeen had to beat Hibs.

One nightmare scenario could no longer happen. Joe Harper could not send Aberdeen down in the manner of Denis Law scoring for Manchester City against United. Hibs fans never viewed Harper as the ideal replacement for Jimmy O'Rourke, and MacLeod had brought him back north for a bargain £50,000. Harper, though, was signed after the transfer deadline and would take no part.

Training at Seaton Park in 1976. From right: Harper, Fleming, Sullivan, Kennedy

Hibs seemed likely to finish third – high enough for admission to the UEFA Cup – and had no other incentive than pride.

The match proved memorable for Dave Robb, who had been scoring goals for Aberdeen for ten seasons, and who at the peak of his prowess, in 1971-72, had been capped five times. Robb had only managed three goals thus far in 1975-76, and his heart must have been in his mouth when referee Anderson awarded the Dons an early penalty. Williamson and Scott were the regular takers, but Scott was on the bench and Robb took the kick. Alas, Hibs' new keeper, Mike McDonald from Stoke, dived to save.

One can scarcely imagine Robb's torment should Aberdeen have lost, but Jarvie netted on the half-hour and in the second half Joe Smith set Pittodrie alight with a scorching volley. Robb himself added a third a minute later.

The points were safe, but now all ears were tuned elsewhere. Hearts had beaten St Johnstone as expected. Ayr had astonishingly won at Parkhead. And though Dundee United had lost to Rangers they could still overtake Aberdeen.

The crucial result was Motherwell 1 Dundee 1. Dundee had led at half-time, but former Hibee Peter Marinello's equaliser left Dundee two points and thirteen goals behind the Dons, with one game left. Barring the proverbial divine intervention, Aberdeen were safe.

SCOTTISH PREMIER DIVISION   1976-77

Premier Division   Third
League Cup   Winners
Scottish Cup   Fourth Round

In football, as in life, the line between success and failure is wafer thin. Had Aberdeen mustered one fewer point they would have gone down and the extraordinary future awaiting Ally MacLeod would never have come to pass. He would instead have been vilified as the first manager to see Aberdeen relegated. Permitted a second chance he immediately sent for reinforcements. Full-back Stuart Kennedy was recruited from Falkirk and midfielder Dom Sullivan from Clyde. Harper was already back on board. After three and a half years King Joey had come home. He was 28 now, young enough to have another hundred goals in him.

The League Cup draw was kind. Ayr, Kilmarnock and St Mirren were all beatable in Section 2, and the Dons cruised through to the last eight. Harper scored in all six group games.

The only hiccup in Aberdeen's march to the final came against Alex Smith's Stirling Albion from Division 2. The two-leg quarter-final finished one goal apiece, with the Dons under the cosh during extra-time at rain-lashed Annfield Park. The decider, at Dens, meant an additional fixture, but it produced a 2-0 victory.

Both the Old Firm were in the hat for the semis, as were Hearts, who had a jinx on the Dons of late. Aberdeen were paired with champions Rangers, who had required *two* replays to get past Clydebank. Aberdeen crushed Rangers 5-1 in one of the shock scores of the decade. Scott's hat-trick and Jarvie's volley were the highlights of that Hampden occasion, which saw MacLeod and coach George Murray hugging each other like chimpanzees. In 1954 Aberdeen had beaten Rangers 6-0 in a Scottish Cup semi but lost the final to Celtic. MacLeod would write his own script.

Progress in the knock-outs would be poor consolation for another struggle in the league. An early 5-0 win at Ayr hinted at better things. Points were tucked away regularly, and as the season took shape it became clear Aberdeen would win more than they lost. Apart from a 0-1 reverse at Ibrox Aberdeen went the first quarter of the season unbeaten. By overcoming Motherwell on 2 November the Dons went top, and by beating Celtic at Hampden four days later capitalised on a change of rules which permitted League Cup winners entry to the UEFA Cup. Aberdeen had been out of Europe for three seasons and MacLeod could seemingly do no wrong.

Ian Fleming misses with this header in the 0-0 draw v Hibs, 9 April 1977

DID YOU KNOW?

Joe Harper scored in 7 consecutive League Cup-ties in 1976. The run ended at Stirling Albion.

The winning ways persisted till January, when four successive draws enabled Celtic to leapfrog the Dons and pull away. The second half of the season was something of a let-down. From 8 January the Dons won just five of nineteen games. Rangers, too, swept past them, and Aberdeen lost at Pittodrie in the Scottish Cup for the third time in four years. The victors were Gordon Strachan's Dundee in a Fourth Round replay. Willie Miller's fluffed back-pass came at a time in the skipper's career when he was still fallible. The crowd did not spare Miller's feelings. They were not to know that in a few years Willie Miller would become to all intents invincible.

In fact, so many Dons had played below par that a match-rigging scandal broke. Certain players had allegedly bet on Dundee at 8-1 to win. It was nonsense, of course, and the affair quickly subsided.

Nevertheless, it left an unpleasant aftertaste to a season in which Aberdeen rediscovered their self-belief and when the first trophy for six years decorated the board-room. MacLeod had made a bigger splash than even he could have anticipated. And his timing was impeccable. When Willie Ormond quit as manager of the Scottish national team the telephone rang at Pittodrie. Ernie Walker of the SFA was on the line and wanted to offer the job to MacLeod.

Match of the Season

Celtic 1   Aberdeen 2

League Cup Final, 6 November 1976

That Aberdeen were the underdogs went without saying. This was Celtic's thirteenth consecutive appearance in League Cup finals, a run that dated back to Jock Stein's arrival at Parkhead. Not that Celtic had fond recent memories: they had lost five of the last six. Aberdeen were appearing in their first final for 21 years.

Willie Garner had taken over from Willie Young in central defence, Stuart Kennedy had displaced Ian Hair at right-back, and Dave Robb had been ousted by the return of wee Joey. Robb was substitute, and would play a vital part in the unfolding drama.

Aberdeen had the worst possible start. All teams contesting cup finals with Old Firm opponents know the peril of conceding a quick goal. Only eleven minutes into the game referee Paterson blew for a penalty against Jarvie for tripping Dalglish. The Dons were furious, and Dalglish was jostled by Harper after converting the kick.

The Dons needed to strike back quickly, and they did when Harper headed Graham's centre across goal for Jarvie to nod past Peter Latchford.

None disputed Celtic's territorial superiority in the second half, but they could find no way through and extra-time was called upon. Robb had replaced Jarvie, and three minutes into the added period put Aberdeen ahead for the first time. There were 27 minutes to survive and Clark's goal had some narrow squeaks. But the Dons held out, encouraged by the vociferous encouragement of 17,000 supporters. Willie Miller was man enough to admit that fortune favoured Aberdeen on the day. Luck is part and parcel of football and Ally MacLeod exploited it to the full. He was that kind of man and that kind of manager. Everything he touched at Pittodrie turned to gold; everything he touched for Scotland would turn sour.

ABERDEEN HONOURS UNDER ALLY MacLEOD

1. Scottish League Cup 1976-77.

SCOTTISH PREMIER DIVISION   1977-78

Premier Division	Runners-Up
League Cup	Third Round
Scottish Cup	Runners-Up
UEFA Cup	First Round

No club tries seriously to block someone who has been offered control of the national team. Though Aberdeen needed a second manager in eighteen months they had the whole summer and did not need to rush.

Three men were short-listed. Alex Stuart had done well as successor to MacLeod at Ayr. He had the advantage of being an Aberdonian, but Ayr did not relish any more disruption. Alex Ferguson was a headstrong young manager who had just guided St Mirren to the First Division championship. His would have been a risky appointment. Billy McNeill had the highest profile of the three. He had been captain of Celtic's Lisbon Lions and, for sure, had been properly schooled under Jock Stein. Though McNeill was short of managerial experience, having only recently taken the job at Clyde, his other qualities – leadership, a natural winner, Stein's tutelage – swung it his way.

Looking ahead, many of the arguments over Willie Miller's appointment were aired over McNeill. Neither had any managerial experience worth mentioning. Both were one-club men, captains of club and country. The fact that one enjoyed a fine managerial career while the other encountered problems suggests that experience was immaterial. McNeill took to the job in the manner born.

In McNeill's case, being a Celtic man might even count against him. Indeed, his first public act at Pittodrie was to stride onto the pitch wearing Aberdeen red, a declaration that loyalty to the green was (temporarily) forgotten.

The transfer front had been quiet of late, though McNeill would have to make do without Arthur Graham, a favourite of the fans, who in July signed for Leeds. Like Willie Young, Graham was serving an international ban. But in Graham's case it was lifted. Though never capped with Aberdeen, the Scotland call-up was not long delayed.

Popular as he was, Graham's loss was not felt so deeply, partly because John McMaster, who took his place, was no slouch, partly because McNeill's team proved even better than MacLeod's. The Dons embarked on a spirited campaign marred only by the absence of silverware to show for their efforts.

SUN SOCCERCARD No 801 · J. FLEMING (Aberdeen)

SUN SOCCERCARD No 717 · D. SULLIVAN (Aberdeen)

SUN SOCCERCARD No 634 · D. JARVIE (Aberdeen)

Popular soccer cards dating from the 1977-78 season

Since its inception after the war, the League Cup had begun on a group basis. But the drawbacks of adding six – often meaningless – fixtures brought about its eventual abandonment. The League Cup now experimented with knock-out principles, two-legged up to and including the quarter-finals. This format enabled the league season to commence in August rather than September.

McNeill's baptism was Rangers at home. Harper and Jarvie got the goals in a 3-1 win and the crowd filed away at the end full of hope. They would not be quickly disabused. On the morning of 28 September Aberdeen stood top of the league with eleven points out of twelve. They were through to Round 3 of the League Cup, where Rangers awaited, and that evening they hoped to finish off the Belgians of RWD Molenbeek in the UEFA Cup. Those longed-for autumn evenings when Pittodrie reverberated to the thrills and spills of European and League Cup football looked to be on their way back.

In the blink of an eye Aberdeen were out of Europe, out of the Cup, and had lost twice in the league. The most crippling loss came at Ibrox in the League Cup. The Dons had not previously conceded more than a goal a game to Scottish opponents, but Rangers hammered six, leaving Aberdeen battered and bruised. They could do little but recoup some pride in the return leg. To lose their grip on the trophy in such fashion shook the Dons to the core.

Celtic's Peter Latchford saves from Drew Jarvie at Pittodrie, 17 September 1977

This was the first major test of McNeill's management. He took a while to sort matters out and it was December before the team began again to play with confidence. By then they had dropped to fourth and had much leeway to make up.

McNeill was not one for chopping and changing. But during that autumn slump he lost one player and acquired another. The one he lost was Joe Smith, his career wrecked by injury against Clydebank. The one he gained was Gordon Strachan, a flame-haired, impudent little scamp who caught the eye when playing for Dundee, most. recently in the Dons' Scottish Cup defeat in March.

Strachan was raw, and far from the finished article. McNeill used him sparingly, as at first would Alex Ferguson. In January 1978 McNeill introduced two more fresh faces, and these, like Strachan, were destined for great things. Steve Archibald had impressed McNeill at Clyde and settled quickly into attack. Alex McLeish, not yet nineteen, and gangly like a colt, was introduced briefly when McNeill saw fit to discipline a couple of players, including Willie Garner, his regular centre-half.

Defeat at Hibs on 17 December proved to be a watershed, for Aberdeen would not lose again till May. In the league they would not lose at all, and in the Scottish Cup coasted – with the exception of the tie with Morton, who commanded a replay – all the way to the final. With a tight defence, and goals spread around all departments, the Dons advanced to a double-headed confrontation with Rangers. In the league they thrashed them twice and briefly overtook them, but Rangers' games in hand proved decisive.

The last match at Pittodrie under McNeill was rich in symbolism and irony. It was against Alex Ferguson's St Mirren, who had found it tough in the Premier League and had barely warded off relegation. In later years Ferguson would swoop on Love St for several of his former starlets, though the only one now to have broken through was Billy Stark. The likes of Peter Weir and Dougie Bell were still coming through the ranks.

St Mirren stunned Pittodrie by taking a two-goal lead inside ten minutes. If Fergie's face was a picture then, imagine it at the end, by which time Aberdeen had scored four. The championship would go to the wire. Rangers led by a point, but had a weaker goal-difference. Even if Aberdeen won at Hibs, which they did not, it would be meaningless if Rangers beat Motherwell at Ibrox – which they did. It was small consolation that, come what may at Hampden, Aberdeen would contest next season's Cup-Winners' Cup.

McNeill had seven days in which to recharge his players. Though the Dons wilted on the day, permitting Jock Wallace to celebrate his second treble, McNeill had built a resilient team. McNeill, not Jock Wallace, was voted Scottish manager of the year. It was therefore a bitter blow for Aberdeen when Jock Stein stood down at Parkhead. McNeill had proved himself worthy and his departure was inevitable. Once again Aberdeen were without a manager.

ABERDEEN HONOURS UNDER BILLY McNEILL

None.
Runners-up in Scottish Championship and Scottish Cup 1977-78.

Match of the Season (1)

Aberdeen 1   RWD Molenbeek 2
UEFA Cup, 1st Round, 2nd Leg, 28 September 1977

Few today, outside Belgium, are familiar with the name of RWD Molenbeek. The mid-70s was a comparative golden age for the Brussels club, claiming their one and only championship in 1974-75. They did not dally in the European Cup, but in 1976-77 challenged hard for the UEFA Cup. Their journey ended in the semi-finals, where they lost to Athletic Bilbao on away goals.

Their recent record suggested Molenbeek might be too strong for Aberdeen, for whom only Clark, Miller, Jarvie and Harper could call upon prior European experience. Judging by the Dons' composed performance in the scoreless first leg, which drew praise from neutrals, Aberdeen had only to keep their heads to progress to Round 2.

Half-time arrived at Pittodrie with the tie still goalless. Seconds after the resumption Miller missed a cross and Gorez headed in. Aberdeen now needed two. Jarvie brought Pittodrie to its feet when keeper Ruiter deflected a cross to his feet, and for six minutes all was pandemonium as the Dons piled forward. Their defence was threadbare when Wellens scored again for the Belgian club. Never before or since have Aberdeen drawn an away first leg in Europe and failed to capitalise.

Molenbeek lost in the next round, to Carl Zeiss Jena of East Germany, on penalties.

Match of the Season (2.)

Rangers 2   Aberdeen 1

Scottish Cup Final, 6 May 1978

It was eight years since Aberdeen had last contested a Scottish Cup Final, and despite the passage of time Bobby Clark and Joe Harper would play in both games. Clark, now 32, held more caps than any other Aberdeen player. Though he would not play, he had also been named in Ally MacLeod's World Cup squad. Two other Dons – Stuart Kennedy and Joe Harper – would see action in Argentina. Willie Miller was held on stand-by, in case of any call-offs, but was not summoned.

With Drew Jarvie having been capped for Airdrie, almost half the Aberdeen side were full internationals. The Final would bypass Archibald, who was ineligible, and Strachan, who was too inconsistent to be considered.

Previous results gave little clue to the outcome. In Rangers' favour was the 6-1 demolition in the League Cup. This was offset by the Dons' 23-game unbeaten run and by having beaten Rangers three times in the league, scoring eleven goals in the process.

As for McNeill, he had been waging war against Rangers in cup finals as long as he could remember. There was no more natural adversary for him, and no team would give him greater pleasure to beat. McNeill knew enough about motivation to ensure the Dons were, in the modern vernacular, 'up for the game'. It is therefore all the more surprising to record that his team flopped, frozen solid by the occasion, and grateful only to the extent that they did not endure another 1-6 debacle.

Duncan Davidson's overhead kick at Pittodrie v Morton, 11 March 1978

2-1 to Rangers sounds close. In truth, it was not. Spurred on by Bobby Russell, Rangers spent most of the game attacking Aberdeen from all angles. Alex MacDonald's glancing header should have been saved. But Clark had strayed from his goal, his weight was on the wrong foot, and he was static as the ball trundled past him.

Rangers' second goal, a header by Derek Johnstone, was remarkable chiefly for the fact that he was left completely alone as Tommy McLean's cross floated into the box.

The contest was dead, the atmosphere as subdued as anyone could remember in a Hampden final. The one remaining incident was so comical that, even though it went in Aberdeen's favour, they could have done without it. Steve Ritchie should have burst the net from six yards. His miscue summed up the Dons that day. The ball looped in the gentlest of arcs, bouncing down and beyond Peter McCloy as the keeper swung monkey-fashion on his crossbar.

Five minutes remained for the Dons to force a replay. Any other team would have camped in the opposition goalmouth, but even that proved beyond Aberdeen, who could not escape quickly enough to the sanctuary of their dressing room. They had played like strangers to one another and no one knew why.

It was a tribute to the team that the Hampden nightmare was forgiven. Thousands turned out to cheer them back home.

4

THE YOUNGER FERGIE 1978-1982

SCOTTISH PREMIER DIVISION   1978-79

Premier Division   Fourth
League Cup   Runners-Up
Scottish Cup   Semi-Final
European Cup-Winners' Cup   Second Round

Once again the search was on for a manager. George Murray had been passed over twice, and McNeill had brought in John Clark as his number two. The fact that the two Macs had gone to bigger jobs so quickly diminished the sense of expectancy at Pittodrie. It was asking much to strike gold three times in a row.

Coincidence now played its hand. Upheavals were going on all over the place, not only at Rangers and Celtic, but also at St Mirren, who joined the merry-go-round by firing Alex Ferguson. Ferguson had been among those considered for the Dons' job a year earlier. He had been recommended by the departing Ally MacLeod, under whom he had played at Ayr in 1973-74. Now that Ferguson was unemployed, he could be offered the post speedily and without complications.

His arrival was not universally applauded in the north-east. He was only 35, had a reputation as a hot-head both as a player and a manager, and the circumstances of his sacking at Love St, whatever the rights and wrongs, suggested he might be difficult to handle. Aberdeen were, and are, a club who likes to do things by the book. Image is important, and rightly so. It says much for the chemistry between manager and chairman Dick Donald that all worked out so well. Ferguson took time to acclimatise, as he would later at Old Trafford. In his first season at Pittodrie he was distracted by his father's illness, which required frequent visits to Glasgow, and the back-lash of his departure from St Mirren, the murky circumstances of which were being thrashed out by a tribunal.

Ferguson inherited McNeill's squad, with the exception of Dave Robb, who went to America. Ferguson also parted with Ian Fleming and Ian Gibson, and temporarily lost the services Bobby Clark with a fractured knuckle. This gave an early baptism for Jim Leighton. McNeill's last signing, Ian Scanlon, laid claim to the No 11 shirt.

The Dons made a good start. Garner's broken leg in Bulgaria opened the way for McLeish and Rougvie, who shared the centre-half responsibilities until Garner returned. A late Sullivan equaliser at building-site Ibrox kept the Dons unbeaten and denied struggling Rangers their first win. A 4-1 victory over Billy McNeill's Celtic was the highlight of those early weeks but, as the season unravelled, points became harder to earn. Whispers from Pittodrie suggested certain players were none too impressed with their new boss.

At one point the Dons won only four of twenty league games, including a three month gap between one victory and the next. By mid-March they had slumped to mid-table. The slide was all the more frustrating, as it was turning into the most open championship in years and would eventually be won with the fewest points.

Most of the winter was lost to inclement weather. Celtic suffered more than anyone, going two and a half months without a league game. They tumbled from first to eighth but capitalised on their games in hand to overhaul Rangers and Dundee United at the death. The Dons could do no better than finish a distant fourth.

What sustained Aberdeen's season was the two domestic cups. Aberdeen enjoyed a clear run through the early rounds of the League Cup, which produced a two-legged quarter-final with Ayr. Ally MacLeod had met his nemesis in Argentina and was now back managing where he started. In the first leg at Somerset Park, which ended 3-3, MacLeod became so agitated that referee Brian McGinlay booked him and ushered him from the stand. Steve Archibald was sent off, too. The Dons came from behind in the return leg to earn a Dens Park semi-final against Hibs. The tie went to extra-time before Hibs' man-of-the-match goalkeeper, Mike McDonald, got in a tizzy and fumbled Stuart Kennedy's cross into his own net.

The Arctic winter delayed the final for three and a half months. In other words, the two domestic cups overlapped, the one starting before the other had finished, contrary to time-honoured practice. In the Scottish Cup quarter-final the Dons needed a meteoric volley by Joe Harper to force a Parkhead replay, which was notable for the ill-grace with which Celtic supporters and players accepted defeat. Skirmishes on the terraces and in the players' tunnel greeted Ferguson's first victory on Old Firm territory.

Harper's penalty is saved by Brcic in this match v Morton, 30 December 1978

In the same match, which Aberdeen lost 1-2, Archibald misses at the far post

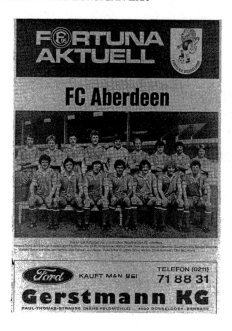

Match programme of Fortuna Dusseldorf v Aberdeen, 18 October 1978

Aberdeen suffered defeat by Rangers in the League Cup Final before Hibs exacted revenge for their earlier semi-final loss, coming from behind to win 2-1 at a dank and misty Hampden to stake a place in the Scottish Cup Final. If Aberdeen no longer feared Ibrox or Parkhead, the same could not be said of the national stadium, which still exerted something of a hoodoo influence. Ferguson began his Aberdeen career with two Hampden defeats, McNeill had lost there too, as had Jimmy Bonthone. Since Turnbull in 1970, only Ally MacLeod knew the exhilaration of winning there.

'Fair, but could do better,' would be any headmaster's report on Alex Ferguson's first term in office. 'Outstanding' would be that same headmaster's verdict on Joe Harper. In the three seasons since his return he had scored 28, 27, and now 33 goals. He ranked – and ranks – as the highest scoring Don in history.

Match of the Season (1)

Aberdeen 2 Fortuna Dusseldorf 0
Cup-Winners' Cup, 2nd Round, 2nd Leg, 1 November 1978

Toppling Rangers and Celtic was Ferguson's pressing ambition, but lurking not far behind was the desire to build a team fit to challenge in Europe. McNeill had bequeathed a place in the Cup-Winners' Cup, plunging Ferguson for the first time into the alien world of international club football.

Three goals by the Petrov brothers earned a narrow first-leg win for Marek Dimitrov in Bulgaria, though the deficit was overturned in an exhilarating second half at Pittodrie. Aberdeen's opponents in Round 2 were nearer to home and immeasurably stronger. West Germany had won the World Cup in 1974 and Bayern Munich had three times lifted the European Cup.

Fortuna Dusseldorf were, on paper, one of Germany's lesser lights. They had not won a domestic trophy since the war, though they would capture the German Cup this season and next. They had lost the 1978 German Cup Final but were admitted to the Cup-Winners' Cup by the same back door as Aberdeen. Cologne, like Rangers, had achieved the double. Fortuna's most recent Euro excursion had been in 1973-74 and 1974-75. Both times they reached Round 3 of the UEFA Cup. The pick of their current players was striker Klaus Allofs, who would score West Germany's winning goal against Scotland in World Cup 86.

There was only one horse at the races in Dusseldorf. On the quarter-hour the ball skidded off John McMaster's head, allowing Gunther the first goal. If the Dons could keep it at that, they might survive, but Gunther burst through to double the lead and nine minutes from time Zimmermann's 25-yard free-kick flew into the net off Leighton's finger-tips.

Ferguson recalls that after the game many of his players went night-clubbing in Dusseldorf. The team paid the price by losing at home to Hearts on Saturday, and Ferguson vowed never again to permit midweek late nights and partying.

Three-goal deficits are considered irretrievable in Europe. Aberdeen have never yet recovered from such a margin. The crowd at Pittodrie was smaller than that to see Marek Dimitrov in Round 1, which suggests supporters knew the game was up. Those who stayed away missed a night of frenzied action. Bobby Clark came in for his first game of the season, and Ferguson judged the situation ripe for the explosive but as yet raw talent of Gordon Strachan.

Strachan was prominent as Aberdeen laid siege to the German goalmouth. It looked all over when half-time arrived scoreless but two goals in three minutes set up a furious finale, with the ball bouncing off defenders and woodwork to the end. Ferguson learned lessons in defeat, notably that teams cannot expect to prosper by conceding three goals in every away leg.

Fortuna advanced to the final, where they lost 3-4 after extra-time to Valencia.

Drew Jarvie is tackled by Celtic's Edvaldsson at Pittodrie, 7 October 1978

Match of the Season (2)

Rangers 2   Aberdeen 1

League Cup Final, 31 March 1979

Alex Ferguson, like MacLeod and McNeill, took Aberdeen to a cup final in his first season. Inevitably, it was one of the Old Firm who awaited. Rangers were not faring well under John Greig. League encounters between the sides had ended all-square. Both clubs were still coming to terms with their new managers.

Ferguson had heard about the big Hampden freeze the previous May. He might not be able to guarantee victory, but he would make sure his players gave of their best. With Sullivan unfit and Scanlon in two minds about going to America, Ferguson played McMaster in midfield behind three front men: Archibald, Harper, and Duncan Davidson. Mark McGhee had just been signed from Newcastle, but Ferguson considered it unwise to launch him into a cup final.

Derek Johnstone enjoyed a chequered Rangers career alternating between centre-half and all-action striker. He was operating in defence when sending Archibald spinning in the first minute, incapacitating the Aberdeen player to such an extent that Archibald remained on the fringes for the rest of the game.

St Mirren's Billy Thomson saves from Mark McGhee at Pittodrie, 28 April 1979

The Dons certainly did not freeze on the day. They scored first, courtesy of Davidson's header, and looked to be holding out comfortably until Rangers levelled out of the blue. John McMaster's heel deflected Alex MacDonald's shot beyond Clark's reach.

Aberdeen were now on the back foot, extra-time the summit of their ambitions. Doug Rougvie had already been one of six players booked when he was involved in an off-the-ball clash with Derek Johnstone, who had switched to attacking mode. Johnstone lay prostrate for several minutes, and – though it is doubtful he had seen what had taken place – referee Ian Foote sent Rougvie off. TV cameras missed the incident, but a tearful Rougvie denied any wrong-doing. Johnstone was accused of conning the ref, and relations between the clubs would be soured in consequence. More to the point, Aberdeen were down to ten men, and of these Clark and Archibald were walking wounded.

To cap it all, six minutes into injury time Aberdonian Colin Jackson planted a header wide of Clark to win the day for Rangers.

SCOTTISH PREMIER DIVISION   1979-80

Premier Division	Champions
Bell's League Cup	Runners-Up
Scottish Cup	Semi-Final
UEFA Cup	First Round

1979-80 was a peculiar, if ultimately memorable season. It was the year that one trophy seemingly destined for Pittodrie slipped away, while another, altogether bigger, prize suddenly ended up in Aberdeen's lap.

Alex Ferguson had had his season of grace, which all managers demand though not all are fortunate enough to enjoy. Fergie's personal difficulties were behind him. The transfer market had been reasonably quiet. Sullivan had gone to Celtic for £82,000. The only players set to break into the side were fringe players, plus Dougie Bell, who Fergie had poached from St Mirren on a free transfer.

The season got off to a dreadful start, a last-minute defeat at Partick brought about by McLeish's handball. It was afterwards that Ferguson uttered his famous remark: 'Don't laugh, but I've got a scent about the way things are going to turn out this season.' Ferguson may have doubted his own words when Aberdeen lost at Morton, then at Arbroath (in a League Cup-tie), and then at home to Celtic, in a match seething with animosity. Tommy Burns was the only player expelled, though half a dozen others might have joined him. Billy McNeill, it seemed, did not like losing, least of all to his former employers.

The fifth defeat of this nascent season ended Aberdeen's interest in Europe for another year. Once again they were brought down by a German team, this time Eintracht Frankfurt, famous for their part in the epic European Cup Final with Real Madrid in 1960. Their currant side contained six internationals, among them Jurgen Grabowski and Bernd Holzenbein, both of whom had been in Germany's World Cup 74 winning team. At Pittodrie in the first leg spectators were treated to the rare sight of Stuart Kennedy, one of the nippiest full-backs in Scottish football, skinned alive by the lightning-fast Korean, Cha Bum Kun.

It was early October and Ferguson's team had yet to find their feet. Nor did fortunes improve in November, when Dundee United and Morton won at Pittodrie on successive Saturdays. In the newly sponsored Bell's League Cup the Dons presented a tougher face. Round 3 paired Aberdeen with Rangers, where Rougvie and Johnstone hoped to settle old scores. Rangers had denied both

McNeill and Ferguson in recent Hampden finals, and nothing could detract from the importance of this tie for Fergie. It was the same in the quarter-final, which pitched Aberdeen against Celtic. History was made, for the Dons defeated both the Old Firm home and away. Though Ally MacLeod's team had beaten the Old Firm back to back in the League Cup, no Aberdeen side had inflicted on Rangers and Celtic *four* successive cup defeats.

If that were not achievement enough, Aberdeen were then asked to surmount Morton in the semis. This was the best Morton team in memory. They topped the league, in which they had already defeated Aberdeen twice, and in Andy Ritchie they boasted one of the game's most maverick match winners. True to form, Morton stretched the Dons to the utmost. Lady Luck was for once with Aberdeen, and now only Dundee United stood between them and Ferguson's first trophy.

Match of the Season (1)

Dundee Utd 3   Aberdeen 0
League Cup Final, Replay, 12 December 1979

This season there was less ice and snow to drag the final back till March, enabling the competition to run its course by Christmas. It was the first time in sixteen years that neither of the Old Firm would contest the League Cup Final. Neither Ferguson nor McLean had won anything yet. One would now do so, the other must wait.

The paths of the two teams to the final were totally opposite. While Aberdeen's could not have been tougher, United had marched to Hampden by stamping on the tiddlers thrown up against them. No Premier Division side barred their route – only the likes of Queen's Park, Raith, and Hamilton – and if there was any justice Aberdeen's Herculean labours would be duly rewarded.

They were not. The final was unexceptional. The Dons had the better of what few good moments there were, but when Willie Garner's header rolled along the goal-line and stopped short in the mud the Dons were obliged to try again in a replay.

Dens Park may be convenient, it may be neutral, but Hampden Park it is not. Yet pressure from both clubs determined that the venue be moved from the west of Scotland to the east. Only 21,000 had turned out at Hampden, while 30,000 did so at Dens, defying one of the filthiest nights of the year. The deluge rendered the pitch all but unplayable, and the game would surely have been called off had it been a routine league fixture. In which case the final might have had to be rescheduled for March, like its predecessors.

The Aberdeen team in 1979-80 that would win the Scottish championship

Aberdeen were unchanged; United stiffened their midfield by bringing in Fleming and Kirkwood for Phillip and Payne. The Dons earned instant unpopularity by trotting out for their kickabout at the United end. Aberdeen tried to play a short game, United played it long, and McLean's tactics were vindicated. Willie Pettigrew scored United's first two goals, Paul Sturrock the third, to present Dundee United with their first ever trophy.

Ferguson admitted he should have changed his team for the replay, to counter the changes he knew McLean would make. Matters were exacerbated by Ferguson's touchline ban, which prevented him directing affairs as he would have wished. He was paralysed into inactivity, and he pledged himself never again to be so indecisive.

So, Alex Ferguson had lost two League Cup Finals. If he was not careful he would a labelled a loser, or – which was worse – a 'nearly man'.

Back in the league, a third defeat by Morton dumped Aberdeen down to sixth. Ferguson was a year and a half into the job and progress seemed slow. Flashes of inspiration in cups were drowned in a sea of inconsistency in the league. Had the team finished in the bottom half, one wonders how Fergie would have been viewed by supporters, and more importantly by his employers. The question would remain hypothetical.

A cruel winter was again playing havoc with the schedule. This, plus Aberdeen's League Cup run, left them seriously adrift in their fixtures. A goalless home draw with Celtic failed to close the daunting ten-point gap, though the Dons had played three games fewer. At that halfway stage Aberdeen had a modest twenty points from eighteen matches, little better than par. It was asking much of any team to mount a serious challenge from that position.

Aberdeen timed their title push to perfection. In this they were assisted by the upheavals that precipitated Ferguson's arrival, for neither Rangers nor Celtic had yet bedded down. Under Greig and McNeill each was rebuilding concurrently, and neither was running away with the championship in the time-honoured manner.

These unusual circumstances, of two transitional Old Firm teams, encouraged others to have a tilt at the title. Aberdeen had to start winning, obviously, but Celtic also needed to scatter points like confetti to be caught.

Incredibly, Celtic fell to pieces. In the space of nineteen days in April they lost 1-5 at lowly Dundee and twice to the Dons at Parkhead. Aberdeen had won *three* times at Celtic in one season; Rangers had also been beaten *five* times, and these unprecedented upsets stamped the Dons' arrival as a power in Scottish football. All they needed was a prize to prove it.

The Scottish Cup option was dashed in a semi-final by Rangers, who all season had been little better than cannon-fodder to the Dons' sharpshooters. Only the league remained, but when Hibs, inflated with an overweight George Best in their ranks, drew at Pittodrie that seemed tantamount to whistling for the moon.

The next game brought Aberdeen's second triumph at Parkhead. It was a night of seething emotion, with Gordon Strachan missing a penalty. The 3-1 win nudged the Dons above Celtic with four games to play – three of them away from home. A year earlier Dundee United had been in the same position. Jim McLean's boys blew it, and there were many who expected Aberdeen to blow it too.

Match of the Season (2)

Hibernian 0   Aberdeen 5

Premier Division, 3 May 1980

On Saturday, 3 May, Aberdeen played at Hibernian, with Celtic engaged at Love St. The Dons also had a crucial match in hand, at Partick. The positions before kick-off were:

		P	W	D	L	F	A	(GD)	Pts
1	Celtic	35	18	10	7	61	38	(+23)	46
2	ABERDEEN	34	18	9	7	62	35	(+27)	45

Easter Road was at that time a bogey ground for Aberdeen, who had yet to win there in the Premier League. Presuming Celtic won, Aberdeen would not be proclaimed champions at Easter Road. They would need a further point or two at Firhill the following Wednesday. Whereas Hibs were bottom of the league and going down, St Mirren were a feisty outfit, already sure of finishing third. They could be banked upon to resist Celtic.

Aberdeen polished off poor Hibs without fuss. The saddest man was Hibs' debutant goalkeeper, Dave Huggins, who was beaten five times and whose first match for Hibernian would also be his last. The points were safe for Aberdeen long before the end; all that mattered was the score at Love St. Thousands of mini-radios were pressed to thousands of ears. Ten minutes from time Celtic, who were drawing 0-0, were awarded a penalty. A groan swept round Easter Road, followed by a mighty cheer. The referee had consulted a linesman and changed his mind. Aberdeen's game finished first, and anxious seconds passed before confirmation of the draw at Love St launched Ferguson's famous dance on the pitch.

Aberdeen were champions of Scotland, the first outside the Old Firm for fifteen years. The title had been won in Edinburgh, or so it seemed. But not to the mandarins of the Scottish League. Partick, who had set the season rolling so miserably all those months ago, could divert the trophy to Celtic if they beat Aberdeen by ten goals. That possibility was judged real enough for the coronation to be deferred till after the game at Firhill, which ended 1-1.

The championship meant different things to different players. For Bobby Clark it was the culmination of his long career, a clean sweep of domestic medals; for Willie Miller it was the beginning of a torrent of trophies under Alex Ferguson. For Gordon Strachan it was the realisation of his gorgeous talent. Ferguson had switched him from centre midfield to the right, and Strachan had blossomed to such an extent that he was voted Scottish Football Writers' Player of the Year. For Steve Archibald the league title was a fitting farewell. Transfer talk had been thick for weeks, and he would shortly be on his way to Spurs for £800,000.

DID YOU KNOW?

Joe Harper scored 14 hat-tricks for the Dons. His first was against Raith in January 1970 and his last against Hamilton in October 1978.

Jarvie celebrates a headed goal at Dens Park v Dundee, 29 September 1979

No more Archibald, and no more Harper either. For wee Joey it was a season of frustration and, later, public criticism. He had been out since November with injury, but that appears to have saved him the indignity of being dropped. Ferguson states in his memoirs that the work-rate demanded of his team could not accommodate someone like Harper, not renowned for grafting, and that away from home Harper could be a luxury. Ferguson wrote: 'I don't think we would have won the League Championship with Joe in the side.' At 32, Harper's time was up. The principal beneficiary of his long absence was Mark McGhee, a £70,000 snip from Newcastle who, like Strachan, took time to adapt, but who would grow into a centre-forward of international stature.

In the wider context, the fact that two of the season's prizes went to east-coast clubs created a new concept in football's glossary – the New Firm. Between them, Jim McLean and Alex Ferguson were set to shift the axis of Scottish soccer.

SCOTTISH PREMIER DIVISION   1980-81

Premier Division   Runners-Up
Bell's League Cup   Quarter-Final
Scottish Cup   Fourth Round
European Champions' Cup   Second Round

Winning the league gave Ferguson security. Deep down, he no longer feared the sack. The nearly-man tag was gone. Aberdeen were Scottish champions for the first time in 25 years. A generation had passed since they *should* have competed in the European Cup. Now the Dons hoped to make up for lost time.

An impartial assessment of the team shows pluses and minuses. None could quibble with their right to be champions: the consistent slaying of the Old Firm brooks no argument. On the downside, facts are facts. The title had been won with just 48 points. No smaller total has ever been so handsomely rewarded. To that extent, sceptics dismissed Aberdeen as the poorest champions Scotland had known, having won just twelve matches more than they lost. Indeed, the Dons would improve on that *seven* times in subsequent seasons yet finish second or lower. The 1979-80 Dons vintage pales alongside Fergie's all-conquering heroes of the mid-80s.

The breakthrough had been made, that was all that mattered. Ferguson could now aim to build a dynasty fit to dominate Scottish football. The club would have a stadium to match, with the South Stand now roofed. Pat Stanton, Ferguson's assistant these past two years, chose to return to his former club, Hibs. In time, Archie Knox arrived from Forfar to replace him. On the playing front, having lost Archibald, Ferguson now lost Bobby Clark, a victim of back trouble. Twenty-year-old Jim Leighton started the season in goal, and stayed there when Clark's intended replacement, Marc de Clerck, was injured himself.

Nor was Fergie yet the shrewd judge in the transfer market that he would become. Of the players bought and introduced in 1980-81 – Angus, Cowan, Dornan, Harrow, McCall – none would be more than fringe players, and some would be quickly moved on. All of which meant Ferguson set out to retain the championship with a weaker pool of players than had won it.

Q	Which Belgian player was signed from a Dutch club and on his competitive Dons debut scored in England?
A	Goalkeeper Marc de Clerck, who scored in the League Cup at Berwick Rangers on 30 August 1980.

The Dons made a best possible start. By December they had opened a lead of three points on Rangers and six on Celtic. In the process Aberdeen won at Parkhead for the fourth time in a row. They also crushed Morton 6-0, which they hoped had put paid to the Greenock curse. But at Cappielow Andy Ritchie's late cross was nodded in by Jim Rooney to inflict on Aberdeen their first league defeat since February, spanning ten months and 31 games.

Form had not been so impressive in the cups. Hopes of a third successive League Cup Final were dashed at the quarter-final stage by Dundee's Cammy Fraser, five minutes from time. As for the European Cup, Aberdeen survived against Austria Memphis in the first round, but been taught one hell of a lesson by Liverpool in the second.

The damage inflicted by Bob Paisley's team was twofold. Any aspirations the Dons might have had of being, or becoming, a great side were rudely shattered. So were John McMaster's ligaments, which deprived the team of one of its most cultured and creative influences for a whole year.

The Dons bounced back to beat Celtic and Rangers yet again, this time in successive visits to Pittodrie. But against Dundee United in the last game of 1980, Gordon Strachan suffered a stomach injury that took months to heal. The loss of McMaster *and* Strachan stripped the midfield of its spark. There was half a season to go, and if Aberdeen were to keep their title they would have to grind out their wins.

This proved beyond them. A sequence of two victories from ten games coincided with Celtic piling win upon win to pass them in the fast lane and open up a decisive lead by late March. The last hope was extinguished at Parkhead, where Aberdeen were bidding for their fifth straight win. They were five minutes from achieving it when George McCluskey hooked Celtic's equaliser and effectively dethroned the Dons.

Nor could solace be found in the Scottish Cup. Aberdeen were drawn to visit the place they most dreaded, Morton, where they were duly beaten by a wonder goal from Andy Ritchie.

When the curtain finally fell, Aberdeen were runners-up with 49 points, one more than when winning the championship. Did that mean they were better or worse? It could be argued both ways, but in sport trophies matter, statistics don't.

One particular player had come of age. No longer overshadowed by Harper and Archibald, Mark McGhee was voted the Scottish Players' Player of the Year for 1980-81, the first Don to be so rewarded in the four years of that honour's existence.

Match of the Season

Aberdeen 0   Liverpool 1

European Cup, 2nd Round, 1st Leg, 22 October 1980

Season 1980-81 may be summed up in one word – Liverpool. Aberdeen's first crack at the European Cup earned them a daunting appointment with the legendary English champions. Both before and afterwards, the shadow of Anfield hung over every match Aberdeen played. Never mind the outcome, Alex Ferguson would have preferred less exalted opponents, simply to avoid the disruption that ensued from the moment the two teams were pulled out of the bag together.

The pairing of the Scottish and English champions caught the imagination of the whole of Britain. At the time, Aberdeen were going well, still full of themselves. But they were far from being the strongest champions Scotland had ever produced (how one would have cherished a rematch in 1985), and they were taking on not just the best team in England but the best in Europe. The very name 'Liverpool' in the 1970s and 80s made opponents shiver. English champions in four of the past five seasons they were establishing themselves as a dynastic power, capable of changing managers and players without interruption to their winning ways. They had won the European Cup in 1977 and 1978, setting in train an era of total dominance when English clubs would claim the Cup for six successive years.

Not the least of Liverpool's strengths were their three great Scots – Hansen, Souness, and Dalglish – two of whom would become distinguished managers in their own right.

Yet none of the three was involved in one the finest goals Pittodrie had ever seen. It arrived after just five minutes, while McMaster was lying injured on the pitch. Had he been able, he would have tracked Terry McDermott as he hared down the inside-left channel in pursuit of David Johnson's pass. No great danger threatened, for by the time McDermott reached the ball he was far from goal near the by-line. Most players in that position would have pulled the ball back; few would have attempted the audacious angled chip that carried the ball over Leighton's head.

Aberdeen looked stunned. If Liverpool could do that, they could do anything. Aberdeen created few chances, and in other circumstances would have been prepared to applaud Liverpool's genius. But a sour taste was left by Ray Kennedy's 'tackle' on McMaster, which raised doubts over whether the Aberdeen player would ever walk again, never mind play.

Aberdeen and Liverpool take the field at Pittodrie, 22 October 1980

Asking any side to win at Anfield was asking much. None had done so for almost three years. Even to score there was beyond most teams. Ferguson rejuggled his side to seek the tiniest advantage. A half-chance fell to McGhee, but that was the only chink of light as Liverpool bided their time. When Willie Miller sliced a corner past Leighton it did two things. It ended Aberdeen's hopes of springing a shock and presented a final glimpse of Miller's vulnerability. The Aberdeen captain would be virtually invincible for the next five or six years.

Phil Neal added another goal before half-time, and from then on Ferguson was faced with damage limitation. The final score – 4-0 (5-0 on aggregate) – failed even to meet that objective.

During all their Scottish travels in 1980-81 Aberdeen never conceded more than one goal a game. This puts Liverpool's achievement in scoring four into true perspective. In May Bob Paisley's team lifted the European Cup for the third time, defeating Real Madrid.

SCOTTISH PREMIER DIVISION   1981-82

Premier Division	Runners-Up
League Cup	Semi-Final
Scottish Cup	Winners
UEFA Cup	Third Round

But for Liverpool and crippling injuries, Alex Ferguson believes Aberdeen would have retained their title. That is easy to say, of course, but anyway it was history.

Some supporters wondered where the £800,000 from the sale of Archibald had disappeared to. Now, belatedly, Ferguson did spend. Though only one player arrived in the summer, he would provide a crucial piece of Ferguson's jigsaw. Peter Weir was nimble and strong, a left winger with four caps already under his belt. Ferguson wanted him badly, and persuaded St Mirren to part in exchange for £200,000 plus Ian Scanlon. The total package was reckoned to create a record fee between Scottish clubs. In his dream team Ferguson wanted Weir on the left, Strachan on the right, and someone to replace Archibald up front. That someone turned out to be two players, both home grown. John Hewitt and Eric Black would take turns to partner Mark McGhee.

Bells no longer sponsored the League Cup, which reverted to its sectional format. With only doomed Airdrie to provide Premier opposition, Aberdeen strolled into the last eight, where Berwick detained them no longer than expected. Now for Dundee United.

Did we but know it, United's win in the 1979-80 final was the start of a relationship verging on the incestuous. So powerful were the New Firm becoming that both reached the latter stages of domestic cups as if by clockwork. And if the frequency with which Aberdeen and Dundee United were paired dismayed supporters, those of United at least had the consolation of most victories – especially at Pittodrie, which shed more than its share of tears when Dundee United came a-calling.

Peter Weir's header gave Aberdeen a one-goal advantage at Tannadice. Few would have bet on any team pulling it back, but Dundee United did so, scoring three times without reply.

It was now late October. The Dons were still alive in the UEFA Cup, having enjoyed a glittering win over holders Ipswich in the first round. In the second they overcame the Romanians of Arges Pitesti – though not before nearly tossing away a three-goal home-leg advantage – to break new ground by advancing past the second round in Europe for the first time.

Harper and Celtic's Edvaldsson in a match from the late 1970s

Having double the number of entrants, the UEFA Cup required an extra round. Instead of a quarter-final held over till the spring, Aberdeen therefore found themselves in Round 3, to be played before Christmas. For much of the home leg with Hamburg, Aberdeen appeared to be heading for the last eight. 36-year-old Franz Beckenbauer oozed class, but the Dons were 3-1 up and Strachan had squandered a penalty. Only three minutes remained when Rougvie crumpled in a heap. Rather than belt the ball off, so that Neale Cooper could come on, the Dons kept playing and Horst Hrubesch found himself unmarked to score. Ferguson was hopping mad, knowing that that goal had turned the tie. He was right: the Dons had no answer in Hamburg, who went all the way to the final, where they were beaten by IFK Gothenburg.

In the league, Celtic, reasserted themselves with a vengeance. By January they had beaten Aberdeen three times and Billy McNeill appeared to have righted wrongs in his personal battle with Ferguson. Celtic led the title race from start to finish.

Aberdeen never fully recovered from losing their first two games (for the first time in 22 years), in which they conceded seven goals. Strachan was fit enough to start the season and McMaster was back by October. But their return was not enough to transform Aberdeen into a winning outfit. At one stage they went six games and three months without beating anyone, and by February were languishing in sixth position. Mark McGhee hadn't scored in the league all season, and press and fans weren't slow to remind him.

These must have been trying times for the Aberdeen manager. He could no longer blame a long casualty list, and had probably resigned himself to having just one prize to show for his four years in charge. This was a far cry from the 'two trophies a season' that would shortly become the norm. Unless they pulled their socks up Aberdeen would not even make the UEFA Cup. Ferguson's teams had a habit of either starting well and falling apart after Christmas (1980-81) or *vice versa* (1979-80). The current season now confirmed the trend.

When Aberdeen set course for the Scottish Cup in January 1982 it was all they had left. John Hewitt set the ball rolling by banging it into the Motherwell net after just 9.6 seconds. A harsh winter meant another backlog of fixtures, but the long layoff seemed to recharge a few batteries. Whatever the cause, everything suddenly came right. February passed without defeat. March too. April would have been equally profitable but for a late goal at Morton. The season would drag on till late May, by which time Aberdeen had defeated Rangers three times and Celtic once. Given another month or so the Dons might even have been champions. As it was, fifteen wins from sixteen games left them breathing down Celtic's neck. Everything hinged on the last match, which saw the Dons needing two points and five goals to make up. The half-time scores – Aberdeen 4 Rangers 0; Celtic 0 St Mirren 0 – kept everyone on tenterhooks, and it was deep into the second-half before Celtic finally broke through. The championship, as expected, was theirs. But Aberdeen would face Rangers again seven days hence in the final of the Scottish Cup.

Aberdeen's had been no easy path to Hampden. Hewitt's overhead kick put out Celtic and prevented three home defeats by McNeill's team in one season. Kilmarnock could not capitalise on a first-minute goal in the quarter-finals. In the semis, St Mirren led at one stage, but paid the price for fragile goalkeeping in the mud and mire of a Dens Park replay.

Match of the Season (1)

Aberdeen 3   Ipswich Town 1
UEFA Cup, 1st Round, 2nd Leg, 30 September 1981

There was something intoxicating about meeting Bobby Robson's Ipswich so soon after the Liverpool debacle. East Anglia must have given a collective chortle when Ipswich's first opponents were named. Liverpool had shown the Dons to be mugs, and passage to Round 2 seemed assured.

In fairness, this Ipswich team was pretty special. Long before the likes of Snelders and Gillhaus descended on Pittodrie, Robson had judged the merit of top class Dutch players who could be bought cheaply and who fitted in like a hand to a glove. Arnold Muhren and Frans Thijsson had helped Ipswich finish second, three places above Liverpool. Ipswich were also defending the UEFA Cup, having in the final defeated AZ 67 Alkmaar of Holland. With Liverpool also having beaten Real Madrid, English football was indulging in a little tub-thumping, an act guaranteed to raise the hackles of any self-respecting Scot.

The question was, had Ferguson and his players learned from the Liverpool experience. The answer was yes. Aberdeen played with aplomb in the first leg, earned their 1-1 draw, and extracted from Robson the unfortunate words 'Aberdeen can't play better'.

The second leg provided another of those sensational Euro nights. Two penalty-kicks in the first half, one to each team, left the tie perfectly balanced and set up an enthralling second period in which Aberdeen found an unlikely hero. Peter Weir had begun his Dons career nervously. Few expected him now to run at England full-back Mick Mills, twist him this way and that, and score two blinding goals, one with his left foot, one with his right. Had Strachan not failed with a twice-taken, last-minute penalty Ipswich would have been confronted with a humiliating scoreline. 3-1 was bad enough, and the ghost of Liverpool had been laid to rest.

Match of the Season (2)

Rangers 1   Aberdeen 4
Scottish Cup Final, 22 May 1982

A Scottish Cup Final was an unexpected treasure in a season that looked to be going nowhere, and at a time when the Falklands War hogged the airwaves. For weeks it looked like Scotland would boycott the coming World Cup. While the threat lasted it could have done nothing for the peace of mind of Leighton, Kennedy, Miller, and McLeish, who had been named in Scotland's 22.

If league form was any guide Aberdeen would beat Rangers handsomely. They had taken seven points out of eight and finished ten points ahead. Rangers were top-heavy with ageing players and had reached the final only after two unconvincing attempts to get past Forfar in the semis.

Yet no one dared write off the Old Firm. Ferguson had only to recall his championship year, when Aberdeen beat Rangers five times but lost in the Cup. Besides, Fergie had lost two (League) cup finals and had never won at Hamden. He was as committed to breaking his duck as was his team.

Both sides were shorn of key players – in Rangers' case Derek Johnstone and Ian Redford, in Aberdeen's Peter Weir. Rangers would include Jim Bett. Only three Dons survived from their last Scottish Cup Final, in Billy McNeill's last game – Miller, Kennedy, and McMaster. Aberdeen's kids – Simpson, Cooper and Hewitt would now come of age.

Fears of another Hampden hoodoo resurfaced when John McDonald stooped to head Rangers in front. Ferguson wouldn't have known and wouldn't have cared that Aberdeen had never yet come from behind to win a Hampden final, and the equaliser came from an unlikely source. Alex McLeish, lurking on the eighteen-yard line, well to the left, curled an exquisite right-footer into the far top corner.

McLeish's goal lit up the ninety minutes, which otherwise saw little in the way of pulsating soccer. Extra-time awaited, the first time a Scottish Cup Final would be settled in this way. Dougie Bell and Eric Black replaced McMaster and Hewitt. Within three minutes Strachan had pitched over a cross and McGhee surged behind John McClelland to direct a header inside the post.

Lesser Dons' sides would have fallen back to protect their lead. But not Ferguson's. So hard did Aberdeen press that one would have thought it was they who were trailing. Alex Miller stumbled over the by-line, permitting McGhee to roll the ball to Strachan – six inches out – who scored extravagantly.

Two goals up with fifteen minutes left, yet the aura of Rangers' long history gnawed at Aberdonian finger-nails. Then came another goal. Jim Stewart's clearance ballooned off Neale Cooper's chest and flew into the stratosphere. With both players searching around like dogs for a tossed bone, the ball dropped sweetly for Cooper to whack it home. 4-1 to Aberdeen, who would have believed it? The nerves disappeared and the celebrations began.

History shows this to have been the victory from which all future glories stemmed. It came not a moment too soon in the career of Alex Ferguson. Imagine for a moment what the future would have held for manager and club had Aberdeen lost yet again. Imagine too the reaction had Willie Miller – the second Don (after Bobby Clark) to boast a complete set of Scottish medals – accepted a desperate bid by vanquished Rangers to sign him.

5

THE ELDER FERGIE 1982-1986

SCOTTISH PREMIER DIVISION   1982-83

Premier Division	Third
League Cup	Quarter-Final
Scottish Cup	Winners
European Cup-Winners' Cup	Winners

Alex Ferguson had become the first Aberdeen manager since Dave Halliday to lead the Dons to two major prizes. But it had taken him four years. In the next four he would mastermind eight more trophies. Willie Miller's decision to stay put, and not defect to Rangers, spoke volumes for Pittodrie's new sense of expectancy. Other than Steve Archibald, Aberdeen had not lost a star player against their wishes for five years. Team-spirit was as high as anyone could remember.

Circumstances conspired to make this the most congested start on record. Aberdeen had drawn the short straw and had to squeeze in a preliminary Cup-Winners' tie with Sion of Switzerland. Eleven goals over two legs would have been unremarkable had the opponents hailed from Iceland or Luxembourg. But the Swiss were no dunces, and four years later would teach the Dons a lesson.

Eighteen League Cup goals in Section 2 carried the Dons into the quarter-finals. Dundee United yet again ensured that Aberdeen got off to a losing start in the league, and then, to rub it in, dumped them from the League Cup. It was the third time in four seasons United had done so. Rangers, meanwhile, won at Pittodrie for the first time in the Premier League, leaving the Dons with three points from four games. It was early days, but with his team out of one competition and lagging in another, Fergie needed to put his finger on the pulse quickly.

Whatever medicine he prescribed it was certainly potent. In Europe four clean sheets against Albanian and Polish opposition kept the Dons alive till the spring quarter-finals, which was uncharted territory. Hibs, Dundee and Partick were barged aside in the Scottish Cup, while in the league Aberdeen were piling up the points. The championship developed early into a three-horse race between Aberdeen, Celtic and Dundee United. Aberdeen showed their mettle in beating Dundee United 5-1 and 3-0, and Celtic 3-1 at Parkhead. Other than Celtic's December revenge at Pittodrie, Aberdeen went five months without losing to anyone.

At one stage they looked on course for a monumental treble. As the players awoke on Wednesday, 16 March 1983 the Dons were top of the league, through to the semis of the Scottish Cup, and that evening had a Pittodrie engagement with Bayern Munich in the quarter-final of the Cup-Winners' Cup. The circumstances of that match would write a chapter in Pittodrie folklore.

Ferguson had been in the game long enough to know that Wednesday's wizards are often Saturday's flops. He needed to bring his players back down to earth quickly for the clash with Dundee United, and no one was more pleased with the Bayern result than Jim McLean. In fact, the Dons lost three out of four, leaving them too far adrift to recover. Two more points and they would have been champions of Scotland.

The explanation for Aberdeen's triumphs in 1982-83 was simple: they had the meanest of defences, coupled with a potent strike-force which saw no fewer than six players score ten goals or more.

Match of the Season (1)

Aberdeen 3   Bayern Munich 2
Cup-Winners' Cup, Quarter-Final, 2nd Leg, 16 March 1983

The roll-call for the 1982-83 Cup-Winners' Cup included Tottenham Hotspur, Real Madrid and Barcelona (the holders) from Spain, Internazionale of Milan, Bayern Munich, Paris St Germain, Austria Vienna. Those who mischievously suggest that the Cup-Winners' is the softest of the three European competitions argue from a false premise. Though many continental countries give lower priority to domestic knock-out tournaments, it does not follow that the winners will be any less formidable on the European stage.

By the quarter-finals all the big guns were still around, with the exception of Spurs, toppled by Bayern Munich in Round 2. It was Bayern who were now paired with the Dons. The draw was made in December; the games were not played till March.

Match programme of Bayern Munich v Aberdeen, 2 March 1983

In their mid-1970s heyday Bayern had been European champions three years in a row. Though relinquishing their German crown in 1981-82 to Hamburg, Bayern would still have contested the Champions Cup had they not lost to Peter Withe's mis-hit from two yards in the 1982 European Cup Final against Aston Villa.

Eight of that Bayern side – including Breitner, Augenthaler, Hoeness and Rummenigge – lined up against the Dons in the Olympic stadium, where Spurs had recently crumbled 1-4. If one detected a certain cockiness in German attitudes, these seemed well-founded. Scottish clubs in recent years had not lingered long in Europe, their record against German sides was poor, and in Aberdeen's case, woeful. Over the years the Dons had lost to Borussia Moenchengladbach, Fortuna Dusseldorf, Eintracht Frankfurt and Hamburg. There were few reasons to suppose Bayern would end their duck.

Aberdeen played with unexpected discipline in Munich – unexpected, that is, to the Germans – and McGhee might even have turned a 0-0 draw into a 1-0 win. Even so, it was probably the most notable result Aberdeen had posted in Europe.

Sceptics were quick to point out that without the cushion of an away goal the Dons still had it all to do. The Germans would go through with a 1-1 draw and were still favourites.

The captains exchange pennants before the Waterschei tie in Belgium, 19 April 1983

What followed was to be the most ecstatic night in Pittodrie's history. It was the manner of the win that was astonishing. Bayern were good enough to snatch an away goal – two, in fact. Leighton's finger-tips were almost severed by Augenthaler's blazing shot, and Pflugler's volley inside the near post, after Neil Simpson had bundled an equaliser, should have extinguished Aberdeen's last hopes.

With fifteen minutes left Aberdeen needed to conjure two goals. A well-practised Strachan-McMaster free-kick led to Alex McLeish heading one of them. With the crowd agog and the TV cameraman distracted, Eric Black powered in another header. Muller plunged the keep it out, only for Hewitt to stab the ball back between his legs.

Pittodrie erupted. It did so again when the final whistle blew, and again when Ferguson ordered his players back on to the pitch to acknowledge the delirious fans.

Match of the Season (2)

Real Madrid 1   Aberdeen 2

Cup-Winners' Cup Final, 11 May 1983

The quarter-finals saw not only the demise of Bayern Munich, but also Barcelona, Internazionale and Paris St Germain. All of a sudden the path looked enticingly clear, especially when Aberdeen drew Waterschei in the semi-final. The Belgian side had recovered from a two-goal deficit to put out Paris St Germain and would be accorded all due respect. For all that, this small provincial team, which had never won the Belgian championship, was there for the taking.

Losing two goals in the first four minutes was a blow from which Waterschei never recovered, enabling Aberdeen to contest their first European final. On paper, Real Madrid versus Aberdeen sounded like the mismatch of all time. The six-times European champions against the two-times Scottish champions, the multi-millionaires of Spain against a homely, tightly-run club most of whose team cost nothing.

Real Madrid were coached by one of their greatest players, Alfredo di Stefano. From his standpoint, facing Aberdeen was a mixed blessing. Real should win, provided he could guard against complacency. It would be the same for Aberdeen if contesting a cup final against a Raith or an Airdrie.

Aside from the Dutchman Metgod and the German Stielike, Real were packed with Spanish internationals. Camacho and Santillana had both faced England in World Cup 82.

Ferguson played every psychological card he knew. In the Dons' favour was the venue, Gothenburg, easily accessible from Scotland, a journey and a half from Spain. The distance, coupled with un-glamorous opposition, encouraged a mere handful of Spanish fans to make the trip. The Ullevi Stadium became Pittodrie for a day.

Jock Stein was invited along to add his massive experience to the Aberdeen cause. A third 'plus' was the weather, hours of pre-match rain leaving the pitch sodden and puddly, conditions with which Dons players were far more familiar than Real's, even if they were not to the liking of tricksters like Strachan and Weir.

In the end, of course, it all came down to players. The loss of Stuart Kennedy through knee injury in Belgium meant Doug Rougvie played right-back and John McMaster left. Both performed so well that Kennedy was barely missed. That spell-binding drib-bler, Dougie Bell, was also missing, though with hindsight the aquatic pitch might have dampened his contribution.

The first action saw Eric Black lean into a volley that crashed back off Augustin's crossbar. One did not know whether to marvel at Black's athleticism or curse his bad luck. With chances likely to be at a premium, that one might prove costly.

The debate was shelved when Aberdeen scored. It was a strange goal. McLeish's header was deflected to Black, who turned it awk-wardly inside a post from six yards. TV evidence suggests Black mistimed his contact, almost screwing the ball wide.

The official programme of the Cup-Winners' Cup Final in Gothenburg, 11 May 1983

But Aberdeen had their goal, and on the evidence of what had passed before it had gone to the better side. Real Madrid carved out little by way of scoring chances, and their equaliser was due not to their enterprise but to the conditions, which Aberdeen had reckoned in their favour. McLeish's back-pass braked sharply in the wet, Leighton brought down Santillana, and Juanito scored from the spot. It is a sobering thought that under today's regulations Leighton would have been sent off for the foul.

For McLeish, whose wondrous cup-final goal had helped make it all possible, his error must have left him close to despair. Should Aberdeen lose he would be inconsolable.

Aberdeen had the better of the second half, but despite the marauding of Weir and McGhee the score remained unchanged. Extra-time saw Black's withdrawal and the introduction of super-sub Hewitt. Eight minutes from a shoot-out which Real confidently expected to win, Peter Weir skirted two players down the left touchline. He chipped the ball on to McGhee, whose cross tempted Augustin off his line. The keeper missed contact by inches and there, rushing in, was John Hewitt to head into an empty net.

'Aberdeen have what money cannot buy – a soul – a team spirit built in a family tradition.' Alfredo di Stefano, manager of Real Madrid.

The jubilant Dons return to Aberdeen after their epic win in Gothenburg

Only once did Real threaten, when from a twice-taken free-kick Salguero drove the ball past Leighton's far post. Then it was over, and players and supporters indulged in celebrations unparalleled in the history of Aberdeen FC. For John Hewitt, whose quick-fire goal at Motherwell set the whole caboodle rolling, his would be a special place in Pittodrie's hall of fame.

As with Celtic in 1967 and Rangers in 1972, Aberdeen's European glory was achieved with a team composed entirely of Scots. The Dons picked up just one yellow card in eleven European ties.

There was icing on the Aberdeen cake. English clubs' six-year monopoly of the European Cup was over, enabling Aberdeen to hog the limelight. It was typical that the Cup-Winners' Cup Final should be televised in 42 countries, but not England.

DID YOU KNOW?

Of the team which won the Cup-Winners' Cup, 6 were at Aberdeen before Ferguson – Leighton, Rougvie, McMaster, McLeish, Miller, Strachan. Only 3 players cost fees – Strachan, McGhee, Weir – which meant the entire team cost less than £400,000.

Willie Miller sprints away from Celtic's Frank McGarvey

Match of the Season (3)

Rangers 0   Aberdeen 1

Scottish Cup Final, 21 May 1983

One would think the Cup-Winners' Cup would satisfy any appetite. But Aberdeen returned from Gothenburg with two games to play and two more trophies to win. First they met Hibs, who graciously applauded them out at Pittodrie before being sunk 5-0. Results elsewhere meant Aberdeen finished third. Their 55 points remains a record for a team finishing in bronze medal position and was seven points more than when winning the title in 1980.

Many considered the championship would have been just reward for Aberdeen's heroic exertions. But the fact that Dundee United had themselves played eight ties in reaching the quarter-finals of the UEFA Cup, not to mention beating the Dons four times out of six, suggests they were not unworthy champions.

Aberdeen's win over a surprisingly physical Celtic had earned them a place in a second successive Scottish Cup Final. Rangers were their opponents yet again. As in 1982 the form book suggested an emphatic Aberdeen win. Ferguson stayed true to the eleven who kicked-off against Real Madrid.

Goalmouth action v Hibs in Aberdeen's first match after Gothenburg, 14 May 1983

Incredible to say, what would have been the highlight of any other season was for Aberdeen just another game. It was a poor final. The Aberdeen players looked lethargic and uncoordinated, unable to raise themselves a second time. They failed to score in ninety minutes and required a slick Leighton save to deny Jim Bett in the dying seconds. An untidy goal four minutes from the end of extra-time decided a game which most neutrals thought Rangers had shaded. McGhee's cross looped off Craig Paterson for Black to head into an unattended goal. For the first time but not the last, Aberdeen had won two trophies in one season.

The manner of victory did not impress the perfectionist in Alex Ferguson. He publicly lambasted his players – 'we were lucky to win' – only to accept that he had spoken in haste. He apologised the next day.

Rangers were unlikely beneficiaries of Aberdeen's success. With the Dons qualifying as holders for next season's Cup-Winners' Cup, Rangers took the place assigned to the Scottish Cup winners. Aberdeen had enjoyed the same in the past, of course. Now they were dishing out favours to the Old Firm. How the worm had turned.

SCOTTISH PREMIER DIVISION   1983-84

Premier Division	Champions
League Cup	Semi-Final
Scottish Cup	Winners
European Cup-Winners' Cup	Semi-Final
European Super Cup	Winners

The European Cup is the summit of achievement for club footballers and managers. Knowing that the club had missed out on qualifying by so little must have hurt Ferguson. He could console himself that – all being well – the club would have to wait just twelve months to rectify matters. In the meantime Aberdeen could bask in being voted the Best Team in Europe by the magazine *France Football*.

Though Ferguson lost Archie Knox to Dundee, and replaced him with Willie Garner, the playing squad was more or less intact. That was bound to change now that the spotlight was on them. The first to show stirrings of discontent was Gordon Strachan. A star in the 1982 World Cup, winner of a European medal in 1983, Strachan served notice that season 1983-84 would be his last in Aberdeen red.

Strachan's leaving allowed Ferguson time to hunt for a successor. Replacing the wee man was not easy, but St Mirren's Billy Stark had qualities of his own. A rangy midfielder, with a taste for wearing his shorts up to his crutch, Stark was as sharp in front of goal as most strikers.

Sooner or later Ferguson also had to address the weakness at full-back. On the left, Rougvie – for all his lion's heart – was really a stopper out of position. On the right, Kennedy career had been terminated by injury. By December Ferguson had brought in Dundee's stylish young Stewart McKimmie, an Aberdonian to boot. McKimmie's was a seamless introduction. His baptism was the stuff of fairy tales. A home debut against Hibs, followed three days later by Hamburg in the European Super Cup.

But this is to fast-forward. The League tinkered with the rules again, introducing an initial round, with the sections to follow. Aberdeen belted nine goals past Raith, topped Section 3 with ease, and found themselves paired with Celtic in a semi-final.

In the league, early defeats by Dundee United and Hibs kept the Dons down to fourth, with Celtic to come. Matches with the Celts, never placid under Billy McNeill, became yet more brutal under Davie Hay. The first encounter, in the league, brought Aberdeen two penalties; the next, in the League Cup semi, an overload of bookings, fisticuffs in the crowd, and a decisive penalty to Celtic.

In late October Pittodrie was rocked by the news that Rangers wanted Ferguson to replace John Greig. Ferguson, of course, had been a former Rangers player. Not so long ago Billy McNeill had had to make similar decision and had chosen to leave. But the choice confronting Ferguson was more complicated. Aberdeen had shown faith in him when others had not. He was genuinely happy at the club, and in his relationship with the board, and was not eager to uproot. Besides, Rangers needed major surgery; Aberdeen were touching greatness.

Not wishing to act in haste and repent at leisure, Ferguson took time to weigh things up. His decision was as surprising as it was welcome. Rangers could look elsewhere; he was staying put, and duly signed a five-year contract.

The players celebrated by rolling off win after win to open up a handsome lead. On the last occasion Aberdeen led the table at New Year, in 1980-81, they had folded. This time they grew in strength. Defeating Celtic, their only realistic challengers, in February opened up a gap of six points, which was to prove conclusive.

By late April Aberdeen were heading for a sweep of trophies to eclipse even their achievements of 1982-83. Porto proved too good in the Cup-Winners' Cup, but otherwise the Dons were invincible. They took the Premier League title with a record 57 points, equalling the best ever defensive record of 21 goals conceded.

DID YOU KNOW?

Against Northern Ireland in December 1983 a record 6 Aberdeen players won Scottish caps. Five started the match and a sixth – McGhee – came on as sub. And Willie Miller missed that game.

Match of the Season (1)

Aberdeen 2   SV Hamburg 0
European Super Cup, 2nd Leg, 20 December 1983

The European Super Cup is not a cup at all, but a plaque. Nor is it necessarily super. It is related in concept to the Charity Shield in England, between league and cup winners, and the World Club Championship between the European and South American title holders. The idea brings cash and kudos to the winners, and the losers promptly forget all about it. In congested timetables extra matches are difficult to squeeze in, and – to underline their scant value – are sometimes dispensed with altogether. Fixture congestion is a particular headache for European champions, since they may challenge both Cup-Winners' Cup holders and South American champions – all in addition to defending their European crown.

Smaller clubs like Aberdeen, new to the exhilarating effects of international success, are understandably more enthusiastic than bigger ones, who could do without the distraction if not the loot. Aberdeen had the additional incentive of becoming the first Scottish club to win the Super Cup. It was established only in 1972 (too late for Celtic), when Rangers were roundly beaten by Ajax.

The Dons' opponents were old adversaries. It was only two years since Hamburg had provided one of Pittodrie's great Euro nights. Since then, Beckenbauer and Hrubesch had gone.

Having drawn 0-0 in Bayern, the Dons did the same in Hamburg. Once again McGhee came closest to scoring a precious away goal.

The atmosphere at Pittodrie could not compare with that for Bayern. Drizzle seemed to depress players as much as supporters. Hamburg played in red, obliging Aberdeen to wear white and black. The match was indifferent too, until Peter Weir scampered down the touchline just after half-time to create a goal for Simpson. Thereafter the fans found their voice and the Dons found their form. McGhee added a second and by the end the Germans had escaped lightly.

It is a moot point: did Aberdeen win the wrong match with Hamburg? Would they have swapped a semi-precious plaque for passage to the 1981-82 UEFA Cup quarter-finals?

Hamburg lost the World Club Championship in Tokyo, 1-2 to Gremio Porto Alegre of Brazil.

Match of the Season (2)

Aberdeen 3   Ujpest Dozsa 0
Cup-Winners' Cup, Quarter-Final, 2nd Leg, 21 March 1984

European opponents used to view Aberdeen as a soft touch. 1982-83 changed all that. They were now up there in lights as they strove to become the first club to retain the Cup-Winners' Cup. This time they were seeded, naturally, and were spared the indignity of a preliminary round. The current crop of entries included Manchester United, Juventus, Barcelona, Porto, Cologne, Paris St Germain – not to mention Rangers. In Round 1 the Dons encountered unexpectedly sturdy opposition from Akranes of Iceland, who squandered a penalty. Round 2 was overshadowed by the Rangers-Alex Ferguson saga. News that Fergie was staying at Pittodrie was announced hours before the second leg with Beveren of Belgium, and the match turned into a pageant of celebration.

Match programme of Ujpest Dozsa v Aberdeen, 7 March 1984

Aberdeen were through once more to the last eight, where they found temselves pitched against Ujpest Dozsa of Budapest. Eastern European teams were hard to assess. On the one hand they seldom won anything, and never the Champions or Cup-Winners' Cup. On the other, they boasted good technical skills. Being paired with teams from communist countries provoked groans, partly because they brought no supporters to generate cash or atmosphere, partly because of visa and other administrative hassles.

Ujpest Dozsa had been doing their stuff in Europe a long time, coming closest in 1968-69 when beaten by Newcastle in the final of the Fairs Cup. That was the beginning of their great age, when Ujpest won the Hungarian championship seven years in a row.

The Dons journeyed to Budapest for the first leg buoyed by an unbeaten run of 27 games. But for inexplicable misses by Strachan and McGhee, they would surely have extended that run. Instead it came to an abrupt halt with a 0-2 defeat.

Aberdeen had never yet pulled back a two-goal deficit in Europe. Of the Hungarian team facing them, Toth, Kiss and No 9 Torocsik had played at Wembley in a 1981 World Cup qualifier. Torocsik's attitude in that game was summed up when he kicked off the second half with his arms folded. He was scarcely more in evidence at Pittodrie. Ujpest seemed unable to escape their half, and for much of the time their penalty area. The game would stand as a personal monument to Mark McGhee, who headed in Strachan's cross in the first half, and in the frenzied closing minutes scored again to take the tie to extra-time. Aberdeen loved extra-time as much as they hated penalty shoot-outs, and it was not long before McGhee completed his hat-trick. It was all too much for goalkeeper Szendrei, who took out his frustration on McLeish and was sent packing.

This season, like last, had any number of worthy candidates for match of the season. Another memorable occasion lay in store, for Manchester United, Juventus and Porto made up the semi-finalists. Porto, having already claimed the scalp of Rangers, made it a Scottish double with a classy display at Pittodrie. In so doing they became the only European opponents – Liverpool aside – to prevent Aberdeen scoring in both legs. Porto lost the final to Juventus.

Match of the Season (3)

Celtic 1   Aberdeen 2

Scottish Cup Final, 19 May 1984

Porto was the only serious disappointment in this phenomenal season. The championship was sewn up at Hearts, on Willie Miller's 29th birthday, with four fixtures in hand.

The path to Hampden in the Scottish Cup was hard work. It took two bites to swallow the Kilmarnock cherry in Round 3, and the pairing with Dundee United in the quarter-final looked ominous, particularly when United forced a goalless draw at Pittodrie. Mark McGhee settled the replay, Dundee were rendered impotent in the semi-final, leaving Aberdeen to contemplate a third successive final. It was the first under McNeill or Ferguson not to involve Rangers. Celtic would take their turn.

Davie Hay's first season in charge at Parkhead had seen Celtic finish runners-up in league and League Cup. The Scottish Cup was therefore their only escape from an unwanted trio of second-places.

McKimmie in, McMaster out, was the only change from 1983, in what would be the Dons' 63rd competitive game of the season – a club record. Aberdeen scored first. McLeish headed on Strachan's corner and Black hooked in, shoulder high, from a position Celtic insisted was offside. Their grievance, expressed most volubly by skipper Roy Aitken, contributed to the flare-up that soon followed. McKimmie, playing at Hampden for the first time, belted a shot from MacLeod off the line. McGhee then burst clear on the right. Aitken raced across and brought him down with a tackle that was, shall we say, neck high. Several minutes were spent fixing up

McGhee, and when he got to his feet referee Valentine flourished a red card. Aitken became the first player to be sent off in a Scottish Cup Final since Rangers' Jock Buchanan in 1929.

Celtic felt doubly aggrieved. They were a goal and a man down. They held Strachan's tongue-wagging responsible for much of their misfortune, and he was singled out for harsh treatment. The ongoing vendettas brought six bookings.

Irrespective of having an extra man there is little rejoicing at the dismissal of an opponent. The reduced team always seem to sprout wings, their team-spirit surges, and they have the perfect excuse in defeat. There is scant praise for beating ten men.

Whatever Ferguson's instructions, his team retreated more and more as the game progressed, seemingly intent on letting Celtic run themselves into the ground. As a tactic it alienated neutrals, but it was four minutes from proving successful when Paul McStay fired a merited equaliser past Leighton.

Unfortunately for Celtic, unless they could conjure a quick winner they would have to contend with extra-time. It was then that Aberdeen regained the ascendancy. Substitute Dougie Bell, uncorked a peach from thirty yards which flew off the junction of post and bar. Strachan squared across goal and McGhee squeezed the ball in from a tight angle. This time Celtic's tank was empty.

Three Scottish Cups, all won in extra-time in the first three years since the extra period's introduction. That was some coincidence. All told, Aberdeen had survived fifteen consecutive ties (plus three replays) and equalled Rangers achievement of three successive Scottish Cups, most recently recorded between 1962 and 1964.

Scottish Champions, Scottish Cup-holders, European Super Cup-winners. No one could argue with that.

SCOTTISH PREMIER DIVISION   1984-85

Premier Division	Champions
League Cup	Second Round
Scottish Cup	Semi-Final
European Champions' Cup	First Round

Hindsight shows the Dons had peaked. A great side by any standards, one that had taken Ferguson six years to build, now suffered the consequences of life in the fast lane. The bids came thick and fast. Ferguson declined an offer to manage Tottenham. As for the players, freedom of contract widened their horizons. It is not surprising that good players should wish to leave a poor team; it was that they should wish to leave one of Aberdeen's eminence, unless of course money, not medals, was the driving factor.

Strachan's impending departure was no secret. 27 years old and a proven international, he had put himself in the shop window. He struck a deal of sorts with Cologne, then changed his mind when Manchester United took an interest. He, at least, could be said to be bettering himself. The same could not be said of Mark McGhee and Doug Rougvie.

McGhee was the same age. A deceptively skilful, hard-working forward with a penchant for burrowing into defences, he too was in his prime. But one sensed that he was tailor-made for Aberdeen's style and would be on the slippery slope elsewhere. Hamburg knew him at first hand and McGhee disappeared into the Bundesliga for two years.

That Doug Rougvie should wish to leave Aberdeen struck many as daft. Not the most skilful of players, he was hugely popular among supporters. It was highly improbable that the 28-year-old, who had picked up a cap against Northern Ireland, would ever strike up the same rapport with any other crowd. And so it proved. A badly-handled wrangle saw him off to Chelsea, from where he quickly disappeared from top-class football. More to the point, Aberdeen had to come to terms with three Scottish internationals – a defender, midfielder, and forward – quitting Pittodrie in a matter of weeks. The team was threatening to come apart at the seams.

DID YOU KNOW?

In June 1984 Aberdeen had EIGHT full internationals at the club:
Willie Miller 33 caps, Alex McLeish 30, Gordon Strachan 28, Jim Leighton 14,
Peter Weir 6, Mark McGhee 4, Neil Simpson 2, Doug Rougvie 1.

Strachan's replacement, Billy Stark, was already *in situ*. Tommy McQueen was signed from Clyde to play left-back. But Ferguson's choice to replace McGhee was inspired. St Mirren had lost too many players to Aberdeen, not to mention managers, to relish any further exodus. In any case, Frank McDougall looked overweight and had little of McGhee's deftness of touch. But at Pittodrie he took wing. For two seasons he was the hottest goalscorer in the business.

In 1982-83 Aberdeen had played 63 competitive matches. In 1983-84 that total dropped to 45, tantamount to losing half a league season. Clearly, their interest in the various cups did not last long.

After years of fiddling, the League Cup had found new sponsors. The Skol Cup, as it became known, did away once and for all with six-game sections and introduced a straight knock-out, Scottish-Cup style, one leg only. This put a smile on the face of Ally MacLeod, now ruling the part-timers of Airdrie in Division 1, for it was they who fired three goals past Jim Leighton to bring about Aberdeen's shortest ever involvement in this competition.

That disappointment counted as nothing compared with the traumas of Berlin in the European Cup. The season was just seven weeks old and already the Dons had been booted from two cups. Defeat at Celtic four days later left Fergie tearing at his hair. Missed penalties cost Aberdeen dear in East Germany and at Parkhead.

The Dons' line-up was in any case unrecognisable. Besides the three summer moves, McMaster was out for the duration, Weir had been crocked pre-season, and Neale Cooper was still match rusty. The new-look team needed time to bed down.

All things considered they had already bedded down pretty well. In the league Aberdeen set the pace with five quick wins. With McDougall firing on all cylinders they shrugged off the Celtic loss to rattle off another eight wins, the last of which, against Celtic at Pittodrie, left supporters hoarse with excitement. Aberdeen won that game 4-2 to widen their lead to six points.

For two worrying weeks over Christmas and New Year it looked like Aberdeen might falter. Archie Knox's Dundee were worth more than a draw, McDougall salvaged a point at Love St, and two goals from Richard Gough inflicted two defeats by Dundee United. The gap over Celtic had closed to two points.

Ferguson sorted out the problem. The next twelve games hauled in 21 points. Celtic could not keep pace and they travelled to Pittodrie on 27 April needing to win to deny the Dons the title.

DID YOU KNOW?

Frank McDougall scored in 8 successive games from 29 September 1984.

DID YOU KNOW?

Between January 1982 and April 1985 Aberdeen survived 23 Scottish Cup-ties. Of these, 18 were won and 5 were drawn.

Aberdeen had by then suffered a huge disappointment. Minus McDougall, injured at Raith, the Dons' hopes of a fourth Scottish Cup were scuppered by Dundee United in a semi-final replay. The Dons did not lie down quietly. Neale Cooper and United's Davie Dodds were sent off and Ferguson lost his cool when Malpas handled unseen.

'Semi-finals are no good to this club,' Ferguson snarled afterwards.

Ironically, Aberdeen had never secured a major prize in front of their own fans. Cups, of course, had been won at Hampden, or Gothenburg, and the Super Cup did not really count. Previous championships had been won at Clyde, Easter Road, and most recently at Tynecastle. Now came the chance to clinch the title at Pittodrie.

Aberdeen gifted Davie Hay's team a penalty when Stark nudged Mo Johnston. Willie Miller headed in a free-kick to equalise. But the two critical moments were still to come. Celtic 'scored' again, only for the referee to blow for a doubtful foul on Leighton. Pittodrie breathed deep, then squealed in anguish as deep into injury time Hewitt missed a gaping goal. The final whistle blew, and Celtic players shook the hands of the champions.

		P	W	D	L	F	A	(GD)	Pts
1	ABERDEEN	34	25	5	4	84	25	(+59)	55
2	Celtic	33	21	7	5	74	28	(+46)	49

Strictly speaking, Aberdeen had *not* sewn up the title. They had two away games left, Celtic three at home. Five games could erode a goal-difference of thirteen, especially as the Scottish League had deferred proclaiming the Dons champions at Hibs in 1980. Then, a goal difference of ten had to be erased in *one* match.

Suppose the championship flag had been unfurled at Pittodrie, only for Aberdeen to lose their last two games 0-1 and for Celtic to win their last three 4-0. Stranger things have happened.

DID YOU KNOW?

In season 1984-85 Aberdeen took 7 or 8 league points from every team in the league except Celtic and Dundee United.

Match of the Season

Dynamo Berlin 2   Aberdeen 1
European Cup, 1st Round, 2nd Leg, 3 October 1984

Among the other seeded teams in the 1984-85 Champions' Cup were Liverpool, Juventus, Benfica, Stuttgart, Red Star Belgrade and Feyenoord. Ferguson admitted to a sinking feeling when learning of Aberdeen's first opponents. Dynamo Berlin had won the East German championship six times in a row and were seasoned campaigners in the European Cup. They had reached the quarter-finals in 1979-80 (when losing to Nottingham Forest) and 1983-84.

Aberdeen had home advantage in the first leg. Weir was still injured and McDougall was serving a ban imposed when playing in a European tie with St Mirren. Ferguson would have settled for the two-goal lead that was Aberdeen's after 82 minutes. Black's twin headers looked to have given a healthy cushion, but Shulz's header from a corner radically changed the complexion of the tie.

In years to come Dons supporters would become familiar with 2-1 home wins in Europe. Opponents only needed a 1-0 victory in the return leg, and they invariably achieved it.

The match in Berlin did not go quite to plan. Fortunes see-sawed every few minutes, which was not easy on the nerves of Dons fans listening at home to live radio transmission. Thom's second-half goal put Dynamo ahead. Ian Angus's thumping shot restored the Dons' advantage. They were six minutes from Round 2 when crazy defending allowed Ernst to force the ball past Leighton. All square, 3-3, with one away goal apiece. Miller chipped against the bar in extra-time but the ball stayed out and Aberdeen were confronted with a dreaded shoot-out. Shades of Honved in 1970.

Aberdeen went first. Porteous, McQueen, Hewitt and Stark sank their kicks, but Schulz drove Dynamo's third against Leighton's crossbar. Willie Miller took responsibility for the fifth and final kick. It was brave, because he was not normally a penalty taker. But his shot was too close to Rudwaleit, who guessed correctly to save.

Now it was sudden death. Those relectant to take a penalty could no longer hide. Black's effort was blocked, whereupon Trielloff fired Aberdeen out of the European Cup.

Dynamo Berlin were beaten by FK Austria in Round 2.

DID YOU KNOW?

Aberdeen improved their points total in each of Ferguson's first 7 seasons.
The Dons' 59 points in 1984-85 was a Premier League record.

SCOTTISH PREMIER DIVISION   1985-86

Fine Fare Premier Division	Fourth
Skol League Cup	Winners
Scottish Cup	Winners
European Champions' Cup	Quarter-Final

1985-86 would prove to be Alex Ferguson's last and most topsy-turvy season. It would also be the complete opposite of its predecessor. Then, Aberdeen were swept from the cups, allowing them tunnel vision in the league. In 1985-86 they struggled to pick up league points, but proved immovable in the knock-outs.

The summer saw one significant import. Ex-Ranger Jim Bett was tempted back to Scotland from Belgian club Lokeren. A languid midfielder, a regular in the Scottish national side, he would in time become Aberden's central playmaker.

Hitherto, the players Ferguson unloaded had gone to England or abroad. Pittodrie was spared the sight of returning heroes wearing opponents' strip. Steve Cowan had never been more than striker's understudy until he transferred to Hibs. But Dougie Bell was different. He was a museum piece, seldom picked except in Europe, when his mazy skills were set loose. Bell wanted to leave and signed for Rangers, the first Don to do so in the European era.

Aberdeen's season was thrown into turmoil in September, when Jock Stein died following Scotland's World Cup-tie in Cardiff. Alex Ferguson was Stein's deputy. With the World Cup finals just nine months away there was no sense in bringing in an outsider. Ferguson was the only real candidate.

Unwilling to take the post permanently, this meant him doing two jobs at once. From Aberdeen's point of view, half a Fergie seemed better than none, though Pittodrie lost much of its buzz without his day-to-day supervision.

Aberdeen did not dally in winning their first trophy. The League Cup was the one Scottish prize to have eluded Ferguson. Better that than any other, but a clean sweep of domestic trophies was something only managers of Rangers and Celtic had achieved in modern times.

Aberdeen's path to the final was distinguished by two factors: preserving their goal throughout, and outsmarting Dundee United in the semi-final. In the final Hibs were simply overwhelmed.

The quest for the European Cup began with a gentle dip. Akranes of Iceland could not capitalise on scoring first. The choppy waters arrived in Round 2. Though the Dons were their efficient selves in Geneva, drawing 0-0, the second leg with Servette was an eye-opener. McDougall headed Aberdeen in front, from which moment Servette teased and tormented the Dons to their wits' end. No previous Continental team had handed out such punishment in Ferguson's time, and he was honest enough to admit it. Aberdeen had the goal, but Servette taught all the lessons.

The Dons faced few comparable hardships on the domestic front. Shrugging off defeat at Parkhead on the Saturday following Stein's death, Aberdeen hit the front in October and stayed there through to December. Outwardly, everything looked smoothly on course. But cracks were showing. Defeats at St Mirren and Clydebank, of all places, were not a sign of champions. Like Liverpool, Ferguson had boasted that the Dons seldom lost twice in a row, and the Kilbowie result sent shock-waves through the Premier League.

Autumn trophies have been known to induce complacency, a sense that the job's been done. The Skol Cup may have had that effect, though Aberdeen also had to contend with Ferguson's divided loyalties. Whatever the cause, league form disintegrated – especially on the road. The Dons went five months without an away win, and even at home the goals dried up alarmingly.

One win in ten games ditched Aberdeen from first to fourth. This was their worst run under Ferguson's management, and in any ordinary season it would have dashed hopes of the championship. But 1985-86 was reverting to a pattern last seen in 1979-80. No team was good enough to pull away. The Old and New Firms were treading water and Hearts stepped into the vacuum.

Aberdeen got their second wind with the arrival of the Scottish Cup. February was a good month: the Dons stepped two rounds nearer Hampden and picked up seven league points. March brought the extra-time defeat of Dundee in one cup but elimination by Gothenburg in another. Aberdeen's league surge came to an anticlimactic end with home defeats by Celtic and Dundee United, but by then they had booked another date at Hampden.

44 league points was Aberdeen's worst for seven years. The team had clearly gone backwards, though two cups in one season offered the best possible disguise.

Match of the Season (1)

Hibernian 0   Aberdeen 3

Skol Cup Final, 27 October 1985

For teams outside the Old and New Firms, getting to any cup final in the 1980s was achievement in itself, since there were now four

Scottish giants to be bypassed *en route*. Hibs' endeavours in seeing off Celtic and Rangers earned plaudits, though the daunting shape of table-topping Aberdeen barred their path in the final.

Hibs presented the Dons with a fresh challenge. Previous cup wins had been against the Old Firm, in which Aberdeen had to withstand the weight of history. Against Hibernian they were such overwhelming favourites that complacency was as big a danger as the opposition. Ex-Don Steve Cowan served as a fifth columnist, but he of all people knew Aberdeen's powers. Hibs, in fact, were a fragile team, still recovering from losing their first six games. They would finish the season avoiding relegation by one place.

The match became dubbed 'the twelve-minute final'. That was the time it took Aberdeen to go two up and kill the contest. Hewitt's ferreting into the heart of Hibs' defence produced goals for Eric Black and Billy Stark which silenced the green end of Hampden and knocked the stuffing from their players.

Aberdeen had never known such luxury so early in a cup final. Hibs hadn't the nous to strike back and when Black scored number three the only question was whether Aberdeen could go the whole tournament without conceding a goal. They could.

DID YOU KNOW?

Aberdeen's triumph in the1985-86 Skol Cup completed a set of domestic medals for Leighton, McKimmie, Stark, Cooper, McLeish, Black and Simpson.

Match of the Season (2)

Aberdeen 2   IFK Gothenburg 2
European Cup, Quarter-Final, 1st Leg, 5 March 1986

The squeaky victory over Servette suggested Aberdeen might go all the way. In the quarter-finals they were happy to avoid Juventus, Barcelona, Bayern Munich and Anderlecht – not to mention the eventual winners, Steaua Bucharest. All things considered, IFK Gothenburg was as kind a draw as Ferguson could have wished. But it had an unpleasant downside. For it meant returning to the Ullevi Stadium, scene of the Dons' greatest triumph. It was asking much to enshrine the Ullevi a second time.

Swedish football is hard to assess. The national team likes to defy the handicaps of small population and part-time league to assert itself in World Cups. Swedish clubs, too, shrug off the effects of selling their best to Germany and elsewhere to challenge for European trophies. Gothenburg won the UEFA Cup in 1982.

Frank McDougall tangles with Paul Hegarty v Dundee United, 9 October 1985

As the Swedish season extends from April to October, the champions must wait a year before competing in the European Cup. Gothenburg were champions in 1982, 83 and 84. Playing in March, a month before their season commenced, was equivalent to making Aberdeen play vital cup-ties in July.

European football in 1986 was far from the multi-nationalism that would sweep the game in the 1990s. Aberdeen were full of Scots, Gothenburg full of Swedes. Sweden still exported her best players. Sweeper Glenn Hysen would arrive at Liverpool in 1989, while quicksilver striker Johnny Ekstrom would do the rounds with a host of great clubs.

The first leg was preceded by a minute's silence for Sweden's assassinated prime minister, Olof Palme. It was a sombre moment before what turned out to be the last of Pittodrie's great European nights.

Aberdeen were minus Leighton in goal and McDougall in attack. The tie was similar to that with Servette. The Dons scored first – Willie Miller's fiftieth European game rewarded with a cracking left-footer – whereupon the visitors did all the pressing. The Dons might have survived but for late goals in each half. When Hewitt made it 2-1 eleven minutes from time it gave Aberdeen a fighting chance. But with the stadium whistling for the referee to blow, Ekstrom slipped through a threadbare defence and rounded Bryan Gunn to level the scores. A match that had begun in silence ended in silence.

Gothenburg second time round was unrecognisable. The scent of late winter hung in the air. Only 17,000 – mostly Dons fans – had attended the Cup-Winners' Final. Now the Ullevi was crammed with 44,000 Swedes. Aberdeen had to win. Experienced teams in this situation play tight rather than hurl men forward. This is what Ferguson prescribed. Alas, the Dons seldom got a sniff of a goal and they exited in a trough of anti-climax.

In the semi-final Gothenburg took a 3-0 lead to Terry Venables' Barcelona, but went out on penalties.

Match of the Season (3)

Hearts 0   Aberdeen 3

Scottish Cup Final, 10 May 1986

March put paid to the European Cup, April to the Scottish championship. The only hiccup on the road to Hampden came in the quarter-final against Dundee, who led twice overall before Weir floated an extra-time winner in a replay. Hibs were despatched in the semi-final 3-0, and must have been heartily sick of Aberdeen.

Hearts were sick of everything. They had come good since October, going 27 league games without loss until the closing minutes of the closing match, when Celtic won handsomely at Love St to pip them. The one consolation for Hearts' players was that they could now focus on Hampden.

Form pointed to a Hearts' win. They had bettered Aberdeen in the league and in head-to-head results. They had reached the final with hard-fought wins over Rangers and Dundee United. Psychology, however, pointed to Aberdeen, whose cup record was awesome, and whose opponents had just lived through the worst day of their footballing lives. In the minds of bookies, psychology outweighed form: Aberdeen were firm favourites, though the whole of neutral Scotland (Hibernian supporters aside) was rooting for Hearts.

Eric Black would not play. He had signed for French club Metz behind Ferguson's back and was dropped. Black had been part of all three previous Cup wins, and had scored twice against Hibs in the Skol Cup Final. He would be missed. There was a welcome place for John McMaster, whose injuries had restricted him to just a handful of games in three years.

Previous finals had been hard work, won in extra-time. Hearts' lax defending, however, presented Aberdeen with a quick goal. Hewitt bored into the danger area unchallenged and shot low inside Henry Smith's left post.

Conceding an early goal was the last thing Hearts needed. They played thereafter with plenty of huff, but Aberdeen were too canny. Hearts created just two real chances, when John Robertson's lob carried too far, and when Neil Berry drove against Leighton's cross-bar. Three minutes after half-time Aberdeen scored a sweet second. Weir's cross, McDougall's dummy, Hewitt's shot.

Defeat for Hearts was made worse by Stark's diving header, and less dignified when Walter Kidd – booked in the first half – was sent off for slinging the ball at Cooper. Kidd thereby joined Roy Aitken in the select register of players sent off in Scottish Cup Finals against Aberdeen.

Ferguson had won his tenth and what would be his final trophy with the Dons, eight of which had come in four years. Now he was off to take charge in Mexico, along with four players – Leighton, Miller, McLeish and Bett.

6

THE HANGOVER
1986-1991

SCOTTISH PREMIER DIVISION   1986-87

Fine Fare Premier Division	Fourth
Skol League Cup	Quarter-Final
Scottish Cup	Third Round
European Cup-Winners' Cup	First Round

The parting of the ways had to come. Alex Ferguson, still in his early forties, had added 'World Cup veteran' to his already formidable *curriculum vitae*. He now commanded the highest profile in the Scottish game.

Wise to the way the wind was blowing, chairman Dick Donald offered him a directorship. Ferguson became, so to speak, a managing director. Yet one sensed the season needed to start well to prevent him day-dreaming of bigger stages.

Aberdeen were still coming to terms with the death of visionary vice-chairman Chris Anderson. The playing squad had been depleted by the loss of Eric Black to the nobodies of Metz and of Neale Cooper to Aston Villa. Cooper's was another move which a cooler head might have resisted. But for brief interludes Cooper was gone from the top class game. The third loss was Frank McDougall. Back trouble ended his career as it would later end Black's.

Between them, Black and McDougall had scored 79 goals in two seasons. There was no way to recoup that kind of return. For the moment, the burden fell on Hewitt and Stark.

This was a new look Premier League. Its high hopes on inception had proved ill-founded. Entertainment had not noticeably increased, nor had standards. Fear ruled. With a twenty percent casualty rate those teams not pursuing the title were peering over their shoulders and playing accordingly.

Match programme of the disastrous Cup-Winners' Cup-tie in Sion, 1 October 1986

Division 1 clubs, too, were chafing at the bit. They demanded their place in the sun. The tail wagged the dog, and with no club being relegated in 1986 the Premier League was extended to twelve teams. The fear-factor was marginally reduced in exchange for a gruelling and, many considered, preposterously long 44-match league season.

For the Dons, the first month passed without alarm. Tannadice, in the first game, saw the only defeat, and Stark quickly took his goal tally to seven.

It couldn't last. September was miserable. Celtic extinguished Aberdeen's hold on the Skol Cup in a Pittodrie shoot-out, Hewitt and Willie Miller failing to score from the spot.

Defeats by Hearts and Rangers left Aberdeen off the pace in the league. Ferguson could no longer delay bringing in reinforcements. He had already introduced Bobby Connor from Dundee into mid-field, and David Robertson was nudging his way into the team at left-back. Now Ferguson bolstered the forward line by signing Davie Dodds for £200,000. Dodds had inflicted enough damage over the years with Dundee United, but a close-season move to Neuchatel Xamax in Switzerland hadn't suited him.

Dodds was no McDougall in the six-yard box and no Black in the air. His signing appeared to be either stop-gap or short-sighted.

Equally unsettling was the idea of poaching players attached to rivals. Aberdeen's prizes had been won by a combination of youth and imports from lesser clubs. Dodds signalled a departure from a well-established practice. More to the point, his four goals from 27 games did little to ease the goal drought.

Dodds' arrival coincided with Aberdeen's darkest moment of the Ferguson era. Four years after Sion's eleven-goal thrashing in the Cup-Winners' Cup, the teams were paired again. The Dons had to come from behind to take a narrow lead to Switzerland. What happened there was the stuff of farce. In four minutes, Sion scored direct from a corner, putting them ahead on away goals. By half-time they had scored another and Jim Bett had been sent off. There would be no reprieve. So elated were the Swiss by their win that they did a lap of honour. That in itself shows how highly Aberdeen were regarded – and how heavily they had fallen.

All the hard-earned lessons had been cast to the winds. Ferguson took the Sion nightmare badly. His yardstick – at Pittodrie and Old Trafford – is success in Europe, the biggest stage. There is little doubt that Aberdeen's early exit stripped the club of one of its few assets when the Manchester United bombshell exploded.

Chairmen of successful smaller clubs live in dread of tremors at big ones. Aberdeen had gone through it before, with Rangers. On Thursday, 6 November 1986 ailing Manchester United fired Ron Atkinson. Almost in the same breath they announced that Ferguson was their man. In football jargon, he had clearly been 'tapped' beforehand.

North-east folk reacted philosophically. Indeed, the reappointment of Archie Knox in the close season as Ferguson's No 2 had the air of a planned succession. Aberdeen supporters could live with Knox in charge; he was widely respected in the game and knew the club from the inside. But Knox was also off. Lieutenant at Old Trafford carried greater kudos than general at Pittodrie, though he agreed to stay on as lame duck president until such time as Aberdeen found someone else.

Knox's decision to follow his master threw the Aberdeen board into disarray. That much is clear from the time it took to appoint a successor. Some supporters urged Willie Miller to step up there and then. Knox was booed as he appeared for the home game against St Mirren, while Miller's every touch brought howls of approval.

ABERDEEN HONOURS UNDER ALEX FERGUSON

10.
3 Leagues, 4 Scottish Cups, 1 League Cup, 1 Cup-Winners' Cup, 1 Super Cup.

The club was rudderless for two weeks. The list of candidates included the Dundee pairing of Jocky Scott and Drew Jarvie, Alex Smith of Stirling Albion, Tommy Craig, Craig Brown (Scotland's number two), and Ally MacLeod. Others mentioned were Billy Bremner, Jim McLean, Bruce Rioch, John Greig and Lou Macari.

Ian Porterfield's name was on nobody's list. He applied on spec, was called to interview, and evidently impressed. Porterfield had made news twice in his life – first, when scoring the winning goal for second-division Sunderland in the 1973 FA Cup final; then when fracturing his skull in a road accident.

The gist of Porterfield's application was that he was a winner, both as player and manager. He had lifted Sheffield United from Division 4 to Division 2. They had then become becalmed. Patience ran out, and following a 2-5 home defeat by Norwich in March 1986 he was shown the door.

His arrival eight months later at Pittodrie overrode inescapable problems. Though born in Dunfermline and playing for Raith, it was in England that Porterfield established his football career. He knew little about the Scottish game and had never managed in the top flight. A gulf existed between English second-division also-rans and a club challenging for honours on all fronts. Stepping into Alex Ferguson's shoes was hard enough as it was. Many thought the appointment unwise, among them Ferguson himself, who later described it as 'ridiculous'.

Pittodrie sportingly rose to acclaim the new man as he took his seat for a home debut against Graeme Souness's Rangers. The Dons won. In fairness, Porterfield made a fist of his first six months, making no changes for changes sake. Senior players, shocked by Ferguson's departure, seemed well disposed to Porterfield's methods. Not until his sixteenth match did he taste defeat, in a Scottish Cup-tie with Celtic. But that was followed by back-to-back losses to St Mirren and Dundee United and the high hopes vanished. The season ended in a trough of despair, two wins from the last seven games. But Porterfield could say, rightly, that this had been Ferguson's team and it had been disintegrating before he arrived. Next season would be the time to judge him.

Match of the Season

Aberdeen 2   Celtic 2
Scottish Cup, 3rd Round, 1 February 1986

This was the first season since 1980-81 in which the Dons won nothing, so there are no cup finals or championship deciders to relive. In fact, few individual games stand out. The defeat in Sion was the most far-reaching, but it would be perverse to dwell upon that.

The Scottish Cup-tie with Celtic came at a time when Ian Porterfield's extended honeymoon was in full swing. He was almost two months into the job, the team were unbeaten, and now came the chance to defend the last trophy masterminded by his predecessor. Table-topping Celtic came out of the hat in Round 3.

The tie was put back to Sunday to accommodate a live TV audience. Grampian was snow-bound, the pitch was unplayably icy, and but for TV referee George Smith would surely have called the match off. He would be glad no serious injuries resulted, but a combination of the pitch, defensive frailties, and two committed teams served up a cocktail of thrills to warm the blood.

First blood to Celtic. Jim Leighton lost his footing and McInally's header looped over his head and went in off the bar. Celtic found their feet, literally, with greater assurance in the first half, and when rookie Robertson slid in on Paul McStay from behind Brian McClair converted the penalty. Aberdeen appeared to lack the wit or sure-footedness to mount a challenge.

That was about to change. With Hewitt replacing young Joe Miller, Porterfield pushed four men up and suddenly the dynamic of the game changed. Danny McGrain eased Paul Wright off the ball and looked aghast when Smith pointed to the spot. Jim Bett did his job, leaving Aberdeen 22 minutes in which to save the tie.

They needed only five before Hewitt kept his balance to round Bonner and level. With Pittodrie in ferment Celtic were forced on their heels. Chances went begging – Paul Wright twice shot past and Conner nearly touched in Hewitt's cross.

The final whistle blew, Willie Miller was voted Mr Superfit man of the match, and fans looked forward to an equally enthralling replay. It was not to be. Safety-first tactics ruled, as they would in the second replay at Dens Park, which was won by Brian McClair in the mud. Porterfield's honeymoon was over.

SCOTTISH PREMIER DIVISION   1987-88

Fine Fare Premier Division	Fourth
Skol League Cup	Runners-Up
Scottish Cup	Semi-Final
UEFA Cup	Second Round

Ian Porterfield had had his six months' grace. Now he was on his own. Defeats could no longer be dismissed as the embers of Alex Ferguson's tired regime.

Billy Stark departed to Celtic in the summer. His style did not please everyone, but his goals would be missed. Hewitt had been quickly disenchanted with the new set up and was open to offers. This season his contribution would be just one goal from 26 games.

Having lost Black and McDougall's goals, Aberdeen now needed to replenish those of Stark and Hewitt. With Davie Dodds missing half the season through injury it required no great insight to see where Aberdeen's deficiencies lay. Porterfields's summer signings – Welsh international Peter Nicholas from Luton and winger Gary Hackett from Shrewsbury – would not beef up the attack, though Nicholas took to his new surroundings like a duck to water and was one of the few plusses in an otherwise mediocre season.

It began well enough. By early October Aberdeen were top of the league, into Round 2 of the UEFA Cup and through to the Skol Cup Final, having disposed of Celtic's challenge along the way. Sixteen games, all told, and not a defeat among them. The signing of Hull's Keith Edwards – whom Porterfield knew at Sheffield United – was hoped to be worth a few goals.

October was Ian Porterfield's nemesis, the month everything turned sour. Defeat by Hearts was followed by tepid goalless draws against both Dundee clubs and a home loss to Celtic. Feyenoord extinguished Aberdeen's European dreams and Rangers snatched the Skol Cup after an epic final. Come November, the Dons were down to fourth with just the Scottish Cup to keep the season alive.

The Dons launched another unbeaten run that carried them into 1988 on the trail of leaders Celtic. The air was heavy with transfer talk. Peter Weir had already gone to Leicester and Joe Miller to Celtic. Miller cost £650,000, the richest deal yet between Scottish clubs. Hackett and Edwards would soon return to England, emasculating what remained of Aberdeen's strike force. One minute it seemed Alex McLeish was bound for Old Trafford to link up with Ferguson. The next, Aberdeen were linked with Kevin Drinkell, a journeyman striker at Norwich who would shortly end up at Ibrox.

The signing Porterfield did make surpassed anything supporters dreamed of. Charlie Nicholas was a Scottish gem. He had been lured away from Celtic by the bright lights of Highbury, where he spent five largely unfulfilled years. He was no longer sure of his place with club or country. Arsenal were so happy to see the back of him that he was available for a song. It says much that a flock of big clubs did not rush for his signature. Celtic were noticeably silent, and for want of any better offers Nicholas signed for Aberdeen for the paltry sum of £400,000.

None of this dampened enthusiasm for his arrival. Nicholas was still only 26: if he knuckled down he could do much to rejuvenate Aberdeen's prospects and his own. Talk of his coming was enough to sell out Pittodrie against Dundee United, the goalless draw extending the Dons' unbeaten run to thirteen games.

Nicholas made his debut at Easter Road on 9 January, taking the place of Davie Dodds, whose cartilage had an appointment with a surgeon's knife. Nicholas had seen no first-team football since August, but despite his rustiness he struck the woodwork twice in a 0-0 draw. Better times looked to be on their way.

They did not arrive. Nicholas himself did not greatly disappoint, but the team could not fashion the chances upon which he thrived. He conjured flashes of magic, but in the hard currency of goals, his was a poor return, just five in 22 games and none at Pittodrie.

Worse, his arrival coincided with a downturn in results. The team that couldn't lose without him became beatable. Aberdeen stumbled against Dundee United in the semi-finals of the Scottish Cup, after two replays, and in the league slithered further behind, finishing a disappointing fourth. Seventeen league draws, ten of them goalless, had taken their toll.

Porterfield had played his last hand. Problems in his private life were already the talk of the town, and once the tabloids aired them he was on borrowed time. Aberdeen FC's proud claim never to have sacked a manager was put under strain, but a formula was reached that enabled Porterfield to leave with dignity and the club to continue its boast. His assistant, Jimmy Mullen, left too. Porterfield teamed up with Peter Nicholas at Chelsea, becoming assistant manager, before taking charge of Reading and then the Zambian national side.

DID YOU KNOW?

According to the Skonto Riga match programme in August 1994, the Scottish Premier League includes the following clubs:
Reindzers, Moteruell, Seltik, Dandi Junaited, Kilmarnol, Patrik Tistl, Sent Dzonston, Rait. The leading scorer is Heitli of Reindzers.

Match of the Season (1)

Aberdeen 2   Feyenoord 1

UEFA Cup, 2nd Round, 1st Leg, 21 October 1987

Like Scotland, Holland is a small country whose football is dominated by a handful of clubs. One of them, Feyenoord, had beaten Celtic in the final of the 1970 European Cup. The Amsterdam club's most recent Dutch honours were the league and cup double in 1984. In 1986-87 Feyenoord had finished a distant third behind PSV Eindhoven and Ajax.

Feyenoord had a virtual season-ticket for Europe, and their team at any given time contained its share of Dutch internationals. This particular side also accommodated Dave Mitchell, once of Rangers, who had led the Australian attack against Scotland in two recent World Cup play-offs.

Porterfield's introduction to European football had produced a stuttering victory over the Irish part-timers Bohemians. Rinus Israel, Feyenoord's coach, saw the Dons surrender their unbeaten start at Tynecastle. Porterfield now faced some hard choices. Hewitt was out of touch, Dodds injured, Edwards ineligible. Willie Falconer was big and strong but not a heavy scorer. Porterfield gambled, playing Falconer at No 3 and bringing in Peter Weir for his first game of the season.

Conceding silly goals at home once again cost Aberdeen dear. Dave Mitchell found himself in the clear, 'collided' with Leighton, and the Dane, Lars Elstrup, scored from the penalty spot.

Deficits are best erased quickly, and it was not long before Weir flighted the free-kick from which Falconer headed Aberdeen level. Early in the second half Feyenoord skipper Wijnstekers treated Weir uncivilly and was ushered from the pitch. Ideally, the Dons needed two more goals to travel in confidence, but they managed just one, when Joe Miller netted at the second attempt.

Aberdeen required a 0-0 or 1-1 draw in Amsterdam, where they adopted one of the most negative formations ever practised by the Dons abroad. Irvine played at right back in place of McKimmie and was partially at fault with the goal that cost Aberdeen the match. The Dons never threatened to pull it back and went out tamely. In Round 3 Feyenoord lost to Bayer Leverkusen, the eventual winners.

ABERDEEN HONOURS UNDER IAN PORTERFIELD

None.
Runners-up in Skol Cup Final 1987-88.

Match of the Season (2)

Rangers 3   Aberdeen 3

Skol Cup Final, 25 October 1987

Four days after the first leg with Feyenoord, the Dons challenged for the Skol Cup. They had disposed of Celtic in the quarter-finals, Dundee in the semis, and now faced a Rangers team revolutionised by Graeme Souness. Ibrox was transforming itself into a home for English expatriates who – on account of the Heysel ban – saw no European prospects back home. Ray Wilkins and Mark Walters had not yet arrived, Terry Butcher had broken his leg and Trevor Francis was on the bench. Rangers' only English representative in the final was former Spurs hard-man Graham Roberts, captain in the absence of Souness.

Rangers had made a poor start to the season and had already lost at Pittodrie, but one statistic stood out. By September, Ally McCoist had scored more goals than any Aberdeen player would do by May. Other than to prefer Simpson to Weir, Porterfield stuck with the team that had struggled against Feyenoord.

Given the rivalry with Rangers and Aberdeen's chronic weakness up front, many expected a war of attrition. Almost everyone was taken aback by the goal-feast that was served up, for this was an exhilarating match, played without rancour by two adventurous teams. It was fired into life inside nine minutes when keeper Nicky Walker – later to sign for Aberdeen – toppled Falconer and Bett lashed home the penalty. McLeish then had an effort cleared off the line. But instead of leading 2-0 the Dons were soon trailing. Willie Miller impeded McCoist in the arc and Davie Cooper's free-kick speared into the top corner. Ian Durrant then sprinted through the middle to score Rangers' second.

With Weir taking over from Simpson, Hewitt's deflected shot levelled the scores. After 81 minutes Bett's cross was spectacularly headed in by Falconer, and the Dons had only to see out time. Few would have bet against them doing so, but Robert Fleck's messy goal sent the final into extra-time.

Those with an eye to history knew what to expect. Aberdeen were kings in extra-time, clowns in penalty shoot-outs. They had better score in the thirty minutes available, or face another exposure to soccer's equivalent of Russian roulette.

The players appeared to ignore the script. Bucking the trend, it was Rangers who were indisputably in control as Willie Miller and Co manned the barricades. It was almost as if Aberdeen wanted the opportunity to redeem themselves in a shoot-out.

They got their chance. Rangers went first; first blood to McCoist. Jim Bett levelled. Davie Cooper made it 2-1, at which point Peter Nicholas's effort grazed the crossbar on its way over. Conversions by Fleck and Weir, Trevor Francis and Hewitt left Ian Durrant to net with the decisive kick. Joe Miller, Aberdeen's scheduled fifth taker, was not needed. Durrant was voted man of the match after this, Rangers' fifteenth win in twenty League Cup Finals.

Sympathy for Nicholas increased when it was disclosed that – despite missing two penalties for Luton last season – he had been press-ganged into service when only four Dons volunteered.

The Final itself had been such a joy that in an unprecedented gesture the Scottish League and the sponsors presented Aberdeen with a trophy to commemorate their part in the occasion.

The principal casualty of the result was Ian Porterfield, he of the self-professed winning habit. Had he won a cup so soon after arriving he would have done much to lay the ghost of Ferguson. Porterfield lost when it mattered so much that he won.

SCOTTISH PREMIER DIVISION   1988-89

B & Q Premier Division	Runners-Up
Skol League Cup	Runners-Up
Scottish Cup	Fourth Round
UEFA Cup	First Round

This time the Aberdeen board did not have to search far and wide for a manager. Alex Smith was already on the payroll. Smith's was an unlikely path to a top job. His playing career saw him scratching around the lower divisions until it was truncated by injury, and his managerial career had only recently taken him out of the shadows.

As with Alex Ferguson, it was St Mirren who gave Smith his big break. In his first season at Love St – 1986-87 – Smith masterminded a Scottish Cup triumph over Dundee United. But friction at the club led to his dismissal in the spring of 1988, at which point he accepted Porterfield's coaching offer at Pittodrie.

Smith was therefore on hand when Porterfield left. But the board evidently had misgivings about allowing him unfettered control and brought in two former Dons to share the workload. Jocky Scott and Drew Jarvie had picked up League Cup winners medals under Ally MacLeod in 1976-77. They were recruited from Dundee, Jarvie as assistant manager and Scott – in a semantic game that confused everyone – co-manager. The buck, however, stopped with Smith.

The priority of this new triumvirate was to build a side which could score as well as prevent goals. This necessitated a hard look at what masqueraded as a forward line. The latest striker to leave was Willie Falconer, who decamped to Watford. In two years Aberdeen had lost the goals of Black, McDougall, Stark, Edwards, Joe Miller, Weir and Falconer. Dodds and Nicholas were the only ones left, unless Hewitt could turn back the clock.

Aberdeen had also lost their goalkeeper. Jim Leighton had won everything going, and the Bermuda Triangle of Leighton, Miller and McLeish had been responsible for many an opposing shipwreck. Leighton was Scotland's undisputed first choice keeper, but had let it be known that he sought fresh challenges. He left the pitch after the last match (Motherwell, 0-0, his 35th clean sheet in 59 matches) applauding the crowd, and they he. At the time, it was assumed he was headed for Europe; instead Leighton landed at Old Trafford, the one Aberdeen player Ferguson managed to entice.

In years to come, Dons' fans would turn against Alex Smith, though he was responsible in his early seasons for much that was good. He was, for example, the architect of the Dutch invasion.

> **Q   Have Aberdeen ever faced a member of Germany's Euro 96 winners?**
> **A   Yes. Matthias Sammer of Dynamo Dresden in the 1988-89 UEFA Cup.**

First to arrive was Theo Snelders from Twente Enschede. In the eyes of many, Leighton was the best No 1 Aberdeen had ever had, or was likely to have. Snelders quickly made them reconsider. He appeared, heaven forbid, even better than Leighton. At the end of his first season he would win the coveted Scottish Players' Player of the Year award.

But Snelders was only the first Dutch import. A lad from Merseyside, Paul Mason, was signed from Groningen. Versatility is seldom appreciated by supporters. Bought as a full-back, Mason played most of his time in midfield, and when, later, he was pushed into service as a striker became top scorer.

Like Porterfield, Smith achieved a good start. The Premier League had reverted to ten teams, allowing midweek games once again to be the preserve of the Skol Cup and Europe. Aberdeen made headway in the first but came a cropper in the second.

In those times UEFA's seeding principle was crude but straightforward. Clubs reaching the semi-finals of any competition were seeded in all for the next five seasons. This meant that, having reached the last four of the Cup-Winners' Cup in 1983-84, Aberdeen were seeded up to and including this season, 1988-89. Seeded teams were kept apart in Round 1. From next season Aberdeen would be thrown to the lions from the start.

The seeded Dons faced the unseeded Dynamo Dresden in Round 1 of the UEFA Cup. Aberdeen had painful memories of East German opponents – missed penalties against Dynamo Berlin had put them out of the competition.

Dresden had done their homework. Pack their defence and it was unlikely Aberdeen had the wit to break through. In this, they were right. Dynamo took a 0-0 draw back to East Germany and won comfortably, aided by the expulsion of David Robertson. The reason for yet another early exit from Europe was glaringly obvious. For the sixth successive tie they had failed to score in the away leg.

The Dons got Dresden out of their system by beating Rangers at Pittodrie (more of which shortly), and a fortnight later took on the same opponents in the final of the Skol Cup. Sadly, Alex Smith fared no better than Porterfield.

DID YOU KNOW?

Aberdeen's Premier League record v Dundee since 1975-76
Played 34, Won 26, Drew 8, Lost 0, For 71, Against 17, Points 60

Pele is photographed at Pittodrie, along with Scott, Jarvie, Teddy Scott and Smith

In the league Aberdeen were proving difficult to beat, but prone to too many low-scoring draws to mount a serious challenge. But it was not till the last day of 1988 that the Dons suffered their second defeat, and then to the most unlikely opponents. Aberdeen's crushing superiority over Dundee had no parallel. Year in, year out, four times a season, Dundee would find themselves hammered into the turf. One had to go back to the inaugural season of the Premier League to find the last occasion on which Dundee triumphed. Since then they had tried and failed 34 times. Now, aided by two goals by Tommy Coyne, they finally won at last.

Dundee United, on the other hand, enjoyed under Jim McLean an unwelcome superiority in the cups. This was underlined in a protracted fourth round Scottish Cup-tie that saw the Dons finally vanquished after three matches and five hours.

It was February, and the season threatened to have an awfully long tail, so it was timely that the Dons embarked on an eight-game winning run that saw them inch closer to Rangers. The pursuit began following the arrival of Smith's second Dutchman, Willem van der Ark, a tall gangling striker from Willem II. Van der Ark scored on his debut, but sceptics feared his inclusion encouraged long ball tactics at the expense of the midfield industry that was a hall-mark of Ferguson's teams.

Defeat at Hearts in late April ended any dreams of overhauling Rangers. But the season had one treasure up its sleeve. The Dons party-pooped the Ibrox title celebrations, winning 3-0.

It would be unfair to conclude this summary without mentioning one unqualified success. Charlie Nicholas had no endure a variety of attacking partners, or sometimes none at all, but still managed eighteen goals. This was more than twice anyone else's total. Without Nicholas, the Dons would have fired blanks all season.

Match of the Season

Rangers 3   Aberdeen 2

Skol Cup Final, 23 October 1988

Deja vu. An October appointment at Hampden with Rangers. To get there Aberdeen had stepped over those bogey-men from Tannadice, which was achievement in itself.

Souness's frantic buying and selling, mostly buying, meant that just three of Rangers' 87 winning team – Gough, McCoist, Ian Ferguson – lined up a year later. Aberdeen's transfer activity did not command the same headlines, but just four Dons lined up for their second final – McKimmie, McLeish, Bobby Connor, and Jim Bett.

Whereas in 1987 both sides prepared without distraction, this time the air was thick with malice. Two weeks previously, the Dons had beaten Rangers in a match whose ramifications linger to this day. It was bad enough seeing Neale Cooper, snarling face and clenched fists, returning to Pittodrie and scoring against the club that nurtured him. But that was immaterial. Neil Simpson and Ian Durrant were in their different ways a credit to Scottish football. Durrant was talked about as a future Scottish great. Simpson was a homespun grafter, the epitome of Aberdeen's spirit.

Simpson's foul on Durrant, for which he was only booked, pro-voked heated exchanges. Injuries are part and parcel, but Durrant's looked likely to end his career. He would be out of the game for two and a half years, never recaptured his earlier form, and eventu-ally sought redress through the law-courts. Simpson was subjected to a witch-hunt. He, too, would never be the player of old.

This was the atmosphere with which the final had to contend. Durrant, of course, could not play. Simpson did. It is to the credit of both teams that they busied themselves with the game rather than indulge in vendettas, though Terry Butcher's public remarks that Rangers wanted to win the cup for Durrant were perhaps better left unsaid.

The final matched its predecessor, without the artificial drama of a penalty shoot-out. Once again the scoring was sparked by a spot-kick, awarded after some daft defending by Aberdeen. Robertson's throw-in to Snelders was short, and in a moment of panic the Dutchman took Drinkell's legs.

If Davie Dodds' first equalising header was bread and butter – connecting with Hewitt's corner – that which cancelled out Ian Ferguson's volley was a rare treat. Bett's angled cross to the far post did not permit firm contact, merely precise placement. Dodds directed the ball in a high arc, back across goal into the one spot Chris Woods could not reach. His two goals were enough to win Dodds the man-of-the-match award, but sadly not the match. For the second year running Aberdeen were floored by McCoist's late strike, missing chances of their own right up to the final whistle.

SCOTTISH PREMIER DIVISION   1989-90

B & Q Premier Division	Runners-Up
League Cup	Winners
Scottish Cup	Winners
UEFA Cup	First Round

Everyone connected with Aberdeen FC knew the club had to bring home a cup or two, to prove that life was possible without Alex Ferguson. Porterfield and Smith had come close in successive Skol Cup Finals, but as yet the cupboard was bare. What particularly irked supporters was that those wonder years, when the Dons trounced Rangers at will, had gone. Souness had turned the tables. Rangers were kings, and they had the trophies to prove it.

It was as if a dynastic transfer had taken place, Fergie lording it for so long, now Souness assuming his mantle. It was no use crying for the moon, but Scottish football needed Fergie. A confrontation between Ferguson's Dons and Souness's Rangers, both at their peak, would have made the mouth water.

Notwithstanding the bullish optimism of Messrs Smith and Scott, prospects in 1989-90 did not seem bright. No new players arrived, other than Ian Cameron from St Mirren, and he did not linger. But the haemorrhaging of Aberdeen's attacking strength continued. Paul Wright joined QPR, Hewitt went to Celtic, and with the season barely underway, Dodds signed for Rangers. The exodus made one scratch one's head in puzzlement. Charlie Nicholas was the only goal-getter left, and one could not be surprised if he queried the extent of Aberdeen's ambition. Van der Ark was an unlikely foil for one of Nicholas's virtuosity, and in any case, the tall Dutchman had been used intermittently.

The consequences were all too predictable. Aberdeen's first nine league games produced just eight goals. No player netted more than two, and Charlie Nicholas, starved of supply and support, failed to score at all.

A shot-shy forward line shifted the balance of priorities. Snelders and his back four could repel most boarders; indeed, the team's defensive resilience now appeared its sole means of picking up points. Tactics reflected this new imperative. Aberdeen acquired the reputation of being dour and defensive – qualities anathema to supporters weaned on the Ferguson era.

Aberdeen tumbled from the UEFA Cup at the first hurdle, to the cynical play of Rapid Vienna, unable to keep a clean sheet at home, unable to score away for the seventh successive tie.

But this season had exhilarating surprises in store, undreamed of in those dispiriting first weeks. The one place the Dons found goals easy to come by was in the Skol Cup. Celtic and Rangers barred their way, but Cameron's fizzing shot saw off the Celts and enabled Paul Mason to make a hero of himself against Rangers.

Fortified by their first post-Ferguson trophy, the Dons picked up momentum. They had climbed to second when Willie Miller's career was effectively terminated by injury in a World Cup qualifier with Norway. It was in that same week that Alex Smith swooped for a genie and his magic lamp.

PSV Eindhoven had won the European Cup in 1988. Wearing No 11 in the final against Benfica was a left-sided striker by the name of Hans Gillhaus (the 'g' pronounced as an 'h') who had scored three goals in earlier rounds. Smith learned via his by-now extensive Dutch connections that PSV were prepared to sell, and at £650,000 Gillhaus became Aberdeen's record signing.

Gillhaus's debut was sensational. An overhead kick in the twelfth minute at Dunfermline was trumped two minutes later by a header that left Aberdeen's travelling support goggle-eyed. News spread, and the thousands that flocked to Pittodrie in midweek were enticed as much by the new boy-wonder as the hope of seeing Rangers beaten. Gillhaus did not disappoint, scoring the only goal to underline Aberdeen's title challenge.

St Mirren and Dundee were hit for five, Dunfermline for four. Gillhaus even sparked Charlie Nicholas into life. Nicholas belatedly opened his season's account, and the pairing of such beguiling talents threatened to unnerve defenders everywhere.

It could not last. One swallow does not make a summer and one superlative foreigner does not make a team. Nicholas's disillusion had eaten too deep. His contract was up in the summer and he had no intention of renewing it. Aberdeen topped the league till mid-December, but away wins were rare and Rangers stepped on the throttle. This was hardly the best of Souness's championship teams. Rangers scored a miserly 48 league goals, a figure even topped by Aberdeen, who improbably finished up highest scorers. Few gloated over this. Standards in the Scottish game were deteriorating year on year, a worrying trend which has yet to be arrested.

What sustained the second half of the season was the Dons' onward march to the final of the Scottish Cup. Two individual awards also came their way. McLeish was voted Scottish Football Writers' Player of the Year, and Jim Bett the Players' Player. Both – plus Stewart McKimmie – would be named in Scotland's World Cup 90 squad for Italy, while Hans Gillhaus would play for Holland against England and the Republic of Ireland.

Match of the Season (1)

Rangers 1   Aberdeen 2

Skol Cup Final, 22 October 1989

For the third year in a row the same teams contested the final. Rangers had been favourites on the first two occasions, but never so overwhelmingly as now. They were quoted at 15–8 on to win their twentieth successive Skol Cup-tie and keep the Cup for the fourth year running. The reasoning was clear. The pre-Gillhaus Dons hadn't the firepower to trouble Rangers, and Ian Cameron, scorer against Celtic in the semis, was missing with a head injury. 1-0 to Rangers was the punters' verdict, with McCoist at 6-1 to score it.

Rangers began in a stampede. They failed to break through and by the end the game had thrown up an unlikely match winner, reminiscent of cup-tie McKay back in 1970. In this season of sterile attacks, Paul Mason had been handed the No 9 shirt. Whether up front or foraging from midfield his goals frequently turned defeats into draws, and draws into victories. The Skol Cup Final was a case in point. After twenty minutes the ball was swung across. Chris Woods seemed rooted to his line, Mason timed his jump better than Munro, and the underdogs were in front.

Not for long. George Smith's award of a penalty when McCoist barged backwards into the stationary Miller would have threatened post-match inquests should Walters' spot-kick have won the Cup.

That it did not was due to Mason. Seven minutes into extra-time Nicholas squared and Mason fired the winner through a ruck of players. Victory was all the sweeter at the third time of asking, even though Aberdeen had performed less impressively in victory than they had twice in defeat. Jim Bett was named man of the match, but this was undoubtedly Mason's finest hour. Aberdeen had won the first Scottish trophy of the 1980s, and the last.

Match of the Season (2)

Celtic 0   Aberdeen 0

Scottish Cup Final, 12 May 1990

Celtic did everyone a favour by knocking out Rangers in Round 4. With the favourites gone there was no logical reason why Aberdeen should not go all the way. A flurry of sixteen goals carried them past Partick, Morton, Hearts and those bugbears of Dundee United, when they were assisted by *two* own-goals by *two* foreigners, Paatelainen and van der Hoorn.

The fact that Aberdeen had drawn United in the semis, while Celtic had claimed Clydebank, had suggested the gods were rooting for the Celts, managed once again by Billy McNeill. Celtic were in a hole, partly caused by internal bickering, partly by Rangers' massive ascendancy. Only four points separated Celtic from next-to-bottom St Mirren. Aberdeen had journeyed to Parkhead for the final league fixture, omitted half the team earmarked for Hampden, and still won at a stroll. Accustomed to playing in Europe, Celtic had to lift the Scottish Cup or face exile for the first time in twelve seasons.

The form book favoured the Dons, who found themselves in the unaccustomed position in the post-Ferguson era of being favourites against one of the Old Firm.

The match would be remembered among other things for players present and absent. Celtic included former Dons Billy Stark and Joe Miller, but appeared never to have recovered from the pre-season shock of Mo Johnston opting for Rangers. Aberdeen would line up without Willie Miller. The old warhorse was feeling his 35 years and, more importantly, his right knee. He had hobbled through the last couple of fixtures but was too much of a gamble in a cup final. Besides, Brian Irvine was more than capable.

With van der Ark ruled out by a groin strain, the partnership of Nicholas and Gillhaus was permitted a final fling. It was Nicholas's last match, though as yet there was no confirmation that he was off back to Parkhead. Such divided loyalties would surely have kept him out of the side. Besides, Nicholas had never won a Scottish Cup-winners' medal. Aberdeen could supply it.

Despite his aberration in the Skol Cup Final, George Smith was given charge of Scotland's showpiece. He would need to be thick skinned, for the granting of another ill-judged penalty was sure to see him pilloried in north-eastern quarters.

On this occasion the players were capable of ruining the match by themselves. Passes went astray and chances were rare. At one end Paul Elliott cleared after Nicholas turned to shoot past Bonner; at the other Stark directed a couple of headers too close for comfort. Celtic substitute Mike Galloway might have been sent off for his first, dreadful foul, but otherwise the game spluttered towards its destiny. Extra-time was even worse than normal time, players fearful of making a mistake from which there could be no reprieve.

Hitherto, both teams would have returned for a replay. But the SFA, who inadvertently assisted Aberdeen in 1982 by introducing extra-time, now decreed that penalties should produce a winner on the day – as was the case with the Skol Cup. This innovation spelled gloom for the Dons, who had never yet won in such fashion. Honved, Dynamo Berlin, Celtic in the Skol Cup in 1986 and

Rangers in the 1988 final had each punished the wayward penalty shooters of Aberdeen.

It took an age for managers and officials to draw up lists and spin coins. The shoot-out would be staged at the Aberdeen end. Celtic's consolation was to go first, but when Wdowczyk blazed high and wide Aberdeen needed only to keep their cool.

Kicks were converted until Aberdeen's fourth, when Brian Grant shot over the bar. Charlie Nicholas dared not, and did not, raise questions by missing, though he took his kick against a background of 'Charlie, Charlie' ringing out from the Celtic end. At 4-4 the shoot-out moved to sudden death. The entire teams, if need be, would take turns. By going last, any Don who missed would hand the Cup to Celtic.

Celtic's tenth taker was left-back Anton Rogan. He struck the ball low to Snelders' left, but the keeper read it correctly and celebrated by gesticulating wildly to the red-bedecked masses behind him.

The cup was not yet won. Willie Miller had missed in similar circumstances in Berlin. The man striding forward with the weight of destiny on his shoulders was Miller's replacement, Brian Irvine. He was the tenth man, the last outfield player left. If he missed, the two goalkeepers would have to take their turn against each other. But Irvine, fortified by strong Christian beliefs, seized the moment to fire the ball past Bonner's shoulder.

The glory days were back. Two trophies in one season may have been par for Ferguson, but it was something special for Alex Smith.

DID YOU KNOW?

Up to 1995-96, 8 Aberdeen players have been voted Scottish Player of the Year.

Football Writers' Player (from 1965)	Players' Player (from 1977-78)	
1971 Martin Buchan	1980-81	Mark McGhee
1980 Gordon Strachan	1983-84	Willie Miller
1984 Willie Miller	1988-89	Theo Snelders
1990 Alex McLeish	1989-90	Jim Bett

SCOTTISH PREMIER DIVISION   1990-91

B & Q Premier Division	Runners-Up
Skol League Cup	Semi-Final
Scottish Cup	Third Round
European Cup-Winners' Cup	Second Round

For Alex Smith to duplicate so soon the triumphs of Fergie's final season thrust Aberdeen back into the limelight. Their success also distracted attention from Graeme Souness's increasingly omnipotent Rangers. The fact that the Dons finished second in the league made them Rangers' obvious challengers in 1990-91.

But the team needed reinforcing. Potential champions know how to win away from home. The Dons in 1989-90 did not. Indeed, they were the first Aberdeen team for eleven years to lose on their travels more than they won.

And what kind of team could Smith assemble? Willie Miller was finished, Neil Simpson was off to Newcastle and Stewart McKimmie had demanded a transfer. As ever it was the ballistics department that invited biggest worries. Nicholas had turned it on only when in the mood, but now he was gone. Paul Mason had done wonders in his improvised attacking role, but it was asking too much to expect him to come up trumps again.

Gillhaus remained the jewel, and was feted all the more following Holland's World Cup exploits. But it looked like he would have to bear the brunt of Aberdeen's scoring single-handed. The only close-season addition to the squad was Peter van de Ven, a workhorse midfielder who brought the tally of Dutch imports up to four – five if one included Mason's previous club, Groningen.

It proved to be a season that, following a string of defeats and injuries, rose from nothing to provide a climax like no other.

There were few early alarms. McKimmie changed his mind about leaving, Brian Irvine looked comfortable in Miller's No 6 shirt, and the Dons logged victories in the league, Skol Cup, and against Famagusta in the Cup-Winners' Cup, where they scored their first goals in eight away legs, since Akranes in 1985.

Then the roof fell in. Rangers barred Aberdeen's path in the Skol Cup for the fourth successive year, this time in the semi-final rather than final. Rangers overturned a Dons side unable to compensate for the absent Gillhaus, on international duty with Holland.

Three days later, Aberdeen journeyed to St Johnstone's new stadium, McDiarmid Park, and were engulfed by a five-goal avalanche. Robertson's expulsion, when the deficit was only one goal, exacerbated rather than eased the shame. Never in modern times had Aberdeen suffered such a league defeat, and it was necessary to go back to 1965 (1-7 at Celtic) to find worse.

Next up were Rangers at Pittodrie. With hindsight it would have been preferable had the torrential rain invited postponement. On the hour Mark Hateley headed down. Snelders rushed out, McCoist rushed in, aquaplaning through the puddles, his studs impacting with Snelders' face.

The seriousness of the situation was apparent from McCoist's agitated reaction to the keeper's motionless form. Snelders had a broken cheekbone and would be out for months. The club had no Bryan Gunn waiting in the wings. With Michael Watt still learning the ropes, Smith had to seek outside assistance. He had done so the previous season, and on-loan Bobby Mimms had not excelled. Andy Dibble would do better, conceding just one goal in five games. Dibble was ineligible for Europe, which saw Watt thrown in against Legia Warsaw in Round 2. Watt was blameless for the goal that divided the sides.

Two possible trophies had gone, but following a 3-2 win at Tannadice Aberdeen displaced Dundee United at the top of the league. All three goals were scored by Eoin Jess, a youthful discard by Rangers, who was proving an exciting replacement for Nicholas. At one stage Jess topped the Premier League scoring charts. 1990 ended on a high. Snelders was back, and Jess scored a last-minute winner against St Mirren to take the Dons through a whole calendar year unbeaten at Pittodrie.

In January Aberdeen lost three vital matches. Dundee United put paid to that unbeaten home run. And when Tommy Coyne scored a late winner for Celtic it left Aberdeen trailing seven points behind Rangers. Retaining the Scottish Cup looked to be the only source of silverware, but frailty in front of goal cost the Dons yet again, and Motherwell's Steve Kirk shattered their dreams when blasting the winner.

The season appeared dead. But behind-the-scenes wrangling had ushered in yet another change to the league set-up, which would see the return of twelve clubs to the Premier Division. For reasons that brought little credit upon those responsible, the change would be implemented at once. To attract enough votes it was decided in mid-season to scrap relegation. Struggling teams woke up one morning to find the threat of the guillotine withdrawn. Their matches, previously frantic, were now to all intents meaningless.

With the title seemingly heading for Ibrox, and no one worrying about relegation, the second half of 1990-91 degenerated into a farcical sequence of friendlies. Crowds at Pittodrie dipped below

10,000. The lack of competitive edge evidently suited the Dons, who belted five goals past Hearts, then took revenge on St Johnstone and Rangers. The gap was closed to six points, Aberdeen having a game in hand.

Aberdeen piled win upon win. Had Rangers stayed on course, this would have counted for little. But Souness's shock departure to Liverpool, and his replacement by Walter Smith – soon to be joined by Archie Knox – made these anxious weeks for the defending champions. Defeat at Pittodrie was followed by defeat at Parkhead and suddenly Rangers were peering over their shoulder. North-east folk, however, appeared fatalistic. As late as 20 April there was little buzz about Pittodrie. Motherwell's visit was notable for empty seats and hushed atmosphere.

On 4 May the destiny of the championship took a dramatic twist. At kick-off Rangers' lead was two points and four goals. On an afternoon of giddy emotions Aberdeen fell behind to St Johnstone but clawed their way back to win. Rangers, meanwhile, trailed at Motherwell, news of which was greeted rapturously on the bush telegraph at Pittodrie.

The final moments at Fir Park was Roy of the Rovers stuff. Chasing an equaliser, Rangers were hit twice by Dougie Arnott. Motherwell 3 Rangers 0. When the sums were done Aberdeen were top of the league, level on points and goal-difference, but having scored two more goals. All now depended on the final game, at Ibrox of all places. The sting in Motherwell's tail meant Aberdeen did not even need to win. A draw and they were champions.

Match of the Season

Rangers 2   Aberdeen 0

Premier Division, 11 May 1991

Last-day trips to Ibrox had a habit of throwing up the unexpected. In 1968 the Dons inflicted Rangers' only defeat and in 1989 they won 3-0 to dampen Rangers' celebration party.

Winning in May 1991 had rather more at stake. Having the title race go to the wire was not uncommon. It had happened as recently as 1983 and again in 1986. But it was necessary to go back to 1965 to find the last 'cup final' championship decider.

The obvious difference – compared to the neutrality and even-handedness of a real cup final – is that in a league showdown one team enjoys home advantage and one side could 'win' with a draw. In 1965, for example, Kilmarnock had to triumph 2-0 at Tynecastle; in 1989 Arsenal ditto at Anfield.

Peter van de Ven takes on two St Mirren players at Pittodrie, 22 September 1990

Aberdeen had won championships at various places but never in the cauldron of Ibrox. They now needed a draw at a stadium where they had lost fewer than half their Premier League matches. Not that Aberdeen needed it, but an extra incentive could be found in the fresh format of next season's European Cup. Rangers had been a driving force behind seeking more games and more revenue, and UEFA had decreed that after two initial rounds a champions' league would replace quarter- and semi-finals.

There are those who, with hindsight, regret that Aberdeen needed only to draw, and who felt that the team had hit the front one match too soon. Minds returned to 1979-80, when in not dissimilar circumstances Aberdeen had won *twice* at Parkhead.

In truth it is always easier to draw than to win. This is partly a matter of common sense. Aberdeen, however, had got where they were by playing three up front. Smith now dismantled the winning formula, omitting van der Ark in favour of van de Ven.

Already without Irvine, who had stomach problems, the team would also be without Snelders, victim of a shoulder injury sustained at Easter Road. He joined in the pre-match stroll onto the pitch, in a desperate game of bluff, but Alex Smith knew, if Walter Smith did not, that Snelders was out. Michael Watt, on the losing side just once in nine appearances, would keep goal.

Paul Mason skips past two Salamina Famagusta players, 30 October 1990

As for Rangers, they had to contend with the absence of skipper Richard Gough, hospitalised with hepatitis. Bravely, Walter Smith kept faith with the team humbled at Fir Park.

The game's first controversy arrived within seconds of kick-off. A high ball came over and Mark Hateley clattered Watt with such force that the goalkeeper required lengthy treatment. Referee Brian McGinlay gave no foul against Hateley.

Aberdeen needed to extract the sting from their hosts, mindful not to concede too many free-kicks in dangerous positions. Rangers had won more penalties than anyone else, and the Dons' defence needed to time their tackles. Ibrox was already getting fidgety when, after eighteen minutes, Jim Bett shot hastily and high. Seconds later van de Ven squandered the best chance of all. With only Chris Woods between him and goal, he tried a chip which plopped straight into the goalkeeper's arms. Aberdeen never again came so close. Five minutes before the interval Hateley powered in a header at the far post and ten minutes after it added a second. Smith threw on Booth and van der Ark, but the game was lost.

Few disputed that on the day the better team had won, or that Mark Hateley's aerial power was beyond anything Aberdeen could muster, but that did little to ease the pain.

St Johnstone's John Inglis watches Hamilton gather the ball, 17 November 1990

Jim Bett hits the post with this penalty against Celtic at Pittodrie, 6 April 1991

Aberdeen's David Robertson tussles with Rangers' Mo Johnston, 11 May 1991

Referee McGinlay separates Eoin Jess from Rangers' John Brown, 11 May 1991

7

CAPTAINS COURAGEOUS 1991-1997

SCOTTISH PREMIER DIVISION 1991-92

B & Q Premier Division	Sixth
Skol League Cup	Third Round
Tennents Scottish Cup	Third Round
UEFA Cup	First Round

Alex Smith had been one match away from bringing to Pittodrie a clean sweep of Scottish trophies in two years. Had he done so he would have been acclaimed as the club's most successful manager bar Alex Ferguson. And it had taken Ferguson far longer to bring his first three prizes to Pittodrie.

Had Smith established a rapport with supporters, the Ibrox setback would have earned him respect and sympathy. That was not the case. Like Porterfield, he had failed to win over hearts and minds. By Ferguson's standards, three second places in three years was tantamount to failure. Had Smith taken over from MacLeod or McNeill, his accomplishments would have been praised to the skies. That they were not, suggested other factors were at work.

For one thing, Ferguson's legacy had proved impossible to escape. He was to Aberdeen what Herbert Chapman was to Arsenal and Jock Stein to Celtic. Such exalted stature can prove impossible for successors to live with. For another, supporters generally prefer charismatic leaders to quiet ones. Where Ferguson was volatile and mercurial, Smith was introspective, at times monosyllabic. A third factor was style. Fergie's Dons played with a rare combination of flair and steel. Smith's teams seemed by comparison regimented and unimaginative. Supporters would traipse away from Pittodrie, another win notched up, yet unexcited by what they had seen. In a word, the Dons were grey, in keeping with the manager.

Eoin Jess and Hans Gillhaus in action against Airdrie at Broomfield, 10 August 1991

Hans Gillhaus shapes to shoot past Celtic's Peter Grant at Pittodrie, 24 August 1991

Stephen Wright lunges to tackle v Hibs at Pittodrie, 21 September 1991

Appearances, of course, are often deceptive. Behind the scenes Smith had clearly earned the respect of his players. But in football, image is everything.

This is why Smith had so little leeway when things began to go wrong. He was not helped by the summer departure of David Robertson, who had long been admired north and south of the border. Having played in the decider at Ibrox, he signed for Rangers. Robertson's loss would be felt for years, as one successor after another tried on the No 3 shirt but was found wanting.

Smith's new intake comprised David Winnie from St Mirren, Gary Smith from Falkirk, and Theo Ten Caat, whose arrival brought the number of Dutch footballers on Aberdeen's books to five. Never before had the club recruited foreigners in such quantity. On 16 November, at Love St, Aberdeen made history by lining up with all five Dutch players.

By then, however, Smith was grateful for any distraction. Despite losing McLeish on the eve of the season with a chipped ankle, Aberdeen had begun well enough. They won their first four in the league, Celtic being among the victims. Then, disaster struck, and the Dons crashed to three home defeats in a row. These pulled the rug from under the manager and set in train the sequence of events from which the club is still recovering.

Paul Mason heads towards goal v Hibs at Pittodrie, 21 September 1991

The first of these defeats was in the Skol Cup against promoted Airdrie. Aberdeen had laboured to beat Airdrie in the league on the opening day of the season. Now, John Watson's goal was enough to see them through.

Next came St Johnstone in the league. It was only a year since the 0-5 debacle at McDiarmid Park, so St Johnstone found themselves with an important say in affairs at Pittodrie. Aberdeen scored first, an opponent was sent off, but the Dons still fell sucker to two second-half headers.

Not since April 1986 had Aberdeen lost at home twice in a row; not since 1968 had the sequence been extended to three. But that was the fate in store following the visit of BK1903 Copenhagen in the UEFA Cup. This team of unknowns, from one of the weakest leagues in Europe, took their name from the year of their foundation – the same as that of Aberdeen FC. The Danes reduced the Dons to impotence, scoring late in the game to spark demonstrations in the ground and outside of a kind never before seen at Pittodrie. Chants of 'Smith Must Go' rent the air, and from that moment it was only a matter of time before he did.

Co-manager Jocky Scott was the immediate casualty. He left to take over at Dunfermline. Now on his own, Smith tried to regroup, and an improbable win at Ibrox briefly lifted spirits. But the reprieve was brief. November brought another plague of defeats. In desperation Smith signed midfielder Paul Kane from Oldham and blooded young Gary Smith. These two, plus the eagerly greeted return of McLeish, constituted Smith's last throw of the dice.

The rot was too deep. Gillhaus wanted away and it showed. He had been playing on half-throttle for some time. His goal against Falkirk on 30 November – which averted another hat-trick of home defeats – would be his last. Defeats piled up. The Dons slumped to sixth and in their first match of 1992 were thrashed 0-4 at Tannadice. When Rangers, in the Cup, and Hibs, in the league, won at Pittodrie there was nowhere for Smith to hide. The team was spiralling out of control and he became the first manager ever to be formally dismissed by Aberdeen Football Club.

Neither Porterfield nor Smith had proved popular, and no one wanted to see the next man quickly hounded out of his job. But this time the solution seemed ready made. Willie Miller's name had been canvassed back in 1986. He was at the time indispensable as a player and he was rightly passed over. Five years later he had hung up his boots, enjoyed a testimonial, and been retained on the staff almost like a crown prince in waiting.

Miller's elevation had obvious advantages. It would galvanise players and supporters alike. He was revered for his ability and his commitment. One thing seemed certain: there would be no shirkers while Miller was in charge.

Yet some voices expressed unease. Greatness as a player is no indication of greatness as a manager. Besides, Miller had little to gain and everything to lose. He was already a living god in the city. Who in his right mind would jeopardise that?

Much was later made of Miller's lack of managerial experience. But the same could be said of Billy McNeill at Aberdeen and Kenny Dalglish at Liverpool. Miller had enjoyed an eighteen-month rest since hanging up his boots. He had learned much, of course, from the six managers he had played for, from Jimmy Bonthone onwards. Now he re-emerged from the shadows to be acclaimed Messiah.

Miller took charge of a team that had won just three of eighteen league games. His immediate aim was to stop the rot. A realistic target was fourth place, which was also being contested by Dundee United and Hibernian. Players with their minds elsewhere could expect little sympathy. Gillhaus was the first to be turfed out, losing his place to Miller's first signing. Mixu Paatelainen a £400,000 buy from Dundee United, was the first major transfer between the clubs in the age of the New Firm. One could never imagine Ferguson and Jim McLean swapping players, any more than Rangers and Celtic, and Paatelainen's arrival, in some eyes, undermined much of what remained of the New Firm's prestige.

Defeat by Rangers in the final match kept the Dons down in sixth, their lowest placing since 1975-76. It meant they would miss out on Europe for the first time in 15 years.

Match of the Season

Hearts 0   Aberdeen 4

Premier Division, 11 January 1992

There were few matches to remember fondly in this sad season. Early exits from the cups, plus a wretched league campaign, shrinks the short list to one or two games. The 4-0 win at Tynecastle stands out from the dross and provided Alex Smith with one of his few treasured moments. Two weeks later he was sacked.

The championship had preoccupied everyone at Tynecastle since that awful day in 1986, and 1991-92 gave them as good a chance as any to exorcise the demons of Dens. Hearts had lost but twice, were top of the league and enjoying a fifteen-game unbeaten roll. They were a miserly lot, specialising in winning home games 1-0. No team had scored more than one at Tynecastle, and only six had managed that. With the Dons in disarray, it looked a home banker.

Smith sprang a surprise by playing three men up. McLeish had to limp off ten minutes before the interval, but before it arrived Jess controlled Gary Smith's long pass, sidestepped McLaren, and fired past Henry Smith from twenty yards.

Aberdeen knew they would need to man the barricades, but they scored again when Booth's effort deflected off Levein. When Mason added a third it confirmed Hearts' first home defeat of the season, and when Jess made it four it credited Aberdeen with their biggest ever win at Tynecastle. The result knocked Hearts off the top and they never recovered, losing three of their next four games.

ABERDEEN HONOURS UNDER ALEX SMITH

2.   Scottish Cup and League Cup 1989-90.
Runners-up in Scottish Championship 1988-89, 1989-90, 1990-91; Skol Cup 1988-89.

Formalities are observed before the home tie with BK1903, 18 September 1991

SCOTTISH PREMIER DIVISION   1992-93

Premier Division	Runners-Up
Skol League Cup	Runners-Up
Tennents Scottish Cup	Runners-Up

In the summer Willie Miller brought in his one-time arch rival, Roy Aitken, as player and assistant manager. Aitken's was an unexpected appointment, inasmuch as managers generally prefer contrasting personalities to assist them, able to dangle carrots and wield sticks. Aitken was in the same mould as Miller, unyielding, loyal, fiercely competitive, a captain courageous. Aitken's real worth to the club would be seen in seasons to come.

Miller's other close-season signing, Duncan Shearer, became an overnight sensation. Just short of his thirtieth birthday, the Fort William-born Shearer had made his name as a sharp-shooter under Ardiles and Hoddle at Swindon. When Kenny Dalglish needed instant success at Division 2 Blackburn, Shearer was one of a multitude of players quickly ushered in, then quickly ushered out. He played just five games for Rovers, but the fact that he was linked with such big-name managers could not be overlooked. Considering the long-term drain on Aberdeen's attacking resources, Shearer's signing was overdue. At £550,000, only Gillhaus had cost more.

Shearer scored two in his first match. By the end of August he had reached eight, by which time Aberdeen were through to play Celtic in the semi-final of the Skol Cup, and briefly topped the table until losing 1-3 at Ibrox.

The September signing of Lee Richardson, also from Blackburn – the Dons' first English player since Paul Mason – was no less enlightened. 'Rico' gave and expected no quarter, and brought welcome steel to midfield. He arrived in time to play at Hampden twice; the first time, joyously, as Aberdeen overcame Celtic; then in the final against Rangers, when the outcome was less favourable.

Having a forward line scoring an average of two goals a game was a novelty, and gave the team a helping hand in its pursuit of Rangers. Unfortunately the timing was wrong, for this looked to be the strongest of Rangers' recent teams. They outscored Aberdeen, conceded fewer, and head to head left no doubt about who called the tune. The teams met six times overall, Rangers winning five. There was no arguing with that.

But the Dons' sparking approach augured well. Were it not for the temporary three-sided stadium – pending the completion of the new stand – disillusioned spectators may have flocked back.

A run of 27 points from fifteen games, spanning October through to February, confirmed the Dons as Rangers' only serious pursuers. Aberdeen needed to beat Rangers at Pittodrie to sustain their challenge, but Mark Hateley's header settled the points and, to all intents, the destiny of the championship. It also extended Rangers' own unbeaten run to 33 games, a figure never approached in Aberdeen's history. From Rangers' lofty perch it was a case of 'Anything you can do, we can do better.'

Pride of place in Aberdeen's goal-machine went to Shearer, whose 28 goals even surpassed Frank McDougall's haul in 1984-85. Paatelainen added a further twenty, and the young guns, Booth and Jess, nineteen and sixteen respectively. Teams capable of attacking on such a wide front are not easily halted, and the loss of Jess in March with a fractured ankle was not therefore so serious as it might otherwise have been.

Jess's injury occurred in a Scottish Cup-tie with Clydebank. Aberdeen had overcome Dundee United in the previous round, and saw off Clydebank in a replay and Hibs in the semis. That brought them up against Rangers. By then, two more Dons – Scott Booth and Stephen Wright – had been added to the list of internationalists, winning their first caps against Germany.

Match of the Season (1)

Rangers 2   Aberdeen 1
Skol Cup Final, 25 October 1992

The Skol Cup was the one domestic trophy not won by Rangers in 1991-92. This was a mere blip on the record of Ally McCoist, who had already picked up *six* Skol Cup winners' medals. Come the final, McCoist had already scored an improbable 25 goals.

Aberdeen enjoyed a leisurely preparation. But Rangers had to face Leeds in the European Cup, and though buoyed by the first-leg result were bound to be suffering aches and bruises.

Willie Miller faced his first cup final as manager with a refreshing bullishness. He had played in twelve finals himself, seven in the League Cup, and knew the psychological ins and outs. He told his team to have a go at Rangers, keeping faith with the 4-3-3 formation that had paid early season dividends.

DID YOU KNOW?

Alex Ferguson had Duncan Shearer at Pittodrie on trial in 1981. In 1987 Ian Porterfield had the chance to sign him from Huddersfield for just £250,000.

DID YOU KNOW?

When Aberdeen beat Partick 2-0 on 19 September 1992, it was the first time Thistle had ever failed to score at Pittodrie in the Premier League (13 games).

The first quarter of an hour was both kind and cruel. Kind, when Ferguson's drive flew off Snelders's left-hand post; cruel, when Aberdeen fell victim to a change in the laws.

FIFA's new back-pass ruling had taken effect in the summer. Goalkeepers and defenders were still adjusting to it, especially how to respond to the unintentional back-pass. This was the dilemma confronting Snelders when Winnie tackled on the edge of the box and the ball reared into the keeper's path. Fearing to catch it, Snelders tried to chest it down, and McCall scored in the confusion.

For the statistically-minded the cup was as good as won. Never under Walter Smith had Rangers lost a match in which they had scored first, a run that stretched back well over a hundred games. After an hour, with Aberdeen still trailing, Miller brought on a fourth striker, Scott Booth, and within seconds they were level – Shearer swivelling to turn Winnie's cross past Goram.

Extra-time was hardly new to Aberdeen in cup finals, and only once – in 1989 – had it rebounded on them. A second back-pass incident caused panic. McLeish's tackle on Hateley was surely that, a tackle not a pass back, but when Snelders gathered the ball in his arms referee David Hope thought otherwise. Mercifully, the indirect free-kick came to nothing.

But Aberdeen's reprieve was short. Gary Smith had been the pick of Aberdeen's defenders, but six minutes from a penalty shoot-out ex-Don David Robertson swung over a cross, Smith's clearing header was all wrong, and the ball flew into Snelders' goal.

Match of the Season (2)

Rangers 2   Aberdeen 1

Scottish Cup Final, 29 May 1993

Aberdeen had already finished runners-up to Rangers in the league and Skol Cup, and only the Scottish Cup was left to avert an unwelcome hat-trick.

DID YOU KNOW?

9 Aberdeen players were called into Scottish international squads during 1992-93. Snelders and Paatelainen were also called up for their countries.

Brian Grant tangles with Rangers' Stuart McCall, Scottish Cup Final, 29 May 1993

Whatever the outcome, the Dons would contest next season's Cup-Winners' Cup. This was their fourteenth Scottish Cup Final, having won seven. It was their fifth against Rangers, the score standing at two wins apiece. Only twice previously had the same teams contested both Scottish finals in the same season.

Owing to redevelopment of the national stadium the final was switched to Parkhead. The last occasion Rangers had played there in a final had been in 1921, when they lost to Partick Thistle.

Walter Smith's team had gone ten matches unbeaten in Europe, and Aberdeen hoped their opponents would be as drained in the final as Aberdeen themselves had been in similar circumstances in 1983.

Nine Rangers players appeared in both Skol and Scottish Cup Finals. One of the absentees would be McCoist, who had taken his season's tally to fifty. He would be badly missed. Aberdeen showed five changes from the Skol final and would include two English players for the first time.

Aberdeen began brightly and Brian Grant – back from a fractured arm – grazed a post during that early ascendancy. The last thing the Dons needed was to lose another soft goal. Falling behind to Rangers was hard enough without giving them a helping hand, but Irvine's sad part in Murray's goal – failing to clear a cross, then deflecting the shot – proved to be a body blow. The Dons seemed to sense the fates were against them and they wilted. Mark Hateley made it 2-0 before half-time and from that point there was no way back.

It was late in the game when Miller brought on Jess – out for two months with a fractured ankle. Hopes were raised briefly when Lee Richardson's shot went in off John Brown, but Aberdeen couldn't square the scores.

Rangers had won their first treble for fifteen years. Alex McLeish picked up his first Scottish Cup losers' medal after five winning ones. Ian Durrant was named man of the match.

DID YOU KNOW?

Two English players have scored for Aberdeen v Rangers in recent finals – Paul Mason (1989 Skol Cup) and Lee Richardson (1993 Scottish Cup).

SCOTTISH PREMIER DIVISION   1993-94

Premier Division	Runners-Up
League Cup	Quarter-Final
Tennents Scottish Cup	Semi-Final
European Cup-Winners' Cup	Second Round

Back in 1989 Aberdeen FC had laid down blueprints for a vast new stand costing £4.5 million to replace the Beach End. Engineering works in 1992-93 had reduced Pittodrie's three-sided capacity to less than 15,000. When finally opened, the Richard Donald Stand seated 6,000. Those in the uppermost seats were not so much in the gods as in the clouds, for the edifice reared 32 metres high. While applauding the go-ahead thinking, opinions were divided as to the wisdom of putting the club heavily in debt for the first time, and whether the new stand improved or impeded the overall contours of the stadium. The SFA bestowed its approval by permitting Pittodrie to stage World Cup qualifiers against Estonia and Switzerland. Aberdeen chairman Dick Donald lived to see his dream creation come true, but died on Hogmanay.

Willie Miller's reign would see three contrasting seasons, each markedly worse than its predecessor. On paper he had reason for high hopes. The main comings and goings saw Mason off to Ipswich for £400,000 and Joe Miller return from Celtic for £250,000. One could see sense in both moves. Miller was sprightly enough to worry full-backs for several more years, while 29-year-old Mason hankered to try his luck in his native England. Aberdeen had enough cover in midfield.

The first weeks suggested the Dons might take up where they left off. August passed without defeat, with five-goal hauls against Clydebank and Motherwell, after extra-time, in the League Cup.

The first day of September brought Aberdeen a quarter-final date at Rangers, against whom in recent years they seemed destined to lose whether they played well or badly. Conceding a soft penalty in the first minute did not help, though yet again Rangers needed extra-time to extinguish Aberdeen's challenge.

Managers look for tell-tale signs after crippling defeats, to gauge how quickly the players pick themselves up. Willie Miller needed to have no worries on that score. Three days later Aberdeen won at Celtic, and followed that – by way of defeat at Hibs – by beating Rangers 2-0 at Pittodrie. A week later Aberdeen went top of the league with a 4-1 win over Raith. It would be the last time Willie Miller had cause to smile.

Lee Richardson on the rampage against Motherwell, 13 November 1991

What distinguished 1993-94 from the five preceding seasons was that Rangers were much more vulnerable. Injuries and poor form meant they dropped points here, there, and everywhere, exposing themselves to any pretenders determined to take them on. With Celtic inspecting their navel, Hearts nowhere, and Dundee United all at sea without Jim McLean, Aberdeen were handed a gift-wrapped opportunity to seize the championship. A repeat of the 64 points earned in 1992-93 would be more than enough.

But Aberdeen weren't up to it. Motherwell, of all teams, were the ones to capitalise most on a season unfondly remembered for its plethora of draws, negativity, and indifferent entertainment – all to some extent the consequence of a bitter relegation struggle that sucked in half the division.

Aberdeen's own problems became apparent in the wake of their 2-3 Cup-Winners' Cup defeat in Torino. They somehow topped the league till mid-December, but an excess of draws and an inability to string together more than three wins pegged them back.

DID YOU KNOW?

When Dundee equalised on 30 April 1994 it brought about their first ever score draw at Pittodrie in the Premier League.

Progress in the Scottish Cup was hard work. Aberdeen needed a late winner to squeeze past Raith and two matches to overcome St Johnstone. Both these opponents were heading for relegation. The semi-final saw the Dons pitched with Dundee United, against whom they had taken seven points out of eight in the league. Aberdeen were two minutes away from the final when Welsh equalised, and Jim McInally's second-half goal in the replay earned Ivan Golac's team – the eventual winners – their reward. A wave of despondency swept through the north-east. Home attendances fell below 8,000, with a state-of-the-art stand eerily empty.

Victories were few, not because of a porous defence – Aberdeen's was the meanest in the league – but because the goals dried up. 87 in the league last season, 58 this, which meant 29 goals had vanished. Booth and Paatelainen played fewer than half the games, Jess hardly scored at all, and Joe Miller seemed too often on the fringes. Duncan Shearer alone exceeded seven in the league.

The team appeared to be relying more on defence, but was that by choice or necessity? Was the manager consciously changing his style, or was he responding to the shortcomings of his forwards? Either way, his team too often appeared to play with two minds, or none at all. The Dons ended the season with more draws than anyone else, and even their victories were achieved without gloss. Few matches had fans on the edge of their seats. Even so, Aberdeen nearly caught up as Rangers stumbled lamely across the finishing line. Cynics suggested the championship might have been withheld in a season that saw standards fall to such a parlous state. The announcement that Willie Miller had been invited to join Craig Brown's national management set-up was a worthy tribute to Miller but a blow to those supporters who remembered the effect of Alex Ferguson taking on additional, international responsibilities. Farseeing students of Aberdeen FC feared for the prospects in 1994-95.

DID YOU KNOW?

Duncan Shearer's missed penalty in the 2-3 home defeat by Hibernian on 29 March 1994 was his first miss from the spot in his career.

Match of the Season

Torino 3   Aberdeen 2
Cup-Winners' Cup, 2nd Round, 1st Leg, 20 October 1993

After one season out of Europe the Dons were back. They enjoyed a kind draw in Round 1 and handsome wins over Valur of Iceland.

Round 2 threw up Torino, who in the dim and distant past were the cream of the Italian crop. In the late 1940s Torino won four Italian championships and provided the bulk of the national team, but in subsequent decades they had been overtaken by their Turin rivals Juventus.

Torino had started the season promisingly, and lay fifth in Serie A, though they would later slip back to mid-table. They employed a fair sprinkling of past and future internationals, but only one – defender Roberto Mussi – would be selected for the Italian squad in World Cup 94. The player best known to Scotland was the 33-year-old Uruguayan Enzo Francescoli, veteran of a spiteful World Cup clash in Mexico 86.

Willie Miller approached the away leg in the Stadio della Alpi with predictable caution. Shearer and Booth were left on the bench, Bobby Connor buttressing the midfield. The Dons expected to be put under early pressure and they were. Snelders pulled off a couple of sharp early saves before the Dons took a shock lead, Paatelainen heading in Kane's inswinging free-kick.

If that was beyond expectation, Aberdeen's second goal – Jess turning in Paatelainen's low cross – left everyone spellbound. Never could Willie Miller have anticipated such a score. At this level, a two-goal away advantage should be decisive. There should have been no way back for Torino, who must have known in their hearts that they were out.

It was imperative for Aberdeen to hang on till half-time, when Willie Miller could plan his second-half strategy. But full-back Sergio broke through in stoppage time and changed the dynamics of the tie.

Aberdeen did not wear the look of winners as they re-emerged. When Serie A's leading scorer, Silenzi, nodded down for Fortunato to volley past Snelders one sensed everything slipping away. Even 2-2 would have been a creditable result, but that was denied the Dons two minutes from time when Irvine fouled Silenzi and substitute Alguilera's free-kick deflected off the defensive wall into the net.

A 1-0 win at Pittodrie would be still be enough for Aberdeen, and Lee Richardson scored the goal they wanted. But two Torino strikes either side of half-time meant the Dons required another two goals just to force extra-time.

In the quarter-finals Torino lost to Arsenal.

Q	**Prior to Torino in September 1993, when was the last occasion the Dons lost a match in which they had led by two goals?**
A	**Never in the European era.**

SCOTTISH PREMIER DIVISION   1994-95

Bell's Premier Division   Ninth
Coca-Cola League Cup   Semi-Final
Tennents Scottish Cup   Fourth Round
UEFA Cup   Preliminary Round

The summer witnessed a radical restructuring of the Scottish League. Not only was the Premier Division shrunk back to ten – inviting that mad dog-fight to escape the *three* relegation places – but an extra division was created and new clubs brought in to fill it. Another innovation, designed to brighten the tarnished face of Scottish football, was the introduction of play-offs. In the Premier League, the bottom team would face automatic relegation, while the team above them would play off against the Division 1 runners-up. For the likes of Aberdeen, these changes seemed of Martian insignificance, of concern only to others.

Another change was the awarding of three points for a win. This had been introduced in England back in 1981, and play-offs in 1986. The Scottish League had insisted on maintaining the *status quo*. But with more and more nations switching over, and FIFA employing 'three points' in World Cup 94, Scottish compliance was only a matter of time.

Not that Aberdeen looked likely to benefit. Three points for a win punishes teams that draw, and no one drew more than Aberdeen. Had the new system been installed one year earlier, they would have finished third instead of second, eight points behind Rangers instead of three.

Whether or not these changes were responsible, Willie Miller wanted a clear-out. Though several players' contracts were up, the extent of the exodus took everyone by surprise. Lee Richardson, feeling hounded by referees, returned to England. Ten Caat's departure reduced the Dutch squad to one – Snelders. Miller's first signing, Mixu Paatelainen, joined Bolton. Most attention focused on the vanishing old guard. Bett had gone to Iceland, McLeish, after seventeen years at Pittodrie, was named manager of Motherwell, and Connor had also played his last game. With McLeish's departure, Stewart McKimmie was named captain.

The intake was just as extensive. Much was expected of £800,000 record signing Billy Dodds, a proven predator at Dundee and St Johnstone. Other arrivals were Peter Hetherston (Raith, £200,000), Colin Woodthorpe (Norwich, £400,000), and – in October – John Inglis (St Johnstone, £400,000). They would enjoy mixed fortunes.

The new broom did not sweep clean. Aberdeen embarked on a season of unsurpassed trauma. Bearing in mind they had finished second to Rangers in five of the previous six seasons, no one could have anticipated that they would fall so fast so quickly.

Aberdeen's first competitive fixture was in the Preliminary Round of the UEFA Cup. Despite being Latvian champions, Skonto Riga had been downgraded into the UEFA Cup. Whatever tournament they were in, they were there to be beaten.

By all accounts the 0-0 draw in Riga was dire. But it was made to look glamorous by Aberdeen's wan display in the return leg, which saw them ousted on the away-goals rule. Never in the European era had the Dons been so embarrassed by such humdrum opponents (who would be beaten 0-3 by Napoli in the next round). Emotions among spectators spilled over after the game, many insisting that what they had seen was beyond compare.

Had they a crystal ball, those same supporters would know to expect more of the same, and worse. Arguments would rage not about the *best* match of the season but the *worst*. And there was no shortage of candidates.

Stranraer in the League Cup – now sponsored by Coca-Cola – would have been a contender but for Duncan Shearer's face-saving winner. Aberdeen's next dose of humble pie was administered by Alex McLeish, Big Eck himself. Motherwell had never won at Pittodrie in the Premier League in thirty attempts. That is, until 15 October when, trailing to Billy Dodds' first-half penalty, McLeish's team struck three times. Defeat at Tynecastle the following Saturday dumped the Dons next to bottom. They had gone nine games without a win and had kept a clean sheet just once.

It was early to start thinking the unthinkable. Pundits dismissed the idea that Aberdeen might be relegated, insisting with famous last words that they were too good to go down. That did not square with what supporters were witnessing. Besides, it was nearly twenty years since the Dons had been in the mire. The players had no experience of scrapping their way to safety and would surely be disadvantaged against the Particks, Falkirks and Kilmarnocks, battle-hardened veterans in the art of survival. Whisper it quietly, but some Aberdeen players appeared docile in defeat. If losing hurt, it did not hurt nearly enough.

DID YOU KNOW?

The Skonto Riga match programme listed these Aberdeen players:
Mihael Vatt, Stepen Rait, Hari Smit, Stjuart Makkimi, Aleksander Makleis,
Dzeims Bett, Dunkan Sirer, Skott But, Eoin Dzess, Andrju Roddi, Dodsas.

Miller had changed not only the personnel but also the tactics, experimenting with modern formations such as 3-5-2 or 5-3-2. Players and supporters alike seemed bemused by the permutations.

A ray of light appeared in the Coca-Cola Cup. Five goals against Partick and four against Falkirk carried the Dons to the last four, where Raith and Airdrie from Division 1 waited pensively. Sadly, Celtic made up the foursome, and it was they who came out of the bag. Brian O'Neil's extra-time header earned Celtic their infamous appointment with Raith.

Whether or not a Coca-Cola Cup triumph would have lifted the Dons we shall never know. The next black day was not long in coming. On 3 December Kilmarnock won at Pittodrie to push Aberdeen down to tenth. They could go no lower.

What needs reminding is that Aberdeen had not known a losing team since 1975-76. Both the Old Firm had experienced hard times since then – for Celtic, defeats outnumbered wins as recently as 1989-90, and Rangers in 1985-86. Prior to 1995, even the weakest Dons teams finished in the top half. What was happening now was beyond comprehension.

Clutching at straws, maybe, but the Dons staged a mini-revival. Six unbeaten games – three wins, three draws, twelve points – hoisted them to the dizzy heights of sixth. True, they were assisted by two own-goals and Pittodrie endured two miserable goalless draws, but at least fear of the dreaded drop was receding.

If only. The defeats returned – 2-4 at Hibs, 1-3 at Kilmarnock. Aberdeen were back down to ninth and at that point the directors decided enough was enough. Miller had to go.

Willie Miller was a fighter, and his departure must have hurt him deeply. Supporters had not directed their frustration at him; they blamed anyone and everyone, which meant their anger was blunted by being unfocused.

This is not to say they were unhappy at Miller's going. No one associated with Aberdeen FC escapes some share of responsibility for the sorry state of affairs the club found itself in. In these times of limited patience and success at all costs, supporters had put unprecedented pressure on the board. Judged purely by results, Porterfield and Smith were not bad managers. They were not judged by results, however, but against Alex Ferguson's record.

One could understand the board's thinking in asking Miller to take charge. He was the people's choice, not necessarily theirs, and if all turned sour it was the people who should take the blame.

Financial factors had to be weighed too. Aberdeen FC prided itself on good housekeeping. Ferguson nurtured success; he had not had to buy it. But in Fergie's time Rangers and Celtic also spent comparatively little. The mega-buck 90s, when Rangers splashed millions on anything that moved, created a market in which Aberdeen self-evidently could not compete. The Richard Donald Stand obliged even more belt-tightening. Supporters retorted that money cannot buy a team. Ferguson had proved that. What the club needed most was a new Ferguson, not a new stand.

Certain players also came in for criticism. McKimmie, as captain, took much of the flak and was provoked into unpleasant exchanges with the crowd. But when the heat was on, he came to the fore and led by example.

The bottom line, of course, rests with Miller himself. He knew the club inside out and had had three years in the job. There was talk of younger players failing to respond to him, of tactics being too complex, of opposing sides coming to Pittodrie with no thought other than to defend. But Miller had been in the game too long to expect others to carry the can. Looking back, everyone was relieved that he was not burdened with driving the club he loved into a lower division.

With twelve matches to play there was little sense in searching for an outsider, even though Roy Aitken was in many eyes too closely associated with Miller. Aitken was give temporary custody of the team till its fate was decided.

His first two games touched heaven and hell. First, Aberdeen beat table-topping Rangers 2-0 at Pittodrie. Then came the result that eclipsed even Skonto Riga. Stenhousemuir from Division 2 won 2-0 in the Scottish Cup. The score made headlines, the Dons had become the laughing stock. If confirmation was needed of their parlous state, this was it.

Aberdeen picked up just two points from their next six games. They were marooned at the bottom and Kilmarnock had achieved what no other club had ever done – beaten Aberdeen four times in the league in one season. When Rangers won 3-2 at Ibrox it seemed as if the patient was beyond resuscitation. Aberdeen's only escape, should the worst come to the worst, seemed to lie with idle gossip about restructuring the league. That would surely happen in the case of the Old Firm, but Aberdeen would probably be left to sink or swim. Besides, the shame of being rescued by bureaucrats would be worse than being relegated.

ABERDEEN HONOURS UNDER WILLIE MILLER

None.
Runners-up in Scottish Championship 1992-93, 1993-94.
Runners-up in Scottish Cup and Skol Cup 1992-93.

A momentary respite came with a home success over Celtic, but cruel defeat at Motherwell, coupled with Dundee United's win at Partick, pitched Aberdeen to the edge. Before kick-off at Hearts on 29 April Aberdeen looked to be beyond recall.

		P	W	D	L	F	A	(GD)	Pts
6	Kilmarnock	33	11	9	13	39	44	(-5)	42
7	Hearts	33	11	7	15	40	46	(-6)	40
8	Partick	32	9	10	13	36	48	(-12)	37
9	Dundee Utd	33	9	9	15	39	52	(-13)	36
10	ABERDEEN	33	7	11	15	37	44	(-7)	32

Partick had aggravated matters, propping up the table for so long, but now pulling clear. Dundee United, however, were tumbling in the opposite direction.

Billy Dodds' late goal earned three precious points at Tynecastle. The rest, as they say, is history. The Dons won all their remaining games to defy the odds and stay in the Premier League.

Match of the Season (1)

Aberdeen 2   Dundee Utd 1

Premier Division, 6 May 1995

The New Firm was a joke in Glasgow eyes. Here were these supposed east coast superstars battling it out just to stay up. It looked likely that both would go down.

Dundee United had lost their cutting edge some years earlier, though it was only when Jim McLean stepped upstairs as chairman that the cracks widened. Winning the Scottish Cup in 1994 had done little to arrest the general decline. As with Aberdeen, a generation of great players in the 80s had gone and never been replaced.

Even so, few expected these two clubs to be where they were. If Aberdeen lost, they would finish bottom and go down. Realistically, both teams were striving to finish ninth, where they would take their chances in the play-offs. United had won once in nine games, Aberdeen twice in nine, so no one could accuse the teams of overconfidence.

The atmosphere inside Pittodrie was electric, unrecognisable from that of even a few weeks earlier. Half-time was approaching when O'Hanlon parried Jess's header, allowing Dodds as easy a goal as he has ever scored. Dodds made the second, squaring for Shearer, unleashing a crescendo of noise that was stilled only when Robbie

Winters pulled one back five minutes from time. The countdown was agonisingly slow, but the roar that erupted told its own story.

Match of the Season (2)

Aberdeen 3   Dunfermline 1

Play-off, 1st Leg, 21 May 1995

Aberdeen have a history of firsts – winning the first Scottish championship that qualified (in theory) for the first European Cup (1955); losing the first ever European tie to be decided on penalties (1970); playing in the first Scottish Cup Final to have extra-time (1982) and penalties (1990); now participating in the first ever play-offs. We should have known all along that this was to be the Dons' destiny.

Winning at Falkirk in the final fixture earned Aberdeen that privilege. Whether the opponents would be Raith, Dundee, or Dunfermline was not determined until the final kick of the final match.

The rules stipulated that the Premier side be at home for the first leg. But in the minds of supporters, though not players, the hard part had been done in beating Dundee United. That had been the one that mattered. The atmosphere for the visit of Dunfermline was in consequence perceptibly less tense, almost as if safety was a foregone conclusion.

Dunfermline had lost only four times all season – the fewest in any Scottish division – and the most recent of those had been back in January. They had missed automatic promotion by just one point and Stewart Petrie and Hamish French had scored 26 league goals between them. Dunfermline, in other words, were not short on confidence, and their preference to play it tight was not necessarily the wisest option.

It took almost forty minutes to break through, Stephen Glass's free-kick eluding the keeper. Craig Robertson did his former club no favours when heading Dunfermline level from a corner, and at that point, survival seemed far from assured. Seven minutes later Shearer nodded in McKimmie's lob, and three minutes from time added a ferocious volley to make it 3-1.

'It's a goal, Duncan Shearer,' roared the faithful. Young Stephen Glass had earlier hung his head, having waltzed through the Pars' defence on his own, only to miss badly. Now all was forgiven.

At East End Park the Dons had too much know-how to let the Pars off the hook. Half-time arrived without inroads into their lead, and after the turnaround Aberdeen turned on a show. It was fitting that Glass should score the third and final goal of this extraordinary season.

DID YOU KNOW?

Dunfermline's last league win over Aberdeen was on 22 January 1972. Since then they had tried and failed 20 times.

SCOTTISH PREMIER DIVISION   1995-96

Bell's Premier Division	Third
Coca-Cola League Cup	Winners
Tennents Scottish Cup	Semi-Final

In 1976 Ally MacLeod's Dons avoided relegation by a whisker and six months later won the League Cup. Punters would have received long odds on Aberdeen revisiting those times in 1995. But the turnaround in the club's fortunes was so swift and dramatic as to reduce the sorry affairs of the spring almost to a bad dream.

Roy Aitken was inevitably promoted from caretaker to full-time manager. He brought in Tommy Craig as coach, 26 years after he left to join Sheffield Wednesday. Other than Stephen Wright's departure for Rangers, and one or two on-loan experiments, the transfer market was quiet. Aitken's attitude to his players was: 'you got us out of the mess; now show what you can really do.'

Aberdeen needed to get out of the starting stalls quickly. This they did, though an early home loss to Celtic might have opened old wounds. Two up in ten minutes in a televised match, they fell away badly. The Dons were 2-3 down at the break and that's the way it stayed. But this was an isolated setback. Thirteen points from their first six games left Aberdeen second only to Rangers.

October was dominated by the men from Ibrox. Rangers won at Pittodrie in the league and expected to repeat the feat at Hampden in the Coca-Cola Cup. For the second year running the Dons had cursed the semi-final pairings, which deprived them of juicy pickings from Division 1. But Rangers fell two goals behind and scored too late in the day to affect the outcome. Aberdeen could enjoy their Division 1 pickings after all, but this time in the final.

Triumphs snatched from disaster are always that bit sweeter, and none could deny McKimmie and his players that special moment when Aberdeen lifted their first trophy in five and a half years.

MacLeod had learned in 1976 and Ferguson in 1985 that November prizes are apt to backfire, and under Aitken, too, the distraction had adverse effects in the league. Home defeats by Hearts and Celtic left the Dons hopelessly adrift of the Old Firm and invited anxious glances behind them at the nether reaches of the league.

DID YOU KNOW?

When Celtic came from behind to win 3-2 in September 1995 it was their first league win at Pittodrie in 15 games.

Aikten had already bought Paul Bernard and Dean Windass, both from lower divisions in England, and in Bernard's case Aberdeen's record signing – £1 million plus. In Stephen Glass, who shone in the play-offs, the Dons appeared to have mined a rare nugget.

Aberdeen had no say in the title race, in which the Old Firm had long-since disappeared over the horizon, but given a kind draw all things were possible in the Scottish Cup. The Dons had twice in recent seasons done the cup double, and with each obstacle inched closer and closer to doing so again. The league's top four all won through to the semi-finals, a case of perfect seeding, but unlike the Coca-Cola Cup the draw winked at Aberdeen. The Old Firm would fight out their own little war. This left the Dons to take on Hearts, who had an unhappy record of collapsing under pressure and who had already lost to Aberdeen twice this season in three meetings.

The team-sheet showed no Jess, who had burst on the scene in the late 1980s as a youngster of wondrous promise. He had shown equal promise in a Scotland shirt. Now in his mid-twenties, and playing more in midfield, he had not quite realised his potential. With Jess's contract expiring in the summer Aitken sold him to Ron Atkinson's Coventry for £1.7 million. No Aberdeen player had ever been sold for more. Before long, Theo Snelders was on his way too, in his case to Rangers.

Despite being favourites against Hearts, and despite happy memories of Hampden, Aberdeen were short of their best. They saw more of the ball, however, and on another day would have done enough to win. The omens appeared to smile on them when Shearer levelled three minutes from the end, but that still left time for Johnston to snatch a last-minute winner. Hearts' hoped-for collapse was left to the final.

Aberdeen and Hearts were also competing for bronze medal position in this league. The Dons won this particular contest on the final Saturday of the season.

Every story has two sides. The upper side showed Aberdeen a creditable third. On the downside, they won just three matches more than they lost. Other than 1994-95, it was necessary to go back to MacLeod's dice with the drop to find a worse record. Put another way, Aberdeen had just completed their second worst campaign of modern times.

DID YOU KNOW?

Up to 1995-96, Aberdeen's Premier League record against Rangers shows 34 wins and 27 losses. But Rangers have finished higher 14 times, Aberdeen only 7. Rangers have finished above the Dons 10 seasons in a row.

Aberdeen had also lost at home *six* times. Apart from Alex Smith in his final season, not since the 1960s had the visitors' changing room reverberated to so many post-match celebrations. Added to which, the Dons, for the first time, failed to notch a single Premier League win over the Old Firm. Aberdeen finished 32 points behind Rangers and only 25 ahead of relegated Partick, which in the language of cold logic says they were nearer to being a relegation side than a championship one.

While no longer terminally ill, talk of Aberdeen's full recovery was premature. They were far from their former selves and faced a long period of recuperation. But in the context of what might have been, it was time to be thankful.

DID YOU KNOW?

Aberdeen have scored more Premier League goals against Dundee United at Tannadice than at Pittodrie.

Match of the Season

Dundee 0   Aberdeen 2
Coca-Cola Cup Final, 26 November 1995

Finding themselves so soon in a cup final was cause for disbelief, though the nature of the opposition invited caution. Had Aberdeen taken on Rangers or Celtic they would have had a ready excuse for defeat. Now, for this first time, they would contest a final against a team from a lower division, whose record against the Dons over the past two decades was simply dreadful. Raith Rovers' humbling of Celtic in 1994 was a stark reminder to Aberdeen of the perils of over-confidence.

Dundee were not doing particularly well even in their own division. Three months into the season they had kept just two clean sheets. Home advantage had helped them overcome Premier sides Kilmarnock and Hearts – the latter on penalties – in earlier rounds. Dundee had last won the League Cup back in 1973, but now, on the occasion of the fiftieth final, found themselves overwhelming underdogs.

Perhaps they hoped to unnerve Aberdeen with their battery of unpronounceable players' names – Pageaud, Wieghorst, Vrto. Of greater concern to the Dons was the absence of Scott Booth, now matured into an international striker of rich promise, but worryingly susceptible to injury. Duncan Shearer, himself capped by Scotland in the autumn of his career, was nowadays employed more as an ageing super-sub, always liable to score. He would play from the start.

Aberdeen clicked almost at once. Their play was sweet and well-orchestrated and Dundee escaped from their own half so rarely that Michael Watt enjoyed a largely idle afternoon. Jess and Glass delivered a ceaseless supply of passes to Dodds and Shearer, and Joe Miller on the wing was also hugely influential.

But goals are the currency of football, and the longer the game progressed without one the greater the danger of Dundee springing a shock. The breakthrough came in 33 minutes. Keeper Pageaud spilled Glass's hard-driven cross and Dodds swept in the loose ball.

Dundee's hopes of rescuing the match were rendered bankrupt within seconds of the change-round. Once again Glass laid on the cross, and Shearer's massive header brooked no argument. Watt's goal enjoyed a couple of close shaves, but none so close as to threaten the outcome.

The new-look, white-shorts, Aberdeen squad.

SCOTTISH PREMIER DIVISION   1996-97

There was more going than coming in the summer, more thunder clouds than sunshine. The exodus included Paul Kane to Norway and Gary Smith to France. Those arriving bore Bulgarian passports, spoke little English, and had much to live up to. Ilian Kiriakov had looked a pearl in Euro 96, and was not wholly unlike Gordon Strachan, though weightier in the tackle.

The club did away with tradition in agreeing to Umbro's new strip, which saw the team revert to white shorts for the first time since 1966, and adopt trendy zebra socks.

A string of defeats in pre-season friendlies, against modest opponents (in Ireland), or by massive margins (0-6 to Olympiakos) darkened the mood of supporters, but left Aitken bullish. 'Wait till the action gets competitive,' he urged.

DID YOU KNOW?

Aberdeen have NEVER beaten European opponents on away goals or penalties, but have lost 6 times: (Honved and Dynamo Berlin in penalty shoot-outs; IFK Gothenburg, Feyenoord, Rapid Vienna and Skonto Riga on away goals.)

Ilian Kiriakov, one of the new breed of foreign stars playing for the Dons

Aitken was right, the only blot on Aberdeen's start being Celtic's last-minute equaliser at Pittodrie in the curtain-raiser.

There was some thrilling action to report in the first weeks of 1996-97. At one stage the Dons were ploughing merrily onwards in the Coca-Cola Cup and Europe, causing palpitations on the way. Who would have believed that the unknowns of Zalgiris would win 3-1 at Pittodrie, the first time Aberdeen had lost at home by more than one goal in Europe? Who would have believed they would win 7-3 at Morton, after being seconds away from defeat?

The Coca-Cola Cup quarter-final at Dundee was a repeat of last year's final and offered ample opportunity for progress to the last four. Dundee had other ideas. Slack defending against Brondby in the UEFA Cup put paid to further advancement in Europe.

By then, more newcomers had arrived, Nicky Walker in goal, and Tony Kombouare, an elegant French presence in central defence. Aberdeen entered November in third place, chasing you know who.

DID YOU KNOW?

**By the close of 1994-95, Aberdeen had a superior head-to-head record over all Premier League opponents.
Celtic's 4 wins in 1995-96 levelled the scores at 27 wins apiece.**

ABERDEEN'S SEASONAL LEAGUE RECORDS 1966-67 TO 1995-96

Division 1	Pos	P	Home					Away					Total					*Pts
			W	D	L	F	A	W	D	L	F	A	W	D	L	F	A	
1966-67	4	34	11	3	3	44	17	6	5	6	28	21	17	8	9	72	38	42
1967-68	5	34	11	1	5	36	17	5	4	8	27	31	16	5	13	63	48	37
1968-69	15	34	6	5	6	26	24	3	3	11	24	35	9	8	17	50	59	26
1969-70	8	34	6	6	5	30	19	8	1	8	25	26	14	7	13	55	45	35
1970-71	2	34	11	6	0	38	7	13	0	4	30	11	24	6	4	68	18	54
1971-72	2	34	13	3	1	54	13	8	5	4	26	13	21	8	5	80	26	50
1972-73	4	34	10	6	1	42	15	6	5	6	19	19	16	11	7	61	34	43
1973-74	4	34	7	9	1	26	9	6	7	4	20	17	13	16	5	46	26	42
1974-75	5	34	9	6	2	42	20	7	3	7	24	23	16	9	9	66	43	41
		306	84	45	24	338	141	62	33	58	223	196	146	78	82	561	337	370
Premier League																		
1975-76	7	36	8	5	5	27	19	3	5	10	22	31	11	10	15	49	50	32
1976-77	3	36	11	4	3	30	18	5	7	6	26	24	16	11	9	56	42	43
1977-78	2	36	14	3	1	43	13	8	6	4	25	16	22	9	5	68	29	53
1978-79	4	36	9	5	4	39	16	4	9	5	20	20	13	14	9	59	36	40
1979-80	1	36	10	4	4	30	18	9	6	3	38	18	19	10	7	68	36	48
1980-81	2	36	11	4	3	39	16	8	7	3	22	10	19	11	6	61	26	49
1981-82	2	36	12	4	2	36	15	11	3	4	35	14	23	7	6	71	29	53
1982-83	3	36	14	0	4	46	12	11	5	2	30	12	25	5	6	76	24	55
1983-84	1	36	14	3	1	46	12	11	4	3	32	9	25	7	4	78	21	57
1984-85	1	36	13	4	1	49	13	14	1	3	40	13	27	5	4	89	26	59
1985-86	4	36	11	4	3	38	15	5	8	5	24	16	16	12	8	62	31	44
1986-87	4	44	13	6	3	32	11	8	10	4	31	18	21	16	7	63	29	58
1987-88	4	44	11	7	4	27	11	10	10	2	29	14	21	17	6	56	25	59
1988-89	2	36	10	7	1	26	10	8	7	3	25	15	18	14	4	51	25	50
1989-90	2	36	12	4	2	33	13	5	6	7	23	20	17	10	9	56	33	44
1990-91	2	36	12	5	1	30	7	10	4	4	32	20	22	9	5	62	27	53
1991-92	6	44	9	6	7	32	23	8	8	6	23	19	17	14	13	55	42	48
1992-93	2	44	13	7	2	41	13	14	3	5	46	23	27	10	7	87	36	64
1993-94	2	44	11	9	2	33	12	6	12	4	25	24	17	21	6	58	36	55
1994-95	9	36	7	7	4	24	16	3	4	11	19	30	10	11	15	43	46	41
1995-96	3	36	11	1	6	31	17	5	6	7	21	28	16	7	13	52	45	55
		796	236	99	63	732	300	166	131	101	588	394	402	230	164	1320	694	1060

* 3 points for a win
from 1994-95

ABERDEEN'S COMPLETE PREMIER LEAGUE RECORD TO 1995-96

	P		Home					Away					Total			
		W	D	L	F	A	W	D	L	F	A	W	D	L	F	A	*Pts
Rangers	84	22	12	8	62	30	12	11	19	41	48	34	23	27	103	78	92
Celtic	84	16	15	11	60	45	11	15	16	48	53	27	30	27	108	98	85
Dundee Utd	80	18	9	13	51	39	14	16	10	55	48	32	25	23	106	87	91
Hibernian	80	24	10	6	75	24	14	16	10	63	45	38	26	16	138	69	104
Hearts	68	17	9	8	65	32	13	11	10	49	35	30	20	18	114	67	85
Motherwell	68	23	9	2	70	24	13	14	7	43	28	36	23	9	113	52	98
St Mirren	60	21	5	4	70	21	14	11	5	48	25	35	16	9	118	46	86
Dundee	52	19	6	1	46	14	17	7	2	52	19	36	13	3	98	33	85
Partick Thistle	40	14	5	1	35	16	7	7	6	30	20	21	12	7	65	36	57
Kilmarnock	28	10	0	4	28	9	8	3	3	25	16	18	3	7	53	25	42
Morton	28	10	1	3	35	9	6	2	6	19	15	16	3	9	54	24	35
St Johnstone	24	7	4	1	23	6	7	3	2	19	10	14	7	3	42	16	35
Falkirk	24	7	5	0	23	11	7	4	1	25	13	14	9	1	48	24	41
Airdrie	16	6	2	0	20	2	5	2	1	16	5	11	4	1	36	7	26
Dunfermline	16	6	2	0	17	5	4	4	0	16	5	10	6	0	33	10	26
Ayr	12	4	1	1	10	5	2	3	1	8	3	6	4	2	18	8	16
Clydebank	12	4	2	0	16	4	5	0	1	19	4	9	2	1	35	8	20
Hamilton	8	2	2	0	6	1	4	0	0	6	0	6	2	0	12	1	14
Raith	8	4	0	0	12	1	1	2	1	5	4	5	2	1	17	5	14
Dumbarton	4	2	0	0	5	0	2	0	0	4	0	4	0	0	9	0	8

* 3 points for a win
from 1994-95

ABERDEEN'S EUROPEAN RECORD – COUNTRY BY COUNTRY – TO 1996-97

	P	W	D	L	F	A	W	D	L	F	A	W	D	L	F	A	W–L
					Home					Away					Total		
Albania	2	1	0	0	1	0	0	1	0	0	0	1	1	0	1	0	1–0
Austria	4	2	0	0	3	1	0	1	1	0	1	2	1	1	3	2	1–1
Belgium	8	3	0	1	12	4	0	2	2	0	4	3	2	3	12	8	2–2
Bulgaria	4	2	0	0	5	0	0	1	1	2	3	2	1	1	7	3	2–0
England	6	1	1	1	4	3	0	1	2	2	9	1	2	3	6	12	1–2
Cyprus	2	1	0	0	3	0	1	0	0	2	0	2	0	0	5	0	1–0
Denmark	4	0	0	2	0	3	0	1	1	0	2	0	1	3	0	5	0–2
Germany East	4	1	1	0	2	1	0	0	2	1	4	1	1	2	3	5	0–2
Germany West	12	4	1	1	13	8	0	2	4	4	13	4	3	5	17	21	2–4
Holland	2	1	0	0	2	1	0	0	1	0	1	1	0	1	2	2	0–1
Hungary	4	2	0	0	6	1	0	0	2	1	5	2	0	2	7	6	1–1
Iceland	8	3	1	0	19	2	4	0	0	12	3	7	1	0	31	5	4–0
Rep Ireland	4	2	0	0	5	1	1	1	0	3	1	3	1	0	8	2	2–0
Italy	4	0	1	1	2	3	0	0	2	2	5	0	1	3	4	8	0–2
Latvia	2	0	1	0	1	1	0	1	0	0	0	0	2	0	1	1	0–1
Lithuania	2	0	0	1	1	3	1	0	0	4	1	1	0	1	5	4	1–0
Poland	4	1	1	0	2	0	1	0	1	1	1	2	1	1	3	1	1–1
Portugal	2	0	0	1	0	1	0	0	1	0	1	0	0	2	0	2	0–1
Romania	2	1	0	0	3	0	0	1	0	2	2	1	1	0	5	2	1–0
Spain	5	2	0	0	3	1	1	0	1	2	3	4	0	1	7	5	2–1
Sweden	2	0	1	0	2	2	0	1	0	0	0	0	2	0	2	2	0–1
Switzerland	6	3	0	0	10	1	1	1	1	4	4	4	1	1	14	5	2–1
Wales	2	1	0	0	3	1	0	1	0	3	3	1	1	0	6	4	1–0
(23 countries)	95	31	8	8	102	38	10	15	22	45	66	*42	23	30	149	105	25-23

ABERDEEN'S EUROPEAN RECORD – BY COMPETITION – TO 1996-97

	P	W	D	L	F	A	W	D	L	F	A	W	D	L	F	A	W–L
					Home					Away					Total		
European Cup	12	4	1	1	10	5	1	3	2	4	7	5	4	3	14	12	3–3
Cup-Winners' Cup	39	15	2	2	56	10	6	3	10	21	26	22	5	12	79	37	13–7
Fairs/UEFA Cup	42	11	5	5	34	23	3	8	10	20	33	14	13	15	54	56	8–13
Super Cup	2	1	0	0	2	0	0	1	0	0	0	1	1	0	2	0	1–0
	94	31	8	8	102	38	10	15	22	45	66	*42	23	30	149	105	25-23

* includes win against Real Madrid in neutral Sweden.

GUIDE TO SEASONAL SUMMARIES

Col 1: Match number (for league fixtures); Round (for cup-ties).
  e.g.   2:1 means 'Second round; first leg.'
  e.g.   4R means 'Fourth round replay.'

Col 2: Date of the fixture and whether Home (H), Away (A), or Neutral (N).

Col 3: Opposition.

Col 4: Attendances. Home gates appear in roman; Away gates in *italics*.
  Figures in **bold** indicate the largest and smallest gates, at home and away.
  Average home and away attendances appear after the final league match.

Col 5: Respective league positions of Aberdeen and their opponents after the match.
  Aberdeen's position appears on the top line in roman.
  Their opponents' position appears on the second line in *italics*.
  For cup-ties, the division and position of opponents is provided.
  e.g.   *2:12* means the opposition are twelfth in Division 2.

Col 6: The top line shows the result: W(in), D(raw), or L(ose).
  The second line shows Aberdeen's cumulative points total.

Col 7: The match score, Aberdeen's given first.
  Scores in **bold** indicate Aberdeen's biggest league win and heaviest defeat.

Col 8: The half-time score, Aberdeen's given first.

Col 9: The top lines shows Aberdeen's scorers and times of goals in roman.
  The second line shows opponents' scorers and times of goals in *italics*.
  A 'p' after the time of a goal denotes a penalty; 'og' an own-goal.
  The third line gives the name of the match referee.

Team line-ups: Aberdeen line-ups appear on the top line, irrespective of whether
  they are home or away. Opposition teams appear on the second line in *italics*.
  Players of either side who are sent off are marked !
  Aberdeen players making their league debuts are displayed in **bold**.

Substitutes: Names of substitutes appear only if they actually took the field.
  A player substituted is marked *
  A second player substituted is marked ^
  A third player substituted is marked "
  These marks do not indicate the sequence of substitutions.

N.B. For clarity, all information appearing in *italics* relates to opposing teams.

SCOTTISH LEAGUE DIVISION 1

Manager: Eddie Turnbull

SEASON 1966-67

No	Date	Att	Pos	Pt	F-A	H-T	Scorers, Times, and Referees	1	2	3	4	5	6	7	8	9	10	11	12 sub used
1	A DUNDEE 10/9	10,000	–	–	L 1-2	0-1	Wilson J 86p / *Cameron 44, Penman 73* / Ref: N Watson. After beating both Dundee clubs twice in the League Cup, Aberdeen lose to one of them as soon as the league gets under way. Billy Little missed a penalty for the Dons at 0-0, so Jim Wilson takes the second spot-kick near the end. Both full-backs, Whyte and Shewan, were booked.	Clark / *Donaldson*	Whyte / *Wilson*	Shewan / *Cox*	Millar / *Selway*	McMillan / *Easton*	Petersen / *Stuart*	Little / *McKay*	Melrose / *Penman*	Winchester / *Cameron*	**Wilson P** / *Murray*	Wilson J / *Campbell*	
2	H ST JOHNSTONE 17/9	7,000		2	W 3-2	1-2	Winchester 28, 71, Smith 52 / *Kemp 25, McPhee 41* / Ref: C Hutton. Aberdeen seem to be meeting their League Cup opponents early in the League. This is the third straight win over St Johnstone. This time they had to do it the hard way and come from behind – twice. Dave Millar blundered for Saint's first goal. Winchester levelled with a scissors kick.	Clark / *McVittie*	Whyte / *McCarry*	Shewan / *Coburn*	Millar / *Whitelaw*	McMillan / *Ryden*	Petersen / *McPhee*	Little / *O'Donnell*	Melrose / *Townsend*	Winchester / *Kilgannon*	Smith / *Duffy*	Wilson J / *Kemp*	
3	A RANGERS 24/9	30,000	13	2	**L 0-3**	0-0	Henderson 50, Johnston 59, McLean 63 / Ref: J Stewart. This dress rehearsal for the League Cup semi-final at Hampden went dreadfully wrong in the second half hence for Aberdeen. Centre-half Tommy McMillan protested so vigorously about McLean's goal, which made it 3-0, that he was booked by referee Stewart.	Clark / *Ritchie*	Whyte / *Johansen*	Shewan / *Provan*	Millar / *Millar*	McMillan / *McKinnon*	Petersen / *Smith D*	Smith / *Henderson*	Melrose / *Greig*	Winchester / *McLean*	Watt / *Smith A*	Wilson J / *Johnston*	
4	H CLYDE 1/10	**5,000**	11 *13*	3	D 1-1	1-0	Winchester 37 / *Stewart 85p* / Ref: R Crockett. Aberdeen's 100% home record in league and league Cup was spoiled by a late penalty converted by former Banks o' Dee player Ian Stewart, after Millar had used his hands to stop Glasgow's header. Staite becomes the first league substitute to take the field against the Dons.	Clark / *Wright*	Whyte / *Glasgow*	Shewan / *Mulherron*	Millar / *McHugh*	McMillan / *Fraser**	Petersen / *Anderson*	Little / *McFarlane*	Melrose / *Soutar*	Winchester / *Gilroy*	Smith / *Stewart*	Wilson J / *Hastings*	*Staite*
5	A DUNFERMLINE 8/10	8,500	11 *13*	4	D 1-1	0-0	Shewan 89 / *Barry 73* / Ref: J Kelly. Plenty of talking points at East End Park. 17-year-old Martin Buchan makes his senior debut for Aberdeen; Harry Melrose is ordered off for protesting Barry's goal; and Shewan heads a last-gasp equaliser. Just one league win to so far, and Aberdeen cannot afford to slip further behind.	Clark / *Martin*	Whyte / *Callaghan W*	Shewan / *Lunn*	Petersen / *Thomson*	McMillan / *Delaney*	**Buchan** / *Callaghan T*	Wilson P / *Edwards*	Melrose! / *Barry*	Winchester / *Hunter**	Smith / *Ferguson*	Wilson J / *Robertson*	*Fleming*
6	H AYR 15/10	7,000	9 *18*	6	W 2-0	0-0	Smith 60, Winchester 74 / Ref: R Wilson. Turnbull gives debuts to Jim Hermiston and Francis Munro. The Dons take an hour to break down a stubborn, winless Ayr team managed by Ally MacLeod. Ernie Winchester nods down for Jim Smith, then seals the points himself with a header, his fourth league goal of the season.	Clark / *Miller*	**Hermiston** / *Malone*	Shewan / *Murphy*	Millar / *Quinn*	McMillan / *Monan*	**Munro** / *Mitchell*	Wilson P / *Grant*	Melrose / *McMillan*	Winchester / *Black*	Smith / *Ingram*	Wilson J / *Hawkshaw*	
7	A AIRDRIE 22/10	4,320	7 *5*	8	W 2-1	1-1	Taylor 12, Wilson J 89p / *Keenan 42p* / Ref: A Crawley. Airdrie are already downcast over losing a League Cup semi-final to Celtic in midweek. They are not made any happier by the sight of Dons' debutant Ian Taylor's 25-yarder flashing past McKenzie to open the scoring. A very late penalty puts the Dons within sight of the leaders.	Clark / *McKenzie*	Hermiston / *Jonquin*	Shewan / *Keenan*	Millar / *Goodwin*	McMillan / *Black*	Munro / *Ramsay*	Wilson P / *Ferguson*	Winchester / *McPheat*	**Taylor** / *Marshall*	Smith / *Murray*	Wilson J / *Irvine*	
8	H HIBERNIAN 29/10	10,000	7 *5*	10	W 2-1	0-0	Winchester 64, Watt 79 / *Cormack 55* / Ref: R Davidson. Aberdeen shrug off the disappointment of losing a League Cup semi-final to Rangers by overtaking the Gers in the league and moving up to third. Winchester replaced Petersen for the second half and he levelled the scores after a goalmouth scramble to set up a rip-roaring climax.	Clark / *Wilson*	Whyte / *Duncan*	Shewan / *Davis*	Munro / *Stanton*	McMillan / *Cousin*	Petersen* / *O'Rourke*	Wilson J / *Cormack*	Melrose / *Stein*	Taylor / *Scott*	Smith / *McGraw*	Winchester / *Stevenson*	
9	H HEARTS 5/11	10,000	4 *11*	12	W 3-1	0-0	Taylor 80, Watt 84, 87 / *Murphy 67* / Ref: T Wharton. Aberdeen set about Hearts as they had Hibs to gain a famous Guy Fawkes victory. Yet again the Dons trail to defensively minded opponents, but their late riposte has the crowd baying in frenzy. Dons' matches have plenty of needle. Melrose, Whyte and Smith now start suspensions.	Clark / *Cruickshank*	Whyte / *Polland*	Shewan / *Peden*	Munro / *Cumming*	McMillan / *Anderson*	Millar / *Gordon*	Little / *Hamilton*	Melrose / *Davidson*	Taylor / *Wallace*	Smith / *Murphy*	Watt / *Traynor*	
10	A ST MIRREN 12/11	5,500	3 *18*	14	W 3-1	0-1	Watt 51, 72, Winchester 75 / *Treacy 40* / Ref: D Small. Five league wins in a row. Once again they save their best efforts till they fall behind. Again the introduction of Winchester at half-time does the trick. They have now scored 15 of 18 league goals in the second half. Five goals in three games for Willie Watt. St Mirren are now bottom.	Clark / *Connachan*	Hermiston / *Murray*	Shewan / *Gemmell*	Millar* / *Clark*	McMillan / *Kiernan*	Petersen / *Pinkerton*	Wilson J / *Hutton*	Melrose / *Taylor**	Munro / *Adamson*	Little / *McLaughlin*	Watt / *Treacy*	*McLardy*

11 | H | PARTICK THISTLE | 3 W | 5-2 | 2-1
19/11 — 9,500 · 13 · 16
Petersen 36, Whyte 41, Wilson 68p, 80
Whyte 44 (og), Rae 88 [Winchester 71]
Ref: J Gordon
Aberdeen: Clark, Whyte, Shewan, Munro, McMillan, Petersen, Little, Winchester, Taylor, Smith, Wilson J
Partick Thistle: Niven, Tinney, Muir, Gibb, McKinnon, O'Neill, McLindon, Rae, Divers, Cunningham, Duncan
Ace marksman Willie Watt is out, injured. In his absence it is Aberdeen's defenders take the initiative in scoring, though Jim Whyte's got so excited at scoring that three minutes later he does so again. This time at the wrong end. Jim Wilson scores his third penalty of the season.

12 | A | DUNDEE UTD | 3 W | 3-1 | 1-1
26/11 — 7,210 · 11 · 18
Winchester 3, Briggs 52 (og), Wilson 84
Wing 38p
Ref: E Thomson
Aberdeen: Clark, Whyte, Shewan, Munro, McMillan, Petersen, Little, Winchester, Taylor, Smith, Wilson J
Dundee Utd: Davie, Millar, Briggs, Neilson, Smith, Wing, Berg, Hainey, Mitchell, Gillespie/Person*, Dossing
Seven wins out of seven, and no let up in the Dons' physical commitment. Both Munro and McMillan were booked - Munro for protesting about the penalty. This is Aberdeen's third win of the season over Dundee United, and United captain Briggs' second own-goal for the Dons.

13 | H | MOTHERWELL | 3 W | 2-1 | 0-0
3/12 — 8,000 · 13 · 20
Wilson J 50, 75p
Hunter 54
Ref: J Stewart
Aberdeen: Clark, Whyte, Shewan, Munro, McMillan, Petersen, Little, Winchester, Taylor, Smith, Wilson J
Motherwell: McCloy, Whiteford, McCallum R, McCallum W, Martis, Campbell, Lindsay, Cairney, Deans, Murray, Hunter
Eight wins on the trot, but still Aberdeen cannot climb into the top two. Unbeaten Celtic lead the way by four points, Rangers holding back the Dons on goal-average. Jimmy Wilson's second, and winning, goal was a disputed penalty after Willie McCallum was adjudged to handle.

14 | A | FALKIRK | 3 L | 0-1 | 0-0
10/12 — 4,565 · 15 · 20
Graham 62
Ref: D Small
Aberdeen: Clark, Whyte, Shewan, Munro, McMillan, Petersen, Little, Winchester, Taylor, Smith, Wilson J
Falkirk: Connachan, Lambie, Hunter, Fulton, Markie*, Barter, Cowan, Rowan, Vincent, Graham, McKinney/Moran
It had to happen. After eight successive wins Aberdeen are sent crashing by struggling Falkirk, who win their first match in eight. The result is a fine start for the Bairns' new manager, John Prentice. This is the kind of result that has Dons' fans tugging at their hair in frustration.

15 | A | STIRLING ALB | 3 W | 6-2 | 3-1
17/12 — 1,375 · 16 · 22
Whyte 15, Wilson 17,27,87p, Johnston 51 [Taylor 73]
Symington 1, Caldow 85
Ref: N Watson
Aberdeen: Clark, Whyte, Shewan, Munro, McMillan, Petersen, Wilson J, Winchester, Johnston, Melrose, Taylor
Stirling Albion: Murray, Dickson, Caldow, Thomson, Rodgerson, Laing, Peebles, McKinnon, Grant, Kerray, Symington
Filthy weather and a first-minute deficit cannot stop Aberdeen roaring to their biggest away win of the season. Dave Johnston - from Nairn County - scores for the Dons on his debut. Now bring on the Celts. Eric Caldow scores a late consolation for Stirling, who will escape the drop.

16 | H | CELTIC | 3 D | 1-1 | 1-1
24/12 — 28,000 · 1 · 23
Melrose 30
Lennox 23
Ref: C Hutton
Aberdeen: Clark, Whyte, Shewan, Munro, McMillan, Petersen, Wilson J, Winchester, Johnston, Melrose, Taylor
Celtic: Simpson, Gemmell, O'Neill, Murdoch, McNeill, Clark, Chalmers, Auld, McBride, Wallace, Lennox
In rock hard conditions Bobby Clark sports track-suit trousers and jacket. He is helpless as the unbeaten leaders score first through Lennox, after McMillan lost control. Munro back-heads Shewan's cross to set up Melrose's firm header. Simpson got a touch but could not save.

17 | H | KILMARNOCK | 3 W | 4-0 | 0-0
31/12 — 14,000 · 8 · 25
Melrose 55, Smith 76, Little 87, Munro 89
Ref: R Gordon
Aberdeen: Clark, Whyte, Shewan, Munro, McMillan, Petersen, Little, Winchester, Johnston, Melrose, Wilson J
Kilmarnock: Ferguson, King, McFadzean, O'Connor, McGrory, Beattie, McLean, McInally, Bertelsen, Queen, McIlroy
Kilmarnock have recently slipped out of the championship race, but their Scottish international keeper, Bobby Ferguson kept them in the game in the first half, when Aberdeen threatened to overrun his team. The massacre was not avoided, only delayed, with two more goals at the death.

18 | H | DUNDEE | 2 W | 5-2 | 3-0
2/1 — 17,000 · 8 · 27
Melrose 13, Smith 15, Wilson 35p, Cameron 60, 69 [Munro 59, 88]
Ref: J Paterson
Aberdeen: Clark, Whyte, Shewan, Munro, McMillan, Petersen, Little, Winchester, Johnston, Melrose, Wilson J
Dundee: Arrol, Hamilton, Cox, Murray, Easton, Stuart, Bryce, Kinninmonth, Cameron, McLean, Scott
Nine goals from two holiday games, and there is an undeniable air of expectancy about Aberdeen. They spread the goals around, not relying on any one marksman. The Dons are now second, behind Celtic, and there seems every chance that they will qualify for Europe for the first time.

19 | A | ST JOHNSTONE | 2 L | 0-1 | 0-1
3/1 — 8,200 · 3 · 27
Whitelaw 37
Ref: R Crockett
Aberdeen: Clark, Whyte, Shewan, Munro, McMillan, Petersen, Little, Winchester, Melrose*, Johnston, Wilson J
St Johnstone: Donaldson, McGarry, Coburn, Townsend, Rooney, McPhee, Clark, Whitelaw, Kilgannon, McDonald, Johnston
In the 1960s a booking was as bad as a sending off today. Jim Smith finds himself cautioned again. So too does Tommy McMillan, in his case after the final whistle for an 'incident' in the players tunnel. Aberdeen were due to face Rangers next Saturday, but the match was postponed.

20 | A | CLYDE | 3 D | 0-0 | 0-0
14/1 — 5,500 · 6 · 28
Ref: B Padden
Aberdeen: Clark, Whyte, Shewan, Munro, McMillan, Petersen, Little, Winchester, Taylor, Melrose, Wilson J
Clyde: McCulloch, Glasgow, Mulherron, Anderson, Staite, McHugh, McFarland, Hood, Gilroy, Stewart, Hastings
An anticlimactic result, Aberdeen's first scoreless match of the season. Clyde will only draw one other home game all season. But the Dons have yet to win at Shawfield since Clyde were promoted to the Division 1 in 1964. Three points dropped and no goals from two away games

21 | H | RANGERS | 3 L | 1-2 | 1-0
18/1 — 31,000 · 2 · 28
Johnston 27
McLean 48, 81
Ref: J Gordon
Aberdeen: Clark, Whyte, Shewan, Munro, McMillan, Petersen, Wilson J, Winchester, Taylor, Melrose, Johnston
Rangers: Martin, Johansen, Provan, Greig, McKinnon, Smith D, Henderson, Smith A, McLean, Forrest, Johnston
Aberdeen's first home defeat, as Rangers inflict the double, plus a Cup KO. Bookings for Winchester and Shewan take the Dons' tally to 14. Nine minutes from time Martin dropped a corner. Provan cleared upfield and McLean exchanged passes with Johnston to score the winner.

SCOTTISH LEAGUE DIVISION 1   Manager: Eddie Turnbull   SEASON 1966-67

No		Date	Att	Pos	Pt	F-A	H-T	1	2	3	4	5	6	7	8	9	10	11	12 sub used	Scorers, Times, and Referees
22	H DUNFERMLINE	21/1	9,000	3 L *(10)*	28	1-2	1-1	Clark	Whyte	Shewan	Munro	McMillan	Petersen	Wilson J*	Smith	Winchester	Melrose	Johnston	Taylor	Winchester 17; Robertson 32, Ferguson 60; Ref: J Callaghan
								Martin	*Totten*	*Lumm*	*Thomson*	*Fraser*	*Barry*	*Edwards*	*Paton*	*Delaney*	*Ferguson*	*Robertson*		
23	A AYR	4/2	3,100	3 W *(18)*	30	5-2	3-2	Clark	Whyte		Munro	McCabe*	Petersen	Robb	Smith	Johnston	Melrose	Wilson J	Watt	Smith 7,21, Robb 15, Johnston 48; Rutherford 23p, Murphy 39 [Whyte 70]; Ref: W Elliott
								Malone*	*Millar*	*Murphy*	*Oliphant*	*Quinn*	*Thomson*	*Rutherford*	*McMillan*	*Ingram*	*Mitchell*	*Paterson*	*Monan*	
24	H AIRDRIE	11/2	8,000	3 W *(11)*	32	7-0	4-0	Clark	Whyte	Shewan	Munro	McMillan	Petersen	Little	Smith	Johnston	Melrose	Wilson J	Phillips	Munro 3, Johnston 4, 43, 77, Smith 36 [Wilson J 52, 83]; Ref: W Mullen
								McKenzie	*Jonquin*	*Keenan*	*Goodwin*	*Black*	*Ramsay*	*Ferguson*	*Murray*	*Menzies*	*Fyfe*	*Phillips*		
25	A HIBERNIAN	25/2	18,500	3 L *(4)*	32	0-1	0-0	Clark	Whyte	Shewan	Munro	McMillan	Petersen	Buchan	Smith	Johnston	Melrose	Wilson J	Stevenson	Cormack 60; Ref: W Syme
								Allan	*Duncan*	*Davis*	*Stanton*	*Madsen*	*Cousin*	*Quinn*	*O'Rourke*	*Scott*	*Cormack*	*Stevenson*		
26	A HEARTS	4/3	12,000	3 W *(10)*	34	3-0	1-0	Clark	Whyte	Shewan	Munro	McMillan	Petersen	Storrie*	Smith	Johnston	Melrose	Wilson J	Robb	Johnston 13, 82, Smith 64; Ref: T Kellock
								Cruickshank	*Polland*	*Shevlane*	*Ferguson*	*Thomson*	*Aitchison*	*Kemp*	*Kerrigan*	*Milne*	*Gordon*	*Hamilton*		
27	A PARTICK THISTLE	18/3	4,000	4 D *(13)*	35	1-1	1-0	Clark	Whyte	Shewan	Munro	McMillan	Buchan	Robb	Storrie	Johnston	Melrose	Wilson J	Gallagher	Storrie 44; McLindon 76; Ref: W Anderson
								Niven	*Campbell*	*Muir*	*McLindon*	*McKinnon*	*Gibb*	*Rae**	*Cunningham*	*Flanagan*	*O'Neill*	*Duncan*	*Gallagher*	
28	H DUNDEE UTD	25/3	13,000	6 L *(9)*	35	0-1	0-1	Clark	Whyte	Shewan	Munro	McMillan	Petersen	Wilson J	Winchester	Storrie	Melrose	Johnston		Graham 39; Ref: R Gordon
								Davie	*Millar*	*Briggs*	*Neilson*	*Smith*	*Wing*	*Hainey*	*Graham*	*Dossing*	*Mitchell*	*Persson*		
29	H ST MIRREN	27/3	10,000	5 D *(17)*	36	0-0	0-0	Clark	Whyte	Shewan	Munro	McMillan	Petersen	Little	Smith	Johnston	Melrose	Wilson J	Hutton	Ref: E Thomson
								Connachan	*Murray*	*Clark*	*Kiernan*	*Heaps*	*Renton*	*Aird*	*Pinkerton*	*Kane*	*Gemmell*	*Hutton*		
30	A MOTHERWELL	4/4	4,500	L	36	2-3	0-1	Clark	Hermiston	Shewan	Millar	Munro	Petersen	Little	Smith	Winchester	Buchan	Johnston		Winchester 60, Smith 82; Deans 26, Campbell 53, Hunter 89; Ref: J Gordon
								McCloy	*Whiteford*	*Thomson M*	*Thomson I*	*Martis*	*McCallum*	*W Moffat*	*Hunter*	*Deans*	*Campbell**	*Weir*	*Murray*	
31	H FALKIRK	8/4	7,000	3 W *(15)*	38	6-1	4-0	Clark	Whyte	Shewan	Munro	McMillan	Petersen	Wilson J	Smith	Storrie	Melrose	Johnston	Cowan	Johnston 7,37p, Smith 15, Munro 41,86, [Melrose 72]; Cowan 66; Ref: I Foote
								Connachan	*Lambie*	*Markie*	*Hunter*	*Gibson*	*Moran*	*McManus*	*Smith*	*Fulton*	*Graham*	*Cowan*		

22. Aberdeen are going through a sticky patch; only one point has been taken from four games. Dunfermline's winner was scored by a gentleman by the name of Alex Ferguson, who earlier in the match had found himself caught repeatedly offside. The Dons are nine points behind Celtic.

23. Ally MacLeod's Ayr United are bottom and still looking for their first win of the season. Aberdeen race into a three-goal lead. Newcomer Dave Robb is the latest Aberdeen player to be booked. Bobby Clark saved Rutherford's last-minute penalty, but by then the score was academic.

24. Five goals last Saturday, seven this, as the Dons make Ayr and Airdrie pay for their bout of poor form. Aberdeen were two up inside as many minutes, and local boy Dave Johnston's hat-trick is the toast of Pittodrie. The following week the Dons hit five past St Johnstone in the Cup.

25. These two sides will soon meet again, in Round 3 of the Scottish Cup. Martin Buchan wore the No 7 shirt but played in defence. Bob Shankly's team won through a goal from Peter Cormack, who followed up to score the only goal when Clark failed to hold Scot's effort.

26. Aberdeen parade new signing Jim Storrie from Leeds United. Storrie enjoys a sprightly debut, wandering across the forward line at will in what looks like a free role. He fails to score, but helps the Dons gain a welcome league double over Hearts. Two more goals for Dave Johnston.

27. Jim Storrie, in oceans of space, scores his first goal for his new club. McLindon's equaliser for Thistle would have counted for nothing but for the intervention of a linesman near the end. The ball ends up in the Partick net, the referee signals a goal, then after consultation disallows it.

28. Aberdeen drop to sixth after this shock home defeat by their future Scottish Cup semi-final opponents. The Dons had scored 11 goals in three previous matches this season against United, but are made to pay when Jimmy Wilson misses a second-half penalty. They create little else.

29. Two home games in three days and Aberdeen are without a goal to show for three hours' endeavour. Aberdeen were chasing doubles over Dundee United and St Mirren, having beaten both away from home. Aberdeen chances of qualifying for a Fairs Cup place are receding.

30. A reshuffled side. Francis Munro captains the side in the absence of the Harry Melrose. Munro spoils his copy book with a slack lob back to Bobby Clark in the final minute. The ball fell short, allowing Hunter to pounce for the winner. Jim Smith had just put the Dons back on terms.

31. Celtic and Rangers are way out in front, and the pursuing pack is so congested that this enormous win lifts the Dons back up to third. Hibs, Kilmarnock and Clyde are breathing down Aberdeen's neck, and most of them have games in hand. The Dons will do well to finish third.

32 H STIRLING ALB 3 W 1-0 | 7,500 16 40

Melrose 58

Ref: E Thomson

Clark	Whyte	Shewan	Munro	McMillan	Petersen	Wilson J	Smith	Storrie	Melrose	Johnston
Murray	*Caldow*	*McGuinness*	*Reid*	*Rogerson*	*Thomson*	*Peebles*	*Smith*	*Grant*	*Kerray*	*Hall*

Aberdeen make dreadfully hard work of beating a team who have conceded more goals than any other - apart from bottom-placed Ayr - but who appear to have avoided the drop. Albion keeper Murray, out of his goal, pushed Melrose's 30-yard shot up, and over his head into the net.

33 A CELTIC 5 D 0-0 | 33,000 1 41

0-0

Ref: R Davidson

Clark	Whyte	Shewan	Munro	McMillan	Petersen	Wilson J	Smith	Storrie	Melrose	Johnston
Simpson	*Craig*	*Gemmell*	*Murdoch*	*McNeill*	*Clark*	*Johnstone*	*Wallace*	*Chalmers*	*Auld*	*Lennox*

Celtic still have not got the league championship sewn up. Rangers could still overtake theme if Aberdeen win this rehearsal for the Scottish Cup Final. In the event, the Dons become the first team to hold Celtic to two draws this season. Celtic's 100-goal forwards can't break through.

34 A KILMARNOCK 4 D 1-1 | 5,500 7 42

McGrory 51 (og)
McLean 78p

Ref: J Callaghan

Clark	Whyte	Shewan	Munro	McMillan	Petersen	Wilson P	Smith	Johnston	Storrie	Taylor
Ferguson	*King*	*McFadzean*	*Murray*	*McGrory*	*O'Connor*	*McLean*	*McInally*	*Bertelsen*	*Queen*	*Watson*

Kilmarnock are two points behind Aberdeen, but their goal average is so poor that they can't overtake them. Aberdeen score when McFadzean handled. Ferguson saved Johnston's penalty, but McGrory slashed the ball into his own net. Munro handles and McLean levels from the spot.

Average Home 11,800   Away 9,800

Scottish League Cup - Section 1

1 H ST JOHNSTONE W 3-0 | 5,000 2

Smith 56, 83, Little 87p

Ref: R Henderson

Clark	Whyte	Shewan	Petersen	McMillan	Millar	Little	Melrose	Smith	Winchester	Wilson J
Donaldson	*Michie*	*Coburn*	*McCarry*	*Ryden*	*McPhee*	*Clark*	*Townsend*	*Littlejohn*	*Duffy*	*Kemp*

Dave Smith's eve-of-season transfer to Rangers deadens interest in this curtain-raiser, as the woeful attendance indicates. His namesake - Jim - fills the gap quite nicely, scoring the first two goals after half-time to put the skids under St Johnstone. The first of four wins over the Saints.

2 A DUNDEE W 4-3 | 9,500 4

Wilson 4, 71, Winchester 52, 80,
Scott 30, McLean 70, 82

Ref: J Gordon

Clark	Whyte	Shewan	Petersen	McMillan	Millar	Little	Melrose	Smith	Winchester	Wilson J
Donaldson	*Hamilton*	*Cox*	*Selway*	*Easton*	*Stuart*	*Penman*	*Murray*	*McLean*	*Scott*	*Cameron*

A seven-goal thriller sets Aberdeen up for a place in the last eight. But Bobby Clark's blunder, when he allowed John Scott's speculative shot from 30 yards to pass over his head to equalise, might have proved expensive. A cracking climax produced four goals in the last 20 minutes.

3 H DUNDEE UTD W 4-1 | 11,000 6

Winchester 25, Briggs 45 (og),
Millar 10 (og) [Smith 49, Melrose 84]

Ref: I Foote

Clark	Whyte	Shewan	Petersen	McMillan	Millar	Little	Melrose	Smith	Winchester	Wilson J
Mackay	*Dick*	*Briggs*	*Neilson*	*Smith*	*Fraser*	*Seemann*	*Munro*	*Dossing*	*Hainey*	*Persson*

A game of two headed own-goals. United defender Briggs, just on the half-time whistle, cancelled out Millar's earlier miscue and put the Dons 2-1 up. Jim Smith and Melrose tightened the screw in the second half. The Dons have a maximum six points at the halfway stage.

4 A ST JOHNSTONE W 3-0 | 5,000 8

Wilson 16, Little 59, Winchester 69

Ref: R Gordon

Clark	Whyte	Shewan	Petersen	McMillan	Millar	Little	Melrose	Smith	Winchester	Wilson J
Donaldson	*McCarry*	*Coburn*	*Townsend*	*Ryden*	*McPhee*	*Clark*	*Kilgannon*	*Rooney*	*Duffy*	*Kemp*

The Dons repeat the score inflicted on Saints in the opening match, to take their tally to 14 in their first four matches. St Johnstone are out of contention, and it looks like Dundee Utd are the only team now capable of denying Aberdeen top spot. The Dons will lose here in the league.

5 H DUNDEE W 2-0 | 12,000 10

Smith 72, Melrose 88

Ref: J Barclay

Clark	Whyte	Shewan	Petersen	McMillan	Millar	Little	Melrose	Smith	Winchester	Wilson J
Donaldson	*Wilson*	*Selway*	*Houston*	*Easton*	*Stuart*	*Kinninmonth*	*Murray*	*McLean*	*Scott*	*McKay*

This is the 67th match between these clubs in all competitions since 1945. Before kick-off, the tally was 27 wins each. Dundee's ultra-defensive methods looked like keeping matters even until Jim Smith found a way through. The result seals Aberdeen's place in the last eight.

6 A DUNDEE UTD W 4-3 | 5,000 12

Wilson 4, Little 13, Whyte 25, 65,
Seemann 10p, Mitchell 16, 69

Ref: A Fleming

Clark	Whyte	Shewan	Petersen	McMillan	Millar	Little	Melrose	Smith	Winchester	Wilson J
Mackay	*Millar*	*Dick*	*Neilson*	*Smith*	*Fraser**	*Seemann*	*Hainey*	*Dossing*	*Mitchell*	*Persson*

The Dons have 10 points already, United six, so the result can affect nothing. A meaningless match for both sides turns into a goal fiesta, the second match won 4-3 by Aberdeen in this group. Jim Whyte scores his first and only goals in the League Cup this season.

Qual							
ABERDEEN	6	6	0	0	20	7	12
Dundee Utd	6	2	2	2	12	12	6
Dundee	6	1	2	3	8	11	4
St Johnstone	6	0	2	4	5	12	2

SCOTTISH LEAGUE DIV 1 (CUP-TIES)   Manager: Eddie Turnbull   SEASON 1966-67

Scottish League Cup

Rd	Venue	Opponent	Date	W/L	F-A	H-T	Att	Scorers, Times, and Referees
QF 1	A	MORTON	14/9	L	1-3	1-2	4,750	Smith 21 / *Mason 27, 78, Gray 35* — Ref: A Webster
QF 2	H	MORTON	21/9	W	3-0	0-0	19,000	Winchester 46, Smith 85, Petersen 89 (Dons win 4-3 on aggregate) — Ref: A Webster
SF	N	RANGERS (at Hampden)	19/10	D	2-2 (aet)	1-2	38,600	Wilson J 24, Shewan 71 / *Henderson 12, 26* — Ref: R Davidson
SF R	N	RANGERS (at Hampden)	24/10	L	0-2	0-2	38,000	*Johnston 4, Smith A 39* — Ref: R Davidson

Line-ups (League Cup)

Match	1	2	3	4	5	6	7	8	9	10	11	12 sub used
Morton (A)	Clark	Whyte	Shewan	Petersen	McMillan	Millar	Little	Melrose	Winchester	Smith	Wilson J	
Morton	*Sorensen*	*Boyd*	*Kennedy*	*Madsen**	*Strachan*	*Gray*	*Harper*	*Arentoft*	*Mason*	*Bolton*	*Stevenson*	*Davin*
Morton (H)	Clark	Whyte	Shewan	Petersen	McMillan	Millar	Little	Melrose	Winchester	Smith	Wilson J	
Morton	*Sorensen*	*Boyd*	*Kennedy*	*Madsen*	*Strachan*	*Gray*	*Harper*	*Arentoft*	*Mason*	*Bolton*	*Stevenson*	
Rangers (SF)	Clark	Whyte	Shewan	Petersen	McMillan	Millar	Little*	Melrose	Winchester	Smith	Wilson J	
Rangers	*Ritchie*	*Johansen*	*Provan*	*Greig*	*McKinnon*	*Smith D*	*Henderson*	*Smith A*	*Millar**	*McLean*	*Johnston*	*Wilson P*
Rangers (SF R)	Clark	Whyte	Shewan	Petersen	McMillan	Millar	Little	Melrose	Winchester	Smith	Wilson J	
Rangers	*Martin*	*Johansen*	*Provan*	*Greig*	*McKinnon*	*Smith D*	*Wilson*	*Watson*	*McLean*	*Smith A*	*Johnston*	

Morton (A): Aberdeen scored first, then tried to mix it with the no-holds-barred Division 2 pacemakers. Two Dons were booked in the second half and the referee left the ground hugely unpopular with the Aberdeen players. Mason's second goal for Morton makes it an uphill struggle to stay afloat.

Morton (H): Bobby Clark watched the game in distant parts as his team-mates tried to bludgeon a way through Morton's massed defence. The Dons were five minutes from elimination when Jim Smith appeared to earn extra-time. Then Petersen chested down Little's lob and hammered the winner.

Rangers (SF): Both sides are criticised for using substitutes in extra-time, when the ruling which introduced them was designed to replace injured players, not to seek tactical advantage. In the 87th minute McLean came nearest to settling the outcome when burrowing through to hit Clark's crossbar.

Rangers (SF R): The dream ends. Rangers' reserve keeper, Norrie Martin, did not have one direct shot to save, such was Aberdeen's inability to make a fist of it. They never recovered from Willie Johnston's early goal for Rangers, who won despite their preferred front line being wrecked by injury.

Scottish Cup

Rd	Venue	Opponent	Date	W/L	F-A	H-T	Att	Scorers, Times, and Referees
1	A	DUNDEE	28/1	W	5-0	1-0	23,000	Smith 15, 86, Wilson 49, Johnston 62, 77 — Ref: J Paterson
2	H	ST JOHNSTONE	18/2	W	5-0	0-0	22,800	Wilson 47, Smith 60, Johnston 65, 88, [Melrose 89] — Ref: T Wharton
QF	A	HIBERNIAN	11/3	D	1-1	0-1	37,200	Smith 86 / *Stevenson 15* — Ref: T Wharton
QF R	H	HIBERNIAN	22/3	W	3-0	2-0	44,000	Winchester 3, 56, Storrie 15 — Ref: T Wharton
SF	N	DUNDEE UTD (at Dens Park)	1/4	W	1-0	1-0	28,000	Millar 4 og — Ref: T Wharton
F	N	CELTIC (at Hampden)	29/4	L	0-2	0-1	126,102	*Wallace 42, 49* — Ref: W Syme

Line-ups (Scottish Cup)

Match	1	2	3	4	5	6	7	8	9	10	11	12 sub used
Dundee (A)	Clark	Whyte	Shewan	Munro	McMillan	Petersen	Robb	Smith	Johnston	Melrose	Wilson J	
Dundee	*Arrol*	*Hamilton*	*Stuart*	*Murray*	*Easton*	*Houston*	*Scott**	*Kinninmonth*	*Cameron*	*McLean*	*Bryce*	*Penman*
St Johnstone (H)	Clark	Whyte	Shewan	Munro	McMillan	Petersen	Little	Smith	Johnston	Melrose	Wilson J	
St Johnstone	*Donaldson*	*McGarry*	*Coburn*	*Townsend*	*Rooney*	*McPhee*	*Clark*	*Whitelaw*	*Kilgannon*	*Weir*	*Johnston*	
Hibernian (QF)	Clark	Whyte	Shewan	Munro	McMillan	Petersen	Storrie	Smith	Johnston	Melrose	Wilson J	
Hibernian	*Allan*	*Duncan*	*Davin*	*Stanton*	*Madsen*	*Cousin*	*Quinn*	*O'Rourke*	*Scott*	*Cormack*	*Stevenson*	
Hibernian (QF R)	Clark	Whyte	Shewan	Munro	McMillan	Petersen	Storrie	Smith	Winchester	Melrose	Wilson J	
Hibernian	*Allan*	*Duncan*	*Davis*	*Stanton*	*Madsen*	*Cousin*	*Quinn*	*O'Rourke*	*Scott*	*Cormack**	*Stevenson*	
Dundee Utd (SF)	Clark	Whyte	Shewan	Munro	McMillan	Petersen	Storrie	Smith	Johnston	Melrose	Wilson J	
Dundee Utd	*Davie*	*Millar*	*Briggs*	*Neilson*	*Smith*	*Wing*	*Gillespie*	*Graham*	*Dossing*	*Mitchell*	*Persson*	
Celtic (F)	Clark	Whyte	Shewan	Munro	McMillan	Petersen	Wilson J	Smith	Storrie	Melrose	Johnston	
Celtic	*Simpson*	*Craig*	*Gemmell*	*Murdoch*	*McNeill*	*Clark*	*Johnstone*	*Wallace*	*Chalmers*	*Auld*	*Lennox*	

Dundee (A): Dave Robb makes his debut on the wing in this demolition. Poor, demoralised Dundee melt away in the second half and leave the stage to Jim Smith. Pick of the Dons' goals was Dave Johnston's second. Smith rolled the ball into his path and the inrushing centre forward hit it. Hard.

St Johnstone (H): The good times are back at Pittodrie. Aberdeen are thrown against the same opponents in the League Cup and Scottish Cup. The rout took a long time coming. Clark saves a Coburn penalty when the score is 3-0, but by then the Saints are past caring. Nothing went right for them.

Hibernian (QF): For much of this match it looked like Hibs would repeat their 1-0 league victory over the Dons at Easter Road. Blustery conditions spoiled the spectacle for the fans. Wilson and McMillan were booked in the second half before Jim Smith headed in the equaliser from a corner.

Hibernian (QF R): A record midweek attendance witnesses transfer-seeking Ernie Winchester shoot his team into a quick lead, prodding the ball home after it had rebounded off Duncan. Then Allan failed to hold Petersen's rocket and Storrie poked in a second. 'Easy, easy' roared the crowd after half-time.

Dundee Utd (SF): Aberdeen's last Scottish Cup semi-final at Dens Park was in 1947, when they went on to win it. The Dons had beaten Dundee 5-0 here in Round 1. United full-back Tommy Millar turns the ball past his keeper. Storrie then fires wide from the spot. Desperation tactics by the close.

Celtic (F): Celtic have yet to secure the league title, so Aberdeen are not sure of a place in Europe. Turnbull is unwell and misses the match. The players arrive late at the stadium. Aberdeen looked like a rudderless ship. A rugged Final was won by two strikes by ex-Hearts poacher Willie Wallace.

	P	W	D	L	Home F	A	W	D	L	Away F	A	Pts
1 Celtic	34	14	2	1	61	17	12	4	1	50	16	58
2 Rangers	34	13	3	1	54	13	11	4	2	38	18	55
3 Clyde	34	10	2	5	29	20	10	4	3	35	28	46
4 ABERDEEN	34	11	3	3	44	17	6	5	6	28	21	42
5 Hibernian	34	10	3	4	43	24	9	1	7	29	25	42
6 Dundee	34	9	5	3	34	16	7	4	6	40	35	41
7 Kilmarnock	34	9	5	3	33	18	4	3	7	26	28	40
8 Dunfermline	34	9	4	4	46	27	5	6	6	26	25	38
9 Dundee Utd	34	7	5	5	36	33	7	4	6	32	29	37
10 Motherwell	34	7	6	4	37	26	3	5	9	22	34	31
11 Hearts	34	7	6	4	22	16	4	2	11	17	32	30
12 Partick This	34	5	5	8	25	21	4	4	9	24	47	30
13 Airdrie	34	7	1	9	27	27	4	5	8	14	26	28
14 Falkirk	34	8	1	8	18	24	3	3	11	15	46	26
15 St Johnstone	34	8	3	6	31	30	2	2	13	22	43	25
16 Stirling Alb	34	3	6	8	18	34	2	3	12	13	51	19
17 St Mirren	34	4	1	12	18	47	0	6	11	7	34	15
18 Ayr	34	1	4	12	11	37	0	3	14	9	49	9
	612	142	68	96	587	447	96	68	142	447	587	612

Odds & ends

Double wins: (4) Ayr, Airdrie, Hearts, Stirling.
Double losses: (1) Rangers.

Won from behind: (6) St Johnstone (h), Hibs (h), Hearts (h), Stirling (a), St Mirren (a), Dundee Utd (LC).
Lost from in front: (3) Rangers (h), Dunfermline (h), Morton (LC).

High spots: 8 successive league wins from 15 October.
The only team to earn two draws against champions Celtic.
Scoring 7 goals against Airdrie and 6 against Stirling and Falkirk.
The first time Aberdeen finished in top four for 11 years.
Reaching semi-final of League Cup and Final of Scottish Cup.

Low spots: 1 point from four matches in January to end title hopes.
Failing to Celtic and Rangers in the cups.
Failing to beat either of the Old Firm in seven attempts.

Losing the Scottish Cup Final.

Ever-presents: (2) Bobby Clark, Ally Shewan.
Hat-tricks: (2) Jim Wilson 1, Dave Johnston 1.
Leading scorer: (20) Jim Smith, Jim Wilson.

	Appearances						Goals			
	Lge	Sub	LC	Sub	SC	Sub	Lge	LC	SC	Tot
Buchan, Martin	4									
Clark, Bobby	34		10		6					
Hermiston, Jim	4									
Johnston, Dave	20					6	10		4	14
Little, Billy	14		10			1	1		3	4
McCabe, Benny	1									
McMillan, Tommy	32		10		6					
Melrose, Harry	27		10		6		5	2	1	8
Millar, Dave	9		10							
Munro, Francis	29				6		6			6
Petersen, Jens	30		10		6		1	1		2
Robb, Dave	2			1		1	1			1
Shewan, Ally	34		10		6		1	1		2
Smith, Jim	30		10		5		10	6	4	20
Storrie, Jim	7				4		1	1		2
Taylor, Ian	12	1		1			3			3
Watt, Willie	4	1		1			5			5
Wilson, Jim	31		10		6		13	5	2	20
Wilson, Pat	5			1						
Winchester, Ernie	15	3	10			1	10	5	2	17
Whyte, Jim	30		10		6		3	2		5
(own-goals)							2	1	1	4
21 players used	404	6	110	1	66		72	26	15	113

SCOTTISH LEAGUE DIVISION 1

Manager: Eddie Turnbull SEASON 1967-68

No	Date	Att	Pos	Pt	F-A	H-T	Scorers, Times, and Referees	1	2	3	4	5	6	7	8	9	10	11	12 sub used
1 H DUNDEE	9/9	15,000		2	W 4-2	3-0	Storrie 7, Munro 22, Taylor 44, 59; *Campbell 48, Stuart 78*; Ref: J Paterson	Clark *Arrol*	Whyte *Wilson R*	Shewan *Cox*	Petersen *Murray*	McMillan *Stewart*	Buchan *Stuart*	Wilson J *Campbell*	Munro *McLean J*	Storrie *Wilson S*	Smith *McLean G*	Taylor *Scott*	
2 A ST JOHNSTONE	16/9	6,400	4	3	D 1-1	0-0	Wilson J 72; *Whitelaw 50*; Ref: R Greenlees	Clark *Donaldson*	Whyte *McGillivray*	Shewan *Coburn*	Petersen *Miller*	McMillan *Rooney*	Buchan *McPhee*	Wilson J *Aird*	Munro *Whitelaw*	Storrie *McCarry*	Smith *McDonald*	Taylor *Wilson*	
3 H CLYDE	23/9	12,000	9	3	L 1-2	1-1	Watt 17; *Hood 25, Gilroy 85*; Ref: R Crawford	Clark *Wright*	Whyte *Glasgow*	Shewan *Soutar*	Munro *McFarlane*	McMillan *Staite*	Buchan *Fraser*	Wilson J *Knox*	Smith *Hood*	Storrie *Gilroy*	Watt *Stewart*	Taylor *Hastings*	
4 A MORTON	30/9	4,500	10	4	D 3-3	0-0	Shewan 78, Watt 89, opp 90 og; *Mason 51, Allan 61, Sweeney 84*; Ref: R Wilson	Clark *Russell*	Whyte *Loughlan*	Shewan *Kennedy*	Millar *Arnott*	McMillan *Strachan*	Munro *Gray*	Wilson J *Jensen*	Smith *Allan*	Taylor* *Mason*	Watt *Stevenson*	Johnston *Sweeney*	Wilson P
5 H DUNFERMLINE	7/10	12,500	13	4	L 0-1	0-1	*Gardner 30*; Ref: R Wilson	Clark *Martin*	Whyte *Callaghan W*	Shewan *Lunn*	Munro *Delaney*	McMillan *Barry*	Petersen *Thomson*	Wilson J! *Hunter*	Smith *Callaghan T*	Storrie *Gardner*	Millar* *Paton*	Johnston *Robertson*	Robb
6 H DUNDEE UTD	14/10	9,000	9	6	W 6-0	2-0	Taylor 12, Munro 38, Johnston 48, 66p, [Smith 62, Robb 88]; Ref: J McKee	Clark *Davie*	Hermiston *Millar T*	Shewan *Briggs*	Munro *Wood*	McMillan *Smith*	Petersen *Gillespie*	Johnston *Seemann*	Smith *Dossing*	Robb *Millar J*	Melrose *Rowland*	Taylor *Mitchell*	
7 A HEARTS	21/10	11,000	11	6	L 1-2	0-1	Storrie 62; *Jensen 9, Ford 85*; Ref: D Small	McGarr *Garland*	Hermiston *Sneddon*	Shewan *Holt*	Munro *Macdonald*	McMillan *Thomson*	Petersen *Miller*	Johnston *Jensen*	Storrie *Townsend*	Robb *Ford*	Melrose *Irvine*	Taylor *Traynor**	Fleming
8 A PARTICK THISTLE	4/11	6,530	12	7	D 2-2	2-1	Smith 8, Little 42; *McParland 3, Rae 71*; Ref: A McKenzie	Clark *Niven*	Hermiston *Campbell*	Shewan *Muir*	Buchan *O'Neil*	McMillan *McKinven*	Petersen *Gibb*	Little *Rae*	Smith *McParland*	Johnston *Cuilston*	Melrose *Flanagan*	Wilson J *Duncan*	
9 H RAITH ROVERS	11/11	8,000	13	9	W 6-2	1-1	J'ston 42p, Little 58, Petersen 69p, 82, Wallace 30, 86 [Mackle 72 og, Wilson 88 og]; Ref: W Anderson	Clark *Reid*	Hermiston *Bolton*	Shewan *Gray*	Buchan *Kinloch*	McMillan *Davidson*	Petersen *Porterfield*	Little *Wallace*	Smith *Stein*	Johnston *Cunningham*	Melrose *Sneddon*	Wilson J *Mackle*	
10 A HIBERNIAN	18/11	11,000	10	9	L 0-1	0-0	*Cormack 56*; Ref: A McKenzie	Clark *Allan*	Hermiston *Duncan*	Shewan *Davis*	Buchan *Stanton*	McMillan *Madsen*	Petersen *McGraw*	Little *Scott*	Smith *Quinn*	Robb* *Stein*	Melrose *Cormack*	Wilson J *O'Rourke*	Munro

Match notes

1. Dundee were on a roll: this is their first defeat in 25 games. After the traumas of Aberdeen's League Cup section, this result is as welcome as it is unexpected. Players to catch the eye included Jimmy Smith and Martin Buchan. The match was virtually over by half-time.

2. It seems to be the case that when Jimmy Smith plays well Aberdeen play well. At Perth, he did not, and neither did they. The Dons faced St Johnstone five times last season, winning four. Not only are they sick of the sight of them, they know this is a point that slipped away.

3. Not much entertainment here. Not many smiles either, unless you were a Clyde supporter. Three minutes before Gilroy's winner, Francis Munro blazed a penalty against the Clyde crossbar. This result takes the gloss off Aberdeen's promising start to the league campaign.

4. Top scorer Jim Storrie is mysteriously omitted from the Dons travelling party. He missed a Roy of the Rovers fightback – sparked by Watt's 20-yard free-kick, and Jim Whyte's fierce cross that was turned in by a defender. Whyte claimed the goal. Morton rued their missed chances.

5. Aberdeen's disciplinary record, bad last season, is becoming embarrassing. Ally Shewan was booked in the second half and Jimmy Wilson ordered off. It is clear why Aberdeen's shirts have numbers on the front as well as back: it is to prevent the ref having to turn the player around.

6. A new-look forward line – with Taylor and Melrose restored – creates countless chances and gains handsome revenge for the 0-5 drubbing inflicted by United at Tannadice in the League Cup. Funny game, football. Just six weeks earlier these side's had played a 2-2 draw at Pittodrie.

7. Jim Storrie was both hero and villain. His superb diving header made it 1-1, but he then blazed frivolously over the bar before Ford restored Hearts' lead. Up in the stand Bill Shankly and Wolves scouts sized up Francis Munro. They also came to see Jim Smith, but he wasn't playing.

8. Bobby Clark resumes in goal, and is watched by a member of the Scottish Selection Committee. Clark chooses this, of all days, to allow Rae's half-hit, second-half shot to deprive the Dons of a point. Clark need not lose any sleep. He will be capped under Bobby Brown before long.

9. For much of the match this result looked impossible. The Dons trailed to a Willie Wallace goal as half-time neared. The turning point was Johnston's equalising penalty, which beat Reid even though Johnston miscued. Then the floodgates opened. The Dons climb above Raith.

10. Hibs have a 100% home record and only they seem able to challenge to the Old Firm this season. Aberdeen lost Robb early on with a cut eye. The match was settled by Peter Cormack's hook, after a corner wasn't cleared. Twice so far the Dons have hit six, then lost their next game.

11 H MOTHERWELL 25/11 — 9,000 — W 2-1 — 10 17 11
Lineup: Clark, Hermiston, Shewan, Buchan*, Munro, Petersen, Johnston, Smith, Robb, Melrose, Wilson J, Little
Opposition: McCloy, Whiteford, Mackay, Forsyth, Martis, Murray, Lindsay, McCall, Deans, Campbell, Moffat*, McCallum W
Wilson 37, Melrose 67 — Murray 79 — Ref: A Crawley
Motherwell are entrenched in the bottom two with only one away point. Aberdeen are now in the mood to travel to Standard Liege in the Cup-Winners' Cup. Motherwell will not survive. As for Aberdeen, how can a team averaging over two goals a game be so low in the league?

12 A FALKIRK 2/12 — 4,500 — D 2-2 — 10 13 12
Lineup: Clark, Devlin, Shewan, Munro, McMillan, Petersen, Johnston, Smith, Robb, Melrose, Wilson J
Opposition: Lambie, Hunter, Markie, Baillie, Gibson, Marshall, Smith, Graham, McLaughlin, Watson
Melrose 43, Smith 44 — Markie 47, Watson 60 — Ref: A McDonald
Falkirk have won just once at home. Aberdeen inflicted a double dose of pain on their opponents, scoring twice in the last seconds before the break. That should have sunk Falkirk, but no sooner do the teams restart than Buchan deflects Markie's shot, and the match is alive.

13 A KILMARNOCK 9/12 — 8,755 — L 0-3 — 12 8 12
Lineup: Clark, McLaughlan, Shewan, Munro, McMillan, Petersen, Little, Smith, Robb, Melrose, Wilson J, Murray
Opposition: Arthur, McFadzean, Murray, McGrory, Beattie, McLean, Queen, Morrison, Sinclair, Cameron, Taylor*, Murray
Queen 20, Morrison 51, 75 — Ref: J Callaghan
Aberdeen are licking their wounds in the Cup-Winners' Cup. One would hope Kilmarnock would be made to pay for Standard Liege's success. Instead the Dons resort to muscle instead of skill. Shewan and Munro were booked in the second half, but the match had already slipped away.

14 H STIRLING ALB 16/12 — 6,000 — W 1-0 — 9 18 14
Lineup: Clark, Murray, Shewan, Munro, McMillan, Petersen, Little, Smith, Storrie, Melrose, Craig
Opposition: Cunningham, McGuinness, Grant, Corrigan, Thomson, Hall, Peebles, Hughes, Laing, Symington
Shewan 72 — Ref: A McDonald
Ally Shewan's run of more than 230 consecutive first-team appearances is crowned with a win, but breaks the tedium of what has gone before. Stirling are propping up the league table, so this victory is laboured. Stirling have now conceded 28 away goals.

15 A AIRDRIE 23/12 — 4,000 — L 0-1 — 11 14 14
Lineup: Clark, McKenzie, Shewan, Munro, McMillan, Petersen, Little*, Smith, Murray, Murray, Craig
Opposition: Jonquin, Caldwell, Goodwin, Black, Whiteford, Wilson, Ramsay, Marshall, Fyfe, Train, Buchanan
Marshall 72 — Ref: R Wilson
Aberdeen's disciplinary record is so bad that there seems to be an unofficial race going on among the players to see who can attract the most cautions. Among the leaders is Francis Munro, who in this match enters the little black book for the fourth time this season.

16 H RANGERS 30/12 — 20,000 — L 1-4 — 12 1 14
Lineup: Clark, Sorensen, Shewan, Munro, McMillan, Petersen, Little, Smith, Johnston, Murray, Craig
Opposition: Johansen, Greig, Watson, McKinnon, Smith D, Penman, Willoughby, Smith A, Johnston, Persson
(Willoughby 83)
Smith 71 — Penman 12, Watson 55, Johnston 77 — Ref: J Paterson
In the League Cup this match finished 1-1. Unbeaten Rangers were rarely in difficulties. Ex-Don Dave Smith swept up majestically at the back. A goal by his namesake Jim - spread hope through Pittodrie after 71 minutes, but Willie Johnston clamped down on any Dons resurgence.

17 A DUNDEE 1/1 — 10,000 — W 2-0 — 11 14 16
Lineup: Clark, Donaldson, Shewan, Petersen, McMillan, Petersen, Little, Buchan, Buchanan, Smith, Craig
Opposition: Wilson R, Houston, Murray, Easton, Stuart, Scott, McLean J, Wilson S, McLean G, Campbell
Johnston 1, Easton 20 og — Ref: E Pringle
This is Aberdeen's first away win in the league since Hearts last March. The conditions made for a farcical match. Dave Johnston scored the first goal of 1968, after 40 seconds. Eddie Buchanan pressured Jim Easton into scoring an own-goal. A sixth straight win against Dundee.

18 A DUNFERMLINE 20/1 — 9,650 — L 2-4 — 13 4 16
Lineup: Clark, Martin, Shewan, Petersen, McMillan, Petersen, Robb, Buchanan, Johnston, Buchanan, Craig
Opposition: Callaghan W Lunn, Fraser, Thomson, Barry, Edwards, Paton, Gardner, Callaghan T Robertson
Johnston 36, Buchanan 85 — Robertson 28, 69p, Paton 48, Fraser 71 — Ref: W Syme
Dunfermline are the form team in the division. They went into this match having taken 13 points from their last seven games. Now it's 15 from eight. The turning point came midway through the second half, when Robertson scored from the spot after Murray had brought down Edwards.

19 A DUNDEE UTD 3/2 — 6,500 — W 3-2 — 10 11 18
Lineup: Clark, Mackay, Shewan, Murray, McMillan, Petersen, Johnston, Smith, Robb, Buchan, Craig
Opposition: Miller, Cameron, Neilson, Smith, Gillespie, Seemann, Rolland, Scott*, Mitchell, Wilson, Wood
Murray 12, Smith 37, Johnston 79 — Seemann 48, Mitchell 87 — Ref: W Elliott
There are no frills about this Dons side, which took both points when Dave Johnston beat goalkeeper Mackay one-on-one. This win brings the unusual distinction of double league wins against both Dundee teams. United's only success had been in the League Cup, when they won 5-0.

20 H HEARTS 10/2 — 12,000 — W 2-0 — 9 8 20
Lineup: Clark, Garland, Shewan, Murray, McMillan, Petersen, Johnston, Smith, Robb, Buchan, Craig
Opposition: Sneddon, Mann, Thomson A, Miller, Thomson E, Ford, Townsend, Moller*, Irvine, Traynor, Fleming
Craig 24, Johnston 66 — Ref: I Foote
Dave Robb is the new victim of the Pittodrie barrackers. Tommy Craig scored his first senior goal for Aberdeen, whose second goal required a helping hand from Hearts' keeper Garland. He failed to clear Craig's corner, and Dave Johnston was on hand to jab the ball over the line.

21 H MORTON 12/2 — 10,000 — D 0-0 (W 1-0) — 9 7 22
Lineup: Clark, Russell, Shewan, Murray, McMillan, Petersen, Johnston, Smith, Robb, Buchan, Craig
Opposition: Loughan, Kennedy, Rankin, Strachan, Gray, Sweeney, Arnetoft, Mason, Allan, Taylor
Robb 82 — Ref: A McKenzie
Boo-boy Robb scores the one and only goal which sustains Aberdeen's revival, capitalising on Buchan's flick-on from Craig's corner-kick. Only eight minutes remained. Aberdeen would have dropped a point but for Clark's thrilling one-handed save from Taylor's strong header.

SCOTTISH LEAGUE DIVISION 1 — Manager: Eddie Turnbull — SEASON 1967-68

No	Date		Att	Pos	Pt	F-A	H-T	Scorers, Times, and Referees	1	2	3	4	5	6	7	8	9	10	11	12 sub used
22	2/3	H PARTICK THISTLE 10	7,000	9	22	0-1	0-0	Gibb 46 / Ref: R Davidson	Clark / Niven	Whyte / Campbell	Shewan / Muir	Petersen / O'Neil	McMillan / Hansen	Murray / Gibb	Johnston / Rae	Smith / McParland	Robb* / Coulston	Buchan / Flanagan	Craig / Duncan*	Watt / Gallagher
23	6/3	A CELTIC 11	28,000	2	22	1-4	0-4	Johnston 70, Lennox 3, 31, 35, McNeill 7 / Ref: W Mullen	Clark / Simpson	Whyte / Gemmell	Shewan / O'Neil	Petersen / Murdoch	McMillan / McNeill	Murray / Brogan	Johnston / Johnstone	Smith / Lennox	Watt / Wallace	Buchan / Gallagher*	Craig / Hughes	Hay
24	9/3	A RAITH ROVERS 11	5,000	15	22	1-3	1-2	Taylor 1, Wallace 36, 45, Gillespie 63 / Ref: R Crawford	Clark / Reid	Whyte / Hislop	Shewan / Gray	Petersen / Stein	McMillan / Polland	Murray* / Millar	Johnston / Wilson	Smith / Falconer	Taylor / Wallace	Buchan / Judge	Craig / Gillespie	Robb
25	16/3	H HIBERNIAN 11	7,000	3	24	5-0	3-0	Johnston 9, 23, Smith 22, opp 85 og, [Buchan 87] / Ref: R Greenlees	Clark / Allan, Simpson	Whyte / Davis	Shewan / Cousin	Petersen / Madsen	McMillan / McGraw	Buchan / Scott	Johnston / Quinn	Cumming / Stein	Taylor / O'Rourke	Buchan / Stevenson	Watt	
26	23/3	A MOTHERWELL 10	2,360	17	26	3-0	0-0	Watt 65, Cumming 76, Smith 87p / Ref: A Crawley	Clark / McCloy	Whyte / Whiteford	Shewan / McKay	Petersen / Campbell	McMillan / Martis	Buchan / McCallum W	Johnston / Beaton	Cumming / McInally	Taylor / Deans*	Smith / Goldthorpe	Watt / Wilson	Forsyth
27	27/3	A CLYDE	5,500		26	0-1	0-0	Knox 52 / Ref: R Greenlees	Clark / Wright	Whyte / Glasgow	Shewan / Soutar	Petersen / McHugh	McMillan / Fraser	Buchan / Staite	Johnston / Knox	Cumming / Anderson	Taylor / Hood	Smith / Stewart	Watt / Hastings	
28	30/3	H FALKIRK 7	5,000	6	28	2-0	1-0	Shewan 43, Johnston 69 / Ref: W Balfour	Clark / Devlin	Whyte / Lambie	Shewan / Hunter	Petersen / Markie	McMillan / Baillie	Buchan / Gibson	Johnston / McManus	Cumming / Smith	Taylor / Graham	Smith / McLaughlin	Watt / Watson	
29	6/4	H KILMARNOCK 7	6,000	8	29	1-1	1-1	Johnston 4, Morrison 6 / Ref: E Thomson	Clark / McLaughlan	Whyte / Arthur	Shewan / King	Petersen / Murray	McMillan / McGrory	Buchan / Beattie	Johnston / McLean	Cumming / Queen	Taylor* / Morrison	Smith / McFadzean	Watt / McIlroy	Little
30	10/4	H CELTIC 7	22,000		29	0-1	0-0	Lennox 60 / Ref: E Thomson	Clark / Simpson	Whyte / Craig	Shewan / Gemmell	Petersen / Murdoch	McMillan / McNeill	Buchan / Brogan	Little / Johnstone	Smith / Lennox	Johnston / Wallace	Robb / Gallagher	Watt / Hughes	
31	13/4	A STIRLING ALB 5	1,600	18	31	3-0	1-0	Petersen 7, Robb 50, Smith 60 / Ref: T Marshall	Clark / Murray	Whyte / Reid	Shewan / Corrigan	Petersen / Grant	McMillan / Rogerson	Buchan / Henderson	Little / Laurie	Smith / Thomson	Johnston / Lynn	Robb / Hughes	Watt / Hall	

22 — Thistle's goal was in keeping with the impoverished state of the match. Gibb's feeble shot was mishandled over the line by Bobby Clark upon the change-round. The result puts an end to Aberdeen's winning spell. The Dons won this fixture 5-2 last season. Partick overtake the Dons.

23 — The Dons were brushed aside, as if so much fluff. Celtic are now four points behind unbeaten Rangers with one game in hand. Lennox's delicate header, followed by McNeill's thumping header, gave Celtic the whip hand after seven minutes. The game was dead by half-time.

24 — Gordon Wallace's two goals make him the league's top scorer. Celtic have apparently bid £50,000 for Jim Smith. In recent weeks Turnbull has sold Jim Storrie to Rotherham, Munro to Wolves, Jim Wilson to Motherwell, Dave Millar and Pat Wilson to Raith. Both line up in this match.

25 — You would never have believed Hibs were third, so badly did they play. Skipper Joe Davis even fluffed a penalty. Ian Cumming has a quiet debut for the Dons. Johnston looked a mite offside when scoring his first goal; he was almost on his knees when heading his second.

26 — Motherwell could not afford to lose this game if they wished to stay up. The pitch had to be sanded before the referee would let the game start. Ally Shewan was made captain to mark his 250th consecutive first-team appearance. Motherwell hold out for over an hour, then collapse.

27 — Ian Cumming hit the post in the first half, but that is the nearest the Dons come to a goal as lively Clyde complete the double over them. Aberdeen have beaten them just once in eight attempts since Clyde were promoted. The season cannot end quickly enough for the feeble Dons.

28 — Even though they have lost more games than they have won, the Dons are on paper still in with a shout for a Fairs Cup place, though nobody knows how many places are up for grabs. They gain two more welcome points against a struggling Falkirk side with little interest in attacking.

29 — Kilmarnock attacked in the first half, defended in the second. Aberdeen were not given long to celebrate Dave Johnston's quick opener. Clark rushed out to gather the ball, McMillan touched it past him, and Morrison was presented with a gift. The Fairs Cup seems yet further away.

30 — In view of Celtic's tightrope finish with Rangers, Lennox's goal is priceless. Overall Celtic were poor value for their win, as the Dons looked the more likely to score. Simpson's save under siege when Shewan miskicked at a Jimmy Johnstone cross, leaving Lennox unmarked.

31 — Before kick-off Aberdeen had lost more game than they'd won. Yet this win lifts them to fifth, which if maintained should secure a place in the Fairs Cup. Scotland team manager Bobby Brown cast a critical eye over Bobby Clark and Jim Smith. Stirling have now conceded 101 goals.

32. H ST JOHNSTONE — 17/4 — W 1-0 — 33 — Att 6,500 (HT 0-0)

Aberdeen: Clark, Whyte, Shewan, Petersen, McMillan, Buchan, Little, Smith, Johnston, Robb, Craig
St Johnstone: *Robertson, McGillivray, Coburn, Miller, Rooney, McPhee, Aird, Gordon, McDonald, McCarry, Aitken*, Whitelaw*

Buchan 80
Ref: R Henderson

Aberdeen beat St Johnstone three times at Pittodrie last season. Desperate Saints hold out this time until 10 minutes from time, when Martin Buchan's head meets Craig's corner. There was still time for McCarry's header to rebound from Clark's goalpost and fly back into play.

33. H AIRDRIE — 20/4 — 5 — W 3-2 — 35 — Att 8,000 — 13 (HT 2-0)

Aberdeen: Clark, Whyte, Shewan, Petersen, McMillan, Buchan, Little, Smith, Johnston, Robb, Craig
Airdrie: *McKenzie, Jonquin, Keenan, Goodwin, Whiteford, Madden*, Jarvie, Marshall, Irvine, Phillips, McPheat*

Little 21, Robb 37, Smith 73p
Goodwin 60, Marshall 65
Ref: S Anderson

Panic for Aberdeen after they appeared to be coasting. Both sides made substitutions at 2-1. Young Drew Jarvie caught the eye for Airdrie with some neat footwork. Jim Smith nets a late penalty to win the game, though it looked as though Black had fouled Dave Robb outside the box.

34. A RANGERS — 27/4 — 5 — W 3-2 — 2 37 — Att 40,000 (HT 1-1)

Aberdeen: Clark, Whyte, Shewan, Petersen, McMillan, Buchan, Little, Smith, Johnston, Robb, Craig
Rangers: *Sorensen, Johansen, Mathieson, Greig, McKinnon, Smith, Henderson, Willoughby, Ferguson, Johnston, Persson, Taylor*

Johnston 29, 58, Taylor 89
Smith D 17, Ferguson 56
Ref: T Kellock

Rangers' first and only league defeat of the season hands the championship to Celtic. When Alex Ferguson was put clear to restore Rangers' lead it looked like curtains. But Little immediately sent Johnston away to level, and substitute Ian Taylor was unmarked for a last-gasp winner.

Average Home 10,300 — Away 9,100

Scottish League Cup - Section 2

1. H RANGERS — 12/8 — D 1-1 — 1 — Att 36,000 (HT 0-1)

Aberdeen: Clark, Whyte, Shewan, Petersen, McMillan, Wilson P, Storrie, Johnston, Buchan, Wilson J
Rangers: *Sorensen, Johansen, Provan, Greig, McKinnon, Henderson, Penman, Ferguson, Smith D, Persson*

Storrie 82
Persson 25
Ref: A McKenzie

A huge turn-out reflects hopes for the new season. Before today Aberdeen had not beaten Rangers in nine matches. Now it is 10. Alex Ferguson makes his first appearance at Pittodrie for Rangers. Aberdeen shirts show the player's number on the front as well as the back.

2. A DUNDEE UTD — 16/8 — L 0-5 — 1 — Att 7,550 (HT 0-0)

[Gillespie 89]
Aberdeen: Clark, Whyte, Shewan, Petersen, McMillan, Munro, Storrie, Johnston, Buchan, Wilson J
Dundee Utd: *Mackay, Millar T, Briggs, Wood, Smith, Berg, Hainey, Gillespie, Wilson*

Hainey 57, Wilson 69, Seemann 72, 86
Ref: W Mullen

It is not often that Turnbull's Dons suffer a result like this. The odd thing is that they held their own for almost an hour. The tidal wave began with Bill Hainey's overhead kick. Two goals in the last four minutes turn a heavy defeat into a massacre. What hopes now for the new season?

3. A CELTIC — 19/8 — L 1-3 — 1 — Att 50,000 (HT 0-0)

Aberdeen: Clark, Whyte, Shewan, Munro, McMillan, Petersen, Storrie, Robb, Buchan, Johnston
Celtic: *Simpson, Craig, Gemmell, Murdoch, McNeill, Clark, Johnstone, Wallace, Chalmers, Auld, Lennox*

Storrie 77
Gemmell 48p, Lennox 78, Auld 89
Ref: J Kelly

This game - Aberdeen's first against the new European champions - turned on a questionable penalty. Bobby Lennox seemed to stumble when challenged by Whyte and Shewan. Storrie gave Aberdeen hope after Jens Petersen's free-kick almost snapped Ronnie Simpson's crossbar.

4. A RANGERS — 26/8 — L 0-3 — 1 — Att 50,000 (HT 0-2)

Aberdeen: Clark, Whyte, Shewan, Petersen, McMillan, Storrie, Smith, Johnston, Melrose, Taylor
Rangers: *Sorensen, Johansen, Provan, Jardine, McKinnon, Greig, Henderson, Penman, Ferguson, Smith D, Persson*

Jardine 23, Penman 30, 80
Ref: T Kellock

The Dons' confidence has drained away. Turnbull has now called upon nine different forwards in four matches. Melrose was booked for fouling Alex Ferguson; Munro for toppling ex-Don Dave Smith. Rangers' first two goals were long-range pile-drivers. Will the Dons ever win?

5. H DUNDEE UTD — 30/8 — D 2-2 — 2 — Att 10,000 (HT 1-0)

Aberdeen: Clark, Whyte, Shewan, Petersen, McMillan, Buchan, Wilson J, Smith, Storrie, Smith
Dundee Utd: *Mackay, Millar T, Briggs, Millar J, Berg, Dossing, Hainey, Mitcell, Wilson*, Graham*

Storrie 23, Munro 55
Hainey 49, Smith 78
Ref: R Gordon

With Celtic coming next, Aberdeen are playing for pride. The have nearly all the play, but dropped a point when Dundee United centre-half Doug Smith scored a goal that went in off Bobby Clark's head. This result makes it likely that Aberdeen will finish bottom of their section.

6. H CELTIC — 2/9 — L 1-5 — 2 — Att 23,000 (HT 1-2)

[Auld 87, Craig 90]
Aberdeen: Clark, Whyte, Shewan, Petersen, McMillan, Buchan, Storrie, Storrie, Robb, Taylor
Celtic: *Craig, Gemmell*, McNeill, Clark, O'Neil, Johnstone, Wallace, Murdoch, McMahon, Lennox*

Smith 7
Gemmell 16p, McMahon 32, J'stone 63, Simpson
Ref: J Gordon

A game remembered for an on-field assault on the referee by a man and a dog. The tension was sparked by a penalty awarded to Celtic after Clark had saved at Lennox's feet. Clark saved from Gemmell, only for the ref to order a retake. Jimmy Johnstone gave an exhibition show.

	P	W	D	L	F	A	Pts
Qual Celtic	6	5	1	0	14	4	11
Rangers	6	3	2	1	10	5	8
Dundee Utd	6	1	1	4	7	8	3
ABERDEEN	6	0	2	4	5	19	2

SCOTTISH LEAGUE DIV 1 (CUP-TIES)   Manager: Eddie Turnbull

Scottish Cup

				F-A				H-T	Scorers, Times, and Referees
1	H	RAITH ROVERS	27/1	13	D	1-1	10,700 17	1-1	Robb 25 / Mackle 20 — Ref: A McKenzie
1R	A	RAITH ROVERS	31/1	13	W	1-0	3,500 17	0-0	Reid 68 og — Ref: A McKenzie
2	A	DUNFERMLINE	19/2	9	L	1-2	14,700 4	1-0	Smith 39 / Robertson 55, Edwards 84 — Ref: T Wharton

Match 1 — Clark, Whyte, Shewan, Buchan, McMillan, Murray, Robb, Buchanan*, Johnston, Smith, Craig / Little
Reid, Selfridge, Hislop, Bolton, Davidson, Gray, Stein, Wallace, Cunningham, Sneddon, Mackle

Raith put the Dons out of the Scottish Cup in 1963 and threaten to do so again. In the league they have won just twice in 20 matches, but do not look inferior. At 1-1 Sneddon's penalty hit the junction of bar and post. Long before the end a slow-handclap reverberated around Pittodrie.

Match 1R — Clark, Whyte, Shewan, Murray, McMillan, Petersen, Johnston, Smith, Robb, Buchan, Craig
Reid, Selfridge, Hislop, Bolton, Davidson, Gray, Stein, Wallace, Cunningham, Sneddon, Mackle

Lucky Aberdeen. In a match played in an Arctic gale, they survive only thanks to a freak goal. Jens Petersen floated over a free-kick which keeper Reid pushed into the air and then punched into his own net. Petersen would be happy to claim it, but it goes down as an own-goal.

Match 2 — Clark, Whyte, Shewan, Murray, McMillan, Petersen, Johnston, Smith, Robb, Buchan, Craig
Martin, Callaghan W Lunn, Thomson, Barry, Callaghan T Edwards, Paton, Gardner, Totten, Robertson, Gordon*

Fourth-placed Dunfermline squeeze past Aberdeen. Jim Smith was the man of the first half. He was booked in the 27th minute, then scored after Martin had spilled Shewan's effort. The Dons would have forced a replay had not Martin been equal to Dave Robb's flying header.

European Cup-Winners' Cup

				F-A				H-T	Scorers, Times, and Referees
1:1	H	KR REYKJAVIK (Iceland)	6/9	10	W	10-0	14,000	4-0	Munro 19,53,62, Storrie 21,56, Smith 32,78, [McMillan 44, Taylor 49, Petersen 72] — Ref: A Aalbrecht (Holland)
1:2	A	KR REYKJAVIK	13/9	10	W	4-1	1,500	2-0	Storrie 42, 59, Buchan 45, Munro 52 / Hafsteinsson 74 — Ref: I Hornstein (Norway) (Dons win 14-1 on aggregate)
2:1	A	STANDARD LIEGE (Belgium)	29/11	10	L	0-3	30,000	0-2	Claessen 7, Cajou 11, Pilot 64 — Ref: S Ellonaro (Portugal)
2:2	H	STANDARD LIEGE	6/12	10	W	2-0	13,000	1-0	Munro 20, Melrose 65 — Ref: M Petursson (Iceland) (Dons lose 2-3 on aggregate)

Match 1:1 — Clark, Whyte, Shewan, Petersen, McMillan, Buchan, Wilson J, Munro, Storrie, Smith, Taylor
Petursson, Jonsson K, Felixson B, Jonsson P, Schram, Kjartansson, Markan, Felixson G, Baldvinsson, Hafsteinsson, Jacobsson

14,000 came to see what continental football is all about, and watched gleefully as Aberdeen inflicted unnecessary suffering on the Icelandic amateurs. Bobby Clark did not have a shot to save until the closing minuutes. Never subsequently have Aberdeen scored 10 goals in Europe.

Match 1:2 — Clark, Whyte, Shewan, Munro, McMillan, Kirkland, Wilson J, Smith, Storrie, Buchan, Taylor
Petursson, Jonsson K, Felixson B, Gudmundsson, Schram, Kjartansson, Felixson G, Jonsson T, Baldvinsson, Hafsteinsson, Lalusson

The tiny stadium was in uproar when Hafsteinsson fired past Bobby Clark. That reduced the deficit to 14-1. Aberdeen players must be thinking European football is a doddle. This baptism would hardly be typical. Never again would the Dons beat European opponents by such a margin.

Match 2:1 — Clark, Whyte, Shewan, Munro, McMillan, Petersen, Johnston, Smith, Robb, Melrose, Wilson J
Nivolay, Onclin, Jeck, Beurlet, Dewalque, Naumovic, Semmeling, Claessen, Galic, Cajou

Standard Liege have in the past reached the semi-finals of two European competitions. Aberdeen's hopes in the Sclessin Stadium were dented in the first 11 minutes. International striker Claessen drove a corner past Bobby Clark. Another corner-kick brought the second goal, for Cajou.

Match 2:2 — Clark, Whyte, Shewan, Munro, McMillan, Petersen, Little, Smith, Robb, Melrose, Wilson J
Nicolay, Beurlet, Jeck, Pilot, Thissen, Dewalque, Naumovic, Semmeling, Claessen, Galic, Cajou

A disappointing crowd. Partly because they think the Dons are out; partly because of the weather - the match began in a snowstorm. Francis Munro's raging volley pulls a goal back, but shortly afterwards Jim Whyte blazed wide with the goal at his mercy. It proved expensive.

Scottish League Division One

	P		Home					Away					Pts
		W	D	L	F	A	W	D	L	F	A		
1 Celtic	34	14	3	0	53	14	16	1	0	53	10		63
2 Rangers	34	14	2	1	50	13	14	3	0	43	21		61
3 Hibernian	34	12	2	3	40	17	8	3	6	27	32		45
4 Dunfermline	34	9	1	7	38	18	8	5	5	26	23		39
5 ABERDEEN	34	11	1	5	36	17	5	8	4	27	31		37
6 Morton	34	10	4	3	35	25	5	2	10	22	28		36
7 Kilmarnock	34	9	4	4	34	23	4	9	4	25	34		34
8 Clyde	34	9	3	5	39	25	6	1	10	16	30		34
9 Dundee	34	8	2	7	44	39	5	5	7	18	20		33
10 Partick This	34	6	5	6	25	28	6	2	9	26	39		31
11 Dundee Utd	34	7	7	3	36	30	3	4	10	17	42		31
12 Hearts	34	9	1	7	24	23	4	3	10	32	38		30
13 Airdrie	34	7	5	5	26	20	3	4	10	19	38		29
14 St Johnstone	34	6	2	9	19	26	4	5	8	24	26		27
15 Falkirk	34	3	6	8	19	25	4	6	7	17	25		26
16 Raith Rovers	34	5	4	8	32	30	4	3	10	26	56		25
17 Motherwell	34	4	3	10	20	32	2	4	11	20	34		19
18 Stirling Alb	34	4	3	10	18	44	0	1	16	11	61		12
	612	147	58	101	588	449	101	58	147	449	588		612

Odds & ends

Double wins: (4) Dundee, Dundee Utd, Motherwell, Stirling A.
Double losses: (3) Clyde, Dunfermline, Celtic.

Won from behind: (2) Raith (h), Rangers (a).
Lost from in front: (4) Clyde (h), Raith (a), (Celtic (LC), Dunfermline (SC).

High spots: Winning last four league games.
Defeating unbeaten Rangers at Ibrox in final match.
Scoring 10 goals at home to KR Reykjavik.

Low spots: Being swamped by 19 goals in League Cup section.
Four straight defeats in league and Scottish Cup from 17 February.

Ever-presents: (1) Ally Shewan.
Hat-tricks: (1) Francis Munro.
Leading scorer: (14) Dave Johnston.

Appearances and Goals

	Appearances								Goals				
	Lge	Sub	LC	Sub	SC	Sub	Eur	Sub	Lge	LC	SC	Eur	Tot
Buchan, Martin	24		5		3		2		2			1	3
Buchanan, Eddie	3	1	1		1								1
Clark, Bobby	33		6		3		4						
Craig, Tommy	13	1			3				1				1
Cumming, Ian	5								1				1
Hermiston, Jim	6												
Johnston, Dave	28		4		3		1		14				14
Kirkland, Jim						1							
Little, Billy	13	2				1	1		3				3
McGarr, Ernie	1												
McMillan, Tommy	33		6		3		4			1			1
Melrose, Harry	8		1				2		2			1	3
Millar, Dave	2												
Munro, Francis	13	1	6				4		2	1		5	8
Murray, George	9	1			3				1				1
Petersen, Jens	32		6		2		3		3			1	4
Robb, Dave	16	2	1	1	3		2		4		1		5
Shewan, Ally	34		6		3		4		3				3
Smith, Jim	33		3		3		4		9	1	1	2	13
Storrie, Jim	6		6				2		2		3	4	9
Taylor, Ian	14	1	3				2		5			1	6
Watt, Willie	10	1											
Whyte, Jim	28		6		3		4						
Wilson, Jim	10		4				4		3				3
Wilson, Pat		1	3										
(own-goals)													3
25 players used	374	11	66	1	33		44		63	5	3	16	87

SCOTTISH LEAGUE DIVISION 1 — Manager: Eddie Turnbull — SEASON 1968-69

No	Date	Att	Pos	Pt	F-A	H-T	1	2	3	4	5	6	7	8	9	10	14	12 sub used
1 A DUNDEE	7/9	10,000		D 1	4-4	2-1	Clark	Hermiston	Shewan	Petersen	McMillan	Craig	**Rae**	Robb	Forrest	Smith	Taylor	12 sub used
							Donaldson	*Wilson*	*Houston*	*Murray*	*Easton*	*Stewart*	*Campbell*	*McLean*	*Duncan*	*Scott*	*Georgeson*	
2 H ST JOHNSTONE	14/9	11,000	5	W 3	2-0	0-0	Clark	Hermiston	Shewan	Petersen	McMillan	Craig	Rae	Robb	Forrest	Smith	Taylor	
							Robertson	*McGillivray*	*Miller*	*Gordon*	*Rooney*	*McPhee*	*Aird*	*Whitelaw*	*McGarry*	*MacDonald*	*Aitken*	
3 H DUNDEE UTD	21/9	13,000	8	L 3	0-1	0-1	Clark	Hermiston	Shewan	Petersen	McMillan	Craig	Rae	Smith	Forrest	Smith	Taylor	
							Mackay	*Rolland*	*Cameron J*	*Gillespie*	*Smith*	*Wood*	*Hogg*	*Reid*	*Cameron K**	*Mitchell*	*Wilson*	*Scott*
4 A CELTIC	28/9	35,000	11	L 3	1-2	1-1	Clark	Hermiston	Shewan	Petersen	McMillan	Craig	Rae	Smith	Forrest	Smith	Taylor	
							Simpson	*Craig*	*Gemmell*	*Murdoch*	*McNeill*	*Brogan*	*Johnstone*	*Lennox*	*Wallace*	*Connelly*	*Hughes*	
5 H HEARTS	5/10	12,000	14	L 3	1-2	0-1	Clark	Hermiston	Shewan	Petersen	McMillan	Buchan M	Rae*	Robb	Hamilton	Smith	Taylor	Johnston
							Cruickshank	*Mann*	*Townsend*	*Thomson E*	*McDonald*	*Ford*	*Hamilton*	*Fleming J**	*Moller*	*Fleming G*	*Miller*	
6 A PARTICK THISTLE	12/10	5,500	16	L 3	0-1	0-0	Clark	Hermiston	Shewan	Petersen	McMillan	Craig	Rae	Robb	Johnston	Smith	Taylor	
							Ritchie	*Cumming*	*McLindon*	*McParland*	*McKinnon*	*O'Neil*	*Flanagan*	*Stewart*	*Coulston*	*Bone*	*Duncan*	
7 H CLYDE	19/10	8,000	16	L 3	0-1	0-0	Clark	Hermiston	Shewan	Petersen	McMillan	Buchan M*	Hamilton	Smith	Forrest	Craig	Taylor	Johnston
							Wright	*Glasgow*	*Mulherron*	*Anderson*	*Fraser*	*McHugh*	*Soutar*	*McFarlane*	*Hood*	*Burns*	*Hastings*	
8 A RANGERS	26/10	40,000	16	W 5	3-2	2-0	Clark	Hermiston	Shewan	Petersen	McMillan	Craig	Johnston	Smith	Forrest	Buchan M	Taylor	
							Martin	*Jackson*	*Mathieson*	*Greig*	*Hynd*	*Smith D*	*Henderson*	*Penman*	*Jardine**	*Johnston*	*Persson*	*Ferguson*
9 H RAITH ROVERS	2/11	8,000	14	W 7	2-1	1-1	Clark	Hermiston	Shewan	Petersen	McMillan	Craig	Johnston	Smith*	Forrest	Robb	Taylor	Buchan M
							Reid	*Hislop*	*Gray*	*Millar*	*McDonald*	*Bolton*	*Wilson*	*Falconer*	*Wallace*	*Judge*	*Gillespie*	
10 A MORTON	9/11	9,000	14	L 7	0-1	0-0	Clark	Hermiston	Shewan	Petersen	McMillan	Craig*	Johnston	Robb	Forrest	Smith	Taylor	Buchan M
							Crawford	*Thorup*	*Sweeney*	*Arnetoft*	*Gray*	*Strachan*	*Coakley*	*Harper*	*Mason*	*Allan*	*McNeill*	

Scorers, Times, and Referees

1. Taylor 19, Robb 23, 83, Shewan 87 — *Scott 38, Campbell 48, Wilson 54, [Duncan 56]*. Ref: W Anderson.
This is not the sort of score commonly associated with Eddie Turnbull's teams. Aberdeen's two-goal lead was transformed into a 2-4 deficit before their late rally. Dave Robb came close to snatching his hat-trick - and the winner - in the final minute. Thrilling stuff.

2. Smith 49, Craig 68p. Ref: R Wilson.
The fixture list traditionally opens with matches against Dundee and St Johnstone. Saints' stuffy defence holds out capably until pierced by Smith's header from Rae's corner. But Aberdeen's minds seem to be distracted by adventures in Europe. They fly to Bulgaria after this match.

3. *Cameron K 8*. Ref: T Wharton.
Aberdeen are perked by their goalless draw in Sofia, so this result comes as a severe anti-climax. Cameron's early misfit shot did not deserve to inflict upon the Dons their first league defeat of the season. A month earlier the Dons had crushed United 4-1 at Pittodrie in the League Cup.

4. Rae 19 — *Connelly 2, Lennox 75*. Ref: B Padden.
Lennox seemed to punch the ball out of Clark's hands for the winner. Uproar followed, as Clark and his team-mates besieged the officials. Earlier George Connelly's 20-yarder had been cancelled out by Tommy Rae's first goal for the Dons, after he glided past three defenders.

5. Robb 34 — *Fleming 5, Hamilton 48*. Ref: J Kelly.
A rough-house match. Aberdeen wore all-white and were handicapped by the absence of Tommy Craig and Jim Forrest. A corner brought Hearts' first goal, after Clark had parried Fleming's effort. Robb levelled from a tight angle. Hearts shut up shop after Willie Hamilton's goal.

6. *Bone 51*. Ref: A Webster.
Four league defeats in a row for dismal Dons. Jimmy Bone will later try his luck down in England. For the moment the Thistle striker is happy with his second-half header that maintains Partick's 100% home record. Perhaps the Dons were unable to get Real Zaragoza out of their minds.

7. *Buchan 20 og*. Ref: R Henderson.
Clyde's third win over the Dons this season comes about when Buchan failed to intercept a Hood through-pass. Aberdeen then hit the woodwork twice, and find themselves not in the best of spirits for the visit of Real Zaragoza. They also have a trip to Ibrox looming.

8. Johnston 3, Forrest 13, 76 — *Ferguson 83, Henderson 85*. Ref: T Kellock.
Aberdeen win at Ibrox for the second year running. This time they are totally in control - except for the last seven minutes. Rangers' John Greig missed a first-half penalty. Later the crowd chanted 'Bring on Fergie', and the substitute immediately cut the Dons' lead.

9. Forrest 23, Craig 60p — *Wallace 24*. Ref: A Crawley.
Teams are frequently at their most vulnerable immediately after they have scored - as Wallace confirms. Fortunately, for Aberdeen, Reid then grabbed hold of Ian Taylor's legs to provide the Dons with a penalty. Two quick wins have momentarily lifted the relegation gloom.

10. *Harper 54*. Ref: W Syme.
Tiny Joseph Harper threatened the Aberdeen goal several times before breaking away to project a shot-cum-cross that eluded Bobby Clark and McNeill, and which went in off the far post. This is Aberdeen's fourth 0-1 league defeat so far this season. There are two more to come.

Match 11 — H ARBROATH, 16/11

Att	Pos	Result	HT
8,000	15 D, 18, 8	2-2	0-0

Aberdeen: Clark, Hermiston, Shewan, Petersen*, McMillan, Craig, Johnston, Robb, Forrest, Smith, Watt, Buchan M
Arbroath: Williamson, Booth, Riddle, Cargill, Stirling, Finnie*, Cant, Jack, Reid, Bruce, Wilkie, Pierson

Scorers: Robb 55, Forrest 88; Jack 50, Bruce 59
Ref: A McKenzie

Arbroath come to Pittodrie with just one point from 10 league outings. They go in front twice and were denied both points only by an own-goal, claimed by Robb, and a late face-saver by Forrest. This result, more than any other, shows the depths to which the Dons have plummeted.

Match 12 — H ST MIRREN, 23/11

Att	Pos	Result	HT
12,000	13 W, 4, 10	2-0	1-0

Aberdeen: Clark, Hermiston, Shewan, Petersen, Craig, Johnston, Smith, Forrest, Buchan M, Taylor
St Mirren: Connachan, Murray C, Connell, Fulton, Murray E, McFadden, Adamson, Hainey, Kane, Pinkerton, Gilshan

Scorers: Forrest 32, 53
Ref: T Marshall

Newly promoted St Mirren are continuing their winning ways, and arrive at Pittodrie undefeated, but have no complaints as Aberdeen's Jekyll and Hyde season continues. This will prove to be no new dawn for the Dons, however, as the next couple of results will indicate.

Match 13 — A DUNFERMLINE, 30/11

Att	Pos	Result	HT
6,500	14 L, 4, 10	1-5	1-2

Aberdeen: Clark, Hermiston, Shewan, Petersen, Murray, Craig, Johnston*, Smith, Forrest, Buchan M, Rae, Robb
Dunfermline: Martin, Callaghan W, Lunn, Fraser, Barry, Renton, Robertson, Paton, Edwards, Gardner, Mitchell, Totten

Scorers: Craig 35; Edwards 5, Paton 6, Gardner 74, 78, 87
Ref: J Callaghan

Dunfermline don't appear unduly fatigued by their midweek encounter in Greece with Olympiakos Piraeus. Two goals within 30 seconds rocked the Aberdeen boat. Tommy Craig steadied things, but then Gardner's hat-trick holed her irreparably. Surely things cannot get worse.

Match 14 — H HIBERNIAN, 7/12

Att	Pos	Result	HT
11,500	15 L, 9, 10	2-6	1-5

Aberdeen: Clark, Whyte, Shewan, Buchan M, Murray, Petersen, Little, Smith, Forrest, Craig, Taylor
Hibernian: Allen, Davis, Shevlane, Cousin, Madsen, Stanton, Scott, Quinn, McBride, Cormack, Stevenson

Scorers: Buchan 14, Forrest 49 (McBride 83); Cormack 9, 27, 29, Davis 33p, Scott 36, Allen
Ref: A Currie

11 goals conceded in two games shows the extent of Aberdeen's problems. Peter Cormack destroyed the Dons virtually single-handed. He began with a fierce half-volley, followed up with a downward header, and finished by imperiously sweeping Scott's centre past Bobby Clark.

Match 15 — A AIRDRIE, 14/12

Att	Pos	Result	HT
3,500	16 L, 12, 10	0-2	0-0

Aberdeen: McGarr, Whyte, Shewan, Buchan M, McMillan, Petersen, Hamilton, Smith*, Forrest, Craig, Johnston, Cumming
Airdrie: McKenzie, Jonquin, Keenan, Goodwin, Black, Whiteford, Wilson, Fyfe, Marshall, McPheat, Jarvie

Scorers: Wilson 49, Goodwin 81p
Ref: W Mullen

Bobby Clark is not the only casualty from the two recent spankings, but his season is over. Ernie McGarr takes over, and the flood becomes a trickle. Hermiston and Rae had been dropped after Dunfermline, and now Taylor, Murray and Little are also axed. Tommy McMillan returns.

Match 16 — H FALKIRK, 21/12

Att	Pos	Result	HT
7,000	13 W, 17, 12	2-0	2-0

Aberdeen: McGarr, Whyte, Shewan, Petersen, McMillan, Murray, Johnston, Smith, Forrest, Buchan M, Craig, Hunter*
Falkirk: Rennie, Lambie, Hunter J, Smith, Markie, Miller, Marshall, McLaughlin, Young, Gibson, Watson*, Hunter

Scorers: Forrest 2, Johnston 43
Ref: E Pringle

Play for some reason began earlier than scheduled, and many spectators were still outside the ground when Jim Forrest capitalised on Markie's stumble inside 90 seconds. With Falkirk inside the bottom two, one place and four points behind the Dons, this is a crucial victory.

Match 17 — A KILMARNOCK, 28/12

Att	Pos	Result	HT
6,500	13 L, 3, 12	1-2	0-1

Aberdeen: McGarr, Whyte, Shewan, Petersen, McMillan, Murray, Johnston, Smith, Forrest, Buchan M, Craig
Kilmarnock: McLaughlan, King, Dickson, Gilmour, McGrory, Beattie, McLean T, Queen, Morrison!, McLean J, McIlroy

Scorers: Johnston 53; McIlroy 10, Morrison 51
Ref: R Wilson

3rd place Killie are stretched in a tempestuous match. Their second goal came when McGarr was challenged by Morrison as he tried to clear. The ball bounced against a post and Morrison poked it in. Later the same forward was ordered off after a further clash with the Dons' keeper.

Match 18 — H DUNDEE, 1/1

Att	Pos	Result	HT
12,000	13 D	0-0	0-0

Aberdeen: McGarr, Whyte, Shewan, Petersen, McMillan, Murray, Johnston, Smith, Forrest, Buchan M, Craig
Dundee: Donaldson, Wilson, Swan, Murray, Stuart, Houston, Campbell, Gilroy, Kinninmonth, Bryce, Scott

The league season began with one sort of draw between these sides - 4-4, and brings in the New Year with another, far less satisfying kind. The one player to hold his head high after this game is Dundee goalkeeper Alistair Donaldson. Dundee are happier with the result than Aberdeen.

Match 19 — A ST JOHNSTONE, 2/1

Att	Pos	Result	HT
7,000	14 L, 13, 13	1-3	1-2

Aberdeen: McGarr, Whyte, Shewan, Petersen, McMillan, Murray, Johnston, Smith, Forrest, Buchan M*, Craig, Robb
St Johnstone: Robertson, Miller, Coburn, Gordon, Rooney, McPhee, Hall, McCarry, Whitelaw, Rennie, Aitken

Scorers: Buchan 12; Aitken 6, Hall 36, 61
Ref: W Anderson

Aberdeen should have handed St Johnstone a first-half pasting, but suffered an attack of squandermania. Worst miss of all was that of Jim Forrest, who dribbled round goalkeeper Robertson, then shot wide. Saints leap-frog over the Dons, who are four points off a relegation place.

Match 20 — A DUNDEE UTD, 4/1

Att	Pos	Result	HT
15,000	14 W, 2, 15	4-1	2-0

Aberdeen: McGarr, Whyte, Shewan, Petersen, Boel, Murray, Johnston, Smith, Forrest, Craig, Robb
Dundee Utd: Mackay, Millar, Cameron J, Markland, Smith, Wood, Hogg*, Reid, Cameron K, Rolland, Wilson

Scorers: Shewan 25, Robb 30, Craig 61, Cameron K 70 [Forrest 79]
Ref: R Gordon

Only goal-average was keeping United behind Celtic at the top. The breakthrough comes when Shewan's header from Craig's corner slipped through Mackay's butter-fingers. At 2-0 Kenny Cameron missed a penalty for United. Aberdeen's latest Dane, Henning Boel, makes his debut.

Match 21 — H CELTIC, 11/1

Att	Pos	Result	HT
31,000	14 L, 1, 15	0-2	0-2

Aberdeen: McGarr, Whyte, Shewan, Petersen, Boel, Murray, Johnston, Smith, Forrest, Craig, Robb
Celtic: Simpson, Craig, Gemmell, Murdoch, Brogan, McNeill, Johnstone, Callaghan, Wallace, Lennox, Hughes

Scorers: Forrest 79; Hughes 3, Wallace 27, Boel 53 og
Ref: W Balfour

The Dons did Celtic a favour against Dundee United. Celtic have enjoyed the breaks against Aberdeen in recent matches. This time there are no complaints: they oozed class and are in control from the moment John Hughes fires in a blistering shot from outside the box.

SCOTTISH LEAGUE DIVISION 1 — Manager: Eddie Turnbull — SEASON 1968-69

Match summary

No	Date	Att	Pos	Pt	F-A	H-T	Scorers, Times, and Referees
22	A HEARTS 18/1	8,000	15 / 7	15	L 2-3	1-1	Robb 29, Johnston 46 / Ford 19, 86, Anderson 52. Ref: R Henderson
23	H PARTICK THISTLE 1/2	8,000	15 / 14	16	D 1-1	1-1	Craig 13 / Duncan 30. Ref: J McKee
24	A ARBROATH 8/3	4,700	15 / 18	16	L 1-2	1-1	Forrest 9 / Bruce 14, Sellars 52. Ref: T Kellock
25	A ST MIRREN 15/3	3,750	15 / 6	18	W 2-1	1-0	Robb 4, Connell 80 og / Kane 66. Ref: R Greenlees
26	A RAITH ROVERS 19/3	5,000		18	L 2-3	1-1	Johnston 5, Forrest 53 / Wallace 4, Millar 61, Sneddon 77. Ref: B Padden
27	H DUNFERMLINE 24/3	7,000		19	D 2-2	1-2	Robb 44, Craig 50p / McLean 32, Callaghan 37. Ref: A Crawley
28	A HIBERNIAN 29/3	6,321	15 / 10	20	D 1-1	0-0	Forrest 60 / Davis 58p. Ref: J Kelly
29	A MORTON 2/4	10,000		22	W 6-3	2-2	P'sen 9, Craig 23, Forrest 50, J'ston 52,65, [Whyte 88] / Mason 4, Oakley 25, Harper 58. Neilson. Ref: R Davidson
30	H AIRDRIE 5/4	11,000	15 / 9	24	W 3-1	3-0	Forrest 7, Johnston 14, Robb 33 / Wilson 48. Ref: R Gordon
31	H RANGERS 9/4	23,000		25	D 0-0	0-0	Ref: W Paterson

Line-ups (positions 1–11, 12 sub used)

No	1	2	3	4	5	6	7	8	9	10	11	12 sub used
22	McGarr	Whyte	Shewan	Petersen	Boel	Buchan M	Rae	Smith	Johnston	Robb	Craig	
	Cruickshank	Holt	McAlpine	Anderson	Thomson A	Thomson E	Fleming J	Hamilton	Ford	Fleming G	Jensen*	Brown
23	McGarr	Whyte	Shewan	Buchan M*	Boel	Petersen	Johnston	Smith	Forrest	Robb	Craig	Paul
	Ritchie	Campbell	Gray	Hansen	McKinnon	O'Neil	McLindon	McParland	Flanagan	Bone	Duncan	
24	McGarr	Whyte	Shewan	Petersen	Boel	Buchan M	Hamilton	Smith	Forrest	Robb	Craig	
	Hodge	Booth	Hughes	Cargill	Stirling	Reid*	Sellars	Cant	Jack	Bruce	Wilkie	Kennedy
25	McGarr	Whyte	Shewan	Petersen	Boel	Buchan M	Johnston	Smith	Forrest	Robb	Craig	Taylor*
	Thorburn	Young	Connell	Fulton	McFadden	Murray E	Adamson*	Urquhart	McLaughlin	Kane	Gilshan	Duffy
26	McGarr	Whyte	Shewan	Petersen	Boel	Buchan M	Johnston*	Buchan G*	Forrest	Robb	Hamilton	
	Reid	McDonald	Gray	Millar D	Poland	Bolton	Miller A	Falconer*	Wallace	Sneddon	Wilson	Judge
27	McGarr	Whyte	Shewan	Petersen	Boel	Buchan M	Robertson	Smith	Forrest	Robb	Hamilton	Murray
	Duff	Callaghan W	Lunn	Fraser	Barry	Renton	McKimmie*	Edwards	McLean	Mitchell	Bailie	Judge
28	McGarr	Whyte	Shewan	Petersen	Boel	Buchan M	Johnston	Smith	Forrest	Robb	Hamilton*	Taylor
	Allan	Shevlane	Davis	Blackley	Madsen	Stanton	Marinello	O'Rourke	Grant*	Cormack	McGraw	
29	McGarr	Whyte	Shewan	Petersen	Boel	Buchan M	Johnston	Smith	Forrest	Robb	Craig	
	Neilson	Ferguson	Laughton	Rankin	Gray	Sweeney	Coakley	Allan	Mason	Harper	Bartram	
30	McGarr	Whyte	Shewan	Petersen	Boel	Buchan M	Johnston	Smith	Forrest	Robb	Craig	
	McKenzie	Jonquin	Caldwell	Goodwin	Black	Whiteford	Bird	Fyfe	Marshall	McPheat*	Wilson	Menzies
31	McGarr	Whyte	Shewan	Petersen	Boel	Buchan M	Johnston	Smith	Forrest	Robb*	Craig	
	Martin	Johansen	Mathieson	Greig	McKinnon	Smith D	Henderson	Jardine*	Ferguson	Johnston	Persson	Conn

Match notes

22 — Hearts: Aberdeen would have deserved a point, and looked set for two when the Hearts defence blundered to let Dave Johnston through, straight after the resumption. And following Anderson's equaliser for the home team Dave Robb sent a shot crashing against a Tynecastle goalpost.

23 — Partick Thistle: Partick have just lost 1-8 to Celtic in the Scottish Cup, so Aberdeen could not have chosen a better time to play them. Unfortunately the game is played in a monsoon, and the pitch is almost totally submerged by the end, having earlier drowned out all possibility of further goals.

24 — Arbroath: Inclement weather and cup-ties mean this is the Dons' first league match in five weeks. Memorable Cup wins at Dunfermline and Kilmarnock are followed by this abject defeat. Arbroath's winner was disputed. McGarr clutched a high cross and was bundled over the line by Sellars.

25 — St Mirren: Aberdeen haven't had too many breaks this season, but they get one when Connell dives full length to head into his own goal. Two minutes earlier the same player had headed against McGarr's post.

26 — Raith Rovers: As a result of this win Aberdeen can see daylight between them and the bottom two. Ernie McGarr has an unhappy match, allowing Millar's indifferent shot from 25 yards to squirm into the net. The goal was scored at a wretched time, for the Dons had come from behind to lead 2-1. This is not the best preparation for the Cup semi-final with Rangers.

27 — Dunfermline: Out of the Cup, Aberdeen must now concentrate on league survival. The game is held up for eight minutes by an intruding Alsatian. The Dons come back from 0-2 when Duff crocked George Buchan, younger brother of Martin. George was carried off and Craig converted the penalty.

28 — Hibernian: The Grand National on television partly accounts for the poor attendance. Those who came did not miss much, though Dave Johnston hit a Hibs' post late on. Boel had earlier handled to concede the penalty. Hibs' starlet Peter Marinello plays against the Dons for the first time.

29 — Morton: Aberdeen virtually banish the relegation clouds with this second-half fiesta. Falkirk are now seven points adrift of the Dons. The match must have felt strange for Joe Harper, who scored for Morton - to make it 4-3 - in the knowledge that Aberdeen are eyeing him keenly.

30 — Airdrie: Aberdeen avenge their earlier defeat at Broomfield and are now mathematically safe. The other good news is the healthy gate of 11,000, who turned out to watch the festivities. There was almost a party atmosphere when Dave Robb put the Dons three up shortly after half an hour.

31 — Rangers: Aberdeen's incentive is a rare league double over Rangers, who beat the Dons 6-1 in the Scottish Cup and who are forlornly chasing Celtic at the top of the table. This latest dropped point means that Rangers can realistically forget about the championship for another season.

Matches 32–34 (League)

32 · A FALKIRK · 12/4 · L 0-1 (HT 0-0) · 25 · 2,500
McGarr, Shewan, Buchan M, Petersen, Boel, Craig, Johnston, Smith, Forrest, Robb, Buchan G
Rennie, Lambie, Hunter J, Gibson, Markie, Miller, Marshall, Smith*, Hunter I, McLaughlin I Watson, Young
Young 52
Ref: W Syme
With the pressure off Aberdeen, the result is a tiresome match. Relegated Falkirk are playing out their last games in the First Division, and a meagre-sized crowd is encouraged to attend. Substitute Young's second-half goal brings Falkirk's first win over the Dons in five attempts.

33 · H KILMARNOCK · 19/4 · L 0-1 (HT 0-1) · 15 · 25 · 8,000 · 4
McGarr, Herniston, Shewar, Petersen, Boel, Buchan M, Johnston, Smith, Forrest, Robb, Craig
McLaughlan King, Dickson, Queen, McGrory, Beattie, Cook, McLean J, Morrison, Evans, McIlroy
Cook 38
Ref: T Marshall
Even though Kilmarnock have had a very good season, they contribute to a dreadful match. It proves to be the last appearance in an Aberdeen shirt for 18-year-old starlet Tommy Craig, who is set to sign for English club Sheffield Wednesday. 26 years later Craig will return as coach.

34 · A CLYDE · 23/4 · D 1-1 (HT 0-1) · 26 · 987
McGarr, Herniston, Shewan, Petersen, Boel, Buchan M, Johnston, Smith, Forrest, Robb, Buchan G
Wright, Glasgow, McGregor, Staite, McVie, McHugh, McFarlane, Anderson, Quinn, Burns, Hastings
Forrest 89
Quinn 15
Ref: E Thomson
The Dons have lost three times already to Clyde this season. Forrest's 25-yard blockbuster rescued a late point. Ally Shewan was making his 350th appearance and 313th consecutive appearance in an Aberdeen shirt. Jim Smith made his his last, following Tommy Craig down to England.

Average Home 11,800 · Away 10,000

Scottish League Cup - Section 3

1 · A CLYDE · 10/8 · L 1-4 (HT 1-2) · – · 5,000
Clark, Whyte, Shewan, Buchan M, McMillan, Petersen, Rae, Robb, Forrest, Craig, Johnston
McCulloch, Glasgow, Mulheron, McHugh, Fraser, Anderson, McFarlane, Hood, Staite, Burns, Hastings
Robb 18
Anderson 38, 42, Hood 47, Burns 61
Ref: E Pringle
Jim Smith misses the first four matches of the new season through suspension. Three of Clyde's goals stem from corner-kicks. Last season they did the league double over the Dons; both matches the previous season were drawn, and this season Clyde won't lose any of four meetings.

2 · H DUNFERMLINE · 14/8 · W 1-0 (HT 0-0) · 2 · 18,000
Clark, Whyte, Shewan, Buchan M, McMillan, Petersen, Rae, Robb, Forrest, Craig, Taylor
Martin, Callaghan W Lunn, Thomson, McGarty, Callaghan T Lister, Paton, Gardner, Robertson, Edwards
Forrest 75
Ref: R Davidson
Striker Jim Forrest has signed from Preston for £25,000. He opens his account with a shot from the edge of the box. The win rectifies the damage inflicted by Clyde and will appear all the more impressive with hindsight, in the light of Dunfermline's splendid season to come.

3 · H DUNDEE UTD · 17/8 · W 4-1 (HT 1-0) · 4 · 16,000
Clark, Whyte, Shewan, Buchan M, McMillan, Petersen, Rae, Robb, Forrest, Craig, Taylor
Mackay, Rolland, Cameron J, Gillespie, Smith, Wood, Hogg, Reid, Cameron K, Dunne, Mitchell
Buchan 5, Craig 50p, Forrest 60, 65
Mitchell 79
Ref: J Paterson
Martin Buchan's thunderous volley after five minutes shows he can score goals as well as make them and prevent them. These two clubs find themselves thrown together frequently in cups as well as the league, and the outcome more often than not is a goal-feast. This is no exception.

4 · H CLYDE · 24/8 · L 0-2 (HT 0-2) · 4 · 19,000
Clark, Whyte, Shewan, Buchan M, McMillan, Petersen, Rae, Johnston, Forrest, Craig, Taylor
McCulloch, Glasgow, Mulheron, Anderson, Fraser, McHugh, McFarlane, Hood, Staite, Burns, McGregor
McFarlane 30, Staite 37
Ref: R Crawford
A healthy gate of 19,000 see part-timers Clyde inflict a second defeat on the Dons with consummate ease. By the end of the season they will not have lost to Aberdeen in eight matches. Clyde now look favourites for the quarter-finals. Aberdeen's chances look very dim.

5 · A DUNFERMLINE · 28/8 · W 2-1 (HT 1-0) · 6 · 8,000
Clark, Whyte, Shewan, Petersen, McMillan, Buchan M, Rae, Robb, Forrest, Smith, Taylor
Martin, Callaghan W Lunn, Thomson, McGarty, Callaghan T* Lister, Paton, Gardner, Renton, Edwards, Mitchell
Smith 25, Taylor 68
Lister 73
Ref: R Gordon
Clyde have lost 0-4 at home to Dundee United. Everything now hinges on the final round of matches. Jim Smith can't keep out of the news. He returns from suspension, midway through the first half sees Martin punch his shot into goal, and is then booked for upending Edwards.

6 · A DUNDEE UTD · 31/8 · L 0-1 (HT 0-0) · 6 · 12,000
Clark, Whyte, Shewan, Petersen, McMillan, Buchan M, Rae, Robb, Forrest, Smith, Taylor
Mackay, Rolland, Cameron J, Gillespie, Smith, Wood, Hogg*, Reid, Cameron K, Wilson, Scott
Smith 61 og
Ref: E Thomson
Jimmy Smith is in the news again. This time for a woeful back-pass, which eludes Bobby Clark and presents the game to Dundee United. It was academic in the end, for the Dons would have needed to win at Tannadice by 4-0 to oust Clyde from a place in the quarter-finals.

Qual	P	W	D	L	F	A	Pts
Clyde	6	4	0	2	13	9	8
Dundee Utd	6	3	0	3	12	11	6
ABERDEEN	6	3	0	3	8	9	6
Dunfermline	6	2	0	4	7	11	4

SCOTTISH LEAGUE DIV 1 (CUP-TIES) Manager: Eddie Turnbull SEASON 1968-69

Scottish Cup

							1	2	3	4	5	6	7	8	9	10	11	12 sub used
1	H	BERWICK RGS	25/1	13,600 2:12	W	3-0 1-0	McGarr	Whyte	Shewan	Petersen	Boel	Buchan M	Forrest*	Smith	Johnston	Robb	Craig	Taylor
							Wallace	*Petterson*	*Haig*	*Smith*	*Coutts*	*Gilchrist*	*Tait*	*Craig*	*Bowron*	*Jones*	*Dowds*	

Forrest 36, 82, Robb 73. Ref: R Henderson

Until keeper Jock Wallace was beaten a second time there was always the risk of an upset. Jim Forrest had been in the Rangers side beaten at Berwick in the Cup two years earlier, and gained belated revenge with two goals. Ex-Don Doug Coutts captained his new side against his old.

							1	2	3	4	5	6	7	8	9	10	11	12 sub used
2	H	DUNFERMLINE	25/2	14,685	D	2-2 1-0	McGarr	Whyte	Shewan	Petersen	Boel	Buchan M	Johnston	Smith	Forrest	Robb	Taylor*	Hamilton
							Duff	*Callaghan*	*W Thomson*	*Fraser*	*Barry*	*Renton*	*Robertson**	*Paton*	*Edwards*	*Gardner*	*Mitchell*	*Baillie*

Johnston 31, Hamilton 47, Fraser 56, Renton 88. Ref: W Syme

Dunfermline are defending the Scottish Cup, they have reached the semi-finals of the Cup-Winners' Cup, and are chasing the Old Firm in the league. Yet only a late goal earns them a replay. Aberdeen's sub, Jim Hamilton, had put the Dons two up with his first touch - a diving header.

							1	2	3	4	5	6	7	8	9	10	11	12 sub used
2R	*A	DUNFERMLINE	26/2		W	2-0 1-0	McGarr	Whyte	Shewan	Petersen	Boel	Buchan M	Johnston	Smith	Forrest	Robb	Hamilton	
							Duff	*Callaghan*	*W Thomson*	*Fraser*	*Barry*	*Renton*	*Robertson*	*Paton*	*Edwards*	*Gardner*	*Mitchell*	

Robb 10, 76. Ref: W Syme

This cup replay takes place just 24 hours after the first match. Robb's first goal came when Fraser lashed the ball at keeper Duff, and it fell to Robb's feet. Thereafter it was all hands to the pump, as Aberdeen resisted manfully. Putting out the Scottish Cup-holders is a famous result.

							1	2	3	4	5	6	7	8	9	10	11	12 sub used
QF	H	KILMARNOCK	1/3	24,000 2	D	0-0 0-0	McGarr	Whyte	Shewan	Petersen	Boel	Buchan M	Johnston	Smith	Forrest	Robb	Hamilton*	Craig
							McLaughlin	*King*	*Dickson*	*Gilmour*	*McGrory*	*Beattie*	*McLean T*	*Evans*	*Morrison*	*McLean J*	*McIlroy*	

Ref: T Wharton

The immovable object comes up against the irresistible force. The result is a stalemate with neither side creating a chance worthy of the name - apart from when McLaughlin turned Dave Johnston's shot against the inside of a post. Once again the Dons will have to win away from home.

							1	2	3	4	5	6	7	8	9	10	11	12 sub used
QF R	A	KILMARNOCK	5/3	17,183 2	W	3-0 1-0	McGarr	Whyte	Shewan	Petersen	Boel	Buchan M	Johnston*	Smith	Forrest	Robb	Hamilton	Craig
							McLaughlin	*King*	*Dickson*	*Gilmour*	*McGrory*	*McFadzean*	*McLean T*	*Queen*	*Morrison*	*McLean J*	*McIlroy*	

Robb 43, Craig 67, Hamilton 85. Ref: T Wharton

Like Dunfermline, Killie are hot on Celtic's heels in the league. This is Aberdeen's fourth cup-tie in nine days on heavy pitches. Again it is Dave Robb with the eye for goal, but the pick of Aberdeen's three goals was Tommy Craig's blistering shot from Jim Forrest's pull-back.

							1	2	3	4	5	6	7	8	9	10	11	12 sub used
SF	N	RANGERS	22/3	39,250 2	L	1-6 1-2	McGarr	Whyte	Shewan	Petersen	Boel	Buchan M	Johnston	Smith	Forrest	Robb	Craig	
	(at Parkhead)						*Martin*	*Johansen*	*Mathieson*	*Greig*	*McKinnon*	*Smith D*	*Henderson*	*Penman*	*Stein*	*Johnston*	*Persson*	

Forrest 45 [Johnston 47, 72, 84] Penman 14, 51, Henderson 39. Ref: W Mullen

Winning the Scottish Cup is Aberdeen's only route back into Europe. They were still in the hunt at half-time, whereupon Jim Smith - under the eyes of countless scouts - presents the ball to Persson, who despatched it to Willie Johnston. An anti-climactic end to an exhilarating cup run.

European Fairs Cup

							1	2	3	4	5	6	7	8	9	10	11	12 sub used
1:1	A	SLAVIA SOFIA	17/9 (Bulgaria)	13,000	D	0-0 0-0	Clark	Hermiston	Shewan	Petersen	McMillan	Craig	Rae	Robb	Forrest	Smith	Buchan M	
							Simeonov	*Alexiev*	*Petrov*	*Jonov*	*Davidov*	*Kristev*	*Haralampiev Dimitrov*	*Haralampiev Vassilov*	*Grigorov*	*Tassev*	*Lukach*	

Ref: S Petri (Hungary)

The draw for the Fairs Cup is unchanged, despite the Soviet invasion of Czechoslovakia. For their first ever trip behind the Iron Curtain Aberdeen adopt a defensive 5-3-2 formation, which neither the Bulgarian forwards not the 85 degree temperature could break down.

							1	2	3	4	5	6	7	8	9	10	11	12 sub used
1:2	H	SLAVIA SOFIA	2/10	29,000	W	2-0 2-0	Clark	Hermiston	Shewan	Petersen	McMillan	Craig*	Rae	Robb	Forrest	Smith	Taylor	Buchan M
							Simeonov	*Petrov*	*Charliev*	*Jonov*	*Davidov*	*Kristev*	*Haralampiev Vassilov*	*Grigorov*	*Tassev*	*Letchov*		

Robb 7, Taylor 39. Ref: C Liedberg (Sweden) (Dons win 2-0 on aggregate)

All-action Aberdeen power their way past Slavia Sofia. Dave Robb side-flicked Forrest's pass beyond keeper Simeonov. Before half-time Petrov slipped while trying to cut out Shewan's lateral pass, allowing Ian Taylor to unleash an unstoppable, unforgettable shot.

							1	2	3	4	5	6	7	8	9	10	11	12 sub used
2:1	H	REAL ZARAGOZA	23/10 (Spain)	25,000	W	2-1 1-0	Clark	Hermiston	Shewan	Petersen	McMillan	Craig	Johnston	Smith	Forrest	Buchan M	Taylor	
							Nieves	*Rico*	*Reija*	*Violeta*	*Gonzales*	*Borras*	*Oliveros*	*Pais**	*Marcelino*	*Tejedor*	*Lapetra*	*Planas*

Forrest 32, Smith 64. McMillan 73 og. Ref: R Schaut (Belgium)

Zaragoza won the Fairs Cup in 1964 and reached the final in 1966. This season they are near the bottom of the Spanish League. Forrest took Buchan's chip on his chest to shoot past Nieves. Jim Smith puts away Taylor's cross, but then McMillan slashes Lapetra's cross past Clark.

							1	2	3	4	5	6	7	8	9	10	11	12 sub used
2:2	A	REAL ZARAGOZA	30/10	30,000	L	0-3 0-2	Clark	Hermiston	Shewan	Petersen	McMillan	Craig	Robb	Smith	Forrest	Buchan M	Taylor	
							Nieves	*Rico**	*Reija*	*Violeta*	*Gonzales*	*Borras*	*Tejedor*	*Santos*	*Marcelino*	*Villa*	*Lapetra*	*Bustillo/Planas*

Marcelino 35, Tejedor 43, Villa 78. Ref: J Rodriguez (Portugal) (Dons lose 2-4 on aggregate)

The Romareda Stadium is awash with noise as Real Zaragoza maintain their record of never having lost to a British team, though they will be beaten by Newcastle in the next round. Hermiston heads wide for Aberdeen before Marcelino heads in Lapetra's corner. Then it all slips away.

League Table

	P	W	D	L	F	A	W	D	L	F	A	Pts
			Home						Away			
1 Celtic	34	12	3	2	50	19	11	5	1	39	13	54
2 Rangers	34	13	3	1	47	12	8	4	5	34	20	49
3 Dunfermline	34	12	4	1	42	20	7	3	7	21	25	45
4 Kilmarnock	34	10	6	1	30	15	5	8	4	20	17	44
5 Dundee Utd	34	12	3	2	40	25	5	6	6	21	24	43
6 St Johnstone	34	11	2	4	39	22	5	3	9	27	37	37
7 Airdrie	34	10	5	2	27	16	3	6	8	19	28	37
8 Hearts	34	7	7	3	26	20	3	7	7	26	34	36
9 Dundee	34	4	8	5	24	23	6	1	9	23	25	32
10 Morton	34	8	5	4	34	27	4	3	10	24	41	32
11 St Mirren	34	7	4	6	24	21	4	6	7	16	33	32
12 Hibernian	34	9	2	6	38	24	3	5	9	22	35	31
13 Clyde	34	6	7	4	20	18	3	6	8	15	32	31
14 Partick This	34	7	3	7	21	24	2	7	8	18	29	28
15 ABERDEEN	34	6	5	6	26	24	3	3	11	24	35	26
16 Raith Rovers	34	6	2	9	23	29	2	3	12	22	38	21
17 Falkirk	34	4	6	7	21	27	1	2	14	12	42	18
18 Arbroath	34	4	3	10	24	34	1	3	13	17	48	16
	612	148	78	80	556	400	80	78	148	400	556	612

Odds & ends

Double wins: (1) St Mirren.

Double losses: (3) Celtic, Hearts, Kilmarnock.

Won from behind: (1) Morton (h).

Lost from in front: (4) Hearts (a), Arbroath (a), Raith (a), Clyde (LC).

High spots: 4 undefeated league games from 24 March.
Reaching semi-final of Scottish Cup.

Low spots: 5 consecutive league defeats from 21 September.
Conceding 11 goals in consecutive league matches, including a 2-6 home defeat by Hibs.
Being crushed 1-6 by Rangers in Scottish Cup semi-final.

Ever-presents: (2) Jens Petersen, Ally Shewan.
Hat-tricks: (0).
Leading scorer: (23) Jim Forrest.

Appearances and Goals

	Appearances								Goals				
	Lge	Sub	LC	Sub	SC	Sub	Eur	Sub	Lge	LC	SC	Eur	Tot
Boel, Henning	15												
Buchan, George	3	1	6										
Buchan, Martin	24	3	6		6		3		2	1			3
Clark, Bobby	14		6		6		4						
Craig, Tommy	30	1	6		2	2	4		7	1	1		9
Cumming, Ian		1											
Forrest, Jim	31		6		6		4		16	3	3	1	23
Hamilton, Jim	6	1	6		3	1				2			2
Hermiston, Jim	14												
Johnston, Dave	25	2	2		6		1		8		1		9
Little, Billy	1												
McGarr, Ernie	20				6								
McMillan, Tommy	16		6				4						
Murray, George	9	1											
Paul, Billy		1											
Petersen, Jens	34		6		6		4		1				1
Rae, Tommy	8	.	6		2		2		1				1
Robb, Dave	24	2	5		6		3		9	1	4	1	15
Shewan, Ally	34		6		6		4		2				2
Smith, Jim	33		2		2				1		1	1	3
Taylor, Ian	13	1	3		2	1	1	3	1		1	1	3
Watt, Willie	1												
Whyte, Jim	19		6		6				1				1
(own-goals)									1				1
23 players used	374	14	66	2	66	4	44	7	50	8	11	4	73

SCOTTISH LEAGUE DIVISION 1 — Manager: Eddie Turnbull — SEASON 1969-70

Match summary

No	Date	Venue	Opponent	Att	Pos (opp)	Pt	Res	F-A	H-T	Scorers, Times	Referee
1	30/8	H	CLYDE	12,500		2	W	6-0	1-0	Robb 14, 46, 66, Forrest 48, 62, [Petersen 61]	R Henderson
2	3/9	A	RANGERS	40,000		2	L	0-2	0-0	Provan 75p, Stein 88	T Kellock
3	6/9	A	AIRDRIE	2,000	17	4	W	4-3	1-1	Robb 44, 68, Forrest 54, Rae 63 / Whiteford J 35, Marshall 49, McPheat 78	R Wilson
4	13/9	H	MORTON	14,000	2	5	D	2-2	2-1	Hamilton 1, Wilson 24 / Laughton 7, Allan 52	A McKenzie
5	20/9	A	ST JOHNSTONE	9,400	5	5	L	1-3	0-2	McCarry 26, Hall 36, Connolly 57	I Foote
6	27/9	H	DUNDEE	13,000	13	6	D	1-1	1-0	Hermiston 32p / Wilson 83	S Anderson
7	4/10	A	AYR	9,100	9	8	W	2-1	0-0	Robb 48, 61 / Malone 49	J Kelly
8	11/10	H	PARTICK THISTLE	12,500	18	10	W	2-1	1-0	Hamilton 24, Harper 85p / Coulston 74	E Pringle
9	29/10	H	CELTIC	25,000		10	L	2-3	1-1	Fallon 34 og, Robb 55 / Auld 5, Johnstone 78, Brogan 83	R Davidson
10	1/11	A	DUNFERMLINE	7,000	2	10	L	1-2	0-1	Forrest 63 / Edwards 20p, 90	A Crawley

Line-ups (1–11, 12 sub used)

No	Team	1	2	3	4	5	6	7	8	9	10	11	12
1	Aberdeen	McGarr	Boel	Hermiston	Murray G*	McMillan	Petersen	Willoughby	Robb	Forrest	Wilson T	Hamilton	Rae
1	Clyde	Wright	Glasgow	Mulherron	Burns	McVie	McHugh	McFarlane	Hay*	Staite	Hulston	McLean	Hastings
2	Aberdeen	McGarr	Boel	Hermiston	Murray G	McMillan*	Petersen	Willoughby	Robb	Forrest*	Wilson T	Hamilton	Clark
2	Rangers	Neef	Johansen	Provan	Greig	McKinnon	Baxter	McDonald	Jardine	Stein	Penman	Johnston	
3	Aberdeen	McGarr	Boel	Hermiston	Murray G	McMillan	Petersen	Rae	Robb	Forrest	Wilson T	Hamilton	
3	Airdrie	McKenzie	Jonquin	Caldwell	Goodwin	Delaney	Whiteford D	Jarvie	Bird*	Marshall	Whiteford J	Stewart	McPheat
4	Aberdeen	McGarr	Boel	Hermiston	Murray G	McMillan	Petersen	Rae	Robb	Forrest	Wilson T	Hamilton	Jensen
4	Morton	Neilsen	Ferguson	Laughton	Sweeney	Gray	Rankin	Harper	Collins	Ferry	Allan*	Gallacher	Jensen
5	Aberdeen	McGarr	Boel	Hermiston*	Petersen	McMillan	Clark	Robb	Murray G	Forrest	Wilson T	Hamilton	Rae
5	St Johnstone	Donaldson	Lambie	Coburn	Gordon	Rooney	Rennie*	Aird	Hall	McCarry	Connolly	Aitken	Whitelaw
6	Aberdeen	McGarr	Boel	Hermiston	Murray G	McMillan	Petersen	Adams	Robb	Forrest	Wilson T	Hamilton	Taylor
6	Dundee	Donaldson	Wilson	Swan	Selway	Stewart	Houston*	Murray	Scott	Gilroy	Bryce	Wallace	Kinninmonth
7	Aberdeen	McGarr	Boel	Hermiston	Murray G	McMillan*	Petersen	Harper	Robb	Forrest	Wilson T	Hamilton	McKay
7	Ayr	Stewart	Malone	Murphy	Fleming	Quinn	Mitchell	Young	Ferguson*	Ingram	McCulloch	Rough	Hood
8	Aberdeen	McGarr	Boel	Hermiston	Murray G	McMillan	Petersen	Harper	Robb	Forrest	Wilson T*	Hamilton	McKay
8	Partick Thistle	Dick	Reid	Gray*	MacLindon	McKinnon	Rowan	Flanagan	Smith	Bone	Hansen	Duncan	Coulston
9	Aberdeen	McGarr	Boel	Hermiston	Kirkland	McMillan	Murray G	Harper*	Robb	Forrest	Willoughby	McIlroy	Petersen
9	Celtic	Fallon	Craig	Hay	Murdoch	McNeill	Clark	Johnstone	Callaghan	Hughes	Hood*	Auld	Brogan
10	Aberdeen	McGarr	Hermiston	Kirkland	Petersen*	McMillan	Murray G	Harper	Robb	Forrest	Willoughby	McIlroy	Hamilton
10	Dunfermline	Martin	Callaghan	Lunn	McGarty	Baillie	Robertson	Mitchell	McKimmie	Edwards	Gardner	McLean	Hamilton

Match notes

1. Some of these goals were fit for a connoisseur: Jim Forrest's left-foot volley, for example; or Jens Petersen's ballistic drive into the roof of the net. The second half was one long party. This is the third meeting between these sides this season, and Clyde still have not scored a goal.

2. McMillan was sent off after 20 minutes for retaliating against Colin Stein. Boel handles as he falls on the ball, and once Provan scores from the spot the Dons' displaced keeper, Clark, comes on as an outfield substitute. Scotland manager Bobby Brown watches McGarr's super show.

3. Broomfield has not been a happy hunting ground for Aberdeen of late. Three minutes from time Hermiston's swallow dive saved a certain equaliser, at the cost of a penalty. McGarr parried Goodwin's spot-kick, and his follow-up. Now for Celtic in the League Cup quarter-final.

4. Morton are second in the table. Aberdeen were keen to buy Morton's Joe Harper last season, after the wee man scored against them twice. Now they are even more interested: his two free-kicks manufacture two goals for his side. They take the gloss off Hamilton's first minute goal.

5. Wonders will never cease. Keeper Bobby Clark plays from the start in defence. He has been described as the best header of a ball at Pittodrie. The following day Ernie McGarr wins his first cap in the 1-1 draw with Ireland in Dublin, where he is taken off injured after 25 minutes.

6. Aberdeen are despondent about their League Cup quarter-final defeat by Celtic, also Bobby Clark, because he has now been dropped as a defender. Aberdeen's goal comes from the penalty spot, after Jim Forrest's goal-bound shot was 'saved' by full-back Wilson with his hands.

7. At last, Aberdeen have taken the plunge and spent £40,000 on Morton's Joe Harper. The Aberdeen Evening Express remarked: 'He had a serviceable start for the Dons and looked as if he will fit in.' It would have been too much to expect him to score on his debut.

8. Partick are bottom and could have done with the point that is denied them by Joe Harper's first goal for Aberdeen. It came with five minutes left to play, with the score 1-1. Aberdeen win a penalty. Harper readily accepts responsibility, and shows he has nerves of steel. Now for Celtic.

9. Having eliminated the Dons from the League Cup, Celtic triumph after a 90-minute thriller. Aberdeen levelled Murdoch's 20-yarder when, pressured by McIlroy, Fallon drops the ball over the line. Robb's header made it 2-1, but super Harper limps off and Aberdeen lose direction.

10. Joe Harper makes a quick recovery from injury and takes his place in attack. A farcical penalty is awarded to pace-setting Dunfermline when Gardner's shot strikes Kirkland on the upper arm. Forrest levels, but Alex Edwards scores his side's second goal, the winner, in injury time.

11 A ST MIRREN 5/11 — 4,000 — L 0-2 (10) — HT 0-0

Clark · Sutherland · Kirkland · Hermiston · Robb · Murray G · Willoughby · Harper · Forrest · Wilson T* · McIlroy · Smith A
Connaghan · Murray · Connell · Cumming · McFadden · Kane · Gilshan · Lister · McLaughlin · Blair · Pinkerton · Urquhart*

Gilshan 50, Blair 75
Ref: A McDonald

With all Aberdeen's central defenders still sidelined, it is the turn of striker Dave Robb to wear the number 5 shirt. Bobby Clark is temporarily back in the side, not on form, but because Ernie McGarr is playing for Scotland in Austria. Clark desperately wanted to keep a clean-sheet.

---

12 H DUNDEE UTD 8/11 — 8,000 — D 0-0 (11) — HT 0-0

McGarr · Sutherland · Kirkland · Hermiston · Robb · McMillan · Murray G · Harper · Forrest · Willoughby · McIlroy
Mackay · Rolland · Cameron · Gillespie · Smith · Henry · Hogg · Reid · Gordon · Mitchell · Scott · Wilson*

Ref: T Wharton

League leaders Dundee United are still unbeaten. Yet they could no more master a swirling wind than could their opponents. The best chance of the game fell to United in the final minute, when McGarr saved splendidly from Rolland. Aberdeen are forgetting how to win matches.

---

13 A HEARTS 15/11 — 11,500 — D 2-2 (8 12) — HT 1-1

McGarr · Cruickshank · Kirkland · Hermiston · Robb · McMillan · Murray G · Harper · Forrest · Willoughby · McIlroy
Cruickshank · Clunie · Oliver · MacDonald · Anderson · Thomson · Jensen · Moller · Ford · Brown · Murray · Fleming*

Robb 3, Forrest 52
Moller 43, Ford 81
Ref: A Currie

Both teams persisted employing the offside trap, which produced much whistle from the referee. It was also a tetchy match, with five players booked. Aberdeen welcomed the return of Martin Buchan, victim of a summer road accident and playing his firs: match of the season.

---

14 H MOTHERWELL 22/11 — 7,000 — W 4-1 (6 14) — HT 1-1

McGarr · McCloy · Kirkland · Hermiston · Robb · McMillan · Murray G · Harper · Forrest · Willoughby · McIlroy* · Hamilton
McCloy · Campbell · Wark · Donnelly · Forsyth · Goldthorpe · Murphy · McInally · Deans · Wilson · Muir · McCrae*

Robb 11, Hermiston 75, Buchan 76, [Forrest 89]
Muir 27
Ref: R Crawford

Motherwell provide Aberdeen with their first win in six games. A miserable day, together with the Dons' poor form, keeps the crowd down. Jim Hermiston's 25-yarder puts Aberdeen ahead for the second time, whereupon Martin Buchan immediately adds a third.

---

15 A KILMARNOCK 29/11 — 5,000 — W 2-0 (9 16) — HT 0-0

McGarr · McLaughlan · Kirkland · Hermiston · Robb · Murray G · Harper · Forrest · Willoughby* · Hamilton · McIlroy
McLaughlan · King · Dickson · Gilmour · McGrory · Beattie · McLean T · Morrison · Mathie · Strachan · Cook

Forrest 62, Harper 66
Ref: T Kellock

Kilmarnock have just returned from a Fairs Cup match in Bulgaria. They are through to Round 3, but they look jaded, and run out of steam in the last third of the game. Joe Harper scores his second goal for the Dons, seven weeks after his first, and his first from open play.

---

16 A CLYDE 13/12 — 2,000 — L 1-2 (15 16) — HT 1-0

McGarr · McCulloch · Kirkland · Hermiston · Boel · Petersen · Harper · Robb · Forrest · Willoughby* · Hamilton · McIlroy
McCulloch · Anderson · Mulherron · Beattie · McHugh · Burns · Glasgow · Hulston · Staite · Stewart · Hastings

Harper 45p
Mulherron 52, Staite 57
Ref: R Greenlees

Clyde are in relegation difficulties and are pleased to scored their first goals of the season against Aberdeen in four attempts. Yet it all seemed to be going the Dons' way. On the stroke of half-time Beattie pulled down Hamilton to allow Harper to shoot home from the penalty spot.

---

17 H RANGERS 20/12 — 22,000 — L 2-3 (2 16) — HT 2-2

McGarr · Neef · Kirkland · Hermiston · Boel · Petersen · Harper · Robb · Forrest · Buchan M · Hamilton
Neef · Johansen · Mathieson · Smith · McKinnon · Greig · Henderson · Baxter · Stein · Settangton · Johnston · Penman*

Robb 3, 28
Stein 10, 41, Johnston 54
Ref: E Pringle

Once again it seems to be Celtic v Rangers for the title. What a start for Aberdeen: the Gers defence stands transfixed as Joe Harper glides the ball across for Dave Robb to score unmolested. But Rangers finally took both points, thanks to Johnston's wheeling shot on the turn.

---

18 A RAITH ROVERS 27/12 — 4,000 — W 1-0 (16 18) — HT 1-0

McGarr · Reid · Kirkland · Hermiston · Boel · Buchan M · Harper · Robb · Forrest · Hamilton · Petersen
Reid · McDonald · Lindsay · Buchanan · Bolton · Hislop · Judge · Sneddon · Miller A · Polland*

Hamilton 5
Ref: W Mullen

Raith Rovers are fighting to avoid the drop and scrap desperately for some reward. The Dons looked punch-drunk by the final whistle, hanging on as best they could to Jim Hamilton's early goal, which looked to be a mis-hit. This is only the Dons' fourth clean-sheet of the season.

---

19 A DUNDEE 1/1 — 12,000 — L 0-2 (18) — HT 0-2

McGarr · Sutherland · Hermiston · Buchan M · Harper · Murray G* · Forrest · Willoughby · Hamilton · Petersen
Donaldson · Wilson · Houston · Murray · Selway · Steele · Kinnimonth · Wallace · Scott · Bryce

Steele 8, Bryce 15
Ref: R Gordon

The first match of the 1970s and Eddie Turnbull springs a tactical surprise, employing Joe Harper wide on the wing. The irony was that this left no one in the middle capable of taking chances, which went begging throughout the match. Dundee's two early strikes win the match.

---

20 H RAITH ROVERS 10/1 — 8,000 — W 5-1 (15 20) — HT 2-1

McGarr · Sutherland · Kirkland · Hermiston · Boel · Buchan M · Willoughby · Harper · Forrest · Robb · Hamilton · Petersen
Reid · Hislop · Lindsay · Cooper · Polland · Buchanan · Bolton · Brand · Millar · Judge · Sinclair · Vincent

Murray 30, Harper 32p, 70, 81, Robb 64
Lindsay 10
Ref: E Thomson

Ernie McGarr makes a hash of Lindsay's cross-cum-shot. Bobby Clark is on the brink of signing for Rangers. Joe Harper doubles his goal tally since arriving at Pittodrie with his first hat-trick. This win completes Aberdeen's first league double of the season. Raith will be relegated.

---

21 A MORTON 17/1 — 6,500 — L 2-3 (20) — HT 2-1

McGarr · Sutherland · Kirkland · Hermiston* · Boel · Buchan M · Willoughby · Harper · Forrest · Murray G · Harper · Wilson T
Neilsen · Ferguson · Laughton · Sweeney · Gray · Rankin · Collins · Osborne · O'Neill · Allan

Ferguson 20 og, Robb 35
Osborne 42p, Ferguson 61, Coakley 89
Neilsen
Ref: H Dempsey

Here was a game to ponder. There was an own-goal by Morton's full-back Ferguson, while attempting a harmless pass-back; a mysterious Morton penalty; a bad ankle injury to Jim Hermiston; and a disallowed Harper equaliser in the last minute. He would love to have scored here.

No	Date	Venue	Opponents	Att	Pos	Pt	Res	F-A	H-T	Scorers, Times, and Referees
22	31/1	H	AIRDRIE	8,500		20	L	0-1	0-0	Jarvie 58. Ref: A McKenzie
23	25/2	H	AYR	8,000		22	W	1-0	0-0	Buchan 90. Ref: R Wilson
24	28/2	A	PARTICK THISTLE	5,500	9	24	W	3-0	2-0	Petersen 11, Forrest 40, 68. Ref: B Padden
25	2/3	H	ST JOHNSTONE	7,000		25	D	0-0	0-0	Ref: T Marshall
26	9/3	H	HIBERNIAN	8,500	3	25	L	0-2	0-2	McBride 28p, Cormack 32. Ref: W Anderson
27	18/3	H	ST MIRREN	9,000		26	D	1-1	1-1	Robb 37, McMillan 24 og. Ref: R Gordon
28	21/3	H	DUNFERMLINE	10,000	9	28	W	2-0	1-0	Forrest 44, 63. Ref: T Kellock
29	25/3	A	CELTIC	33,000	1	30	W	2-1	0-0	Murray G 49, Graham 65. Gemmell 87. Ref: J Paterson
30	28/3	A	DUNDEE UTD	8,000	4	30	L	0-2	0-0	Mitchell 49, Cameron K 75. Ref: R Crawford
31	4/4	H	HEARTS	10,000	4	30	L	0-1	0-1	Moller 34. Ref: R Davidson

Line-ups (Aberdeen / Opponent):

No	1	2	3	4	5	6	7	8	9	10	11	12 sub used
22	McGarr / McKenzie	Boel / Jonquin	Kirkland / Caldwell	Petersen* / Menzies	McMillan / Delaney	Buchan M / Whiteford	Hamilton / Wilson	Robb / Jarvie	Forrest / Marshall	Murray G / Goodwin	Harper / Cowan	Willoughby
23	Clark / Stewart	Boel / Malone	Murray G / Murphy	Petersen* / McAnespie	McMillan / Fleming	Buchan M / Mitchell	McKay / Young	Robb / Reynolds	Forrest / Hood*	Hamilton / McCulloch	Harper / McCall	Wilson T / McGregor
24	Clark / Ritchie	Boel / Reid	Murray G / Holt	Petersen / Clark	McMillan / Gray	Buchan M / Johnston	McKay / Rae	Robb / Smith*	Forrest / Flanagan	Hamilton / Bone	Buchan G / Lawrie	/ Hansen
25	Clark / Robertson	Boel / Millar	Murray G / Coburn	Petersen / Gordon	McMillan / Rooney	Buchan M / McPhee	McKay / Aird	Robb / Hall	Forrest / McCarry	Hamilton / Whitelaw	Buchan G / Aitken	
26	Clark / Marshall	Boel / Shevlane	Murray G / McEwan	Petersen / Blackley	McMillan / Black	Buchan M / Stanton	McKay / Graham	Robb / Hamilton	Forrest / McBride	Hamilton / Cormack	Harper / Stevenson	
27	Clark / McGarr	Boel / Murray	Murray G / Connell	Murray S / Fulton	McMillan / McFadden	Buchan M / Palmer	McKay / Gilshan	Robb / Lister	Forrest / Hamilton	Hamilton / Blair	Harper / Pinkerton	
28	Clark / Arrol	Boel / Callaghan	Murray G / Lunn	Murray S / Fraser	McMillan / McNicoll	Buchan M / Renton	McKay* / Mitchell	Robb / McLaren*	Forrest / Edwards!	Hamilton / McLean	Harper / Gillespie	Graham / Gardner
29	Clark / Williams	Boel / Craig	Murray G / Gemmell	Murray S / Murdoch	McMillan / McNeill	Buchan M / Brogan	McKay / Johnstone	Hermiston / Connelly	Robb / Wallace	Willoughby / Lennox	Graham / Auld	
30	Clark / Mackay	Boel / Rolland	Murray G / Cameron J	Murray S / Gillespie	McMillan / Smith	Buchan M / Henry*	Harper / Wilson	Hermiston* / Stevenson	Robb / Cameron K	Willoughby / Mitchell	Forrest / Dunne	McKay / Markland
31	Clark / Cruickshank	Boel / Clunie	Murray G / Oliver	Murray S / Veitch	McMillan / Anderson	Buchan M / Thomson	McKay / Traynor	Robb / Winchester	Forrest / Irvine	Willoughby / Townsend*	Graham / Moller	Ford

Match notes:

22. Possibly Aberdeen's worst display of the season, as the Dons slip to their third defeat in four games in 1970. Drew Jarvie's header for Airdrie earned the points, leaving the Pittodrie crowd to jeer their own players. This match proves to be the end of the road for Ernie McGarr in goal.

23. This Wednesday match provided a night of frustration. Many of the small crowd had drifted away by the time Henning Boel back-heads across goal and Martin Buchan fires a last-gasp winner. Clark celebrates his recall with a welcome shut-out. Derek McKay's first start of the season.

24. Partick are staring relegation in the face; the more so following this result, which brings their fourth straight defeat. Aberdeen are in that no-man's land in mid-table and casually took the chances that came their way. Aberdeen's minds are clearly focused on the Scottish Cup.

25. The white pitch and strange yellow ball evidently disconcerted Aberdeen, who did everything but score. Martin Buchan almost repeated his late winner against Ayr, but this time he lifted his shot too high. Just one point from St Johnstone this season, the fewest since 1965-66.

26. Not the result Aberdeen wanted on the eve of a Scottish Cup semi-final. Hibs, third in the league, enjoyed their first win in five games. A rough match saw a dubious penalty awarded against McMillan, for the first goal, and a misdirected pass by Buchan to Cormack, for the second.

27. A game of three Murrays. Aberdeen have two of them, now that they have picked up midfielder Steve from Dundee for a Dons record fee of £50,000. He is, though, cup-tied, and ineligible for the Scottish Cup Final. McMillan's own-goal follows the penalty he conceded against Hibs.

28. More stars of the future come along. This time it's 17-year-old Arthur Graham, who makes his debut as a second-half substitute. Following Jim Forrest's second goal, Dunfermline's Alex Edwards was ordered off for his protests to the referee. Dunfermline had no chance after that.

29. Celtic need two points for the championship. Young Arthur Graham teed the ball up for George Murray for the first goal, and then had the cheek to head the second. This is the Dons' first win over Celtic in 13 matches, since January 1966, and their first at Parkhead since 1962-63.

30. It is asking too much to expect two inspired performances in a row. Dundee United's season has collapsed. A boring first half is followed by United taking control of the second, and having the nerve to indulge in some exhibition pretty stuff by the end.

31. Aberdeen's minds are somewhere else. Hampden perhaps? The only goal of this untidy match belonged to Hearts' Rene Moller, whose free-kick was politely left to one another by Aberdeen's defenders. Joe Harper has been relegated to the reserves. Should he be recalled?

32 | H | KILMARNOCK | 6/4 | 6,500 | D | 2-2 | 31 | Buchan G 66, Graham 84 / *McLean 23, Morrison 61* | Ref: S Anderson

Clark · Whyte · Murray G · Hermiston · Boel · Murray S · Buchan G · Harper · Robb · Willoughby* · Graham · Hamilton
McLaughlan · King · Dickson · Gilmour · Rodman · McGrory · McLean T · Morrison · Mathie · MacDonald · Cook

Arthur Graham to the rescue. His shot (or was it a cross?) from the wing leaves keeper McLaughlan flapping in mid-air to give the Dons a draw. Harper justifies his recall to the first team with a fine display. Heartbreak for Willoughby, whose injury will keep him out of the final.

---

33 | A | HIBERNIAN | 13/4 | 10,000 | W | 2-1 | 33 | Robb 37, Forrest 76 / *Stevenson 41* | Ref: G Anderson

Clark · Whyte · Murray G · Hermiston · Boel · Murray S · McKay · Robb · Harper · Buchan G* · Forrest
Allan · Duncan · Jones · Blackley · Black · McBride · Graham · Hamilton · O'Rourke · Stevenson · Cropley

Aberdeen have won the Scottish Cup. Hibs' players sportingly line up to applaud the Dons out at Easter Road. Aberdeen respond in the best possible way, by beating them. The championship belongs to Celtic, but this result will ultimately deny Hibs runners-up spot ahead of Rangers.

---

34 | A | MOTHERWELL | 18/4 | 6,100 11 | 35 | W | 2-0 | Forrest 47, 69 | Ref: J Grant

McGarr · Whyte · Murray G · Hermiston · Boel! · Buchan M · McKay · Robb · Forrest · Harper · Graham
McCrae · Whiteford · Wark · Forsyth · McCallum · Watson · Wilson · Muir · Deans! · McInally · Heron

At the final whistle Henning Boel and Motherwell's John Deans had a bust-up in the players tunnel. Both were retrospectively 'sent off' by the referee. This headline grabbing incident was the last thing Aberdeen needed to detract from their wonderful achievements in the Scottish Cup.

Average Home 11,100 — Away 10,300

Scottish League Cup - Section 2

1 | H | DUNFERMLINE | 9/8 | 16,000 | D | 2-2 | 1 | Forrest 37, Smith A 87 / *Mitchell 50, Petersen 73 og* | Ref: R Gordon

McGarr · Whyte* · Hermiston · Smith A · McMillan · Petersen · Willoughby · Robb · Forrest · Wilson T · Buchan G · Hamilton
Martin · Callaghan · Lunn · Fraser · Barry · Renton · Mitchell · Paton · Edwards · McLean · Thomson*

Aberdeen have lost Tommy Craig and Jim Smith, and Martin Buchan, who broke his ankle in a car crash. Turnbull signs two Rangers Alec's, Smith and Willoughby. Now, Jim Whyte ruptures an Achilles tendon, and Dunfermline's Jim Fraser breaks a leg when colliding with Petersen.

---

2 | A | CLYDE | 13/8 | 4,000 | D | 0-0 | 2 | Ref: R Crawford

McGarr · Boel · Hermiston · Smith A · McMillan · Petersen · Willoughby · Robb · Forrest · Wilson T · Buchan G
Wright · Glasgow · McGregor · Anderson · McVie · Burns · Hay · Hulston · McLean · Hastings

Both sets of forwards weren't allowed to breathe, let alone score. Clyde were paired with Aberdeen in the League Cup last season, too, winning twice, and are due for another confrontation in the Scottish Cup. It is now nine matches since the Dons last beat these doughty opponents.

---

3 | H | HIBERNIAN | 16/8 | 16,000 | D | 2-2 | 3 | Hermiston 35p, Hamilton 62 / *McBride 43, Grant 63* | Ref: T Marshall

McGarr · Boel · Hermiston · Smith A · McMillan · Petersen · Willoughby · Robb · Forrest · Wilson T · Hamilton
Marshall · Shevlane · Davis · Wilkinson · Black · Stanton · Grant · McBride · O'Rourke · Stevenson · Hamilton

Aberdeen were twice in front. They might have stayed that way, too. But Dave Robb's flick crashed off the Hibs' post and nestled in keeper Marshall's arms. Three draws out of three would ordinarily eliminate a team from contention, but in Section 2 no one has yet pulled away.

---

4 | H | CLYDE | 20/8 | 13,500 | W | 3-0 | 5 | Wilson 35, 61, 68 | Ref: E Thomson

McGarr · Boel · Hermiston · Murray G · McMillan · Petersen · Willoughby · Robb · Forrest · Wilson T · Hamilton
Wright · Glasgow · Mulherron · Anderson · McVie · McHugh · McFarlane · Hay · Hulston · Burns · Hastings

A memorable hat-trick for 18-year-old Tommy Wilson, a local lad who hails from Sandyhills Youth Club. His second goal was the best - a pile-driver from 22 yards. Aberdeen's first win over Clyde in 10 meetings gives them a chance of qualifying for the quarter-finals.

---

5 | A | DUNFERMLINE | 23/8 | 8,000 | W | 1-0 | 7 | Willoughby 15 | Ref: R Davidson

McGarr · Boel · Hermiston · Murray G · McMillan · Petersen · Willoughby · Robb · Forrest · Wilson T · Hamilton
Duff · Callaghan · Lunn · McGarty · Barry · Renton · McFarlane · Hay · Mitchell · Paton · Edwards · Gardner · McLaren*

Alec Willoughby's header from Hamilton's corner-kick earns two more points and sets up an eagerly awaited match with Hibs. The Dons also faced Dunfermline in both cups last season, gaining all four points in the League Cup and winning a Scottish Cup replay against the holders.

---

6 | A | HIBERNIAN | 27/8 | 18,300 | D | 0-0 | 8 | Ref: J Paterson

McGarr · Boel · Hermiston · Murray G · McMillan · Petersen · Willoughby · Robb · Forrest · Wilson T · Hamilton
Marshall · Shevlane · Davis · Wilkinson · Black · Stanton · Marinello · O'Rourke · McBride · Cormack · Stevenson

Goal difference has replaced goal average this season. Aberdeen can afford to lose by one goal and still reach the quarter-finals. Jock Stein sent three players to spy on Celtic's next opponents. They noted another resolute defensive display and the third Dons shut-out in three away ties.

Qual							
ABERDEEN	6	2	4	0	8	4	8
Hibernian	6	2	2	2	10	9	6
Dunfermline	6	1	3	2	5	6	5
Clyde	6	1	3	2	4	8	5

SCOTTISH LEAGUE DIV 1 (CUP-TIES)   Manager: Eddie Turnbull   SEASON 1969-70

Scottish League Cup

	F-A	H-T		Scorers, Times, and Referees
QF 1 H CELTIC 10/9 33,000	D 0-0	0-0		Ref: J Mullen
QF 2 A CELTIC 24/9 37,500	L 1-2	1-0		Forrest 31 — Lennox 52, Wallace 55. Ref: W Mullen. (Dons lose 1-2 on aggregate)

	1	2	3	4	5	6	7	8	9	10	11	12 sub used
QF 1	McGarr	Boel	Hermiston	Murray G	McMillan	Petersen	Rae	Robb	Forrest	Wilson T	Hamilton	
	Fallon	*Hay*	*Gemmell*	*Murdoch*	*McNeill*	*Clark*	*Hood**	*Chalmers*	*Wallace*	*Callaghan*	*Lennox*	*Brogan*
QF 2	McGarr	Boel	Hermiston	Murray G	McMillan	Petersen	Adams	Robb	Forrest	Wilson T	Hamilton	
	Fallon	*Hay*	*Gemmell*	*Brogan*	*McNeill*	*Clark*	*Johnstone*	*Chalmers*	*Wallace*	*Hood*	*Lennox*	

Aberdeen desperately wanted a first-leg lead to take to Parkhead. The nearest they came was when Jim Hamilton struck Celtic's crossbar in the first half. Celtic only came out of their defensive shell after half-time. It is now a long, long time since Aberdeen beat these opponents.

A shock for Celtic as Jim Forrest ran on to Wilson's pass to bang Aberdeen in front. At half-time Jock Stein switched Jimmy Johnstone to centre-forward. It was he who manufactured Celtic's equaliser for Lennox. Then Wallace outwitted Aberdeen's offside trap to fire the winner.

Scottish Cup

		F-A	H-T	Scorers, Times, and Referees
1 H CLYDE 24/1 9 12,229 15	W	4-0	3-0	Harper 6, 36, Robb 20, 51. Ref: R Henderson
2 H CLYDEBANK 11/2 13,082	W	2-1	2-1	Forrest 5, Robb 32 — McGhee 11. Ref: R Wilson
QF A FALKIRK 21/2 13 13,500 2:7	W	1-0	0-0	McKay 66. Ref: J Paterson
SF N KILMARNOCK 14/3 10 25,812 6 (at Muirton Pk)	W	1-0	1-0	McKay 21. Ref: J Paterson
F N CELTIC 11/4 9 108,434 1 (at Hampden)	W	3-1	1-0	Harper 27p, McKay 83, 90 — Lennox 89. Ref: R Davidson

	1	2	3	4	5	6	7	8	9	10	11	12 sub used
1	McGarr	Boel	Kirkland	Petersen	McMillan	Buchan M	Hamilton	Robb	Forrest	Murray G	Harper	
	McCulloch	*Anderson*	*Soutar*	*Beattie*	*McHugh*	*Burns*	*Glasgow*	*Hulston*	*Staite**	*Stewart*	*Hastings*	*McFarlane*
2	Clark	Boel	Kirkland	Murray G	McMillan	Buchan M	Willoughby	Robb	Forrest	Hamilton	Harper	
	McDonald	*Mitchell*	*Gray*	*Ruddy*	*Fallon*	*Hay*	*Caskie*	*Love*	*Munro*	*McGhee**	*O'Brien*	*MacMillan*
QF	Clark	Boel	Murray G	Petersen	McMillan	Buchan M	McKay	Hermiston	Forrest	Hamilton	Harper	
	Rennie	*Abel*	*Miller*	*Ford*	*Markie*	*Gibson*	*Hoggan*	*Roxburgh**	*Young*	*Ferguson*	*Watson*	*Scott*
SF	Clark	Boel	Murray G	Hermiston*	McMillan	Buchan M	McKay	Robb	Forrest	Hamilton	Harper	Buchan G
	McLaughlan	*King*	*Dickson*	*Gilmour*	*McGrory*	*McDonald*	*McLean T*	*Morrison*	*Mathie*	*McLean J*	*Cook*	
F	Clark	Boel	Hermiston	Murray G	McMillan	Buchan M	McKay	Robb	Forrest	Harper	Graham	
	Williams	*Hay*	*Gemmell*	*Murdoch*	*McNeill*	*Brogan*	*Johnstone*	*Wallace*	*Connelly*	*Lennox*	*Hughes**	*Auld*

These two teams are thoroughly sick of one another. Clyde are never in with a shout once Joe Harper and Dave Robb had given the Dons a picture-book start. This result follows home wins over Clyde (3-0) in the League Cup and (6-0) in the league.

This Wednesday night cup-tie had to be postponed from the Saturday because of snow. Aberdeen are a shambles. The crowd cheered Second Division Clydebank's spirited efforts to equalise. Perhaps Pittodrie did not recognise its own players, kitted out in unfamiliar striped shirts.

Derek McKay, a free transfer from Dundee, plays his first full match. Against the Division 2 title chasers he provides the decisive touch after a bout of head tennis in the Falkirk goalmouth. His goal sends Aberdeen into the Scottish Cup semi-finals for the fourth time in five seasons.

For the second successive season Kilmarnock block Aberdeen's path in the Scottish Cup. McKay's goalscoring knack is maintained. By the end there were plenty of chewed finger nails. Like most semi-finals, this was no classic. But Derek McKay pounces.

Celtic were 11-4 on, Aberdeen 5-1 against. McKay's cross struck Murdoch's arm. Penalty said the referee. Gemmell flung the ball at him and was booked. Harper scores. Seven minutes from time Williams blocks Forrest's drive and McKay pounces. Then comes the sensational climax. Hooligans also let fly with bottles and cans.

League Table

	P	Home					Away					Pts
		W	D	L	F	A	W	D	L	F	A	
1 Celtic	34	12	2	3	54	18	15	1	1	42	15	57
2 Rangers	34	13	1	3	38	17	6	6	5	29	23	45
3 Hibernian	34	12	2	3	40	17	7	4	6	25	23	44
4 Hearts	34	6	7	4	28	19	7	5	5	22	17	38
5 Dundee Utd	34	10	3	4	36	23	6	3	8	26	41	38
6 Dundee	34	11	2	4	29	15	4	9	4	20	29	36
7 Kilmarnock	34	10	5	2	37	21	5	1	11	25	36	36
8 ABERDEEN	34	6	6	5	30	21	6	5	6	25	26	35
9 Morton	34	9	5	3	33	21	5	2	10	19	31	35
10 Dunfermline	34	12	2	3	32	17	3	3	11	13	28	35
11 Motherwell	34	8	4	5	25	18	4	4	9	24	33	32
12 Airdrie	34	8	3	6	33	26	2	8	7	26	38	32
13 St Johnstone	34	9	4	4	35	28	2	5	10	15	34	31
14 Ayr	34	10	3	4	26	20	2	3	12	11	32	30
15 St Mirren	34	6	5	6	28	28	2	4	11	11	26	25
16 Clyde	34	8	4	5	21	18	1	3	13	13	38	25
17 Raith Rovers	34	4	6	7	15	24	1	5	11	17	43	21
18 Partick This	34	4	4	9	22	33	1	3	13	19	49	17
	612	158	69	79	562	382	79	69	158	382	562	612

Appearances and Goals

Player	Appearances						Goals			
	Lge	Sub	LC	Sub	SC	Sub	Lge	LC	SC	Tot
Adams, George	1			1						
Boel, Henning	28		7		5					
Buchan, George	4		2				1			1
Buchan, Martin	19				5		2			2
Clark, Bobby	13		8		4					
Forrest, Jim	31	1	1		5		15	2	1	18
Graham, Arthur	4	1		1			2			2
Hamilton, Jim	19	3	6	1	4		3	1		4
Harper, Joe	24				5		6		3	9
Hermiston, Jim	26		8		3		2	1		3
Kirkland, Jim	13				2					
McGarr, Ernie	22		8		1					
McIlroy, Brian	6	1								
McKay, Derek	10	3			3				4	4
McMillan, Tommy	24		8		5					
Murray, George	34		5		5		2			2
Murray, Steve	7									
Rae, Tommy	2	2	1				1			1
Petersen, Jens	17	3	8		2		2			2
Robb, Dave	34		8		4		16		3	19
Smith, Alex	5	1	3						1	1
Sutherland, Ian	1									
Taylor, Ian	3		1							
Whyte, Jim	9	2	8							
Wilson, Tom	18	1	6		1		1	3		4
Willoughby, Alec								1		1
(own-goals)							2			2
26 players used	374	19	88	1	55	1	55	9	11	75

Odds & ends

Double wins: (4) Ayr, Partick, Motherwell, Raith.

Double losses: (1) Rangers.

Won from behind: (2) Airdrie (a), Raith (h).

Lost from in front: (5) Celtic (h), Clyde (h), Rangers (h), Morton (a). Celtic (LC).

High spots: 4 unbeaten league games from 8 November. Winning at champions Celtic in the league. Winning Scottish Cup Final against Celtic. Derek 'cup-tie' MacKay's four Scottish Cup goals.

Low spots: 3 straight league defeats from 29 October. Losing League Cup quarter-final to Celtic after taking the lead.

Ever-presents: (2) Dave Robb, George Murray (league only).

Hat-tricks: (3): Dave Robb (1), Joe Harper (1), Tom Wilson (1).

Leading scorer: (19) Dave Robb.

SCOTTISH LEAGUE DIVISION 1 — Manager: Eddie Turnbull — SEASON 1970-71

Match summary

No		Opponent	Date	Att	Pos	Pt	F-A	H-T	Scorers, Times, and Referees
1	H	AIRDRIE	29/8	9,000	D	1	1-1	1-0	Harper 26 / Busby 86 — Ref: R Henderson
2	A	DUNDEE	5/9	8,000	6 W (9)	3	2-1	2-0	Harper 33, Hamilton 45 / Duncan 75 — Ref: A Webster
3	H	ST JOHNSTONE	12/9	10,000	6 D (5)	4	0-0	0-0	Ref: R Davidson
4	A	KILMARNOCK	19/9	6,000	3 W (17)	6	4-0	4-0	Arthur 16 og, Hamilton 34, Harper 35, [Boel 39] — Ref: R Gordon
5	H	HIBERNIAN	26/9	13,000	2 W (7)	8	3-0	1-0	Forrest 43, Robb 58, Harper 85p — Ref: J Paterson
6	A	MORTON	3/10	7,000	5 L (8)	8	0-2	0-1	Mason 31, 78 — Ref: H Dempsey
7	H	DUNFERMLINE	10/10	10,000	4 W (18)	10	3-2	2-1	Buchan M 20, Graham 29, 66 / Mitchell 25, Fraser 75 — Ref: R Wilson
8	A	RANGERS	17/10	44,000	3 W (4)	12	2-0	1-0	Jackson 44 og, Harper 58 — Ref: A McKenzie
9	A	ST MIRREN	24/10	3,000	2 W (11)	14	3-1	1-0	Robb 19, Murray S 55, Forrest 73 / Hamilton 79 — Ref: J Callaghan
10	H	DUNDEE UTD	31/10	10,000	2 W (13)	16	4-0	1-0	Robb 44, Murray S 62, Harper 80, 89 — Ref: A McDonald

Line-ups (Aberdeen top, opponents in italics)

No	1	2	3	4	5	6	7	8	9	10	11	12 sub used
1	Clark	Boel	Murray G	Hermiston*	McMillan	Buchan M	Forrest	Murray S	Robb	Harper	Graham	Hamilton
	McKenzie	*Jonquin*	*Caldwell*	*Menzies*	*Delaney*	*Whiteford*	*D Wilson*	*Jarvie*	*Busby*	*McPheat*	*Cowan**	*Bird*
2	Clark	Boel	Murray G	Murray S	Young	Buchan M	McKay	Robb	Hamilton	Harper	Buchan G	
	Donaldson	*Wilson R*	*Johnston*	*Selway*	*Stewart*	*Houston*	*Kinninmonth Bryce*		*Duncan*	*Scott*	*Wilson J*	
3	Clark	Boel	Murray G	Murray S	Young	Buchan M	McKay	Robb	Hamilton	Harper	Buchan G	Forrest
	Donaldson	*McManus*	*Argue*	*Rooney*	*Gordon*	*Rennie*	*Leslie**	*Hall*	*Connolly*	*McPhee*	*Muir*	*Lambie*
4	Clark	Boel	Hermiston	Murray S	Young	Buchan M	Hamilton	Buchan G	Harper	Robb	Graham	
	Hunter	*Dickson*	*Swan*	*Maxwell*	*McGrory*	*Arthur*	*McLean*	*Morrison*	*Mathie*	*McSherry*	*Cook**	*McCulloch*
5	Clark	Boel	Hermiston	Murray S	Young	Buchan M	Forrest	Buchan G	Robb	Harper	Willoughby	
	Marshall	*Shevlane*	*Schaedler*	*Blackley*	*Black*	*Stanton*	*Hamilton**	*Graham*	*McBride*	*McEwan*	*Cropley*	*Blair*
6	Clark	Boel	Hermiston	Murray S	Young	Buchan M	Willoughby	Robb*	Forrest	Harper!	Graham	Murray G
	Nielsen	*Murray*	*McDerment*	*Sweeney*	*Gray*	*O'Neill*	*Hannigan*	*Collins*	*Osborne**	*Mason*	*Anderson*	*Jordan*
7	Clark	Boel	Hermiston	Murray S	Young	Buchan M	Buchan G*	Hamilton	Forrest	Harper	Graham	Willoughby
	Arrol	*Callaghan*	*Lunn*	*Fraser*	*Cushley*	*Thomson J*	*Gardner*	*Robertson*	*Mitchell*	*Walsh*	*McKimmie**	*Scott*
8	Clark	Boel	Hermiston	Murray S	McMillan	Buchan M	Taylor	Harper	Forrest	Robb	Graham	
	McCloy	*Jardine*	*Miller*	*Greig*	*McKinnon*	*Jackson*	*Henderson*	*Frye*	*Stein*	*MacDon'ld A**	*Johnston*	*Smith*
9	Clark	Boel	Hermiston	Murray S	McMillan	Buchan M	Taylor	Harper	Forrest	Robb	Graham	
	McCann	*McFadden*	*Brown*	*Fulton*	*Murray C*	*Munro*	*McKean*	*Gilshan*	*Knox*	*Hamilton*	*Lister*	
10	Clark	Boel	Hermiston	Murray S	McMillan	Buchan M	Taylor	Robb	Forrest	Harper	Graham	
	McAlpine	*Markland*	*Cameron J*	*Stevenson*	*Smith*	*Henry*	*Wilson*	*Reid A*	*Cameron K*	*Gordon**	*Traynor*	*Gillespie*

Match notes

1. Airdrie — It is only seven days since Aberdeen beat Airdrie 7-3 in the League Cup, so this result takes some explaining. It all began well enough, with Joe Harper adding to his five goals scored in the League Cup. Busby's late equaliser came when the Dons failed to clear a free-kick.

2. Dundee — Turnbull introduces the team's new 18-year-old centre-half, Willie Young, who gets himself booked on his debut. Aberdeen went in front thanks to Joe Harper's header. Keeper Donaldson got both hands to it, but could not keep it out. It is seven goals already for wee Joey.

3. St Johnstone — Aberdeen exert a lot of huff and puff against St Johnstone - who like themselves are unbeaten in the league - yet achieve very little. They have now let slip two precious home points. Strangely, Aberdeen beat the Saints twice in the League Cup. Two more Dons are booked in this match.

4. Kilmarnock — Kilmarnock were barracked by their own crowd throughout the second half, as Aberdeen cruised to a comfortable win. Things started dreadfully for Killie, Arthur running the ball into his own net when the game was goalless. Three more goals in six minutes killed the match.

5. Hibernian — Aberdeen gain revenge for their humiliating elimination from the League Cup. Three Hibs players were booked. Harper's penalty was the result of Willoughby being sandwiched between two defenders. This result sets up Aberdeen for their midweek Cup-Winners' trip to Hungary.

6. Morton — Nothing goes right for the Dons, who are still suffering the effects of Jim Forrest's penalty miss in Budapest. Dave Robb is injured early on at Cappielow, and Joe Harper is sent off after Morton's second goal. This is Aberdeen third successive defeat at Greenock.

7. Dunfermline — Dunfermline, so powerful in recent seasons, are bottom of the league without a win. Yet they take advantage of Joe Harper's rare penalty miss to put the Dons defence under sustained pressure for the last fifteen minutes. Now begins Aberdeen's phenomenal winning sequence.

8. Rangers — Aberdonian Colin Jackson, the Rangers pivot, slices the ball over keeper McCloy's head to put his home-town club ahead. If either side deserved a bit of good fortune it was Aberdeen, for they looked the better team. Another goal for Joe Harper settles the outcome.

9. St Mirren — When Hamilton scored for St Mirren, by dribbling the ball around Bobby Clark, it made no difference to this match - since Aberdeen were leading 3-0 - but it would prove to be the last goal Clark would concede until 16 January. Harper leaves the goalscoring to others in this match.

10. Dundee Utd — The Dons turn out in royal blue shirts and white socks - imitating Chelsea perhaps. With United playing in tangerine the two kits should have been dazzling, but the filthy weather made both strips an insipid grey. The Dons are introduced to keeper Hamish McAlpine for the first time.

No		Date	Att		Pos	Pts	FT	HT	Scorers	
11	H CLYDE	7/11	13,000	2 W	13	18	3-0	1-0	Harper 15, 52, Hermiston 55	Ref: E Pringle

Aberdeen: Clark, Boel, Hermiston, Murray S, McMillan, Buchan M, Taylor*, Robb, Forrest, Harper, Graham, Willoughby
Clyde: Wallace, Burns, Mulherron*, Beattie, McGoldrick, McHugh, Sullivan, Hay, Hulston, Flanagan, Hastings, McColligan

Such was Aberdeen's early dominance that the crowd expected a feast of goals. They had to make do with Harper's morsel in the first half, and two more goals in the second. The third goal is Jim Hermiston's one and only goal of the season. The Dons are breathing down Celtic's necks.

| 12 | A AYR | 14/11 | 11,000 | 2 W | 16 | 20 | 1-0 | 1-0 | Harper 44 | Ref: P Hunter |

Aberdeen: Clark, Boel, Hermiston, Murray S, McMillan, Buchan M, Willoughby, Robb, Forrest, Harper, Graham
Ayr: Stewart, Filippi, Murphy, McAnespie, Fleming, Mitchell, Young, McFadzean, McLean, Whitehead*, McGovern, Reynolds

Aberdeen took just one of the many chances that came their way against Ally MacLeod's struggling Ayr. Three players were booked, including Aberdeen's Dave Robb and Tommy McMillan. It took a while for Joe Harper to settle in last season, but now he just can't stop scoring.

| 13 | H HEARTS | 21/11 | 13,500 | 2 W | 14 | 22 | 1-0 | 0-0 | Harper 60p | Ref: J McRoberts |

Aberdeen: Clark, Boel, Hermiston, Murray S, McMillan, Buchan M, Willoughby, Robb, Forrest, Harper, Graham
Hearts: Cruickshank, Clunie, Oliver, Thomson, Anderson, Brown*, Winchester, Townsend, Ford, Wood, Fleming, Young

Hearts are at the wrong end of the table, but they stretch Aberdeen all the way. Harper is pulled down from behind in the box and needed attention before getting to his feet to score. With Celtic only drawing at Falkirk, the Dons are just one point behind them.

| 14 | A MOTHERWELL | 28/11 | 10,000 | 2 W | 9 | 24 | 2-0 | 0-0 | Boel 48, Taylor 77 | Ref: I Foote |

Aberdeen: Clark, Boel, Hermiston, Murray S, McMillan, Buchan M, Taylor, Robb, Forrest, Harper, Graham
Motherwell: McCrae, Whiteford, Wark, Forsyth, McCallum, Donnelly, Campbell, Watson, Deans, Muir, Heron

It took the Dons half the match to get accustomed to the opposition and to the mud. Once they had become acclimatised they were always likely winners. The breakthrough came from full-back Henning Boel, with his second league goal of the season. The Dons' eighth straight win.

| 15 | H COWDENBEATH | 5/12 | 14,000 | 2 W | 18 | 26 | 7-0 | 3-0 | Kinnell 26 og, 83 og, Graham 28, [Harper 34, 79, 89, Murray 60] | Ref: A Crawley |

Aberdeen: Clark, Boel, Hermiston, Murray S, McMillan, Buchan M, Taylor, Robb, Forrest, Harper, Graham
Cowdenbeath: Wyllie, McLaughlin, Bostock, Taylor, Kinnell, Moore, McCullie, Dickson, Thomson, Kennedy*, Ross, Laing

Cowdenbeath's first visit to Pittodrie in 30 years, and their stay in the top division will be brief. It is all too much for centre-half Andy Kinnell, who bags two own-goals in one match. Harper's third hat-trick for the Dons. Next Saturday's clash with Celtic cannot come quickly enough.

| 16 | A CELTIC | 12/12 | 63,000 | 1 W | 2 | 28 | 1-0 | 0-0 | Harper 53 | Ref: A Webster |

Aberdeen: Clark, Boel, Hermiston, Murray S, McMillan, Buchan M, Taylor, Robb, Forrest*, Harper, Graham, Willoughby
Celtic: Fallon, Craig, Gemmell, Murdoch, McNeill, Brogan, Johnstone, Connolly*, Macari, Hay, Hughes, Hood

Aberdeen surge past Celtic to claim pole position after this momentous win, their 10th in succession, and third in a row over Jock Stein's team. Bobby Clark's goal was under siege after Harper's impertinent header. Dave Robb back-headed and Harper sprang forward to beat Fallon.

| 17 | H FALKIRK | 19/12 | 19,000 | 1 W | 5 | 30 | 1-0 | 1-0 | Harper 19p | Ref: R Davidson |

Aberdeen: Clark, Boel, Hermiston, Murray S, McMillan, Buchan M, Taylor, Robb, Forrest, Harper, Graham
Falkirk: Rennie, Abel, McLaughlin, Markie, Miller, Gibson, Hoggan, Roxburgh, Ferguson, Shira, Setterington

Aberdeen faced two future Scotland managers - Alex Ferguson and Andy Roxburgh - playing for Falkirk, who were unbeaten since September. Their captain, George Miller, was booked for disputing the penalty, awarded when the ball struck Markie's arm. Fergie often upset the referee.

| 18 | A AIRDRIE | 26/12 | 8,000 | 1 W | 12 | 32 | 4-0 | 1-0 | Taylor 35, Murray S 57, Harper 65, 80 | Ref: J Paterson |

Aberdeen: Clark, Boel, Hermiston, Murray S, McMillan, Buchan M, Taylor*, Robb, Forrest, Harper, Graham, Willoughby
Airdrie: McKenzie, Jonquin, McKay, Menzies, Goodwin, Whiteford, Wilson, McKinlay, Busby*, Jarvie, Cowan, Bird

It wasn't that Airdrie were bad, it was simply that Aberdeen were better - much better. This is the fourth match between the sides this season: two ended all square, and the two that Aberdeen won in a landslide. Two more goals for Harper. At this rate he could break Dons' scoring record.

| 19 | H DUNDEE | 1/1 | 24,000 | W | 3 | 34 | 3-0 | 2-0 | McMillan 11, Murray S 27, Graham 89 | Ref: R Gordon |

Aberdeen: Clark, Boel, Hermiston, Murray S, McMillan, Buchan M, Willoughby, Robb, Forrest, Harper, Graham
Dundee: Donaldson, Wilson R, Soutar, Selway, Phillip, Houston, Gilroy, Kinninmonth, Wallace, Scott, Johnston*, Falconer

A standing ovation from Pittodrie after this scintillating performance, which was summed up by Arthur Graham's last-minute goal. He veered 25 yards infield from the wing to beat keeper Donaldson from long range. It is now 10 matches since Aberdeen let in a goal, never mind lost.

| 20 | A ST JOHNSTONE | 2/1 | 21,500 | W | 3 | 36 | 1-0 | 0-0 | Forrest 76 | Ref: B Padden |

Aberdeen: Clark, Boel, Hermiston, Murray S, McMillan, Buchan M, Willoughby, Robb, Forrest, Harper, Graham
St Johnstone: Donaldson, Lambie, Argue, Rooney, Gordon, Rennie, Aird, Hall, Connelly, McPhee, McCarry

St Johnstone were in third position, 10 points behind the Dons. Now the gap is 12 points. Joe Harper did not score, but he did the next best thing, flashing the ball across goal for Jim Forrest to net. Thereafter there were 21 players camped in the Dons' half of the pitch.

| 21 | H KILMARNOCK | 9/1 | 18,000 | 1 W | 15 | 38 | 3-0 | 1-0 | Robb 25, Forrest 64, Willoughby 71 | Ref: E Thomson |

Aberdeen: Clark, Boel, Hermiston, Murray S, McMillan, Buchan M, Willoughby, Robb, Forrest, Harper, Graham
Kilmarnock: Hunter, Whyte, Dickson, Gilmour, McGrory, McDonald*, McLean, Graham, Mathie, Cairns, Cook, Morrison

The facts are astonishing. This is Aberdeen 15th straight win and 12th without conceding a goal. A minute's silence precedes this match, out of respect for the victims of the Ibrox tragedy. Jim Whyte has transferred to Kilmarnock, but he did little to trouble his former team-mates.

SCOTTISH LEAGUE DIVISION 1

Manager: Eddie Turnbull

SEASON 1970-71

Match summary

No	Date	Att	Pos	R	Opp Pos	Pt	F-A	H-T	Scorers, Times, and Referees
22	A HIBERNIAN 16/1	23,400	1	L	8	38	1-2	0-0	Robb 84 / *Stanton 64, Baker 68* / Ref: J McKee
23	H MORTON 30/1	18,000	1	W	11	40	3-1	3-1	Harper 30, Taylor 35, 40 / *Bartram 14* / Ref: T Marshall
24	A DUNFERMLINE 6/2	9,000	1	L	17	40	0-1	0-1	*Robertson 42* / Ref: A Crawley
25	H RANGERS 20/2	36,000	1	D	4	41	0-0	0-0	Ref: A McKenzie
26	H ST MIRREN 27/2	15,000	1	D	16	42	1-1	0-1	Forrest 63 / *Munro 20* / Ref: S Anderson
27	A DUNDEE UTD 10/3	7,000	1	W		44	2-0	1-0	Buchan M 22, Forrest 64 / Ref: E Pringle
28	A CLYDE 13/3	4,500	1	W	14	46	2-1	2-1	McGoldrick 4 og, Forrest 7 / *Flanagan 33* / Ref: J Grant
29	H AYR 24/3	18,000	1	W		48	4-1	1-0	Robb 43, Graham 52, Forrest 55, [Murray 86] / *Ingram 65* / Ref: W Mullen
30	A HEARTS 27/3	13,500	1	W	6	50	3-1	0-1	Robb 46, 60, 85 / *Ford 8* / Ref: R Henderson
31	H MOTHERWELL 3/4	13,000	1	D	8	51	0-0	0-0	Ref: J Callaghan

Line-ups

No	Team	1	2	3	4	5	6	7	8	9	10	11	12 sub used
22	Aberdeen	Clark	Boel	Murray G	Murray S	McMillan	Buchan M	Willoughby	Robb	Forrest	Harper	Graham	
22	*Hibernian*	*Baines*	*Brownlie*	*Jones*	*Blackley*	*Black*	*Stanton*	*Duncan*	*O'Rourke*	*Baker*	*Hamilton*	*Davidson**	*Blair*
23	Aberdeen	Clark	Boel	Hermiston	Murray S	McMillan	Buchan M	Taylor	Robb	Forrest	Harper	Graham	
23	*Morton*	*Sorensen*	*Murray*	*Laughton*	*Sweeney*	*Gray*	*Rankin*	*Hannigan*	*O'Neill*	*Bartram*	*Masch*	*Thomson*	
24	Aberdeen	Clark	Boel	Hermiston	Murray S	McMillan	Buchan M	Taylor*	Robb	Forrest	Harper	Graham	Willoughby
24	*Dunfermline*	*McGarr*	*Thomson*	*Lunn*	*Fraser*	*Cushley*	*McNichol*	*Edwards*	*Mitchell*	*McBride*	*Gardner*	*Robertson*	
25	Aberdeen	Clark	Boel	Hermiston	Murray S	McMillan	Buchan M	Taylor	Robb	Forrest	Hamilton*	Graham	Willoughby
25	*Rangers*	*McCloy*	*Jardine*	*Mathieson*	*Greig*	*McKinnon*	*Jackson*	*Henderson*	*McDonald*	*Johnstone**	*Smith*	*Johnston*	*Conn*
26	Aberdeen	Clark	Boel	Hermiston	Murray S	McMillan	Buchan M	Taylor*	Robb	Forrest	Harper	Graham	Willoughby
26	*St Mirren*	*Connaghan*	*Connell*	*McLaughlin*	*Murray*	*McQueen*	*Fulton*	*McKean*	*Blair*	*Knox*	*Munro*	*Lawson*	*Henry*
27	Aberdeen	Clark	Boel	Hermiston	Buchan M	McMillan	Young	Forrest*	Murray S	Buchan G	Taylor	Graham	Willoughby
27	*Dundee Utd*	*McAlpine*	*Rolland*	*Cameron J*	*Smith W*	*Smith D*	*Stevenson*	*Wilson*	*Reid A*	*Copland*	*Gordon*	*Traynor**	*Henry*
28	Aberdeen	Clark	Boel	Hermiston	Buchan M	McMillan	Young	Buchan G*	Murray S	Forrest	Robb	Graham	Taylor
28	*Clyde*	*McCulloch*	*Anderson*	*Mulheron*	*Beattie*	*McGoldrick*	*McHugh*	*Sullivan*	*Hay*	*Flanagan*	*Burns*	*Hastings*	
29	Aberdeen	Clark	Boel	Hermiston	Murray S	McMillan	Buchan M	Forrest	Robb	Harper	Graham	Buchan G	
29	*Ayr*	*Stewart*	*Filippi*	*Murphy*	*Fleming*	*Quinn*	*Mitchell*	*Young*	*McGovern*	*Ingram*	*McCulloch**	*Rough*	*Doyle*
30	Aberdeen	Clark	Boel	Hermiston	Murray S	Young	Buchan M	Forrest	Robb	Harper	Graham	Buchan G	
30	*Hearts*	*Cruickshank*	*Clunie*	*Kay*	*Thomson*	*Anderson*	*Brown*	*Carruthers**	*Fleming*	*Wood*	*Ford*	*Lynch*	*Veitch*
31	Aberdeen	Clark	Boel	Hermiston	Murray S*	McMillan	Buchan M	Forrest	Robb	Harper	Graham	Buchan G	Taylor
31	*Motherwell*	*MacCrae*	*Whiteford*	*Wark*	*Forsyth*	*McCallum*	*Goldthorpe*	*Martin*	*Watson*	*Lawson*	*Muir*	*Heron*	

Match notes

22 — Hibernian: All good things must come to an end. Pat Stanton's raging cross-shot ends Aberdeen's run of clean sheets. Four minutes later Joe Baker - captain for the day on his return to the club - is unmarked to head past Clark. Hibs' colourful side contains a Black, a Blackley, and Brownlie.

23 — Morton: This otherwise insignificant result means that Aberdeen have now beaten every team in the league this season. Morton's goal was the first conceded at Pittodrie since 10 October. The following Wednesday, Jim Forrest comes on as a substitute for Scotland against Belgium in Liege.

24 — Dunfermline: Dunfermline are next to bottom. Their goalkeeper is former Don Ernie McGarr. He is not overworked. Fortunately for Aberdeen, Celtic lost at St Johnstone. Unfortunately, fire engulfed Pitodrie's main stand while the players were away. Joe Harper will not score again this season.

25 — Rangers: A vital point dropped, for Celtic are now one point behind with a game in hand. The match deteriorated into a midfield struggle. Neither keeper was extended, and neither side gained any psychological advantage for their coming Scottish Cup-tie. Robb and Jackson were booked.

26 — St Mirren: The Dons are wobbling. Struggling St Mirren snatch a first-half lead and then defend it by fair means or foul. Aberdeen have failed to win in three games. But it could have been worse: Celtic can only draw at Hearts. Eddie Turnbull has now been manager of Aberdeen for six years.

27 — Dundee Utd: Minus goal aces Harper and Robb, Aberdeen are still too strong for Dundee United. Martin Buchan abandons his sweeper's role and turns goalscorer. The finishing tape is in sight, and already it looks clear that the crunch match with Celtic holds the destiny to the championship.

28 — Clyde: Dave Robb's shot is wickedly deflected by McGoldrick to send Aberdeen on their way. Within minutes Jim Forrest dribbles round McCulloch to put the Dons two up. Aberdeen then fall back on an unpopular offside trap. These tactics provoke a slow hand-clap at Shawfield.

29 — Ayr: Ally MacLeod's Ayr are hovering above the relegation places. Three quick goals either side of half-time settle the outcome. Jim Forrest's goal is his 200th in senior football in Scotland. Joe Harper returns to the Dons side, but his goalscoring touch seems to have deserted him.

30 — Hearts: A blood and thunder match. Ford dispossessed Martin Buchan to put Hearts in front. This provokes a famous hat-trick for Dave Robb and less than famous bookings for Boel and Hermiston. The Dons are indebted to Hearts' fluffed penalty at 1-0. Fleming fired wide with his spot-kick.

31 — Motherwell: This could be the result that deprives Aberdeen of the title. Aberdeen could not come to terms with a swirling wind or the knowledge that Scotland manager Bobby Brown was watching them. The nearest they came was when George Buchan's late header hit the crossbar.

32 A COWDENBEATH 10/4 — 1 W 18 53 — 2-1 — 4,000

Clark	Williamson	Hermiston	Buchan M	Boel	McMillan	Forrest	Robb	Buchan G	Harper*	Graham	Willoughby
McArthur	*Bostack*	*Taylor*	*Kinnell*	*Moore*	*McCullie**	*Dickson*	*Laing*	*Kennedy*	*Thomson*	*Judge*	

Bostock 4 og, Buchan G 76 / Boel 11 og
Ref: P Hunter

Aberdeen make hard work of beating bottom-placed Cowdenbeath, but are rejuvenated with the post-match news that Celtic have dropped a home point to Dundee United. George Buchan headed on to the bar against Motherwell. Now, his late winning header could prove decisive.

33 H CELTIC 17/4 — D 1-1 54 — 36,000

Clark	Williams	Hermiston	Murray S	McMillan	Buchan M	Forrest	Willoughby	Robb	Graham	Buchan G*	Harper
Craig	*Brogan*	*Connelly*	*McNeill*	*Hay*	*Johnstone*	*Lennox*	*Wallace*	*Callaghan*	*Hood**	*Quinn*	

Willoughby 38 / Hood 3
Ref: W Anderson

The Dons are three points ahead but have played two games more. A home win would therefore secure the title. Harry Hood, Scotland's top scorer, hooked home Johnstone's corner. After the Dons levelled, Arthur Graham rounded Williams but Billy McNeill cleared off the line.

34 A FALKIRK 24/4 — L 0-1 54 — 8,000
Average Home 17,000 Away 14,500

Clark	Rennie	Hermiston	Murray S	McMillan	Buchan M	Forrest	Robb	Harper	Graham	Willoughby
Abel	*McLaughlin*	*Markie*	*Gibson*	*Hoggan*	*Ferguson*	*McLeod*	*Shirra*	*Setterington*		

Miller 22p
Ref: J McRoberts

Aberdeen had to win to exert maximum pressure on Celtic. But midway through the first half Dave Robb handled Miller's free-kick, and the Dons fuel tanks had run dry. The Dons' first defeat in 10 games could not have come at a worse time. Celtic will be champions by two points.

Scottish League Cup - Section 4

1 A AIRDRIE 8/8 — D 1-1 1 — 3,500

Clark	McKenzie	Hermiston	Murray G	Whyte	McMillan	Buchan M	Forrest	Murray S	Robb	Harper	Graham
Jonquin	*Caldwell*	*Goodwin*	*Delaney*	*Whiteford*	*Wilson*	*Jarvie*	*Marshall**	*McPheat*	*Cowan*	*Menzies*	

Murray S 44 / Menzies 78
Ref: E Pringle

Steve Murray is on hand to put the Dons in front after Jim Hermiston's shot was saved. Airdrie's substitute saved the day for the home team. Last season, Jim Whyte was injured in this corresponding fixture, and was out for six months. Now he plays his last game for the Dons.

2 H ST JOHNSTONE 12/8 — W 2-1 3 — 13,500

Clark	Donaldson	Hermiston	Murray G	Boel	McMillan	Buchan M	Forrest	Murray S	Robb	Harper*	Graham
McManus	*Argue*	*Rooney*	*Rennie**	*Aird*	*Hall*	*Whitelaw*	*Connolly*	*Leslie*	*McPhee*	*Buchan G*	

Harper 17, Robb 58 / Hall 68
Ref: J Gordon

Aberdeen are so much on top that it is an hour before Bobby Clark has a shot to save. At the other end, Saints Jim Donaldson performs wonders to keep his team in the hunt. St Johnstone are set to have a wonderful season, but they will be consistently second best to the Dons.

3 H HIBERNIAN 15/8 — D 1-1 4 — 16,000

Clark	Marshall	Hermiston	Murray G	Boel	McMillan	Buchan M	Forrest	Murray S	Robb	Harper	Graham
Brownlie	*Schaedler*	*Blackley*	*Black*	*Stanton*	*Stevenson*	*Graham*	*McBride*	*Hamilton*	*Duncan*		

Robb 46 / Duncan 41
Ref: T Marshall

Scotland manager Bobby Brown took in this hard-fought affair. Hibernian are set to hang over Aberdeen's season like a shroud. Though Dave Robb equalises with a deft back-header, the draw leaves the Edinburgh club favourites to qualify from Section 4.

4 A ST JOHNSTONE 19/8 — W 1-0 6 — 3,300

Clark	Donaldson	Hermiston	Murray G	Boel	McMillan	Buchan M	Forrest	Murray S*	Robb	Willoughby	Buchan G	Hamilton
McManus	*Argue*	*Rooney*	*Rennie*	*Gordon*	*Muir*	*Hall*	*Connolly*	*McPhee*	*Aitken*			

Forrest 44
Ref: R Greenlees

Alec Willoughby's inspired pass prises open St Johnstone's defence for Jim Forrest to nab the only goal. The home team had to contend with Aberdeen's offside trap, which four times in the second half required Bobby Clark to rush from his goal to clear outside his penalty area.

5 H AIRDRIE 22/8 — W 7-3 8 — 12,000

Clark	McKenzie	Hermiston	Murray G	Boel	McMillan	Buchan M	Forrest	Hamilton	Robb	Harper	Graham
Jonquin	*Caldwell*	*Goodwin*	*Delaney*	*Whiteford D*	*Wilson*	*Jarvie*	*Busby*	*McPheat*	*Cowan*		

Harper 18,20,36p,89, Robb 25, Boel 35 / Jarvie 23, Cowan 63, Busby 77 (Jonq 86og)
Ref: A McDonald

For the first 45 minutes Aberdeen were irresistible. For the second they fell apart, as if at the flick of a switch. But two more goals in the last four minutes mean that Aberdeen have overtaken rivals Hibs on goal difference. Joe Harper claims his first foursome for the Dons.

6 A HIBERNIAN 26/8 — L 0-4 8 — 24,900

Clark	Marshall	Hermiston	Murray G	Boel	McMillan	Buchan M	Forrest	Murray S	Robb	Harper	Graham
Brownlie	*Schaedler*	*Blackley*	*Black*	*Stanton*	*Stevenson*	*Graham*	*McBride*	*McEwan*	*Duncan*		

Stanton 7, Graham 24, Duncan 31, [McBride 40]
Ref: J Callaghan

Aberdeen need a draw to book a quarter-final appearance with Rangers. They held out for just seven minutes, whereupon McBride drove a free-kick across the box and Pat Stanton hooked the ball in off a post. The rest of the first half was a nightmare; the second became academic.

Qual							
Hibernian	6	4	2	0	16	7	10
ABERDEEN	6	3	2	1	12	10	8
Airdrie	6	2	1	3	10	15	5
St Johnstone	6	0	1	5	3	9	1

Scottish Cup

		Scorers, Times, and Referees	1	2	3	4	5	6	7	8	9	10	11	12 sub used
3 H ELGIN CITY W 5-0 2-0	25/1 24,136	Taylor 30, Forrest 35, 84, Harper 72, 89 — Ref: J Gordon	Clark	Boel	Hermiston	Murray S	McMillan	Buchan M	Taylor*	Robb	Forrest	Harper	Graham	Willoughby
			Lawtie	*Gerrard*	*Cowie*	*Soutar*	*Grant*	*Shewan*	*Duncan*	*Douglas*	*McArthur*	*Graham*	*Macdonald**	*Thom*
4 A DUNDEE UTD D 1-1 0-1	13/2 24,000 12	Forrest 75 / Smith D 40p — Ref: R Davidson	Clark	Boel	Hermiston	Murray S	McMillan	Buchan M	Willoughby*	Robb	Forrest	Harper	Graham	Taylor
			McAlpine	*Rolland*	*Cameron J*	*Smith W*	*Smith D*	*Stevenson*	*Wilson*	*Reid A*	*Gordon*	*Henry*	*Traynor*	
4R H DUNDEE UTD W 2-0 0-0	17/2 29,000 12	Boel 67, Robb 88 — Ref: R Davidson	Clark	Boel	Hermiston	Murray S	McMillan	Buchan M	Taylor	Robb	Forrest	Harper*	Graham	Willoughby
			McAlpine	*Rolland*	*Cameron*	*Smith W*	*Smith D*	*Stevenson*	*Wilson*	*Reid**	*Gordon*	*Henry*	*Traynor*	*Scott*
QF A RANGERS L 0-1 0-0	6/3 65,000 4	Jackson 67 — Ref: W Mullen	Clark	Boel	Hermiston	Murray S	McMillan	Buchan M	Taylor*	Robb	Forrest	Harper	Graham	Willoughby
			McCloy	*Jardine*	*Mathieson*	*Greig*	*McKinnon*	*Jackson*	*Henderson*	*Conn**	*Stein*	*Smith*	*Johnston*	*McDonald*

Match 3 notes: This Monday match was postponed from the Saturday because of torrential rain. At 0-0 this north-east clash might have turned Elgin's way had McArthur done better than shoot straight into Clark's arms when in the clear. Pittodrie welcomed back Ally Shewan, sold to Elgin for £3,000.

Match 4 notes: An all-ticket match. Aberdeen conceded a penalty when Boel rugby-tackled Alan Gordon. After Forrest levelled, Harper took the ball round McAlpine, only to see Walter Smith clear off the line. Both teams wore black armbands out of respect for late Dons' director Douglas Philip.

Match 4R notes: Aberdeen's biggest gate so far this season. Harper collides with keeper Hamish McAlpine at the start of the second half and retires to have eight stitches in his gashed shin. United hold the Dons at bay until Henning Boel swoops upon Dave Robb's header to score off a post.

Match QF notes: A scrappy game, but Rangers were worth their win. It was skipper Martin Buchan's 22nd birthday. John Greig's effort bounced off the bar for Aberdonian Colin Jackson to poach the winner. The Dons had won at Ibrox in the league, but sadly relinquish their hold on the Scottish Cup.

European Cup-Winners' Cup

		Scorers, Times, and Referees	1	2	3	4	5	6	7	8	9	10	11	12 sub used
1:1 H HONVED (Hungary) 6 W 3-1 2-1	16/9 21,500	Graham 14, Harper 34, Murray S 83 / Pusztai 9 — Ref: A Bucheli (Switzerland)	Clark	Boel	Hermiston	Murray G*	Boel	Buchan M	McKay	Robb	Forrest	Harper	Graham	H'ton/Buchan G
			Bicskei	*Molnar*	*Ruzsinszky*	*Pusztai**	*Vari*	*Vagi*	*Tajfi*	*Toth*	*Kocsis*	*Komora*	*Szurgent*	*Pinter*
1:2 A HONVED 2 L 1-3 0-1	30/9 18,500 (aet)	Murray S 77 / Kocsis 17, 67, Kosma 59 — Ref: C Lo Bello (Italy) (Dons lose on penalties)	Clark	Boel	Hermiston	Murray G*	Young*	Buchan M	Robb	Harper	Forrest	Murray S	Graham	Willoughby
			Bicskei	*Tajfi*	*Ruzsinszky*	*Marosi*	*Vari**	*Vagi*	*Pusztai*	*Kocsis*	*Pinter*	*Kosma*	*Karakas**	*Toth/Tichy*

Match 1:1 notes: A night to remember. The white-clad Hungarians go in front when Clark turns Kocsis's 25-yarder against a post, but Pusztai reacts quickest. The Dons hit back, though Honved complain that Harper's goal was offside. Steve Murray held off two challenges before scoring the third.

Match 1:2 notes: Honved halve the deficit despite a linesman's raised flag. Kosma chips Clark to put Honved ahead on away goals. A twice-taken free-kick makes it 3-1 Steve Murray's deflected goal earns extra-time. Then penalties. At 2-2 Forrest hits the bar. The goalkeeper takes the winning kick.

League Table

	P	W	D	L	F	A	W	D	L	F	A	Pts
			Home						Away			
1 Celtic	34	15	1	1	43	7	10	5	2	46	16	56
2 ABERDEEN	34	11	6	0	38	7	13	0	4	30	11	54
3 St Johnstone	34	10	3	4	33	20	9	3	5	26	24	44
4 Rangers	34	10	5	2	33	10	6	4	7	25	24	41
5 Dundee	34	9	2	6	30	23	8	4	5	23	22	38
6 Dundee Utd	34	8	4	5	34	29	6	4	7	19	25	36
7 Falkirk	34	8	5	4	24	20	5	4	8	22	33	35
8 Morton	34	9	4	4	25	17	4	4	9	19	27	34
9 Motherwell	34	7	4	6	30	27	6	4	7	13	20	34
10 Airdrie	34	8	3	6	33	26	5	5	7	27	39	34
11 Hearts	34	8	5	4	24	16	5	2	10	17	24	33
12 Hibernian	34	8	4	5	33	24	2	6	9	14	29	30
13 Kilmarnock	34	5	6	6	26	31	5	2	10	17	36	28
14 Ayr	34	7	5	5	22	15	2	3	12	15	39	26
15 Clyde	34	5	5	7	19	23	3	5	9	14	36	26
16 Dunfermline	34	6	5	6	26	19	0	6	11	18	37	23
17 St Mirren	34	4	3	10	20	30	3	6	8	18	26	23
18 Cowdenbeath	34	1	2	14	13	39	6	1	10	20	38	17
	612	139	72	95	506	383	95	72	139	383	506	612

Odds & ends

Double wins: (7) Dundee, Dundee U, Kilmarnock, Clyde, Ayr, Hearts, Cowdenbeath.

Double Losses: (0).

Won from behind: (3) Morton (h), Hearts (a), Honved (h).

Lost from in front: (0).

High spots: 15 successive league wins from 10 October.

12 successive defensive clean sheets from 31 October.

Highest league position since 1955-56.

Twice scored 7 goals in a match (v Airdrie in Cup and Cowdenbeath).

Fewest league defeats (4) since World War II.

Fewest league goals (18) ever conceded.

Using just 19 players in all matches.

Low spots: Defeat at Hibs to end 15-game winning run.

Failure to beat Celtic in title decider at Pittodrie

Ever-presents: (3) Martin Buchan, Clark, Henning Boel (league only).

Hat-tricks: (3) Joe Harper (2), Dave Robb (1).

Leading scorer: (27) Joe Harper.

Appearances and Goals

			Appearances							Goals				
	Lge	Sub	LC	Sub	SC	Sub	Eur	Sub	Lge	Sub	LC	SC	Eur	Tot
Boel, Henning	34		5		4		2		2		2			4
Buchan, George	12		1	1					1					1
Buchan, Martin	34		6		4		2		2					2
Clark, Bobby	34		6		4		2							
Forrest, Jim	31	1	6		4		2		8		1	3		12
Graham, Arthur	31		5		4		2		5				1	6
Hamilton, Jim	5	1	1	1					2					2
Harper, Joe	30	1	5		4		2		19		5	2	1	27
Hermiston, Jim	31		6		4		2		1					1
McKay, Derek	2													
McMillan, Tommy	27		6		4		2		1					1
Murray, George	4	1	6				2		6		1		2	9
Murray, Steve	33		5		4		2		9		3	1		13
Robb, Dave	32		6		4		2		4			1		5
Taylor, Ian	14	2			3	1								
Whyte, Jim			1											
Williamson, Billy	1													
Willoughby, Alec	10	9	1			3			2	1				2
Young, Willie	9				1				6			1		7
(own-goals)														
19 players used	374	15	66	2	44	4	22	3	68	3	12	8	4	92

SCOTTISH LEAGUE DIVISION 1 — Manager: Jimmy Bonthrone — SEASON 1971-72

1. H DUNDEE — 4/9 · Att 13,188 · W · Pt 2 · F-A 3-0 · H-T 0-0
Scorers, Times, and Referees: Willoughby 59, Robb 68, Harper 69 — Ref: E Pringle

	1	2	3	4	5	6	7	8	9	10	11	12 sub used
Aberdeen	Clark	Boel	Hermiston	Murray S*	Young	Buchan M	Forrest	Robb	Harper	Willoughby	Graham	Taylor
Dundee	Hewitt	Wilson	Johnston	Steele	Phillip	Houston	Duncan*	Kinninmonth	Wallace	Scott	Lambie	Bryce

The third meeting between the clubs this season and Aberdeen's first win. They struggled early on, and Alec Willoughby's header only just got the better of goalkeeper Hewitt. But Joe Harper's goal was a gem. He beat two players out on the left before cutting in to score.

---

2. A ST JOHNSTONE — 11/9 · Att 7,930 · D · Pos 10 · Pt 3 · F-A 1-1 · H-T 1-1
Scorers, Times, and Referees: Robb 30; Hall 10 — Ref: R Gordon

	1	2	3	4	5	6	7	8	9	10	11	12 sub used
Aberdeen	Clark	Boel	Hermiston	Murray S	Young	Buchan M	Forrest	Robb	Harper	Taylor	Graham	
St Johnstone	Donaldson	Lambie	Coburn	Rennie	Gordon	Rooney	Aird	Hall	Pearson	Connolly	Aitken	

Dave Robb entered the referee's book twice; once for his goal - one for a naughty foul. Aberdeen deserved both points for their second-half offensive, but Jim Forrest's aim was wanting and Joe Harper was thwarted by a goalpost. The Dons can't afford to drop points like this.

---

3. H AIRDRIE — 18/9 · Att 14,133 · W · Pos 9 · Pt 5 · F-A 5-0 · H-T 2-0
Scorers, Times, and Referees: Harper 12, 15, Graham 71, Robb 72, 78 — Ref: J Gordon

	1	2	3	4	5	6	7	8	9	10	11	12 sub used
Aberdeen	Geoghegan	Boel	Hermiston	Murray S	Young	Buchan M	Forrest	Robb	Harper*	Willoughby	Graham	Taylor
Airdrie	Gourlay	Jonquin	McKay	Delaney	Goodwin	Whiteford	Wilson	Menzies	Busby	Jarvie	Cowan	

Aberdeen follow up their good result in Spain in the UEFA Cup with this demolition of Airdrie. An injury to Bobby Clark gives Geoghegan his first taste of the big time. Harper scores twice before being substituted in the second half. Drew Jarvie will sign from Airdrie in the summer.

---

4. A RANGERS — 25/9 · Att 41,236 · W · Pos 14 · Pt 7 · F-A 2-0 · H-T 1-0
Scorers, Times, and Referees: Murray S 37, Harper 78 — Ref: A McKenzie

	1	2	3	4	5	6	7	8	9	10	11	12 sub used
Aberdeen	Geoghegan	Boel	Hermiston	Murray S	Young	Buchan M	Forrest	Robb	Harper	Willoughby*	Miller R	Taylor
Rangers	McCloy	Jardine	Mathieson	Greig	Jackson	Smith	Penman	Conn	Stein	McDonald*	Johnston	McLean

Rangers have made a rocky start. This is their third defeat in four league matches. It was also the fourth time Aberdeen have won at Ibrox in the league in the past five seasons. Rangers did not take kindly to this embarrassment - they forced umpteen corners in their efforts to score.

---

5. H DUNFERMLINE — 2/10 · Att 14,885 · W · Pos 12 · Pt 9 · F-A 2-0 · H-T 1-0
Scorers, Times, and Referees: Harper 23p, Murray S 81 — Ref: J Callaghan

	1	2	3	4	5	6	7	8	9	10	11	12 sub used
Aberdeen	Geoghegan	Boel	Murray G	Murray S	Young	Buchan M	Forrest	Robb	Harper	Willoughby	Miller R	
Dunfermline	McGarr	Callaghan	Mercer	Fraser	Cushley	McNicoll	Scott	Mitchell	Edwards	O'Neill	Gillespie*	McBride

Joe Harper sends Ernie McGarr the wrong way with a spot-kick: Steve Murray leaves the keeper equally helpless with his effort. The key Dons player is Bertie Miller, playing only his second game, who is involved in both goals. With Celtic losing and Hibs drawing, Aberdeen go top.

---

6. A KILMARNOCK — 9/10 · Att 8,500 · W · Pos 15 · Pt 11 · F-A 3-0 · H-T 0-0
Scorers, Times, and Referees: Harper 62, Murray S 75, Forrest 86 — Ref: R Davidson

	1	2	3	4	5	6	7	8	9	10	11	12 sub used
Aberdeen	Clark	Murray G	Hermiston	Murray S	Young	Buchan M	Forrest	Robb	Harper	Willoughby	Miller R	
Kilmarnock	Hunter	Whyte	Cairns	Maxwell	Rodman	McGrory	Morrison	Gilmour	McCulloch	McSherry	Cook	

A Juventus spy sitting in the stand at Rugby Park must have left impressed with Aberdeen. So was Bobby Brown, the Scotland international manager. The following Wednesday Martin Buchan won his first full cap as a substitute in the 2-1 Hampden Park win over Portugal.

---

7. H HIBERNIAN — 16/10 · Att 24,450 · W · Pos 4 · Pt 13 · F-A 2-1 · H-T 0-1
Scorers, Times, and Referees: Harper 57, Young 65; Duncan 39 — Ref: J Paterson

	1	2	3	4	5	6	7	8	9	10	11	12 sub used
Aberdeen	Clark	Murray G	Hermiston	Murray S	Young	Buchan M	Forrest	Robb	Harper	Willoughby	Miller R	
Hibernian	Herriot	Brownlie	Schaedler	Stanton	Black	Blackley	Duncan	Hamilton	Baker	Gordon	Cropley	

A grudge match! Eddie Turnbull's new team versus his old. His new team take the first round: his old one the second and third. Joe Harper has struck a rich vein of form, scoring in Aberdeen's last five league matches. Willie Young's first ever goal wins the game for the Dons.

---

8. A MORTON — 23/10 · Att 4,843 · W · Pos 11 · Pt 15 · F-A 1-0 · H-T 1-0
Scorers, Times, and Referees: Murray S 1 — Ref: W Anderson

	1	2	3	4	5	6	7	8	9	10	11	12 sub used
Aberdeen	Clark	Murray G	Hermiston	Murray S	Young	Buchan M	Forrest	Robb	Harper	Willoughby	Graham	
Morton	Sorensen	Hayes	Laughton	Lumsden	McDerment	Clark	Chalmers	Mason	Osborne	Murphy	Smith	

Steve Murray's goal, seconds after kick-off, concludes the scoring and sends Aberdeen three points clear of Celtic. It is as well that Aberdeen scored when they did. They did not look like doing so afterwards. Harper fails to score in the league for the first time since early September.

---

9. H PARTICK THISTLE — 30/10 · Att 19,304 · W · Pos 8 · Pt 17 · F-A 7-2 · H-T 3-1
Scorers, Times, and Referees: Forrest 4, Robb 25, Harper 29, 89, 90, Young 40 og, Bone 64 (Willoughby 53, 80) — Ref: R Greenlees

	1	2	3	4	5	6	7	8	9	10	11	12 sub used
Aberdeen	Clark	Murray G	Hermiston	Murray S	Young	Buchan M	Forrest	Robb	Harper	Willoughby	Graham	
Partick Thistle	Rough	Hansen	Forsyth	Clark	Campbell	Strachan*	McQuade	Coulston	Bone	Rae A	Lawrie	

Partick Thistle are the new holders of the League Cup - but reputations get them nowhere in this match. Alan Rough bungles Forrest's early shot, letting it slip under his body. The best goal of all was Willie Young's bullet header - into his own goal. The Dons were 3-0 up at the time.

---

10. A CELTIC — 6/11 · Att 61,385 · D · Pos 2 · Pt 18 · F-A 1-1 · H-T 0-0
Scorers, Times, and Referees: McNeill 78 og; Hood 60 — Ref: J McRoberts

	1	2	3	4	5	6	7	8	9	10	11	12 sub used
Aberdeen	Clark	Murray G	Hermiston	Murray S	Young	Buchan M	Forrest	Robb	Harper	Willoughby	Graham	
Celtic	Connachan	Craig	Brogan	Hay	McNeill	Connelly	Johnstone	Hood	Dalglish	Macari	Callaghan	

Territorially, the Dons take an absolute battering from Celtic, and capitulate when Johnstone's cross is fired past Clark by Harry Hood. That goal would have taken Celtic top, but for Billy McNeill's own-goal, when under no pressure. Kenny Dalglish faced the Dons for the first time.

11 H EAST FIFE 13/11 — 1 W 5-0 — 14,298 18 20

Young 21, Robb 50, Harper 56, Taylor 75, [Hermiston 84] *Gorman*
Ref: R Valentine

Clark	Murray G	Hermiston	Taylor	Young	Buchan M	Forrest	Robb	Harper	Willoughby*	Graham	Miller R
Duncan	*McQuade*	*Cairns*	*Martis*	*Clarke*	*Honeyman*	*Hamilton*	*Barthwick*	*Hughes*	*Dailey**	*Bernard*	

Top versus bottom, so Aberdeen are on a hiding to nothing. They don't slip up, in fact they hardly raise a sweat. At the back of their minds is the prospect of mighty Juventus' visit on Wednesday. Yet again, centre-half Willie Young scores an important goal for the Dons.

12 A MOTHERWELL 20/11 — 1 W 4-0 — 5,000 12 22

Murray S 5, 85, Forrest 33, Harper 80
Ref: R Crawford

Clark	Murray G	Hermiston	Murray S	McMillan	Buchan M	Forrest	Robb	Harper	Willoughby*	Graham	Miller R
MacCrae	*Gillespie*	*Main*	*Forsyth*	*Muir, John*	*Campbell*	*McInally*	*Wark*	*Muir, Jim*	*Goldthorpe*	*Heron**	*Lawson*

Aberdeen show no ill-effects after the lessons handed out by Juventus. Joe Harper had one shot kicked off the line. He was then booked, and at long last scored. The Dons have now won on their last four league visits to Motherwell, and are averaging three goals a game this season.

13 H HEARTS 27/11 — 2 L 2-3 — 19,754 3 22

Harper 69, Robb 73
Ford 54, 86, 87
Ref: T Marshall

Clark	Murray G	Hermiston	Murray S	McMillan	Buchan M	Forrest	Robb	Harper	Willoughby	Graham*	Miller R
Cruickshank	*Sneddon*	*Kay*	*Brown*	*Anderson*	*Thomson*	*Townsend!*	*Benton*	*Ford*	*Winchester*	*Murray T*	

Disaster for Aberdeen. They lose their first home league match for two seasons. Donald Ford began by putting Hearts ahead with an angled drive. Hearts' pivot, Townsend, was sent off for dissent when Robb made it 2-1. Ford replied with two late headers for 10-man Hearts.

14 A AYR 4/12 — 2 W 5-1 — 7,582 12 24

Miller 14, Robb 23, Murray S 47, [Harper 67, 78] Graham 88p
Graham 88p
Ref: J Grant

Clark	Murray G	Hermiston	Murray S	McMillan	Buchan M	Forrest	Robb	Harper	Willoughby	Graham	Miller R
Stewart	*Filippi*	*Murphy*	*Fleming*	*Campbell*	*Reynolds*	*Doyle*	*Graham*	*Ingram*	*McGovern*	*Stevenson*	

Ally MacLeod's Ayr had only two draws to show from their past seven games. They start the match in sprightly fashion, but then Bertie Miller scores direct from a corner-kick and the flood-gates open. Robb gets himself booked for the second successive week. Harper can't stop scoring.

15 H CLYDE 11/12 — 2 W 4-1 — 13,194 17 26

Willoughby 29, Harper 30, Murray G 39, [Buchan M 75] McBride 17
Ref: E Thomson

Clark	Murray G	Hermiston*	Murray S	McMillan	Buchan M	Forrest	Robb	Harper	Willoughby	Graham	Miller R
Cairney	*Anderson*	*Swan*	*Burns*	*McHugh*	*Glasgow*	*Sullivan*	*McGrain*	*McBride*	*Hay*	*Ahern**	

Lowly Clyde have the nerve to go in front, and are made to pay for their temerity. Bertie Miller was involved in three of Aberdeen's four goals. Joe Harper has scored in each of his last five matches, and is set to extend this rich sequence. Martin Buchan scores his last goal for the Dons.

16 A DUNDEE UTD 18/12 — 2 W 3-0 — 13,707 11 28

Murray S 24, Willoughby 67, Harper 89p
Ref: A Crawley

Clark	Murray G	Hermiston*	Murray S	McMillan	Buchan M	Forrest	Robb	Harper	Willoughby	Graham	Miller R
McAlpine	*White J*	*Cameron*	*Markland**	*Smith D*	*Henry*	*Traynor*	*Smith W*	*Copland*	*Rolland*	*White A*	*Reid*

United's Walter Smith, wearing No 8, tries to mark Joe Harper out of the game. Hamish McAlpine is establishing himself as a bit of a nuisance at Pittodrie, and his gritty performances, but his defenders are less resilient than he. A last-minute penalty extends Harper's scoring sequence.

17 A FALKIRK 25/12 — W 3-0 — 6,885 30

Harper 51, 89, Miller 80
Ref: J Paterson

Clark	Murray G	Hermiston	Murray S	McMillan	Buchan M	Miller R	Robb	Harper	Willoughby	Graham
Rennie	*Gibson*	*Jones*	*Markie*	*Miller*	*Shirra*	*Hoggan*	*Young*	*Somner*	*Ferguson*	*Setterington*

A match played on Christmas Day. Aberdeen are due a victory over Falkirk. They lost at Brockville in the last game of last season, and also in the League Cup in September. Joe Harper is making a habit of scoring last-minute goals. The season is half over and the Dons have 30 points.

18 A DUNDEE 1/1 — 2 D 1-1 — 18,680 5 31

Harper 65p
Duncan 26
Ref: J Callaghan

Clark	Murray G	Hermiston	Murray S	McMillan	Buchan M	Miller R	Robb	Harper	Willoughby	Graham	
Hewitt	*Wilson R*	*Johnston*	*Stewart*	*Phillip*	*Ford**	*Duncan*	*Lambie*	*Wallace*	*Scott J*	*Wilson T*	*Kinninmonth*

Aberdeen were having the better of the exchanges when Duncan broke away to score for Dundee. The Dons deservedly equalised from the penalty-spot after Bertie Miller had his legs whipped from under him. This is a point won rather than a point lost, as Dundee are going well.

19 H ST JOHNSTONE 3/1 — W 4-2 — 24,235 33

Harper 5, Graham 15, 54, Murray S 19
Aitken 20, 88
Ref: J Gordon

Clark	Murray G	Hermiston*	Murray S	McMillan	Buchan M	Forrest*	Robb	Harper	Willoughby	Graham	Buchan G
Robertson	*Coburn*	*Argue*	*Rennie*	*Gordon*	*Rooney*	*Aird*	*Mercer*	*Connolly*	*Hall*	*Aitken*	

A large holiday crowd enjoy a Pittodrie goal-spree. Best of Aberdeen's goals was the first, scored by Joe Harper from a near-impossible angle. It extends his goal-scoring sequence to nine matches. It was about that his goal-supply dried up. Fingers crossed.

20 A AIRDRIE 8/1 — 2 W 2-1 — 5,681 18 35

Robb 1, Willoughby 59
Wilson 65
Ref: S Anderson

Clark	Murray G	Hermiston	Taylor	Young	Buchan M	Miller R	Robb	Harper	Willoughby	Graham	
McKenzie	*Jonquin*	*Clark*	*Menzies*	*McKinlay*	*Whiteford D*	*Cowan*	*Walker J*	*Whiteford**	*Jarvie*	*Wilson*	*Busby*

This win brings Aberdeen their first league double. They opened with a flourish, but by the end were hanging on by their finger-nails. Willie Young made his comeback after injury against Juventus. Harper's crosses produced both goals, and sent Airdrie to the bottom of the league.

21 H RANGERS 15/1 — 2 D 0-0 — 33,608 3 36

Ref: E Pringle

Geoghegan	Murray G	Hermiston	Murray S	Young	Buchan M	Miller R	Robb	Harper	Willoughby	Graham
McCloy	*Jardine*	*Mathieson*	*Greig*	*Johnstone D Smith*	*McLean*	*McDonald A Stein**	*Johnston W McDonald / Jackson*			

As had happened last season, this fixture ended goalless. A miserable day and a miserable afternoon for Dave Robb, booked for the fourth time this season. McCloy becomes the first goalkeeper to prevent the Dons scoring this season. Their usually rampant attack was stilled.

No	Date	Att	Pos	Pt	F-A	H-T	Scorers, Times, and Referees	1	2	3	4	5	6	7	8	9	10	11	12 sub used
22	A DUNFERMLINE 22/1	7,243	2	L 17 36	0-1	0-1	Gillespie 40 — Ref: R Gordon	Geoghegan	Murray G	Hermiston	Murray S	Young	Buchan M	Miller R	Robb	Harper	Willoughby*	Graham	Taylor
	opponents							*Arrol*	*Callaghan*	*Mercer*	*Fraser*	*McNicoll*	*O'Neill*	*Paterson*	*Scott*	*Millar*	*Mitchell*	*Gillespie*	

Two points behind Celtic before kick-off, Aberdeen now slip further behind. Last season Dunfermline's 1-0 home win over the Dons enabled them to escape relegation. This time it brings their first win in 13 games. Steve Murray's back-pass stopped short in the mud for the goal.

No	Date	Att	Pos	Pt	F-A	H-T	Scorers, Times, and Referees	1	2	3	4	5	6	7	8	9	10	11	12 sub used
23	H KILMARNOCK 29/1	12,981	2	W 10 38	4-2	2-1	Harper 18, 30, Graham 57, Murray S 76 / Fleming 35, Cook 64 — Ref: A McKenzie	Marshall	Murray G	Hermiston	Murray S	Young	Buchan M	Miller R	Robb	Harper	Willoughby	Graham	Taylor
	opponents							*Hunter*	*Whyte*	*Dickson*	*Maxwell*	*Rodman*	*McGrory*	*McSherry*	*Gilmour*	*Mathie*	*Fleming*	*Cook*	

When Joe Harper stopped scoring Aberdeen wobbled. The one was inevitably linked to the other. Now Joey gets back to scoring ways, helped by McSherry's inattentive back-pass to his goalkeeper. Killie never get back on terms. Former Don Jim Whyte makes a return to Pittodrie.

No	Date	Att	Pos	Pt	F-A	H-T	Scorers, Times, and Referees	1	2	3	4	5	6	7	8	9	10	11	12 sub used
24	A HIBERNIAN 12/2	21,389	2	D 4 39	2-2	1-1	Harper 39, 71 / O'Rourke 30, Duncan 62 — Ref: R Davidson	Marshall	Murray G	Hermiston	Murray S	Young	Buchan M	Miller R	Robb	Harper	Willoughby	Graham	
	opponents							*Herriot*	*McEwan*	*Schaedler*	*Stanton*	*Black*	*Blackley*	*Hamilton*	*O'Rourke*	*Gordon*	*Cropley*	*Duncan*	

New Scotland manager Tommy Docherty takes in this pulsating match. Joe Harper takes his personal tally to six goals in three league and cup games. O'Rourke scored for Turnbull's new team, firing round a defensive wall. O'Rourke later struck Gordon Marshall's crossbar.

No	Date	Att	Pos	Pt	F-A	H-T	Scorers, Times, and Referees	1	2	3	4	5	6	7	8	9	10	11	12 sub used
25	H MORTON 19/2	14,230	2	W 14 41	1-0	1-0	Willoughby 5 — Ref: A Webster	Marshall	Murray G	Hermiston	Murray S	Young	Buchan M	Miller R	Robb	Harper	Willoughby	Graham*	Forrest
	opponents							*Sorensen*	*Thorup*	*Shevlane*	*Clark*	*Anderson*	*Rankin*	*Booth*	*Lumsden*	*Gillies*	*Mason*	*Murphy*	

These two sides will meet again in the Scottish Cup. It is hoped that the cup-tie will offer better entertainment than this dreary spectacle, redeemed only by Willoughby's goal. Anderson kept Joe Harper in his pocket throughout, and not many defenders have done that this season.

No	Date	Att	Pos	Pt	F-A	H-T	Scorers, Times, and Referees	1	2	3	4	5	6	7	8	9	10	11	12 sub used
26	A PARTICK THISTLE 4/3	11,340	2	L 6 41	0-2	0-2	Forsyth 11p, Glavin 31 — Ref: B Padden	Marshall	Boel	Hermiston	Murray S	Young	Murray G	Miller R*	Robb	Harper	Willoughby	Graham	Taylor
	opponents							*Rough*	*Hansen*	*Forsyth*	*Smith*	*Clark*	*Strachan*	*McQuade**	*Glavin*	*Coulston*	*Rae A*	*Lawrie*	*Gibson*

The whole of north-east Scotland is shattered by the transfer of Martin Buchan to Manchester United. Without their captain the Dons look a listless crew. Willoughby headed against the bar and Alan Rough made saves beyond the call of duty. Thistle's penalty was a farce.

No	Date	Att	Pos	Pt	F-A	H-T	Scorers, Times, and Referees	1	2	3	4	5	6	7	8	9	10	11	12 sub used
27	H CELTIC 11/3	32,853	2	D 1 42	1-1	0-0	Harper 82 / Lennox 73 — Ref: J Gordon	Marshall	Boel	Hermiston	Murray S	Young	Murray G	Forrest	Robb	Harper	Willoughby	Graham	
	opponents							*Williams*	*McGrain*	*Brogan*	*Murdoch*	*McNeill*	*Connelly*	*Hood*	*Hay*	*Dalglish**	*Macari*	*Lennox*	*Callaghan*

The loss of Martin Buchan and defeat at Partick took the edge off this match. Aberdeen have a fine recent record against Celtic, but fell behind when George Connelly made a goal for Bobby Lennox. Joe Harper's equaliser deprived Celtic of only their second point in 17 games.

No	Date	Att	Pos	Pt	F-A	H-T	Scorers, Times, and Referees	1	2	3	4	5	6	7	8	9	10	11	12 sub used
28	A EAST FIFE 21/3	4,850	2	W 44	1-0	0-0	Harper 49 — Ref: A Patterson	Marshall	Boel	Hermiston	Murray S	Young	Buchan M	Miller R	Robb	Harper	Taylor	Graham*	Walker
	opponents							*Gorman*	*Duncan*	*McQuade*	*McLaren*	*Martis*	*Clarke*	*Bernard*	*Borthwick*	*Hughes*	*Love**	*McPhee*	*Walker*

Three days previously the Dons had been put out of the Scottish Cup by Hibs. Their season is effectively over, and the morale among the players is visibly crumbling. Joe Harper's phenomenal goal-tally deserves better. East Fife will escape relegation by one point.

No	Date	Att	Pos	Pt	F-A	H-T	Scorers, Times, and Referees	1	2	3	4	5	6	7	8	9	10	11	12 sub used
29	H MOTHERWELL 25/3	9,391	2	W 10 46	4-1	1-1	Forrest 20, Harper 53p, 87, Robb 79 / McInally 37 — Ref: R Valentine	Marshall	Boel	Hermiston	Murray S	Young	Wilson	Forrest*	Robb	Harper	Taylor	Graham	Willoughby
	opponents							*Fallon*	*Muir*	*Whiteford*	*Forsyth*	*McCallum*	*Watson*	*Campbell*	*McInally*	*McCabe*	*Lawson*	*Heron**	*Main*

Referee Bob Valentine refuses two clear-cut penalty awards - in addition to the one he did give - for Aberdeen. He also sends Jim Hermiston off, which provokes some unseemly crowd disturbances. Pittodrie is not a happy place to be: the place is still seething over Martin Buchan.

No	Date	Att	Pos	Pt	F-A	H-T	Scorers, Times, and Referees	1	2	3	4	5	6	7	8	9	10	11	12 sub used
30	A HEARTS 1/4	7,189	2	L 5 46	0-1	0-0	Renton 52 — Ref: T Kellock	Clark	Boel	Hermiston	Murray S	Young	Wilson	Miller R	Robb	Harper	Taylor	Graham*	Willoughby
	opponents							*Garland*	*Clunie*	*Jefferies*	*Thomson*	*Anderson*	*Wood*	*Murray T*	*Brown*	*Ford*	*Carruthers*	*Renton*	

Edinburgh is becoming a graveyard for Aberdeen this season. Knocked out of the Cup at Easter Road, they are now beaten a second time in the league by Hearts - Aberdeen's first double loss for two seasons. Behind the scenes they have signed up 16-year-old winger John McMaster.

No	Date	Att	Pos	Pt	F-A	H-T	Scorers, Times, and Referees	1	2	3	4	5	6	7	8	9	10	11	12 sub used
31	H AYR 8/4	8,240	2	W 13 48	7-0	2-0	Harper 27, 38, 61, 83, Miller 55, [Taylor 64, Young 68]Stewart — Ref: J Paterson	Clark	Boel	Hermiston	Murray S	Young	Wilson	Miller R	Robb	Harper	Taylor	Graham	Stevenson
	opponents							*Stewart*	*McFadzean*	*Murphy*	*Fleming*	*Quinn*	*Filippi*	*Graham*	*McLean*	*Ingram*	*McGregor**	*Doyle*	

'Joey for Scotland' sing the Pittodrie faithful, and the wee man confirms his place as the country's leading marksman. It is not the first time he has scored four in one match; he did so against Airdrie in the League Cup last season. The players are now off for a short holiday in Greece.

32. A CLYDE 15/4 — 2 D 0-0 0-0 — 1,535 17 49

| Clark | Boel McCulloch | Hermiston McHugh | Murray S Beattie | Young McVie | Wilson Burns | Miller R* McGrain | Robb Millar | Harper Flanagan | Taylor Hulston | Graham Ahern* | Purdie Sullivan |

Ref: R Anderson

Clyde are desperate for points to escape the drop. Their fight goes on. But at the other end two things are settled. Celtic are confirmed as champions yet again, while Aberdeen have clinched runners-up spot ahead of Rangers. This is the smallest crowd to see the Dons this season.

33. A DUNDEE UTD 22/4 — 2 L 0-2 0-2 — 4,743 9 49

| Clark | Boel Rolland | Hermiston Cameron J | Murray S Copland | Young Smith D | Wilson Gray | Forrest Fleming | Robb Kopel | Harper Gardner | Taylor Mitchell | Graham* Cameron K | Willoughby |

Mitchell 25, Smith D 32p
Ref: I Foote

You would never believe that Aberdeen won 4-0 on the same ground in February in the Scottish Cup. No wonder Dons' officials are off hunting new players. For the second successful season the team have run out of puff in the late winter and spring. Three hours without a goal.

34. H FALKIRK 29/4 — 2 D 0-0 0-0 — 8,771 14 50

| Clark | Boel Kennedy S | Hermiston Shirra | Murray S Cattanach | Young Markie | Wilson Kennedy J | Forrest Hoggan | Robb Harley | Harper Jack | Taylor Ferguson | Graham Somner | |

Ref: G Smith

Pittodrie is not amused by this apology of a football match. The high hopes of the autumn are replaced by a palpable lack of heart and spirit. The crowd boo and slow-handclap the players, astonishing really, when they have finished second in the championship. Falkirk avoid the drop.

Average Home 17,130
Away 13,300

Scottish League Cup - Section 2

1. H DUNDEE 14/8 — D 1-1 0-1 — 19,053

| Clark | Williamson Wilson | Murray G Johnston | Murray S Steele | McMillan Phillip | Buchan M Houston | Buchan G Duncan | Robb Scott I | Harper Wallace | Willoughby Scott J | Graham Lambie* | Bryce |

Robb 57
Duncan 17
Ref: E Thomson

George Buchan holds his head in despair as he shoots against the goalpost and watches the ball fly across the goalmouth before swerving out of play for a goal-kick. Dropping a home point at the outset does not enhance Aberdeen's chances of qualifying. They will look to win at Clyde.

2. A CLYDE 18/8 — W 2-0 2-0 — 2,027

| Clark | Boel McCulloch | Murray G Glasgow | Murray S Burns | McMillan McVie | Buchan M McHugh | Buchan G* Thomson | Robb McGrain | Harper Hulston | Willoughby Ahern | Graham McColligan* Flanagan | Williamson |

Harper 18, 33
Ref: W Mullen

Aberdeen - or rather Joe Harper - do the business in the first half. They ended the match relieved that Clyde's Hulston missed the second-half chances that came his way. This is the Dons' fourth win over Clyde in succession, and sets them up nicely for the game with Falkirk.

3. H FALKIRK 21/8 — W 1-0 1-0 — 17,339

| Clark | Boel Rennie | Hermiston Jones | Murray G* Markie | McMillan Miller | Buchan M Gibson | Murray S Hoggan | Robb Young | Harper Jack | Willoughby Ferguson | Graham Shirra | Williamson |

Harper 78
Ref: I Foote

Aberdeen tried to beat Falkirk with the heavy artillery, but with time running out had to rely on a moment of Joe Harper magic to take both points. Aberdeen had lost at Brockville in the final league match of last season. They now have a fighting chance of making the quarter-finals.

4. H CLYDE 25/8 — W 5-0 0-0 — 15,542

| Clark | Boel 79 McCulloch | Hermiston Anderson | Murray S Swan | McMillan Burns | Buchan M Beattie | Robb Sullivan | Robb McDonald | Harper Thomson* | Willoughby McGrain | Graham McColligan McHugh | |

Graham 56, 64, 83, Harper 62, Willoughby 79
Ref: J Grant

The Dons spent nearly an hour knocking at the door before it caved in. Arthur Graham's volley paved the way for his first ever hat-trick. This result means little, in reality, since Clyde will lose to everybody else. It is a three-horse race at the top of Section 2 with everything to play for.

5. A DUNDEE 28/8 — L 1-3 1-1 — 11,875

| Clark | Boel Hewitt | Hermiston Wilson R | Murray S Johnston | McMillan* Phillip | Buchan M Houston | Forrest Duncan | Robb Kinninmonth Wallace | Harper Wallace | Willoughby Scott | Graham Wilson J | Buchan G |

Willoughby 38
Wallace 26, 48, Houston 55
Ref: J McRoberts

Aberdeen have two away matches to come. Two points, or maybe even one, should see them through, so this result is disappointing though not fatal to their chances. Alec Willoughby gave away Dundee's first goal, then headed an equaliser. In the league Aberdeen will draw at Dens Pk.

6. A FALKIRK 1/9 — L 1-3 1-0 — 11,865

| Clark | Boel Rennie | Hermiston Jones | Murray S McLaughlin | Young Miller | Buchan M Shirra | Forrest Hoggan | Robb Jack* | Harper Young | Willoughby Ferguson | Graham Setterington Gibson | |

Forrest 19
McLaughlin 46, Ferguson 60, 65
Ref: T Marshall

Dundee are sure to beat Clyde, but by how many goals? A draw at Brockville will keep Aberdeen above Falkirk on goal-difference, and in all probability edge out Dundee too. A quarter-final with Hibs awaits, but Aberdeen are sunk by the pace and power of Alex Ferguson.

Qual					
Falkirk	6	4	1	1	12	6	9
Dundee	6	3	2	1	10	5	8
ABERDEEN	6	3	1	2	11	6	7
Clyde	6	0	0	6	2	17	0

Scottish Cup

3 A DUNDEE UTD 2 W 4-0 H-T 1-0
5/2   12,974 13
Scorers: Miller 7, Harper 64p, 67, Young 90
Ref: A McKenzie

1	2	3	4	5	6	7	8	9	10	11	12 sub used
Clark	Murray G	Hermiston	Murray S	Young	Buchan M	Miller R	Robb	Harper	Willoughby	Graham	
McAlpine	Rolland	Cameron J	Markland	Smith D	Smith W	Cameron K	Knox	Copland*	Gardner*	Mitchell	Traynor

A repeat of last season's cup draw. The end result makes it look easier for Aberdeen than it was. With the Dons ahead 1-0 United were given a penalty when Martin Buchan handled. Kenny Cameron's spot-kick was saved by Clark. Joe Harper then scored from the spot for Aberdeen.

4 H MORTON 2 W 1-0 H-T 1-0
26/2   18,277 14
Scorer: Willoughby 42
Ref: R Davidson

1	2	3	4	5	6	7	8	9	10	11	12 sub used
Marshall	Murray G	Hermiston	Murray S	Young	Buchan M	Forrest	Robb	Harper	Willoughby	Miller R*	Graham
Sorensen	Thorup	Shevlane	Clark	Anderson	Rankin	Chalmers	Lumsden	Gillies*	Mason	Murphy	Osborne!

A carbon copy of last week's league match. Both times Alec Willoughby nabs the one and only goal. Morton substitute Osborne was sent off two minutes after coming on, following an exchange of views with Willie Young. Pittodrie fears Martin Buchan is headed for Old Trafford.

QF A HIBERNIAN 2 L 0-2 H-T 0-1
18/3   25,936 5
Scorers: O'Rourke 1, Baker 49
Ref: W Mullen

1	2	3	4	5	6	7	8	9	10	11	12 sub used
Marshall	Boel	Hermiston	Murray S*	Young	Murray G	Forrest	Taylor	Harper	Willoughby	Graham	Wilson
Herriot	Brownlie	Schaedler	Stanton	Black	Blackley	Hamilton	O'Rourke	Baker	Gordon	Duncan	

After 17 seconds O'Rourke snaps up Gordon's pass and fires left-footed past Marshall. The Dons are not in the game. Joe Baker, at the second attempt, doubles Hibs' lead. Steve Murray, Dons' new skipper, was substituted after 75 minutes and did not like it. Joe Harper was carried off.

UEFA Cup

1:1 A CELTA VIGO 4 W 2-0 H-T 0-0
15/9 (Spain)   35,000
Scorers: Harper 51, Forrest 73
Ref: R Ellis (France)

1	2	3	4	5	6	7	8	9	10	11	12 sub used
Clark	Boel	Hermiston*	Murray S	Young	Buchan M	Forrest	Robb	Harper	Willoughby	Graham	Murray G
Gost	Pedrito	Dominguez	Hidalgo	Manolo	Rivera	Lezcano	Juan	Rodilla	Almargo*	Jiminez	Rivas

The Fairs Cup has been renamed the UEFA Cup. The Spanish club went all last season unbeaten at home. Aberdeen employed the offside trap, despite the fact that the linesmen helping the French referee were Spanish. Harper lobbed the first goal and Forrest scored direct from a corner.

1:2 H CELTA VIGO 3 W 1-0 H-T 0-0
29/9   20,000
Scorer: Harper 89
Ref: K Wahlen (Norway)
(Dons win 3-0 on aggregate)

1	2	3	4	5	6	7	8	9	10	11	12 sub used
Geoghegan	Boel	Murray G	Murray S	Young	Buchan M	Forrest	Robb	Harper	Willoughby	Buchan G	Rivera/Jimenez
Alarcia	Pedrito	Navarro	Manolo	Dominguez	Rivas	Lezcano	Juan	Rodilla	Almargo*	Suco*	

Aberdeen had it won in Spain. They knew it, and so did their opponents. The match marked Joe Harper's 100th first team appearance for Aberdeen. He proceeded to waste a penalty-kick before crashing the ball home from 25 yards in the final minute. A rare win over the Spanish.

2:1 A JUVENTUS 1 L 0-2 H-T 0-1
27/10 (Italy)   35,000
Scorers: Anastasi 5, Capello 55
Ref: P Nicolov (Bulgaria)

1	2	3	4	5	6	7	8	9	10	11	12 sub used
Clark	Murray G	Hermiston	Murray S	Young*	Buchan M	Forrest	Robb	Harper	Willoughby	Graham	Taylor
Carmignani	Spinosi	Marchetti	Morini*	Salvadore	Furino	Haller	Savoldi	Anastasi	Capello	Bettega	Roveta

Franco Caussio was sent off in Round 1, against Malta, and is banned from the Stadio Communale. The world's most expensive player, Pietro Anastasi, runs from the halfway line to score. Capello's free-kick is deflected for No 2. Bonthrone hauls off Willie Young before he is sent off.

2:2 H JUVENTUS 1 D 1-1 H-T 0-0
17/11   29,500
Scorer: Harper 77
Anastasi 50
Ref: T Boosten (Holland)
(Dons lose 1-3 on aggregate)

1	2	3	4	5	6	7	8	9	10	11	12 sub used
Clark	Murray G	Hermiston*	Murray S	Young*	Buchan M	Forrest	Robb	Harper	Willoughby	Graham	Buchan G/Taylor
Carmignani	Spinosi	Marchetti	Furino	Morini	Salvadore	Haller	Causio	Anastasi	Capello	Bettega	Roveta

Last week Pittodrie staged a full international against Belgium. Now it hosts the might of Juventus, top of the Italian League. The pitch was sprinkled with snow. Anastasi beats Martin Buchan and shoots inside Clark's near post. The Dons need four, but get one, from Harper's head.

League Table

	P	W	D	L	F	A	W	D	L	F	A	Pts
		Home					Away					
1 Celtic	34	15	1	1	48	14	13	3	1	48	14	60
2 ABERDEEN	34	13	3	1	54	13	8	5	4	26	13	50
3 Rangers	34	11	0	6	41	21	10	2	5	30	17	44
4 Hibernian	34	11	2	4	34	13	8	4	5	28	21	44
5 Dundee	34	8	6	3	30	14	6	7	4	29	24	41
6 Hearts	34	10	5	2	29	17	3	8	6	24	32	39
7 Partick This	34	9	5	3	35	23	3	5	9	18	31	34
8 St Johnstone	34	7	5	5	26	21	3	3	9	26	37	32
9 Dundee Utd	34	7	5	5	36	37	5	2	10	19	33	31
10 Motherwell	34	9	3	5	33	26	2	4	11	16	43	29
11 Kilmarnock	34	7	3	7	27	28	4	3	10	22	36	28
12 Ayr	34	5	6	6	20	19	4	3	10	20	39	28
13 Morton	34	5	5	7	23	20	5	0	12	23	32	27
14 Falkirk	34	7	4	6	26	23	3	3	11	18	37	27
15 Airdrie	34	4	6	7	25	37	3	6	8	19	39	26
16 East Fife	34	2	7	8	19	34	3	8	6	15	27	25
17 Clyde	34	5	4	8	16	26	2	6	9	17	40	24
18 Dunfermline	34	5	5	7	19	24	2	4	11	12	26	23
	612	140	77	89	541	410	89	77	140	410	541	612

Appearances and Goals

	Appearances								Goals					
	Lge	Sub	LC	Sub	SC	Sub	Eur	Sub	Lge	Sub	LC	SC	Eur	Tot
Boel, Henning	14		5		1		2							
Buchan, George		1	2					1		1				1
Buchan, Martin	25		6		2		3							
Clark, Bobby	22		6		1		4							
Forrest, Jim	21	1	3		2		4		4		1		1	6
Geoghegan, Andy	5						1	1						
Graham, Arthur	27	2	6	1	2		3		4		3			7
Harper, Joe	34		6		3		4		33		4	2	3	42
Hermiston, Jim	33		4		3		3		1					1
McMillan, Tommy	8		5		2									
Marshall, Gordon	7													
Miller, Bertie	20	3			2		1	1	3			1		4
Murray, George	23		3		3		3		1	1				1
Murray, Steve	32		6		3		4		10					10
Purdie, Ian		1						1						
Robb, Dave	34		6		2		4		10		1			11
Taylor, Ian	10	5	1	2	1	1			2	2				2
Williamson, Billy		3	1			1								
Willoughby, Alec	26		6		3		4		7		2	1		10
Wilson, Tom	7													
Young, Willie	26				3		4		3			1		4
(own-goals)														1
21 players used	374	16	66	3	33	2	44	4	80	4	11	5	4	100

Odds & ends

Double wins: (6) Airdrie, Kilmarnock, Morton, E Fife, Motherwell, Ayr.
Double losses: (1) Hearts.

Won from behind: (2) Hibs (h), Clyde (h).
Lost from in front: (2) Hearts (h), Falkirk (LC).

High-spots: 7 consecutive league wins from 18 September.
Unbeaten in first 12 league games.
Scoring in every match until the 21st league game.
Joe Harper scoring 42 goals in all competitions.
Never losing to either of the Old Firm.

Low spots: mediocre second half to the season.
Early elimination from both domestic cups.
Transfer of Martin Buchan to Manchester Utd in February.

Ever-presents: (2) Joe Harper, Dave Robb (league only).
Hat-tricks: (3) Joe Harper (2), Arthur Graham (1).
Leading scorer: (42) Joe Harper.

SCOTTISH LEAGUE DIVISION 1

Manager: Jimmy Bonthrone — SEASON 1972-73.

No	Date	Att	Pos	Pt	F-A	H-T	Scorers, Times, and Referees	1	2	3	4	5	6	7	8	9	10	11	12 sub used
1	H 2/9 HIBERNIAN	16,947		2	W 1-0	0-0	Harper 48 — Ref: A McKenzie	Clark	Murray G	Hermiston	Murray S*	Boel	Young	Willoughby	Robb	Harper	Jarvie	Taylor	Buchan G
								Herriot	*Brownlie*	*Schaedler*	*Stanton*	*Black*	*Blackley*	*Edwards*	*Hazel*	*Gordon*	*Cropley**	*Duncan*	*McEwan*
2	A 9/9 DUNDEE	10,100	5	3	D 0-0	0-0	Ref: R Davidson	Geoghegan	Willoughby	Hermiston	Murray S	Boel	Young	Forrest	Robb	Harper	Jarvie*	Taylor	Graham
								Hewitt	*Wilson R*	*Houston*	*Robinson*	*Philip*	*Stewart*	*Wilson J*	*Duncan*	*Wallace*	*Scott J*	*Scott!**	*Ford*
3	H 16/9 ST JOHNSTONE	9,917	7	4	D 0-0	0-0	Ref: J Paterson	Clark	Willoughby	Hermiston	Murray G	Boel	Young	Buchan G*	Robb	Harper	Jarvie	Taylor	Graham
								Donaldson	*Lambie*	*Argue*	*Kinnell*	*Rennie*	*Rooney*	*Hall*	*Muir*	*Pearson*	*McPhee*	*Aitken*	
4	A 23/9 DUMBARTON	6,854	5	6	W 2-1	0-1	Jarvie 49, Harper 52; Wilson D 32 — Ref: R Henderson	Clark	Willoughby	Hermiston	Murray S	Boel	Young	Buchan G	Robb	Harper	Jarvie	Graham*	Miller R
								Williams	*Menzies*	*Wilkinson*	*Cushley*	*Bolton*	*Graham*	*Coleman**	*Jenkins*	*McCormack*	*Wilson K*	*Wilson D*	*Paterson*
5	H 30/9 MOTHERWELL	11,351	2	8	W 7-2	5-1	Robb 2, Harper 12,18p,79, Jarvie 21, McClymont 44p, Gray 55 [Murray S 86]; (Dons' other goal: Whiteford 20 og) — Ref: I Foote	Clark	Willoughby	Hermiston	Murray S	Murray G	Young	Graham*	Robb	Harper	Jarvie	Taylor	Miller R
								MacCrae	*Whiteford*	*Wark*	*Forsyth*	*McCallum*	*Muir*	*Gray*	*Murray**	*Lawson*	*McClymont*	*Martin*	*Goldthorp!*
6	A 7/10 HEARTS	11,763	3	8	L 1-2	0-1	Harper 79; Carruthers 35, Ford 51 — Ref: R Gordon	Clark	Willoughby	Hermiston	Murray S	Murray G	Young	Forrest	Robb	Harper	Jarvie	Graham*	Miller R
								Garland	*Clunie*	*Oliver*	*Kay*	*Anderson*	*Wood*	*Murray*	*Brown*	*Ford*	*Carruthers*	*Lynch*	
7	H 14/10 FALKIRK	14,165	4	9	D 2-2	1-2	Taylor 40,81; Scott 16, Willoughby 45 og — Ref: R Marshall	Clark	Willoughby	Hermiston	Murray S	Young	Taylor	Graham*	Robb	Harper	Jarvie	Miller R*	Graham
								Donaldson	*Kennedy S*	*Shirra*	*Markie*	*McMillan*	*McLeod*	*Setterington*	*Harley**	*Scott*	*Young*	*Jack*	*Somner*
8	A 21/10 AYR	7,823	4	11	W 3-2	3-1	Jarvie 8, Harper 18, 40; McLean 23, Fleming 88 — Ref: T Kyle	Clark	Willoughby	Hermiston	Murray S	Young	Taylor	Varga	Robb	Harper!	Jarvie	Mitchell	
								Stewart	*Filippi*	*Murphy*	*Fleming*	*McAnespie*	*McCulloch*	*Doyle*	*Graham!*	*Ingram*	*McLean*	*Stevenson**	*McGovern*
9	H 28/10 CELTIC	34,262	4	11	L 2-3	1-2	Varga 25, 83; Deans 13, Macari 16, Dalglish 67 — Ref: E Pringle	Clark	Willoughby	Hermiston	Murray S	Young*	Taylor	Varga	Robb	Harper!	Jarvie	Mitchell	Graham
								Williams	*McGrain*	*McCluskey*	*Hay*	*McNeill*	*Connelly*	*Dalglish*	*Macari*	*Deans*	*Callaghan*	*Lennox*	
10	A 4/11 PARTICK THISTLE	8,962	4	13	W 2-0	1-0	Harper 29, Miller 80 — Ref: J Gordon	Clark	Murray G	Hermiston	Murray S	Mitchell	Taylor	Varga	Robb	Harper	Jarvie	Miller R	Graham
								Rough	*Forsyth*	*Ralston*	*Glavin*	*Clark*	*Strachan*	*Gibson*	*Coulston*	*Craig*	*Rae A*	*McQuade**	*Chalmers*

Match notes

1. Having put himself in the headlines in midweek with a hat-trick against Queen's Park, Joe Harper now accepts Taylor's pass to send Eddie Turnbull's boys home pointless. It is at Easter Road that the Dons seem to flounder these days. We shall see what happens later in the season.

2. This game had its moments. But there were not many of them. Geoghegan made two splendid saves from Duncan, one in each half. It is early days, but there is not much sign of Aberdeen's rapier attacks this season. Drew Jarvie will net his share of goals once he settles in.

3. Aberdeen have still to concede a league goal. Trouble is they still don't look like scoring themselves. George Buchan was stretchered off in this match. After four and a half hours of league football, just one goal has been scored at either end. The Dons won't challenge Celtic at this rate.

4. Willie Young concedes countless free-kicks as Aberdeen back-pedal in the closing stages. Harper's winner is a delightful left-footed shot on the turn. Drew Jarvie nets his first league goal for his new club, having already bagged five in the League Cup section matches.

5. The Dons have just lost 3-6 to Borussia. This is Motherwell's first league defeat of the season. They don't take too kindly to it. Their principal tormentor is Dave Robb. He was treated harshly, especially by Goldthorp, who was sent off near the end. After 21 minutes the score was 5-0.

6. Hearts have been a thorn in Aberdeen's side in recent seasons. And they continue to be so. Carruthers missed a hatful of chances before finally opening the scoring. Joe Harper's counter came too late to save the day. He had earlier hit a post. Had it gone in the Dons might have survived.

7. This game comes alive just before half-time. Taylor levels for Aberdeen; then Shirra pulls down Jarvie but Donaldson saves Harper's penalty. Willoughby then turns Harley's cross into his own net. Zoltan Varga makes his debut. In midweek Clark and Harper are capped in Denmark.

8. Zoltan Varga must wonder what kind of football Scottish fans appreciate. Harper and Ayr's Graham are sent off after a touchline tussle spotted by a linesman. Several other players are booked in an altogether unpleasant match. Not much chance for Varga to show his skills here.

9. This is the stage Zoltan Varga needed. His first goal was a swerving 20-yarder; his second is an exquisite lob. Too bad they were not enough to protect Aberdeen from their first defeat by Celtic since October 1969, seven games ago. Bobby Clark almost signs for Stoke after the match.

10. Partick are back in Division 1 after two years in Division 2. They belie their lowly position to play their part in a cracking match that is once again illuminated by Varga's extravagant skills. Aberdeen were never sure of both points until Bertie Miller's late header went in off a post.

11 H EAST FIFE 11/11 — Att 10,651 — Pos 3 (opp 8) — Pts 15 — **W 4-3** (HT 0-2)

Scorers: Jarvie 48, Will 60, McQuade 68 og, Robb 70p — McGarr / McPhee 21, Honeyman 32, Hegarty 85
Ref: A McDonald

Aberdeen: Clark, Willoughby, Hermiston, Murray S, Mitchell, Taylor, Varga, Robb, Forrest, Jarvie, Miller R
East Fife: *Duncan, McQuade, Borthwick, Martis, Clarke, Hegarty, Hamilton, Honeyman, McPhee, Bernard*

This is the stuff to have the fans roaring. Two down at the break, Aberdeen besiege East Fife's goalmouth. The suspended Harper was hardly missed. But he scores for Scotland against Denmark in midweek.

---

12 H KILMARNOCK 18/11 — Att 10,234 — Pos 3 (opp 17) — Pts 17 — **W 3-0** (HT 1-0)

Scorers: Taylor 28, Harper 50, Jarvie 54
Ref: G Smith

Aberdeen: Clark, Willoughby, Hermiston, Murray G, Murray S, Taylor, Robb, Harper, Forrest, Jarvie, Miller R
Kilmarnock: *Hunter, Whyte, Robertson, Maxwell, McSherry, Lee, Dickson, Morrison, Smith, Cook*, Cairns*

Joe Harper scored one, and hit the post twice. Of Scotland's two international goalkeepers on view, Kilmarnock's Alistair Hunter was much the busier. The Dons have now won three league games in a row. They will not match that league consistency throughout the rest of the season.

---

13 A DUNDEE UTD 25/11 — Att 8,173 — Pos 4 (opp 6) — Pts 17 — **L 2-3** (HT 0-1)

Scorers: Varga 58, Murray S 86 / Gardner 29, 70, Copland 48
Ref: W Mullen

Aberdeen: Clark, Willoughby, Hermiston, Murray S, Mitchell, Taylor, Varga, Robb, Harper, Jarvie, Miller R
Dundee Utd: *McAlpine, Rolland, Markland, Copland, Smith D, Henry, Kopel, Fleming, Mitchell, Gardner, White*

Aberdeen look jittery in defence and are a well-beaten side by the close. United's second goal was the killer blow. Bobby Clark came for a cross and was left stranded as Copland put it in. Clark held his head in his hands. Steve Murray's goal made the result look closer than it was.

---

14 A AIRDRIE 2/12 — Att 4,059 — Pos 4 (opp 18) — Pts 18 — **D 1-1** (HT 0-0)

Scorers: Murray S 54 / Wilson 77
Ref: J Grant

Aberdeen: Clark, Willoughby, Hermiston, Murray S, Young, Taylor, Varga, Robb, Harper, Jarvie, Miller R*
Airdrie: *McKenzie, Jonquin, Clarke, Menzies, Fraser, Whiteford, Wilson, Walker, Busby, McRoberts*, Cowan, Thomson*

Bottom of the league Airdrie have won just once all season. After Wilson heads them level they look the more likely side to add a second goal. This proves to be Harper's last match before transferring to Everton. Steve Murray is scoring useful goals from midfield, and they are needed.

---

15 H ARBROATH 9/12 — Att 8,354 — Pos 5 (opp 14) — Pts 19 — **D 0-0** (HT 0-0)

Ref: D Syme

Aberdeen: Clark, Willoughby, Hermiston, Murray S, Young, Taylor, Varga, Robb, Forrest, Jarvie, Miller R*
Arbroath: *Marshall, Milne, Rylance, Cargill, Waddell, Winchester, Sellars, Cant, Pirie, Stanton, Payne*

Hours before kick-off Joe Harper was transferred to Everton for £180,000. He does not think Aberdeen will win trophies. The supporters learn of his departure only as they reach the stadium. They boo and jeer throughout the match. Alec Willoughby later describes them as 'diabolical'.

---

16 A RANGERS 16/12 — Att 26,375 — Pos 5 (opp 4) — Pts 20 — **D 0-0** (HT 0-0)

Ref: E Thomson

Aberdeen: Clark, Willoughby, Hermiston, Murray S, Young, Wilson, Varga, Smith, Forrest, Jarvie, Miller R — (sub Buchan G)
Rangers: *McCloy, Jardine, Mathieson, MacDonald, Johnstone, Smith, McLean, Conn*, Parlane, Mason, Young, Fyfe*

One star goes; another is born. Following the departure of Joe Harper another Joe - Joe Smith, brother of former Don, Jim - makes his debut. Aberdeen took some punishment in the first half, but handed out some in the second. The Dons second back-to-back 0-0 draws this season.

---

17 H MORTON 23/12 — Att 7,031 — Pos 4 (opp 13) — Pts 22 — **W 3-0** (HT 3-0)

Scorers: Varga 10, 12, Mitchell 36
Ref: R Henderson

Aberdeen: Clark, Willoughby, Hermiston, Murray S, Young, Wilson, Varga, Smith, Forrest, Jarvie, Miller R* — (sub Buchan G)
Morton: *Baines, Shevlane, Laughton, Reid, Anderson, Clark, Christensen, Townsend, Gillies, Murphy, Rankin*, Lavelle*

These would be dark days for Aberdeen FC were they not illuminated by Zoltan Varga. After 10 minutes he sweeps past Gillies to score an unstoppable shot from 30 yards. Two minutes later he scores with a header - and the crowd loves him. If only Buchan and Harper had stayed.

---

18 A HIBERNIAN 30/12 — Att 21,279 — Pos 6 (opp 2) — Pts 22 — **L 2-3** (HT 1-1)

Scorers: Jarvie 35, Miller 75 / Stanton 24, O'Rourke 50, Gordon 60
Ref: J Paterson

Aberdeen: Clark, Willoughby*, Hermiston, Graham, Young, Wilson, Varga, Smith, Mitchell, Jarvie, Miller R* — (sub Buchan G)
Hibernian: *Brownlie, Schaedler, Stanton, Black, Blackley, Edwards, O'Rourke, Gordon, Cropley, Duncan*

Aberdeen slip to sixth after this enthralling encounter. In the absence of Steve Murray, Willie Young is temporarily made captain. The best goal of the match was Hibs' third - a diving header by Gordon. One draw is all the Dons have to show from their last six visits to Easter Road.

---

19 H DUNDEE 1/1 — Att 13,576 — Pts 24 — **W 3-1** (HT 1-0)

Scorers: Hermiston 28, Varga 52, Jarvie 76 / Scott J 60
Ref: R Gordon

Aberdeen: Clark, Willoughby, Hermiston, Graham, Young, Wilson, Varga, Smith*, Mitchell, Jarvie, Miller R — (sub Buchan G)
Dundee: *Allan, Wilson R, Johnston, Houston, Stewart, Pringle, Scott J, Wallace, Duncan, Scott J, Lambie*

Pittodrie is the place to be for New Year drama. It is a party for Zoltan Varga, and not just to celebrate his 28th b.rthday. Hermiston fired the first goal in off the bar, and then everyone sat back and watched Varga go through his repertoire. Near the end Dundee's Pringle was sent off.

---

20 H HEARTS 27/1 — Att 13,282 — Pos 5 (opp 7) — Pts 26 — **W 3-1** (HT 2-1)

Scorers: Jarvie 17, 24, Varga 71 / Renton 15
Ref: J Callaghan

Aberdeen: Clark, Willoughby, Hermiston, Murray S, Young, Wilson, Varga, Graham, Mitchell, Jarvie, Miller R — (sub Buchan G)
Hearts: *Garland, Clunie, Jefferies, Thomson, Anderson, Kay, Park*, Renton, Ford, Brown, Murray T, Carruthers*

Bad weather has ruined three successive Saturdays. The crowd turn up just to see Zoltan Varga, it seems. Word of mouth has spread the news about him. He shines like a beacon light, scoring a superlative goal to crown a memorable match. The Dons have games in hand to make up.

---

21 A MOTHERWELL 7/2 — Att 4,000 — Pts 26 — **L 0-2** (HT 0-0)

Scorers: Lawson 47, Campbell 49
Ref: A Webster

Aberdeen: Clark, Willoughby, Hermiston, Murray S, Young, Wilson, Varga*, Graham, Mitchell, Jarvie, Miller R — (sub Smith)
Motherwell: *MacRae, Whiteford, Wark, Watson, McCallum, Goodwin, Campbell, McCabe, Goldthorp*, Lawson, Millar, Martin*

Aberdeen come to Fir Park with four straight wins under their belt in league and cup. But they lose Zoltan Varga after 15 minutes with a pulled hamstring. As Motherwell then discovered, the Dons are not the same side without him. They have become almost a one-man team.

Results summary (columns as printed: No | Date | Att | Pos | Pt | F-A | H-T | Scorers, Times, and Referees)

No	Date	Att	Pos	Pt	F-A	H-T	Scorers, Times, and Referees
22	A FALKIRK 10/2	4,897	6	27	D 0-0	0-0	[opp pos 12] Ref: A McCririck. If the Scottish Cup-tie between these sides is as shoddy as this no one will turn up. Ian Taylor was sent off for a silly foul on Sonner. Falkirk's player-coach Alex Ferguson was booked for back-chatting to the ref. Bobby Clark lets in five goals for Scotland against England in midweek.
23	H AYR 17/2	8,538	4	29	W 1-0	0-0	[opp pos 7] Jarvie 90. Ref: A McDonald. Jim Hermiston misses a penalty, leaving it to Drew Jarvie to bag the last-gasp winner. Ayr manager Ally MacLeod jumped to his feet in rage, jabbing his finger at his watch. Time was up ages ago, he seems to say. Jarvie's late strike prevents three pairs of goalless draws this season.
24	H DUMBARTON 20/2	7,852		31	W 6-0	2-0	Purdie 8, 65, Forrest 35, Jenkins 67 og, Varga 79, Jarvie 88. Ref: R Greenlees. This is promoted Dumbarton's first visit to Pittodrie since World War II. Aberdeen complete the double over them with such ruthlessness they may never want to come back. They will avoid relegation, so they have to. Happiest man was Ian Purdie, scoring twice on a rare appearance.
25	A CELTIC 3/3	36,245	5	31	L 0-2	0-0	[opp pos 1] Lennox 60p, Dalglish 83. Ref: A McKenzie. Aberdeen forced just one save from Alistair Hunter throughout the match. The Dons seemed concerned only to protect their own goal. This they achieved until the hour, when Young handled. By then Ian Purdie has been booked for three tough fouls on McGrain in quick succession.
26	A ST JOHNSTONE 7/3	4,389		31	L 0-1	0-0	Muir 54. Ref: C Huton. St Johnstone had not won since Hogmanay, a barren run o[f] eight games. Yet this win is no fluke. The Saints fully deserve it. The Dons had done well in Perth the last couple of seasons. These are the first consecutive league defeats Aberdeen have suffered this season.
27	H PARTICK THISTLE 10/3	8,994	5	32	D 0-0	0-0	[opp pos 13] Ref: J Gordon. Aberdeen have forgotten how to score. Three games without a goal is their worst sequence since the end of last season. The Dons are forced to concede defeat to Alan Rough - who will play for Scotland in Wales next week. Now for Celtic in the Cup. But can Aberdeen score?
28	A KILMARNOCK 24/3	4,000	6	34	W 2-0	0-0	[opp pos 17] Robb 70, Young 88. Ref: R Marshall. Two scoreless games against Celtic in the Scottish Cup takes the Dons' barren run to five matches - their worst sequence since World War II. With 20 minutes to play against Kilmarnock it looked like the run would continue. Ex-Hearts skipper Eddie Thomson makes his Dons debut.
29	A EAST FIFE 27/3	4,594	4	36	W 1-0	1-0	Varga 19. Ref: E Thomson. The two points lift Aberdeen from sixth to fourth. The match was settled, and Aberdeen completed the double over East Fife, thanks to Zoltan Varga's side-footed goal from close range. The only thing Aberdeen have left to play for is a place in next season's UEFA Cup.
30	H DUNDEE UTD 31/3	8,831	4	37	D 0-0	0-0	[opp pos 6] Ref: E Thomson. Both teams are seeking a place in Europe and have to battle against each other and against a blustery wind. The wind wins. This is Aberdeen's seventh goalless draw in the league this season. No wonder they are failing to excite in the way they did over the last couple of years.
31	H AIRDRIE 7/4	6,500	4	39	W 5-1	2-1	[opp pos 18] Jarvie 22, 30, 62, Robb 79, Murray 87; McKinley 13. Ref: R Greenlees. Before today Aberdeen have scored just three goals in eight league and cup games. Bottom-placed Airdrie, saying farewell to the First Division, allow the Dons' marksmen some practice - after Airdrie had taken the lead. How Airdrie must be missing Drew Jarvie.

Line-ups (columns 1–11 plus 12 sub used; Aberdeen in roman, opponents in *italics*)

No	Team	1	2	3	4	5	6	7	8	9	10	11	12 sub used
22	Aberdeen	Clark	Willoughby	Hermiston	Murray S	Young	Wilson	Buchan G	Graham	Mitchell	Jarvie	Taylor†	Willoughby
22	*Falkirk*	*Donaldson*	*Kennedy S*	*Young*	*McMillan*	*Markie*	*Kennedy J*	*Hoggan*	*Eadie*	*Sonner*	*Ferguson*	*Setterington*	*Wilson*
23	Aberdeen	Clark	Williamson	Hermiston	Murray S	Young	Wilson	Varga	Graham	Mitchell	Jarvie	Buchan G	McCulloch
23	*Ayr*	*Stewart*	*Wells*	*Murphy*	*McAnespie*	*Fleming*	*Filippi*	*Doyle*	*Graham*	*Ingram*	*McGregor*	*McCulloch*	
24	Aberdeen	Clark	Williamson	Hermiston	Murray S	Young	Wilson	Varga	Graham*	Forrest	Jarvie	Purdie	Willoughby
24	*Dumbarton*		*Jenkins*	*McKay*	*Cushley*	*Bolton**	*Graham*	*Coleman*	*Kidd*	*Mathie*	*Wallace*	*Heron*	*Livingstone*
25	Aberdeen	Clark	Williamson	Hermiston	Murray S	Young	Willoughby	Varga	Graham	Forrest	Jarvie	Purdie	
25	*Celtic*	*Hunter*	*McGrain*	*Quinn*	*Murdoch**	*McNeill*	*Connelly*	*Johnstone*	*Dalglish*	*Deans*	*Hood*	*Lennox*	*McCluskey*
26	Aberdeen	Clark	Williamson	Hermiston	Smith	Young	Taylor	Varga	Graham	Forrest	Jarvie	Purdie*	Willoughby
26	*St Johnstone*	*Donaldson*	*McManus*	*Argue*	*Kinnell*	*MacDonald*	*Rennie*	*Hall*	*Hotson*	*Muir*	*Rooney*	*Aitken*	
27	Aberdeen	Clark	Williamson	Hermiston	Murray S	Young	Smith	Varga	Graham	Forrest	Jarvie*	Purdie*	Street
27	*Partick Thistle*	*Rough*	*Hansen*	*Gray*	*Glavin*	*Campbell*	*Strachan*	*Gibson*	*Coulston*	*Craig**	*Rae A*	*Lawrie*	
28	Aberdeen	Clark	Williamson	Hermiston	Thomson	Young	Smith	Murray S	Robb	Forrest	Jarvie	Graham	Willoughby
28	*Kilmarnock*	*Stewart*	*Whyte*	*Robertson*	*Dickson*	*Rodman*	*Maxwell*	*McSherry*	*Morrison*	*Fleming*	*Smith*	*Cook*	
29	Aberdeen	Clark	Williamson	Hermiston	Thomson*	Young	Smith	Murray S	Robb	Forrest	Jarvie	Graham	Varga
29	*East Fife*	*McGarr*	*Duncan*	*Printy*	*Hamilton*	*Martis*	*Clarke*	*Hegarty*	*Love*	*Dailey*	*McPhee*	*Bernard*	
30	Aberdeen	Clark	Williamson	Thomson	—	Young	Smith	Murray S*	Robb	Forrest	Varga	Graham	Willoughby
30	*Dundee Utd*	*Davie*	*Kopel*	*Cameron J*	*Copland*	*Smith D*	*Cameron K*	*Wilson*	*Smith W*	*Gardner*	*Mitchell*	*Traynor*	*Busby*
31	Aberdeen	Clark	Williamson	Hermiston	Thomson	Young	Smith	Murray S	Robb	Varga	Jarvie	Graham*	Willoughby
31	*Airdrie*	*McKenzie*	*Jonquin*	*Caldwell*	*Fraser*	*McKinley*	*Whiteford*	*Wilson*	*McRoberts*	*Busby*	*Walker*	*Cowan*	

32 A ARBROATH 14/4   4,757 13 40   D 4   1-1   1-1

Varga 12

Sellars 33

Ref: G Smith

Clark | Williamson | Boel | Thomson | Young | Smith | Murray S | Street | Jarvie | Varga | Forrest* | Miller R
Marshall | Milne | Rylance | Cargill | Waddell | Winchester | Sellars | Penman | Pirie | Fletcher | Payne

Bertie Miller was about to come on as substitute, but found he had forgotten his shorts. He had to dash off to find them. At the time Aberdeen were leading 1-0 through a delicately curled free-kick by Zoltan Varga, who was later booked. Two draws with Arbroath this season says it all.

33 H RANGERS 21/4   32,000 2 41   D 5   2-2   0-1

Hermiston 67p, Taylor 85

McLean 22, Conn 87

Ref: J Paterson

Clark | Williamson | Boel | Thomson | Young | Smith* | Murray S | Taylor | Jarvie | Varga | Graham | Boel
McCloy | Jardine | Mathieson | Greig | Dickson | Smith | McLean | Forsyth | Parlane | McDonald A | Conn

Rangers must win if they want to deprive Celtic of the title. Calamity for them when Derek Johnstone hauls down Ian Taylor in the box, and again when Taylor slips the ball past McCloy with time running out. But then Conn exchanges passes with Parlane for a clever equaliser.

34 A MORTON 28/4   3,000 12 43   W 4   2-1   0-1

Young 61, Jarvie 62

Anderson 35

Ref: R Henderson

Clark | Williamson | Boel | Thomson | Young | Smith | Murray S | Taylor | Jarvie | Varga | Graham* | Miller W
Baines | Hayes | Ritchie | Rankin | Boel | Clark | Brown | Lavelle | Murray | Armstrong | Hepburn | McNab*

Aberdeen complete their fifth league double. With 37 minutes of the season remaining, Jimmy Bonthrone gives young Willie Miller his first taste of league football. It is also Zoltan Varga's last match, so these two great players share the same stage for a fleeting moment in time.

Average   Home 13,087   Away 10,075

Scottish League Cup - Section 2

1 A QUEEN OF SOUTH 12/8   4,673 2   W 2   4-0   1-0

Buchan G 39, Jarvie 50, Hermiston 80, Clark [Robb 88]Ball

Ref: J Callaghan

Clark | Willoughby | Hermiston | Murray S | Young | Buchan G | Robb | Harper | Jarvie | Taylor
Ball | Totten | Connell | Easton | Dickson | Dempster | Hamilton | Malcolmson Hannigan | Bryce | Donald*

There has been a change of format in the League Cup: now the top two teams qualify for the next stage. Drew Jarvie plays his first match for the Dons since signing from Airdrie and bags his first goal. Dave Robb and Joe Harper set up the chance. Robb claims a late own-goal as his.

2 H HIBERNIAN 16/8   20,673 4   W 4   4-1   3-0

Jarvie 28, 41, Harper 39, 62

Edwards 54

Ref: J McRoberts

Clark | Willoughby | Hermiston | Murray G | Young | Buchan G | Robb | Harper | Jarvie | Taylor
Herriot | Brownlie | Schaedler | Stanton | Blackley | Hamilton | Edwards | Higgins | Cropley | Duncan

Eddie Turnbull did not like this. Strangely, Hibs looked the better side until Aberdeen hit them with a triple blow. The most spectacular goal was the Dons' fourth, scored by Harper, who lobbed the stranded Herriot from way out near the touchline. The Dons can hardly fail to qualify.

3 H QUEEN'S PARK 19/8   11,464 6   W 6   5-1   1-0

Young 40, 50, Harper 78, 88, Jarvie 81

Scott 54

Ref: E Thomson

Clark | Willoughby | Hermiston | Murray S | Murray G | Buchan G* | Robb | Harper | Jarvie | Miller R
Purvis | Barr | Thomson | Robertson | Hunter | Morrison | Campbell | Scott | McKay | Borland | Molloy*

13 goals in just three games - four to Drew Jarvie. Queen's Park hold out, not without alarms, for most of the first half, but are then dashed to two replica goals. Ian Taylor swings over two corner-kicks and Willie Young powers in two headers. The league will be harder than this.

4 A HIBERNIAN 23/8   17,133 6   L 6   1-2   0-1

Jarvie 80

Cropley 28, O'Rourke 66

Ref: T Marshall

Clark | Willoughby | Hermiston | Murray S | Boel | Young | Buchan G* | Robb | Harper | Jarvie | Miller R
Herriot | Brownlie | Schaedler | Stanton | Black | Blackley | Edwards | O'Rourke | Gordon | Cropley | Duncan | Hamilton*

Under the previous rules this would have been a mighty showdown. Now it means nothing as both sides are bound to go through. Seven players are booked as Hibs exact revenge for their earlier Pittodrie setback. Drew Jarvie has scored in all four matches he has played in.

5 H QUEEN OF SOUTH 26/8   10,144 8   W 8   2-1   1-0

Taylor 13, Purdie 85

Dickson 68

Ref: R Greenlees

Clark | Willoughby | Hermiston | Murray G | Young | Purdie | Robb | Harper | Jarvie | Taylor
Ball | Totten | Thorburn | Connell | Boyd | Dempster | Dickson | Malcolmson McChesney Donald

At 1-0 Aberdeen are awarded a penalty, which Harper squanders. It is his second miss from the spot so far this season. He was grateful for Ian Purdie's late winner. Without it there would have been cat-calls descending on the players' heads as they trooped off the pitch at the end.

6 A QUEEN'S PARK 30/8   1,029 10   W 10   3-0   1-0

Harper 11, 53, 60

Ref: E Pringle

Clark | Willoughby | Hermiston | Murray S | Murray G | Purdie | Robb | Harper | Jarvie | Taylor
Taylor | Barr | Thomson | Hastie | Hunter | Robertson | Mackay | Gibson | Scott | Whyte | Colgan

Hampden Park is eerily empty with barely one thousand spectators. Aberdeen don't let the lack of atmosphere affect them, and win as they please. By topping their section they would have qualified for the next stage under the old rules. It is Hibs who have most to be thankful for.

	P	W	D	L	F	A	Pts
Qual ABERDEEN	6	5	0	1	19	5	10
Qual Hibernian	6	5	0	1	14	8	10
Queen of South	6	2	0	4	5	13	4
Queen's Park	6	0	0	6	4	16	0

SCOTTISH LEAGUE DIV 1 (CUP-TIES) Manager: Jimmy Bonthrone SEASON 1972-73

Scottish League Cup

			F-A	H-T	1	2	3	4	5	6	7	8	9	10	11	12 sub used
2:1	H	FALKIRK	W 8-0	0-0	Clark	Willoughby	Hermiston	Murray S	Boel	Young	Graham	Robb	Harper	Jarvie	Taylor*	Forrest
		20/9 9,939				Kennedy S	Shira*	Markie	McMillan		Hoggan	Harley		Young	Kennedy J	McLeod	Setterington

Forrest 50, Jarv 63, 74, Harper 63,77p,86, Clark [Graham 87, Robb 88]Donaldson
Ref: E Thomson

The newly introduced Round 2 of this competition sees Aberdeen establish a new club record. Goalless at half-time, the Dons smash eight goals in the space of 38 minutes in the second half. The massacre was sparked by Jim Forrest, who came on as a half-time substitute.

			F-A	H-T	1	2	3	4	5	6	7	8	9	10	11	12 sub used
2:2	A	FALKIRK	L 2-3	2-0	Clark	Willoughby	Hermiston	Murray S	Murray G	Young	Forrest	Taylor	Harper	Jarvie	Miller R	Eadie
		4/10 4,000			Donaldson	Kennedy S	Shira	Markie	McMillan	Kennedy J*	Hoggan	Harley	Scott	Young	McLeod	

Harper 30, 40
Harley 49, Hoggan 63, Young 79
Ref: E Thomson
(Dons win 10-3 on aggregate)

This second leg was pointless. Aberdeen are on a hiding to nothing. Bonthrone fields his strongest side, watches them open up a 10-0 aggregate lead by the interval, then suffer the humiliation of losing on the day. This goes down in the record books as a defeat, even though it wasn't.

			F-A	H-T	1	2	3	4	5	6	7	8	9	10	11	12 sub used
QF	H	EAST FIFE	W 3-0	2-0	Clark	Willoughby	Hermiston	Murray S	Young	Taylor*	Forrest	Robb	Harper	Jarvie	Miller R	Graham
1		11/10 13,605			Gorman	Duncan	McQuade	McIvor		Clarke	Honeyman	Hegarty	Dailey*	Borthwick	McPhee	Green

Taylor 24, Jarvie 38, Harper 75
Ref: A Webster

Quarter-finals are now two-leg affairs. There is no doubt about the hero of this match - East Fife goalkeeper David Gorman. Without him his team would doubtless have gone the same way as Falkirk. His performance leaves East Fife with a glimmer of hope for the second leg.

			F-A	H-T	1	2	3	4	5	6	7	8	9	10	11	12 sub used
QF	A	EAST FIFE	W 4-1	2-0	Clark	Willoughby*	Hermiston	Murray S	Mitchell	Taylor	Varga	Robb	Harper	Jarvie	Miller R	Forrest
2		1/11 4,492			Gorman	Printy	McQuade	McIvor		Clarke	Hegarty	Hamilton	Honeyman	McPhee	Bernard	

Harper 22, Jarvie 32, 55, Clarke 57 og
Hegarty 80
Ref: A Webster
(Dons win 7-1 on aggregate)

East Fife did their best, but it was not good enough. Joe Harper's head-flick ended the tie as a contest. The Dons will also do a league double over East Fife this season, inflicting six league and cup defeats in two seasons. Yet the Fifers will finish in mid-table respectability.

			F-A	H-T	1	2	3	4	5	6	7	8	9	10	11	12 sub used
SF	N	CELTIC	L 2-3	1-1	Clark	Willoughby	Hermiston	Murray S	Young	Taylor	Varga	Robb	Harper	Jarvie	Miller R	
		27/11 39,682			Williams	McGrain	Brogan	McCluskey	Connelly	Hay	Johnstone	Deans	Dalglish	Hood	Callaghan	

Harper 30, Robb 74
Hood 33p, Johnstone 75, Callaghan 80
Ref: J Paterson
(at Hampden)

Driving rain could not spoil this thrilling contest. When Robb headed the Dons 2-1 in front from Varga's corner things looked good. Within seconds Johnstone - possibly offside - beat Clark from close range, and Callaghan volleyed the winner. Williams parried Taylor's late effort.

Scottish Cup

			F-A	H-T	1	2	3	4	5	6	7	8	9	10	11	12 sub used
3	A	BRECHIN	W 4-2	3-0	Clark	Williamson	Hermiston	Smith	Young	Wilson	Varga	Graham	Mitchell	Jarvie	Miller R	Britton
		3/2 8,123			McEwan	Kidd	Gillespie	Donnelly	Milne	Clark	Miller*	Coutts	Reid	Cunningham Dow		

Mitchell 16, 44, Jarvie 33, Milne 64 og
Miller 73, Clark 87p
Ref: J Gordon

There was a hint of crowd trouble before the match, and more than a hint of bother from Brechin, who were effectively buried by half-time. But they never stopped fighting, sometimes literally. Two late Brechin goals gave them something to smile about. Clark scored against Clark.

			F-A	H-T	1	2	3	4	5	6	7	8	9	10	11	12 sub used
4	H	FALKIRK	W 3-1	1-0	Clark	Williamson	Hermiston	Murray S	Young	Wilson	Varga	Graham	Forrest	Jarvie	Purdie	
		28/2 17,730			Donaldson	Kennedy S	Kennedy J	McMillan	Markie	McLeod	Hoggan	Harley	Sonner	Ferguson!	Setterington	

Forrest 44, Purdie 47, Murray 75
Harley 68
Ref:J Gordon

Falkirk must be dreading a repeat of the 8-0 humiliation handed out to them in the League Cup. Seconds after Jim Forrest put the Dons in front, just before half-time, Falkirk player-coach Alex Ferguson was involved in a skirmish with Willie Young and was ordered off.

			F-A	H-T	1	2	3	4	5	6	7	8	9	10	11	12 sub used
QF	A	CELTIC	D 0-0	0-0	Clark	Williamson	Hermiston	Murray S	Young	Smith	Varga*	Robb	Forrest	Graham	Taylor	Jarvie
		17/3 40,032			Hunter	McGrain	Brogan	Murdoch	McNeill	Connelly	Johnstone	Dalglish	Deans	Hay	Lennox	

Ref: R Davidson

Aberdeen grit their teeth and hold out for 90 minutes in the face of pulsating Celtic attacks. More than 20 corner-kicks were conceded by the desperate Dons. Celtic's cause was hindered by Jimmy Johnstone being sent off following a clash with Hermiston. Three Dons were booked.

			F-A	H-T	1	2	3	4	5	6	7	8	9	10	11	12 sub used
QF	H	CELTIC	L 0-1	0-0	Clark	Williamson	Hermiston	Murray S	Young	Smith	Forrest	Robb*	Jarvie	Graham	Miller R	Buchan G
R		21/3 33,465			Hunter	McGrain	Brogan	Murdoch	McNeill	Connelly	Johnstone*	Hood	Deans	Hay	Lennox	Davidson

McNeill 86
Ref: R Davidson

When Billy McNeill headed in Hood's corner four minutes from time it brought about Aberdeen's first home defeat in the Scottish Cup since Ayr in 1964. It was a pity either side had to lose this epic battle. But Celtic exerted the greater pressure, forcing 14 corners to Aberdeen's six.

1:1 H BORUSSIA MG	L	2-3	0-2	Harper 55, Jarvie 67
13/9 (W Germ) 21,000				Kulik 20, Heynckes 38, Jensen 76
				Ref: R Machin (France)
1:2 A BORUSSIA MG	L	3-6	3-2	Jarvie 23, Willoughby 26, Murray S 45
27/9 19,000				Rupp 3, Heynckes 40p, 74, 88, Vogts 70, Kleff
				Ref: F Rion (Belgium) [Danner 83p]
				(Dons lose 5-9 on aggregate)

Match 1 / Match 2 line-ups (Aberdeen / Borussia):

Match 1 – Aberdeen	Borussia	Match 2 – Aberdeen	Borussia
Geoghegan	Kleff	Clark	Kleff
Willoughby	Michallik	Willoughby	Michallik
Hermiston	Rosenthal	Hermiston	Rosenthal
Taylor	Kulik*	Murray S 45	Kulik
Boel	Vogts	Boel*	Vogts
Young	Bonhof	Young	Bonhof
Forrest	Rupp	Taylor	Rupp*
Robb	Wimmer	Robb	Wimmer
Harper	Heynckes	Harper	Heynckes
Jarvie	Netzer*	Jarvie	Danner
Graham*	Jensen	Graham	Jensen^ Furmann/Bleidik
Miller R	Bleidik/Danner	Murray G	

Netzer, Heynckes, Vogts, Bonhof - just some of the illustrious names that enthral Pittodrie. The majestic Gunther Netzer projects the slide-rule pass that makes it 0-2, but is subbed at half-time with a thigh injury. Pandemonium when Jarvie heads an equaliser, but the joy did not last.

Aberdeen shrug off the loss of an early goal and the loss of Henning Boel to launch a series of attacks that square the aggregate scores at 5-5 on the stroke of half-time. It took a surging run and shot by Bertie Vogts to break Aberdeen's resistance. Then the Dons collapse badly.

	P	W	D	L	F	A	W	D	L	F	A	Pts
			Home						Away			
1 Celtic	34	14	3	0	47	10	12	2	3	46	18	57
2 Rangers	34	14	2	1	36	10	12	2	5	38	20	56
3 Hibernian	34	12	2	3	43	17	7	5	5	31	16	45
4 ABERDEEN	34	10	6	1	42	15	6	5	6	19	19	43
5 Dundee	34	13	4	0	45	10	4	5	8	23	33	43
6 Ayr	34	11	4	2	33	21	5	4	8	17	30	40
7 Dundee Utd	34	11	3	3	32	24	6	2	9	24	27	39
8 Motherwell	34	5	6	6	20	23	6	3	5	18	25	31
9 East Fife	34	8	3	6	26	21	3	5	9	20	33	30
10 Hearts	34	7	4	6	15	17	5	2	10	24	33	30
11 St Johnstone	34	8	3	6	35	30	2	6	9	17	37	29
12 Morton	34	8	4	5	33	21	2	4	11	14	32	28
13 Partick This	34	4	5	8	17	25	6	3	8	23	28	28
14 Falkirk	34	6	4	7	24	26	1	8	8	14	30	26
15 Arbroath	34	8	3	6	31	23	1	5	11	8	40	26
16 Dumbarton	34	3	9	5	26	30	3	2	12	17	42	23
17 Kilmarnock	34	6	3	8	23	30	1	5	11	17	41	22
18 Airdrie	34	2	4	11	16	35	2	4	11	18	40	16
	612	150	72	84	544	388	84	72	150	388	544	612

Appearances and Goals

Player	App Lge	Sub	LC	Sub	SC	Sub	Eur	Sub	Gls Lge	LC	SC	Eur	Tot
Boel, Henning	6	1	4										1
Buchan, George	4	4	4								1		1
Clark, Bobby	33		11	4									
Forrest, Jim	11		2	2	3				1	1		1	3
Geoghegan, Andy	1												
Graham, Arthur	19	4	11	1	4	2			10	15		1	26
Harper, Joe	13		11	1					2	1			3
Hermiston, Jim	33		11		4				2	2			3
Jarvie, Drew	33	1	11	3	1				15	10	1	2	28
Miller, Bertie	13	4	4	2	2	1		1	2				2
Miller, Willie	1												
Mitchell, Barrie	12	1	1						1		2		3
Murray, George	7		6										
Murray, Steve	29		11	3		1			4	1	1		6
Purdie, Ian	3		2	1					2	1	1		4
Robb, Dave	19		10	2					4	3			7
Smith, Joe	13	1											
Street, Bobby	1	1											
Taylor, Ian	18		11	1					4		2		6
Thomson, Eddie	7												
Varga, Zoltan	26		2	3					10				10
Williamson, Billy	12			3									
Willoughby, Alex	22	4	9	1					1			1	2
Wilson, Tom	9			2									
Young, Willie	30		10	4					2		2		4
(own-goals)									3		1	1	5
25 players used	374	21	121	5	44	2	22	2	61	38	7	5	111

Odds & ends

Double wins: (5) Dumbarton, Ayr, East Fife, Kilmarnock, Morton.
Double losses: (1) Celtic.

Won from behind: (5) Dumbarton (a), East Fife (h), Hearts (h), Airdrie (h), Morton (a).
Lost from in front: (3) Falkirk (LC), Celtic (LC), Borussia (a).

High spots: Unbeaten in first 5 league games. 3 consecutive league wins in early November, and up to 3rd. Reaching semi-final of League Cup, and scoring 38 goals in all rounds.

Low spots: 4 league games without a win from 25 November. Losing to Celtic twice in the league and in both cups. Losing at home in Europe for the first time.

Ever-presents: (0).
Hat-tricks: (4) Joe Harper (3), Drew Jarvie (1).
Leading scorer: (28) Drew Jarvie.

SCOTTISH LEAGUE DIVISION 1   Manager: Jimmy Bonthrone   SEASON 1973-74

No	Date	Att	Pos	Pt	F-A	H-T	Scorers, Times, and Referees	1	2	3	4	5	6	7	8	9	10	11	subs used
1	A MOTHERWELL 1/9	6,083	D	1	0-0	0-0	Ref: R Gordon	Clark	Hair	Willoughby	Thomson	Young	Miller W	Smith	Graham	Taylor	Jarvie	Miller R*	Purdie
2	H DUNDEE 8/9	9,517	8 D	2	0-0	0-0	Ref: A McKenzie	Clark	Hair	Hermiston	Thomson	Young	Miller W	Smith	Graham	Taylor	Jarvie	Purdie*	Miller R
3	A ST JOHNSTONE 15/9	4,000	6 W	4	2-1	2-0	Miller R 17, Hair 42; Smith 71; Ref: J Paterson	Clark	Hair	Hermiston	Thomson	Young	Miller W	Willoughby	Graham*	Taylor	Jarvie	Miller R	Craig
4	A CLYDE 29/9	2,375	5 W	6	3-1	2-0	Robb 20, 89, Jarvie 40; McVie 54; Ref: W Anderson	Clark	Hair	Hermiston	Thomson	Young	Miller W	Willoughby	Robb	Taylor	Jarvie	Purdie	
5	H HIBERNIAN 6/10	13,954	6 D	7	1-1	1-1	Jarvie 29; Gordon 8; Ref: R Valentine	Clark	Hair	Hermiston	Thomson	Young	Miller W	Graham	Robb	Taylor	Jarvie	Miller R	Higgins
6	A DUMBARTON 13/10	3,000	5 W	9	1-0	0-0	Jarvie 61; Ref: T Muirhead	Clark	Hair	Hermiston	Thomson*	Young	Miller W	Willoughby	Robb	Taylor^	Jarvie	Miller R	Graham
7	H DUNFERMLINE 20/10	7,351	4 D	10	0-0	0-0	Ref: A McDonald	Clark	Hair	Hermiston	Thomson	Young	Miller W	Willoughby*	Robb	Taylor^	Jarvie	Graham	Miller R/Craig
8	H DUNDEE UTD 27/10	7,081	3 W	12	3-1	1-0	Graham 33, Robb 65, Jarvie 76; Gray 54; Ref: E Thomson	Clark	Hair	Hermiston	Thomson	Young	Miller W	Graham	Robb	Taylor	Smith	Taylor	Gray/Cameron K
9	A MORTON 3/11	4,000	3 L	12	0-2	0-0	Thomas 46, Osborne 89; Ref: R McGinlay	Clark	Hair	Hermiston	Thomson	Young	Mitchell	Graham	Robb	Jarvie	Willoughby	Miller R*	Taylor
10	A FALKIRK 10/11	3,500	3 W	14	3-1	1-0	Robb 11, 52, Jarvie 84; Fowler 64; Ref: R Gordon	Clark	Hair	Hermiston	Thomson	Young	Miller W	Willoughby	Robb	Jarvie	Smith	Graham*	Miller J

Opponent line-ups (italic), by match:

1. *MacCrae, Muir (John Wark), Watson, Muir Jim, Goodwin*, Campbell, Millar, Lawson^, McCabe, McClymont, Goldthorp/Martin*
2. *Allan, Ford, Johnston, Robinson, Stewart*, Gemmell, Anderson^, Duncan, Wallace, Scott, Lambie, Pringle/Wilson*
3. *Donaldson, Lambie, Argue, Rennie, MacDonald, Rooney^, Hall, Smith, Muir^, Aitken, Ritchie/McGregor*
4. *Cairney, McHugh, Swan, Beattie, McVie, Sullivan, Ahern, Burns!, Miller, McGrain, Boyle*
5. *McKenzie, Brenner, Schaedler, Stanton, Black, Blackley, Edwards, O'Rourke*, Gordon, Cropley, Duncan*
6. *Williams, McKay, Wilkinson, Menzies, Cushley, Ruddy, Coleman*, Wallace, McCormack, Paterson, McAdam^, Graham/Jenkins*
7. *Arrol, Leishman, Wallace, Thomson, McNicoll*, Kinninmonth, Campbell, Scott, Mackie, Shaw, Gillespie, Nelson*
8. *McAlpine, Rolland, Kopel, Copland, Smith D, Smith W, Henry^, Knox^, Gardner, Fleming, Traynor*
9. *Baines, Hayes, Ritchie, Townsend, Anderson, Nelson, Osborne, Reid, McIlmoyle, McCallion, Thomas*
10. *Donaldson, Whiteford, D Cameron, Markie, Gibson, McLeod, Thomas, Fowler, Lawson, Shira, Mitchell*, Young*

Match notes:

1. Not since 1966-67 have the Dons lost their opening league fixture. Jimmy Bonthrone's emphasis on defence is clear. In four away matches in League Cup and league Aberdeen have yet to concede a goal. Willie Miller is at this early stage of his career playing in midfield.
2. It seems ages since Aberdeen have been involved in a goal - at either end. They were involved in two back-to-back 0-0 draws at the league last season. Including the League Cup game at Motherwell, the Dons have now played three successive goalless games. This won't win the league.
3. St Johnstone wiped off the smile off Bobby Clark's face: he has conceded his first goal in six League Cup and league games. Bertie Miller has the distinction of scoring Aberdeen first league goal of 1973-74, after 197 minutes of football. New full-back Ian Hair added a second.
4. Promoted Clyde made the mistake of unfurling the Second Division championship flag before this match. They had little to celebrate during it, and had Burns ordered off for crocking Ian Taylor. Dave Robb's first goals of the season secure the points. McVie will score at Pittodrie too.
5. Willie Miller makes a howler. He passes back to a goalkeeper who was not there. Miller's error goes to his head and his game falls apart. Drew Jarvie's equaliser eases his torment. It is one defeat in a dozen league and League Cup games so far, but too many of them have been drawn.
6. A bread and butter match settled by a bread and butter goal. Willie Miller's cross eluded goalkeeper Williams, came back off the far post, and was tucked in by Drew Jarvie. But without Joe Harper the front line looks impotent. Dumbarton are keeping their heads above water so far.
7. Dunfermline have just lost 0-4 at home to Ayr, and set their sights on a goalless draw. They indulge in numerous 30-yard back-passes to their goalkeeper. The Dons have now lost just once in 15 League Cup and league games, but are scoring at just one league goal per game.
8. Goals at last. This is Aberdeen's first home game. They are the last unbeaten side in Scotland, and have the best defensive record. For a while, bustling Andy Gray threatened Aberdeen's winning prospects. The Dons are just one point behind Celtic and Hearts at the top.
9. Aberdeen present Morton with their second win of the season and their first at Cappielow. The Dons left their concentration behind in the dressing room at half-time. Coming just three days after defeat at Celtic in the League Cup, Aberdeen are rudely reacquainted with losing.
10. Falkirk are still looking for their first win. All these Millers are becoming confusing. Aberdeen have one of them on from the start - Willie - and two more on the bench - Jimmy and Bertie. It is Jimmy - making his league debut - who takes over from Arthur Graham.

11 H HEARTS 17/11 — 11,000 — 3 W 3-1 2 16

Anderson 21 og, Miller W 75, Jarvie 89 / Ford 27 — Ref: T Kellock

Clark, Hair, Hermiston, Thomson, Young, Miller W, Miller J, Robb, Jarvie, Smith*, Graham, Craig
Garland, Kay, Clunie, Cant, Anderson, Jefferies, Park, Ford, Busby, Stevenson, Prentice, Craig

A top of the table clash. More of the same please. Both sides looked good: Aberdeen looked better. A minute after John Craig came on as a substitute his cross was knocked out to Willie Miller, who hit a screamer from 20 yards past Garland. It is Miller's first goal for Aberdeen.

---

12 A EAST FIFE 24/11 — 2,597 — 3 D 2-2 17 17

Hermiston 63p, Robb 67 / Borthwick 9, Hegarty 64 — Ref: D Ramsay

Clark, Boel, Hermiston, Thomson, Young, Miller W, Miller J*, Robb, Jarvie, Craig, Graham
McGarr, Duncan, Printy, Hamilton, Martis, Clarke, Love, Hegarty, Borthwick, McPhee, Ritchie, McIvor*

Dave Robb is both saint and sinner in this match. His inattentive back-pass was gobbled up by Hegarty to restore the Fifers' lead. Minutes later he was on the receiving end of Willie Miller's through ball to level the scores. To cap a day to remember, Robb had earlier been booked.

---

13 A ARBROATH 22/12 — 2,711 — 6 W 3-1 13 19

Taylor 55, 73, 77, Sellars 72 — Ref: I Muirhead

Clark, Boel, Hermiston, Thomson, Young, Miller W, Miller J*, Taylor, Jarvie, Craig, Graham, Willoughby
Marshall, Milne, Rylance, Cargill, Waddell, Murray, Sellars, Cant, Pirie, Penman, Fletcher, Walker*

A look at the scoresheet shows a hat-trick for Ian Taylor. These are the only goals he will score throughout the season. They are also the last goals he will ever score for Aberdeen, and they maintain the Dons' surge up the table. Taylor will remember Gayfield Park with affection.

---

14 H MOTHERWELL 29/12 — 8,000 — 5 D 0-0 8 20

Ref: J Gordon

Clark, Boel, Hermiston, Thomson, Young, Miller W, Taylor, Graham, Jarvie, Craig, Graham, Willoughby
Rennie, Muir, John, Wark, Watson R, Muir, Jim, McCabe, Campbell, Graham, Goldthorp, Martin, McClymont

Motherwell are now unbeaten in seven games, but tedium reigns. This is the third goalless draw fought out between these sides this season. Motherwell came nearest to a goal when McCabe struck Bobby Clark's upright near the end. Motherwell only draw one other away game.

---

15 A DUNDEE 1/1 — 9,451 — D 1-1 21

Graham 44 / Wilson J 26 — Ref: G Smith

Clark, Boel, Hermiston, Thomson, Young, Miller W, Williamson, Jarvie*, Craig*, Graham, Purdie/Smith
Allan, Wilson R, Johnston, Ford, Gemmell, Phillips, Wilson J, Robinson, Duncan, Scott J, Lambie

Arthur Graham's sweet goal - switching the ball from right foot to left before bending his shot inside the far post - brought a smile to Jimmy Bonthrone. Former Don Jimmy Wilson's crunching tackle on John Craig, which broke the Aberdeen player's leg, wiped it off again.

---

16 H ST JOHNSTONE 5/1 — 6,000 — 6 L 0-1 15 21

Hall 74 — Ref: D Syme

Clark, Boel, Hermiston, Thomson, Young, Miller W, Graham*, Taylor, McCall, Smith, Purdie, Willoughby
Donaldson, Ritchie, Argue, Rennie, MacDonald, Cramond, Muir, Smith, Pearson, Hall, Hotson

If he had played his cards right Henry Hall would have been an Aberdeen player. Instead Pittodrie casts its critical eye on debutant Walker McCall. Their verdict comes with their chant of 'We want Joey Harper', who Everton want to sell. St Johnstone's first win in nine games.

---

17 A RANGERS 12/1 — 16,000 — 6 D 1-1 3 22

Purdie 31 / McLean 51 — Ref: R Davidson

Clark, Boel, Hermiston, Thomson*, Young, Miller W, Graham, Smith, Taylor, Henry, Purdie, Williamson
McCloy, Jardine, Mathieson, Greig, Johnstone, Forsyth, McLean, O'Hara, Parlane, MacDonald, Young, Fyfe*

It is now four years since Aberdeen last lost at Ibrox. They were prevented from winning by McLean's back-header from a free-kick with Bobby Clark off his line. The Dons' goal was scored by Ian Purdie, his first and last of the season. Three games without a win for Rangers.

---

18 H CLYDE 19/1 — 7,000 — 5 D 1-1 14 23

Jarvie 41 / McVie 90 — Ref: C Hutton

Clark, Boel, Hermiston, Thomson, Young, Miller W*, Taylor, Robb, Jarvie, Henry, Purdie, Smith
Cairney, Anderson, Swan, McHugh, McVie, Ahern, Sullivan, Burns, Miller, McGrain, Beattie, Boyle*

In the third minute of injury-time McVie heads in a Clyde corner to prevent a fifth successive defeat and deny Aberdeen the first league double of the season. The Dons are fifth, 11 points behind Celtic, who have scored twice as many goals as Aberdeen. Clyde score only 29 all season.

---

19 A HIBERNIAN 2/2 — 15,700 — 5 L 1-3 2 23

Robb 17 / O'Rourke 4, 49, Gordon 35 — Ref: R Valetine

Clark, Williamson, Hermiston, Smith, Young, Miller W, Graham, Smith, Robb, Jarvie, Taylor, Street
McArthur, Brownlie, Schaedler, Stanton, Black, Blackley, Edwards, O'Rourke, Gordon, Cropley, Duncan

Aberdeen have now gone seven league and cup games without a win. Aberdeen supporters are frustrated to hear that Hibs have just signed Joe Harper from Everton. He sits up in the stand to watch his new team demolish his old. Hibs are the only team within striking distance of Celtic.

---

20 H DUMBARTON 9/2 — 4,000 — 5 W 3-0 11 25

Young 50, Robb 86, Jarvie 88 — Ref: B McGinlay

Clark, Hermiston, McLelland, Smith, Young, Miller W*, Street*, Robb, Jarvie, Henry, Graham, Thomson
Williams, McKay, Black, Menzies, Cushley, Ruddy, McAdam, Wallace, McCormack, Mathie, Paterson, McIntyre*

Aberdeen's poor form is reflected in the gate - their lowest for about 16 years. Bobby Street breaks his leg just five minutes into his first full come-back game. Chic McLelland has an uneventful debut. Dumbarton substitute Williams, their goalkeeper. Their first defeat in four games.

---

21 A DUNFERMLINE 24/2 — 6,959 — 5 D 0-0 15 26

Ref: A McCririck

Clark, Hermiston, McLelland, Thomson, Young, Miller W, Smith*, Robb, Jarvie, Henry, Graham, Craig
Karlsen, Brown, Wallace, Thomson, McCallum, Kinninmonth/Cameron, Scott, Mackie, Shaw, Sinclair

Aberdeen's goal held out as if by magic in the dying minutes, as relegation-haunted Dunfermline did everything but score. In fact, the one point Dunfermline did earn will keep them up - on goal-difference. This is the second 0-0 draw between the sides this season.

SCOTTISH LEAGUE DIVISION 1 — SEASON 1973-74

Manager: Jimmy Bonthrone

Results

No	Date	V	Opponents	H-T	F-A	Res	Pos	Opp	Pt	Att	Scorers, Times & Referee
22	3/3	A	DUNDEE UTD	1-0	3-0	W	5	9	28	6,500	Robb 18, Addison 63 og, Narey 77 og — Ref: A Webster
23	9/3	H	MORTON	0-0	0-0	D	5	16	29	5,000	Ref: R Greenlees
24	16/3	H	FALKIRK	2-0	6-0	W	4	18	31	5,500	Young 7, Jarvie 36, 61, 73, 77, Robb 74 — Ref: R Henderson
25	23/3	A	HEARTS	0-0	0-0	D	4	7	32	13,500	Ref: T Kellock
26	30/3	H	EAST FIFE	0-0	2-0	W	4	16	34	5,000	Graham 72, Jarvie 77 — Ref: A McKenzie
27	6/4	A	AYR	0-0	0-0	D	4	5	35	5,000	Ref: E Thomson
28	8/4	A	PARTICK THISTLE	0-0	0-2	L			35	3,500	Craig 65, Glavin 88 — Ref: R Henderson
29	13/4	H	PARTICK THISTLE	1-0	2-0	W	4	13	37	6,000	Robb 40, Smith 87 — Ref: W Anderson
30	17/4	H	RANGERS	0-0	1-1	D	4	2	38	18,000	McDougall 56 og, Greig 75 — Ref: E Pringle
31	20/4	A	CELTIC	0-1	0-2	L	4	1	38	31,000	Deans 4, Lennox 85 — Ref: G Smith

Line-ups (Aberdeen above; opponents in italics below)

No	1	2	3	4	5	6	7	8	9	10	11	subs used
22	Clark	Hermiston	McLelland	Thomson	Young	Miller W	Smith	Robb	Jarvie	Henry	Graham	
	Davie	*Addison*	*Kopel*	*Copland*	*Smith D**	*Smith W*	*Payne*	*Sheehy**	*Cameron*	*Gardner*	*Traynor*	*Narey/Holt*
23	Clark	Hermiston	McLelland	Thomson	Young	Miller W	Smith	Robb	Jarvie	Henry	Graham	Townsend
	Baines	*Hayes*	*Ritchie*	*Anderson**	*Nelson*	*Rankin*	*Murray*	*Reid*	*McIlmoyle*	*Hepburn*	*McCallion*	
24	Clark	Hermiston	McLelland	Thomson	Young	Miller W*	Smith	Robb	Pirie	Jarvie	Graham	Taylor
	Donaldson	*Whiteford*	*D Cameron*	*Markie*	*Gibson*	*Wheatley*	*Hoggan*	*Fowler**	*Lawson*	*Smith*	*Shirra**	*Thomas/Harley*
25	Clark	Hermiston	McLelland	Thomson	Young	Hair	Smith*	Robb	Pirie	Jarvie	Graham	Taylor
	Cruickshank	*Sneddon*	*Clunie*	*Jefferies*	*Anderson*	*Brown*	*Aird*	*Ford*	*Busby*	*Stevenson*	*Prentice*	
26	Clark	Hermiston	McLelland	Thomson	Young	Hair	Smith	Robb	Pirie	Jarvie	Graham	McPhee
	McGarr	*Printy*	*Gillies*	*Clarke*	*Martis*	*Rae*	*Miller*	*Borthwick*	*Kinnear*	*O'Connor*	*Love**	
27	Clark	Hermiston	McLelland	Thomson	Young	Miller W	Smith	Robb	Pirie	Jarvie	Graham	McCulloch
	McLean A	*Wells*	*Filippi*	*McAnespie*	*Fleming*	*Tait*	*Doyle*	*Graham*	*Ingram*	*McLean G*		
28	Clark	Hermiston	McLelland	Thomson	Young	Miller W*	Smith	Robb	Pirie	Jarvie	Graham	McCall/Davidson
	Rough	*Houston*	*Kellachan*	*Glavin*	*Campbell*	*Anderson*	*Chalmers*	*McDowell**	*Craig*	*Rooney*	*Lawrie*	*Gibson*
29	Clark	Hermiston	McLelland	Thomson	Young	Miller W	Smith	Robb	Hair	Jarvie	Graham	
	Rough	*Houston*	*Kellachan*	*Glavin*	*Campbell*	*Anderson*	*Chalmers*	*McDowell**	*Craig*	*Rooney*	*Lawrie*	*Gibson*
30	Clark	Hermiston	McLelland	Thomson	Young	Miller W*	Smith	Robb	Pirie	Jarvie	Graham	McCall
	McCloy	*Jardine*	*Greig*	*MacDougall*	*Johnstone*	*Jackson*	*Young*	*Scott*	*Parlane*	*MacDonald*	*Fyfe*	
31	Clark	Hermiston	McLelland	Thomson	Young	Miller W*	Smith	Hair	Pirie	Jarvie	Graham	Davidson/McCall
	Connaghan	*McGrain*	*Brogan*	*Hay*	*McNeill*	*McCluskey*	*Johnstone**	*Murray*	*Deans**	*Hood*	*Dalglish*	*Lennox/Callaghan*

Match reports

22 — Dundee United (A). United contributed to their own downfall in the second half. Joe Smith's flashing cross was turned into his own net by Addison, under pressure from Jarvie; and when Drew's shot banged against a post, Narey ran the ball over the line. Earlier Robb had scored his 100th goal for the Dons.

23 — Morton (H). Once again Aberdeen have forgotten how to score goals and how to concede them. This is their ninth goalless draw of the season, and the fans are staying away in their thousands. It is no good having a well-organised defence if the front line can't score. Morton don't score many either.

24 — Falkirk (H). No wonder Falkirk are bottom of the league. Aberdeen parade new signing Billy Pirie, and he helps inspire Drew Jarvie to a four-goal bonanza. He is far and away the Dons' leading scorer, and will top the scoring charts for the second successive season. No goals from Pirie this season.

25 — Hearts (A). Not a game to remember. Three players were booked, among them Aberdeen's Dave Robb. Billy Pirie fails to score again, and in fact will fail to do so all season. The main question in Dons' fans minds is how many goalless draws will the team finish up with. It is 10 so far.

26 — East Fife (H). Are you watching Willie Ormond? With the World Cup finals just two months away, goalkeepers Bobby Clark and Ernie McGarr are the best players on the pitch. Clark has now kept seven clean sheets in a row. East Fife had just won three in a row, but they will be relegated.

27 — Ayr (A). Bobby Clark's eighth successive shut-out. He has not been beaten since 2 February. But Aberdeen have won just four of those eight matches. Billy Pirie comes the closest yet to scoring a goal, but his header hits a post. Ally MacLeod's Ayr are having a surprisingly good season.

28 — Partick Thistle (A). For over an hour it looked like Aberdeen would record their ninth game in a row without conceding a goal. But then Glavin's shot was parried by Clark, and Craig swooped on the loose ball. Glavin's late goal seals what is only the Dons' fourth league defeat of the season.

29 — Partick Thistle (H). Back-to-back games with Partick Thistle. Quick revenge for Aberdeen, though Dave Robb looked suspiciously offside as he collected McLelland's lob before netting. Joe Smith then scores his first league goal for Aberdeen. Pittodrie's attendances are going from bad to worse.

30 — Rangers (H). Aberdeen are grateful to young Ranger Ian McDougall for a back-pass which completely nonplussed McCloy. It looked like giving Aberdeen their first home win over Rangers in the league for nine seasons. But then came John Greig's raging shot-on-the-run from 25 yards to level.

31 — Celtic (A). Celtic are almost home and dry for their ninth successive championship. They are on their way to winning this match after just four minutes, when Johnstone cut the ball in front of Deans. Aberdeen stopper Willie Young was booked for toppling ex-Don Steve Murray.

32 H AYR 24/4 — 4 W 5 40 — 3,945 — **1-0**
Thomson 22, McCall 75 / McLean 64
Ref: R Henderson

Clark · Hermiston · McLelland · Thomson · Young* · Miller W · Smith · Hair* · McCall · Jarvie · Graham! [sub: Williamson/Davidson]
McLean A · Wells · Filippi · McAnespie · Fleming · Tait · Doyle · Graham* · Ingram · McLean G* · McCulloch! [sub: Docherty/Donald]

Ayr's McCulloch was ordered off, for speaking out of turn, shortly after Aberdeen's first goal. At 1-1 Arthur Graham was also dismissed for hacking down Wells off the ball. When everything had calmed down Walker McCall scored his first senior goal for the Dons to win the game.

33 H ARBROATH 27/4 — 4 D 11 41 — 4,000 — **2-2**
McLelland 1, McCall 83 / Sellars 74, Cant 80p
Ref: R Davidson

Clark · Hermiston · McLelland · Thomson · Young · Miller W · Smith · McCall · Pirie* · Jarvie · Graham
Marshall · Milne · Buchan · Cargill · Carson · Murray · Sellars · Cant · Fletcher · Rylance · Walker [sub: Davidson]

When Willie Young handled the ball in the act of falling, the resultant penalty meant that Aberdeen had conceded two goals at Pittodrie for the first time in the league this season. If only their attack was as strong as their defence. Attendances are now becoming embarrassingly small.

34 H CELTIC 29/4 — 4 D 1 42 — 14,000 — **0-0**
Ref: R Valentine

Clark · Hermiston · McLelland · Hair · Young · Miller W · Smith · McCall · Pirie* · Jarvie · Graham
Hunter · McGrain · Quinn · McCluskey · Welsh · Brogan · Dalglish · Hay · Deans* · Davidson · Callaghan [sub: Hood]

Not even the visit of Celtic can half-fill Pittodrie these days. Once the Dons had lined up to applaud Celtic's ninth consecutive championship, the match ends with Aberdeen's 12th goalless draw of the season. Both sides wasted good chances to win. Celtic will draw their last four.

Average Home 8,000 · Away 8,000

Scottish League Cup - Section 4

1 H MOTHERWELL 11/8 — W 3-1 — 10,722 — 2
Hermiston 21p, Smith 54, Graham 61 / Lawson 53
Ref: E Thomson

Clark · Williamson · Hermiston · Thomson · Young · Boel* · Graham* · Taylor · Jarvie · Smith · Purdie
MacCrae · Muir, John · Wark · Watson · McCallum · Muir, Jim · Campbell · Millar · Lawson · McCabe · McClymont

The latest Aberdeen star to leave Pittodrie is skipper Steve Murray, who has signed for Celtic. Aberdeen's first goal of the new season is a penalty conceded by McCallum. As with last season, with two teams qualifying, much of the edge has been lost to the new format League Cup.

2 A DUNDEE UTD 15/8 — D 0-0 — 6,000 — 3
Ref: T Kellock

Clark · Williamson · Hermiston · Thomson · Young · Miller W · Smith · Graham* · Taylor · Jarvie · Purdie R
McAlpine · Rolland · Kopel · McLeod · Smith D · Cameron K* · Gardner · Payne · Henry · Traynor · Fleming

Representatives of Finn Harps - Aberdeen's UEFA Cup opponents from Ireland - watch as the Dons bang their heads against a tangerine wall. Without Drew Jarvie's goals they will be in a mess. The wall held firm. This is the first of a dozen 0-0 draws the Dons will contest this season.

3 H EAST FIFE 18/8 — D 1-1 — 8,188 — 4
Williamson 72 / McIvor 31
Ref: J Gordon

Clark · Williamson · Hermiston · Thomson · Young · Miller W · Smith · Graham* · Taylor · Jarvie · Miller R
McGarr · Duncan · Printy · Love · Martis · Clarke · Hegarty · McIvor · Dailey* · Hamilton · McPhee^

Billy Williamson's face-saving equaliser was no more than a prod over the goal-line after his first effort had been blocked. Former Don Ernie McGarr stood tall in the East Fife goal. This dropped point is going to make qualification more difficult, and in fact makes all the difference.

4 H DUNDEE UTD 22/8 — L 0-2 — 8,912 — 4
Knox 49, Cameron K 74
Ref: R Davidson

Clark · Williamson · Hermiston · Thomson · Young* · Miller W · Smith · Graham · Fleming · Cameron K · Gardner [sub: Willoughby]
McAlpine · Rolland · Kopel · Copland · Smith D · Knox* · · · · · McLeod · Henry

Archie Knox is the man who pulls the rug from under Aberdeen, rifting home an angled shot which was deflected past Bobby Clark by Willie Young. This will be one of just three home defeats for the Dons this season. It looks as if they will miss out on Round 2 of the League Cup.

5 A EAST FIFE 25/8 — W 2-0 — 4,153 — 6
Miller R 43, Graham 58
Ref: R Henderson

Clark · Williamson · Hermiston · Thomson · Young · Miller W · Smith · Graham · Taylor · Jarvie · Miller R
McGarr · Duncan · Printy* · Love · Rutherford · Clarke · Hegarty · McIvor* · Honeyman · McPhee · Ritchie [sub: Walker/Noble]

With Aberdeen two goals up, Willie Miller fouls Hegarty in the box, but Bobby Clark is equal to McPhee's penalty. This result eliminates East Fife from contention, setting up a grandstand finish for the other three. Aberdeen will also take three points from East Fife in the league.

6 A MOTHERWELL 29/8 — D 0-0 — 9,808 — 7
Ref: G Smith

Clark · Williamson · Hermiston* · Thomson · Young · Miller W · Smith · Graham · Taylor · Jarvie · Miller R [sub: Willoughby]
MacCrae · Muir, John · Wark · Watson · Goodwin · Muir, Jim · Campbell · Millar* · Lawson · McCabe · McClymont [sub: Goldthorp]

Aberdeen know that a draw will take them through behind Motherwell, unless Dundee United beat East Fife by six clear goals. But the incentive for the group winners is a money-spinner with one of the Old Firm. Both teams want to win. MacCrae saves Bertie Miller's penalty.

	P	W	D	L	F	A	Pts
Qual Motherwell	6	3	1	2	13	6	7
Qual ABERDEEN	6	2	3	1	6	4	7
Dundee Utd	6	3	1	2	9	10	7
East Fife	6	1	1	4	7	15	3

SCOTTISH LEAGUE DIV 1 (CUP-TIES) Manager: Jimmy Bonthrone SEASON 1973-74

Scottish League Cup

			F-A		H-T	Scorers, Times, and Referees	1	2	3	4	5	6	7	8	9	10	11	subs used
2:1 H STIRLING ALB	8 W	3-0			1-0	Graham 24, Jarvie 71, 80	Clark	Hair	Hermiston	Thomson	Young	Miller W	Smith*	Graham	Taylor	Jarvie	Miller R	Willoughby
12/9	7,500					Ref: R Valentine	*Young*	*Jones*	*McAlpine*	*Clark**	*McAleer*	*Carr*	*McPhee^*	*Steele*	*Lawson*	*McMillan*	*Murphy*	*Christie/Downie*

Such is Aberdeen's historical dominance over Stirling Albion that this is their 21st victory in 26 meetings, and Aberdeen's goal tally now stands at 95. The second leg ought to be a formality, and the Dons can look forward to a place in the quarter-finals.

			F-A		H-T	Scorers, Times, and Referees	1	2	3	4	5	6	7	8	9	10	11	subs used
2:2 A STIRLING ALB	6 W	3-0			2-0	Jarvie 22, 30, 64	Clark	Hair	Hermiston	Thomson	Young	Miller W	Smith*	Robb	Taylor	Jarvie	Miller R	Lawson
10/10	3,000					Ref: R Valentine	*Young*	*Jones*	*McAlpine*	*Duffin*	*McAleer*	*Carr*	*McPhee**	*Steele*	*McMillan*	*Clark**	*Downie*	

(Dons win 6-0 on aggregate)

A hat-trick for Drew Jarvie, including two headers. He has now scored five times against poor Stirling. If he goes on at this rate Aberdeen supporters will forget all about Joe Harper. Now for a two-leg tie against Celtic in the quarter-final. Stirling will finished seventh in Division 2.

			F-A		H-T	Scorers, Times, and Referees	1	2	3	4	5	6	7	8	9	10	11	subs used
QF A CELTIC	3 L	2-3			1-2	Jarvie 4, 55	Clark	Hair	Hermiston	Thomson	Young	Miller W	Graham	Robb	Jarvie	Smith*	Taylor^	Willoughby/Miller R
1 31/10	26,000	1				Dalglish 15, 16, McCluskey 56	*Hunter*	*McGrain*	*Brogan*	*McCluskey McNeill*	*Connelly*	*Hood*	*Murray*	*Deans*	*Hay*	*Dalglish*	*Johnstone*	
						Ref: J Paterson												

Aberdeen's first away defeat in any competition this season. Graham's knock-down enabled Jarvie to pick his spot. Kenny Dalglish poked an equaliser through Clark's legs, and within seconds blasted a second. Jarvie directed Robb's shot past Hunter. McCluskey scored off the wood.

			F-A		H-T	Scorers, Times, and Referees	1	2	3	4	5	6	7	8	9	10	11	subs used
QF H CELTIC	3 D	0-0			0-0		Clark	Hair*	Hermiston	Thomson	Young	Miller W	Graham	Robb	Jarvie	Craig	Graham^	Williamson/Miller R
2 21/11	15,500	1				Ref: J Paterson	*Hunter*	*McGrain*	*Brogan*	*McCluskey McNeill*	*Murray*	*Lennox*	*Hood*	*Deans**	*Callaghan*	*Dalglish*	*Johnstone*	*Johnstone*

(Dons lose 2-3 on aggregate)

47 free-kicks but no goals. That was the sum of achievement of this Wednesday afternoon match. The Dons' only real opening fell to Jimmy Miller in the first half. His first effort was blocked and his follow-up was headed behind by McGrain. A third Miller - Bertie - came on, too.

Scottish Cup

			F-A		H-T	Scorers, Times, and Referees	1	2	3	4	5	6	7	8	9	10	11	subs used
3 H DUNDEE	5 L	0-2			0-1	Johnston 32, Robinson 73	Clark	Williamson*	Hermiston	Smith	Young	Miller W*	Graham	Robb	Jarvie	Henry	Purdie	Thomson/Taylor
3/1	23,574	9				Ref: G Smith	*Allan*	*Wilson R*	*Johnston*	*Ford*	*Phillip*	*Gemmell*	*Wilson J*	*Robinson*	*Duncan*	*Scott J*	*Lambie*	

Scotland stages official matches on a Sunday for the first time, producing Pittodrie's biggest gate of the season. Robb's debut was in the Cup at Dens six years ago, when Dundee's Jimmy Wilson played for Aberdeen. Johnston's goal is deflected in by Henry. Graham's shot hits a post.

UEFA Cup

			F-A		H-T	Scorers, Times, and Referees	1	2	3	4	5	6	7	8	9	10	11	subs used
1:1 H FINN HARPS	6 W	4-1			3-0	Miller R 33, Jarvie 36, 82, Graham 38	Clark	Hair	Hermiston	Thomson	Young	Miller W	Willoughby	Graham	Taylor	Jarvie	Miller R	
19/9 (Rep Ireland)	10,700					Harkin 87	*Murray*	*McGrory*	*Hutton*	*McDowell*	*Sheridan*	*McDermott*	*Smith*	*Nicholl*	*Bradley*	*Harkin*	*Ferry*	
						Ref: E Axelryd (Sweden)												

The Donegal team had never won the Irish championship or the FAI Cup, and are playing in Europe for the first time. How Aberdeen failed to score 20 is a mystery. The luck of the Irish may have had something to do with it. So might Aberdeen's profligate finishing.

			F-A		H-T	Scorers, Times, and Referees	1	2	3	4	5	6	7	8	9	10	11	subs used
1:2 A FINN HARPS	5 W	3-1			2-0	Robb 21, Jarvie 28, Miller R 89	Clark	Hair	Hermiston	Thomson*	Young	Miller W	Willoughby	Graham^	Jarvie	Jarvie	Miller R	Smith/Purdie
3/10	5,500					Harkin 66	*Murray*	*McDowell*	*Hutton*	*O'Docherty Sheridan*	*McDermott Smith*		*Nicholl*	*Bradley*	*Harkin*	*Ferry*		*McGrory*
						Ref: F Geluck (Belgium)												

(Dons win 7-2 on aggregate)

Finn Park, Ballybofey, proves to be an amenable little vacation for Aberdeen. The appreciative Irish crowd would have welcomed a display of Aberdeen's superior skills - but the Dons couldn't be bothered. Alex Harkin, who scored in both legs, will later become Finn Harps' manager.

			F-A		H-T	Scorers, Times, and Referees	1	2	3	4	5	6	7	8	9	10	11	subs used
2:1 H TOTTENHAM	4 D	1-1			0-1	Hermiston 87p	Clark	Hair	Hermiston	Thomson*	Young	Miller W	Graham	Robb	Jarvie	Smith	Miller R	Naylor/Neighbour
24/10 (England)	30,000					Coates 15	*Daines*	*Evans*	*Kinnear**	*Pratt*	*England*	*Beal*	*Gilzean*	*Perryman*	*McGrath*	*Peters*	*Coates**	
						Ref: S Patterson (N Ireland)												

Aberdeen's first competitive home match against an English club. Spurs have won the Cup-Winners' and UEFA Cup, but are 15th in the English First Division. Willie Miller tackles McGrath and the ball breaks to Ralph Coates. Evans fells Bertie Miller from behind for a penalty.

			F-A		H-T	Scorers, Times, and Referees	1	2	3	4	5	6	7	8	9	10	11	subs used
2:2 A TOTTENHAM	3 L	1-4			0-2	Jarvie 54	Clark	Hair	Hermiston	Thomson*	Young	Miller W*	Graham	Robb	Jarvie	Smith	Graham	Mitchell/Miller R
7/11	21,785					Peters 13, Neighbour 36, McGrath 80, 89/Jennings	*Evans*	*Knowles*	*Pratt*	*England*	*Beal*	*Gilzean*	*Perryman*	*Chivers*	*Peters*	*Neighbour**	*McGrath*	
						Ref: K Tshenscher (W Germany)												

(Dons lose 2-5 on aggregate)

Peters punishes Willie Miller's weak clearance. Three minutes later Jarvie is pulled down. The ref says penalty, but Spurs' protests make him consult a linesman, who says no. Thomson's miskick lets in Jimmy Neighbour. Jarvie hooks a goal, but Spurs sub Chris McGrath settles it.

League Table

			Home					Away					
	Team	P	W	D	L	F	A	W	D	L	F	A	Pts
1	Celtic	34	12	4	1	51	15	11	3	3	31	12	53
2	Hibernian	34	14	2	1	46	18	6	7	4	29	24	49
3	Rangers	34	9	3	5	32	17	12	3	2	35	17	48
4	ABERDEEN	34	7	9	1	26	9	6	7	4	20	17	42
5	Dundee	34	9	7	1	32	25	4	4	9	35	23	39
6	Hearts	34	6	6	5	26	20	8	4	5	28	23	38
7	Ayr	34	9	4	4	23	16	4	4	7	21	24	38
8	Dundee Utd	34	7	3	7	30	25	5	4	8	25	26	37
9	Motherwell	34	8	5	4	28	20	6	2	9	17	17	35
10	Dumbarton	34	7	3	7	23	23	4	4	9	20	35	29
11	Partick This	34	7	4	6	19	16	2	6	9	14	30	28
12	St Johnstone	34	3	6	8	20	31	6	4	7	21	29	28
13	Arbroath	34	5	5	10	24	32	5	5	7	28	37	27
14	Morton	34	4	5	8	20	27	4	5	8	17	22	26
15	Clyde	34	5	2	10	13	26	3	7	7	16	39	25
16	Dunfermline	34	3	5	9	28	37	5	3	9	15	28	24
17	East Fife	34	3	2	12	9	30	6	4	7	17	21	24
18	Falkirk	34	1	11	5	17	21	3	3	11	16	37	22
		612	117	79	110	467	405	110	79	117	405	467	612

Odds & ends

Double wins: (3) Dumbarton, Dundee Utd, Falkirk.

Double losses: (0).

Won from behind: (0).

Lost from in front: (1) Celtic (LC).

High spots: Unbeaten in first 8 league games.
Best defensive record - 26 - in the league.

Low spots: Being knocked out of Scottish Cup at first hurdle.
7 league and cup matches without a win from 29 December.
11 home draws in league and cups.
Most league draws - 16 - of any club.
Failure to beat Celtic in 4 attempts.

Ever-presents: (2) Bobby Clark, Willie Young.

Hat-tricks: (3) Drew Jarvie 2, Ian Taylor 1.

Leading scorer: (24) Drew Jarvie.

Appearances and Goals

	Appearances								Goals				
	Lge	Sub	LC	Sub	SC	Sub	Eur	Sub	Lge	LC	SC	Eur	Tot
Boel, Henning	7	1											
Clark, Bobby	34		10		1		4						
Craig, John	4	4	1	1									
Davidson, Duncan		5											
Graham, Arthur	31	1	9		1		4		3	3		1	7
Hair, Ian	18		4				4		1				1
Henry, Jim	6				1								
Hermiston, Jim	33		10		1		4		1	1		1	3
Jarvie, Drew	32		10		1		4		13	7		4	24
McCall, Walker	4	3							2				2
McLelland, Chic	15								1				1
Miller, Bertie	5	2	5				2		1	1		2	4
Miller, Jimmy	4	1	1										
Miller, Willie	31		9				4		1				1
Mitchell, Barrie	1	1										1	
Pirie, Billy	9												
Purdie, Ian	6	2	3				3		1				1
Robb, Dave	21	3	3		1		3	1	11	1			12
Smith, Joe	23	2	8		1		2		1	1			2
Street, Bobby	1	1											
Taylor, Ian	14	3	9	1			2		3				3
Thomson, Eddie	31	1	10				4		1				1
Williamson, Billy	2	2	6	1									
Willoughby, Alec	8	3	1	4	3					1			1
Young, Willie	34		10		1		4		2				2
(own-goals)									4				4
25 players used	374	30	110	11	11	2	44	5	46	14		9	69

Each match is shown on two lines: the upper (bold) line is Aberdeen, the lower (italic) line is the opponents.

No	Date	Opp (H/A)	Att	Pos	Pt	F-A	H-T	Scorers, Times, and Referees	1	2	3	4	5	6	7	8	9	10	11	subs used
1	31/8	HIBERNIAN (H)	13,000	—	—	L 2-3	1-1	Purdie 17, Pirie 77 / Cropley 32, 90, Harper 86 — Ref: A McKenzie	Clark	Hermiston^	McLelland	Smith	Young	Miller	Purdie	Hair	Thomson	Jarvie*	Graham	Pirie
									McArthur	Bremner	Schaedler	Stanton	Spalding	Blackley*	Cropley	Smith*	Harper	Gordon	Duncan	Munro/Edwards
2	7/9	DUNDEE (A)	6,396	10	2	W 1-0	1-0	Purdie 12 — Ref: E Pringle	Clark	Hermiston^	McLelland	Smith	Young	Miller	Purdie	Hair	Thomson^	Pirie	Graham	Jarvie/Williamson
									Allan	Wilson R	Johnston	Ford*	Stewart	Gemmell	Wilson J	Robinson	Hutchinson	Scott J	Scott I	Lembie
3	14/9	ST JOHNSTONE (H)	7,000	6	4	W 3-1	0-0	Jarvie 68, Hair 70, Graham 82 / Cramond 59 — Ref: R Henderson	Clark	Hermiston	McLelland	Smith^	Young	Miller	Purdie	Hair	Thomson	Pirie^	Graham	Jarvie/Williamson
									Nicoll	Smith	Argue	Rennie	Macdonald	Finnell	Muir	O'Rourke	McGregor*	Cramond*	Hall	Hotson
4	21/9	KILMARNOCK (A)	5,000	8	4	L 0-1	0-0	McDicken 58 — Ref: E Thomson	Clark	Williamson	McLelland	Smith	Young	Miller	Purdie^	Hair	Thomson^	Jarvie	Graham	Davidson/Pirie
									Stewart	Maxwell	Robertson	McCulloch	Rodman	McDicken	McSherry	Fleming	Morrison	Sheed	Smith	
5	28/9	AIRDRIE (H)	5,000	8	6	W 1-0	1-0	Young 24 — Ref: A Webster	Clark	Williamson	McLelland	Smith	Young	Miller	Purdie	Hair	Pirie	Jarvie	Graham	McCall
									McWilliams	Jonquin	Menzies	Black	McKinley	Whiteford	Reynolds	Cowan	McCulloch	Walker	Wilson*	McCann
6	5/10	HEARTS (A)	8,500	4	8	W 4-1	3-1	Purdie 35, Graham 38, Smith 43, [McCall 72] / Park 45 — Ref: B McGinlay	Clark	Williamson	McLelland	Smith	Young	Miller	Purdie	Craig	Pirie*	Jarvie	Graham	Hair/McCall
									Garland	Kay	Burrell	Jefferies	Anderson	Brown	Aird	Ford	Busby	Park	Murray	
7	12/10	AYR (H)	6,000	4	10	W 3-0	2-0	Jarvie 9, Purdie 23p, McCall 57 — Ref: K Hope	Clark	Williamson	McLelland	Smith	Young	Miller	Purdie	Craig	McCall	Jarvie	Graham	McCulloch/Ingram
									McLean	Wells*	Murphy	McAnespie	Fleming	Fippi	Doyle	Lannon	Sommer	Dickson	Cameron	
8	19/10	DUMBARTON (A)	4,000	3	12	W 3-2	1-1	McCall 10, Jarvie 52, Graham 62 / Wallace 19p, Cook 70 — Ref: J Gordon	Clark	Williamson	McLelland	Smith*	Young	Miller	Purdie	Craig	McCall	Jarvie	Graham	Thomson
									Williams	Mullen	Watt	Cushley*	Muir	Ruddy	Cook	Wallace	Bourke	McAdam	Graham	Coleman
9	26/10	ARBROATH (H)	7,000	3	14	W 5-1	3-1	Williamson 16, 70, McCall 27, 61, [Purdie 32] / Wells 40 — Ref: R Henderson	Clark	Williamson	McLelland	Smith	Young	Miller	Purdie	Craig	McCall	Jarvie	Graham	Thomson
									Marshall	Milne	Rylance	Cargill	Carson	Murray	Sellars*	Cant*	Wells	Fletcher	Yule	Reid/Buchan
10	2/11	CELTIC (A)	29,000	3	14	L 0-1	0-1	Wilson 42 — Ref: G Smith	Clark	Williamson	McLelland	Smith	Young	Miller	Purdie	Craig	McCall	Jarvie	Graham	
									Hunter	McDonald	Brogan	Murray	McNeill	McCluskey	Johnstone*	Dalglish	Deans	Hood	Wilson	Lennox

Match notes:

1. They came in their thousands to Pittodrie to witness the painful sight of Joe Harper in a green and white jersey. Four minutes from time Harper fires a free-kick past Bobby Clark to level the scores at 2-2. In injury-time Harper has another shot blocked, but the ball falls to Cropley.

2. Not since 1959-60 have Aberdeen lost their first two opening league fixtures. Bobby Clark's clearance was carried on by Ian Hair and Eddie Thomson for the unmarked Ian Purdie to outmanoeuvre Allan. Aberdeen have not lost at Dens Park in the league since season 1969-70.

3. St Johnstone have won their first two league games. They looked to be maintaining their 100% record until Jimmy Bonthrone made two inspired substitutions. One of them, Jarvie, put the Dons level with an unstoppable header past Nicoll. Two minutes later Hair scored a second.

4. Kilmarnock players are earning the displeasure of referees this season. Against Kilmarnock Ian Purdie was booked for the fourth time and Willie Miller for the third. Kilmarnock lost their opening match 0-5 to Celtic and will lose their next 0-6 to Rangers, so the Dons had little to beat.

5. Airdrie have won their past three games and are fourth at start of play. Dons' acting skipper Willie Young plays a captain's part and scores a captain's goal. Keeper McWilliams might have saved Young's header but for the distraction of Billy Pirie's looming presence.

6. Eddie Thomson is Dons' acting captain on his old Tynecastle stomping ground. Not a good day for Hearts fans, whose team have yet to win. After Joe Smith put the Dons 3-0 up they chanted 'Seith must go'. Best of Aberdeen's goals was Arthur Graham's thunderous angled drive.

7. Ally MacLeod's Ayr are having a tough time. They have only recently won their first match of the season. The player making the greatest impact is Drew Jarvie, who scores once, is brought down for Aberdeen's penalty, and who in the last minute hits the Ayr goalpost.

8. Willie Young nudged Tom McAdam in the air to concede the penalty from which Dumbarton equalise. Jarvie and Graham restored Aberdeen's advantage. Dumbarton had a goal disallowed before Cook halved the deficit, but cannot prevent a third consecutive league defeat.

9. Five goals in four matches for lanky Walker McCall as Aberdeen extend their winning sequence to five and set up a visit to Celtic. Poor Arbroath have started the season respectably, but this defeat starts the rot that will eventually see them finish adrift at the bottom.

10. Celtic are about to be dethroned, though they will head the table going into the New Year. For the second successive game Ian Purdie fails from the spot. Graham had been impeded by Brogan, but Purdie hit a post. Harry Hood had earlier chipped a pass to the unmarked Wilson.

11 H PARTICK THISTLE 3 D 1-1 8,000 14 15 — 0-0

Purdie 77
Prudham 68
Ref: J Paterson

Clark, Williamson, McLelland, Smith, Young, Miller, Purdie, Craig, McCall, Jarvie, Graham, Davidson
Rough, Hansen J, Anderson, Campbell, Hansen A, Clark, Lawrie, Houston, Glavin, Prudham, Gray*, Coulston

Two men deny Aberdeen a comfortable victory - Eddie Prudham, on loan to Thistle from Sheffield Wednesday, and goalkeeper Alan Rough. Ian Purdie, villain at the penalty spot in Aberdeen's last two matches, rescues a point. Thistle are enduring a winless run of seven games.

12 H MORTON 5 D 3-3 7,500 14 16 — 0-1

McCall 47, Young 85, Graham 87
Stovdam 6, Reid 59, Taylor 89
Ref: W Mullen

Clark, Williamson, McLelland, Smith*, Young, Miller, Davidson, Craig*, McCall, Jarvie, Graham, Hermiston/Pirie
Baines, Hayes, Ritchie, Lumsden, Anderson, Rankin, Taylor, Reid, Harley, Stovdam*, McGhee, Murray

Three goals in the final five minutes sends the Pittodrie fans home in a daze. Two headers seemed to have given the Dons both points, but still left time for Taylor to rescue a draw for Morton which they fully deserved and which prevented a fifth consecutive league defeat.

13 A DUNDEE UTD 5 L 0-4 8,000 4 16 — 0-2

[Williamson 88 og]/Geoghegan
Fleming 11, 37, Narey 65,
Ref: R Hopkins

Williamson, McLelland, Smith*, Young, Miller, Purdie, Craig*, McCall, Jarvie, Graham, Hermiston/Davidson
McAlpine, Rolland, Kopel, Smith W, Houston, Traynor, Narey, Gray, Fleming, McDonald

A virus keeps out Bobby Clark. In steps Andy Geoghegan, himself not fully fit, to play the worst game of his life - brushing Fleming's cross over his own goal-line to make it 2-0 to United. This is Dundee United's ninth game in a row without defeat, but the run will now end at Ibrox.

14 A MOTHERWELL 5 L 1-2 3,472 11 16 — 1-0

Graham 45
McIlwraith 55, Goodwin 80
Ref: I Foote

Clark, Hair, Hermiston, Young, Miller, Purdie, Davidson, McCall, Jarvie, Graham, Graham*
Lloyd, Watson W, Wark*, Watson R, McLaren, Goodwin, McIlwraith, Millar, Taylor, Gardner, Graham*, McClymont/Goldthorp

Drew Jarvie and Willie Miller are booked. Arthur Graham gives Aberdeen an interval lead, but they still lost. Scotland manager Willie Ormond watches the Dons for the first time this season. Ultimately, these two points will secure Motherwell a place in next season's Premier League.

15 H RANGERS 5 L 1-2 25,000 1 16 — 0-1

Hair 75
Johnstone 30, McLean 87
Ref: D Ramsay

Clark, Hermiston, Hermiston, Young, Miller, Purdie, Thomson, Jarvie, Street, Graham
Kennedy, Jardine, Greig, Johnstone, Jackson, Forsyth, McLean, Parlane, McKean, MacDonald, Young

Before kick-off Rangers fans charge across the pitch towards the Beach End. Willie Waddell and Jock Wallace appeal for order. Johnstone chests the ball down and fires past Clark. Ian Hair levels, then Willie Young is dispossessed by Parlane: he squares for the inrushing McLean.

16 A CLYDE 5 D 1-1 2,053 13 17 — 1-1

Purdie 34
Boyle 40
Ref: J Grant

Clark, Hair, Hermiston*, Young, Miller, Purdie, Street, Jarvie, Graham, Williamson
Williams, Anderson, Swan, Ahern, McVie, Burns, Sullivan, Ward, Boyle*, Burns, John Millar*, Ferris

Clyde are drawing a lot of games recently. Aberdeen's Ian Hair was sent off in the first half: Clyde's goalscorer, Peter Boyle, in the second. This will be the smallest attendance to view the Dons this season. This is the Dons' seventh league game without a win, and the run isn't over.

17 H DUNFERMLINE 5 D 1-1 5,000 9 18 — 0-1

Hair 71
Forrest 8
Ref: D Syme

Clark, Thomson, Young, Miller, Purdie, Henry*, Street, Graham, Williamson/Davidson
Karlsen, Scott, Markey, Thomson, Evans, Kinninmonth Watson*, McNicoll, Forrest, Shaw, Cameron, Sinclair

Aberdeen have now gone eight games and two months without a win. If Bonthrone cannot stop the rot they will lose their place in next season's 10-team Premier Division. It is also Dunfermline's fourth game without a win, so there is not much confidence on display out there.

18 A HIBERNIAN 5 W 1-0 13,190 3 20 — 1-0

Pirie 18
Ref: R Marshall

Clark, Hair, Thomson, Thomson, Miller, Purdie, Henry*, Pirie*, Williamson, Graham, Jarvie/Davidson
McArthur, Brownlie, Schaedler, Stanton, Bremner, Blackley, Edwards, McLeod, Harper, Munro, Duncan

After five minutes Hibs are awarded a penalty, saved by Clark. Hibs' keeper McArthur blocks Williamson's shot, but Billy Pirie pounces. Joe Harper was harshly treated throughout by Willie Young. In a tempestuous match Chic McLelland and Hibs' Alec Edwards were sent off.

19 H DUNDEE W 4-0 12,000 22 — 1-0

Caldwell 14 og, Pirie 54, Jarvie 77, [Hair 79]Allan
Ref: E Pringle

Clark, Hair, Thomson, Thomson, Miller, Purdie, Henry*, Pirie*, Williamson, Graham, Jarvie/Davidson
Wilson R, Gemmell, Ford, Stewart*, Phillip, Gordon, Robinson, Wallace*, Scott J, Caldwell, Johnston Hutchinson

Aberdeen record their biggest winning margin in a New Year derby with Dundee since World War II. Jarvie's goal - his first in 11 games - was a peach. Coming on as substitute he swerved past two Dundee defenders and whacked the ball past Allan. He won't be dropped again.

20 A ST JOHNSTONE 5 D 1-1 4,500 11 23 — 0-0

Davidson 82
Macdonald 57
Ref: F Phillip

Clark, Hair, Thomson, Thomson, Miller, Purdie, Henry*, Pirie*, Williamson, Graham, Jarvie/Davidson
Robertson, Smith*, Argue, Rennie, Macdonald Kinnell, Muir, O'Rourke, Hall, Cramond, Lambie*, Ritchie/Aitken

St Johnstone have won just one match in 12. Drama at the death at Muirton Park. Saints' Jim O'Rourke is pulled down, picks himself up and sees his penalty smartly saved by a limping Bobby Clark. According to the statistics, Aberdeen are the dirtiest team in the First Division.

21 H KILMARNOCK 4 W 4-0 8,500 14 25 — 2-0

Jarvie 24, Young 43, Pirie 72p, Graham 89Clark
Ref: B McGinlay

Clark, Hair, Thomson, Miller, Purdie, Henry*, Pirie*, Williamson* Graham, Jarvie, Pirie/Davidson
McCulloch A McLean, Robertson, McCulloch I* Rodman, Maxwell, Provan, Smith, Morrison E* Sheed, Falls, Whyte/Morrison D

Kilmarnock have won just one game in 10. This is a bleak day for Killie, who have two players stretchered off in the first half within minutes of each other. This easy win stretches Aberdeen's unbeaten run to six. They are now in the right frame of mind to take on Rangers in the Cup.

No	Date		F-A	Pos	Pt	H-T	Scorers, Times, and Referees
22	H HEARTS	1/2	2-2 (D)	5	26	2:1	McLelland 22, Jarvie 32 / Gibson 15, Callachan 70. Ref: T Kyle

Aberdeen: Clark, Hair, McLelland, Thomson, Young, Miller, Purdie, Henry*, Jarvie, Williamson, Graham — sub: Smith
Hearts: Cruickshank, Kay, Clunie, Jefferies, Anderson, Brown, Park*, Busby, Gibson, Murray T, Callachan, Aird

A terrific match. Hearts deserved their early lead, which was cancelled out when McLelland hit the ball on the drop. After Jarvie's low shot put the Dons in front, Callachan levelled with a meteoric shot which went in off the crossbar. Aberdeen are now unbeaten in eight games overall.

No	Date		F-A	Pos	Pt	H-T	Scorers, Times, and Referees
23	A AYR	8/2	0-2 (L)	5	26	0-0	Doyle 71, Graham 79p. Ref: D Downie

Aberdeen: Clark, Hair, McLelland, Thomson, Young, Miller, Purdie*, Henry, Jarvie, Williamson*, Graham — subs: Smith/Davidson
Ayr: McLean, Taylor, Murphy, McAnespie, Fleming, Filippi, Doyle, Graham, Ingram, Phillips, McCulloch*, Dickson

The Dons' unbeaten run comes to an end. Smiles for Ayr manager Ally MacLeod, but not for Ian Hair, whose attempted header back to Bobby Clark fell nicely for Doyle. Aberdeen have 48 hours to put this result out of their system before taking on Rangers in a Scottish Cup replay.

No	Date		F-A	Pos	Pt	H-T	Scorers, Times, and Referees
24	H DUMBARTON	22/2	1-1 (D)	5	27	1:1	Graham 9 / Bourke 32. Ref: J Gordon

Aberdeen: Clark, Hair, McLelland, Thomson*, Young, Miller, Purdie*, Henry, Jarvie, Williamson, Graham — subs: Smith/Davidson
Dumbarton: McGregor, Muir, Watt, McAdam C, Cushley, Ruddy, Coleman, Bourke, McAdam T, Graham, Wallace

Dumbarton have just enjoyed their biggest win of the season - 5-1 v Arbroath. They now claw their way back into a match they should have lost by a mile. Arthur Graham scored one goal and had two more disallowed for offside. The Dons have their minds on Motherwell in the Cup.

No	Date		F-A	Pos	Pt	H-T	Scorers, Times, and Referees
25	A ARBROATH	1/3	2-1 (W)	5	29	1-0	Williamson 11, Graham 49 / Cargill 74. Ref: J Paterson

Aberdeen: Clark, Hair, McLelland, Smith, Young, Miller, Purdie*, Henry, Jarvie, Williamson, Graham — sub: Davidson
Arbroath: Wilson, Milne, Murray, Cargill, Carson, Smith, Reid, Rylance, Bone, Penman, Fletcher

Aberdeen coasted through the first half against the basement team, and panicked their way through the second. At 2-1 Fletcher's header thumped against Clark's post and flew back into the keeper's arms. The Dons are 15 points behind leaders Rangers and can't catch them.

No	Date		F-A	Pos	Pt	H-T	Scorers, Times, and Referees
26	A AIRDRIE	4/3	2-2 (D)		30	0-1	Graham 61, Davidson 77 / McCann 28, Jonquin 88p. Ref: J Callaghan

Aberdeen: Clark, Hair, McLelland, Smith, Young, Miller, Purdie*, Henry*, Jarvie, Williamson, Graham — subs: Davidson/Cooper
Airdrie: McWilliams, Jonquin, Cowan, Menzies, Black, Whiteford, McCann, Reynolds, McCulloch*, Walker*, Wilson, Lapsley/Anderson

Neil Cooper, a former schoolboy international, makes his debut for the Dons. He is denied his win bonus by Willie Young's reckless challenge on Whiteford. Referee Callaghan took an age before deciding that the tackle merited a penalty-kick. Seven games without a win for Airdrie.

No	Date		F-A	Pos	Pt	H-T	Scorers, Times, and Referees
27	H CELTIC	12/3	3-2 (W)		32	1-0	Williamson 17, 57, 78p / Lynch 53, 62. Ref: G Smith

Aberdeen: Clark, Hair, McLelland, Thomson, Young, Miller*, Purdie, Smith, Jarvie, Williamson*, Graham* — subs: McCall/Davidson
Celtic: Latchford, McGrain, McCluskey, Glavin, McNeill, Connelly, Hood, Wilson, Dalglish, Callaghan, Lynch

Skipper Jim Hermiston is dropped and announces his retirement from the end of the season. Billy Williamson brings about Celtic's first league defeat at Pittodrie in nine seasons. At 2-2 Aberdeen were given a penalty. Williamson took responsibility, completing his hat-trick off the post.

No	Date		F-A	Pos	Pt	H-T	Scorers, Times, and Referees
28	A PARTICK THISTLE	15/3	0-1 (L)	5	32	0-0	McQuade 78. Ref: R Keggie

Aberdeen: Clark, Hair, Hermiston, Thomson*, Ward, Miller, Purdie, Smith, McCall, Williamson, Graham — sub: Davidson
Partick Thistle: Rough, Hansen J, Kellachan, Campbell, Hansen A, Aaderson, Houston, Rae, Craig, Sommer, McQuade

Under normal circumstances Partick's mid-table position might see them less than committed. But they are desperate to finish in the top 10. Having eight teams to go down changes the complexion of title and relegation issues. Chic McLelland misses this game through suspension.

No	Date		F-A	Pos	Pt	H-T	Scorers, Times, and Referees
29	A MORTON	22/3	3-0 (W)	5	34	1-0	Robb 17, Williamson 53, Graham 67. Ref: A McKenzie

Aberdeen: Clark, Hair*, McLelland, Hermiston, Ward, Miller, Purdie, Robb, McCall, Williamson, Graham — sub: Campbell
Morton: Baines, Hayes, Ritchie, Townsend, McNeill, Irvine, Hudson, Lumsden, Hazel, Skovdam, Harley*, Taylor

Dave Robb celebrates his return after almost a whole season out with a knee injury. He scores the first goal, a neat effort set up by Joe Smith's lob. This is Morton's fifth defeat on the trot. Without any chance of their getting into the top 10, there seems little for Morton to play for.

No	Date		F-A	Pos	Pt	H-T	Scorers, Times, and Referees
30	H DUNDEE UTD	29/3	2-0 (W)	5	36	1-0	Williamson 43, Hermiston 62p. Ref: R Davidson

Aberdeen: Clark, Hair, McLelland, Hermiston, Young, Miller, Purdie, Robb, Jarvie, Williamson, Graham — sub: Robb
Dundee United: McAlpine, Rolland, Forsyth*, Copland, Houston, Narey, Sturrock, Hegarty, Gray, Smith W, Payne*, Addison/Traynor

David Narey conceded two penalties for Dundee United. Hamish McAlpine saved Robb's, but not Hermiston's. Willie Young kept Andy Gray in his pocket all through the game, which end's United's six-match winning streak. Both clubs are chasing a UEFA Cup place.

No	Date		F-A	Pos	Pt	H-T	Scorers, Times, and Referees
31	A RANGERS	12/4	2-3 (L)	5	36	0-0	Williamson 55, Hermiston 61p / Johnstone 57, Stein 59, Miller 76p. Ref: R Valentine

Aberdeen: Clark, Kennedy, McLelland, Hermiston, Young, Smith, Purdie, Robb, Jarvie, Williamson, Graham — sub: Robb
Rangers: Jardine, Miller, McKean, Jackson, Forsyth, McLean*, Stein, Parlane, MacDonald, Johnstone, Fyfe

Four goals in six minutes. Rangers are guaranteed the title and Aberdeen have booked their place in the Premier Division, but their first league defeat at Ibrox since 1969-70 keeps them out of Europe. Miller conceded Rangers' penalty; Williamson was booked for protesting about it.

League matches

32   H   CLYDE   19/4 | 5 W 16 38 | 3-0
Hermiston 8p, Jarvie 32, 37, Miller 83
Harvey 85
Ref: F Phillips   3,300

Clark — Cairney — Hair — McLelland — Hermiston — Young — Miller — Smith — Robb — Jarvie — Williamson* — Graham — **McMaster**
Anderson — Swan — Ahern — McVie — Boyd — Sullivan^ — Millar — Ferris — Harvey — Boyle — Burns JimHutchison*

Playing without tension, Aberdeen inflict a demolition job on Clyde, who have no chance of making the top 10. Jim Hermiston's penalty is his third in three games. Pittodrie draws another terribly small crowd. Drew Jarvie's two goals are not enough to make him top scorer this season.

33   H   MOTHERWELL   23/4 | D 2-2 | 39
Jarvie 8, Graham 51
Pettigrew 17, Graham 40
Ref: J Gordon   8,000

Clark — Rennie — Hair — McLelland — Hermiston — Young — Miller — Smith — Robb — Jarvie — Williamson — Graham — **McCall**
Watson W — Wark — Watson R — McLaren — Hamilton — Pettigrew — Millar — Graham — Goodwin — Taylor — Gardner*

Motherwell love playing at Pittodrie this season. Having won 1-0 in the Scottish Cup, they now need a point to virtually guarantee their place in the Premier Division. In the last minute Robb 'scored' from Graham's cross, but after consultation the referee annulled the effort for offside.

34   A   DUNFERMLINE   26/4 | 5 W 15 41 | 3-1
Robb 6, 69, 90
Shaw 14
Ref: A Paterson   3,500

Clark — Karlsen — Hair — McLelland — Hermiston — Young — Miller — Smith — Robb — Jarvie — Williamson* — Graham — **McCall**
Scott — Markey — Thomson — Evans — KinninmonthWatson — Campbell* — Smith — Reid — Shaw — Hamilton/Cameron*

Dunfermline have won just once since early January and have little fight in them. Dons' skipper Jim Hermiston plays his last game for the club and comes within inches of an own-goal with a downward header past Clark's post. Willie Miller is booked for the second time in four days.

Average   Home 9,500   Away 8,500

Scottish League Cup - Section 3

1   H   HEARTS   10/8 | L 0-1 | —
Ford 52
Ref: R Valentine   11,000

Geoghegan — Hermiston — McLelland — Smith — Hair — Davidson* — Henry* — Jarvie — Graham — Campbell — **McCall/Purdie**
Garland — Sneddon — Jefferies — Cant — Gallagher — Brown — Aird — Ford — Busby — Stevenson — Prentice

The two-year experiment of having two teams qualify from each section has been abandoned. Now only the top team goes throught to the semis, which makes it difficult for Aberdeen after this. Their youthful, makeshift side was beaten by Donald Ford's wheeling cross-cum-shot.

2   A   MORTON   14/8 | L 1-3 | —
Hermiston 86
McGhee 23, Skovdam 41, Hegarty 72
Ref: J Paterson   2,000

Geoghegan — Hermiston — McLelland — Smith — Hair — Davidson — Graham — Jarvie — Graham — Campbell — **Davidson**
Hayes — Ritchie — Townsend — Anderson — Rankin — Brown — Reid — Hazel — Pirie — Skovdam* — Murray*

Morton adapted themselves to the swamp conditions much better than Aberdeen. Morton's opener came when McGhee fended off Willie Miller's challenge to unleash an angled shot from 15 yards. This second defeat virtually eclipses Aberdeen's chances of staying alive.

3   A   DUNFERMLINE   17/8 | D 1-1 | —
Jarvie 30
Sinclair 27
Ref: J Gordon   4,500

Clark — Hermiston — McLelland — Smith* — Purdie — Hair — Jarvie — Thomson — Graham — Campbell — **Davidson**
Karlsen — Thomson — Wallace — Campbell R Leishman — KinninmonthWatson — Campbell I — Mackie — Shaw — Sinclair — Davidson*

Both teams brought on a substitute named Davidson. But all the scoring had already been done. Drew Jarvie scores the first goal of what will be a disappointing season for him. The Dons might finish bottom of their section, and that would not augur well for the league.

4   H   MORTON   21/8 | W 4-0 | 3
Purdie 24, Thomson 53, Jarvie 53, [Young 75]Baines
Ref: F Phillips   5,000

Clark — Hermiston — McLelland — Smith — Hair — Purdie — Jarvie — Thomson — Graham — Campbell — **Hunter**
Hayes — Ritchie — Townsend — Nelson — McGhee — Reid — Hazel — Hegarty — Skovdam — Prentice*

All things are relative. Morton had lost five goals to Hearts on Saturday, so this is an improvement. In the first match between these sides McGhee had got the better of Willie Miller. Not this time. Morton will finish next to bottom in Division 1, so the result means little.

5   H   DUNFERMLINE   24/8 | W 3-0 | 5
Jarvie 65, Williamson 69, Purdie 71
Ref: T Muirhead   7,000

Clark — Hermiston — McLelland — Smith* — Young — Miller — Purdie — Williamson Thomson — Jarvie — Graham* — **Pirie/McMaster**
Karlsen — Thomson — Wallace — Campbell R McNicoll — KinninmonthWatson — Campbell I Davidson^ — Shaw — Sinclair — Evans/Scott*

For over an hour Dunfermline's Norwegian keeper, Geir Karlsen, is the most grudgingly admired man at Pittodrie. Six minutes later all his earlier brilliance was forgiven. Among the Aberdeen substitutes was a youthful John McMaster, who came on for the last few minutes.

6   A   HEARTS   28/8 | L 1-2 | 5
Hermiston 55p
Aird 16, 72
Ref: D Syme   14,000

Clark — Hermiston — McLelland* — Smith* — Young — Purdie — Williamson Thomson — Jarvie — Graham — **Pirie/McMaster**
Garland — Sneddon — Jefferies — Cant — Gallagher — Brown — Aird — Ford — Busby — Stevenson Callachan

Hearts survive the League Cup section stage for the first time in 14 seasons. In the event, had the Dons won they would have gone through instead, though they did not play with any urgency. They are beaten by two Kenny Aird goals, but have earned seven bookings in six matches.

	P	W	D	L	F	A	Pts
Qual Hearts	6	4	0	2	13	6	8
Dunfermline	6	2	3	1	8	9	7
ABERDEEN	6	2	1	3	10	7	5
Morton	6	1	2	3	5	14	4

SCOTTISH LEAGUE DIV 1 (CUP-TIES)

Manager: Jimmy Bonthrone

SEASON 1974-75

Scottish Cup		F-A	H-T	Scorers, Times, and Referees	1	2	3	4	5	6	7	8	9	10	11	subs used
3 H RANGERS	30,000	D 1-1	0-0	Miller 87	Clark	Hair	McLelland	Thomson	Young	Miller	Purdie*	Henry	Jarvie	Williamson	Graham	Davidson
	1			Scott 67	*Kennedy*	*Jardine*	*Miller*	*McDougall*	*Jackson*	*Forsyth*	*McLean*	*Johnstone* *Parlane*		*MacDonald* *Scott*		*McKean*
				Ref: R Davidson												

An all-ticket match with the league leaders and champions-elect. Ian Purdie's free-kick hit the Rangers' post in the first half; Scott hit the Dons' net in the second. Then, with time running out, Willie Miller chipped a dramatic lob over Kennedy to earn Aberdeen a replay.

3R A RANGERS	52,000	W 2-1	1-1	Graham 2, Davidson 112	Clark	Hair	McLelland	Thomson	Young	Miller	Purdie	Henry*	Jarvie	Williamson*	Graham	Davidson/Smith
	1		*(aet)*	McKean 30	*Kennedy*	*Jardine*	*Miller*	*Johnstone* *Jackson*		*Forsyth*	*McKean*	*McLean*	*Parlane*	*MacDonald* *Scott*		*O'Hara/Fyfe*
				Ref: R Davidson												

Extra-time brings Aberdeen's first-ever Scottish Cup win over Rangers at Ibrox. The Gers have to play in all-white. Graham side-stepped Forsyth to shoot low past Kennedy. McKean's close-range header. 1-1. Joe Smith heads Graham's centre against a post and Davidson scores.

4 A DUNDEE UTD	22,000	W 1-0	1-0	Jarvie 14	Clark	Hair	McLelland	Thomson	Young	Miller	Purdie	Henry*	Jarvie	Williamson	Graham	Smith
	4				*McAlpine*	*Rolland*	*Kopel*	*Copland*	*Smith W.*	*Houston*	*Traynor*	*Narey*	*Gray*	*Fleming* *	*McDonald* *	*Hegarty/McLeod*
				Ref: J Paterson												

Tragedy for Jim McLean's United as Frank Kopel's back-pass was intercepted by Williamson. McAlpine blocked, but Jarvie followed up. Purdie hits the bar but Aberdeen live on their nerves. On 85 minutes Willie Miller handles, but the luckless Kopel blazes the penalty wide.

QF H MOTHERWELL	23,400	L 0-1	0-1		Clark	Hair	McLelland	Thomson	Young	Miller*	Purdie	Henry*	Jarvie	Williamson	Graham	Davidson/Smith
	10			Graham 44	*Rennie*	*Watson W*	*Wark*	*Watson R*	*McLaren*	*Miller*		*McIlwraith* *Pettigrew*	*Graham*	*Gardner*	*Goldthorp*	*Goodwin*
				Ref: I Foote												

Motherwell are beating everyone in sight at the moment, so are not really underdogs. Just before half-time referee Foote awarded Motherwell an indirect free-kick just outside the Aberdeen area. Gardner flipped over the ball and Bobby Graham blasted the Dons out of the Scottish Cup.

League Table

#	Team	P	Home					Away					Pts
			W	D	L	F	A	W	D	L	F	A	
1	Rangers	34	14	1	2	39	15	11	5	1	47	18	56
2	Hibernian	34	12	2	3	41	16	8	7	2	28	21	49
3	Celtic	34	11	2	4	47	20	8	2	5	34	21	45
4	Dundee Utd	34	10	5	2	41	19	9	2	6	31	24	45
5	ABERDEEN	34	9	6	2	42	20	7	3	7	24	23	41
6	Dundee	34	11	1	5	32	17	5	5	7	16	25	38
7	Ayr	34	9	5	3	29	27	5	3	9	21	34	36
8	Hearts	34	8	6	3	24	16	3	7	7	23	36	35
9	St Johnstone	34	8	4	5	27	20	3	8	6	14	24	34
10	Motherwell	34	8	2	7	30	23	6	3	8	22	34	33
11	Airdrie	34	7	7	3	26	20	4	2	11	17	35	31
12	Kilmarnock	34	5	7	5	26	29	3	6	8	26	39	31
13	Partick This	34	7	5	5	27	31	3	5	9	21	31	30
14	Dumbarton	34	5	5	9	19	24	4	5	8	25	31	24
15	Dunfermline	34	3	6	8	24	32	4	3	10	22	34	23
16	Clyde	34	4	6	7	25	30	2	4	11	15	33	22
17	Morton	34	4	5	8	17	28	5	2	10	14	34	22
18	Arbroath	34	4	5	8	20	27	1	2	14	14	39	17
		612	137	80	89	536	414	89	80	137	414	536	612

Odds & ends

Double wins: (2) Dundee, Arbroath.

Double losses: (1) Rangers.

Won from behind: (1) St Johnstoae (h).

Lost from in front: (3) Hibs (h), Motherwell (a), Rangers (a).

High spots: 5 successive wins from 28 September.

Beating Celtic at home in the league for the first time in 9 seasons.

Low spots: 8 games without a win, which followed 5 straight wins.

Home defeat by Motherwell in Scottish Cup.

Ever-presents: (2) Arthur Graham, Willie Miller.

Hat-tricks: (2) Billy Williamson, 1 Dave Robb.

Leading scorer: (13) Drew Jarvie.

Appearances & Goals

Name	Appearances						Goals			
	Lge	Sub	LC	Sub	SC	Sub	Lge	LC	SC	Tot
Campbell, George	33		2	1						
Clark, Bobby	33		4		4					
Cooper, Neil		1								
Craig, John	8									
Davidson, Duncan	2	14	1	2		3	2		1	3
Geoghegan, Andy	1		2							
Graham, Arthur	34		6		4		11	1		12
Hair, Ian	26	1	4		4		4			4
Henry, Jim	11		1		4					
Hermiston, Jim	13	2	6				3	2		5
Jarvie, Drew	27	5	6		4		9	3	1	13
McCall, Walker	10	4		1			6			6
McLelland, Chic	33		6		4		1			1
McMaster, John		1		2						
Miller, Willie	34		6		4			1	1	2
Pirie, Billy	7	4		2			4			4
Purdie, Ian	27	5	5	1	4		7	2		9
Robb, Dave	6						4			4
Smith, Joe	23	3	6			3	1			1
Street, Bobby	3									
Thomson, Eddie	16	1	4		4		1			1
Ward, Noel	2									
Williamson, Billy	27	4	2		4		9	1		10
Young, Willie	31		4		4		3		1	4
(own-goals)							1			1
24 players used	374	41	66	8	44	6	66	10	4	80

No	Date	Att	Pos	Pt	F-A	H-T	Scorers, Times, and Referees	1	2	3	4	5	6	7	8	9	10	11	subs used
1	A DUNDEE			L	2-3	2-1	Smith 3, Williamson 37	Clark	Hair	McLelland	Scott	Young	Miller	Smith	Robb	McMaster*	Williamson	Graham	Jarvie
	30/8	*6,067*		-			*Ford 2, Gemmell 79p, Hoggan 86*	*Allan*	*Wilson*	*Johnston**	*Ford*	*Stewart^*	*Phillip*	*Hoggan*	*Martin*	*Gordon*	*Anderson*	*Purdie*	*Sinclair/Gemmell*
							Ref: W Patson	Aberdeen looked to have the game won. But former Don, Ian Purdie won a fortuitous penalty - scored by Gemmell. Then Purdie appeared to foul Ian Hair, but was allowed by the referee to carry on and cross for Hoggan's winner. The Dons haven't won their first game for four years.											
2	H MOTHERWELL		9	D	2-2	2-1	Robb 17, Williamson 38	Clark	Hair*	McLelland	Scott	Young	Miller	Smith	Robb	McMaster^	Williamson	Graham	Pirie/Thomson
	6/9	5,500	*4*	1			*Pettigrew 19, 73*	*Rennie*	*Watson W*	*Wark*	*Watson R**	*McVie*	*Stevens*	*McAdam*	*Pettigrew*	*Graham*	*Davidson*	*Taylor^*	*McLaren/Millar*
							Ref: A McKenzie	Having knocked the Dons out of last season's Scottish Cup, Motherwell claimed the last vacant position in the new Premier Division. Willie Pettigrew is the man of the moment. It is he who denies Aberdeen their first league win. Pittodrie offers the new division a paltry attendance.											
3	H DUNDEE UTD		10	L	1-3	1-2	Scott 25	Geoghegan	Hair	McLelland	Scott	Young*	Miller	Smith!	Robb	Jarvie	Williamson	Graham	Pirie
	13/9	5,500	*2*	1			*Sturrock 22, Hegarty 45, Copland 67*	*McAlpine*	*Rolland*	*Kopel*	*Copland*	*Smith W**	*Narey^*	*Rennie*	*Payne*	*Gray*	*Houston*	*Sturrock*	*Hegarty/Traynor*
							Ref: D Syme	When did this last happen? Aberdeen are left propping up the table. Shortly after half-time Joe Smith is sent off for a flash of temper directed at Paul Hegarty. Later, Willie Young is substituted. He tore off his shirt, storms out of the ground and never plays for Aberdeen again.											
4	A HEARTS		8	D	2-2	2-2	Scott 7, Williamson 8	Geoghegan	Hair	McLelland	Scott	Ward	Miller	Smith*	Robb	Jarvie	Williamson	Graham	Thomson
	20/9	*9,500*	*7*	2			*Gibson 4, Prentice 5*	*Cruickshank*	*Clunie*	*Kay*	*Brown**	*Anderson*	*Murray*	*Park*	*Busby*	*Gibson*	*Callachan*	*Prentice*	*Aird*
							Ref: R Davidson	Miller is at fault for Hearts' first goal; Geoghegan for their second. But then Scott beat Cruickshank with a low shot and Williamson's effort trickled through the keeper's legs. 2-2, and only eight minutes played. Robb had a chance near the end, but his shot threatened the corner flag.											
5	H AYR		7	W	3-1	1-0	Williamson 33, Scott 48, 77	Geoghegan	Hair	McLelland	Scott	Ward	Miller	Smith*	Robb	Jarvie	Williamson	Graham	**Hather**
	27/9	**4,500**	*6*	4			*Graham 75*	*Sproat*	*Wells*	*Murphy*	*Paton**	*McAnespie*	*McSherry*	*Doyle*	*Graham*	*Ingram*	*McCulloch*	*Dickson^*	*Cameron/McDonald*
							Ref: W Mullen	A nostalgic moment for older Aberdeen fans. Jimmy Bonthrone brings on John Hather as a second-half sub. He is the son of flying Jack Hather from the 1950s. John's debut is a happy one, coinciding with the Dons' first Premier win. Ayr manager Ally MacLeod will soon move north.											
6	A RANGERS		7	L	0-1	0-1		Geoghegan	Hair	McLelland	Scott	Ward	Miller	Thomson	Robb	Jarvie	Williamson*	Graham	Cooper
	4/10	*22,000*	*1*	4			*McDougall 16*	*McCloy*	*Jardine*	*Dawson*	*Greig*	*Jackson*	*Miller*	*McLean*	*McDougall*	*Parlane*	*Johnstone*	*Young*	
							Ref: R Davidson	Rangers are top of the Premier League, but it is difficult to see why, on the evidence of this dreary affair. As for Aberdeen, they looked aimless and dreadful. McDougall's goal was a messy affair, the ball going in after McLean's shot had spun off a post. Troubled times for the Dons.											
7	H CELTIC		9	L	1-2	0-2	Scott 59	Clark	Thomson	McLelland*	Hair	Ward^	Miller	Scott	Robb	Jarvie	Henry	Graham	Williamson/Pirie
	11/10	17,900	*1*	4			*Dalglish 15, Deans 43*	*Latchford*	*McGrain*	*Lynch*	*McCluskey*	*MacDonald*	*Edvaldsson*	*Wilson!*	*Dalglish*	*Deans**	*Callaghan*	*Hood^*	*Lennox/Ritchie*
							Ref: G Smith	Willie Miller's crazy back-pass was snapped up by Dalglish. It put 10-man Celtic ahead - Paul Wilson having been sent off for throwing the ball into Thomson's face. Aberdeen had been playing above themselves, but now Celtic funnelled back. Jimmy Bonthrone quits after the game.											
8	H ST JOHNSTONE		9	W	2-0	0-0	Pirie 55, 63	Clark	Hair	Williamson	Smith	Thomson	Miller	Scott	Robb	Pirie	Jarvie*	Graham	**Rougvie**
	18/10	5,100	*10*	6				*Robertson*	*Smith G*	*Smith S*	*Ritchie**	*McDonald*	*Kinnell*	*Muir*	*O'Rourke*	*Thomson*	*Cramond*	*Lambie*	*Hotson*
							Ref: E Thomson	Goal-difference keeps the Dons above St Johnstone off the bottom, so this is a classic four-pointer. Managerless Dons see off their basement rivals - but it wasn't easy. Three cheers for the forgotten man - Billy Pirie. Pittodrie is buzzing with speculation about the new manager.											
9	A HIBERNIAN		9	L	1-3	0-1	Robb 47	Clark	Hair	Williamson	Smith	Thomson	Miller	Scott	Robb	Pirie	Jarvie*	Graham	McMaster
	25/10	*11,133*	*3*	6			*Jarvie 32 og, Bremner 48, Smith 87*	*McArthur*	*Brownlie*	*Schaedler*	*Stanton*	*Barry*	*Blackley*	*MacLeod**	*Bremner*	*Harper*	*Munro*	*Duncan*	*Smith*
							Ref: H Alexander	Eddie Thomson kept Hibs' Joe Harper quiet throughout. Until the 87th minute. Then Thomson's 'push' on the wee man gave Hibs a free-kick. It was taken quickly by Harper, who rolled the ball into the path of substitute Bobby Smith. Things are getting desperate for struggling Dons.											
10	H DUNDEE		8	W	2-0	0-0	Scott 72, Williamson 74p	Clark	Hair	Williamson	Smith	Thomson	Miller	Scott	Robb	Pirie*	Jarvie	Graham	McMaster
	1/11	6,312	*9*	8				*Allan*	*Wilson*	*Johnston**	*Robinson*	*Stewart*	*Ford*	*Laing*	*Strachan^*	*Wallace*	*Gordon*	*Purdie*	*Caldwell/Phillip*
							Ref: A Ferguson	Dundee's Gordon Strachan looks a nifty little player, especially in the first half when Dundee were going well. But then Jocky Scott netted against his old club. When goalkeeper Allan pulled down Arthur Graham, Ford was cautioned for disputing the resulting penalty award.											

11 — A MOTHERWELL   9   L   0-3   8
8/11   6,294   1   8

Taylor 17, Graham 39, Millar 78p
Ref: J Gordon

Aberdeen: Clark, Hair, Williamson, Smith, Thomson, Miller, Scott, Robb, Jarvie, Rougvie, Graham
Motherwell: Rennie, Millar, Wark, Watson R, McVie, McLaren, McAdam*, Pettigrew, Graham, McIlwraithe/Taylor, Gardner/Ward

Ally MacLeod has been appointed new manager of Aberdeen. He oversees his new players for the first time, and does not like what he sees. He sits in the stand for the first half and comes down to the dug-out to yell instructions in the second. All to no avail. The Dons look dreadful.

---

12 — A DUNDEE UTD   9   W   2-1   10
15/11   4,704   8   10

Williamson 3p, Scott 60
Hegarty 52
Ref: R Marshall

Aberdeen: Clark, Hair, Williamson, Smith, Thomson, Miller, Scott, Robb, Jarvie, McMaster*, Graham
Dundee Utd: McAlpine, Rolland, Fleming*, Rennie, Houston, Narey, Holt, Payne, Hegarty, McAdam/Sturrock, Traynor

Down goes Jarvie; Williamson bangs in the penalty. After Hegarty heads United level, Scott restores the Dons' lead - at the second attempt. Jarvie is then sent off for pole-axing Rennie. Hamish McAlpine wrestles Jocky Scott to the ground 40 yards out from goal, but is only booked.

---

13 — H HEARTS   8   D   0-0   11
22/11   11,390   5   11

Ref: C Hutton

Aberdeen: Geoghegan, Hair, Williamson, Smith, Thomson, Miller, Scott, Robb, Jarvie, McMaster*, Graham
Hearts: Cruickshank/Clunie, Jefferies, Brown, Gallacher, Murray, Park, Busby, Gibson, Callachan, Prentice*, Fraser/Pirie

'Come along to see the rejuvenated Dons,' was Ally MacLeod's hype. What a joke. This bore-draw wouldn't have satisfied anyone. Still this is a better result than when Hearts played at Pittodrie in the League Cup. Then the Dons lost 1-2. Eddie Thomson is still filling in at centre-half.

---

14 — A AYR   8   L   0-1   11
29/11   6,000   6   11

Murphy 50
Ref: T Kyle

Aberdeen: Geoghegan, Hair, Williamson, Smith, Thomson, Miller, Scott, Robb, Jarvie*, McMaster, Graham
Ayr: Sproat, McDonald, Murphy, McAnespie, Fleming, McSherry, Doyle, Graham, Ingram, Phillips*, McCulloch/McCall/McLelland, Dickson

Ayr are still recovering from a 2-7 home defeat by Celtic. When full-back John Murphy tossed in an aimless centre, Geoghegan took a swipe and missed the ball. On the evidence of this match, MacLeod's old team look better than his new. But the Dons won't lose again for 10 games.

---

15 — H RANGERS   8   W   1-0   13
6/12   19,565   4   13

Jarvie 83
Ref: J Paterson

Aberdeen: Geoghegan, Williamson, McLelland, Smith, Thomson, Miller, Scott, Robb, Jarvie, McMaster, Graham
Rangers: Kennedy, Jardine, Greig, Forsyth, Jackson, MacDonald, McKean, Hamilton, Henderson, McLean, Johnstone

Great stuff. MacLeod earns a stiff finger-wagging from the referee in the second half. The ref might have called upon one of the police dogs who entertained the crowd before kick-off and at half-time. Jarvie's goal was set up by McMaster. A great result for new skipper Willie Miller.

---

16 — A CELTIC   7   W   2-0   15
13/12   24,000   1   15

Jarvie 6, Graham 33
Ref: D Syme

Aberdeen: Geoghegan, Williamson, McLelland, Smith*, Thomson, Miller, Scott*, Robb, Jarvie, McMaster*, Graham
Celtic: Latchford, McGrain, Lynch, McCluskey, MacDonald, Edvaldsson, Wilson*, Dalglish, Deans, Callaghan/Lennox, Hood

League leaders Celtic suffer a surprise defeat. Successive wins over the Old Firm can't be bad - but Willie Young's temporary successor, Eddie Thomson, is booked for the third match in a row. Not since December 1970 have the Dons won at Parkhead. Ally is weaving his magic.

---

17 — A ST JOHNSTONE   7   D   1-1   16
20/12   3,500   10   16

Williamson 80
O'Rourke 83
Ref: W Mullen

Aberdeen: Geoghegan, Williamson, McLelland, Smith, Thomson, Miller, Scott*, Robb, Jarvie, McMaster*, Graham
St Johnstone: Robertson, Smith G, Ritchie, MacDonald, Anderson, Smith C, O'Rourke, Muir, Cramond, Lambie, Hair/Pirie

Wins over Rangers and Celtic are followed by near defeat by hopeless St Johnstone, who were heading for their 11th straight loss until Lambie's shot came back off the bar and O'Rourke headed it back in. Williamson had just scored his seventh goal of the season for the Dons.

---

18 — H HIBERNIAN   6   D   2-2   17
27/12   17,630   4   17

McMaster 18, Williamson 56
Bremner 10, Duncan 20
Ref: D Syme

Aberdeen: Geoghegan, Williamson, McLelland, Smith, Thomson, Miller, Scott, Robb, Jarvie, McMaster*, Graham
Hibernian: McArthur, Brownlie, Schaedler*, Stanton, Barry, Blackley, Edwards!, Bremner, Harper, Smith, Duncan/Spalding

Pittodrie certainly got its money's-worth in this thriller. Billy Williamson wasted a penalty for the Dons, while Hibs' Alec Edwards was later ordered off for clattering Eddie Thomson. When Williamson made it 2-2 it was his eighth goal of the season. It would also be his last.

---

19 — A DUNDEE   W   3-1   19
1/1   10,009   19

Robb 14, Scott 28, Graham 62
Hutchinson 4
Ref: E Thomson

Aberdeen: Geoghegan, Williamson, McLelland, Smith*, Thomson, Miller, Scott, Robb, Jarvie, McMaster*, Graham
Dundee: Allan, Caldwell, Gemmell*, Ford, Stewart, Phillip, Laing, Strachan, Wallace, Mackie, Hutchinson*/Robinson/Purdie

Sleet and snow discouraged spectators from turning out for this traditional New Year fixture. Dundee look a fragile team, having already lost 3-6 at home to Motherwell. This is the only away match Aberdeen win from behind. It also begins Aberdeen's great winning run at Dens Park.

---

20 — H MOTHERWELL   6   D   0-0   20
3/1   16,177   3   20

Ref: H Alexander

Aberdeen: Geoghegan, Williamson, McLelland, Smith*, Thomson, Miller, Scott, Robb*, Jarvie, McMaster*, Graham
Motherwell: Rennie, Watson W, Wark, Watson R, McVie, Stevens, McAdam, Pettigrew, Davidson*, McLaren, Marinello/Taylor/Hair/Pirie

No goals, but Geoghegen makes a super penalty save from Willie Watson early on. Before the start Ally MacLeod put into effect his personal style of public relations. All the players carried placards on to the pitch bearing the words: 'Happy New Year'. These were tossed to the crowd.

---

21 — H DUNDEE UTD   5   W   5-3   22
10/1   9,581   9   22

Graham 23, 88, Scott 25p, 52p, 72
Reid 62, 80p, Hegarty 66
Ref: B McGinlay

Aberdeen: Geoghegan, Williamson, McLelland, Smith*, Thomson, Miller, Scott, Robb*, Jarvie, McMaster, Graham
Dundee Utd: McAlpine, Rolland, Kopel, Rennie*, Narey, Houston, Fleming, Hegarty, McAdam, Reid, Steele/Hair/Pirie

Ally MacLeod believes in manager participation. He was to be seen urging his side forward in the second half as United threatened to steal a point in this thriller. Reid's penalty set up a furious finish, and Arthur Graham's late riposte is a rare lucky break for the Dons this season.

SCOTTISH PREMIER DIVISION

Manager: Bonthrone → Ally MacLeod — SEASON 1975-76

Column key (player rows): 1–11 = line-up, then **subs used**. Aberdeen in roman type, opponents in *italic*.

---

22. A HEARTS — 17/1

1	2	3	4	5	6	7	8	9	10	11	subs used
Geoghegan	Williamson	McLelland	Smith	Garner	Miller	Scott	Robb	Jarvie*	McMaster*	Graham	Hair/Pirie
Graham	*Clunie*	*Jefferies*	*Callachan*	*Anderson*	*Kay*	*Aird*	*Park**	*Gibson*	*Shaw**	*Prentice*	*Fraser/Brown*

Att 10,300 · Pos 5 · D · 6 · Pt 23 · F-A 3-3 · H-T 1-1

Scorers: McMaster 13, Scott 58, Pirie 84 / *Gibson 26, Anderson 73, Prentice 87 Graham 84* · Ref: R Davidson

Hearts have lost their last three. Willie Garner makes his debut. Three times Aberdeen led, and three times they were pegged back. With the Dons 2-1 ahead, Andy Geoghegan managed to keep out Prentice's penalty, but this served only to delay, not deny Hearts' second equaliser.

---

23. H AYR — 31/1

1	2	3	4	5	6	7	8	9	10	11	subs used
Geoghegan	Williamson	McLelland	Smith	Thomson	Miller	Pirie	Robb	Jarvie	McMaster	Graham	Graham
Sproat	*Wells*	*Murphy*	*McAnespie*	*Fleming*	*McDonald**	*Doyle*	*Graham*	*Ingram*	*McSherry*	*Robertson*	*McCulloch*

Att 9,920 · Pos 5 · W · 8 · Pt 25 · F-A 2-1 · H-T 1-0

Scorers: Pirie 43, McMaster 61 / *Graham 79p* · Ref: W Anderson

The MacLeod magic seems to be working. Ayr were the last team to beat Aberdeen, nine league games ago. The Dons are entrenched in fifth position, with Dundee United, who occupy the fatal ninth spot, 11 points behind. This appears to offer a huge safety margin, but it does not.

---

24. A RANGERS — 7/2

1	2	3	4	5	6	7	8	9	10	11	subs used
Geoghegan	Williamson*	McLelland*	Smith	Thomson	Miller	Scott	Robb	Jarvie*	McMaster	Graham	Pirie/Fleming
McCloy	*Miller*	*Greig*	*Forsyth*	*Jackson*	*MacDonald*	*McKean*	*Hamilton**	*Henderson^*	*McLean*	*Johnstone*	*Jardine/Parlane*

Att **30,000** · Pos 5 · L · 2 · Pt 25 · F-A 1-2 · H-T 0-2

Scorers: Pirie 77 / *Henderson 24, MacDonald 45* · Ref: E Thomson

Ranges are unbeaten in eight since losing at Pittodrie. The Dons' good run comes to an end. Aberdeen will have to improve for next week's Scottish Cup clash.

---

25. H CELTIC — 21/2

1	2	3	4	5	6	7	8	9	10	11	subs used
Clark	Hair	McLelland	Smith	Garner	Miller	Pirie	Williamson	Jarvie*	McMaster	Graham	Robb
Latchford	*McGrain*	*Lynch*	*McCluskey*	*Aitken*	*Edvaldsson*	*Ritchie**	*Dalglish*	*Deans*	*Glavin*	*Wilson*	*Lennox*

Att 18,221 · Pos 5 · L · 1 · Pt 25 · F-A 0-1 · H-T 0-0

Scorers: *Lennox 80* · Ref: J Paterson

This fixture took a long time to warm up, and was finally settled by Bobby Lennox, the last of the Lisbon Lions still with Celtic. He put the final touch to Kenny Dalglish's net-bound ball, when the Dons had looked set for a point. Celtic are midway through a nine-game winning run.

---

26. H ST JOHNSTONE — 28/2

1	2	3	4	5	6	7	8	9	10	11	subs used
Clark	Hair	McLelland	Smith	Garner	Miller	Pirie	Williamson*	Pirie*	Fleming	Campbell	Scott/Street
Robertson	*Smith G*	*Ritchie*	*Anderson*	*Hamilton*	*Kinnell*	*Muir*	*O'Rourke*	*Smith S*	*Lambie**	*Thomson*	

Att 5,920 · Pos 5 · W · 10 · Pt 27 · F-A 3-0 · H-T 1-0

Scorers: Pirie 25, 75, Scott 56 · Ref: T Kyle

St Johnstone have taken just two draws from 20 games, and long ago accepted that theirs was a lost cause. Ally MacLeod experiments with a new striking partnership of Billy Pirie and Ian Fleming. They do quite well in this match, but St Johnstone's defence does not extend them.

---

27. H DUNDEE — 13/3

1	2	3	4	5	6	7	8	9	10	11	subs used
Clark	Williamson	McLelland	Docherty	Thomson	Miller	Graham	Scott	Pirie*	Fleming	Campbell	Jarvie
Allan	*Wilson*	*Johnstone*	*Robinson*	*Phillip*	*Caldwell*	*Mackie*	*Gordon*	*Wallace*	*Hutchinson^*	*Laing^*	*Strachan*

Att 6,460 · Pos 5 · L · 6 · Pt 27 · F-A 0-1 · H-T 0-0

Scorers: *Hutchinson 88* · Ref: G Smith

The rot starts here. There never was a derby between these two sides as boring as this, settled by Hutchinson's bullet header. In recent weeks Hearts, Celtic, and now Dundee have plundered late points off Aberdeen. This will be Dundee's last league win over Aberdeen for 12 years.

---

28. A MOTHERWELL — 20/3

1	2	3	4	5	6	7	8	9	10	11	subs used
Clark	Hair	McLelland	Smith	Thomson	Miller	Scott	Williamson	Jarvie*	Fleming	Graham	Gibson
Rennie	*Millar*	*Wark*	*Watson R*	*McLaren*	*Stevens*	*Gardner**	*Pettigrew*	*Graham*	*Taylor*	*Marinello*	*Davidson*

Att 5,908 · Pos 5 · L · 4 · Pt 27 · F-A 1-2 · H-T 0-1

Scorers: Fleming 72 / *Pettigrew 5, Davidson 88* · Ref: E Thomson

Aberdeen just cannot come to terms with Motherwell of late. Fleming's rising shot looked like securing a point - but once again a late, late goal defeats them. Every time a match enters its closing minutes the Dons start to get edgy, and with good reason. That's four late points lost now.

---

29. A DUNDEE UTD — 27/3

1	2	3	4	5	6	7	8	9	10	11	subs used
Clark	Williamson	McLelland	Smith	Thomson	Miller	McMaster	Robb	Pirie*	Fleming	Graham*	Gibson
McAlpine	*Rolland*	*Kopel*	*Forsyth*	*Houston*	*Narey*	*Hall*	*Fleming**	*Hegarty*	*McAdam**	*Reid*	*Steele*

Att 4,875 · Pos 5 · L · 8 · Pt 27 · F-A 0-1 · H-T 0-0

Scorers: *Fleming 64* · Ref: W Mullen

When Aberdeen beat Ayr on 31 January all looked rosy in the Pittodrie garden. But a sequence of odd-goal defeats, coupled with United's revival - this is their fifth straight win - is threatening to push the Dons to the brink. Hamish McAlpine saved at least three shots with his legs.

---

30. A HIBERNIAN — 31/3

1	2	3	4	5	6	7	8	9	10	11	subs used
Clark	Hair	McLelland	Smith	Thomson	Miller	Scott	Jarvie	Pirie*	Fleming	Graham*	Gibson
McDonald	*Brownlie*	*Schaedler*	*Stanton*	*Spalding*	*Blackley*	*Edwards**	*Murray*	*Wilson*	*Bremner*	*Duncan*	*Muir*

Att 4,082 · Pos 5 · L · 3 · Pt 27 · F-A 2-3 · H-T 1-1

Scorers: Scott 15, Fleming 49 / *Murray 26, Muir 48, Blackley 90* · Ref: C Hutton

Relegation clouds are overing over the Dons after yet another defeat suffered in the closing seconds. Murray's corner-kick bobbled about crazily until the ball fell at Blackley's feet just inches from the goal-line. Four straight losses, and worse is to come.

---

31. H HEARTS — 7/4

1	2	3	4	5	6	7	8	9	10	11	subs used
Clark	Williamson	McLelland	Smith	Thomson	Miller	Scott	Fleming	Jarvie	Hair*	Graham*	Robb
Cruickshank	*Brown*	*Jefferies*	*Callachan*	*Gallacher*	*Kay**	*Aird*	*Busby*	*Shaw*	*Gibson*	*Prentice*	*Fraser*

Att 8,500 · Pos 5 · L · 6 · Pt 27 · F-A 0-3 · H-T 0-2

Scorers: *Gibson 7, 84, Aird 40* · Ref: C Hutton

Demoralisation pervades Pittodrie after this fifth straight loss. Hearts eased their own relegation worries, and left the home crowd chanting 'Harper, Harper'. Gibson's insulting first goal, hooked over his shoulder, put Aberdeen on the slippery slope. Where will it all end?

32 A AYR 10/4 — 5 D 8 28 — 1-1 — 0-0 — 5,700

Jarvie 86 / Graham 50 — Ref: D Syme

Clark · Williamson! McLelland · Smith* · Thomson · Miller · Robb · Hair · Jarvie · Fleming · Graham* · Garner/Scott
Sproat · Wells · Murphy · Fleming · Tait · Filippi · McSherry · Ingram* · Cramond · Robertson · Phillips

Ayr had won their last three. At long last a late goal for Aberdeen. But the price is high. Williamson is sent off for bringing down Robertson. Aberdeen were down to 10 men when Drew Jarvie scrambled the ball over the line to prevent what would have been a sixth straight defeat.

---

33 H RANGERS 14/4 — 5 D 1 29 — 0-0 — 0-0 — 17,968

Ref: E Pringle

Clark · Hair · Thomson · Garner · Miller · Robb! · Williamson · Jarvie · Fleming · Graham* · Smith
McCloy · Miller · Forsyth · Jackson · MacDonald McKean* · Hamilton · Henderson McLean* · Johnstone · Parlane/Jardine

Two Dons sent off in two games. After half-time Dave Robb commits a crazy tackle on Hamilton and is ordered off. Yet 10-man Dons fight to a standstill. The Pittodrie crowd appreciate the effort if not the skill, and treat the players to a standing ovation. Gers had won their last seven.

---

34 A CELTIC 17/4 — 5 D 2 30 — 1-1 — 1-1 — 29,000

Edvaldsson 40 og / Dalglish 25 — Ref: J Gordon

Clark · Hair · Thomson · Garner · Miller! · Robb · Williamson · Jarvie · Fleming · Graham* · Smith
Latchford · McGrain · Edvaldsson Glavin · Aitken · Callaghan · Doyle* · Dalglish · Deans · Burns · Lennox* · Ritchie/Wilson

Dons skipper Willie Miller makes it a hat-trick - but not one to be proud of. Early in the second half he sends Roy Aitken into orbit and becomes the third Aberdeen player to be dismissed in successive games. Edvaldsson's error could yet provide a lifeline to the Dons.

---

35 A ST JOHNSTONE 21/4 — 5 L 10 30 — 0-2 — 0-1 — 2,500

Hotson 35, Thomson 62 — Ref: D Ramsay

Clark · Hair · Cooper* · Garner · Miller · Robb · Williamson · Jarvie · Fleming · Smith · Scott/McMaster
Robertson · Smith G · Anderson · Roberts · Kinnell · Henderson* O'Rourke · McGregor · Thomson · Hotson · Muir

Two matches to go. Aberdeen are in the top half of the table, yet are one of five clubs who will go down with St Johnstone, who before today had played 29 games in league and cup without the taste of victory. Their deserved success looks like pushing Aberdeen over the brink.

---

36 H HIBERNIAN 24/4 — 5 W 3 32 — 3-0 — 1-0 — 10,985

Jarvie 30, Smith 67, Robb 68 — Ref: W Anderson

Clark · Hair · Smith · Garner · Miller · Robb · Williamson · Jarvie · Fleming* · McCall · Scott
McDonald · Smith · Schaedler · Stanton · Spalding · Blackley · Murray · McGhee · MacLeod · Duncan* · Paterson

Pity Dave Robb who, with responsibility for a make-or-break first-half penalty, watches it saved by McDonald. His guilt was eased when Jarvie netted from close in, and vanished completely when Joe Smith after half-time volleyed the goal of the season. Robb then scored himself.

Average Home 11,000 / Away 10,900

Scottish League Cup - Section 3

1 A CELTIC 9/8 — L – — 0-1 — 0-1 — 32,000

Dalglish 10 — Ref: J Gordon

Clark · Thomson* · McLelland · Hair · Young · Miller · Smith · Robb · Jarvie · Rougvie · Graham* · Williamson/Campbell
Latchford · McGrain · Lynch · McCluskey · MacDonald · Edvaldsson Hood* · Dalglish · Wilson · Glavin · Lennox · McNamara

Celtic may have lost the league title for the first time in nine years, but they hold the League Cup. Following a Celtic corner the Dons defence moves out, but Dalglish springs the offside trap. The Dons' best chance fell to Drew Jarvie, but he hoofed the ball over the bar from four yards.

---

2 H DUMBARTON 13/8 — W 2 — 2-0 — 2-0 — 6,000

Graham 7, Jarvie 37 — Ref: T Muirhead

Clark · McLelland · Gibson · Young · Miller · Smith · Rougvie · Jarvie* · Graham · Williamson/Thomson
Williams · Brown · Watt · Ruddy · Muir · Graham · Cook · McLean · Wallace* · McKinlay · Bourke · Coleman/McAdam

Dumbarton did not qualify for the Premier League and must adjust to life in the new Division 1. Aberdeen won this match more comfortably than the scoreline would suggest. All four teams in Section 3 have two points, with everything to play for, though Celtic must be favourites.

---

3 H HEARTS 16/8 — L 2 — 1-2 — 0-0 — 8,400

Williamson 50 / Ford 72, Hancock 77 — Ref: R Valentine

Clark · McLelland · Gibson* · Young · Miller · Smith · Robb · Williamson · Graham · Henry
Cruickshank Kay* · Clunie · Callachan · Anderson · Murray · Brown · Busby · Hancock · Ford · Prentice · Park

Heavy rain had washed away the white lines. Sawdust was sprinkled everywhere. Dave Robb's first-half penalty rebounded from the Hearts' crossbar, and that effectively cost the match and their chance of reaching the quarter-finals. Hearts had three players booked.

---

4 A DUMBARTON 20/8 — W 4 — 1-0 — 1-0 — 2,400

Hair 72 — Ref: T Kellock

Clark · Hair · McLelland · Scott · Young · Miller · Smith · Robb · Jarvie · Williamson* Campbell · Pirie
Williams · Brown · Watt · Bennett* · Muir · Graham · Cook · McLean · Bourke · McAdam* · Wallace · Coleman

Full-back Ian Hair landed the decisive touch in a goalmouth scramble. This result keeps alive Aberdeen's faint chances of qualifying for the quarter-finals, but they have two tough games to come. A posse of English scouts take notes on centre-half Willie Young's performance.

---

5 A HEARTS 23/8 — L 4 — 0-1 — 0-1 — 11,000

Prentice 2 — Ref: H Alexander

Clark · Hair · Scott · Young · Miller · Smith · Robb · Jarvie* · Pirie · Graham · Rougvie
Cruickshank Kay · Clunie · Jefferies · Anderson · Murray · Brown · Busby · Hancock · Ford · Prentice* · Callachan

Brown's second-minute corner-kick was headed out to Prentice. There seemed to be too many bodies between him and the goal to score. But somehow the ball squeezed through. Losing to Hearts twice does not augur well.

SCOTTISH PREMIER (CUP-TIES)   Manager: Bonthrone → Ally MacLeod   SEASON 1975-76

Scottish League Cup - Section 3

		1	2	3	4	5	6	7	8	9	10	11	subs used
6 H CELTIC L 0-2 H-T 0-1 13,000 4		Clark	Hair	McLelland	Scott	Young	Miller	Smith*	Robb	Pirie	McMaster	Graham	Rougvie
		Latchford	*McGrain*	*Lynch*	*McCluskey**	*MacDonald*	*Edvaldsson*	*McNamara*	*Wilson^*	*Dalglish*	*Callaghan*	*Lennox*	*Connelly/Ritchie*

Scorers, Times, and Referees: *Lennox 5, Ritchie 86*   Ref: E Pringle

Even if Celtic lost they would probably qualify. In fact, they won with style, taking an early lead after Dalglish squared the ball to Bobby Lennox. Celtic substitute Ritchie had only been on the pitch two minutes before he raced through without hindrance to score number two.

	P	W	D	L	F	A	Pts
Qual Celtic	6	5	0	1	17	4	10
Hearts	6	4	0	2	13	8	8
ABERDEEN	6	2	0	4	4	6	4
Dumbarton	6	1	0	5	5	21	2

Scottish Cup

		1	2	3	4	5	6	7	8	9	10	11	subs used
3 A ALLOA W 4-0 H-T 2-0 6,312 2:3		Geoghegan	Williamson	McLelland	Smith	Garner	Miller	Scott	Robb	Jarvie	McMaster	Graham	
		Thomson A	*McCann*	*Wilkinson*	*McGarry*	*Stewart*	*Miller*	*Low*	*Thomson J*	*Wilson*	*Campbell*	*Russell**	*Marrison*

Scorers: Scott 38, McMaster 42, Miller 64, [Robb 72]   Ref: A Paterson

Alloa from the new Division 2 (in reality the third division) had to suffer an invasion by Aberdeen thugs. Players were instructed by the referee to seek the safety of the dressing rooms for 15 minutes. Spectators sought refuge from the bricks and bottles by spilling onto the pitch.

		1	2	3	4	5	6	7	8	9	10	11	subs used
4 A RANGERS L 1-4 H-T 0-1 52,000 2		Geoghegan	Williamson	McLelland	Smith	Thomson*	Miller	Scott	Robb	Jarvie	McMaster*	Graham	Hair/Pirie
		McCloy	*Miller*	*Greig*	*Forsyth**	*Jackson*	*MacDonald*	*McKean*	*Hamilton^*	*Henderson*	*McLean*	*Johnstone*	*Parlane/Jardine*

Scorers: Smith 68 [Henderson 75, Parlane 86] Johnstone 43, McDonald 46,   Ref: J Gordon

Defeats in league and cup at Ibrox on successive Saturdays have brought the Dons down to earth. Aberdeen were always chasing the improbable in this cup-tie, except for a few minutes following Joe Smith's fierce shot midway through the second half that halved the deficit.

League Table

			Home					Away				
	P	W	D	L	F	A	W	D	L	F	A	Pts
1 Rangers	36	15	2	1	38	12	8	4	6	21	12	54
2 Celtic	36	10	5	3	35	18	11	1	6	36	24	48
3 Hibernian	36	13	2	3	37	15	5	5	8	18	28	43
4 Motherwell	36	11	4	3	29	18	5	4	9	28	31	40
5 Hearts	36	7	5	6	23	19	6	4	8	16	25	35
6 Ayr	36	10	3	5	29	24	4	2	12	17	35	33
7 ABERDEEN	36	8	5	5	27	19	3	5	10	22	31	32
8 Dundee Utd	36	9	3	6	27	20	3	5	10	19	28	32
9 Dundee	36	8	5	5	31	26	3	5	10	18	36	32
10 St Johnstone	36	3	4	11	19	34	0	1	17	10	45	11
	360	94	38	48	295	205	48	38	94	205	295	360

Cup Record

	P	W	D	L	F	A	Pts
v St Johnstone	4	2	1	1	6	3	5
v Ayr	4	2	1	1	6	4	5
v Dundee	4	2	0	2	7	5	4
v Dundee Utd	4	2	0	2	8	8	4
v Hibernian	4	1	1	2	8	8	3
v Celtic	4	1	1	2	4	4	3
v Rangers	4	1	1	2	2	3	3
v Hearts	4	0	3	1	5	8	3
v Motherwell	4	0	2	2	3	7	2
	36	11	10	15	49	50	32

	Cup	W	D	L
v Celtic	LC	0	0	2
v Rangers	SC	0	0	1
v Hearts	LC	0	0	2

Appearances and Goals

	Appearances						Goals			
	Lge	Sub	LC	Sub	SC	Sub	Lge	LC	SC	Tot
Campbell, George	2			1		1				
Clark, Bobby	20		6							
Cooper, Neil	1	1								
Docherty, John	1									
Fleming, Ian	11	1	1				2			2
Garner, Willie	7	1				1				
Geoghegan, Andy	16					2				
Gibson, Ian		2	2							
Graham, Arthur	31		5		2		4		1	5
Hair, Ian	24	5	6			1		1		1
Hather, John		1								
Henry, Jim	1			1						
Jarvie, Drew	30	2	4		2		4	1		5
McCall, Walker	1	1								
McLelland, Chic	29	1	6		2					
McMaster, John	18	3	1		2		3		1	4
Miller, Willie	36		6		2				1	1
Pirie, Billy	8	10	2	1		1	7			7
Robb, Dave	30	1	6		2		4		1	5
Rougvie, Doug	1	1	3	2	2					
Scott, Jocky	28	4	3		2		14		1	15
Smith, Joe	33		6		2		2	1		3
Street, Bobby		1								
Thomson, Eddie	26	2	1	1	1					
Ward, Noel	4	1								
Williamson, Billy	35	1	2	2	2		8	1		9
Young, Willie	3		6							
(own-goals)							1			1
27 players used	396	40	66	8	22	2	49	4	5	58

Odds & ends

Never lost to: (0).
Never beat: (2) Motherwell, Hearts.

Won from behind: (1) Dundee (a).
Lost from in front: (3) Dundee (a), Hibs (a), Hearts (LC).

High spots: Back to back wins over Rangers and Celtic in December. These were Aberdeen's only consecutive wins all season, and set in train a sequence of 9 games without defeat.
Beating Hibs in final match to stay up.

Low spots: Failing to win in first 4 league matches.
5 straight defeats, leading to 9 games without a win in March and April.

18 of the 27 players used came on as substitutes.

Bogey teams: Motherwell (league) and Hearts (league and cups).
Ever-presents: (1) Willie Miller.
Hat-tricks: (1) Jocky Scott.
Leading scorer: (15) Jocky Scott.

SCOTTISH PREMIER DIVISION

Manager: Ally MacLeod

SEASON 1976-77

No	Date	Att	Pos	Pt	F-A	H-T	Scorers, Times, and Referees	1	2	3	4	5	6	7	8	9	10	11	subs used
1	H HEARTS 4/9	11,727	1		D 2-2	1-1	Fleming 6, Robb 86 / Busby 1, Park 88 / Ref: K Hope	Clark *Cruickshank/Brown*	Hair *Kay*	McLelland *Jefferies**	Smith *Gallagher*	Garner *Clunie*	Miller *Park*	Sullivan* *Busby*	Williamson *Gibson*	Harper *Callachan*	Fleming *Prentice*	Graham *Shaw*	Robb
2	A AYR 11/9	4,800	2	3	W 5-0	2-0	Fleming 27, Sullivan 40, Harper 60, 85 / Ref: G Smith	Clark *Sproat*	Kennedy *Filippi*	McLelland *Murphy*	Smith *Fleming*	Garner *McDonald*	Miller *McSherry*	Sullivan *Phillips*	Fleming *Graham**	Harper *McCulloch*	Robb *Cramond*	Campbell *Robertson*	Ingram*/Gray
3	H KILMARNOCK 18/9	8,712	2	5	W 2-0	0-0	Jarvie 83, Gibson 88 / Ref: A McFaull	Clark *Stewart*	Williamson *McLean*	McLelland *Robertson*	Smith *Murdoch*	Garner *Clarke*	Miller *Welsh*	Sullivan *Provan*	Fleming* *McCulloch*	Harper *Fallis*	Robb* *Sheed*	Graham *Smith*	Jarvie/Gibson
4	A HIBERNIAN 25/9	9,278	2	6	D 0-0	0-0	Ref: B McGinlay	Clark *McDonald*	Thomson *Brownlie*	McLelland *Smith*	Smith* *Bremner*	Garner *Stewart*	Miller *Blackley*	Sullivan *Murray*	Fleming *Muir**	Harper *Scott*	Robb *McNamara*	Graham *Duncan*	Scott Spalding
5	A PARTICK THISTLE 2/10	5,000	2	7	D 2-2	2-1	Harper 10, Fleming 43 / Sommer 23p, McQuade 62 / Ref: W Mullen	Clark *Rough*	Thomson *Mackie*	McLelland *Whittaker*	Smith *Hansen A*	Garner *Campbell*	Miller *Anderson*	Sullivan *Houston*	Fleming* *Gibson**	Harper *McQuade*	Robb *Sommer*	Graham *Johnston*	Scott Love
6	A RANGERS 16/10	22,000	3	7	L 0-1	0-0	MacDonald 77 / Ref: J Gordon	Clark *Kennedy*	Kennedy *Jardine*	McLelland *Miller*	Williamson *Greig*	Garner *Jackson*	Miller *Danny*	Sullivan *McLean*	Robb *Hamilton**	Thomson* *Parlane*	Fleming *MacDonald*	Graham* *Johnstone**	Rougvie/Campbell McKean/Henderson
7	H CELTIC 23/10	19,370	3	9	W 2-1	0-0	Harper 63, 77p / Dalglish 56p / Ref: G Smith	Clark *Latchford*	Williamson *McGrain*	McLelland *Lynch*	Smith *Stanton*	Garner *MacDonald*	Miller *Aitken*	Sullivan* *Doyle*	Scott *Glavin*	Harper *Craig*	Shirra *Dalglish*	Graham *Wilson*	Jarvie
8	H DUNDEE UTD 30/10	18,577	3	11	W 3-2	1-1	Jarvie 22, Harper 46, Williamson 57 / Sturrock 11, Wallace 84 / Ref: D Syme	Clark *McAlpine*	Kennedy *Rolland*	Williamson *Kopel*	Shirra *Fleming*	Garner *Forsyth*	Miller *Narey*	Sullivan *Sturrock*	Scott *Wallace*	Harper *Hegarty*	Jarvie *McAdam*	Graham *Payne*	Wilson
9	H MOTHERWELL 2/11	15,207	1	13	W 3-1	0-0	Jarvie 64, Sullivan 71, Harper 85 / O'Rourke 89 / Ref: H Alexander	MacLean *Rennie*	Kennedy *McLaren*	Williamson *Wark*	Smith *Millar*	Garner *McVie*	Miller *Stevens**	Sullivan *Marinello*	Scott *Pettigrew**	Harper *Graham*	Jarvie *Davidson*	Graham *Kennedy*	McAdam/O'Rourke
10	A HEARTS 10/11	10,500		13	L 1-2	0-1	Harper 65 / Jefferies 40, 52 / Ref: A Ferguson	Clark *Wilson*	Kennedy *Brown*	Williamson *Kay*	Smith *Jefferies**	Garner *Gallacher*	Miller *Clunie*	Sullivan* *Shaw*	Scott *Busby*	Harper *Gibson*	Jarvie* *Park*	Graham *Prentice*	Robb/Shirra

Match narratives:

1. Just 24 seconds have been played when Busby drills Prentice's cross past Bobby Clark. Joe Harper then provides Fleming with a chance he cannot miss. Near the end Dave Robb also manages a simple goal, but within two minutes it is cancelled out by Park's grass-trimming drive.

2. Ayr are another of those teams which avoided relegation by a whisker, but home defeats by this huge margin do not augur well for the months ahead. Once Ian Fleming had headed over the stranded Sproat, Ayr were always chasing a lost cause. New boy Dom Sullivan bags a brace.

3. Arthur Graham skips past full-back McLean for the umpteenth time. This time he pulls the ball back for substitute Drew Jarvie to sweep low past Stewart. Killie defenders are mad about something and besiege the referee. But the goal stands, and is shortly followed by another.

4. The most predictable feature of this match is that Joe Harper is booed by the home crowd every time he touches the ball. He would have loved to score for the Dons on his return, but is happy to settle for a goalless draw, which preserves Aberdeen's unbeaten start to the new season.

5. Joe Harper's goal is his 12th of the season so far. After Sommer levels from the penalty spot Fleming restores the Dons' lead with a completely miscued shot that left Alan Rough looking disgusted. McQuade's far-post header in the second half puts a smile back on Rough's face.

6. With Joe Harper sidelined through injury, Rangers' Alex MacDonald is probably the smallest man on the pitch. Derek Parlane's back-header finds him in sweet isolation, and MacDonald heads wide of Bobby Clark for the only goal. This is the Dons' first defeat in any competition.

7. A game of two penalties. Willie Miller trips Wilson on the edge of the box, enabling Dalglish to open the scoring. Joe Harper equalises by dribbling the ball round keeper Latchford, and the Dons take both points when Stanton upends Arthur Graham.

8. Aberdeen are already celebrating their place at Hampden for the League Cup final as they inflict this defeat on the league leaders. Sturrock's overhead kick took Clark by surprise, but Jarvie's point-blank header, followed by Joe Harper's wheeling shot-on-the-turn, turned the tables.

9. Clark is injured. Motherwell resisted in the first half - and were executed, clean and simple, in the second. Both Joe Harper and Aberdeen are now top of their respective charts. Four days later table-topping Aberdeen will take on Celtic in the League Cup final at Hampden Park.

10. Aberdeen have won the League Cup. They are vulnerable to this kind of result, though Hearts had previously failed to win in the league all season. The Dons fell victim to two identical goals: two pull-backs by Brown; two fine strikes by Jefferies. Harper's goal is mere consolation.

11 · A KILMARNOCK — 20/11
Att: 5,000 · **Pos:** 10 · **Pts:** 15 · **Result:** W 2-1 (HT 0-1)
Scorers: Scott 55, Kennedy 80 — Smith 42p
Ref: K Hope

	1	2	3	4	5	6	7	8	9	10	11	Sub
Aberdeen	Clark	Kennedy	Williamson	Smith	Garner	Miller	Sullivan*	Scott	Harper	Jarvie	Graham	Shirra
Kilmarnock	Stewart	Maxwell	Robinson	Murdoch	Clarke	Welsh	Provan	McLean	Fallis	Sheed	Smith	

Bobby Clark gives away a rare penalty when diving at Gordon Smith's feet. Jocky Scott levels and full-back Stuart Kennedy scores his first goal for Aberdeen. Newly promoted Kilmarnock are finding it tough in the Premier Division, having only won once — 6-1 against Ayr.

---

12 · H AYR — 24/11
Att: 10,581 · **Pos:** 9 · **Pts:** 17 · **Result:** W 1-0 (HT 0-0)
Scorer: Harper 71p
Ref: G Smith

	1	2	3	4	5	6	7	8	9	10	11	Sub
Aberdeen	Clark	Kennedy	Williamson*	Smith	Garner	Miller	Shirra	Scott	Harper	Jarvie	Graham	Sullivan
Ayr	Geoghegan	Wells	Murphy*	Fleming	Filippi	McAnespie	McCall	McSherry	Masterton	McCulloch	Cramond	Kelly

The score is deceptive. Ayr could hardly get the ball out of their own penalty area, but the solitary goal which takes Aberdeen back to the top of the league is determined by a penalty. It brings about Ayr's 11th consecutive league defeat at Pittodrie. Wee Harper is deadly from the spot.

---

13 · H HIBERNIAN — 27/11
Att: 14,788 · **Pos:** 6 · **Pts:** 19 · **Result:** W 1-0 (HT 1-0)
Scorer: Harper 35
Ref: W Anderson

	1	2	3	4	5	6	7	8	9	10	11	Sub
Aberdeen	Clark	Kennedy	McLelland	Smith*	Garner	Miller	Sullivan	Scott	Harper	Jarvie	Graham	Thomson
Hibernian	McDonald	Brownlie	Schaedler	Bremner	Stewart	Spalding	Duncan*	McGhee	Scott	Smith	Fyfe	Murray

Harper slaloms round three Hibs defenders with the ball glued to his toes, and then whacks it past McDonald from 20 yards. Hibs supporters don't appreciate it. Aberdeen will win 1-0 five times this season: on each occasion Harper scores. This is Hibs' sixth game without a win.

---

14 · A CELTIC — 26/12
Att: 47,000 · **Pos:** 2 · **Pts:** 20 · **Result:** D 2-2 (HT 2-2)
Scorers: Jarvie 22, 37 — Craig 32, 45
Ref: H Alexander

	1	2	3	4	5	6	7	8	9	10	11
Aberdeen	Clark	Kennedy	McLelland	Smith	Garner	Miller	Sullivan*	Shirra	Harper	Jarvie	Graham
Celtic	Latchford	McGrain	Burns	Stanton	MacDonald	Aitken	Doyle	Glavin	Craig	Dalglish	Wilson

On a pitch more suitable to ice-hockey, both teams give their all. Man-of-the-match was Drew Jarvie, for his two goals. In the second half Celtic's Craig comes within a whisker of a hat-trick, but Clark turns his effort onto a post. This is the only point Celtic will drop in 14 games.

---

15 · H HEARTS — 3/1
Att: 18,761 · **Pos:** 5 · **Pts:** 22 · **Result:** W 4-1 (HT 3-0)
Scorers: Harper 21, 38, 58, Jarvie 44 — Callachan 60p
Ref: T Kyle

	1	2	3	4	5	6	7	8	9	10	11	Sub
Aberdeen	Clark	Kennedy	McLelland	Smith	Garner	Miller	Shirra	Brown	Harper	Jarvie	Graham*	Robb
Hearts	Cruickshank	Clunie	Kay	Jefferies	Gallacher	Fraser*	Shaw	Gibson	Callachan	Prentice		

The Hearts hoodoo is finally burst. Aberdeen last beat the Jam Tarts at Pittodrie in November 1973. Joe Harper's memorable hat-trick provided a slap in the face for his marker, Gallacher, who was left floundering for both Harper's openers. Nine points from five games for the Dons.

---

16 · A AYR — 8/1
Att: 5,600 · **Pos:** 9 · **Pts:** 23 · **Result:** D 0-0 (HT 0-0)
Ref: A Ferguson

	1	2	3	4	5	6	7	8	9	10	11
Aberdeen	Clark	Kennedy	McLelland	Smith	Garner	Miller	Sullivan	Scott	Harper	Jarvie	Graham
Ayr	Geoghegan	Wells	Murphy	Fleming	Filippi	McAnespie	McCall	McSherry	Masterton	McCulloch	Cramond

Struggling Ayr knocked Aberdeen out of their stride. Ex-Don keeper Andy Geoghegan frustrated the Dons' few scoring efforts, becoming the first keeper to stop the Dons scoring in 13 league and League Cup games. He also keeps Ayr's first clean sheet since the first day of the season.

---

17 · H PARTICK THISTLE — 12/1
Att: 9,898 · **Pos:** 8 · **Pts:** 24 · **Result:** W 1-0 (HT 1-1)
Scorers: Harper 29 — Sommer 84
Ref: G Smith

	1	2	3	4	5	6	7	8	9	10	11	Subs
Aberdeen	Clark	Kennedy	Williamson	Smith*	Garner	Miller	Sullivan*	Scott	Harper	Jarvie	Graham	Shirra/Robb
Partick	Rough	Mackie	Whittaker	Hansen J	Campbell	Hansen A	Houston	Sommer	Marr*	Melrose	Craig*	Kelly/Love

Aberdeen needed to win to go back above Celtic to the top of the league. But six minutes from time Love takes a Thistle corner-kick and Sommer outjumps the Dons' defenders. This will be Thistle's elegant defender, Alan Hansen's, last season before transferring to Liverpool.

---

18 · H RANGERS — 19/1
Att: 21,591 · **Pos:** 3 · **Pts:** 25 · **Result:** D 3-3 (HT 1-1)
Scorers: Jarvie 40, Scott 60, Smith 64 — Miller 44, MacDonald 80, Johnstone 86
Ref: R Valentine

	1	2	3	4	5	6	7	8	9	10	11	Subs
Aberdeen	Clark	Kennedy	McLelland	Smith*	Garner	Miller	Sullivan	Scott	Fleming	Jarvie	Graham	Kennedy 86
Rangers	Kennedy	Jardine	Miller	Forsyth	Jackson	Watson	McLean	O'Hara*	Parlane*	Greig	Johnstone	MacDonald/McLean

Joe Smith's thunderbolt was rapturously received. It put the Dons 3-1 ahead and should have sealed the match. But MacDonald's 20-yarder and Johnstone's header from McLean's corner salvage a point for Rangers. The Dons are a point ahead of Celtic, who have two games in hand.

---

19 · A HIBERNIAN — 22/1
Att: 11,480 · **Pos:** 5 · **Pts:** 26 · **Result:** D 0-0 (HT 0-0)
Ref: D Syme

	1	2	3	4	5	6	7	8	9	10	11	Subs
Aberdeen	Clark	Kennedy	McLelland	Smith*	Garner	Miller	Sullivan	Scott	Fleming	Jarvie	Graham	Shirra/Robb
Hibernian	McDonald	Brownlie	Spalding	Bremner	Stewart	Blackley	McLean	Edwards	Scott	McGhee	Duncan	

Four straight draws is not championship form — and Celtic leapfrog above the Dons. Without the injured Joe Harper, Aberdeen's firepower is greatly restricted. But at least Easter Road cannot boo him. Hibernian will draw 18 league matches this season, exactly half their fixtures.

---

20 · A PARTICK THISTLE — 5/2
Att: 9,000 · **Pos:** 7 · **Pts:** 26 · **Result:** L 1-2 (HT 0-1)
Scorers: Jarvie 69 — Melrose 25, Sommer 49
Ref: E Thomson

	1	2	3	4	5	6	7	8	9	10	11	Subs
Aberdeen	Clark	Kennedy	McLelland	Smith*	Garner	Miller	Sullivan	Scott	Fleming	Jarvie	Graham	Shirra/Robb
Partick	Rough	Mackie	Whittaker	Hansen A	Campbell	Houston	Sommer	Love	McGhee	Melrose*	Craig	McQuade

Harper returns from injury. Ally MacLeod opts for a 4-4-2 formation, but it fails to unpick Thistle, who score the all-important first goal from a Craig corner-kick. Aberdeen have won only once in their last six games — against First Division Dunfermline in the Scottish Cup.

---

21 · H KILMARNOCK — 7/2
Att: 7,650 · **Pos:** 10 · **Pts:** 28 · **Result:** W 2-0 (HT 0-0)
Scorers: McLelland 73, Graham 85
Ref: R Valentine

	1	2	3	4	5	6	7	8	9	10	11	Subs
Aberdeen	Clark	Kennedy	McLelland	Smith*	Garner	Miller	Sullivan*	Scott	Harper	Jarvie	Graham	Scott/Robb
Kilmarnock	Stewart	Maxwell	Robertson	Murdoch	Clarke	McDicken	Provan	McCulloch	Fallis	Sheed	McLean	

Doomed Kilmarnock provide the Dons with their first win in seven games. The Dons did everything but score for most of the match. Then Chic McLelland tried a hopeful pot-shot from 30 yards. The ball flew past Stewart for McLelland's first and only goal of the season.

SCOTTISH PREMIER DIVISION   Manager: Ally MacLeod   SEASON 1976-77

---

22. A RANGERS — 19/2
Att 17,000 · Pos 3 · Pt 28 · Result L · H-T 0-0 · F-A 0-1
Scorers: Miller 89p. Ref: H Alexander

	1	2	3	4	5	6	7	8	9	10	11	Subs used
Aberdeen	Clark	Kennedy	McLelland	Smith	Garner	Miller	Sullivan	Scott*	Harper	Jarvie*	Graham	Thomson/Shirra
Rangers	*Kennedy*	*Jardine*	*Miller*	*Greig*	*Jackson*	*Watson*	*McLean**	*Hamilton^*	*Parlane*	*MacDonald*	*Johnstone*	*McKean/McDougall*

Aberdeen slip from second to third, and exchange places with Rangers, as a result of Willie Miller's late blunder. He fails to control a pass from McLelland. Derek Johnstone streaks away and Miller drags him down. Willie's namesake - Alex - performed the honours from the spot.

---

23. H CELTIC — 5/3
Att 21,656 · Pos 3 · Pt 30 · Result W · H-T 1-0 · F-A 2-0
Scorers: Graham 21, Harper 89. Ref: J Gordon

	1	2	3	4	5	6	7	8	9	10	11	Subs used
Aberdeen	Clark	Kennedy	McLelland	Smith	Garner	Miller	Davidson*	Fleming*	Harper	Shirra*	Graham	Sullivan/Scott
Celtic	*Latchford*	*McGrain*	*Lynch*	*Stanton*	*Edvaldsson*	*McCluskey**	*Doyle*	*Glavin*	*Craig*	*Aitken*	*Dalglish*	*Conn*

Aberdeen have lost to Dundee in the Scottish Cup. They survived Celtic's second-half onslaught by hook or by crook. At one point Lynch nearly tore Arthur Graham's shirt off his back. Harper's late goal ended his recent famine. 'Easy, easy' chanted Pittodrie. It was anything but.

---

24. H DUNDEE UTD — 12/3
Att 12,620 · Pos 4 · Pt 30 · Result L · H-T 0-1 · F-A 0-1
Scorers: Sturrock 14. Ref: I Foote

	1	2	3	4	5	6	7	8	9	10	11	Subs used
Aberdeen	Clark	Kennedy	McLelland	Smith	Garner	Miller	Sullivan*	Davidson	Harper	Shirra^	Graham	Scott/Thomson
Dundee Utd	*McAlpine*	*Rolland*	*Williamson*	*Fleming*	*Smith*	*Narey*	*Sturrock*	*Houston*	*Hegarty*	*McAdam**	*Payne*	*Kopel*

The Dons slip down to fourth, changing places with United, after this latest reverse. Although this is Aberdeen's first home defeat in the league, at the back of everyone's minds is the fear that last season's dramatic spring collapse is about to be revisited upon the Dons.

---

25. A DUNDEE UTD — 16/3
Att 7,176 · Pos 4 · Pt 30 · Result L · H-T 1-3 · F-A 2-3
Scorers: Smith 9, Harper 72, Narey 2, Hegarty 6, McAdam 35. Ref: E Thomson

	1	2	3	4	5	6	7	8	9	10	11	Subs used
Aberdeen	Clark	Kennedy	McLelland	Smith	Garner	Miller	Campbell*	Fleming	Harper	Shirra^	Graham	McMaster/Davidson
Dundee Utd	*McAlpine*	*Rolland*	*Williamson*	*Fleming G**	*Smith W*	*Narey*	*Sturrock*	*Houston*	*Hegarty*	*McAdam**	*Payne*	*Wallace/Addison*

A game to savour, even though it brought Aberdeen's second defeat in four days. David Narey outwitted Aberdeen's offside trap for the first goal. The match might have ended 3-3, but for Hamish McAlpine saving Willie Miller's deflected header on the line.

---

26. A HEARTS — 19/3
Att 8,000 · Pos 4 · Pt 31 · Result D · H-T 1-0 · F-A 1-1
Scorers: Fleming 5, Park 78. Ref: W Anderson

	1	2	3	4	5	6	7	8	9	10	11	Subs used
Aberdeen	Clark	Kennedy	McLelland	Smith	Garner	Miller	Campbell*	Fleming*	Harper	Shirra	Graham	Davidson
Hearts	*Cruickshank/Brown*	*Kay*	*Bannon^*	*Gallacher*	*Clunie*	*Robertson*	*Busby*	*Gibson*	*Park*	*Prentice*		*Shaw*

Hearts are fighting a losing battle to stay in the Premier League. Fleming scores for Aberdeen after his header flies back to him off a post. In the closing stages Park levelled, then hit Clark's crossbar. The Dons have won just twice in 11 league games, and the season is tailing away.

---

27. H MOTHERWELL — 23/3
Att 7,489 · Pos 4 · Pt 33 · Result W · H-T 0-1 · F-A 2-1
Scorers: Davidson 76, Graham 88, Wark 20. Ref: B McGinlay

	1	2	3	4	5	6	7	8	9	10	11	Subs used
Aberdeen	Clark	Kennedy	McLelland	Smith	Garner	Miller	Campbell*	Fleming*	Harper	Shirra	Graham	Sullivan/Davidson
Motherwell	*Rennie*	*Watson*	*Wark*	*McAdam*	*McLaren*	*Stevens*	*Miller J*	*Pettigrew*	*Graham R*	*Miller P*	*O'Rourke**	*Marinello*

Motherwell scored out of the blue in the first half and elected to protect their lead at all costs in the second. Super-sub Duncan Davidson chested down Miller's lob to equalise. Arthur Graham claimed the winner, two minutes from time, scoring through a packed penalty box.

---

28. H AYR — 26/3
Att 6,057 · Pos 4 · Pt 33 · Result L · H-T 0-1 · F-A 0-2
Scorers: McCall 2, Masterton 66. Ref: W Mullen

	1	2	3	4	5	6	7	8	9	10	11	Subs used
Aberdeen	Clark	Kennedy	McLelland*	Smith	Garner	Miller	Sullivan*	Davidson	Harper	Shirra	Graham	Scott/Rougvie
Ayr	*Sproat*	*Wells*	*Brogan*	*Fleming*	*Filippi*	*McAnespie*	*McSherry*	*McCall*	*Masterton*	*McCulloch*	*Cramond^*	*Phillips/Kelly*

Aberdeen booked their place in Europe by virtue of winning the League Cup. They therefore have little to play for in the league. And it shows. Walker McCall, scorer of Ayr's first goal, had just been transferred from Aberdeen. This is Ayr's first league win at Pittodrie in 12 attempts.

---

29. A KILMARNOCK — 2/4
Att 5,000 · Pos 4 · Pt 35 · Result W · H-T 1-1 · F-A 2-1
Scorers: Graham 44, Davidson 10, McCulloch 10. Ref: D Murdoch

	1	2	3	4	5	6	7	8	9	10	11	Subs used
Aberdeen	MacLean	Kennedy	Shirra	Smith	Garner	Miller	Reilly*	Davidson	Harper	Shirra*	Graham	Fleming/Rougvie
Kilmarnock	*Stewart*	*Maxwell*	*Robertson*	*McCulloch*	*Clarke*	*McDicken*	*Provan*	*Jardine*	*Fallis**	*Murdoch*	*Smith*	*Sharp*

Bottom club Kilmarnock have just beaten Rangers. A reshuffled Dons side overcame them after falling behind early on. In the second half Kilmarnock's Fallis missed a good chance to equalise and was promptly substituted. John Reilly plays his one and only game for Aberdeen.

---

30. A MOTHERWELL — 5/4
Att 5,523 · Pos 4 · Pt 36 · Result D · H-T 0-0 · F-A 1-1
Scorers: Harper 89, Pettigrew 67. Ref: I Foote

	1	2	3	4	5	6	7	8	9	10	11	Subs used
Aberdeen	MacLean	Kennedy	McLelland	Smith	Garner	Miller	Sullivan	Davidson	Harper	Shirra*	Graham	Fleming
Motherwell	*Hunter*	*Watson*	*Wark P*	*Millar*	*McLaren*	*Stevens*	*Miller J*	*Pettigrew*	*Graham R*	*Davidson*	*O'Rourke*	

Aberdeen reserve keeper Ally MacLean kept out Davidson's penalty with his knees, and even got a touch to Pettigrew's effort which put Motherwell one up. But there is no one better at bagging late goals than Joe Harper. The point dropped does not help Well's relegation fight.

---

31. H HIBERNIAN — 9/4
Att 7,910 · Pos 4 · Pt 37 · Result D · H-T 0-0 · F-A 0-0
Ref: K Stewart

	1	2	3	4	5	6	7	8	9	10	11	Subs used
Aberdeen	MacLean	Kennedy	McLelland	Smith	Garner	Miller	Sullivan*	Fleming*	Harper	Robb	Graham	Thomson/Davidson
Hibernian	*McDonald*	*Brownlie*	*Schaedler*	*Bremner*	*Stewart*	*Blackley*	*Brazil*	*MacLeod*	*Scott*	*Smith*	*Duncan*	

Duncan Davidson earns his second booking and Ally MacLean saves his second penalty of the week. Mind you, it was MacLean himself who brought down Hibs' MacLeod. This is the third 0-0 draw between the sides this season; the fourth had been settled by Harper's solitary goal.

#							
32	A	DUNDEE UTD 4	W	3-2	4,500	3	39	13/4

Scott 5, Rougvie 55, Smith 65
Sturrock 6, Rolland 40
Ref: W Mullen

MacLean	Kennedy	Shirra	Smith	Garner	Miller	Sullivan	Scott	Harper	Rougvie	Graham
McAlpine	*Rolland*	*Kopel*	*Rennie*	*Smith**	*Narey*	*Sturrack**	*Houston*	*Hegarty*	*McAdam*	*Payne*

Aberdeen lost by the same score last month. The reason Harper's name is not on the score-sheet is because Hamish McAlpine flung himself to save the wee man's late penalty. This is the result that helps the Dons finish above United this season.

| 33 | H | PARTICK THISTLE 3 | L | 0-2 | 5,836 | 6 | 39 | 16/4 |

Deans 36, 51
Ref: G Smith

MacLean	Kennedy	Shirra	Smith	Garner	Miller	Sullivan*	Scott	Harper	Rougvie*	Graham
Rough	*Hansen J*	*Whittaker*	*Campbell*	*Mar*	*Hansen A*	*Houston*	*Deans*	*Gibson*	*Somner*	*Craig*

Partick have now taken six points out of eight off Aberdeen this season. Former Celtic star Dixie Deans did the damage. Silky Alan Hansen took the eye in defence, as he has done for some seasons. In a few days he will sign for Liverpool. Runners-up spot might be beyond the Dons.

| 34 | A | CELTIC 3 | L | 1-4 | 27,000 | 1 | 39 | 20/4 |

Jarvie 29
Conn 19, Glavin 37, Craig 61, Delglish 85
Ref: D Ramsay

MacLean	Kennedy	McLelland	Smith*	Garner	Miller	Sullivan	Davidson	Harper	Graham	Rougvie
85Latchford	*McGrain*	*Lynch*	*Stanton*	*MacDonald*	*Aitken*	*Doyle*	*Glavin*	*Craig*	*Dalglish*	*Conn*

Celtic clinch the Premier Division title in style, inflicting in the process their first victory in five attempts over Aberdeen this season. The Dons sportingly applauded Jock Stein's team onto the pitch. This is the first time Aberdeen have conceded four in the league since November 1974.

| 35 | A | MOTHERWELL 3 | W | 3-1 | 4,209 | 7 | 41 | 23/4 |

Davidson 79, 85, Graham 84
Kennedy 30
Ref: A McGunnigle

MacLean	Kennedy	Smith	Garner	Miller	Shirra	Davidson	Harper	Jarvie*	Graham	Fleming
Hunter	*Mungall*	*Wark*	*McAdam*	*MacLaren*	*Stevens*	*Miller J*	*Pettigrew*	*Kennedy**	*Davidson*	*O'Neill*	*Graham*

Lucky, lucky Aberdeen. They had taken a mauling for the first 79 minutes, and looked like earning nothing from the match. Joe Harper laid on the last two goals, but by then the Dons should have been dead and buried. That's seven points out of eight from Motherwell this season.

| 36 | H | RANGERS 3 | W | 2-1 | 13,484 | 2 | 43 | 30/4 |

Harper 10p, Davidson 34
Johnstone 25
Ref: R Valentine

MacLean	Kennedy	McLelland	Smith	Garner	Miller	Davidson*	Fleming*	Jarvie	Graham	Sullivan/Shirra
Kennedy	*Jardine*	*Greig!*	*Forsyth*	*Jackson*	*Watson**	*McLean*	*Hamilton*	*Parlane*	*MacDonald*	*Johnstone*	*Armour*

A testy end-of-season match. John Greig was ordered off and five other players booked. The Premier Division's top scorer, Joe Harper, netted from the spot after Hamilton's foul on Stuart Kennedy. Harper's free-kick squirmed out of Kennedy's hands for Davidson to tap the winner.

Average Home 12,884 Away 11,560

Scottish League Cup - Section 2

| 1 | H | KILMARNOCK | W | 2-0 | 10,866 | 2 | 14/8 |

Harper 4, Graham 27
Ref: T Kelloch

MacLean	Kennedy	McLelland	Smith	Garner	Cooper	Sullivan	Fleming	Harper	McMaster*	Jarvie
Stewart	*McLean*	*Robertson*	*Murdoch*	*Clarke*	*Welsh*	*Provan*	*McCulloch*	*McDicken**	*Sheed*	*Smith*	*Maxwell*

Joe Harper is appointed captain for the day to anoint his return to Pittodrie. Hibs' loss is Aberdeen's gain. Within four minutes his neat header puts him back on the goal trail. Section 2 looks pretty undemanding, and the Dons must fancy themselves to reach the quarter-finals.

| 2 | A | ST MIRREN | W | 3-2 | 4,500 | 4 | 2-1 | 18/8 |

Fleming 14, 44, Harper 53
Borthwick 24p, Hyslop 61
Ref: T Muirhead

MacLean	Kennedy	McLelland	Smith	Garner	Cooper	Sullivan	Fleming*	Harper	McMaster	Jarvie
Hunter	*Johnstone*	*Mowatt*	*Fitzpatrick*	*Reid**	*Young*	*Stark*	*Borthwick*	*McGarvey*	*Richardson**	*Hyslop/Gibson*

Paisley's floodlights are not the brightest in the world. But Ian Fleming peers through the gloom to limp off. Young Billy Stark twice came close to an equaliser for the First Division side, Joe Harper scores his second goal in two matches.

| 3 | H | AYR | W | 1-0 | 9,695 | 6 | 0-0 | 21/8 |

Harper 63p
Ref: I Foote

MacLean	Kennedy	McLelland	Smith	Garner	Cooper	Sullivan	Jarvie*	Harper	McMaster*	Williamson/Robb
Sproat	*Filippi*	*Murphy*	*Fleming*	*Hyslop*	*McDonald*	*Gray**	*Graham*	*Phillips*	*McCulloch*	*Cramond*	*Ingram*

McDonald handles, Joe Harper nets from the spot, and that's good enough for two more points. The path to the last eight looks tantalisingly clear. But Neil Cooper has played his last game of the season for the Dons, and John McMaster will be out of action for seven months.

| 4 | H | ST MIRREN | W | 4-0 | 8,212 | 8 | 3-0 | 25/8 |

Harper 4p, 41, Williamson 39, 66
Ref: W Mullen

Clark	Kennedy	McLelland	Smith	Garner	Miller	Sullivan	Williamson	Harper	Scott	Graham
Hunter	*Johnstone*	*Mowatt*	*Fitzpatrick*	*Reid*	*Young*	*Stark**	*Borthwick*	*McGarvey*	*Richardson*	*Gibson*

Bobby Clark and Willie Miller return to the team. Aberdeen are all but through to the quarter-finals after this emphatic win over Alex Ferguson's St Mirren. Harper gained a penalty after being tripped by Reid. Harper took it himself, scored, then added another before half-time.

| 5 | A | AYR | D | 1-1 | 4,800 | 9 | 0-1 | 28/8 |

Harper 79
Phillips 2
Ref: D Syme

Clark	Kennedy	Smith	Garner	Miller	Sullivan	Williamson	Harper	Scott	Graham	Fleming
Sproat	*Filippi*	*Murpay*	*Fleming**	*McDonald*	*McSherry*	*Phillips*	*Graham*	*Ingram*	*McCulloch**	*Robertson*	*Gray/Hyslop*

Ayr full-back Filippi missed a cross: Joe Harper, lurking behind him, did not. Aberdeen might have taken both points but for Harper's extraordinary late boob, missing in front of a begging goal. It is not an expensive miss, as Aberdeen have booked their place in the last eight.

Scottish League Cup – Section 2

6 A KILMARNOCK — L 1-2 (H-T 0-1) — 1/9 — 2,700
Scorers: Harper 87 / Smith 40, 67. Ref: W Anderson

	1	2	3	4	5	6	7	8	9	10	11	subs used
Aberdeen	Clark	Kennedy*	McLelland	Smith	Garner	Miller	Sullivan^	Williamson	Harper	Scott	Graham	Thomson/Fleming
Kilmarnock	*Stewart*	*McLean*	*Robertson*	*Murdoch*	*Clarke*	*Welsh*	*Provan*	*McCulloch*	*Falls*	*Sheed^*	*Smith*	*Maxwell*

However badly Aberdeen play, it seems no one can stop Joe Harper scoring. He has netted in every League Cup match so far. Of the starting line-up, all but Chic McLelland will play in the final. This result is meaningless. The Dons will beat Killie four times out of four in the league.

Qualifying – Section 2 (final table)

Team	P	F	A	Pts
ABERDEEN	6	12	4	9
Ayr	6	8	8	6
Kilmarnock	6	8	8	5
St Mirren	6	1	12	4

QF 1 H STIRLING ALB — W 1-0 (H-T 0-0) — 22/9 — 7,185
Scorers: Harper 65. Ref: E Pringle

	1	2	3	4	5	6	7	8	9	10	11	subs used
Aberdeen	Clark	Thomson	McLelland	Smith	Garner	Miller	Sullivan	Gibson*	Harper	Scott*	Graham	Fleming/Robb
Stirling Alb	*Young*	*Nicol*	*Steedman*	*Burns*	*Kennedy*	*Carr*	*McPhee*	*Clark*	*Downie^*	*Steele*	*Armstrong*	*Thomson*

This is the kindest of quarter-final draws, yet all Aberdeen could show for their intense pressure against the Second Division side was Harper's solitary goal, when he latched on to Ian Fleming's headed pass into the box. A poor result, but surely Albion can't score twice in the return.

QF 2 A STIRLING ALB — L 0-1 (aet) (H-T 0-0) — 6/10 — 3,700
Scorers: Gray 50. Ref: E Pringle (Dons draw 1-1 on aggregate)

	1	2	3	4	5	6	7	8	9	10	11	subs used
Aberdeen	Clark	Kennedy	McLelland	Smith	Garner	Miller	Sullivan*	Fleming^	Harper	Robb	Graham	Scott/Williamson
Stirling Alb	*Young*	*Burns*	*Steedman*	*Clarke*	*Kennedy*	*Carr*	*McPhee*	*Duffin*	*Gray*	*Thomson*	*Armstrong*	*Steele*

Why Scotland boss Willie Ormond should want to brave a howling rainstorm to take in this match is a mystery. Aberdeen could not have impressed him, failing to overturn Gray's header from Duffin's free-kick. Extra-time failed to produce a goal, so a third match is necessary.

QF R STIRLING ALB — W 2-0 (H-T 2-0) — 18/10 — 4,027 (at Dens Park)
Scorers: Scott 9, Smith 40. Ref: E Pringle

	1	2	3	4	5	6	7	8	9	10	11	subs used
Aberdeen	Clark	Kennedy	McLelland	Smith	Garner	Miller	Sullivan*	Scott	Harper	Thomson*	Graham	Jarvie/Campbell
Stirling Alb	*Young*	*Burns*	*Steedman*	*Clark*	*Kennedy*	*Carr*	*McPhee**	*Duffin*	*Gray^*	*Thomson*	*Armstrong*	*Nicol/Steele*

When Jocky Scott ran Harper's cross into the net Aberdeen seized the initiative for the first time in this protracted tie. When Joe Smith's daisy-trimmer flashed through a dozen pairs of legs, the Dons were safely through. What should have been a canter had turned into a nightmare.

SF N RANGERS — W 5-1 (H-T 2-1) — 27/10 — 20,990 (at Hampden)
Scorers: Scott 2, 14, 73, Harper 64, Jarvie 66 / MacDonald 15. Ref: W Anderson

	1	2	3	4	5	6	7	8	9	10	11	subs used
Aberdeen	Clark	Kennedy	Williamson	Smith*	Garner	Miller	Sullivan	Scott	Harper	Jarvie	Graham	Thomson
Rangers	*Kennedy*	*Jardine*	*Miller*	*Greig*	*Jackson*	*Watson*	*McLean*	*McKean^*	*Parlane*	*MacDonald*	*Henderson*	*Hamilton*

Ally MacLeod and coach George Murray hug each other on the running track like chimpanzees. They are happy to forget the uncomfortable 50 minutes when Rangers threatened to equalise. They prefer to celebrate Drew Jarvie's screaming long-range volley which makes it 4-1.

F N CELTIC — W 2-1 (aet) (H-T 1-1) — 6/11 — 69,679 (at Hampden)
Scorers: Jarvie 24, Robb 93 / Dalglish 11p. Ref: J Paterson

	1	2	3	4	5	6	7	8	9	10	11	subs used
Aberdeen	Clark	Kennedy	Williamson	Smith	Garner	Miller	Sullivan	Scott	Harper	Jarvie*	Graham	Robb
Celtic	*Latchford*	*McGrain*	*Lynch*	*Edvaldsson*	*MacDonald*	*Aitken*	*Doyle*	*Glavin*	*Dalglish*	*Burns***	*Wilson*	*Lennox*

Celtic's 13th consecutive appearance in the League Cup Final - Aberdeen's first since 1955. Jarvie's foul on Dalglish yields a penalty. Dalglish scores it and exchanges unpleasantries with Harper, who then heads across goal for Jarvie to level. Sub Dave Robb bags the extra-time winner.

Scottish Cup

3 A DUNFERMLINE — W 1-0 (H-T 0-0) — 29/1 — 11,899 (2:6)
Scorers: Harper 58. Ref: J Gordon

	1	2	3	4	5	6	7	8	9	10	11	subs used
Aberdeen	Clark	Kennedy	McLelland	Smith	Garner	Miller	Sullivan	Scott	Harper	Jarvie	Graham	
Dunfermline	*Whyte*	*Thomson*	*Markey*	*Scott*	*Salton*	*Meakin*	*Watson*	*Bowie*	*Georgeson*	*Evans*	*Donaldson*	*MacLeod*

Dunfermline are sixth in Division 2. As against Alloa a year ago, this cup-tie is marred by hooligan violence. The match itself is played on an ice rink of a pitch, and is settled by Joe Harper's mis-hit shot which is deflected past Whyte. The Dons fancy two cup finals in one season.

4 A DUNDEE — D 0-0 (H-T 0-0) — 26/2 — 16,999 (1:3)
Ref: K Stewart

	1	2	3	4	5	6	7	8	9	10	11	subs used
Aberdeen	Clark	Kennedy	McLelland	Smith	Garner	Miller	Sullivan*	Davidson	Harper	Jarvie*	Graham	Robb
Dundee	*Donaldson*	*Ford*	*Johnston*	*Caldwell*	*Phillip*	*McPhail*	*Hogan^*	*Strachan*	*Pirie*	*Hutchinson**	*Purdie*	*Sinclair/Robinson*

Dundee were relegated on the last day of last season. It could so easily have been Aberdeen in their place. The most noticeable feature of this match was the tension. Aberdeen had a lot of defending to do, and are glad of the chance to replay the tie at Pittodrie.

4R H DUNDEE — L 1-2 (H-T 0-1) — 2/3 — 18,375 (1:3)
Scorers: Davidson 52 / Hutchinson 11, 76. Ref: K Stewart

	1	2	3	4	5	6	7	8	9	10	11	subs used
Aberdeen	Clark	Kennedy	McLelland	Smith	Garner	Miller	Sullivan*	Davidson	Harper	Shirra	Graham	Robb
Dundee	*Donaldson*	*Ford*	*Johnston*	*Caldwell^*	*Phillip*	*McPhail*	*Robinson*	*Strachan*	*Pirie^*	*Hutchinson*	*Purdie*	*Laing/Sinclair*

Willie Miller might be emerging as one of Scotland's great defenders, but he will have nightmares after this. The Dons had fought back from Hutchinson's headed opener. Duncan Davidson pounced when Donaldson failed to hold Scott's drive. Miller then fluffed a simple back-pass.

League Table

	P	W	D	L	F	A	W	D	L	F	A	Pts
			Home						Away			
1 Celtic	36	13	5	0	44	16	10	4	4	35	23	55
2 Rangers	36	12	4	2	36	16	6	6	6	26	21	46
3 ABERDEEN	36	11	4	3	30	18	6	7	6	26	24	43
4 Dundee Utd	36	8	5	5	26	17	8	4	6	28	28	41
5 Partick This	36	9	5	4	27	24	4	8	8	13	20	35
6 Hibernian	36	4	10	4	14	12	8	6	6	20	23	34
7 Motherwell	36	8	7	3	38	25	2	5	11	19	35	32
8 Ayr	36	4	5	9	23	36	7	3	8	21	32	30
9 Hearts	36	5	6	7	26	28	2	7	9	23	38	27
10 Kilmarnock	36	4	5	9	21	30	0	4	14	11	41	17
	360	78	56	46	285	222	46	56	78	222	285	360

	P	W	D	L	F	A	Pts	Cup	W	F	A	L
v Kilmarnock	4	4	0	0	8	2	8	LC	1	1	0	1
v Motherwell	4	3	1	0	9	4	7					
v Ayr	4	2	1	1	6	2	5	LC	1	1	0	
v Celtic	4	2	1	1	7	7	5	LC	1	1	0	0
v Hibernian	4	1	3	0	8	6	5					
v Hearts	4	2	0	2	8	8	4					
v Dundee Utd	4	2	1	1	8	6	4	LC				
v Rangers	4	1	1	2	5	7	3					
v Partick This	4	0	2	2	4	7	2					
	36	16	11	9	56	42	43		1	1	0	0

Odds & ends

Never lost to: (3) Kilmarnock, Motherwell, Hibs.

Never beat: (1) Partick.

Won from behind: (8) Celtic (h & LC), Dundee Utd (h & a), Kilmarnock (h & a), Motherwell (h & a).

Lost from in front: (0).

High spots: 6 league wins out of 7 from 23 October, holding first place. Winning League Cup, and disposing of both Rangers and Celtic.

Low spots: Poor New Year, winning 2 matches out of 10 from 8 Jan, and losing at home to 1st Division Dundee in Scottish Cup.

Bogey-team: Partick Thistle.

Ever-presents: (2) Willie Garner, Willie Miller (league only).

Hat-tricks: (2) Joe Harper 1, Jocky Scott 1.

Leading scorer: (28) Joe Harper.

Appearances and Goals

Player	Lge	Sub	LC	Sub	SC	Sub	Lge	LC	SC	Tot
Campbell, George	4	1		1						
Clark, Bobby	27		8		3					
Cooper, Neil			3							
Davidson, Duncan	8	5			2		5		1	6
Fleming, Ian	13	4	3	3			4	2		6
Garner, Willie	36		11		3					
Gibson, Ian		1	1				1			1
Graham, Arthur	35		11		3		5	1		6
Hair, Ian	1									
Harper, Joe	34		11		3		18	9	1	28
Jarvie, Drew	18	2	3	3	1		9	2		11
Kennedy, Stuart	32		10		3		1			1
MacLean, Ally	9		3		3					
McLelland, Chic	25		9		3		1			1
McMaster, John	1	1	3							
Miller, Willie	36		8		3		1	1		2
Robb, Dave	6	7	1	3		2	1	1		2
Reilly, John	1									
Rougvie, Doug	2	4								
Scott, Jocky	13	6	7	1	2		3	4		7
Shirra, Jim	20	6			2					
Smith, Jim	35		11		3		3	1		4
Sullivan, Dom	28	4	11		2		3			3
Thomson, Eddie	3	4	2	2						
Williamson, Billy	9	5	5	2			1	2		3
25 players used	396	45	121	15	33	2	56	22	2	80

SCOTTISH PREMIER DIVISION

Manager: Billy McNeill

SEASON 1977-78

No	Date	Att	Pos	Pt	F-A	H-T	Scorers, Times, and Referees	1	2	3	4	5	6	7	8	9	10	11	subs used
1	H RANGERS 13/8	21,500	1	2	W 3-1	1-1	Jarvie 11, 60, Harper 62	Clark	Kennedy	McLelland	Smith*	Garner	Miller	Jarvie	Shirra	Harper	Fleming	McMaster	Davidson
							Russell 31 — Ref: T Muirhead	*McCloy*	*Jardine*	*Miller*	*Forsyth*	*Jackson*	*MacDonald McKay**	*Russell*	*Parlane*	*Robertson*	*Cooper*	*McKean*	
							For an ex-Celtic man, this was just the start Billy McNeill wanted to his career as Dons manager. He strolled onto the pitch before kick-off wearing a red shirt, which brought a rapturous ovation from the Dons' fans. Harper and Jarvie carry on where they left off - scoring goals.												
2	A CLYDEBANK 20/8	7,000	1	4	W 3-1	0-1	Garner 71, Harper 77, Davidson 78	Clark	Kennedy	McLelland	Shirra	Garner	Miller	Jarvie	Sullivan	Harper	Fleming	McMaster*	Davidson
							Lamach 27 — Ref: D Downie	*Gallacher*	*Hall**	*Abel*	*Fallon*	*McLaughlin*	*Houston*	*O'Brien*	*McColl*	*Lamach*	*McCallan*	*Lumsden*	*Ronald*
							Whatever Billy McNeill said to his troops at the interval must have been potent. From being totally outwitted by newly promoted Clydebank in the first half, Aberdeen administered the KO punch in the second. Joe Harper's goal was scored not with his foot, but with his stomach.												
3	H DUNDEE UTD 27/8	16,100	1	5	D 0-0	0-0	Ref: G Smith	Clark	Kennedy	McLelland	Shirra	Garner	Miller	Jarvie	Sullivan*	Harper	Fleming	McMaster	Davidson
								McAlpine	*Rolland*	*Kopel*	*Robinson**	*Hegarty*	*Narey*	*Sturrock*	*Wallace GG Kirkwood*	*Addison*	*Fleming*	*McAdam*	
							Ally MacLeod returns to Pittodrie, this time - as befits the manager of Scotland - looking objectively at both sets of players. Both sides kicked off the match with unbeaten records, and seemed determined to safeguard them. Not a pretty spectacle for the fans of either side.												
4	A AYR 10/9	4,700	1	7	W 1-0	0-0	Harper 89	Clark	Kennedy	McLelland	Shirra	Garner	Miller	Jarvie	Robb	Harper	Fleming	McMaster	Davidson
							Ref: B McGinlay	*Sproat*	*Rodman*	*Kelly*	*Fleming*	*McInespie*	*Brogan**	*Phillips*	*McCall*	*Masterton*	*McCulloch*	*Camond*	*Filippi*
							Back from his stint playing in USA, Dave Robb is ineligible for next week's UEFA Cup match in Molenbeek. The watching Belgian spies are relieved, for he was Aberdeen's best performer on the day. Having beaten Celtic, Ayr are starting a run of five defeats without scoring a goal.												
5	H CELTIC 17/9	25,800	1	9	W 2-1	0-0	Fleming 58, 67	Clark	Kennedy	McLelland	Shirra	Garner	Miller	Davidson	Jarvie	Harper	Fleming	McMaster*	Doyle
							Garner 49 og — Ref: J Paterson	*Latchford*	*McGrain*	*Lynch*	*Edvaldsson*	*McDonald*	*McWilliams*	*Glavin*	*McAdam*	*Craig**	*Aitken*	*Wilson*	
							If Billy McNeill had mixed feelings about this result he didn't show it. This is Celtic's fourth defeat on the trot. They looked like ending that sequence with Willie Garner's spectacular header past Bobby Clark. Fleming's equaliser went in off a post; his winner was a thumping header.												
6	H PARTICK THISTLE 24/9	11,900	1	11	W 2-1	1-1	Harper 32p, 49	Clark	Kennedy	McLelland	Shirra	Garner	Miller	Davidson	Jarvie	Harper	Fleming	McMaster	McQuade
							Houston 7 — Ref: J Gordon	*Rough*	*Mackie*	*Whittaker*	*Gibson*	*Marr*	*Campbell*	*Houston*	*Melrose**	*Love*	*Somner*	*Craig*	
							Considering Aberdeen's all-round dominance, Thistle escaped ridiculously lightly. They cannot be that bad, however; they will shortly embark on a long winning run - dropping just one point in eight games - that will carry them to second place when these two teams meet again.												
7	A MOTHERWELL 1/10	6,466	2	12	D 1-1	1-0	McMaster 20	Clark	Kennedy	McLelland	Robb*	Garner	Miller	Davidson	Jarvie	Harper	Fleming	McMaster	Sullivan
							O'Neill 53 — Ref: K Hope	*Rennie*	*Watson*	*Wark*	*Miller*	*McVie*	*Stevens*	*McLaren*	*O'Neill*	*McAdam**	*Davidson*	*Purdie*	*O'Rourke/Marinello*
							Willie Miller collects his third caution in the course of the season as Aberdeen protect their unbeaten league record. McMaster's delicious volley might have brought the Dons two points, but they are pegged back by O'Neill, who starts his first match of the season and scores his one and only goal.												
8	A ST MIRREN 8/10	12,919	5	14	W 4-0	2-0	Jarvie 24, 41, 83, Fleming 65	Clark	Kennedy	McLelland	Smith	Garner	Miller	Sullivan	Jarvie	Harper	Fleming	McMaster	
							Ref: E Thomson	*Hunter*	*Beckett**	*Young*	*Fitzpatrick*	*Reid*	*Copland*	*Docherty*	*Stark*	*McGarvey*	*Richardson*	*Hyslop*	*Abercrombie*
							Alex Ferguson's St Mirren don't relish entertaining the Dons. His promoted team's last home defeat was over a year ago - in the League Cup - and was also against Aberdeen. After this crushing win, the Dons are two points clear of Dundee Utd at the top, and are the last unbeaten team.												
9	H HIBERNIAN 15/10	11,900	1	14	L 1-2	1-1	Jarvie 12	Clark	Kennedy	McLelland	Smith	Garner	Miller	Sullivan*	Jarvie	Harper	Fleming	McMaster	Davidson/Scott
							Smith 22 og, MacLeod 66 — Ref: T Muirhead	*McDonald*	*Brownlie*	*Smith*	*Brazil*	*Stewart*	*McNamara*	*MacLeod*	*Bremner*	*Henderson*	*Higgins*	*Duncan*	
							Tragedy for Joe Smith as Aberdeen's unbeaten record goes up in smoke. He sticks out his foot towards Bobby Smith's inswinging corner and prods the ball past Clark. There is no argument about Hibs' winner - a raging 30-yarder from MacLeod. Hibs won't win any of their next six.												
10	A RANGERS 22/10	37,000	2	14	L 1-3	1-1	Harper 37p	Clark	Kennedy	McLelland	Smith	Garner	Miller	Jarvie	Shirra	Harper	Fleming	McMaster*	Sullivan
							Jardine 31p, Smith 68, MacDonald 72 — Ref: H Alexander	*Kennedy*	*Jardine*	*Greig*	*Forsyth*	*Jackson*	*MacDonald*	*McLean*	*Russell*	*Johnstone*	*Smith*	*Cooper*	*Sullivan*
							Rangers leap-frog over Aberdeen to the top of the league after this gruelling battle. Bobby Clark faced two Sandy Jardine penalties, and saved the second of them. In between, Harper netted from the spot himself and Chic McLelland was ordered off for his challenge on Davie Cooper.												

11 H CLYDEBANK 29/10   2 D 1-1   9,400 10 15

Clark Kennedy McLelland Smith Garner Miller Jarvie Shirra* Harper Fleming McMaster Davidson
Gallacher Hall Abel Fallon McCormack Hay McColl McLaughlan McColl Lamach McCallan Colgan Lumsden*

Harper 52 / McCallan 64   Ref: D Murdoch

Bottom of the table Bankies are there for the taking. The Dons are coasting at 1-0 when Clydebank send over a free-kick. Bobby Clark finds himself clutching at mid-air, and McCallan accepts the gift. It is his first goal of the season, in which no Bankie player scores more than five.

---

12 A DUNDEE UTD 5/11   2 W 1-0   10,000 3 17

Clark Kennedy McLelland Smith Garner Miller Jarvie* Harper Fleming Strachan McMaster
McAlpine Rolland Kopel Fleming Hegarty Narey Addison Bourke* Kirkwood Wallace GG Payne Holt/Wallace G Campbell*

Fleming 89   Ref: I Foote

The most notable feature of this match is the quick return to Tayside for Aberdeen debutant Gordon Strachan, signed from Dundee. United's David Narey was left cursing his late, inattentive back-pass which handed the game to the Dons. United have lost four of their last five games.

---

13 H AYR 12/11   2 D 0-0   9,350 9 18

Clark Kennedy McLelland Smith* Garner Miller Robb Jarvie Harper Fleming Strachan Sullivan
*Sproat Radman Kelly Fleming Hyslop McAnespie McLaughlin*McCall Masterton Hannah* Cramond/ McAllister/Christie*

Ref: G Smith

Ayr have won three of the last five. 16 minutes into this match Joe Smith collides with Hyslop, is carried off, his career permanently wrecked. Later in the first half Ayr's Cramond was sent off for a foul on Stuart Kennedy. Back-to-back home draws with the two teams to be relegated.

---

14 A CELTIC 19/11   2 L 2-3   27,000 5 18

Clark Kennedy Sullivan Garner Miller Robb Jarvie Harper Fleming* Strachan McMaster
Filippi Lynch Munro McDonald Aitken Doyle Edvaldson Craig McAdam Conn Wilson*

Jarvie 15, Harper 70p / Lynch 32p, Aitken 48, Edvaldsson 75 Latchford   Ref: E Pringle

Whether Celtic would have won without a debatable equalising penalty, we shall never know. Filippi's shot struck Garner and a linesman flagged. Edvaldsson settled the dispute with a swivelling shot that nearly ripped the net off its rigging. Nine points from the last 10 for Celtic.

---

15 A PARTICK THISTLE 26/11   4 L 0-1   12,800 2 18

Clark Kennedy McLelland Sullivan Garner Miller Robb Jarvie Fleming McMaster* Strachan Grant
Rough Mackie Whittaker Gibson Anderson Marr Houston Sommer O'Hara Melrose Craig

Sonner 8   Ref: W Mullen

Aberdeen's slide continues. Literally. The soggy pitch was virtually unplayable. But after Sommer's early header, Thistle weren't complaining about the conditions. They have now taken 15 points from eight games, and this win lifts them to second, with two points more than the Dons.

---

16 H MOTHERWELL 3/12   2 W 4-1   9,500 7 20

Clark Kennedy McLelland Strachan Garner Miller Robb Jarvie Harper* McMaster* Fleming
Rennie Watson Wark Miller J McLaren Stevens Marinello Pettigrew O'Rourke Millar P Purdie*

Robb 12, 51, 73, Strachan 16 / Pettigrew 32   Ref: B McGinlay

Motherwell had won one of their previous 10 games. Aberdeen had won one of their previous seven. Not much confidence here. The chief question on this freezing day was which of Robb's stunning three goals was the best. Each of them was an example of power-house shooting.

---

17 H ST MIRREN 10/12   2 W 3-1   9,000 6 22

Clark Kennedy Glennie Strachan* Garner Miller Sullivan Fleming Harper* Robb Fleming
Hunter Beckett Munro Fitzpatrick Reid Copland Richardson Stark McGarvey Abercrombie Hyslop Leonard/Young*

Robb 7, Gibson 47, 53 / Hyslop 84   Ref: E Thomson

More great goals to savour. Dave Robb's free-kick fairly demolished St Mirren's defensive wall. But even Robb was upstaged by Ian Gibson's two efforts. One Saint to guard against was young midfielder Billy Stark, who had scored five goals in St Mirren's previous seven games.

---

18 A HIBERNIAN 17/12   2 L 0-2   6,601 7 22

Clark Kennedy Glennie Cooper Garner Miller Sullivan Jarvie Harper Gibson* Robb*
McDonald Brownlie Smith McNamara Stewart Brazil Murray MacLeod Hutchinson Duncan McGhee Fleming/ Davidson

Murray 33, Duncan 54   Ref: J Gordon

It is two wins out of two for Hibernian over the Dons this season. Hibs brought about Aberdeen's first defeat of the season; now they inflict their last. Curiously, McNeill played Willie Miller in midfield. Hibs are embarking on a spirited run that will lift them from ninth to third.

---

19 H RANGERS 24/12   2 W 4-0   21,000 1 24

Clark Kennedy McLelland McMaster Garner Miller Sullivan Jarvie Harper Gibson* Robb
Kennedy Jardine Greig Forsyth Jackson MacDonald McLean Russell Johnstone Smith McLaughrin*McCall Cooper Parlane*

Gibson 30, Robb 40, Harper 76, Jarvie 85   Ref: J Paterson

Aberdeen declare that the title race is not yet decided, by inflicting on Rangers their first league defeat since August. Last season John Greig was sent off here; this time his ferocious tackles earn a booking. The Dons are now three points behind Rangers, and have played a game more.

---

20 A CLYDEBANK 31/12   2 W 1-0   2,800 10 26

Clark Kennedy McMaster Garner Miller Sullivan Jarvie Harper Gibson* Robb
*King Hall Colgan Fallon McCormack Houston O'Brien McCall McLaughrin*McCallan Lumsden Davidson/Fleming Bradbury*

McMaster 35   Ref: D Syme

A Hogmanay present to John McMaster from the Bankies' goalkeeper King, who - wide of his own goal - miscues a clearance straight to McMaster's feet. This earns Clydebank their sixth successive defeat. Good new from Ibrox, where Rangers have dropped a point to Hibernian.

---

21 H DUNDEE UTD 2/1   W 1-0   23,000 28

Clark Rougvie McLelland McMaster McLeish Miller Sullivan Jarvie Harper Gibson* Robb
McAlpine Rolland Kopel Rennie Hegarty Narey Sturrock Addison Dodds Fleming Payne* Kirkwood/Wallace GG*

Fleming 80   Ref: G Smith

Alex McLeish, not yet 19, makes a surprise debut after both Willie Garner and Bobby Glennie are fined and dropped by Billy McNeill for misdemeanours. Four matches between these sides this season will yield just two goals. The Dons' substitute gets the vital goal.

SCOTTISH PREMIER DIVISION Manager: Billy McNeill SEASON 1977-78

No	Date	Scorers, Times, and Referees	Att	Pos	Pt	F-A	H-T	1	2	3	4	5	6	7	8	9	10	11	subs used
22	A AYR 7/1	McMaster 1 / McCall 63 — Ref: I Foote	5,966	9	29	1-1	1-0	Clark / Sproat	Glennie / Rodman	McLelland / Kelly	McMaster* / Fleming	Garner / Hyslop*	Miller / McAnespie	Sullivan" / McCall	Archibald / McSherry	Harper / Masterton	Gibson / McLaughlin	Jarvie / Cramond	Fleming/Watson / Hannah
23	H CELTIC 14/1	Sullivan 31, 71 / McDonald 75 — Ref: W Mullen	24,600	7	31	2-1	1-0	Clark / Latchford	Kennedy / Filippi	McLelland / Lynch	McMaster / Aitken	Garner / McDonald	Miller / Munro	Sullivan / Glavin	Davidson / Edvaldsson	Gibson / McCluskey	Jarvie / McAdam	Robb / Wilson*	/ Burns
24	A MOTHERWELL 4/2	— Ref: D Downie	8,845	5	32	0-0	0-0	Clark / Rennie	Kennedy / Watson	McLelland / Wark	McMaster / Millar P	Garner / McVie	Miller / Stevens	Strachan / Marinello	Archibald / Pettigrew	Harper / O'Rourke	Davidson / Miller J*	Davidson / Clinging	
25	H HIBERNIAN 25/2	Stewart 21 og, Davidson 49, Miller 71 — Ref: K Hope	11,200	7	34	3-0	1-0	Clark / McDonald	Kennedy / Brownlie	McLelland / Smith	McMaster / Bremner	Garner / Stewart*	Miller / McNamara	Sullivan / Murray	Archibald / MacLeod	Harper / Hutchinson	Strachan / Duncan	Davidson / McGhee	McGhee/Brazil / Brazil
26	A RANGERS 4/3	Archibald 22, 78, Harper 38 — Ref: T Muirhead	34,500	1	36	3-0	2-0	Clark / Kennedy	Kennedy / Miller	McLelland / Greig	McMaster / Forsyth	Garner / Jackson	Miller / MacDonald	Sullivan / McLean	Archibald / Russell*	Gibson / Johnstone	Jarvie / Smith"	Davidson / Cooper	Dawson/Parlane
27	A DUNDEE UTD 18/3	— Ref: E Pringle	9,671	3	37	0-0	0-0	Clark /	McAlpine / Rennie	McLelland / Kopel	McMaster / Fleming	Garner / Hegarty	Miller / Narey	Sullivan / Sturrock	Archibald / Addison	Fleming* / Wallace G	Jarvie / Holt	Davidson / Payne	Strachan / Strachan
28	H CLYDEBANK 21/3	Davidson 58, Archibald 67 — Ref: I Foote	9,600	3	39	2-0	0-0	Clark / Gallacher	Kennedy / Gourlay	Ritchie / Abel	McMaster / Fallon	Garner / McCormack	Miller / Hauston	Strachan / O'Brien	Archibald / McColl	Gibson* / Miller	Jarvie / Lumsden	Davidson / Ronald*	Grant/Bradbury
29	H AYR 25/3	Davidson 17, Archibald 34, Jarvie 49, 74 / Masteron 62 — Ref: D Murdoch	11,000	9	41	4-1	2-0	Clark / Sproat	Kennedy / Wells	Ritchie / Sim*	McMaster / Tait	Garner / Fleming	Miller / Kelly	Strachan* / McCall	Archibald / McSherry	Harper / Masterton	Jarvie / Cramond	Davidson / McLaughlin	McCulloch Sullivan
30	A ST MIRREN 29/3	Davidson 36, Archibald 66 / Stark 52 — Ref: I McGunnigle	9,300	3	43	2-1	1-0	Clark /	McCulloch / Beckett	Ritchie / Munro	McMaster / Fitzpatrick	Garner / Reid	Miller / Copland	Sullivan / Abercr'mbie*	Archibald / Stark	Harper / Bone	Jarvie / Richardson	Davidson / McGarvey	Leonard/Hyslop
31	A CELTIC 1/4	Davidson 57, Sullivan 66 / Glavin 34, Edvaldsson 58 — Ref: W Anderson	24,000	6	44	2-2	0-1	Clark / Latchford	Kennedy / Sneddon	Ritchie / Lynch	McMaster / Aitken	Garner / McDonald	Miller / Dowie	Sullivan / Glavin	Archibald / Edvaldsson	Harper / McAdam	Jarvie / Burns	Davidson / Doyle*	McCluskey

Match commentaries

22 — Struggling Ayr have won their last two, including victory over Celtic. This match sees two more Dons' baptisms: one for Steve Archibald, the other for substitute Andy Watson. It is former-Don Walker McCall who deprives Aberdeen of both points. Rangers won to extend their lead.

23 — A fourth consecutive defeat plunges Celtic into the relegation mire. Late in the game Willie Garner handles in the box, but Lynch's penalty hits a post. This was the match where Celtic tried to play two centre-forwards. Two players wore No 9. The ref told McAdam to change into No 10.

24 — Under Roger Hynd's management Motherwell are having a good run. They have won their last four and climbed from eighth to fifth. That winning run comes to an end, but Well were certainly not second best in this match. Motherwell won't do so well next time these sides meet.

25 — The spooky fog which enveloped Pittodrie had a peculiar effect on Hibs' skipper George Stewart, who floated a header over his keeper into the net. His counterpart, Willie Miller, played his part in a four-man move which climaxed with his thunderous goal. Rangers' lead is six points.

26 — Rangers have won their last six, but their lead is cut to four points after this heroic win. Harper scored one and made two others for Archibald. The most articulate comment on the match was made by Rangers' supporters, who started streaming away from Ibrox long before the end.

27 — The conditions were perfect, but the game was a flop. Both teams know each other too intimately to produce surprises. Future Don Davie Dodds has come on as United sub several times recently, but not this time. Rangers' win extends their lead at the top to five points.

28 — Clydebank have now won just once in 15 league games. They hold out for nearly an hour, but are undone by Strachan' inch-perfect pass to Duncan Davidson, who outpaced keeper Gallacher to score the first. Davidson's header off the crossbar fell to Archibald for the second.

29 — Celtic and Rangers kicked off at 1 pm. Their lead over the Dons is cut to one point, though Aberdeen have played a game more. As for Ayr, they haven't won since 2 January, and they know they are doomed. Drew Jarvie's goals are his first since Christmas.

30 — St Mirren are not yet safe from the drop. Paisley's new super-powered floodlights are reflected in the pools of water which had already submerged the pitch by half-time. Billy Stark's top-spin lob set the game up for a furious finish. Archibald's winner takes the Dons to the top.

31 — Four wins in their last five appear to have made Celtic safe. Aberdeen earn their point with a stunning goal by Dom Sullivan, who exchanges passes with Joe Harper before letting fly. Rangers have drawn two games in four days, and are now second, but they have games in hand.

32 H PARTICK THISTLE 16,000 4/4 — W 2-1 46

Harper 13, 16
Frame 27
Ref: R Valentine

| Clark | Kennedy | Ritchie | McMaster | Garner | Sullivan | Archibald* | Harper | Jarvie | Davidson | Strachan |
| Rough | McAdam | Whittaker | Campbell | Marr | Love | O'Hara | Frame | Sommer | McQuade | Mackie |

Thistle's good autumn run has been followed by a dreadful spring. They have now taken just one point from their last six games. Five days later these teams meet again. Harper did his stuff in the first half; his defenders did theirs in the second, as Thistle threatened to snatch a point.

---

33 A PARTICK THISTLE 1 9,000 8/4 — W 2-0 48

Harper 17, McMaster 22
Ref: E Thomson

| Clark | Kennedy | Ritchie | McMaster | Garner | Sullivan | Archibald | Harper | Jarvie | Davidson | |
| Rough | McAdam | Whittaker | Gibson | Campbell | Marr* | Houston | Frame | Love | Sommer | Craig* | Mackie/O'Hara |

Four points from Partick in five days; that's six points out of eight. Now the Dons meet the Jags again in the Scottish Cup semi-final. As the league reaches its climax, Aberdeen find themselves two points ahead of Rangers, who have two games in hand. The title is in Rangers' hands.

---

34 H MOTHERWELL 1 16,280 15/4 — W 5-0 50

Jarvie 8, 14, Harper 13p, Davidson 32, 55
Ref: D Syme

| Clark | Kennedy | Ritchie | McMaster | Garner | Sullivan | Fleming | Harper | Jarvie | Davidson | Kennedy/McVie |
| Rennie | Watson | Wark | Miller | McLaren | Marinello* | Petigrew | Clinging* | Davidson | Mungall | |

Motherwell's biggest defeat and Aberdeen's biggest win of the season gives the Dons a healthy goal-difference advantage over Rangers. The league and cup double is on! The standing ovation at the finish was just reward for a devastating display. But Rangers won too.

---

35 H ST MIRREN 2 17,250 22/4 — W 4-2 52

Harper 42, 61, 82, Miller 49
McGarvey 2, 10
Ref: T Kyle

| Clark | Kennedy | Ritchie | McMaster | Garner | Sullivan | Fleming | Harper | Jarvie | Davidson | Young |
| McCulloch | Beckett | Munro | Fitzpatrick | Dunlop | Copland | Abercrmbie* Stark | Bone | Richardson | McGarvey | |

What a shock for the Dons as they find themselves 2-0 down to Alex Ferguson's much-improved side. Each of Joe Harper's three goals was netted from close in. A tumultuous reception greets the Dons as they troop off. They have also beaten Ferguson's team four times out of four.

---

36 A HIBERNIAN 2 11,250 29/4 — D 1-1 53

Scanlon 79
Duncan 87
Ref: I Foote

| Clark | Kennedy | Ritchie | McMaster | Garner | Sullivan | Fleming* | Harper | Jarvie | Davidson | Scanlon |
| McDonald | Brownlie | Smith | McNamara | Stewart | Bremner | MacLeod | Rae | Murray | Duncan | Higgins |

Aberdeen need to take one point more from Hibs than Rangers take at home to Motherwell. The Dons 23rd game without defeat was not enough. Substitute Ian Scanlon, on his debut, takes the ball round McDonald to score, but Arthur Duncan heads an equaliser. Rangers won 2-0.

Average Home 15,250 Away 13,320

Scottish League Cup

1:1 H AIRDRIE 10,600 17/8 — W 3-1

Fleming 43, 71, Shirra 78
Kerr 77
Ref: W Mullen

| Clark | Kennedy | McLelland | Smith* | Garner | Miller | Sullivan | Shirra | Harper | Fleming | Jarvie | Davidson |
| Brian | Jonquin | Lapsley | Black | Collins | Cowan | McGowan* McVeigh | Kerr | McCulloch | Clark | Wilson | |

The League Cup has a new format. Gone are the group sections of the past 30 years, replaced by two-legged knock-outs up to and including the quarter-finals. This tie was held up for several minutes in the first half when Airdrie won a corner. None of their players wanted to take it.

1:2 A AIRDRIE 2,500 24/8 — W 2-0

McMaster 23, 57
Ref: W Mullen
(Dons win 5-1 on aggregate)

| Clark | Kennedy | McLelland | Shirra | Garner | Miller | Sullivan | Jarvie | Harper* | Fleming | Davidson |
| McWilliams | Jonquin | Cowan | Anderson | Collins | McCulloch | Wilson | McVeigh | Kerr | Walker | Lapsley |

Airdrie are headed for a poor season in Division 1. John McMaster comes close to registering his first senior hat-trick. His late free-kick beat goalkeeper McWilliams, but was chalked off for an infringement by others on the goal-line. A comfy ride for Aberdeen into Round 2

2:1 H COWDENBEATH 1 8,250 31/8 — W 5-0

Harper 1, 43, 81, Fleming 83, 84
Ref: D Ramsay

| Clark | Kennedy | McLelland | Smith* | Garner | Miller | Jarvie | Shirra | Harper | Fleming | Davidson |
| McGarr | Thomson | Carpenter | Purdie | Aitken | Fair | Hunter | Graham | Steele | Marshall* | Jobson |

Against honest but limited Second Division opposition, Joe Harper breaks Harry Yorston's all-time scoring record for Aberdeen, with a hat-trick that began in the first seconds of the match. Cowdenbeath have won only once against Division 2 opponents, and have little chance here.

2:2 A COWDENBEATH 1 1,780 3/9 — W 5-0

Davidson 16, McMaster 20,
[Harper 45p, 61, 72] McGarr
Ref: D Ramsay
(Dons win 10-0 on aggregate)

| Clark | Kennedy | McLelland | Shirra | Garner | Miller | Jarvie | Davidson | Harper | Fleming* | McMaster |
| McGarr | Ward | Carpenter | Thomson* | Aitken | Fair | Hunter | Harley | Marshall* | Steele | Caithness | Purdie/Graham |

There is no competitive edge to this match, which was settled at Pittodrie. Joe Harper casually wraps up his second successive hat-trick against the Fifers. But this time he was a naughty boy and got himself booked as well. Two cushy rounds have taken Aberdeen into the next stage.

3:1 A RANGERS 2 25,000 5/10 — L 1-6

Davidson 80
[MacDonald 85] Smith 3, 44, 72, Johnstone 30, Miller 45p, MacDonald 85
Ref: G Smith

| Clark | Kennedy | McLelland | Robb | Garner | Jarvie | Davidson | Harper | Fleming* | McMaster | Sullivan |
| Kennedy | Jardine | Miller | Forsyth | Jackson | MacDonald | McLean | Russell | Johnstone | Smith | Cooper |

What a surprise; what an humiliation. Rangers look brilliant, especially Gordon Smith. Billy McNeill is honest enough to describe them as the best Rangers team he has ever seen. Enough said. Two goals in the closing seconds of the first half effectively end the tie as a contest.

SCOTTISH PREMIER (CUP-TIES) Manager: Billy McNeill SEASON 1977-78

Scottish League Cup

3:2 H RANGERS — 26/10 · 2 · W 3-1 · H-T 1-1 · Att 15,600 *1*
Scorers: Smith J 38, Jarvie 59, 65 / *Smith G 30* / Ref: G Smith / (Dons lose 4-7 on aggregate)

1	2	3	4	5	6	7	8	9	10	11	subs used
Clark	Kennedy	McLelland	Smith	Garner	Miller	Jarvie	Shirra	Harper	Fleming	McMaster	Davidson
Kennedy	*Jardine*	*Miller**	*Forsyth*		*MacDonald*	*McLean*	*Russell*	*Johnstone*	*Smith^*	*Cooper*	*Parlane/McKean*

Rangers lost their first two games of the season and since then have not looked back. Gordon Smith extends their aggregate lead to 7-1 before the Dons restore some pride. Aberdeen will beat Rangers three times out of four in the league, but finish behind them in all three competitions.

Scottish Cup

3 H AYR — 6/2 · 2 · W 2-0 · H-T 1-0 · Att 14,244 *9*
Scorers: Harper 18p, 83 / Ref: J Gordon

1	2	3	4	5	6	7	8	9	10	11	subs used
Clark	Kennedy	McLelland	McMaster	Garner	Miller	Davidson	Sullivan	Harper	Strachan	Jarvie	
Sproat	*Wells*	*Murphy*	*Fleming*	*Hyslop*	*Rodman**	*McSherry*	*Masterton*	*Hannah*	*Christie^*		*Sim/McLelland*

Doomed Ayr have drawn their last two against Aberdeen in the league, but there was never a sniff of an upset in the puddles at Pittodrie once Joe Harper has sent goalkeeper Sproat the wrong way from the penalty spot. The only surprise was how long it took Harper to add a second.

4 H ST JOHNSTONE — 27/2 · 2 · W 3-0 · H-T 1-0 · Att 15,597 *1:8*
Scorers: Davidson 11, Harper 75, Jarvie 89 / Ref: R Valentine

1	2	3	4	5	6	7	8	9	10	11	subs used
Clark	Kennedy	McLelland	McMaster	Garner	Miller	Davidson	Fleming	Harper	Strachan^	Davidson	Jarvie
Geoghegan	*Mackay*	*Houston*	*Rutherford*	*O'Brien*	*Clunie*	*Pelosi*	*Brogan*	*O'Connor*	*Thomson*	*Ross**	*Lawson*

St Johnstone beat Brechin 1-0 in Round 3, and find themselves midway in Division 1. Duncan Davidson put Aberdeen ahead amid the lashing feet, but the Dons then stood around like wallflowers as St Johnstone rallied. It was that man Joe Harper again who settled the nerves.

QF H MORTON — 11/3 · 2 · D 2-2 · H-T 1-0 · Att 17,394 *1:2*
Scorers: Davidson 31, Jarvie 85 / *Ritchie 87, Goldthorp 90* / Ref: J Gordon

1	2	3	4	5	6	7	8	9	10	11	subs used
Clark	Kennedy	McLelland	McMaster	Garner	Miller	Strachan	Sullivan	Gibson*	Jarvie	Davidson	Fleming
Connaghan	*Lynch*	*Holmes*	*Anderson*	*Orr*	*Veitch**	*McNeil*	*Brown^*	*Evans*	*Goldthorp*	*Ritchie*	*Mitchell/Thomas*

Morton are headed for the Division 1 title, and accounted for Albion Rovers and Meadowbank in previous rounds. They now pull off a super escape act. When Jarvie made it 2-0 with just five minutes to play, all seemed over. But that man Ritchie will hurt Aberdeen in the future, too.

QF R MORTON — 15/3 · 2 · W 2-1 · H-T 2-1 · Att 10,500 *1:2*
Scorers: McMaster 27p, Fleming 31 / *McNeil 45* / Ref: J Gordon

1	2	3	4	5	6	7	8	9	10	11	subs used
Clark	Kennedy	McLelland	McMaster	Garner	Miller	Strachan	Sullivan	Fleming	Davidson	Jarvie	
Connaghan	*Lynch^*	*Holmes*	*Anderson*	*Orr*	*Veitch**	*McNeil*	*Brown*	*Evans*	*Goldthorp*	*Ritchie*	*Thomas/Mitchell K*

In heavy sleet Aberdeen survive a cliff-hanger. Davidson is felled by Holmes and up steps McMaster - in Harper's absence - to score. Fleming makes it 2-0 with an explosive volley. With the last kick of the first half McNeil's dazzling solo goal sets up a pulsating second period.

SF N PARTICK THISTLE — 12/4 (at Hampden) · 1 · W 4-2 · H-T 2-0 · Att 12,282 *8*
Scorers: Fleming 32, 39, 77, Harper 71p / *Melrose 64, 88* / Ref: D Syme

1	2	3	4	5	6	7	8	9	10	11	subs used
Clark	Kennedy	Ritchie	McMaster	Garner	Miller	Sullivan	Fleming	Harper	Jarvie	Davidson	McLelland
Rough	*Anderson*	*Whittaker*	*Campbell*	*Marr*	*Craig^*	*Houston*	*O'Hara*	*Somner*	*Gibson*	*McQuade*	*Melrose*

Three matches between these sides in the first two, in the league. In all three games the Dons start off with a bang, opening up 2-0 leads, and are then forced to live dangerously. Thistle sub Melrose's overhead kick, to make it 2-1, gave the Dons the flutters.

F N RANGERS — 6/5 (at Hampden) · 2 · L 1-2 · H-T 0-1 · Att 61,563 *1*
Scorers: Ritchie 85 / *MacDonald 35, Johnstone 57* / Ref: B McGinlay

1	2	3	4	5	6	7	8	9	10	11	subs used
Clark	Kennedy	Ritchie	McLelland	Garner	Miller	Sullivan	Fleming*	Harper	Jarvie	Davidson	Scanlon
McCloy	*Jardine*	*Greig*	*Forsyth*	*Jackson*	*MacDonald*	*McLean*	*Russell*	*Johnstone*	*Smith*	*Cooper**	*Watson*

Rangers three titles, Aberdeen none. Having beaten the Gers three times in the league, the Dons froze on the big day. MacDonald's header passes through Clark's hands. Johnstone's firm header makes it 2-0. Ritchie's consolation was a mis-hit from six yards that went in off the bar.

UEFA Cup

1:1 A RWD MOLENBEEK (Belgium) — 14/9 · 1 · D 0-0 · H-T 0-0 · Att 14,000
Ref: M Bjorck (Sweden)

1	2	3	4	5	6	7	8	9	10	11	subs used
Clark	Kennedy	McLelland	Shirra	Garner	Miller	Davidson	Jarvie	Harper	Fleming	McMaster	
Ruiter*	*Dumon*	*Den Haase*	*Ahinho*	*Desanghere*	*Boskamp*	*Cordiez*	*Olsen*	*Gorez*	*Wellens*	*Van Heecke^*	*Leonard/Weissmann*

Molenbeek reached the semis of last season's UEFA Cup, beaten on the away-goals rule by Athletic Bilbao. Of the Dons, only Clark, Miller, Jarvie, and Harper can call upon European experience. The Dons worst scare comes after 84 minutes, when Clark scoops the ball off the line.

1:2 H RWD MOLENBEEK — 28/9 · 1 · L 1-2 · H-T 0-0 · Att 26,000
Scorers: Jarvie 78 / *Gorez 46, Wellens 84* / Ref: A Delmer (France) / (Dons lose 1-2 on aggregate)

1	2	3	4	5	6	7	8	9	10	11	subs used
Clark	Kennedy	McLelland	Shirra*	Garner	Miller	Davidson	Jarvie	Harper	Fleming	McMaster	Sullivan
Ruiter	*Dumon*	*Lafont*	*Ahinho*	*Desanghere*	*Boskamp*	*Cordiez*	*Olsen*	*Gorez*	*Wellens**	*Weissmann*	*Reygaeart*

The Dons' first defeat of the season in any competition, in their 12th match. Miller misses a cross and Gorez is unmarked to head past Clark. Ruiter punches a cross to Jarvie, but the Dons still trail on away goals. Piling forward they expose themselves at the back and pay the price.

League table

	P	W	D	L	F	A	W	D	L	F	A	Pts
			Home						**Away**			
1 Rangers	36	12	4	2	35	18	12	3	3	41	21	55
2 ABERDEEN	36	14	3	1	43	13	8	6	4	25	16	53
3 Dundee Utd	36	9	4	5	28	17	7	4	7	14	15	40
4 Hibernian	36	10	5	3	35	16	5	2	11	16	27	37
5 Celtic	36	11	3	4	36	19	4	3	11	27	35	36
6 Motherwell	36	8	3	7	28	24	5	4	9	17	28	33
7 Partick This	36	10	2	6	25	23	4	3	11	27	41	33
8 St Mirren	36	7	5	6	29	25	4	3	11	23	38	30
9 Ayr	36	5	3	10	17	28	4	3	11	19	40	24
10 Clydebank	36	5	3	10	16	33	1	4	13	7	31	19
	360	91	35	54	292	216	54	35	91	216	292	360

Aberdeen's record against each club

	P	W	D	L	F	A	Pts	Cup
v St Mirren	4	4	0	0	13	4	8	LC
v Clydebank	4	3	1	0	7	2	7	SC
v Motherwell	4	2	2	0	10	2	6	SC
v Rangers	4	3	0	1	11	4	6	SC
v Ayr	4	2	2	0	6	2	6	
v Partick This	4	3	0	1	6	3	6	
v Dundee Utd	4	2	2	0	2	0	6	LC
v Celtic	4	2	1	1	8	7	5	
v Hibernian	4	1	1	2	5	5	3	
	36	22	9	5	68	29	53	

Cup ties: LC = League Cup, SC = Scottish Cup.

Appearances and Goals

	Lge	*Sub*	LC	*Sub*	SC	*Sub*	Eur	*Sub*	Lge	LC	SC	Eur	Tot
			Appearances							**Goals**			
Archibald, Steve	10								5				5
Campbell, George		*1*											
Clark, Bobby	36		6		6		2						
Cooper, Neil	1		2										
Davidson, Duncan	17	*7*	2		6		2		8	2	2		12
Fleming, Ian	20	*5*	6		6		2		5	4	4		13
Garner, Willie	35		6		6		2		1				1
Gibson, Ian	9		6		1				3				3
Glennie, Bobby	3												
Grant, Alex		*2*											
Harper, Joe	31		6		4		2		17	6	4		27
Jarvie, Drew	35		6		5	*1*	2		12	2	2	1	17
Kennedy, Stuart	34		6		6		2						
McLeish, Alex	1												
McLelland, Chic	25		6		4	*1*	2		3	2			5
McMaster, John	30	*2*	5		6		2		2				2
Miller, Willie	36		6		6		2		1				1
Ritchie, Steve	9		1		4				5				5
Robb, Dave	13									3			3
Rougvie, Doug	1		1										
Scanlon, Ian		*1*	1						1				1
Scott, Jocky		*1*				*1*							
Shirra, Jim	8		5		3						1		1
Smith, Joe	7		3								1		1
Strachan, Gordon	10	*2*	2		4		2		1				1
Sullivan, Dom	25	*4*	2	*1*	6		1		3				3
Watson, Andy		*1*											
(own-goals)									1				1
27 players used	396	*26*	66	*5*	66	*4*	22	*1*	68	19	14	1	102

Odds & ends

Never lost to: (5) St Mirren, Clydebank, Motherwell, Ayr, Dundee Utd.

Never beat: (0)

Won from behind: (4) Clydebank (a), Celtic (h), Partick (h), St Mirren (h).

Lost from in front: (2) Hibs (h), Celtic (a).

High spots: Ending the season unbeaten in 18 games. Beating champions Rangers three times out of four. Reaching the Scottish Cup Final.

Low spots: 1 win in seven league games from 15 October. Being crushed 1-6 by Rangers in League Cup. Freezing on the day during the Scottish Cup Final.

Bogey teams: Hibernian in the league, Rangers in cups.

Ever-presents: (2) Bobby Clark, Willie Miller.

Hat-tricks: (6) Harper 3, Jarvie 1, Robb 1, Fleming 1.

Leading scorer: (27) Joe Harper.

No	Date	Venue/Opp	Att	Pos	Pt	F-A	H-T	Scorers, Times, and Referees	1	2	3	4	5	6	7	8	9	10	11	subs used
1	12/8	A HEARTS	11,500	2	W	4-1	2-1	Davidson 23, Harper 37, Archibald 64, 86; Ref: D Syme	Leighton	Kennedy	McLelland	McMaster	Garner	Miller	Sullivan	Archibald	Harper	Jarvie	Davidson*	Scanlon
								Bannon 4	Dunlop	Kidd	Fraser	McNicoll	Jefferies	Liddell	Park	Bannon	Gibson*	Shaw	Robertson*	Prentice/Tierney
2	19/8	H MORTON	14,500	9	W 4	3-1	1-1	Harper 2, 56, 82; Ref: I Foote	Leighton	Kennedy	McLelland	McMaster	Garner	Miller	Sullivan	Archibald	Harper	Jarvie	Davidson*	Scanlon
								Ritchie 39	Connaghan	Hayes	Holmes	Anderson	Orr	Rooney	Russell	Miller	McLean*	Scott	Ritchie	Rae
3	26/8	A DUNDEE UTD	10,000	5	D 5	1-1	1-0	Harper 20; Ref: D Ramsay	Leighton	Kennedy	McLelland	McMaster	Garner	Miller	Sullivan	Archibald*	Harper	Jarvie	Davidson*	Scanlon/Fleming
								Hegarty 78	McAlpine	Stark*	Stewart	Fleming	Hegarty	Narey	Sturrock	Addison	Frye	Holt	Payne	Kopel
4	9/9	H MOTHERWELL	12,200	9	W 7	4-0	1-0	Harper 39, 50p, Archibald 67, 72; Ref: A McFaull	Leighton	Kennedy	McLelland	McMaster	Garner	Miller	Sullivan*	Archibald*	Harper	Jarvie	Scanlon	Strachan
									Latchford	Millar	Wark	Boyd*	McVie	Stevens	Marinello	Pettigrew	Larnach	McLaren	Clinging*	McLeod/Lindsay
5	16/9	A RANGERS	27,000	7	D 8	1-1	0-1	Sullivan 90; Ref: W Anderson	Leighton	Kennedy	McLelland	McMaster	McLeish	Miller	Sullivan*	Archibald	Harper	Jarvie	Scanlon*	Strachan/Rougvie
								Forsyth A 39p	McCloy	Jardine	Forsyth A	Forsyth T	Jackson	MacDonald	McLean	Russell	Parlane	Johnstone	Smith	Smith
6	23/9	A HIBERNIAN	12,086	2	L 8	1-2	1-2	Jarvie 19; Ref: J Gordon	Leighton	Kennedy	McDonald	McMaster	McLeish	Miller	Sullivan*	Archibald	Harper	Jarvie	Scanlon*	Rougvie/Davidson
								Rae 9, MacLeod 41p	McDonald	Duncan	Smith	Rae	Fleming	McNamara*	Temperley	MacLeod	Hutchinson*	Callachan	Higgins	Stewart/O'Brien
7	30/9	H PARTICK THISTLE	11,100	5	D 9	1-1	0-1	Archibald 56; Ref: A Smith	Leighton	Kennedy	McLelland	McMaster	McLeish	Miller	Strachan	Archibald	Harper	Jarvie	Scanlon*	Fleming
								Sommer 43p	Rough	McKinnon	Whittaker	Campbell	Marr	Houston		Park*	Sommer	Melrose*	Love	O'Hara/McAdam
8	7/10	H CELTIC	24,000	1	W 11	4-1	2-1	Archibald 21, 54, Harper 23p, Jarvie 53; Ref: J Gordon	Leighton	Kennedy	McLelland	McMaster	McLeish	Miller	Strachan	Archibald	Harper	Jarvie	Scanlon*	Sullivan
								McAdam 43	Latchford	Filippi	Sneddon	Aitken	McDonald	Edvaldson*	Provan	Conroy	McAdam	Burns*		McCluskey Glavin/Lennox
9	14/10	A ST MIRREN	10,973	11	L 11	1-2	0-0	Harper 84; Ref: D Syme	Leighton	Kennedy	McLelland*	McMaster	McLeish	Miller	Strachan*	Archibald	Harper	Jarvie	Sullivan	Rougvie/Scanlon
								Bone 60, McGarvey 66	Thomson	Young	Munro	Fitzpatrick	Dunlop	Copland	Richardson	Stark	Bone	Abercrombie	McGarvey	
10	21/10	H HEARTS	12,750	9	L 11	1-2	0-1	Harper 59p; Ref: T Kyle	Leighton	Kennedy*	McLelland	McMaster*	McLeish	Miller	Sullivan	Archibald	Harper	Jarvie	Scanlon	Fleming/Strachan
								O'Connor 1, McQuade 78	Dunlop	Kidd*	Jefferies	McNicoll	Liddell	Fraser	Gibson	Bannon	O'Connor	Busby	Robertson*	Brown/McQuade

1. A HEARTS — Young goalkeeper Jim Leighton did not wish to lose a goal so early in his senior baptism. But thereafter Aberdeen slowly steam-rollered the opposition. Hearts' Dunlop had a much worse game than Leighton. This result will sum up the dreadful season awaiting poor Hearts.

2. H MORTON — Joe Harper has now passed the 200-goal mark in all matches for Aberdeen. He shows how to take them aafter just 90 seconds, controlling Sullivan's pass on his chest and shooting on the run past Connaghan. Earlier in the week Pat Stanton joined the Dons as assistant manager.

3. A DUNDEE UTD — A nasty, heated match which ended with fighting on the pitch and on the terraces. This is United's third draw to open the new season, in which they will top the league for months on end. It is fitting that Joe Harper and his marker, Paul Hegarty, should finish honours even, a goal apiece.

4. H MOTHERWELL — It is going to be a long hard season for Motherwell. They have just lost 1-5 to Celtic and are now turned over by Aberdeen. Harper is a marked man. Two defenders sent him into orbit. Both were booked, and Harper was lucky to escape similar punishment for his furious retaliation.

5. A RANGERS — Ibrox is reduced to a bomb-site as reconstruction begins. Rangers have still to register their first win of the season. They are on their way to doing so when McLeish gives away a penalty. But deep in to injury time Sullivan pops up to meet Strachan's cross. Rangers are denied again.

6. A HIBERNIAN — Three draws, followed by three wins have lifted Hibs to second. Both teams scored with early headers before Willie Miller's reckless challenge decided the game. Miller upended Smith for a penalty. The Dons had held their own in the first half, but were mostly outplayed in the second.

7. H PARTICK THISTLE — A game which started as a bore and ended with a roar. Aberdeen were up against it when Jim Leighton grassed Melrose for Thistle's penalty. After Archibald's equaliser, the game focused on the Thistle and Scotland goalkeeper. The 'Alan Rough Show' was hard on Dons supporters.

8. H CELTIC — Celtic had won all but one match before today. Their fans are in good voice, even at the end, with their chants of 'we're going to win the league'. But not even the late introduction of Lisbon Lion - Bobby Lennox - could avert this crushing defeat. The Dons will lose the next three.

9. A ST MIRREN — Last season, under Alex Ferguson, St Mirren lost four out of four to Aberdeen. Now the tables are turned. St Mirren won comfortably. The Dons won't beat them all season. they won, but Fergie's return to Love St leaves him looking a worried man.

10. H HEARTS — Perhaps Aberdeen drank poisoned beer in Dusseldorf. They were dreadful. Hearts' sub McQuade had only been on for four minutes when he unleashed the kind of 25-yarder that footballers dream about. Hearts will win their next two games, too, before the rot sets in again.

11 · A MORTON · 28/10 — Att 6,500 — 5 L *8* 11 — **1-2**
Scorers: Jarvie 18 / *Ritchie 19, Russell 21*
Ref: M Delaney

Aberdeen: Leighton, Rougvie, Ritchie*, McMaster, McLeish, Miller, Sullivan, Archibald, Harper, Jarvie, Scanlon^; subs Fleming/Smith
Morton: Connaghan, Hayes, Holmes, Evans, Orr, Rooney, Russell*, Miller, Thomson, Scott, Ritchie; sub Tolmie

The Dons are on a losing run. Andy Ritchie is performing wonders for Morton, whose equaliser swirled in front of Jim Leighton for his sixth goal of this prolific season. Ritchie's cross, five minutes later, was nudged in by Russell. It is one defeat in eight games for Morton now.

12 · H DUNDEE UTD · 4/11 — Att 13,850 — 2 W *1* 13 — **1-0**
Scorers: Harper 7p
Ref: K Hope

Aberdeen: Clark, Rougvie, McLelland, Fleming*, McLeish, Miller, Strachan, Archibald, Harper, Jarvie*, Sullivan; subs Scanlon/Smith
Dundee Utd: McAlpine, Stewart, Kopel, Fleming, Hegarty, Narey, Stark, Sturrock, Payne*, Kirkwood, Addison^; subs Dodds/Robinson

United's second defeat of the season. Yet they are undeniably unlucky here. The better team by far, United trailed to Harper's penalty when the wee man was flattened by Hegarty. Paul Stewart missed from the spot for United, who fritter away other chances. Yet they still top the league.

13 · A MOTHERWELL · 11/11 — Att 5,448 — 3 D *10* 14 — **1-1**
Scorers: Scanlon 56 / *Wilson 55*
Ref: J Renton

Aberdeen: Clark, Kennedy, McLelland, McMaster*, McLeish, Miller, Strachan, Fleming*, Harper, Jarvie, Sullivan; subs Scanlon/Considine
Motherwell: Rennie, Carr, Wark, McLaren, McVie, Stevens, Marinello, Pettigrew!, Larnach, Millar*, Wilson; sub Clinging

Motherwell haven't won at home all season, but when Willie Miller fluffs a back-pass to Clark the duck looks like being broken. Within seconds Scanlon swivels to hit an instant equaliser. Rougvie is ordered off for an off-the-ball incident - but soon Pettigrew is walking too.

14 · H RANGERS · 18/11 — Att 24,000 — 3 D *6* 15 — **0-0**
Ref: G Smith

Aberdeen: Clark, Kennedy, McLelland, McMaster*, Rougvie!, Miller, Strachan, Archibald, Harper, Sullivan, Scanlon^; sub Fleming
Rangers: McCloy, Jardine, Dawson, Johnstone, Jackson, MacDonald, McLean, Russell, Parlane, Smith, Watson

Rangers have played 14, and won just three. Yet how on earth did they leave Pittodrie with a point? Joe Harper slid a penalty-kick wide of a post, and Peter McCloy in goal saved thrillingly from Archibald and Fleming. Rangers created almost nothing in front of Jim Leighton.

15 · H HIBERNIAN · 25/11 — Att 13,250 — 2 W *8* 17 — **4-1**
Scorers: Fleming 19, Sullivan 36, Harper 69, 80 / *Hutchinson 85*
Ref: A McGunnigle

Aberdeen: Clark, Kennedy, McLelland, McMaster*, Rougvie, Miller, Strachan, Fleming, Harper, Sullivan, Davidson^; subs Jarvie/Cooper
Hibernian: McDonald, Duncan, Smith, Bremner, Fleming, McNamara, Mathison, MacLeod, Refvik, Callachan, Hutchinson

Aberdeen at last get their act together. Their first three goals were scorching drives. Their fourth was a leaping header - by Joe Harper. The Dons are one point behind Dundee Utd. Fans might as well enjoy it while it lasts: Aberdeen won't win again in the league for three months.

16 · A CELTIC · 9/12 — Att 24,000 — 3 D *4* 18 — **0-0**
Ref: W Anderson

Aberdeen: Clark, Kennedy, McLelland, McMaster*, Rougvie, Miller, Strachan, Fleming, MacLeod, Sullivan, Archibald
Celtic: Baines, Filippi, Lynch, Aitken, McDonald, Edvaldsson, Provan, MacLeod, McAdam*, Burns, Doyle; sub Conn

Celtic's worst run in memory sees them topple from first to fourth. Three matches later-they will be down to eighth. This was hardly the best of games between these sides. Parkhead's biggest cheer of the afternoon greeted the announcement that Rangers were trailing at Tannadice.

17 · H ST MIRREN · 16/12 — Att 11,700 — 3 D *5* 19 — **1-1**
Scorers: McMaster 55 / *Stark 19*
Ref: R Cuthill

Aberdeen: Clark, Kennedy, McLelland, McMaster*, Rougvie, Miller, Strachan, Archibald*, Cooper, Sullivan, Scanlon^; sub Fleming
St Mirren: Thomson, Beckett, Munro, Fitzpatrick, Dunlop, Copland, Richardson, Stark, Bone, Abercrombie, McGarvey*; sub Hyslop

John McMaster saves a point for Aberdeen with a glancing header that didn't go where he intended - except that it ended up in the net. No one is saying it louder than a whisper, but St Mirren look better under the management of Jim Clunie than they did under Alex Ferguson.

18 · A HEARTS · 23/12 — Att 9,500 — 3 D *9* 20 — **0-0**
Ref: I Foote

Aberdeen: Clark, Kennedy, McLelland, McMaster*, Rougvie, Miller, Strachan, Archibald*, Harper, Sullivan*, Scanlon; subs Fleming/Considine
Hearts: Dunlop, Kidd, Fraser, McNicoll, Jefferies, Craig, Gibson*, Bannon, O'Connor, Busby, Robertson; sub McQuade

Hearts have lost their last two games 0-4 and 3-5, so their defence is short of confidence. This was a festive bore. Harper was so bad that when he aimed a kick at Bannon he missed. McQuade had burst the net when coming on as sub at Pittodrie: he had no such opportunities this time.

19 · H MORTON · 30/12 — Att 8,700 — 3 L *5* 20 — **1-2**
Scorers: Harper 88 / *Ritchie 59, McNeil 67*
Ref: A McFaull

Aberdeen: Clark, Kennedy, McLelland, McMaster*, Rougvie, Miller, Strachan*, Archibald, Harper, Sullivan, Scanlon^; subs Fleming/Cooper
Morton: Brce, Hayes, Anderson, McLaren, Orr, Rooney, McNeil, Hutchinson, Thomson, Scott, Ritchie

Morton took it on the chin for an hour, and then allowed Andy Ritchie to lay Aberdeen out. The languid striker robbed Chic McLelland and squeezed the ball past Clark. Earlier Joe Harper had squandered a penalty. On the pitch and on the terraces, everyone froze in the snow.

20 · A HIBERNIAN · 20/1 — Att 4,100 — 3 D *8* 21 — **1-1**
Scorers: Harper 15 / *Duncan 51*
Ref: J Renton

Aberdeen: Clark, Kennedy, McLelland, Strachan*, McLeish, Miller, Sullivan, Scanlon, Harper, Jarvie, Davidson*; subs Archibald/Cooper
Hibernian: McArthur, Brazil, Duncan, Bremner, Stewart, McNamara, Refvik*, MacLeod, Callachan, Hutchinson, Lambie; sub Higgins

Joe Harper silences the Easter Road boo-boys when scoring from Ian Scanlon's cut-back. But when Bobby Clark punches out Higgins' header, Arthur Duncan his it sweetly back from 30 yards. This is Hibs' 11th league game without a win, a bad run they end in their next match.

21 · A ST MIRREN · 24/2 — Att 11,500 — 4 D *1* 22 — **2-2**
Scorers: Archibald 23, Strachan 58 / *McGarvey 61, Copland 83*
Ref: D Murdoch

Aberdeen: Clark, Kennedy, Considine, McMaster*, Rougvie, Miller, Sullivan, Archibald, Harper, Jarvie*, Scanlon!; subs Strachan/Davidson
St Mirren: Thomson, Young, Munro, Fitzpatrick, Dunlop, Copland, Richardson, Stark, Bone, Torrance, McGarvey

This result takes St Mirren to the top. Two volleys had put Aberdeen in control, but McGarvey soon chipped Clark. Ian Scanlon was sent off, then Miller too for taking revenge on McGarvey. Copland's equaliser against the nine-Dons was the final blow. Alex Ferguson's father dies.

No	Date		Att	Pos	Pt	F-A	H-T	Scorers, Times, and Referees	1	2	3	4	5	6	7	8	9	10	11	subs used
22	H	PARTICK THISTLE			W	2-1	0-0	McMaster 73, Archibald 86	Clark	Kennedy	Considine	McMaster	Rougvie	McLeish	Sullivan	Archibald	Scanlon	Jarvie*	Strachan^	Harper/McLelland
	28/2		11,500		24			*Gibson 84*	*Rough*	*McKinnon*	*Whittaker*	*Anderson*	*McAdam**	*Campbell*	*Houston*	*Somner*	*Marr*	*O'Hara*	*Park*	*Gibson*
								Ref: W Anderson	Thistle were second in November but will be eighth in March. They look a negative side, devoid of attacking ideas. Their equaliser, a first-time shot by Gibson, looked to have earned them a barely-deserved point, until Archibald stole it back with Alan Rough rooted to his goal-line.											
23	A	CELTIC		2	L	0-1	0-0		Clark	Kennedy	McLelland	McMaster	Rougvie	Miller	Sullivan	Archibald	Scanlon	Jarvie*	Strachan^	Harper/Considine
	3/3		*26,000*	*8*	24			*Conn 65*	*Latchford*	*McGrain*	*Lynch*	*Aitken*	*McDonald*	*Edvaldsson*	*Provan*	*MacLeod*	*Conn*	*Burns**	*Doyle*	*Filippi*
								Ref: J Renton	This is Celtic's first league match for two and a half months, since before Christmas. With four games in hand their position is deceptive. This was a ragged game, settled by Alfie Conn on his comeback. Aberdeen looked more likely to lose a second goal than to score one themselves.											
24	H	DUNDEE UTD		4	L	**0-2**	0-0		Clark	Kennedy	McLelland	McMaster*	Rougvie	Miller	Sullivan	Archibald	Harper*	Jarvie	Davidson	Strachan/McLeish
	17/3		10,200	*1*	24			*Sturrock 55, Fleming 71*	*McAlpine*	*Stewart*	*Stark*	*Phillip**	*Hegarty*	*Narey*	*Holt*	*Sturrock*	*Dodds*	*Fleming*	*Kirkwood*	*Addison*
								Ref: I Foote	The Dons could hardly be seen, wearing an all-white strip on a snow-covered pitch. Paul Sturrock scored United's first goal and crossed on to Fleming's head for their second. The win takes United back to the top, but half the division is contesting the leadership, the most open in years.											
25	H	MOTHERWELL			W	**8-0**	3-0	Harper 20, 44, 47, McMaster 39, [Arch'd 51, 86, Strachan 77, D'dson 89]	Clark	Kennedy	McLelland	McMaster	Rougvie	Miller	Sullivan*	Archibald	Harper	Jarvie	Davidson	Strachan
	26/3		6,300		26				*Rennie*	*Kennedy*	*Wark*	*Kane**	*Dempsey^*	*McLeod*	*Smith*	*Wilson*	*Larnach*	*Clinging*	*Donnelly*	*Mungall/Somerville*
								Ref: A McGunnigle	Motherwell have taken one point from eight games and scored one goal, so Aberdeen's victory is hardly surprising. When Duncan Davidson led a posse of pursuing defenders to bag No 8, it established a new Premier Division scoring record. Motherwell lose their next four, too.											
26	A	MORTON			W	1-0	1-0	Cooper 24	**Gardiner**	Kennedy	McLelland	Cooper	McLeish	Miller	**McGhee***	Watson	Harper	Jarvie^	Strachan	**Hamilton**/McMaster
	4/4		*6,500*		28				*Baines*	*Hayes*	*Holmes*	*Anderson*	*Orr*	*Thomson*	*McNeil*	*Miller*	*Hutchison**	*Tolmie*	*Ritchie*	*Russell*
								Ref: E Pringle	Dons' new signing Mark McGhee makes a quick return to one of his former clubs, and misses two first-half sitters. Not the most impressive of debuts. Goalkeeper Gardiner did better. At least he kept a clean sheet. He is the third keeper Alex Ferguson calls upon this season.											
27	H	HIBERNIAN		5	D	0-0	0-0		Gardiner	Kennedy	McLelland	Cooper*	McLeish^	Miller	McGhee	Watson	Harper	Jarvie	Strachan	Hamilton/Rougvie
	7/4		10,000	*4*	29				*McArthur*	*Brazil*	*Duncan*	*Bremner*	*Stewart*	*McNamara*	*Rae*	*MacLeod*	*Campbell*	*Callachan*	*Brown*	
								Ref: D Syme	In four days' time these two teams will meet in the Scottish Cup semi-final. For the first 70 minutes this contest was staged as a gentle sparring session. When Aberdeen finally woke up, they were frustrated by Hibs' keeper McArthur. That's one win each and two draws in the league.											
28	A	PARTICK THISTLE		3	W	1-0	1-0	McGhee 4	Clark	Kennedy	Hamilton	McLeish	Rougvie	Miller	McGhee	Archibald	Sullivan*	Strachan	Scanlon	McMaster
	14/4		*6,000*	*8*	31				*Rough*	*McKinnon*	*Whittaker*	*Anderson*	*Marr*	*Gibson**	*Houston*	*Melrose*	*Love^*	*Somner*	*Park*	*O'Hara/Campbell*
								Ref: T Muirhead	Mark McGhee scores his first goal for Aberdeen, picking up Gordon Strachan's shrewd pass. Thistle haven't the wit to break down the Dons' defence. They are only one place above the relegation line, but Motherwell and Hearts are so far behind that Thistle appear safe enough.											
29	A	MOTHERWELL			D	1-1	0-0	McLeish 77	Clark	Kennedy	Hamilton	McLeish	Garner	Miller	McGhee	Archibald	Sullivan*	Strachan	Scanlon	Jarvie
	18/4		***2,672***		32			*Stevens 70*	*Rennie*	*Hare*	*Wark*	*Carberry**	*Mackin*	*Stevens*	*Larnach*	*Pettigrew*	*Clinging*	*Irvine*	*Donnelly*	*Wilson*
								Ref: A McGunnigle	Having lost nine in a row, including an 0-8 hiding by Aberdeen, relegated Motherwell have just beaten Rangers. They looked like adding Aberdeen's scalp too, but for Alex McLeish's sweet 20-yard drive. Shortly afterwards McLeish committed a crass tackle and was booked.											
30	H	CELTIC		4	D	1-1	1-1	Strachan 24	Clark	Kennedy	Hamilton	McLeish	Garner	Miller	McGhee	Archibald	Sullivan	Strachan	Scanlon	
	21/4		18,400	*3*	33			*Lynch 40p*	*Latchford*	*McGrain*	*Lynch*	*Aitken*	*Edvaldsson*	*MacLeod*	*Provan*	*Conroy*	*Davidson**	*Burns*	*McCluskey^*	*McAdam/Doyle*
								Ref: E Pringle	A draw was no good to either side's title aspirations. Strachan converted Sullivan's pass to give Aberdeen the lead, but they paid the penalty for Miller's reckless foul on Conroy in the box. Celtic stay a point ahead of the Dons, with two games in hand and five on leaders Dundee Utd.											
31	H	RANGERS			W	2-1	1-0	Archibald 5, McGhee 82	Clark	Hamilton	McLelland	McLeish	Garner	Miller	McGhee	Archibald	Sullivan*	Strachan	Scanlon	McMaster
	25/4		19,000		35			*Smith 61*	*McCloy*	*Miller**	*Dawson*	*Jardine*	*Johnstone*	*MacDonald*	*McLean*	*Russell*	*Parlane*	*Smith*	*Cooper*	*Urquhart*
								Ref: T Kellock	When Gordon Smith teased his way along the bye-line to shoot between Bobby Clark and his near post it seemed Aberdeen had blown it. But Mark McGhee frees himself from defenders' shackles in the box to drive past McCloy. This result is fatal to Rangers' championship hopes.											

League

32 H ST MIRREN — 28/4 — Att 10,400 — HT 1-0 — L 1-2 — Pts 35

Aberdeen: Clark, Kennedy, Hamilton, McLeish, Garner, Miller, McGhee, Archibald, Sullivan, Strachan, McMaster*, Harper
St Mirren: *Thomson, Young, Munro*, Fitzpatrick! Dunlop, Copland, Stark, Weir, McGarvey, Abercrombie Torrance, Docherty/Richardson*

Archibald 16
Torrance 67, Stark 69
Ref: R Valentine

Harper's fourth penalty miss of the season - near the end - cost the Dons a point, and probably a place in Europe. Saints' Billy Stark continues to score useful goals against the Dons. Fitzpatrick was sent off for fouling Strachan. Six points out of eight for St Mirren against Aberdeen.

33 H HEARTS — 2/5 — Att 6,000 — HT 2-0 — W 5-0 — Pts 37

Aberdeen: Clark, Kennedy, Hamilton, Strachan, Garner, Miller, McGhee, Archibald, Sullivan, Strachan, Scanlon, [Sullivan 79]
Hearts: *Brown, Black, Fraser, Liddell, More, Gibson, Tierney*, Stewart*, Craig*, McQuade, Jefferies/Scott*

McGhee 24,71, Strachan 31, Scanlon 55, [Sullivan 79]Allan
Ref: H Alexander

Hearts lose their last 10 games of the season, of which this is the seventh. Doomed Hearts had no heart, so to speak. Mark McGhee scored one goal with his left foot, one with his right, and might have had more. He is evidently seen as an eventual replacement for the absent Joe Harper.

34 A DUNDEE UTD — 5/5 — Att 7,822 — HT 0-1 — D 2-2 — Pts 38

Aberdeen: Clark, Kennedy, Hamilton, McLeish, Garner, Miller, McGhee, Archibald, Strachan, Jarvie, Scanlon, Sullivan
Dundee Utd: *McAlpine, Stewart, Fleming, Hegarty, Narey, Addison*, Sturrock, Dodds, Holt, Payne, Kirkwood*

Jarvie 58, Strachan 82p
Payne 37, Stewart 68
Ref: C White

This is United's final match. The title will slip away from them as Celtic and Rangers haul in their games in hand. The most unpopular man at Tannadice was referee White, for giving Aberdeen a late penalty when Ray Stewart was alleged to have handled.

35 A RANGERS — 7/5 — Att 30,000 — HT 0-0 — L 0-2 — Pts 38

Aberdeen: Clark, Kennedy, Hamilton, McLeish, Garner, Miller, McGhee, Archibald, Sullivan*, Strachan, Scanlon*, Jarvie/Rougvie
Rangers: *McCloy, Jardine, Dawson, Johnstone, Jackson, MacDonald, McLean, Russell, Parlane, Smith, Cooper*

Smith 59, Cooper 62
Ref: D Syme

Rangers have just beaten Celtic. They stand on the brink of another championship after this win. Davie Cooper split the Dons' defence for the Gers' first goal, and then gathered the loose ball after Miller had driven it against him for the second. Rangers lose to Celtic in their next game.

36 A PARTICK THISTLE — 11/5 — Att 4,000 — HT 1-0 — W 2-1 — Pts 40

Aberdeen: Clark, Hamilton, Considine, Sullivan, Garner, Miller, McGhee*, Archibald, Harper, Strachan, Scanlon*, Cooper
Partick Thistle: *Rough, McKinnon*, Whittaker, Marr, McAdam, Doyle, Melrose, Gibson, O'Hara, Sonner, Park^, Clarke/Campbell*

Harper 24, Sullivan 89
O'Hara 76
Ref: T Kellock

Joe Harper announces his return to the first team with a typical goal - prodding the ball into the net from six yards. In the final minute Neil Cooper hit the Thistle crossbar, and Dom Sullivan, following up, poked it in. Aberdeen have taken seven points out of eight taken off Thistle.

Average Home 13,200
Away 12,000

Scottish League Cup

2:1 A MEADOWBANK — 30/8 — Att 1,600 2:12 — 2 W — HT 3-0 — 5-0

Aberdeen: Gardiner, Kennedy, McLelland, McMaster, Garner, Miller, Sullivan, Archibald*, Jarvie*, Scanlon, Jarvie*, Fleming/Strachan
Meadowbank: *Sinclair, O'Rourke, Fraser, Stewart, Wight, Carr, Leetion, Hancock J* Adair*, Davidson, Hancock S, Johnstone/Downie*

Sullivan 18, Jarvie 26, Kennedy 29,
[Archibald 63, Fleming 73]Sinclair
Ref: J Gordon

Meadowbank have not won any of their first three league games, and have scored just one goal. Against Aberdeen all they seemed to want to do was score, never mind how many they let in. Five different Dons get on the scoresheet. The second leg is now of interest to nobody.

2:2 H MEADOWBANK — 2/9 — Att 6,850 2:12 — 2 W — HT 2-0 — 4-0

Aberdeen: Leighton, Kennedy, McLelland, McMaster*, Garner, Miller, Sullivan*, Archibald, Hancock J, Harper, Strachan, Scanlon
Meadowbank: *Sinclair, O'Rourke, Fraser, Stewart*, Wight!, Carr, Leetion, Hancock J, Hancock S, Graham, Davidson*, Mooney/Johnston*

Archibald 16, Harper 44, 50, Scanlon 87
Ref: J Gordon
(Dons win 9-0 on aggregate)

Meadowbank did manage to get an entry in referee Gordon's notebook. Not for a goal, but for Wight's ugly foul on Jim Leighton which got him dismissed. The only question was whether or not the Dons would reach double figures, but Meadowbank avoided that humiliation.

3:1 A HAMILTON — 4/10 — Att 5,000 1:9 — 3 W — HT 1-0 — 1-0

Aberdeen: Leighton, Kennedy, McLelland, Rougvie*, McLeish, Strachan, Miller, Archibald*, Davidson, Fleming, Jarvie, Scanlon
Hamilton: *Ferguson, Grant, Fairlie, Dempsey, Alexander, Young*, Graham, Howie, Glavin, Reilly, McGrogan*

Scanlon 19
Ref: D McFaull

Hamilton are a mediocre team from Division 1. This was a miserable, drizzly evening. A miserable match, too, apart from Fleming and Scanlon's exchange of passes which led to the only goal. The narrowness of the score at least keeps the tie alive for the second leg at Pittodrie.

3:2 H HAMILTON — 11/10 — Att 10,000 1:9 — 3 W — HT 5-1 — 7-1

Aberdeen: Leighton, Kennedy, McLelland, Rougvie*, McLeish, Strachan, Miller, Archibald, Sullivan, Harper, Fleming, Scanlon*
Hamilton: *Ferguson, Grant*, Fairlie, Dempsey, Alexander, Young, Graham, Howie, Glavin, Reilly, McDowell/Wright*

Rougvie 3, Harper 9, 36p, 80, 86p,
Fairlie 2 [Sullivan 22, Kennedy 31]
Ref: E Pringle
(Dons win 8-1 on aggregate)

For 60 seconds or so Hamilton dreamed of a sensation, as Fairlie ran 20 yards with the ball to level the aggregate scores. It was just what the tie needed: Hamilton were then hung, drawn and quartered. Rougvie scored instantly. Five Dons goals by half-time, four to Harper by the end.

QF A AYR — 8/11 — Att 6,300 1:3 — 2 W — HT 2-1 — 3-3

Aberdeen: Clark, Kennedy, McLelland, McMaster*, Miller, Strachan, McLeish!, Archibald!, Harper, Jarvie, Sullivan, Fleming/Rougvie
Ayr: *Wells, Connor, McCall, McAllister, McSherry, McCall, McLaughlin, McLelland, Cramond, Christie*

Sullivan 8, Harper 40, 71
Cramond 3, McCall 48, McLelland S 60|Sproat
Ref: B McGinlay

Ayr are enjoying a long winning run in Division 1. Plenty of goals here, and plenty of bookings, including one for Ayr manager Ally MacLeod, who wouldn't sit still in his dugout. 10 minutes after the interval Steve Archibald was sent off for battering Ayr goalkeeper Sproat.

SCOTTISH PREMIER (CUP-TIES)

Manager: Alex Ferguson

SEASON 1978-79

				F-A	H-T	Scorers, Times, and Referees	1	2	3	4	5	6	7	8	9	10	11	subs used
Scottish League Cup																		
QF	H	AYR	3 W	3-1	2-1	McLelland 25, Harper 44, Archibald 85	Gardiner	Kennedy	McLelland	McMaster	Rougvie	Miller	Strachan	Archibald	Fleming*	Harper	Sullivan	Scanlon
2	15/11		13,000 1:3			McLaughlin 9	Sproat	Wells	Connor	McColl	McAllister	McSherry	McColl	McLaughlin Cramond*	Fleming	Christie	Phillips
						Ref: T Muirhead												
						(Dons win 6-4 on aggregate)												

Ayr followed Hamilton's example in the previous round, and hit Aberdeen while they were still cold. Ayr were looking forward to their 14th match without defeat until Aberdeen gradually exerted their superiority. Chic McClelland's surging overlap brought the Dons level at 4-4.

				F-A	H-T	Scorers, Times, and Referees	1	2	3	4	5	6	7	8	9	10	11	subs used
SF	HIBERNIAN		3 W	1-0	0-0	Kennedy 106	Clark	Kennedy	McLelland	Sullivan	Rougvie	Miller	Strachan	Archibald	Harper	Jarvie*	Scanlon*	McMaster/Cooper
13/12	21,048 7	(aet)					McDonald	Duncan	Kilgour	Bremner	Stewart	McNamara	Smith	MacLeod	Refvik*	Callachan	Hutchinson Higgins
(at Dens Park)						Ref: T Muirhead												

The match was in the second period of extra-time when full-back Stuart Kennedy flighted an angled lob over McDonald's straining fingers. The Hibs' keeper had been the main reason the tie had gone into extra-time - most notably when he touched Joe Harper's volley against a post.

				F-A	H-T	Scorers, Times, and Referees	1	2	3	4	5	6	7	8	9	10	11	subs used
F	RANGERS		4 L	1-2	0-0	Davidson 58	Clark	Kennedy	McLelland	McMaster	Rougvie!	Miller	Strachan	Archibald	Harper	Jarvie	Davidson*	McLeish
31/3	54,000 3					McMaster 77 og. Jackson 90	McCloy	Jardine	Dawson	Johnstone	Jackson	MacDonald McLean	Russell	Urquhart*	Smith	Cooper	Miller/Parlane
(at Hampden)						Ref: I Foote												

This time the Dons did not freeze in a cup final with Rangers. Davidson's header eluded McCloy to put them ahead. McMaster then deflected MacDonald's shot into goal. Six players were booked, and Rougvie sent off for allegedly assaulting Johnstone. Jackson headed the late winner.

				F-A	H-T	Scorers, Times, and Referees	1	2	3	4	5	6	7	8	9	10	11	subs used
Scottish Cup																		
3	A	HAMILTON	3 W	2-0	0-0	Miller 75, Harper 80	Clark	Kennedy	Considine	Strachan	Rougvie	Miller	Sullivan	Archibald	Harper	Jarvie*	Scanlon	McMaster
27/1	9,400 1:5						Ferguson	Frew	Kellachan	Fairlie	Dempsey	Alexander	Grant	Graham	Howie	McDowell*	McManus	Morrison
						Ref: I Foote												

Hamilton will shortly be temporarily top Division 1. Gordon Strachan takes the ball towards goal in an attempt to outwit Hamilton's stifling offside trap. Keeper Ferguson can't hold his shot, and Willie Miller's follow-up screams into the net. Harper capitalises to add a quick second.

				F-A	H-T	Scorers, Times, and Referees	1	2	3	4	5	6	7	8	9	10	11	subs used
4	H	AYR	3 W	6-2	4-0	Arch'd 4,44, McMaster 12, Scanlon 34,70,Clark	Clark	Kennedy	Considine	McMaster	Rougvie	Miller	Sullivan*	Archibald*	Scanlon	Jarvie	Strachan	Harper/Cooper
21/2	11,500 1:3					Phillips 67, McLaughlin 87p [Harper 77]Sproat	Sproat	Wells	Kelly*	Fleeting	McAllister	McSherry!	Phillips	McLaughlin	Cramond	Christie*	Hannah/McLelland
						Ref: R Valentine												

Aberdeen did not find it this easy when the teams met in the League Cup in November. Mind you, Ayr had 11 men then. This time Jim McSherry was expelled six minutes from the end. It was 6-1 at the time, and 10-man Ayr went upfield and nicked a goal themselves.

				F-A	H-T	Scorers, Times, and Referees	1	2	3	4	5	6	7	8	9	10	11	subs used
QF	H	CELTIC	2 D	1-1	1-1	Harper 26	Clark	Kennedy	McLelland	McMaster	McLeish	Miller	Sullivan	Archibald	Harper	Scanlon*	Strachan	Davidson
10/3	23,000 8					Doyle 25	Latchford	McGrain	Lynch	Aitken	McDonald	Edvaldsson	Provan	MacLeod	Conn	Burns	Doyle
						Ref: I Foote												

Celtic won 1-0 in the league last week. Edvaldsson's header fell to Doyle to net from close in. Within seconds Kennedy despatched the ball into Harper's path, and King Joey volleyed an unforgettable goal past the advancing Latchford. Five players were booked in this tough affair.

				F-A	H-T	Scorers, Times, and Referees	1	2	3	4	5	6	7	8	9	10	11	subs used
QF R	A	CELTIC	2 W	2-1	2-0	Davidson 2, Archibald 13	Clark	Kennedy	McLelland	McMaster	Rougvie	Miller	Sullivan*	Archibald*	Harper*	Jarvie	Davidson	McLeish/Scanlon
14/3	36,000 8					Lennox 63	Latchford	McGrain	Lynch	Aitken	McDonald	Edvaldsson	Provan	MacLeod	Conn*	Burns	Doyle/Lennox
						Ref: I Foote												

Harper guides the ball into the path of Davidson for the first goal. Archibald pops the ball over the stranded Latchford for the second. Lennox was played onside by a ricochet between Rougvie and Miller. Missiles later rained down from the terraces. Argy-bargy in the players' tunnel.

				F-A	H-T	Scorers, Times, and Referees	1	2	3	4	5	6	7	8	9	10	11	subs used
SF	HIBERNIAN		5 L	1-2	1-2	Archibald 28	Gardiner	Kennedy	McLelland*	Watson*	Rougvie	Miller	Strachan	Archibald	Harper	Jarvie	Scanlon	Hamilton/McLeish
11/4	9,837 4					Rae 37, MacLeod 43p	McArthur	Brazil	Duncan	Bremner	Stewart	McNamara	Rae	MacLeod	Campbell	Callachan	Brown
(at Hampden)						Ref: R Valentine												

Sweet revenge for Hibs, who lost to Aberdeen at the same stage of the League Cup. Hampden was mist-shrouded and almost empty, and remains a hoodoo stadium for the Dons. Rougvie made a hash of tackling MacLeod for the penalty. Harper later missed from about 12 inches.

				F-A	H-T	Scorers, Times, and Referees	1	2	3	4	5	6	7	8	9	10	11	subs used
European Cup-Winners' Cup																		
1:1	A	MAREK DIMITROV	2 L	2-3	1-0	Jarvie 5, Harper 76	Leighton	Kennedy	McLelland	McMaster	Garner*	Miller	Sullivan	Archibald	Harper	Jarvie	Scanlon	Rougvie
13/9	(Bulgaria)	20,000				Petrov V 66, 70, Petrov I 90	Stoinov	Sevdin	Kolev	Karatolev	Palev*	Rainov	Pargov	Tomov	Petrov I	Petrov V	Ventislav/Vukov
						Ref: J Van Melkebeke (Belgium)												

Scottish double-winners Rangers are in the European Cup. The Petrov brothers slayed the Dons. In aquatic conditions Verislav Petrov headed two goals from twin Ivan's crosses. In injury-time Leighton was impeded as Ivan scrambled a goal for himself. Willie Garner broke a leg.

				F-A	H-T	Scorers, Times, and Referees	1	2	3	4	5	6	7	8	9	10	11	subs used
1:2	H	MAREK DIMITROV	3 W	3-0	0-0	Strachan 63, Jarvie 75, Harper 81	Leighton	Kennedy	McLelland	McMaster	McLeish	Miller	Sullivan*	Archibald	Harper	Jarvie	Scanlon	Rougvie
27/9	21,100						Stoinov	Sevdin	Kolev	Karatolev	Palev	Rainov	Pargov*	Tomov	Petrov I	Petrov V	Dimitrov*	Brankov/Vutov
						Ref: J Keizer (Holland)												
						(Dons win 5-3 on aggregate)												

A 1-0 win was all Aberdeen needed, but it took them over an hour to break down a packed Bulgarian defence. Substitute Gordon Strachan raced in to meet John McMaster's chip. Stoinov almost saved it, but not quite. Forced to come out, the Bulgarians then left gaps at the back.

2:1 A FORT DUSSELDORF	4	L	0-3	0-1:	Gunther 15, 58, Zimmermann 81
18/10 (W Germ) 10,000					Ref: S Thune (Norway)

The ball skidded off McMaster's head in front of Gunther, who claims Dusseldorf's first goal. The Dons' back four statically appealed for offside as Gunther burst through for the second. Zimmermann's 25-yard free-kick through the 'wall' was touched, but not saved, by Leighton.

Leighton	Kennedy	McLelland	McMaster*	McLeish	Miller	Rougvie	Archibald	Harper	Jarvie^	Sullivan	Scanlon/Strachan
Woyke	Brei	Zewe	Zimmermann/Baltes	Kohnen	Fanz	Lund*	Gunther^	Allofs	Seel	Bonmer/Schmitz	

2:2 H FORT DUSSELDORF	5	W	2-0	0-0	McLelland 54, Jarvie 57
1/11 16,800					Ref: C Correia (Portugal)
					(Dons lose 2-3 on aggregate)

Clark	Rougvie	McLelland	McMaster*	McLeish	Miller	Strachan^	Archibald	Harper	Jarvie	Sullivan	Scanlon/Fleming
Woykl	Brei	Zewe	Zimmermann/Baltes	Kohnen	Weikl	Lund	Gunther	Allofs	Seel^	Zimmer	

Clark is recalled for his first match of the season after breaking his thumb, but he was largely idle. How Dusseldorf held out in the second half was a mystery, as the ball flew everywhere except in the net. Jarvie shot against Woyke, then into the side-netting. Archibald headed over, etc.

		Home					Away						
	P	W	D	L	F	A	W	D	L	F	A		Pts
1 Celtic	36	13	3	2	32	12	8	3	7	29	25		48
2 Rangers	36	12	5	1	32	10	6	4	8	20	25		45
3 Dundee Utd	36	12	4	2	33	16	6	4	8	23	20		44
4 ABERDEEN	36	9	5	4	39	16	4	9	5	24	20		40
5 Hibernian	36	8	3	7	23	16	5	4	9	21	32		37
6 St Mirren	36	8	4	5	23	20	7	3	8	22	21		36
7 Morton	36	9	4	5	34	23	3	8	7	18	30		36
8 Partick This	36	10	2	6	31	21	3	6	9	11	18		34
9 Hearts	36	5	5	8	19	25	3	2	13	20	46		23
10 Motherwell	36	2	5	11	20	38	3	2	13	13	48		17
	360	87	45	48	286	197	48	45	87	197	286		360

	P	W	D	L	F	A	Pts	Cup	W	D	L
v Partick This	4	3	1	0	6	3	7				
v Motherwell	4	2	2	0	14	2	6				
v Hearts	4	2	1	1	10	3	5				
v Hibernian	4	1	2	1	6	4	4	LC	1	0	0
								SC	0	0	1
								SC	1	1	0
v Celtic	4	1	2	1	5	3	4				
v Morton	4	1	0	2	6	6	4				
v Dundee Utd	4	1	2	1	4	5	4				
v Rangers	4	1	2	1	3	4	4	LS	0	0	1
v St Mirren	4	0	2	2	5	7	2				
	36	13	14	9	59	36	40				

Appearances / Goals

	Lge	Sub	LC	Sub	SC	Sub	Eur	Sub	Lge	LC	SC	Eur	Tot
Archibald, Steve	30	2	7		5		4		13	3	4		20
Clark, Bobby	23		3		4		1						
Considine, Doug	3	3			2								
Cooper, Neil	3	4		1		1			1				1
Davidson, Duncan	7	2	2		1	1			2	1	1		4
Fleming, Ian	4	8	3		2		1		1		1		2
Gardiner, John	2		2										
Garner, Willie	12	2	2		1								
Hamilton, Derek	9	2		1									1
Harper, Joe	25	3	7		4	1	4		19	9	3	2	33
Jarvie, Drew	24	3	6		4		5		4	1		3	8
Kennedy, Stuart	32		8		3		3		3			3	3
Leighton, Jim	11		3										
McGhee, Mark	11								4				4
McLelland, Chic	25	1	8		4		3		2				2
McLeish, Alex	18	1	3	1	1	2	3		1			1	1
McMaster, John	24	3	6	1	3	1	4		3			1	4
Miller, Willie	34		8		5		4						1
Ritchie, Steve	1												
Rougvie, Doug	16	5	4		2		4		2		1		1
Scanlon, Ian	22	6	5	1	4	1			2	1	2		6
Simpson, Neil	1				1								
Smith, Joe		2											
Strachan, Gordon	26	5	5		3		4	1	2	5		1	6
Sullivan, Dom	32	6	6		4		4		4	3			7
Watson, Andy	2		1										
26 players used	396	50	88	12	55	8	44	6	59	25	12	7	103

Odds & ends

Never lost to: (2) Partick, Motherwell.
Never beat: (1) St Mirren.

Won from behind: (3) Hearts (a), Hamilton (LC), Ayr (LC).
Lost from in front: (5) Morton (h), St Mirren (h), Rangers (LC), Hibs (SC), Rangers (LC).
Marek Dimitrov (a).

High spots: Reaching final of Scottish Cup and semi-final of League Cup.

Recording their highest ever Premier League win, 8-0 over Motherwell.

Low spots: Never won more than two games in a row.
Losing three league games in a row in October.

Bogey-team: St Mirren.
Ever-presents: (0).
Hat-tricks: (3) Joe Harper.
Leading scorer: (33) Joe Harper.

SCOTTISH PREMIER DIVISION

Manager: Alex Ferguson **SEASON 1979-80**

The top (non-italic) line of each fixture is Aberdeen's XI; the lower line is the opponents' XI. An asterisk (*) marks a player who was substituted.

No	Date	Venue / Opponent	Att	Pos	Pt	Res	F-A	H-T	Scorers, Times, and Referees	1	2	3	4	5	6	7	8	9	10	11	subs used
1	11/8	A PARTICK THISTLE	7,500	–	–	L	0-1	0-0	McAdam 89p. Ref: H Robertson	Clark	Rougvie	Considine	Cooper*	Garner	McLeish	McGhee*	Archibald	Sullivan	McMaster	Davidson	Jarvie/Bell
										Rough	McKinnon	Whittaker	Gibson	Campbell*	Anderson	Park	Doyle	McAdam	Melrose	O'Hara	Wilson
2	18/8	H HIBERNIAN	10,300	4	2	W	3-0	1-0	Archibald 44, McMaster 73, 89. Ref: M Delaney	Clark	Kennedy	McLeish	Garner	Miller	McGhee	Archibald	Strachan	McMaster	Davidson*		Jarvie
										McArthur	Brazil	Duncan	Brenner	Paterson	McNamara	Callachan	Campbell	Hutchinson	Brown J*	Higgins*	Rae/Brown
3	25/8	A DUNDEE UTD	10,982	2	4	W	3-1	1-0	McGhee 24, Harper 59, Archibald 63. Sturrock 89. Ref: M Delaney	Clark	Kennedy	Considine	McLeish	Garner	Miller	Archibald	McGhee	Harper*	McMaster*	Strachan	Jarvie/Davidson
										Bonetti	Stewart	Kopel	Phillip*	Stark	Narey	Addison	Sturrock	Dodds*	Pettigrew	Payne	Kirkwood/Ballantyne
4	8/9	A MORTON	5,540	6	4	L	2-3	1-1	Archibald 34, McMaster 74. Thomson 20, 64, Ritchie 60p. Ref: A McGunnigle	Clark	Kennedy	Considine*	McLeish	Garner	Miller	Archibald	McGhee*	Harper	McMaster	Strachan	Jarvie/Sullivan
										Baines	Hayes	Holmes	Anderson	Orr	Rooney	McNeil	Hutchison	Thomson*	Tolmie*	Ritchie	McLaren/Scott
5	15/9	H RANGERS	23,000	2	6	W	3-1	1-1	McMaster 19, Strachan 75p, Rougvie 80. Johnstone 35. Ref: A McFaull	Clark	Kennedy	Considine*	Garner	Miller	McLeish	Strachan	Archibald	McGhee	McMaster	Scanlon	Rougvie/Harper
										McCloy	Jardine	Dawson*	Stevens	Jackson	Watson	Cooper	Russell	Johnstone	MacDonald*	Smith	McLean/Miller A
6	22/9	H CELTIC	23,000	4	6	L	1-2	1-1	Strachan 2. Aitken 40, Doyle 74. Ref: T Muirhead	Clark	Kennedy	Considine*	Garner	Miller	McLeish	Strachan	Archibald	McGhee	McMaster	Scanlon	Rougvie/Davidson
										Latchford	Sneddon	McGrain	Aitken	MacDonald	McAdam	Doyle	Conroy	Lennox	MacLeod	Burns!	
7	29/9	A DUNDEE	11,817	3	8	W	4-0	2-0	Jarvie 8, 9, Harper 77, Archibald 80. Ref: T Kellock	Clark	Kennedy	Considine*	Bell*	Garner	McLeish	Sullivan	Archibald	Harper	McMaster	Jarvie	Scanlon
										Donaldson	Turnbull	Schaedler	Watson*	Glennie	McGeachie	Murphy	Miller	Sinclair	McLaren	Shira	Fletcher
8	6/10	A ST MIRREN	9,163	4	9	D	2-2	1-1	Archibald 7, Harper 68. Stark 14, McDougall 89. Ref: D Murdoch	Clark	Kennedy	Considine*	McLeish	Garner	Miller	Strachan	Archibald	Harper	McMaster	Scanlon	Sullivan
										Thomson	Munro	Beckett	Dunlop*	Young	Richardson	McDougall	Torrance	Dempster*	Abercrombie	Stark	Sonner/Bone
9	13/10	A KILMARNOCK	12,000	3	11	W	3-1	2-1	Scanlon 34, Strachan 40p, Jarvie 89. Houston 11. Ref: K Hope	Clark	Kennedy	Considine*	McLeish	Garner	Miller	Strachan	Archibald	Harper	McMaster*	Scanlon	Sullivan/Jarvie
										McCulloch	Robertson	Clark	McDicken	Clarke	Gibson	Maxwell	Bourke	Mauchlen	Houston		Street/Carnie
10	20/10	H PARTICK THISTLE	12,000	3	12	D	1-1	0-1	Davidson 62. Doyle 44. Ref: H Alexander	Clark	Kennedy	McMaster	McLeish	Garner	Miller	Strachan	Archibald	Harper	Jarvie*	Scanlon*	Bell/Davidson
										Rough	McKinnon	Whittaker	Campbell	Marr	O'Hara*	Park	Gibson	McGregor*	Love	McAdam	Doyle/Melrose

Match reports

1. The referee was about to blow for time when Alex McLeish handled the ball for a penalty. Earlier, Rougvie had grabbed Park by the shirt to prevent him bursting clear. Said Alex Ferguson: 'Don't laugh, but I've got a scent about the way things are going to turn out this season.'

2. Hibs gesture of defiance in the first half came when Campbell's shot hit the junction of post and bar. Steve Archibald's header made it 1-0; McMaster's long-range drive made it 2-0; and McMaster dribbled round the keeper for the third. Hibs go bottom of the league and stay there.

3. Much interest surrounds the appearance in the United goal of 37-year-old Peter Bonetti, famous for his 'Weetabix' save against West Germany in the 1970 World Cup. Bonetti makes a mess of Aberdeen's second goal, losing an aerial duel to Archibald from which Joe Harper netted.

4. Andy Ritchie destroyed Aberdeen virtually single-handedly, though team-mate Thomson took the credit for Morton's first two goals. Thomson was also tripped in the box by McLeish for Ritchie's penalty. After four games Ritchie and Thomson have scored nine goals between them.

5. Eintracht spies are given plenty to think about by this Dons' performance. Mischief-makers can't wait to see what happens if Doug Rougvie comes up against Derek Johnstone, after their clash in the League Cup final. When Rougvie comes on as a sub he sends Johnstone into orbit.

6. This was a shameful match, full of hatred. Strachan streaked through the middle to give Aberdeen the perfect start, but was later the victim of a dreadful foul by Tommy Burns, who was duly expelled. Kennedy then tripped Lennox. Clark blocked MacLeod's penalty but Aitken swooped.

7. Two quick headers from Drew Jarvie's balding head settled the destiny of this match. Dundee have conceded 20 goals already, and are clearly in for a hard season. The Dons now travel to West Germany to face Eintracht Frankfurt in the UEFA Cup, first round, second leg.

8. Alex Ferguson was just seconds from seeing his new club beat his old for the first time when, in a hectic goalmouth scramble, Frank McDougall fired a dramatic equaliser. Bottom of the league after four games, St Mirren are climbing fast. They will be second by early March.

9. The Dons threw everything at Killie from the start and left themselves open to the counter-punch when Houston scored. After Ian Scanlon equalised Willie Miller did something unusual: he won a penalty instead of giving one away. This will be the Dons' last win for five weeks.

10. Partick are as mean as ever. They don't score many, nor do they let many in. They take the lead when Campbell volleyed John McMaster's weak clearance past Bobby Clark. Jarvie then headed across goal for Dons' sub Davidson's equaliser. Thereafter Alan Rough took the honours.

11. A HIBERNIAN 27/10 — 3 D 1-1 10 13 — 7,000
Watson 89 / Hutchinson 17
Ref: J Renton
Clark, Kennedy, Considine*, McLeish, Strachan, Miller, Garner, Archibald, Jarvie*, McMaster, Scanlon — Harper/Watson
McArthur, Brazil, Brown J, Brown S, Callachan, Rae, Paterson, Ward, Hutchinson, MacLeod, Higgins — Campbell*
Hibs are rooted to the bottom of the league. They seem headed for their second win of a depressing season when, with a minute to go, Gordon Strachan sets up Andy Watson to score from 10 yards. Joe Harper's appearance as a substitute did not go down well with Easter Road fans.

12. H DUNDEE UTD 3/11 — 3 L 0-3 6 13 — 12,500
Pettigrew 11, Phillip 13, Bannon 81
Ref: I Foote
Clark, Kennedy, Considine, McLeish, Strachan, Miller, Garner*, Archibald, Harper*, McMaster, Scanlon — Jarvie/Davidson
McAlpine, Stark, Kopel, Phillip, Narey, Hegarty, Sturrock, Petigrew, Fleming, Payne — Dodds*
Tangerine-scarfed United fans were chanting 'easy, easy' by the end. And it was. A Newcastle Utd scout came to look at Steve Archibald. He could have saved his train fare. Aberdeen's inconsistency would make a mockery of any suggestion that this is a championship-winning team.

13. H MORTON 10/11 — 4 L 1-2 1 13 — 10,400
McLeish 4 / Thomson 15, Ritchie 77
Ref: M Delaney
Clark, Kennedy, Rouguie, McLeish, Strachan, Miller, McLeish, Jarvie, Watson, McMaster, Scanlon* — Harper
Baines, Hayes, Holmes, Anderson, McLaughlin, Orr, McNeil, Hutchison, Thomson, Russell*, Ritchie — McLaren/Tolmie*
Eight games without defeat and Morton are top. Andy Ritchie did his usual. Ambled about, looked bored, put the ball on Thomson's instep for Morton's equaliser, and then controlled the ball with his left foot and scored a gem with his right. McLeish's early rocket counted for nothing.

14. A RANGERS 17/11 — 3 W 1-0 7 15 — 18,500
Archibald 87
Ref: D Ramsay
Clark, Kennedy, Rouguie, McLeish, Strachan, Miller, McLeish, Archibald, Harper, McMaster, Scanlon* — McGhee
McCloy, Forsyth A, Dawson, Stevens, Jardine, Watson, McLean, Miller, Johnstone, MacDonald A, Smith — MacDonald J*
An untidy game on an unhelpful pitch. Rangers have won just two of their last eight. Archibald's late winner was all the more enjoyable for the Dons, all the more painful to Rangers, because when he poked the ball past McCloy it stuck in the mud on the line. It needed a second stab.

15. H ST MIRREN 15/12 — 4 W 2-0 5 17 — 5,000
McLeish 65, Hamilton 69
Ref: D Syme
Clark, Kennedy, McMaster*, McLeish, Strachan, Miller, Garner, Archibald, Hamilton*, Jarvie, Hewitt — Rouguie/McGhee
Thomson, Young, Abercrombie, Richardson, Fulton, Copland, Bone*, Stark, Sommer, McDougall, Weir — Torrance/Beckett*
St Mirren go from strength to strength. This is their first defeat in eight games. John Hewitt makes his Aberdeen debut in a match against three future Dons - Stark, McDougall and Weir. Billy Thomson has a nightmare match for St Mirren, allowing both goals to slip through his legs.

16. A MORTON 5/1 — 6 L 0-1 2 17 — 6,000
McLaren 80
Ref: B McGinlay
Clark, Kennedy, Considine, McLeish, Strachan, Miller, Garner, Archibald, Hamilton*, McMaster, Jarvie — McGhee
Baines, Hayes, Holmes, Anderson, McLaughlin, Orr, McLaren, Craig, Hutchison, Scott, Ritchie — Tolmie*
The Cappielow pitch was so dreadful that during the interval a workman came on to try to fill in the pot-holes. This was Aberdeen's third league defeat by their bogey-team this season, but they will not lose another game on their league travels for the remainder of the season.

17. H RANGERS 12/1 — 5 W 3-2 4 19 — 18,600
Strachan 2, Archibald 70, Hamilton 89 / MacDonald J 11, Jackson 49
Ref: R Valentine
Clark, McCloy, Rouguie, Considine, Strachan, Rouguie, Garner, Archibald, Hamilton*, McMaster, Scanlon* — Hewitt
Jardine, Dawson, Forsyth, Aitken, McLean*, Stevens, Jackson, Russell, Parlane, MacDonald A/MacDonald J, Smith/Cooper — Murphy*
Aberdeen capped and tailed an enthralling match with two delicious goals. Strachan opened the way with a 20-yard rocket. After Rangers had gone ahead Derek Hamilton squared for Archibald to level. Hamilton himself bagged the winner. Rangers have a bad away record this season.

18. H CELTIC 19/1 — 4 D 0-0 1 20 — 24,000
Ref: T Muirhead
Clark, Latchford, Considine, McLeish, Strachan, Rouguie, Garner, Archibald, Hamilton*, McMaster, Scanlon* — Jarvie
Sneddon, McGrain, Aitken, Provan, McAdam, Sullivan, Lennox, MacLeod, Doyle
A point suits Celtic more than Aberdeen. The gap between them remains 10 points - though Aberdeen have three games in hand. The match started brightly but soon slumped. It needed a goal but didn't get one. Dom Sullivan makes his first visit to Pittodrie since his transfer.

19. A DUNDEE 2/2 — 3 W 3-1 8 22 — 7,661
Jarvie 2, 84, Hamilton 71 / Redford 20
Ref: D Syme
Clark, Donaldson, Rouguie, Considine, Strachan, Miller, Garner, Archibald, Hamilton*, Jarvie, Scanlon — Hewitt
Barr, Schaedler, Millar, Glennie, Shirra, Fletcher, Mackie, Pirie, Bell, Redford — Murphy
This is the only Premier Division match to go ahead in snow-covered Scotland. Late headers by Derek Hamilton and Drew Jarvie on the straw-strewn pitch secured two priceless points. Although Dundee are down in the depths they have lost just twice at Dens. Both times to Aberdeen.

20. A ST MIRREN 9/2 — 3 D 1-1 4 23 — 7,900
Strachan 47 / Stark 55p
Ref: A Harris
Clark, Kennedy, McMaster, McLeish, Strachan, Miller, Garner, Archibald, Hamilton*, Jarvie, Scanlon* — McGhee/Hewitt
Thomson, Young, Munro, Richardson, Copland, Bone, Fulton, Stark, Sommer, McDougall, Weir — Bell
Billy Stark's goals against Aberdeen are becoming a nuisance. This time it's a penalty, after Willie Garner took the legs from under Peter Weir. Near the end Bobby Clark stuck out a foot to stop Frank McDougall snatching a winner. The Dons head St Mirren by goal-difference only.

21. H KILMARNOCK 23/2 — 4 L 1-2 5 23 — 9,600
Archibald 88 / Street 4, Garner 42 og
Ref: K Hope
Leighton, Kennedy, Hamilton, McLeish, Strachan, Miller, Garner*, Archibald, Scanlon, Jarvie, Hewitt* — Watson/Davidson
McCulloch, Welsh, Clark, Clarke, McDicken, Houston, Mauchlen, Gibson, Cramond, Street, Cairney*
The Dons are in total disarray after Jim Leighton - playing his first game of the season - pushes Cramond's cross to the feet of Street. To make matters worse Willie Garner stabs another cross into his own goal. Though they don't know it, the Dons won't be beaten again this season.

22   H PARTICK THISTLE   1/3 — Att 9,000 · Pos 4 *7* · D · Pt 24 · F-A 1-1 · H-T 1-1
Scorers, Times: Jarvie 41 / Melrose 28 · Ref: E Pringle

	1	2	3	4	5	6	7	8	9	10	11	subs used
Aberdeen	Clark	Kennedy	McMaster	McLeish	Rougvie	Miller	Strachan*	Archibald	Hamilton	Jarvie	Scanlon	Watson
Opponents	*Rough*	*McKinnon*	*Whittaker*	*Campbell*	*McAdam*	*O'Hara*	*Doyle*	*Gibson*	*Jardine*	*Melrose*	*Wilson**	*Wilson / McDonald*

Thistle are drawing most of their matches of late. They were encouraged when Melrose headed the ball through Clark's hands. Jarvie equalised after McKinnon had cleared off the line. Next week these two teams meet in the Scottish Cup. After that the Dons' league winning run begins.

---

23   H DUNDEE UTD   15/3 — Att 10,000 · Pos 6 *9* · W · Pt 26 · F-A 2-1 · H-T 1-0
Scorers, Times: Jarvie 41, Watson 72 / Kirkwood 56 · Ref: A McGunnigle

	1	2	3	4	5	6	7	8	9	10	11	subs used
Aberdeen	Clark	Kennedy	Rougvie	Watson*	McLeish	Miller	Strachan	Archibald	Hamilton*	McMaster	Jarvie	Bell / McGhee
Opponents	*McAlpine*	*Stark*	*Kopel*	*Fleming**	*Hegarty*	*Narey*	*Bannon*	*Sturrock*	*Petrigrew*	*Holt**	*Kirkwood*	*Kirkwood / Mline / Addison*

United have won just one of their last eight, and needed this point in their relegation battle. They seemed to have earned it when Kirkwood's harmless cross was cleared by a trance-like Clark to swing into the net. Mark McGhee dragged defenders away to give Watson space to score.

---

24   H DUNDEE   19/3 — Att 7,000 · W · Pt 28 · F-A 3-0 · H-T 1-0
Scorers, Times: Watson 29, Jarvie 80, Miller 87 · Ref: B McGinlay

	1	2	3	4	5	6	7	8	9	10	11	subs used
Aberdeen	Clark	Kennedy	Rougvie	Watson	McLeish	Miller	Strachan	Archibald	Hamilton*	McMaster	Jarvie	Scanlon
Opponents	*Donaldson*	*Barr*	*Schaedler*	*McLaren*	*Glennie*	*McGeachie*	*Mackie*	*Millar*	*Fleming*	*Sinclair**	*Murphy**	*Corrigan / Ferguson*

Aberdeen never looked likely to lose. But they were not sure of winning until John McMaster turned the ball into the path of Drew Jarvie - who has now scored six goals in three matches against Dundee this season. It is one win in eight for them now, and they are sinking fast.

---

25   H MORTON   22/3 — Att 7,250 · Pos 2 *3* · W · Pt 30 · F-A 1-0 · H-T 0-0
Scorers, Times: Jarvie 51 · Ref: C White

	1	2	3	4	5	6	7	8	9	10	11	subs used
Aberdeen	Clark	Kennedy	Rougvie	Watson*	McLeish	Miller	Strachan	Archibald	Jarvie	McMaster	Scanlon	McGhee
Opponents	*Baines*	*Orr*	*Holmes*	*Anderson*	*McLaughlin*	*Pooney*	*Scott*	*McLaren*	*Thomson*	*Hutchison**	*Ritchie*	*Tolmie*

Morton's early season bubble has burst and they are losing regularly now. The goal came after Mark McGhee's fifth goal in successive games. The goal came after Mark McGhee's effort had hit the post and Archibald's follow-up was cleared off the line.

---

26   A RANGERS   29/3 — Att 20,000 · Pos 2 *5* · D · Pt 31 · F-A 2-2 · H-T 1-1
Scorers, Times: Archibald 35, Jarvie 84 / Jardine 44p, MacDonald J 60 · Ref: K Hope

	1	2	3	4	5	6	7	8	9	10	11	subs used
Aberdeen	Clark	Kennedy	McMaster*	Rougvie	McLeish	Miller	Strachan	Archibald	McGhee	Jarvie	Scanlon	Bell
Opponents	*McCloy*	*Jardine*	*Dawson*	*Forsyth*	*Jackson*	*Stevens*	*McLean*	*Russell*	*Cooper*	*Smith*	*MacDonald J*	

This is the sixth meeting of the sides this season, and Rangers have yet to win one. Alex McLeish's tackle on Gordon Smith provided the penalty for Rangers' equaliser. John MacDonald steered home Russell's shot, but Drew Jarvie - the Dons' man in form - rescued a point.

---

27   A KILMARNOCK   1/4 — Att 5,000 · Pos 2 · W · Pt 33 · F-A 4-0 · H-T 1-0
Scorers, Times: Clarke 26 og, Strachan 69, Kennedy 78, McGhee 56 [McGhee 86] · Ref: A Ferguson

	1	2	3	4	5	6	7	8	9	10	11	subs used
Aberdeen	Clark	Kennedy	Rougvie	Watson*	McLeish	Miller	Strachan	Archibald	McGhee	McMaster	Scanlon	Scanlon / Jarvie
Opponents	*McCulloch*	*Welsh*	*McLean*	*Maxwell*	*Clarke*	*McDicken*	*Houston*	*Mauchlen*	*Doherty*	*Cramond**	*Street*	*Gibson*

Kilmarnock beat the Dons in February and haven't won since. Paul Clarke got in the way of McGhee's effort for the first goal. Best of the lot was Stuart Kennedy's surging run from his own half, outpacing defenders. Overall, Aberdeen's most irresistible performance of the season.

---

28   A CELTIC   5/4 — Att 40,000 · Pos 2 *1* · W · Pt 35 · F-A 2-1 · H-T 1-1
Scorers, Times: Jarvie 19, McGhee 56 / Doyle 23 · Ref: K Stewart

	1	2	3	4	5	6	7	8	9	10	11	subs used
Aberdeen	Clark	Kennedy	Rougvie	Watson*	McLeish	Miller	Strachan	Archibald	McGhee	Jarvie	Scanlon	Bell / McMaster
Opponents	*Latchford*	*Sneddon*	*McGrain*	*Aitken*	*MacDonald*	*McAdam**	*Doyle*	*McGarvey*	*MacLeod*	*Burns*		*Lennox*

McGhee took the ball round Latchford for Jarvie's opener. Doyle's back-header made it all-square. Scanlon's shot is blocked, but McGhee thumped the rebound past Latchford. Then Clark pushed McGarvey. Penalty - but Clark saves from Lennox to inflict Celtic's first home defeat.

---

29   H DUNDEE   7/4 — Att 11,600 · Pos 2 *9* · W · Pt 37 · F-A 2-1 · H-T 0-1
Scorers, Times: Strachan 60p, Jarvie 74 / Fleming 3 · Ref: K Stewart

	1	2	3	4	5	6	7	8	9	10	11	subs used
Aberdeen	Clark	Kennedy	Rougvie*	Watson	McLeish	Miller	Strachan	Archibald	McGhee	Jarvie	Scanlon	Corrigan
Opponents	*Donaldson*	*Barr*	*Millar*	*McLaren*	*Glennie*	*McGeachie*	*Mackie*	*Sinclair**	*Fleming*	*Shirra*	*Ferguson*	*Corrigan*

Former Don, Ian Fleming, does Aberdeen no favours with his quick-fire volley past Clark. McGhee worms through the Dundee defence and lands on his bottom: Strachan obliges from the spot. This win lifts the Dons to within three points of Celtic, from the same number of games.

---

30   H HIBERNIAN   16/4 — Att 15,000 · Pos 2 *10* · D · Pt 38 · F-A 1-1 · H-T 0-0
Scorers, Times: Watson 80 / Rae 66 · Ref: D Murdoch

	1	2	3	4	5	6	7	8	9	10	11	subs used
Aberdeen	Clark	Kennedy	McNamara	Rougvie	McLeish	Miller	Strachan	Archibald	McGhee*	Jarvie	Scanlon*	Hamilton / Watson
Opponents	*McArthur*	*Duncan*	*Paterson*	*Stewart*	*Rae*	*Callachan*	*Lambie*	*Torrance**		*Hutchinson*	*Best*	*MacLeod*

Pittodrie is rocked by rumours that Steve Archibald is about to sign for Spurs. For the second time this season the Dons fail to beat sad, dejected Hibs, who paraded 33-year-old George Best on the wing. He did nothing, except get himself booked. This is a vital point dropped.

---

31   A KILMARNOCK   19/4 — Att 3,800 · Pos 2 *8* · W · Pt 40 · F-A 3-1 · H-T 3-1
Scorers, Times: Strachan 13p, McGhee 24, Archibald 25 / Gibson 15p · Ref: I Foote

	1	2	3	4	5	6	7	8	9	10	11	subs used
Aberdeen	Clark	Kennedy	McMaster	Hamilton	Rougvie	Miller	Strachan	Archibald	McGhee*	Jarvie	Watson	Scanlon
Opponents	*McCulloch*	*Welsh*	*Robertson*	*Clark*	*Clarke*	*McDicken*	*Gibson*	*Mauchlen*	*Bourke*	*McLean*	*Street*	*Scanlon*

Killie's sixth successive defeat is less surprising than the news from Dens Park, where Celtic have lost 1-5. Dons hero is Willie Miller. He concedes Kilmarnock's equalising penalty and in the second half takes a bad knock. Alex Ferguson calls him to come off, but Miller refuses.

32. A CELTIC 23/4 — 1 W 2 42 — 3-1 — 48,000 (HT 2-1)

Archibald 9, McGhee 45, Strachan 65
McCluskey 11p
Ref: D Downie

Celtic's fourth defeat in five games and their second to Aberdeen. This match provided a contrast in emotions for Gordon Strachan, who saw a penalty saved by Latchford at 1-1 before side-footing the third goal when Latchford dropped the ball. The Dons go top on goal-difference.

Aberdeen: Clark, Kennedy, Rougvie, Watson, McLeish, Miller, Strachan, Archibald, McGhee, McMaster, Scanlon
Celtic: Latchford, McGrain, MacLeod, Aitken, MacDonald, Provan, Conroy*, McCluskey, Doyle, McGarvey — McAdam, Burns

33. H ST MIRREN 26/4 — 1 W 3 44 — 2-0 — 19,000 (HT 2-0)

Scanlon 25, Rougvie 42
Ref: R Valentine

Pittodrie senses the incredible. St Mirren can win the title themselves, being just three points behind the Dons at the start of play. McGhee's scintillating run earned a corner, headed in by Scanlon. Thomson then dives to parry Archibald's flick, but Doug Rougvie is in the right spot.

Aberdeen: Clark, Kennedy, Rougvie, Watson, McLeish, Miller, Strachan, Archibald, McGhee, McMaster, Scanlon
St Mirren: Thomson, Young, Abercrombie, Fulton, Copland, Bone, McGhee, Sommer, Logan, Weir — Munro

34. A DUNDEE UTD 29/4 — 1 D 4 45 — 1-0 — 12,954 (HT 1-0)

Strachan 16
Holt 49
Ref: D Downie

Aberdeen use up their game in hand over Celtic to move one point clear. Scotland's 'Player of the Year', Gordon Strachan, fires the first goal. United have conceded at Tannadice since 10 November, 12 matches earlier. It flew in from 25 yards and would have deserved both points.

Aberdeen: Clark, Kennedy, Rougvie, Watson, McLeish, Miller, Strachan, Archibald, McGhee*, McMaster, Scanlon — Jarvie*, Hamilton/Watson
Dundee Utd: Graham, Kirkwood, Stark, Phillip, Hegarty, Narey, Bannon, Sturrock, Pettigrew*, Holt, Dodds, Milne

35. A HIBERNIAN 3/5 — 1 W 10 47 — 5-0 — 12,921 (HT 2-0)

Archibald 26, Watson 28, Scanlon 67, 88, McGhee 84
Ref: B McGinlay

Young Dave Huggins makes his Hibs debut in goal. Doon fans' radios are tuned into Love St. Aberdeen will be almost assured of the title if they win and Celtic draw. Celtic were given a late penalty, but the referee changed his mind. That game finished 0-0: the Dons have done it.

Aberdeen: Clark, Kennedy, Rougvie, Watson, McLeish, Miller, Strachan, Archibald, McGhee, McMaster, Scanlon — Huggins
Hibernian: Brown, Duncan, Paterson, Stewart, Callachan, Murray, McNamara, Torrance, Brazil*, Cormack, Tierney

36. A PARTICK THISTLE 7/5 — 1 D 7 48 — 1-1 — 7,000 (HT 1-1)

McKinnon 23 og
Melrose 22
Ref: T Kellock

This incredible season began at Partick and ends there. Thistle aren't impressed by the Dons' championship credentials, not losing to them once in the league (only in the Scottish Cup). Aberdeen needed to lose this match by 10 clear goals to lose the title. Only their pride is at stake.

Aberdeen: Clark, Kennedy, Rougvie, Watson, McLeish, Miller, Jarvie, Archibald, McGhee, McMaster, Scanlon* — Bell
Partick Thistle: McNab, McKinnon, Whittaker, Higgins, Campbell, Anderson, Park, Melrose, McAdam*, O'Hara, Jardine/Gibson

Average Home 13,290
Away 13,430

Bell's League Cup

1:1 H ARBROATH 15/8 — W 4-0 — 6,700 (HT 3-0)

McGhee 6, Davidson 16, McMaster 26, Jarvie 62
Ref: W Waddell

Aberdeen players wore black armbands, and a minute's silence was observed, in memory of William Gauld, the Pittodrie groundsman, who died at the weekend. Arbroath will be relegated to Division 2 at the end of this season, so they hardly provide the stiffest of opponents.

Aberdeen: Clark, Kennedy, Considine, McLeish, Garner, McGhee, Archibald*, Strachan, McMaster, Davidson, Jarvie
Arbroath: Lister, McKenzie, Rylance, Cargill, Carson, Stark*, Gavine, Mylles, Kidd, Yule*, Forsyth/Copeland

1:2 A ARBROATH 22/8 — L 1-2 — 2,174 (HT 1:1) (HT 1-2)

Harper 36
Wilson 16, Mylles 33
Ref: T Muirhead

(Dons win 5-2 on aggregate)

When Mylles headed past Clark to halve Aberdeen's four-goal advantage, the match took on added urgency. Try as they might, the Dons could not achieve a face-saving draw, though their place in Round 2 was safe. Arbroath won't win at home in the league till late September.

Aberdeen: Clark, Kennedy, Considine, McLeish, Garner, McGhee, Strachan*, Archibald, Harper, McMaster, Bell
Arbroath: Lister, Scrimgeour, Rylance, Cargill, Kydd, Wilson, Wilson, Gavine, Kidd, Yule*, Stark

2:1 A MEADOWBANK 29/8 — W 5-0 — 1,200 (HT 1-0)

McGhee 26, Strachan 70, McMaster 75, 85, Garner 80
Ref: K Stewart

Aberdeen repeated the margin of victory they recorded at Meadowbank in the same competition last season. Thistle gave a good account of themselves until their legs gave out in the last quarter of the match. They are headed for a poor season, though, finishing third from bottom.

Aberdeen: Clark, Kennedy, Considine, McLeish, Garner, McGhee, Archibald, Harper*, Strachan, McMaster, Davidson
Meadowbank: Johnston, Dunn, Fraser, Brown, Wight, Leetion, Small, Boyd, Jobson, Conroy, Davidson

2:2 H MEADOWBANK 1/9 — D 2-2 — 6,000 (HT 0-0)

McMaster 47, Strachan 71p
Jobson 65, 84
Ref: A Harris

(Dons win 7-2 on aggregate)

Meadowbank succeeded in producing a few blushes, if not an upset. Jobson's second equaliser was an insulting free-kick that he bent round Aberdeen's defensive wall six minutes from time. Last season the aggregate score was 9-0; at least Thistle improve upon that this time.

Aberdeen: Clark, Kennedy, Considine, McLeish*, Garner, McGhee*, Archibald, Harper, McMaster, Strachan, Jarvie/Davidson
Meadowbank: Johnston, Dunn, Fraser*, Forte*, Brown, Leetion, McKenna, Boyd, Jobson, Conroy, Ross^ — Wight/McGauran

3:1 H RANGERS 26/9 — W 4-3 — 18,000 (HT 2-0)

Garner 27, Harper 35, McLeish 66
Johnstone 73
Ref: R Valentine

Joe Harper headed on to Willie Garner, who headed the Dons in front. Ian Scanlon hit the bar, the rebound hit McCloy, and Harper poked a second. Alex McLeish's 20-yard effort flew out of McCloy's hands and over the line. Derek Johnstone's lob set up an enthralling second leg.

Aberdeen: Clark, Kennedy, Considine, McLeish, Garner, Miller, Strachan, Archibald, Harper, McMaster*, Scanlon — Rougvie
Rangers: McCloy, Jardine, Dawson, Stevens, Jackson, Watson, Cooper, Johnstone, Miller, MacDonald*, Smith — McLean

SCOTTISH PREMIER (CUP-TIES) Manager: Alex Ferguson SEASON 1979-80

Bell's League Cup

3:2 · A RANGERS · 4 W 2-0 · (H-T 2-0) — 10/10, 28,000
Harper 33, Strachan 36. Ref: E Pringle. (Dons win 5-1 on aggregate)
Aberdeen tormented Rangers, publicly humiliated them and made partial amends for the controversial defeat in last year's final. Harper's one-two with Archibald ended Rangers' hopes, and Strachan's blistering shot left them without anywhere to hide. Three wins over Rangers already.

QF · H CELTIC · 3 W 3-2 · (H-T 2-1) — 31/10, 24,000
Archibald 6, 29, 61 / Edvaldsson 1, Provan 70. Ref: G Smith.
An all-ticket crowd saw an all-ticket cracker, and the sight of Willie Miller changing his torn shorts in the dugout. Hat-trick hero Archibald scores his first with his left foot, his second with his head, his third with his right foot. If he had a fourth it would have been with his backside.

QF · A CELTIC · 3 W 1-0 · (H-T 0-0) — 24/11, 39,000
McGhee 50. Ref: B McGinlay. (Dons win 4-2 on aggregate)
Joe Harper was carried off early, and his replacement - Mark McGhee - relieved the pressure around Clark by being in the right place to collect Garner's knock-down. There were four bookings, including Harper, McLeish, and Rougvie of Aberdeen. The first of three wins at Parkhead.

SF · N MORTON · 3 W 2-1 · (H-T 2-0) — 1/12, 11,896 (at Hampden)
McGhee 14, Strachan 44p / Ritchie 81p. Ref: A Waddell.
It looked so easy for the Dons in the first half. But in the second the league leaders came back strongly. Andy Ritchie's prodigious shot came back off the bar, and Orr's thunderbolt was mysteriously disallowed. Aberdeen somehow held out to the end, but it was desperately tight.

F · N DUNDEE UTD · 3 D 0-0 · (aet) (H-T 0-0) — 8/12, 27,173 (at Hampden)
Ref: B McGinlay.
Dundee United have not had to play a single Premier Division opponent. Hampden's smallest ever crowd for a League Cup final saw Aberdeen in undisputed command. But they fritter their chances, notably Garner's header which rolled along the goal-line before stopping in the mud.

FR · N DUNDEE UTD · 3 L 0-3 · (H-T 0-1) — 12/12, 28,933 (at Dens Park)
Pettigrew 14, 66, Sturrock 76. Ref: B McGinlay.
Both clubs insist the Bell's Cup final replay be transferred to Dens Park. The pitch was hardly playable and the Dons were sunk. At the start they trotted out to the 'United' end. Willie Pettigrew, United's £100,000 signing, sprang the leak in the Dons' bows. United's first-ever trophy.

Match	1	2	3	4	5	6	7	8	9	10	11	subs used
RANGERS (A)	Clark	Kennedy	Considine	McLeish	Garner	Miller	Strachan*	Archibald*	Harper	Jarvie	Scanlon	Sullivan/McMaster
RANGERS	*McCloy*	*Jardine*	*Dawson*	*Stevens*	*Jackson*	*Watson* *	*McLean* *	*MacDonald*	*Johnstone*	*Parlane*	*Cooper*	*Smith/MacKay*
CELTIC (H)	Clark	Kennedy	Considine	McLeish	Garner	Miller	Strachan	Archibald*	Harper*	McMaster*	Scanlon*	Jarvie/Bell
CELTIC	*Latchford*	*Sneddon*	*McGrain*	*Aitken*	*MacDonald*	*MacLeod*	*Provan*	*Edvaldsson*	*Conroy*	*Doyle* *	*Lennox*	
CELTIC (A)	Clark	Kennedy	Considine	McLeish	Garner	Miller	Strachan	Archibald*	Harper*	McMaster*	Scanlon	McGhee/Jarvie
CELTIC	*Latchford*	*Sneddon*	*McGrain*	*Aitken*	*McAdam*	*MacLeod*	*Provan*	*McCluskey* *	*Edvaldsson*	*Conroy*	*Lennox*	*MacDonald*
MORTON (N)	Clark	Kennedy	Rougvie	McLeish	Garner	Miller	Strachan	Archibald*	McGhee	McMaster*	Scanlon	Tolmie/Scott
MORTON	*Baines*	*Holmes*	*Hayes*	*Anderson*	*McLaughlin*	*Orr*	*McNeil* *	*Miller* *	*Thomson*	*Hutchison*	*Ritchie*	
DUNDEE UTD (N)	Clark	Kennedy	Rougvie	McLeish	Garner	Miller	Strachan	Archibald	McGhee*	McMaster*	Scanlon	Jarvie/Hamilton
DUNDEE UTD	*McAlpine*	*Stark*	*Kopel*	*Phillip* *	*Hegarty*	*Narey*	*Bannon*	*Sturrock*	*Pettigrew*	*Holt*	*Payne* *	*Fleming/Murray*
DUNDEE UTD (N)	Clark	Kennedy	Rougvie	McLeish	Garner	Miller	Strachan	Archibald	McGhee*	McMaster*	Scanlon*	Jarvie/Hamilton
DUNDEE UTD	*McAlpine*	*Stark*	*Kopel*	*Fleming*	*Hegarty*	*Narey*	*Bannon*	*Sturrock*	*Pettigrew*	*Holt*	*Kirkwood*	

Scottish Cup

3 · A ARBROATH · 4 D 1-1 · (H-T 1-1) — 26/1, 5,764 (1:13)
Archibald 25 / Stark 45. Ref: D Ramsay.
Five months earlier Aberdeen lost 1-2 at Arbroath in the League Cup. Once again, the Dons are too awful to believe, and will have to try again in a replay caused by Considine being caught in possession by Stark. First Division Bristol City's scout takes in Willie Miller's performance.

3R · H ARBROATH · 4 W 5-0 · (H-T 1-0) — 30/1, 9,127 (1:13)
Hamilton 3, Scanlon 50, 66, 86p, Archibald 62 / Lister. Ref: D Ramsay.
Aberdeen's defence are permitted the day off as Arbroath summon all hands to man the barricades. They could not prevent Ian Scanlon from scoring his first hat-trick for Aberdeen. Poor Arbroath are so bruised by this result that they won't win another match till late March.

4 · H AIRDRIE · 3 W 8-0 · (H-T 4-0) — 16/2, 10,410 (1:3)
Archibald 11, 15, 43, 45, Miller 79, Strachan 80, McMaster 86, Scanlon 90 / McGarr. Ref: R Valentine.
Airdrie are headed for promotion to the Premier Division, so the margin of victory takes everyone by surprise. Airdrie's cause was not helped by having McCulloch and March sent off. Goal of the match was Willie Miller's airborne scissors-kick. Steve Archibald records a foursome.

QF · A PARTICK THISTLE · 4 W 2-1 · (H-T 0-0) — 8/3, 8,584 (7)
Jarvie 62, Archibald 83 / McAdam 88. Ref: J Renton.
For the first half Aberdeen operated with a five-man defensive screen, imitating Thistle. Then Jarvie's head connected with Archibald's flick-on. Kennedy and Watson both hit Rough's woodwork before the game produced a late flurry. The Dons' only success over Thistle this season.

Match	1	2	3	4	5	6	7	8	9	10	11	subs used
ARBROATH (A)	Clark	Kennedy	Considine*	McLeish	Rougvie	Miller	Strachan*	Archibald*	Hamilton	McMaster	Scanlon	Bell/Davidson
ARBROATH	*Lister*	*McKenzie*	*Scrimgeour* *	*Cargill*	*Wells*	*Kidd*	*Stark*	*Myles*	*Barbour*	*Gavine*	*Wilson*	*Durno/Yule*
ARBROATH (H)	Clark	Kennedy	McMaster	McLeish	Rougvie	Miller	Strachan*	Archibald*	Hamilton	Jarvie	Scanlon	Bell/Hewitt
ARBROATH	*McKenzie*	*Scrimgeour*	*Cargill*	*Wells*	*Kidd*	*Stark*	*Myles*	*Gavine*	*Barbour*	*Wilson*		*Durno/Yule*
AIRDRIE (H)	Clark	Kennedy	Leighton	McMaster	Garner	Miller	Strachan	Archibald	Hamilton!	Jarvie	Scanlon	Davidson/Watson
AIRDRIE	*Erwin*	*McGarr*	*Lapsley*	*Walker*	*March!*	*Anderson* *	*McClymont*	*McCulloch!*	*Gordon*	*McKeown* *	*Wilson*	*Hamilton/McGuire*
PARTICK THISTLE (A)	Clark	Kennedy	McMaster	McLeish	Rougvie	Miller	Strachan	Archibald	Hamilton	Jarvie	Watson*	Bell
PARTICK THISTLE	*Rough*	*McKinnon*	*Whittaker*	*Campbell*	*McAdam*	*Anderson* *	*Doyle*	*Melrose*	*O'Hara*	*Gibson*	*Wilson* *	*Jardine/McDonald*

SF

SF	N	RANGERS	2	L	0-1	0-0	Johnstone 75
12/4	44,000	5					
(at Parkhead)						Ref: D Downie	

Aberdeen: Clark, Kennedy, Rougvie, Watson*, McLeish, Miller, McGhee*, Strachan, Archibald, Jarvie, Scanlon (McMaster/Bell)
Rangers: McCloy, Jardine, Miller, Forsyth, Jackson, Stevens, Cooper, Russell, Johnstone, Smith, McDonald J

Lucky '7' for Rangers, as they beat the Dons for the first time in seven attempts this season. They had four players booked in recording this distinction. Derek Johnstone's only contribution to the match was to hook a low shot past Bobby Clark from the edge of the penalty box.

UEFA Cup

1:1	H	EINTRACHT	2	D	1-1	0-1	Harper 52
19/9	20,000	(W Germ)					Cha Bum Kun 13
						Ref: L Agnolin (Italy)	

Aberdeen: Clark, Kennedy, Considine, Sullivan, Garner, Miller, Strachan, Archibald, Harper*, McMaster, Scanlon (Jarvie/Davidson)
Eintracht: Funk, Muller, Neuberger, Korbel, Pezzey, Lorant, Holzenbein, Trapp, Lottermann*, Grabowski, Cha Bum Kun (Karger)

Eintracht lost the 1960 European Cup final 3-7 to Real Madrid. Their current side includes six internationals. South Korean Cha Bum Kun seized on Holzenbein's misplaced header for the first goal. Harper then chested down Scanlon's cross and fended off two challenges to level.

1:2	A	EINTRACHT	3	L	0-1	0-0	Holzenbein 50
3/10	20,000						
						Ref: A Castillo (Spain)	

Aberdeen: Clark, Kennedy, Considine*, Jarvie, McLeish, Miller, Strachan, Archibald, Harper, McMaster*, Scanlon (Garner/Sullivan)
Eintracht: Funk, Muller, Neuberger, Korbel, Pezzey, Lorant, Holzenbein, Nachtweih, Karger*, Grabowski, Cha Bum Kun (Garner/Karger)

In the Wald Stadium it took a goal from 33-year-old Bernd Holzenbein to put Aberdeen out of Europe for another year. Strachan's shot had earlier struck keeper Funk's body. John McMaster's point-blank shot was also kept out. At the close, Cha Bum Kun wobbled Clark's crossbar.

League Table

	Team	P	W	D	L	F	A	W	D	L	F	A	Pts
			Home					**Away**					
1	ABERDEEN	36	10	4	4	30	18	9	6	3	38	18	48
2	Celtic	36	13	3	2	44	17	5	8	5	17	21	47
3	St Mirren	36	11	5	2	37	23	4	7	7	19	26	42
4	Dundee Utd	36	9	7	2	23	16	3	6	9	20	24	37
5	Rangers	36	11	5	2	29	16	4	2	12	21	30	37
6	Morton	36	9	4	5	24	16	5	4	9	27	21	36
7	Partick This	36	6	8	4	24	22	5	6	7	19	25	36
8	Kilmarnock	36	7	6	5	19	19	4	5	9	17	33	33
9	Dundee	36	9	3	6	33	30	1	3	14	6	43	26
10	Hibernian	36	6	4	8	23	31	0	2	16	6	36	18
		360	91	49	40	286	198	40	49	91	198	286	360

Results versus each club

	P	W	D	L	F	A	Pts	Cup	W	D	L	F	A
v Dundee	4	4	0	0	12	2	8						
v Rangers	4	3	1	0	9	5	7	LC	2	0	0	2	0
								SC					
v Hibernian	4	2	2	0	10	2	6	LC					
v Kilmarnock	4	3	0	1	11	4	6	LC					
v St Mirren	4	2	2	0	7	3	6	LC					
v Celtic	4	2	1	1	6	4	5	LC					
v Dundee Utd	4	2	1	1	6	6	5	LC					
v Partick This	4	0	3	1	3	4	3	SC					
v Morton	4	1	0	3	4	6	2						
	36	19	10	7	68	36	48						

Appearances and Goals

	Lge	Sub	LC	Sub	SC	Sub	Eur	Sub	Lge	LC	SC	Eur	Tot
		Appearances								**Goals**			
Archibald, Steve	34		11		5		2		12	3	7		22
Bell, Dougie	4	6		2		4							
Clark, Bobby	35		11		4		2						
Considine, Doug	14		7		1		2						
Cooper, Neil	1												
Davidson, Duncan	2	5	1	2				1	1				2
Garner, Willie	20		11				1		1	1			2
Hamilton, Derek	11	2		2		4			3		1		4
Harper, Joe	8	3	7		2			2	3	3	1		7
Hewitt, John	2	2		1									
Jarvie, Drew	22	8	2	6	4		1	1	7	5	1	1	14
Kennedy, Stuart	35		11		5		2		1				1
Leighton, Jim	1				1								
McGhee, Mark	15	6	6	1			1		6	4			10
McLeish, Alex	35		11		4		2		2	1			3
McMaster, John	32	2	10	1	4	1	2	2	4	4	1		9
Miller, Willie	31		8		5		2		2				2
Rougvie, Doug	25	3	7		4		2		2				2
Scanlon, Ian	25	4	7		4		2		4	4			8
Strachan, Gordon	33		11		5		2		10	4	1		15
Sullivan, Dom	2	3		1									
Watson, Andy	12	5	2		2	1		1	5				5
(own-goals)									2				2
22 players used	396	49	121	16	55	9	22	4	68	23	16	1	108

Odds & ends

Never lost to: (4) Dundee, Hibs, St Mirren, Rangers (in the league).
Never beat: (1) Partick (in the league).

Won from behind: (4) Kilmarnock (h), Rangers (h), Dundee (h), Celtic (LC).
Lost from in front: (2) Celtic (h), Morton (h).

High spots: Winning first championship since 1955.
Unbeaten in final 15 league games.

Almost total dominance over both Celtic and Rangers.

Low spots: 4 games without a win since 20 October.
Losing to Dundee Utd in replayed League Cup final.

Bogey-team: Morton.
Ever-presents: (0).
Hat-tricks: (3) Steve Archibald 2, Ian Scanlon 1.
Leading scorer: (22) Steve Archibald.

SCOTTISH PREMIER DIVISION

Manager: Alex Ferguson

SEASON 1980-81

No	Date	Att	Pos	Pt	F-A	H-T	Scorers, Times, and Referees	1	2	3	4	5	6	7	8	9	10	11	subs used
1	A ST MIRREN 9/8	7,067	W	2	1-0	1-0	Jarvie 23 — Ref: A McFaull	Leighton / *Thomson*	Kennedy / *Young*	McMaster / *Beckett*	Watson / *Richardson*	McLeish / *Fulton*	Miller / *Copland*	Strachan / *Abercrombie*	Hewitt* / *Stark*	McGhee / *Sommer*	Jarvie / *Weir*	Scanlon / *Logan**	Cowan / *McDougall*
2	H DUNDEE UTD 16/8	13,729	4 D	6 3	1-1	1-1	Strachan 29p / *Hegarty 23* — Ref: R Cuthill	Leighton / *McAlpine*	Kennedy / *Kirkwood*	McMaster / *Stark*	Watson* / *Phillip*	McLeish / *Hegarty*	Miller / *Narey*	Strachan / *Milne**	Cowan / *Sturrock*	McGhee / *Payne*	Jarvie* / *Addison*	Scanlon / *Bannon*	Bell, Hewitt / *Kopel*
3	A AIRDRIE 23/8	5,000	2 W	5 5	4-0	2-0	McGhee 1, Cowan 8, Jarvie 70, [Scanlon 74] — Ref: A Waddell	Leighton / *McGarr*	Kennedy / *Erwin*	McMaster / *Rodger*	Watson* / *Walker*	McLeish / *March*	Miller / *Anderson*	Strachan / *McKeown*	Cowan* / *Clark*	McGhee / *Russell*	Jarvie / *Gordon*	Scanlon / *McGuire*	Considine, Hewitt
4	H MORTON 6/9	9,485	1 W	10 7	6-0	1-0	Miller 14, Scanlon 46, 57, Hewitt 84, [Strachan 86, McMaster 87] — Ref: D Syme	Leighton / *Baines*	Kennedy / *Wilkie*	McMaster / *Holmes*	Watson* / *Anderson**	McLeish / *Orr*	Miller / *McLaren*	Strachan / *McNeil*	McMaster* / *Rooney*	McGhee / *Thomson*	Jarvie* / *Cochrane*	Scanlon / *Ritchie**	Bell, Hewitt / *Hutchison, Tolmie*
5	A RANGERS 13/9	30,000	1 D	3 8	1-1	1-1	Strachan 29p / *McAdam 38* — Ref: B McGinlay	Leighton / *McCloy*	Kennedy / *Jardine*	McMaster / *Miller*	Watson* / *Forsyth**	McLeish / *Jackson*	Miller / *Bett*	Strachan / *Cooper*	McMaster* / *McLean**	McGhee* / *McAdam*	Hewitt* / *Redford*	Scanlon / *Johnston W*	Hamilton, Bell / *Johnstone, McDon'd*
6	A PARTICK THISTLE 20/9	6,000	2 W	9 10	1-0	0-0	McGhee 76 — Ref: G Smith	Leighton / *Rough*	Kennedy / *Doyle*	McMaster / *Whittaker*	Bell / *Campbell*	McLeish / *O'Hara**	Miller / *Welsh*	Strachan / *Park*	McMaster* / *Gibson*	McGhee / *Higgins*	Hewitt* / *Watson*	Scanlon / *McDonald**	Hamilton / *Scott, Lapsley*
7	H CELTIC 27/9	23,000	2 D	3 11	2-2	0-2	McGhee 72, McAdam 74 og / *Nicholas 7p, Burns 17* — Ref: R Valentine	Leighton / *Bonner*	Kennedy / *Sneddon*	Hamilton* / *McGrain*	Watson / *McAdam*	McLeish / *MacDonald*	Miller / *Conroy*	Strachan / *Provan*	McMaster / *Sullivan*	McGhee / *McGarvey**	Bell / *Burns**	Hewitt* / *Nicholas*	Scanlon, McCall / *Doyle, MacLeod*
8	A HEARTS 4/10	10,873	2 W	8 13	1-0	0-0	Rougvie 65 — Ref: P McLeish	Leighton / *Brough*	Kennedy / *Jefferies*	Rougvie / *Shields*	Bell / *Denny**	Garner* / *McVie*	Miller / *Kidd*	Strachan / *Bowman*	McCall* / *Gibson*	McGhee / *O'Connor*	Jarvie / *Robertson*	Hewitt* / *MacDonald*	Watson, Scanlon / *Robinson*
9	H KILMARNOCK 11/10	11,000	2 W	10 15	2-0	0-0	Scanlon 48, Jarvie 77 — Ref: J Renton	Leighton / *Brown*	Kennedy / *Robertson*	Rougvie / *Cockburn*	Watson / *Clark*	Cooper* / *Clarke*	Miller / *McDicken*	Strachan / *Houston*	McMaster / *Mauchlen*	McGhee* / *Gibson**	Jarvie / *Cramond**	Scanlon / *Street*	Bell, Cowan / *Doherty, Wilson*
10	H ST MIRREN 18/10	11,000	1 W	7 17	3-2	1-0	McMaster 34, McGhee 70, 72 / *Copland 62, McDougall 63* — Ref: E Pringle	de Clerck / *Thomson*	Kennedy / *Young*	Rougvie / *Beckett*	Watson / *Richardson*	McLeish / *McCormack*	Miller / *Copland*	Strachan / *Stark*	McMaster / *Sommer*	McGhee / *Weir*	Jarvie / *Abercrombie*	Scanlon / *McDougall*	Watson

Match notes

1. This is Alex Ferguson's first win at Paisley since his move to Pittodrie. The Saints thought they had scored first, but Billy Stark's goal was disallowed for offside. Bobby Clark's back injury gives Leighton his chance in goal. He takes it well. The perfect start to defending the title.

2. Matches between these two often end in stalemate. Paul Hegarty had nobody near him as he headed United in front. Fortunately for the Dons, Eamonn Bannon then chopped down Mark McGhee in full flight. After the match Archie Knox joins Aberdeen as assistant manager.

3. Aberdeen had thrashed promoted Airdrie 8-0 in the League Cup last season. Here, it takes just 23 seconds after kick-off for John McMaster to thread his pass to Mark McGhee to put the Dons one goal up. Then it was Mark McGhee's turn to make a goal for Ian Scanlon.

4. Morton have only taken one point so far. The Premier League championship flag flutters over the Paddock End. Willie Miller anoints it by bulging the net from 25 yards. Then his forwards take over. Next Wednesday, Strachan scores for Scotland against Sweden in Stockholm.

5. This top-of-the-table clash produced a penalty for Aberdeen when Tom Forsyth downed Doug Rougvie, and an equaliser for Rangers when McAdam's head connected with Dave Cooper's cross. The Dons stay top of the league, ahead of Celtic and Rangers on goal-difference.

6. Not the best of matches. Not the best of goals - poached by Mark McGhee in a goalmouth scramble. But at least it sets up a league win over Partick, something that was beyond the Dons in the season they won the championship. Partick have only won once so far this season.

7. Aberdeen appeared out for the count. Miller sent Tommy Burns into orbit and Charlie Nicholas scored his 12th goal in nine games. Burns headed a second with John Hewitt off the pitch receiving treatment. Then Mark McGhee prods past Bonner and McAdam adds an own goal.

8. Hearts are having another heart-breaking season. Aberdeen play as though they are still in Vienna, in mind if not in body. But they are thankful to big Doug Rougvie, who cushions a pass on his chest before banging his first goal of the season. Rangers top the league for the moment.

9. Kilmarnock are halfway through a nine-game losing streak. They lost their last two homes 1-8 and 1-6, yet they were the last team to beat the Dons in the league, 24 matches ago. Aberdeen now establish a new record. Neale Cooper, just 16, makes his debut, along with Mark de Clerck.

10. What a turnaround. St Mirren turn a 0-1 deficit into a 2-1 lead as Copland's effort is deflected by Andy Watson, and seconds later Leighton, Miller and Frank McDougall collide in a heap of bodies. The ball ends up in the net. That is the cue for McGhee to charge to the rescue.

No.		Opponent	Date					Score	HT	Scorers	Opp. scorers	Referee
11	A	DUNDEE UTD	25/10	10,043	7	19	W	3-1	2-1	Strachan 10, McGhee 24, Hewitt 86	Sturrock 4	Ref: J Wales
12	H	AIRDRIE	1/11	9,000	5	21	W	4-1	3-0	McCall 5, 27, 48, McGhee 40	Miller 82 og	Ref: A Harris
13	A	CELTIC	8/11	29,000	3	23	W	2-0	1-0	McCall 31, 56		Ref: B Robertson
14	H	PARTICK THISTLE	15/11	12,000	4	25	W	2-1	0-0	Bell 61, Strachan 76p	O'Hara 58	Ref: E Pringle
15	A	KILMARNOCK	22/11	3,200	10	26	D	1-1	0-1	McLeish 89	Miller 35 og	Ref: A Waddell
16	A	MORTON	6/12	5,000	8	26	L	0-1	0-0		Rooney 85	Ref: H Alexander
17	H	RANGERS	13/12	22,500	3	28	W	2-0	0-0	McGhee 67, Johnstone 79 og		Ref: D Downie
18	A	PARTICK THISTLE	20/12	4,000	6	29	D	1-1	1-1	McCall 20	Watson 8p	Ref: D Ramsay
19	H	CELTIC	27/12	24,000	2	31	W	4-1	2-0	McLeish 9, Miller 40, McCall 47, Nicholas 71 [Strachan 69p]	Nicholas 71	Ref: D Ramsay
20	H	DUNDEE UTD	30/12	23,000	4	32	D	1-1	0-1	Scanlon 81p	Dodds 38	Ref: A Waddell
21	A	ST MIRREN	3/1	11,100	5	33	D	1-1	0-0	Scanlon 69p	Bone 55	Ref: A McGunnigle

11 – Dundee Utd (A)
Aberdeen: Leighton, Kennedy, Rougvie, Bell, McLeish, Miller, Strachan, Cowan*, McGhee, Jarvie, Scanlon, Hewitt
Dundee Utd: McAlpine, Kirkwood, Kopel, Holt, Hegarty, Narey, Pettigrew, Gibson*, Payne^, Sturrock, Bannon, Milne/Ward

Aberdeen ought to have been demoralised by Liverpool's regal performance in midweek. But they weren't. They avenge Sturrock's thumping drive with a Strachan one-two with Mark McGhee, followed by a moment of McGhee magic, as he leaves defenders flapping in mid-air.

12 – Airdrie (H)
Aberdeen: Leighton, Dornan, Rougvie, Watson, McLeish*, Miller, Strachan, McCall, McGhee^, Jarvie, Scanlon, Hewitt
Airdrie: Martin, Walker, Rodger, McCluskey, Marchl, Anderson, N Thompson*, Clark, Russell, Gordon, McKeown, Anderson G

Airdrie had only lost one of their previous eight. Walker McCall's first full game since returning from Atlanta Chiefs brings him a memorable hat-trick. Airdrie's Jim March gets so exasperated that he clatters McCall and gets sent off. Now for the visit to Parkhead on Saturday.

13 – Celtic (A)
Aberdeen: Leighton, Kennedy, Rougvie, Watson, McLeish, Cooper, Strachan, McCall, McGhee, Bell, Scanlon, Considine/Hewitt
Celtic: Bonner, Sneddon, McGrain, Aitken, McAdam, Conroy^, Provan, Sullivan, Burns, Nicholas, McCluskey/Doyle

Celtic have just lost to Rangers for the second time, so this is a critical defeat for them. This was the famous match in which Mark McGhee twice loaded the gun for Walker McCall to fire two lethal bullets, and which saw Gordon Strachan attacked on the pitch by a lunatic Celtic fan.

14 – Partick Thistle (H)
Aberdeen: Leighton, Rougvie, Considine, Watson, McLeish, Miller, Strachan, McCall, McGhee, Bell, Scanlon*, Hewitt
Partick Thistle: Rough, Doyle, Lapsley*, Campbell, Welsh, Whittaker, Park, O'Hara, Clark, Watson, Jardine, Torrance/McDonald

O'Hara scores for Thistle from 25 yards. Dougie Bell equalises for the Dons from one fifth that distance, but they all count. Campbell handles Walker McCall's shot for the penalty. Only Aberdeen and Rangers remain unbeaten, but Aberdeen are looking a good bet to hang to their title.

15 – Kilmarnock (A)
Aberdeen: Leighton, Kennedy, Considine, Watson, McLeish, Miller, Strachan, McCall*, McGhee, Jarvie, Scanlon^, Hewitt/Hamilton
Kilmarnock: Wilson, McLean, Robertson, Mauchlen, Clarke, Houston, McNeil^, Maxwell, McBride, Cramond, Street

Kilmarnock had taken just one point from 11 games, but so nearly took two here. Willie Miller's fourth own-goal in five weeks looked to have done the damage. Alex McLeish's thumping header preserved the Dons' long-standing unbeaten record - for one more match.

16 – Morton (A)
Aberdeen: Leighton, Kennedy, Considine, Watson, McLeish, Miller, Strachan, McCall*, McGhee, Jarvie', Scanlon, Hewitt*
Morton: Baines, Hayes, Holmes, Rooney, McLaughlin, Orr, McNeil', Cochrane, Thomson, Busby, Ritchie

Struggling Morton beat Rangers last week and Aberdeen this. The substitute's cross landed on the head of Jim Rooney to bring about Aberdeen's first league defeat in 31 games. Ritchie who schemes it.

17 – Rangers (H)
Aberdeen: Leighton, Kennedy, Considine, Watson, Garner*, Miller, Strachan, McCall*, McGhee, Angus, Scanlon, Simpson/Davidson
Rangers: McCloy, Miller, Dawson, Johnstone, D Jackson, Redford*, McLean^, Russell, McAdam, Johnston, W Cooper/McKay

Rangers are in the middle of a terrible run. Ian Angus plays his first full game as Rangers extend their losing sequence at Pittodrie. McCloy has no chance with McGhee's flashing shot, or with Walker McCall's chip, which Derek Johnstone unwittingly heads into his own net.

18 – Partick Thistle (A)
Aberdeen: Leighton, Kennedy, Considine, McLeish, Garner*, Miller, Strachan, McCall*, McGhee, Angus, Scanlon, Simpson/Davidson
Partick Thistle: Rough, Doyle, Whittaker, Campbell, Anderson, Watson, Park, Jardine, Torrance^, O'Hara, Clark, Lapsley

Now it's Neil Simpson's turn to be introduced to the first team. He is not impressed by Premier League refereeing. Both sides are awarded ridiculously soft penalties. Partick's Watson netted his; Aberdeen's Strachan missed. That denies the Dons a third league win over Thistle.

19 – Celtic (H)
Aberdeen: Leighton, Kennedy, Considine, Watson, McLeish, Miller, Strachan, McCall*, McGhee, Angus, Scanlon^, Hewitt/Angus
Celtic: Bonner, McGrain, Reid, Aitken, MacDonald McAdam, Conroy*, Weir, McGarvey, Burns, Provan/Nicholas

This is a four-pointer Celtic cannot afford to lose. On a sandy, frosted pitch, the defensive duo of Miller and McLeish put the skids under Celtic. Aberdeen now stand three points clear with a game in hand. But Celtic, who had won their last four, will win their next nine games.

20 – Dundee Utd (H)
Aberdeen: Leighton, Kennedy, Considine, Watson, McLeish, Miller, Strachan, McCall*, McGhee, Angus, Scanlon, Hewitt/Angus
Dundee Utd: McAlpine, Holt, Kopel, Phillip, Hegarty, Narey, Bannon, Milne, Dodds, Gibson, Sturrock, Stark

Scotland boss Jock Stein assesses a fine competitive match. Davie Dodds' header was only cancelled out by a debatable penalty, awarded when Mark McGhee collided with David Narey. Crucially, Gordon Strachan suffers the injury that will keep him out for the next nine games.

21 – St Mirren (A)
Aberdeen: Leighton, Kennedy, Rougvie, Watson, McLeish, Miller, Simpson, McCall*, McGhee, Angus, Scanlon, Hewitt
St Mirren: Thomson, Young, Beckett, McCormack, Fulton, Copland, Bone, Stark, Somner, Richardson, Weir

Seven games now without defeat for St Mirren. This match offered a goal to savour, scored by St Mirren's Jimmy Bone, who ran half the pitch before beating Leighton. But then McCormack felled Simpson, and for the second successive game Scanlon rescued the Dons from the spot.

SCOTTISH PREMIER DIVISION — Manager: Alex Ferguson — SEASON 1980-81

Each match lists Aberdeen's line-up (positions 1–11, subs used) on the top line and the opponents on the line below (in italics).

No	V	Date	Team	Att	Pos	Res	Pt	F-A	H-T	1	2	3	4	5	6	7	8	9	10	11	subs used
22	A	10/1	HEARTS	7,999	1	W	35	2-0	1-0	Leighton	Kennedy	Rougvie*	Watson	McLeish	Miller	Simpson	McCall	McGhee	Angus	Scanlon	Considine/Jarvie
			Hearts							*Brough*	*Hamilton*	*Shields*	*More*	*Liddell F*	*Masterton**	*Hamill*	*Gibson*	*Conn**	*O'Brien*	*MacDonald*	*Robinson/O'Connor*
23	A	31/1	RANGERS	32,500	2	L	35	0-1	0-0	Leighton	Hamilton	Rougvie	Watson*	McLeish	Cooper*	Jarvie	McCall	McGhee	Angus	Scanlon	Harrow/Davidson
			Rangers							*McCloy*	*Jardine*	*Dawson*	*Stevens*	*Jackson*	*Bett*	*Johnston W Russell*		*Johnstone D Redford*		*McDonald**	*Cooper*
24	H	7/2	MORTON	11,000	2	L	35	0-1	0-0	Leighton	Hamilton	Considine	Simpson	McLeish	Rougvie	Bell*	Harrow*	McGhee	Angus	Scanlon	Watson/McCall
			Morton							*Baines*	*Hayes*	*Holmes*	*Rooney*	*McLaughlin Orr*		*Busby*	*Marr*	*Thomson*	*Tolmie*	*Ritchie*	
25	A	21/2	AIRDRIE	2,600	2	D	36	0-0	0-0	Leighton	Kennedy	Rougvie	Watson*	McLeish	Miller	Simpson	Harrow	McGhee	Jarvie	Scanlon*	Angus/Considine
			Airdrie							*Gardiner*	*Cairney*	*Rodger*	*Walker*	*Anderson G McCluskey Flood*			*Russell**	*Anderson N Gordon*	*Clark*	*March*	
26	H	28/2	ST MIRREN	9,500	2	L	36	1-2	1-1	Leighton	Kennedy	Rougvie	Watson	McLeish	Miller	Simpson	Harrow*	McGhee*	Jarvie	Scanlon	Angus/Hewitt
			St Mirren							*Thomson*	*Beckett*	*McCormack Richardson*		*Fulton*	*Copland*	*McDougall Stark*		*Sommer*	*Abercrombie Weir*		
27	H	7/3	HEARTS	9,500	2	W	38	4-1	2-0	Leighton	Kennedy	Hamilton*	Angus	McLeish	Miller	Simpson	McCall	McGhee	Jarvie	Scanlon	Rougvie/Hewitt
			Hearts							*Brough*	*Hamilton*	*Shields*	*More*	*Liddell F*	*Hamill*	*Mackay**	*Gibson*	*McShane**	*Liddell G*	*Kidd*	*Bowman/O'Brien*
28	A	14/3	KILMARNOCK	2,400	2	L	38	0-1	0-0	Leighton	Kennedy	Hamilton*	Angus	McLeish	Miller	Simpson	McCall*	McGhee	Jarvie	Scanlon	Rougvie/Watson
			Kilmarnock							*McCulloch*	*Robin*	*Cockburn*	*Clark*	*Armstrong McDicken*	*McBride*	*McLean*		*Bourke*	*Mauchlen*	*Doherty*	
29	A	28/3	CELTIC	35,200	2	D	39	1-1	1-0	Leighton	Kennedy	Rougvie	Watson	McLeish	Miller	Simpson	Bell*	McGhee	Harrow*	Scanlon	Jarvie/McCall
			Celtic							*Bonner*	*McGrain*	*Reid*	*Sullivan*	*McAdam*	*Aitken*	*Provan*	*MacLeod*	*McGarvey*	*Burns*	*Nicholas**	*McCluskey*
30	H	1/4	PARTICK THISTLE	8,000	2	W	41	3-1	1-0	Leighton	Kennedy	Rougvie	Watson	McLeish	Miller	Simpson	Angus	McGhee	Harrow	Scanlon	Cooper
			Partick Thistle							*McNab*	*McKinnon**	*Whittaker Welsh*	*Welsh*	*Campbell*	*Watson**	*Park*	*McDonald*	*Higgins*	*Lapsley*	*Clark*	*Doyle/Jardine*
31	A	4/4	MORTON	4,500	2	W	43	3-1	1-0	Leighton	Kennedy	Rougvie	Watson	McLeish	Miller	Simpson	Angus	McGhee	Harrow*	Scanlon*	Jarvie/Davidson
			Morton							*Baines*	*Hayes*	*Holmes*	*Rooney*	*McNeil*	*Wilkie*	*Busby*		*Thomson*	*Tolmie*	*Ritchie**	*McNab*

Scorers, Times, and Referees

- **22** — McCall 34, McGhee 57. Ref: W Anderson
- **23** — *Johnstone 64.* Ref: R Valentine
- **24** — *Busby 73.* Ref: I Foote
- **25** — Ref: H Alexander
- **26** — Jarvie 40. *Richardson 6, McDougall 58.* Ref: J Timmons
- **27** — McCall 38, Hamilton 42, Jarvie 53, [Angus 65]. *Hamil 69.* Ref: D Syme
- **28** — *Doherty 59.* Ref: C White
- **29** — Harrow 17. *McCluskey 85.* Ref: K Hope
- **30** — Simpson 2, McGhee 64, McLeish 75. *Watson 58.* Ref: T Muirhead
- **31** — McGhee 21, Rougvie 50, Simpson 89. *Tolmie 58.* Ref: B McGinlay

Match notes

22. Things could hardly get worse for Hearts. This is their fourth successive defeat. They cause Aberdeen so few scares in attack that it comes as no surprise that by season's end no Hearts player will have scored more than four league goals. Aberdeen stay one point ahead of Celtic.

23. At long last Aberdeen are knocked off their perch by Celtic. The Dons' barricade finally cracked when Derek Johnstone outmanoeuvred Doug Rougvie before scoring. The Dons still have a game in hand over Celtic, but the momentum has transferred dramatically in Celtic's favour.

24. Oh no! Morton again with a late winner. This time it's Drew Busby to head home Holmes' cross. The nearest Aberdeen came was when Ian Scanlon headed against the bar. Aberdeen's unbeaten home record goes up in smoke. This is the match where the championship was lost.

25. Last Saturday Morton knocked the Dons out of the Scottish Cup. Aberdeen can't even beat Airdrie these days. Former Dons goalkeeper John Gardiner hardly had a shot to save as Aberdeen's goal famine extends to six and a half hours. These are desperate weeks for Aberdeen fans.

26. St Mirren have now lost just once in 11 games, as they inflict more misery on Aberdeen's crumbling season. Frank McDougall's glancing header marks his first ever goal against Aberdeen. Liverpool scouts eye up Saints' winger Peter Weir. Celtic are pulling right away at the top.

27. Ferguson wields the axe and drops three players - Rougvie, Watson, and Harrow - as he tries desperately to get back to winning ways. The result is a first win in any competition for eight weeks. Hearts were the victims then, and now, but Hearts have long since given up the ghost.

28. Surely this result cannot be true. Kilmarnock's third win of the season leaves Aberdeen wondering where it all went wrong. It is impossible to believe that this team is the same that led the table in the New Year. Celtic have one hand on Aberdeen's crown, and Ferguson is at a loss.

29. A win at Parkhead would have kept Aberdeen's spirits up, but even that was denied them by McCluskey's hook over Leighton. Leighton had kept out MacLeod's penalty, as Aberdeen tried to hang on to Andy Harrow's first goal for the Dons. Celtic's lead is still eight points.

30. Aberdeen lost their way after Neil Simpson banged in a rebound to give them a two-minute lead. A scrambled equaliser forced the Dons to regroup, which they did with two headers. April will proved to be a super month for the Dons, earning them 10 points from six matches.

31. Morton have the cheek to let Aberdeen win this one, when it doesn't matter a hoot. Morton always win the ones that matter, having been the principal wreckers of Aberdeen's season. The Dons start each match with Morton almost expecting to lose 0-1, so McGhee's opener is a tonic.

League matches

32. H HEARTS — 11/4 — 2 W 1-0 — 5,600 · 9 · 45
Rougvie 85
Ref: W Knowles
Team: Leighton · Kennedy · Rougvie · Watson* · Cooper* · Miller · Simpson · Angus · McGhee · Harrow · Scanlon
Subs: Brough · Denny · Shields · Bowman · Liddell F · Hamill · Mackay · Gibson · Liddell G · Robertson · Kidd · Jarvie/Hewitt
Hearts can't save themselves from relegation. Doug Rougvie's glancing header maintains Aberdeen's mathematical chances of keeping their title, but they require Celtic to slip up badly, and that is not likely to happen. Eight points out of eight from Hearts, for the loss of just one goal.

33. H AIRDRIE — 18/4 — 2 W 3-0 — 7,000 · 8 · 47
McGhee 26, 78, McCall 27
Ref: D Downie
Team: Leighton · Kennedy · Rougvie · Bell · McLeish · Miller · Simpson · McCall · McGhee · Angus* · Hewitt
Subs: Gardiner · Cairney* · Radger · Erwin · Anderson G · McCluskey · Flood · Clark* · Anderson N · McKeown · McGuire · Thompson/McCaffry
Hoping against hope that Rangers beat Celtic, Aberdeen set out to play relaxed, delightful football. This is typified by Mark McGhee, whose twinkling footwork steals the show. Airdrie's danger-man, Sandy Clark, has now failed to score in 14 games. Alas, Celtic beat Rangers 1-0.

34. H RANGERS — 22/4 — 2 D 0-0 — 15,000 · 3 · 48
Ref: D Ramsay
Team: Leighton · Kennedy · Rougvie · Bell · McLeish · Miller · Simpson* · Scanlon* · McGhee · Angus · Hewitt
Subs: Stewart · Jardine · Miller · Stevens · Forsyth · Bett · Russell · Johnstone · Redford · McLean · Watson/Harrow
Aberdeen had most of the play, but Rangers had more of the shots at goal. It ended up as a stalemate. Even had Rangers won they could not have overhauled Aberdeen in second place. As for the championship, that is Celtic's, though the Dons equal last season's points total of 48.

35. A DUNDEE UTD — 25/4 — 2 D 0-0 — 6,369 · 5 · 49
Ref: G Smith
Team: Leighton · Kennedy · Rougvie · Bell · McLeish · Miller · Simpson · Scanlon · McGhee · Angus* · Hewitt
Subs: McAlpine · Holt · Murray · Kirkwood · Hegarty* · Stark · Bannon · Milne · Petigrew · Sturrack · Payne/Gibson
Beset by injuries, the Aberdeen line-up is remodelled at Tannadice. The third draw between the sides. How ironic that despite their wretched spring, Aberdeen have now overtaken last season's title-winning points tally. Does that mean they are a better team this season than last?

36. H KILMARNOCK — 2/5 — 2 L 0-2 — 6,300 · 9 · 49
McDicken 53, McCready 56
Ref: M Delaney
Team: Leighton · Kennedy · Rougvie · Watson* · McLeish · Miller · Simpson · McGhee · Harper · Angus* · Jarvie/Harrow
Subs: McCulloch · Robin* · Cockburn · Clark · Armstrong · McDicken · McCready · McLean · Bourke · Mauchlen · Eadie · Robertson
An emotional return for Joe Harper in his first and last appearance of the season. Kilmarnock are not impressed. This win cannot avert the drop, but it does mean they finish 9th rather than 10th. It also brings Aberdeen's third home defeat in the final three months of the season.

Average Home 12,315 · Away 11,900

Bell's League Cup

2:1 H BERWICK RGS — 27/8 — 2 W 8-1 — 7,570
McGhee 7, 31, 82, Jarvie 11, 19, Egan 63 [Watson 46, 86, Bell 90]
Ref: R Valentine
Team: Leighton · Kennedy · McMaster · Watson · McLeish · Miller · Strachan* · Cowan* · McGhee · Jarvie · Scanlon
Subs: McCann · Deakin · McDougall · McDowell · Wheatley · Davidson · Romaines · Smith G · Tait* · Egan* · Bell/Rougvie · Dixon/Smith D
Berwick will finish bottom of Division 1. Their best player was goalkeeper Ian McLaren, whose highlight was stopping a Mark McGhee penalty. That would have given McGhee a haul of four goals. As happens with this kind of result, the second leg is now a total waste of time.

2:2 A BERWICK RGS — 30/8 — 2 W 4-0 — 1,188 · 1:14
Strachan 3, Hewitt 7, de Clerck 22, [Kennedy 89]
Ref: M Delaney
(Dons win 12-1 on aggregate)
Team: de Clerck · Kennedy · Rougvie · Garner* · McLeish* · Miller · Strachan · Bell · McGhee · Hewitt · Scanlon
Subs: McCann · McGann · Deakin · Gregson* · McDowell · Moyes · Davidson · Smith D · McLeod · Tait · Cowan · Smith G
Goal of the season, perhaps. Aberdeen's Belgian goalkeeper, Mark de Clerck, drop-kicked a clearance which bounced over Davidson's head into the Berwick goal. It is the first goal ever scored by an Aberdeen goalkeeper in a competitive fixture. Poor Berwick had suffered enough.

3:1 A RANGERS — 3/9 — 2 L 0-1 — 30,000
McAdam 1
Ref: K Hope
Team: Leighton · Kennedy · McMaster · Watson · McLeish · Miller · Strachan* · Cowan · McGhee · Jarvie* · Scanlon
Subs: McCloy · Jardine · Miller · Forsyth · Jackson · Bett · MacDonald* · McMaster* · Redford · Cooper · Hewitt/Bell · Stevens/Johnston!
Rangers' Willie Johnston is sent off for the 13th time in his career, just 12 minutes after coming on as a substitute, for a horrendous stamping foul on John McMaster. Altogether, eight players are booked. The goal, incidentally, was a McAdam header after just 45 seconds.

3:2 H RANGERS — 24/9 — 2 W 3-1 — 23,926 · 1
McMaster 5, Strachan 29p, 90p, McAdam 47
Ref: G Smith
(Dons win 3-2 on aggregate)
Team: Leighton · Kennedy · McMaster · Watson · McLeish · Miller · Strachan · McMaster* · McGhee · Bell* · Scanlon
Subs: McCloy · Jardine · Miller · Forsyth · Jackson · Bett · Cooper* · Johnstone · McAdam · Redford · Johnston* · Hewitt
McMaster levels the tie from 25 yards. Strachan puts the Dons ahead from the spot after Jardine involuntarily handled. McAdam burst through to level. Jim Bett hit the Aberdeen bar, and in injury time Colin Jackson toppled Hewitt. Referee and linesman conferred and said penalty.

QF A DUNDEE — 8/10 — 2 D 0-0 — 10,500 · 1:12
Ref: B McGinlay
Team: Leighton · Kennedy · Geddes · Rougvie · Watson · McLeish · Miller · Strachan · Jarvie* · McGhee · Scanlon
Subs: Barr · Williamson · Fraser · Glennie · McLaren · Mackie · McGeachie · Sinclair · Fleming* · Shira · Considine/Cowan · Murphy
The last time Aberdeen played a League Cup match at Dens Park was in the Final 10 months earlier. They are probably satisfied with this first-leg result, but not with their profligate finishing. Dundee haven't started the season very well, though promotion will be gained at the end.

SCOTTISH PREMIER (CUP-TIES) Manager: Alex Ferguson SEASON 1980-81

Bell's League Cup

		F-A	H-T	Scorers, Times, and Referees	1	2	3	4	5	6	7	8	9	10	11	subs used
QF H DUNDEE 29/10	2 L	0-1	0-0	14,060 7	Leighton	Kennedy*	Rougvie	Bell	McLeish	Miller	Strachan	Cowan	McGhee	Jarvie	Scanlon	Watson
				Fraser 85 *Ref: T Muirhead* *(Dons lost 0-1 on aggregate)*	*Geddes*	*Barr*	*Schaedler Fraser*	*Ford*	*Glennie*	*McLaren*	*Murphy*	*McGeachie Sinclair*	*Sinclair*	*Mackie**	*Williamson Fletcher*	

Dundee's defence remains intact for the sixth time in this competition. Aberdeen are harried into mistakes, and are stunned when Cammy Fraser - a newcomer from Hearts - pounces on Rougvie's headed clearance to score off the post. This takes the wind out of Aberdeen's sails.

Scottish Cup

		F-A	H-T	Scorers, Times, and Referees	1	2	3	4	5	6	7	8	9	10	11	subs used
3 A RAITH ROVERS 24/1	1 W 2-1	1-0		10,000	Leighton	Rougvie	Considine	Watson	McLeish	Cooper	Bell	McCall	McGhee	Jarvie	Hewitt*	Scanlon
				Jarvie 10, 68 *Harris 62* *Ref: R Valentine*	*McDermott*	*McDonough Candlish*	*Ford*	*Forsyth*	*Steele*	*Lawson*	*Urquhart*	*Harris*	*Steen*	*Mitchell*		

Raith have lost just once in 13 games in Division 1, and lie second behind Hibernian. They therefore present a stern test to the Dons, who have cause to be thankful to veteran Drew Jarvie. One goal with his head, another with his foot, eventually sees Aberdeen through to Round 4.

		F-A	H-T	Scorers, Times, and Referees	1	2	3	4	5	6	7	8	9	10	11	subs used
4 A MORTON 14/2	2 L 0-1	0-1		8,350	Leighton	Kennedy	Considine	Watson	McLeish	Miller	Bell*	McCall*	McGhee	Harrow	Angus	Davidson/Hamilton
				Ritchie 21 *Ref: H Alexander*	*Baines*	*Hayes*	*Holmes*	*Rooney*	*McLaughlin*	*Orr*	*Busby*	*Marr*	*Thomson*	*McNeil*	*Ritchie**	*Houston*

Morton's second 1-0 win over Aberdeen in a week and their third in two months. This cap-tie is settled by a sensational goal from Andy Ritchie, who tied up several defenders in knots before scoring. It will prove to be Aberdeen's last defeat in the Scottish Cup until April 1985.

European Champions' Cup

		F-A	H-T	Scorers, Times, and Referees	1	2	3	4	5	6	7	8	9	10	11	subs used
1:1 H AUSTRIA MEMPHIS (Austria) 17/9	1 W 1-0	1-0		20,000	Leighton	Kennedy	Rougvie	Watson*	McLeish	Miller	Strachan	McMaster	McGhee	Jarvie	Scanlon*	Bell/Hewitt
				McGhee 31 *Ref: R Nyhus (Norway)*	*Koncilia*	*Sara R*	*Obermayer*	*Pospischil*	*Baumeister*	*Sara J*	*Dihanich*	*Daxbacher*	*Furst**	*Gasselich*	*Schachner* Zore/Borgan	

Miller leads the Dons into the European Cup for the first time. By half-time they have a McGhee goal to their credit, but should have been a couple of goals behind. Chief culprit of the star-studded Austrians is Walter Schachner. The visitors forgot about attacking in the second half.

		F-A	H-T	Scorers, Times, and Referees	1	2	3	4	5	6	7	8	9	10	11	subs used
1:2 A AUSTRIA MEMPHIS 1/10	2 D 0-0	0-0		37,000	Leighton	Kennedy	Rougvie	Watson	Garner	Miller	Strachan	McMaster	McGhee	Bell	Scanlon	Pfeiler/Borgan
				(Dons win 1-0 on aggregate) *Ref: E Azim-Zaide (Soviet Union)*	*Koncilia*	*Sara R*	*Obermayer**	*Zore**	*Baumeister*	*Sara J*	*Dihanich*	*Daxbacher*	*Furst*	*Gasselich*	*Schachner*	

No wonder Alex Ferguson is proud of his players as they draw the sting from their hosts. Mark McGhee might have popped one in near the end. This is probably Aberdeen's biggest European scalp to date. When the draw is made for Round 2, Aberdeen get the shock of their lives.

		F-A	H-T	Scorers, Times, and Referees	1	2	3	4	5	6	7	8	9	10	11	subs used
2:1 H LIVERPOOL (England) 22/10	1 L 0-1	0-1		24,000	Leighton	Kennedy	Rougvie	Watson	McLeish	Miller	Strachan	McMaster*	McGhee	Jarvie*	Scanlon	Bell/Hewitt
				McDermott 5 *Ref: A Jarguz (Poland)*	*Clemence*	*Neal*	*Kennedy A Thompson*	*Thompson*	*Kennedy R*	*Hansen*	*Dalglish*	*Lee**	*Johnson*	*McDermott*	*Souness* Case	

McMaster, off the pitch receiving treatment, is unable to prevent McDermott haring into space to chip David Johnson's pass over Jim Leighton from an almost impossible angle. The Dons don't let their heads drop, but Liverpool look far too wise in the ways of European football.

		F-A	H-T	Scorers, Times, and Referees	1	2	3	4	5	6	7	8	9	10	11	subs used
2:2 A LIVERPOOL 5/11	1 L 0-4	0-2		36,182	Leighton	Dornan	Rougvie*	Watson	McLeish	Miller	Strachan	Bell*	McGhee	Jarvie	Scanlon	Cooper/Hewitt
				Miller 37 og, Neal 43, Dalglish 58, *[Hansen 70]* *Ref: A Prokop (E Germany)* *(Dons lose 0-5 on aggregate)*	*Clemence*	*Neal*	*Kennedy A* Thompson*	*Thompson*	*Kennedy R*	*Hansen*	*Dalglish*	*Lee*	*Johnson*	*McDermott*	*Souness* Cohen	

Out of the League Cup last week and out of the European Cup tonight. This second leg turned on two moments - when Mark McGhee beat two defenders but failed to beat Clemence; and when Willie Miller sliced a corner into his own net. The second half was simply embarrassing.

League Table

		Home					Away					
	P	W	D	L	F	A	W	D	L	F	A	Pts
1 Celtic	36	12	3	3	47	18	14	1	3	37	19	56
2 ABERDEEN	36	11	4	3	39	16	8	7	3	22	10	49
3 Rangers	36	12	3	3	33	10	4	9	5	22	27	44
4 St Mirren	36	9	6	3	28	20	9	2	7	28	27	44
5 Dundee Utd	36	8	5	5	34	24	9	4	5	32	18	43
6 Partick This	36	6	6	6	17	17	4	4	10	15	31	30
7 Airdrie	36	6	5	7	19	25	4	4	10	17	30	29
8 Morton	36	7	2	9	24	28	3	6	9	12	30	28
9 Kilmarnock	36	3	5	10	14	31	2	4	12	9	34	19
10 Hearts	36	3	4	11	10	27	3	2	13	17	44	18
	360	77	43	60	265	216	60	43	77	216	265	360

Cup Record

	P	W	D	L	F	A	Pts	Cup	W	D	L
v Hearts	4	4	0	0	8	1	8				
v Airdrie	4	3	1	0	11	3	7				
v Partick This	4	3	1	0	7	3	7				
v Celtic	4	2	2	0	9	4	6				
v Dundee Utd	4	1	3	1	5	3	5				
v St Mirren	4	2	1	1	6	5	5				
v Morton	4	2	0	2	9	3	4	SC	0	0	0
v Rangers	4	1	2	1	3	2	4	LC	1	0	1
v Kilmarnock	4	1	1	2	3	4	3				
	36	19	11	6	61	26	49				

Appearances and Goals

	Appearances								Goals				
	Lge	Sub	LC	Sub	SC	Sub	Eur	Sub	Lge	LC	SC	Eur	Tot
Angus, Ian	15	4	4	2	1				1				1
Bell, Dougie	13	4	4	2	2	2	2		2	1	1		2
de Clerck, Mark	1		1								1		1
Considine, Doug	8	4	1	2									
Cooper, Neale	4	2	2	1			1						
Cowan, Steve	3	2	2	2					1				1
Davidson, Duncan		4			1								
Dornan, Andy	2												
Garner, Willie	2		1		1					1			1
Hamilton, Derek	5	3	1		1				1				1
Harper, Joe	7	3	1				1		1				1
Harrow, Andy	9	12	1	2	1			3	2	1			3
Hewitt, John	16	7	4	1	1			3	5	2	1	2	9
Jarvie, Drew	31	6	6	1	1			3	10		1		1
Kennedy, Stuart	35	5	5		2			3					
Leighton, Jim	15	4			2			4					
McCall, Walker													10
McGhee, Mark	36	5	5		2			4	13		3	1	17
McLeish, Alex	32	5	5		2			3	3				3
McMaster, John	10	4	4	1				3	2		1		3
Miller, Willie	33	6	6	1	1			4	2				2
Morrison		1											
Rougvie, Doug	25	3	5	1	1	1		4	3				3
Scanlon, Ian	32	2	5			1		4	6				6
Simpson, Neil	15	1		1					2				2
Strachan, Gordon	20		6					4	6		3		9
Watson, Andy	26	4	4	1	2			4			2		2
(own-goals)									2				2
27 players used	396	59	66	9	22	3	44	6	61	15	2	1	79

Odds & ends

Never lost to: (5) Hearts, Airdrie, Partick, Celtic, Dundee Utd.

Never beat: (0).

Won from behind: (3) St Mirren (h), Dundee Utd (a), Partick (h).

Lost from in front: (0).

High spots: Undefeated in first 15 league games, establishing new record of 30 unbeaten league games.

7 successive league wins in October and November.

Top of the league until February.

Never losing to champions Celtic.

Never conceding more than one goal away from home in domestic competition.

Low spots: 1 point from four games from 31 January.

Home defeat by Division 1 Dundee in Scottish Cup.

Humiliation by Liverpool in European Cup.

Bogey-team: Morton - who beat the Dons three times in all.

Ever-presents: (1) Mark McGhee (league only).

Hat-tricks: (2) Mark McGhee 1, Walker McCall 1.

Leading scorer: (17) Mark McGhee.

SCOTTISH PREMIER DIVISION   Manager: Alex Ferguson   SEASON 1981-82

No			Date	Att	Pos	Pt		F-A	H-T	Scorers, Times, and Referees
1	A	DUNDEE UTD	29/8	10,598	–	–	L	1-4	0-3	McLeish 49 [Bannon 60p] / Sturrock 8, Holt 10, Pettigrew 33 — Ref: D Ramsay
2	H	CELTIC	5/9	18,825	10	1	L	1-3	1-2	Strachan 2p / Burns 8, McGarvey 26, 55 — Ref: B McGinlay
3	A	PARTICK THISTLE	12/9	3,606	8	2	W	2-0	0-0	McCall 71, Cowan 88 — Ref: A Waddell
4	H	HIBERNIAN	19/9	10,852	8	4	W	1-0	0-0	Simpson 85 — Ref: T Muirhead
5	A	AIRDRIE	26/9	3,000	3	6	W	4-0	3-0	McLeish 26, Weir 39, 58, Hewitt 41 — Ref: D Galloway
6	H	MORTON	3/10	11,007	2	8	W	2-0	0-0	Watson 69, Rougvie 77 — Ref: K Hope
7	A	RANGERS	10/10	28,000	2	9	D	0-0	0-0	Ref: J Renton
8	A	ST MIRREN	17/10	6,870	2	11	W	2-1	1-1	Watson 17, 57 / McAvennie 32 — Ref: A Ferguson
9	H	DUNDEE	24/10	11,506	2	13	W	2-1	2-0	McCall 40, Rougvie 41 / Stephen 76 — Ref: B Robertson
10	H	DUNDEE UTD	31/10	11,035	2	14	D	1-1	1-0	Black 9 / Milne 56 — Ref: G Smith
11	A	CELTIC	7/11	29,326	2	14	L	1-2	0-1	Strachan 90 / McGarvey 40, McCluskey 72 — Ref: D Ramsay

Match details

1. Dundee Utd (A) 1-4 — Positions 1-11 / subs used
Aberdeen: Leighton, McAlpine*, Rougvie*, Cooper, Kennedy, Miller, Strachan, Bell*, McGhee, Hewitt, Weir — subs Watson / Jarvie
Opponents: Stark, Bannon, Kirkwood, Pettigrew*, Sturrock, Dodds — sub Milne
Scotland manager Jock Stein takes in this entertaining match, which sees United on top of their game. Aberdeen's defence could not come to grips with Paul Sturrock's trickery. No other team will score four goals past Jim Leighton this season, and this will stand as the heaviest defeat.

2. Celtic (H) 1-3
Aberdeen: Leighton, Cooper, Watson, McLeish, Miller, Strachan, Bell*, McGhee*, McCall, Hewitt — subs McMaster / Cowan
Opponents: Bonner, McGrain, Reid, Aitken, McAdam, MacLeod, Provan, Sullivan, Burns, McCluskey
Penalty for Aberdeen as McAdam crashes into Walker McCall. Gordon Strachan nets, but is then assaulted by a Celtic fan who rushes onto the pitch. Police arrived just in time. Thereafter Celtic turn on the style. Not since 1959-60 have the Dons lost their first two league games.

3. Partick Thistle (A) 2-0
Aberdeen: Leighton, Watson, Rougvie, Cooper, McLeish, Miller*, Strachan, Cooper, McCall, McMaster, Hewitt — subs Simpson / Cowan
Opponents: Rough, Doyle, Lapsley, Kay, Dunlop, Miller*, Park, Higgins, Sweeney, McDonald, Clark
Neither team has a point to their name, so this is a battle to claim bottom spot. Partick win that battle, though it took a while to be settled. The chief difference between the sides is the aerial power of Walker McCall and Steve Cowan. Partick go on to lose their first five matches.

4. Hibernian (H) 1-0
Aberdeen: Leighton, Kennedy, Rougvie, Flavell*, McLeish, Miller, Strachan, Watson*, McGhee, Hewitt*, Weir — subs Simpson / McCall, Schaedler
Opponents: McArthur, Sneddon, Flavell*, McNamara, Paterson, McLaren, Callachan, Rae, MacLeod, Duncan, Murray
The crowd were growing restive, but they eventually leave contented, thanks to Neil Simpson's crisp goal, which sends Hibs to their first defeat. Celtic have a 100 per cent record at the top of league, so the Dons cannot afford any more dropped points. They stay four points behind.

5. Airdrie (A) 4-0
Aberdeen: Leighton, Rougvie, Watson, McLeish, Miller, Strachan, Cooper, McGhee*, Hewitt*, Weir — subs Cowan / Flood, Thompson
Opponents: Martin, Erwin, Rodger, Walker, March, McCluskey, McKeown*, Campbell, McGuire, Gordon, Anderson
Torrential rain cannot dampen Aberdeen's spirits has they give Airdrie a good hiding, and put themselves in the right mind for the UEFA Cup visit of Bobby Robson's Ipswich Town. Alex McLeish's header, Weir's volley, and Hewitt's thunderbolt settled the issue before half-time.

6. Morton (H) 2-0
Aberdeen: Leighton, Hayes, Watson, McLeish*, Miller, Strachan, Simpson, Cochrane, McCall, Cowan*, Weir — subs Cooper / McGhee, McNeil, McNab
Opponents: Baines, Holmes, Rooney, McLaughlin, Orr, Houston, Busby*, Hutchison, McNeil
Every one of Morton's matches so far has been goalless at half-time. This game is no exception. As so often in the recent past, Morton did not appear to have any desire to score. The difference is that this time they didn't. This will be the Dons' only success against Morton this season.

7. Rangers (A) 0-0
Aberdeen: Leighton, Rougvie, Watson, Cooper, Forsyth, Bett, Strachan, Simpson*, McCall, Hewitt*, Weir — subs McMaster / McGhee, Harrow, Redford
Opponents: Stewart, Jardine, Dawson, Stevens, Russell, McAdam, McDonald, Johnston*
No skill on show at Ibrox. Just muscle, and five bookings. There should have been more, too. On the hour Jim Leighton saved a John McDonald penalty, given away by Willie Miller. Leighton has now gone seven league and League Cup matches without conceding a goal.

8. St Mirren (A) 2-1
Aberdeen: Leighton, Rougvie, Watson, McCormack, Miller, Strachan, Simpson*, McGhee, Hewitt, Weir — subs McMaster / Abercrombie, Scanlon, Logan
Opponents: Thomson, Young, Beckett, Fulton*, Cooland, McAvennie, Stark, Bone
Andy Watson sets things moving with a long-range shot past keeper Thomson. The combination of Billy Stark and Frank McAvennie brings St Mirren's equaliser. Substitute John McMaster's slide-rule pass sets up Watson's winner. Aberdeen will overcome St Mirren again and again.

9. Dundee (H) 2-1
Aberdeen: Leighton, Simpson, Cooper, Glennie, Miller, Strachan, Bell*, McGhee, Cowan*, McCall, Weir — subs Watson / Stephen
Opponents: Geddes, Barr, Cameron, Kidd*, McDonald, Ferguson, Mackie, McGeachie, Murphy
This is Dundee's fifth successive defeat, following a 2-3 reverse against Rangers. They may be dunces, but they made Aberdeen sweat after Ray Stephen connected with Murphy's corner. Leaders Celtic lost at Easter Road, and have now dropped three points in their last two games.

10. Dundee Utd (H) 1-1
Aberdeen: Leighton, Rougvie, McMaster, Cooper, Miller, Strachan, Black, McGhee, Black*, Simpson, Weir — subs Watson / Gough
Opponents: Graham, Holt, Murray, Phillip*, Hegarty, Narey, Bannon, Milne, Kirkwood, Sturrock, Dodds
Three days earlier Jim McLean's men won 3-0 at Pittodrie to end the Dons' interest in the League Cup. In the league, it's a different tale. United have won just twice all season. Ferguson introduces another kid, 17-year-old Eric Black, who climbs highest to meet Strachan's corner.

11. Celtic (A) 1-2
Aberdeen: Leighton, Cooper, Watson*, McLeish, Miller, Strachan, Black, McGhee, Black*, Simpson, Weir — subs Watson / Hewitt, McMaster, Conroy
Opponents: Bonner, Moyes, Reid, Aitken, McAdam, MacLeod, Provan, Sullivan, McGarvey, Burns*, McCluskey
Celtic were the last team to beat the Dons in the league, over two months earlier. Aberdeen put on a good show, but McGarvey's exquisite lob puts Celtic ahead. McCluskey exploits Neale Cooper's poor clearance to double the lead. This result widens Celtic's lead to three points.

Aberdeen season log — matches 12–23

12. H PARTICK THISTLE — 14/11
Aberdeen pos 2 · W 2-1 · Pts 16 · Att 11,193 · Opp pos 9 · HT 1-0
Scorers: Harrow 10, Watson 84 / Clark 60 — Ref: D Galloway

Aberdeen: Leighton, Kennedy, McMaster, Cooper, McLeish*, Miller, Strachan, Black*, Harrow, Simpson, Weir, Watson/McGhee
Partick Thistle: Rough, Murray, Lapsley, Dunlop, Whittaker, Watson, Park, McDonald, Johnston*, Doyle, Clark, O'Hara

Two recent wins, including one over Rangers, have lifted Thistle off the bottom. They look set for another point here, and may have got it but for Andy Watson. The Dons substitute flashed home a late header from Mark McGhee's cross. Thistle won't win again till February.

13. A HIBERNIAN — 21/11
Aberdeen pos 2 · D 1-1 · Pts 17 · Att 7,600 · Opp pos 6 · HT 0-1
Scorers: Simpson 63 / Callachan 27 — Ref: T Timmons

Aberdeen: Leighton, Kennedy, McMaster, Cooper*, McLeish, Miller, Strachan, McCall*, McGhee, Simpson, Weir, Cowan/Harrow
Hibernian: McArthur, Sneddon, Schaedler, Brazil, Paterson, Duncan, Callachan, Rae, MacLeod*, Rodier*, Flavell, McLaren/Murray

Several representatives from SV Hamburg make notes on their future UEFA Cup opponents. For a long time it looks like they will be reporting on an Aberdeen defeat, but Simpson saves the day during a hectic goalmouth scramble. This will be Hibs' only point off Aberdeen this season.

14. H AIRDRIE — 28/11
Aberdeen pos 2 · D 0-0 · Pts 18 · Att 8,030 · Opp pos 8 · HT 0-0
Ref: C White

Aberdeen: Leighton, Kennedy, McMaster, Cooper, McLeish, Miller, Strachan, Bell, McGhee, Harrow*, Weir, Simpson/Black
Airdrie: Martin, Erwin*, Rodger, Walker, March, McCluskey, McGuire, Clark, Anderson, Gordon, Frood, McKeown

Airdrie have the worst defensive record in the Premier League. They lost 0-4 to Dundee United in their last match and have yet to keep a league clean sheet. They did manage a 0-0 against Aberdeen in the League Cup, and repeat the score. Sandy Clark even hit Leighton's post.

15. A MORTON — 5/12
Aberdeen pos 4 · L 1-2 · Pts 18 · Att 3,102 · Opp pos 6 · HT 0-0
Scorers: Hewitt 64 / McNeil 58, Houston 72 — Ref: D Syme

Aberdeen: Leighton, Kennedy, McMaster*, Watson, McLeish, Miller, Strachan, Black, McGhee*, Simpson, Weir, Cooper/Hewitt
Morton: Baines, Hayes, Holmes, Rooney, McLaughlin, Orr, McNeil, Docherty, Busby, Hutchison, Houston

Morton are back to their old tricks. Aberdeen have won just once in their last six visits to Cappielow. The Dons might have been 2-1 up, but then Willie Miller attempted a back-pass which fell short. Eric Black headed against Morton's crossbar.

16. H CELTIC — 30/1
Aberdeen pos 6 · L 1-3 · Pts 18 · Att 20,000 · Opp pos 1 · HT 1-1
Scorers: McMaster 2 / McCluskey 28p, McLeod 71, McGarvey 76 — Ref: R Valentine

Aberdeen: Leighton, Kennedy, McMaster, Reid?, McLeish, Miller, Strachan, Bell, McGhee*, Hewitt, Weir, Black
Celtic: Bonner, McGrain, Reid, Aitken, McAdam, MacLeod, Sullivan, McStay, McGarvey, Burns

Bad weather means this is the Dons' first league match for nearly two months. Celtic have now taken six points out of six from Aberdeen, and stretch their lead over them to nine points. The Dons drop to sixth despite the wonderful start given them by McMaster's left-footed drive.

17. A PARTICK THISTLE — 3/2
Aberdeen pos 6 · D 0-0 · Pts 19 · Att 2,317 · Opp pos 10 · HT 0-0
Ref: R Cuthill

Aberdeen: Leighton, Kennedy, Rougvie, Anderson?, McLeish, Miller, Strachan, Bell*, Hewitt, Doyle?, Weir, Black
Partick Thistle: Rough, McKinnon, Whittaker, Anderson, Dunlop, Watson, McDonald, Jardine, Higgins, Doyle, Clark, Park/Johnston

The nearest that Aberdeen came to a goal was John Hewitt's header that came back off Alan Rough's crossbar. Maurice Johnston, later to sign for Watford, brought a full-length save from Jim Leighton. This is the only match between these sides that Aberdeen fail to win this season.

18. H MORTON — 6/2
Aberdeen pos 6 · D 0-0 · Pts 20 · Att 7,217 · Opp pos 7 · HT 0-0
Ref: E Pringle

Aberdeen: Leighton, Kennedy, Rougvie, Watson, McLeish, Miller, Strachan, Bell*, Hewitt, Simpson, Weir, McMaster/Harrow
Morton: Baines, Hayes, Holmes, Rooney, McLaughlin, Duffy, Houston, Docherty, Slavin, Doyle, Ritchie

Poor form and wretched weather means it is now three months since Aberdeen last won a league match. Morton have won just one of their last 10, but are not in charitable mood. Are they ever? Their main problem is they have no one to score goals. No player will exceed six all season.

19. A AIRDRIE — 20/2
Aberdeen pos 4 · W 3-0 · Pts 22 · Att 3,500 · Opp pos 9 · HT 0-0
Scorers: Hewitt 47, McGhee 74, 75 — Ref: B Robertson

Aberdeen: Leighton, Kennedy, Rougvie, McMaster, McLeish, Miller, Strachan, Simpson, McGhee, Hewitt, Weir, Cooper/Cowan
Airdrie: Martin, McCluskey, Rodger, Campbell, Anderson G, Anderson N/McKeown, Clark, Kidd, McDonagh, Gordon, Flood*, McGuire

Believe it or not, these are the first league goals Mark McGhee has scored all season. His two-in-a-minute confirms Aberdeen's first away win since 17 October. Airdrie look dispirited and will shortly embark on a 12-game losing streak.

20. H DUNDEE — 27/2
Aberdeen pos 4 · D 0-0 · Pts 23 · Att 8,961 · Opp pos 10 · HT 0-0
Ref: A Waddell

Aberdeen: Leighton, Kennedy, McMaster, Bell*, McLeish, Miller, Strachan, Simpson, McGhee, Jarvie, Weir, Cooper/Cowan
Dundee: Geddes, McKimmie, McLelland, Fraser, Smith, Glennie, Ferguson, Kidd, Fleming, McGeachie*, Mackie, Stephen/Cameron

Dundee are propping up the league, and travel north with five straight defeats to their name. More frustration for the Dons, who have won one of their last eight games and who watch Celtic disappearing over the horizon. Now begins Aberdeen's incredible sprint to the finishing line.

21. H HIBERNIAN — 10/3
W 3-1 · Pts 25 · Att 8,691 · HT 1-1
Scorers: Cooper 1, Strachan 48p, Jarvie 83 / Rae 28 — Ref: K Hope

Aberdeen: Leighton, Kennedy, Hamilton*, McMaster, McLeish, Miller, Strachan, Cooper, McGhee, Simpson*, Weir, Watson/Jarvie
Hibernian: McArthur, Sneddon, Duncan, McLaren, Paterson, McNamara, Callachan, Murray, MacLeod, Rae, Flavell

Following Neale Cooper's cracking goal after 35 seconds, Hibs find themselves under such pressure that they pass the ball back to goalkeeper McArthur no fewer than 14 times in the first half. Gordon Rae scores for the fourth successive match, and does so in his next game too.

22. A RANGERS — 13/3
Aberdeen pos 3 · W 3-1 · Pts 27 · Att 20,000 · Opp pos 2 · HT 2-0
Scorers: Cowan 9, Cooper 34, Watson 83 / Johnstone 63 — Ref: H Alexander

Aberdeen: Leighton, Kennedy, Rougvie, McMaster*, McLeish, Miller, Strachan, Simpson, McGhee, Cowan, Weir, Cooper
Rangers: Stewart, Jardine, Dawson, Jackson, Bett, Cooper, Russell, Johnstone, Redford, Miller*, Radford, McDonald

Rangers have lost only one of their last 11 games. Man-of-the-match Jim Leighton saved Aberdeen by keeping out Jim Bett's penalty when the Dons led 1-0. Steve Cowan's volley and Neale Cooper's header seal Aberdeen's victory. This is the start of a run of Dons wins over Rangers.

23. A DUNDEE — 17/3
Aberdeen pos 2 · W 3-0 · Pts 29 · Att 6,126 · HT 1-0
Scorers: Simpson 13, Hewitt 53, Cowan 73 — Ref: D Syme

Aberdeen: Leighton, Kennedy, Rougvie, Watson, McLeish, Miller, Strachan, Simpson, McGhee, McMaster, Weir, Cooper
Dundee: Geddes, Cameron, McLelland, Fraser, Smith, Glennie, Mackie, Kidd, Fleming, McGeachie*, Hewitt, Cowan/Murphy/Sinclair

Dundee have just won their first game in eight. It is not often that Willie Miller is unable to carry on after injury. But he is led off the pitch after a crushing tackle by Bobby Glennie. But by then, the Dons are coasting to their third victory in three games, scoring three goals in each.

SCOTTISH PREMIER DIVISION

Manager: Alex Ferguson

SEASON 1981-82

No	Date	Att	Pos	Pt	F-A	H-T	Scorers, Times, and Referees	1	2	3	4	5	6	7	8	9	10	11	subs used
24	H DUNDEE UTD 20/3	12,056	6	W 31	2-1	1-0	Hewitt 43, McLeish 74; Dodds 47; Ref: K Hope	Leighton	Kennedy	Rougvie	Watson*	McLeish	Miller	Strachan	Cooper	McGhee	Simpson	Hewitt*	McMaster/Cowan
								McAlpine	*Holt*	*Stark*	*Gough*	*Hegarty*	*Narey*	*Bannon*	*Gibson*	*Kirkwood*	*Sturrock*	*Dodds*	*Reilly/Malpas*
25	A CELTIC 27/3	30,080	1	W 33	1-0	0-0	Kennedy 69; Ref: D Ramsay	Leighton	Kennedy	Rougvie*	Simpson	McLeish	Miller	Strachan	Cooper	McGhee	Hewitt*	Weir	Cowan/McMaster
								Bonner	*McGrain*	*Reid**	*Aitken*	*McAdam*	*MacLeod*	*Craine*	*Sullivan*	*McGarvey*	*McCluskey*	*Burns*	*Moyes*
26	A HIBERNIAN 10/4	8,000	6	W 35	3-0	1-0	Jarvie 7, Strachan 61, McGhee 85; Ref: W McLeish	Leighton	Mitchell	Rougvie	McMaster*	McLeish	Miller	Strachan	Watson	McGhee	Jarvie*	Weir	Simpson/Black
								McArthur	*Sneddon*	*Flavell*	*McNamara**	*Paterson*	*Brazil*	*McLaren*	*Jamieson*	*MacLeod*	*Rae*	*Duncan*	*Schaedler/Rodier*
27	H ST MIRREN 14/4	12,119	5	W 37	4-1	0-0	Rougvie 62, 85, Strachan 72, Simpson 77; Stark 49; Ref: B McGinlay	Leighton	Rougvie	McMaster	Watson*	McLeish	Miller	Strachan	Simpson	McGhee	Cowan*	Weir	Cooper/Jarvie
								Money	*Walker*	*Fulton*	*Fitzpatrick*	*Copland*	*Abercrombie*	*Stark*	*Curran**	*McEachran*	*McAvennie*	*Scanlon**	*Bone/Logan*
28	A MORTON 17/4	3,000	7	L 37	1-2	0-1	McGhee 81; McNeil 4, Rooney 90; Ref: B McGinlay	Leighton	Kennedy	Rougvie	Cooper	McLeish	Miller	Jarvie*	Watson*	McGhee	Hewitt	Weir	Simpson/McMaster
								Baines	*Hayes*	*Holmes*	*Rooney*	*McLaughlin*	*Duffy*	*McNeil*	*Docherty**	*Cochrane*	*Hutchison*	*Ritchie**	*Slaven/Busby*
29	H RANGERS 21/4	15,700	3	W 39	3-1	2-0	McGhee 7, Rougvie 34, Black 56; Johnstone 69; Ref: E Pringle	Leighton	Kennedy	Rougvie	Cooper*	McLeish	Miller	Black	Simpson	McGhee*	Bell	Weir	McMaster/Jarvie
								Stewart	*Dawson*	*Black*	*Jardine*	*McLelland*	*Bett*	*Dalziel*	*Russell*	*Johnstone*	*McDonald*	*Lyall**	*McAdam*
30	H AIRDRIE 24/4	8,000	10	W 41	2-0	0-0	McGhee 55, Black 73; Ref: A Waddell	Leighton	Kennedy	Rougvie	McMaster	McLeish	Miller	Black	Simpson	McGhee*	Bell*	Weir	Jarvie/Watson
								Martin	*Cairney*	*Rodger*	*Anderson*	*March*	*Gordon*	*Walker*	*Clark*	*Campbell**	*Flood*	*McKeown*	*Erwin*
31	A DUNDEE 1/5	6,415	8	W 43	5-0	2-0	McLeish 21, Harrow 27, Glennie 48 og, [Bell 51, McCall 59]; Ref: E Pringle	Leighton	Kennedy	Rougvie	McMaster	McLeish	Miller	Black*	Simpson	Harrow	Bell	Weir	Watson/McCall
								Geddes	*Barr*	*McKimmie*	*Fraser*	*Smith*	*Glennie*	*Ferguson**	*Stephen*	*Sinclair*	*Kidd*	*McGeachie*	*Markie*
32	H PARTICK THISTLE 3/5	6,000	9	W 45	3-1	2-1	McCall 16, Watson 31, Hewitt 88; Doyle 39; Ref: D Downie	Leighton	Kennedy	Rougvie	Watson	McLeish	Miller	Black	Bell	McCall*	Angus	Weir*	Cooper/Hewitt
								Rough	*Murray*	*Lapsley*	*Whittaker*	*Dunlop*	*Watson**	*Park*	*Jardine*	*Johnston*	*Doyle*	*O'Hara*	*McDonald**/McDowell*
33	A DUNDEE UTD 5/5	6,587	4	W 47	2-1	2-1	Hewitt 15, 37; Hegarty 43; Ref: E Pringle	Leighton	Kennedy	Rougvie	McMaster	McLeish	Miller	Strachan*	Cooper	McGhee	Simpson*	Hewitt	Cooper/Watson
								McAlpine	*Holt*	*Stark**	*Gough*	*Hegarty*	*Narey*	*Bannon*	*Milne*	*Kirkwood**	*Sturrock*	*Dodds*	*Malpas/Reilly*
34	H ST MIRREN 8/5	9,000	5	W 49	5-1	3-1	Strachan 6, 24, McGhee 12, 76, Cooper 59; Speirs 38; Ref: J Duncan	Leighton	Kennedy	Rougvie	McMaster	McLeish*	Miller	Strachan	Simpson	McGhee	Simpson	Weir	Bell
								Thomson	*Stark*	*Beckett*	*Fitzpatrick*	*Fulton*	*Copland*	*McDougall**	*Richardson**	*Sommer*	*McAvennie*	*Speirs*	*Logan/Bone*

24 — United scored five goals last time out (against Partick) and score five next time too (versus Morton). Against Aberdeen they are not so prolific. Stuart Kennedy's marauding run down the right touchline culminates with a perfect cross and a perfect header from Alex McLeish.

25 — At start of play Celtic are six points ahead of Aberdeen. The league needed this result to keep the championship race open. Stuart Kennedy's lob from the touchline sailed over Pat Bonner's head. Near the end Celtic wasted a penalty when Miller tackled McCluskey, who shot wide.

26 — Drew Jarvie does not play too often these days. In this match he heads in Peter Weir's corner for the first goal. Gordon Strachan collected a return pass from Mark McGhee for a superb second. Hibs have taken five points out of six off Celtic, but only one from eight off Aberdeen.

27 — It is not often that Doug Rougvie scores - let alone scores two. But it's his long leg that equalises for Aberdeen in a goalmouth scramble, and his head adds another. Goal of the match was Neil Simpson's thunderbolt. Billy Stark has been scoring goals against Aberdeen for many years.

28 — Seven wins on the trot for the Dons. Morton have just won their first game in eight. They end the Dons' long unbeaten run, just as they did last season. This time the match is into injury time when the ball rebounds off the referee into the path of Rooney - his third goal of the season.

29 — Rangers have gone 20 games at Pittodrie since their last win, back in December 1974, before the Premier League was set up. Keeper Stewart could not quite keep out McGhee's opener. Stewart then failed to gather Eric Black's cross for the second, or Black's volley for the third.

30 — The talk is that Airdrie striker Sandy Clark is heading to Pittodrie. He never does transfer to Aberdeen - ending up at West Ham - and his glaring misses in this match is one reason Ferguson's interest cooled. This is Airdrie's 12th straight defeat, a run that ends in their next game.

31 — Aberdeen's highest score of the season - and Dundee's heaviest defeat - does the relegation-threatened Taysiders no favours. Dundee keeper Bobby Geddes made a present of the first three goals, all of which came from corners. Aberdeen have won 10 of their last 11 league games.

32 — Thistle look resigned to the drop. Pittodrie lowest league crowd of the season seems resigned to the championship heading for Parkhead. Today, however, Celtic draw 0-0 at home to St Mirren. The Dons need to win all their remaining fixtures to equal Celtic's current 53 points.

33 — Three games in five days, and you would never believe it was the end of the season as Aberdeen continue to pick up steam. United have not won in five and the season cannot end quickly enough. Two-goal hero John Hewitt will fail by one goal to be the Dons' top scorer overall.

34 — Celtic are still not quite home and dry. They lose 0-3 at Tannadice today. Aberdeen can only become champions is they secure big wins in their last two matches while Celtic lose at home in their last game - also against St Mirren. St Mirren look so poor that seems unlikely.

35 A ST MIRREN 12/5 — 2 W 2-0 (5) 51 — 3,942

Scorers: McLeish 34, Rougvie 61
Ref: M Delaney

Aberdeen	Leighton	Kennedy	Rougvie	McMaster*	McLeish	Miller	Strachan*	Cooper	McGhee	Simpson	Hewitt	Bell*/Watson
St Mirren	*Thomson*	*Beckett*	*Walker*	*Fitzpatrick*	*Fulton*	*Copland*	*McEachran**	*Stark*	*Bone*	*McAvennie*	*Richardson*	*Logan*

Aberdeen certainly have the Indian sign over St Mirren. The Dons' tall defenders, McLeish and Rougvie, move upfield to score with headers. 12 days earlier they drew there 0-0. The Dons now have to hope that these same feeble opponents can somehow overturn Celtic at Parkhead.

36 H RANGERS 15/5 — 2 W 4-0 (3) 53 — 18,000

Scorers: Jackson 23 og, Hewitt 28, 39, 43
Ref: R Valentine

Aberdeen	Leighton	Kennedy	Rougvie	Cooper	McLeish	Miller	Strachan*	Simpson	McGhee	Simpson	Hewitt	Weir*	Watson/McLean
Rangers	*Stewart*	*Jardine**	*Dawson*	*McLelland*	*Jackson*	*Bett*	*Cooper*	*Miller*	*Dalziel*	*Redford*	*McDonald*	*Redford*	*McDonald McLean*

Aberdeen meet Rangers in next week's Scottish Cup Final, and are well served by John Hewitt's hat-trick. That's seven points out of eight this season over Rangers. Had Celtic lost 0-2 at home to St Mirren the Dons would have been crowned champions. But Celtic won 3-0.

Average Home 11,360 — Away 10,115

Scottish League Cup - Section 3

1 H KILMARNOCK 8/8 — W 3-0 (2) — 9,000

Scorers: McGhee 4, 27 Kennedy 48
Ref: D Downie

Aberdeen	Leighton	Kennedy	McMaster	Cooper	McLeish	Miller	Strachan	Harrow	McGhee	Bell	Weir
Kilmarnock	*McCulloch*	*McLean*	*Cockburn*	*Clark**	*Armstrong*	*McDicken*	*Gallagher*	*Mauchlen*	*Bourke*	*Bryce*	*McCready McBride*

Four-team round robins have been reintroduced into the League Cup. Relegated in May, Kilmarnock will come back up at the first attempt. They have little to show against the Dons. Only a goalpost denied Mark McGhee a hat-trick on the first day of the new season.

2 A HEARTS 12/8 — L 0-1 (2) — 10,500

Scorers: Robertson 65
Ref: A Ferguson

Aberdeen	Leighton	Kennedy	McMaster	Cooper	McLeish	Miller	Strachan	Bell	McGhee	McGhee* Harrow	Weir
Hearts	*Smith*	*More*	*Shields*	*Byrne*	*MacDonald RMcLaren*	*Bowman*	*Bowman*	*Robertson G Liddell*	*Robertson G Liddell*	*MacDonald AHamill*	*Hewitt/Jarvie*

Hearts were relegated alongside Kilmarnock, but instant promotion will elude them. The goal that undermines Aberdeen's chances of qualifying from Section 3 was scored by Chris Robertson, whose wheeling shot-on-the-turn beat Jim Leighton and went in off a post.

3 H AIRDRIE 15/8 — W 3-0 (4) — 7,000

Scorers: Hewitt 12, Weir 37, Strachan 89p
Ref: G Smith

Aberdeen	Leighton	Kennedy	Hamilton	Cooper	McLeish	Miller	Strachan	Harrow	McGhee	Bell*	Weir	Jarvie/Cowan
Airdrie	*Martin*	*Walker*	*Rodger*	*McCluskey March*	*Anderson N Kerr**	*Clark*	*Campbell**	*Gordon*	*Bourke*	*Flood*	*McGuire/Erwin*	*McGuire/Erwin*

Airdrie are the only other Premier League team in section 3, but they will finish bottom of both. Headers by John Hewitt and Peter Weir in the first half ended Airdrie's challenge, and set up the crunch return with Hearts.

4 H HEARTS 19/8 — W 3-0 (6) — 8,600

Scorers: Bell 35, Strachan 62p, Hewitt 72
Ref: R Valentine

Aberdeen	Leighton	Kennedy	McMaster*	Cooper*	McLeish	Miller	Strachan	Bell*	McGhee	Weir	Watson/McCall
Hearts	*Smith*	*More*	*Shields*	*Byrne**	*MacDonald RMcLaren*	*Bowman*	*Bowman*	*Robertson*	*McCoy*	*MacDonald AKamill*	*Kidd/O'Connor*

First-division Hearts could not repeat the upset of last week. Dougie Bell's long-range drive was poor reward for Aberdeen's first-half dominance. Strachan's second penalty in two games settled all doubts. Barring upsets, the quarter-finals are now within reach.

5 A KILMARNOCK 22/8 — W 3-0 (8) — 3,100

Scorers: Strachan 26p, 33, McGhee 78
Ref: M Delaney

Aberdeen	Leighton	Rougvie*	McCulloch	Watson	McLeish	Miller	Strachan	Bell*	McGhee	Weir	McMaster/Watson
Kilmarnock	*Martin*	*Cockburn*	*McLean*	*McCluskey*	*Armstrong*	*McDicken*	*Gallagher*	*Mauchlen*	*Bourke*	*Cramond**	*McCready McBride*

Coupled with Hearts' loss to Airdrie, this result takes Aberdeen through to the knock-out stages with a game to spare. Gordon Strachan's third penalty in as many matches sets things rolling. Aberdeen's final section match is rendered meaningless.

6 A AIRDRIE 26/8 — D 0-0 (9) — 3,000

Ref: E Pringle

Aberdeen	Leighton	Rougvie	Angus	Watson	McLeish	Miller	Harrow*	Bell*	McCall	McMaster	Hewitt/Jarvie
Airdrie	*Martin*	*Gordon*	*Rodger*	*McCluskey*	*Erwin*	*Kerr*	*Flood*	*Clark*	*Anderson N McGuire*	*McCall McKeown*	

Ipswich manager Bobby Robson assesses his team's future UEFA Cup opponents. Alex Ferguson shrewdly rested four first-team regulars. This result looks odd in retrospect, as Airdrie fail to keep another clean sheet for 14 matches, when their opponents are again Aberdeen.

Qual			W	D	L	F	A
ABERDEEN	9	6	4	1	1	12	1
Kilmarnock	6	6	2	2	2	5	8
Hearts	6	6	2	1	3	5	9
Airdrie	4	6	1	2	3	4	8

QF 1 H BERWICK RGS 2/9 — W 5-0 (4-0) — 6,500

Scorers: Cooper 27, Strachan 33, 43p, Bell 40, [McCall 87] McGhee, Harrow
Ref: R Valentine

Aberdeen	Leighton	Kennedy	McMaster	Cooper*	McLeish	Miller	Strachan	Bell	McGhee	Hewitt	Weir*	Jarvie/McCall
Berwick	*McDermott McCann*	*McCann*	*Black**	*McCulloch/*	*Dixon*	*Muirl*	*Davidson*	*Moyes*	*Lawson*	*Tait**	*Armstrong*	*McGlinchey/Romaines*

Berwick Rangers are in Division 2. Their cause is not helped by their indiscipline. They play the whole of the second half with 10 men - and the last 10 minutes with nine - following expulsions for McCulloch and Muir. Strachan has so far netted four penalties in this competition.

QF 2 A BERWICK RGS 23/9 — W 3-0 (2-0) — 1,200 2:2

Scorers: McMaster 21, McGhee 38, Harrow 87
Ref: T Muirhead
(Dons win 8-0 on aggregate)

Aberdeen	Leighton	Rougvie	Angus	Watson	McLeish	Miller	Simpson	McCall	McGhee*	McMaster*	Weir	Harrow/Jarvie
Berwick	*Glynn*	*Moyes*	*McCann*	*Marshall*	*Dixon*	*Muir*	*Romaines*	*Lawson**	*Armstrong*	*Tait*	*Black*	*Krawiec*

All Berwick had to play for was their pride. At 8-0 on aggregate it is doubtful whether they achieved even that objective. At least they finished the game with 11 players, which is more than could be said of them at Pittodrie.

SCOTTISH PREMIER (CUP-TIES) Manager: Alex Ferguson SEASON 1981-82

Scottish League Cup

Match	1	2	3	4	5	6	7	8	9	10	11	subs used
SF 1 — A DUNDEE UTD 2 W 1-0 H-T 1-0 — 15,000 *6*	Leighton	Kennedy	Rougvie	Watson	Cooper	Miller	Strachan	Simpson*	McGhee	Hewitt*	Weir*	McMaster/Harrow
7/10	*McAlpine*	*Stark*	*Kopel*	*Phillip*	*Hegarty*	*Narey*	*Bannon*	*Milne*	*Kirkwood*	*Sturrock*	*Dodds*	*Gough*

Weir 23 — Ref: B McGinlay

Dundee United are aiming to lift the League Cup for the third successive year. Peter Weir heads the all-important goal at a time when United's Davie Dodds is off the field having stitches inserted in a head gash. Surely the Dons won't blow it in the second leg, in front of their own fans.

Match	1	2	3	4	5	6	7	8	9	10	11	subs used
SF 2 — H DUNDEE UTD 2 L 0-3 H-T 0-2 — 21,000 *7*	Leighton	Kennedy	Rougvie	Watson	Cooper	Miller	Strachan	Simpson*	McGhee	Hewitt	Weir*	Bell/McCall
28/10	*McAlpine*	*Holt*	*Murray*	*Phillip*	*Hegarty*	*Narey*	*Bannon*	*Milne*	*Kirkwood*	*Sturrock*	*Dodds*	

Sturrock 7, 83, Milne 38 — Ref: K Hope — (Dons lose 1-3 on aggregate)

Unlucky 13 for Aberdeen, as their long unbeaten run comes to a painful end. Mistakes by Willie Miller and Jim Leighton cost Aberdeen the first two goals – and as the Dons pressed to square the tie Paul Sturrock streaked away for the killer third. United lose the final to Rangers.

Scottish Cup

Match	1	2	3	4	5	6	7	8	9	10	11	subs used
3 — A MOTHERWELL 6 W 1-0 H-T 1-0 — 12,679 *1:1*	Leighton	Kennedy	Rougvie	Cooper	McLeish	Miller	Strachan*	Bell	McGhee*	Hewitt	Weir	McMaster/Black
23/1	*Sproat*	*McLeod*	*Wark*	*McLelland*	*Carson*	*Forbes*	*McLaughlin*	*Rafferty*	*Irvine*	*O'Hara*	*Gahagan*	*Corne/Cleland*

Hewitt 1 — Ref: G Smith

Alex Ferguson has turned down the chance to manage Wolves. Motherwell are unbeaten in 18 Division 1 matches, but concede the fastest goal in the history of the Scottish Cup. Kennedy's deep cross finds John Hewitt, who picks his spot in 9.6 seconds. Brian McLaughlin is sent off.

Match	1	2	3	4	5	6	7	8	9	10	11	subs used
4 — H CELTIC 6 W 1-0 H-T 1-0 — 24,000 *1*	Leighton	Kennedy	Rougvie	McMaster	McLeish	Miller	Strachan*	Simpson*	McGhee	Hewitt	Weir	Bell
13/2	*Bonner*	*McGrain*	*Reid*	*Aitken*	*McAdam*	*MacLeod*	*Sullivan*	*McStay*	*McGarvey*	*Burns*	*McCluskey*	*Halpin*

Hewitt 19 — Ref: K Hope

Twice in the league this season Aberdeen have come from behind to win at Pittodrie. But not this time. John Hewitt follows up his record-breaking goal at Hamilton with an acrobatic flick to beat Pat Bonner. Thereafter chances came and went at both ends.

Match	1	2	3	4	5	6	7	8	9	10	11	subs used
QF — H KILMARNOCK 4 W 4-2 H-T 2-2 — 12,000 *1:4*	Leighton	Kennedy	Rougvie	Hamilton	McLeish	Miller	Strachan*	Cooper	McGhee	Simpson	Watson	
6/3	*McCulloch*	*McLean*	*Robertson*	*Clark*	*Armstrong**	*Clarke*	*Gallagher*	*McLeod**	*Bourke*	*Mauchlen*	*McGivern*	*McDicken/Bryson*

McGhee 20, Simpson 35, Strachan 60p, Simpson 64 — McGivern 1, Gallagher 36 — Ref: R Valentine

Aberdeen beat Killie 3-0 twice in the League Cup. The Division 1 side take a first-minute lead from a whipped centre. They strike again after the Dons go in front. In the second half McLean retaliated against Cooper and was sent off. Both penalties are for Mauchlen fouls on Strachan.

Match	1	2	3	4	5	6	7	8	9	10	11	subs used
SF — N ST MIRREN 2 D 1-1 H-T 0-0 — 16,782 *4* (at Hampden)	Leighton	Kennedy	Rougvie*	McMaster	McLeish	Miller	Strachan	Cooper	McGhee	Simpson	Weir*	Bell/Jarvie
3/4	*Thomson*	*Beckett*	*Abercrombie/Richardson*	*McCormack*	*Copland*	*Bone*	*Stark*	*McDougall*	*McAvennie*	*Scanlon*		

Strachan 66p — McDougall 61 — Ref: H Alexander

Chances are created and scored at both ends before Saints' Frank McDougall forces a corner and then scores from it. Within minutes Thomson pulls down Mark McGhee and Gordon Strachan levels from the spot. Abercrombie takes his revenge on the scorer and is ordered off.

Match	1	2	3	4	5	6	7	8	9	10	11	subs used
SF R — N ST MIRREN 2 W 3-2 H-T 2-1 — 15,663 *4* (at Dens Park)	Leighton	Rougvie	McMaster	McLeish	Cooper	Miller	Strachan	Simpson	McGhee	Hewitt*	Weir*	Watson
7/4	*Thomson*	*Beckett*	*McCormack/Richardson*		*Fulton**	*Bett*	*Copland*	*Stark^*	*Sommer*	*McAvennie*	*Scanlon*	*Fitzpatrick/Bone*

McGhee 6, Simpson 35, Weir 74 — McAvennie 17, Sommer 56 — Ref: H Alexander

Thomson couldn't hold McGhee's shot. Nor Neil Simpson's. Peter Weir hit the winner with a first-time shot. Aberdeen enjoy playing cup semi-finals at Dens Park. This is their fourth such win there since 1945. The waterlogged pitch threatened to make a lottery of the outcome. Billy Thomson couldn't hold McGhee's shot. Nor Neil Simpson's. Peter Weir hit the winner with a first-time shot.

Match	1	2	3	4	5	6	7	8	9	10	11	subs used
F — N RANGERS 2 W 4-1 (aet) H-T 1-1 — 53,788 *3* (at Hampden)	Leighton	Kennedy	Rougvie	McMaster*	McLeish	Miller	Strachan	Cooper	McGhee	Simpson*	Hewitt*	Black/Bell
22/5	*Stewart*	*Jardine*	*Dawson*	*McClelland*	*Jackson*	*Bett*	*Cooper*	*Russell*	*Dalziel**	*Miller*	*McDonald*	*McAdam/McLean*

McLeish 32, McGhee 93, Strachan 103, [Cooper 110] — McDonald 15 — Ref: B McGinlay

Weir is out, injured. John McDonald heads in Dalziel's cross. McLeish levels with an exquisite curler. In extra-time McGhee heads in on the run. McGhee then squares the ball across goal and Strachan scores from six inches out. Neale Cooper nets a rebound off Stewart.

UEFA Cup

Match	1	2	3	4	5	6	7	8	9	10	11	subs used
1:1 — A IPSWICH TOWN (England) 8 D 1-1 H-T 0-1 — 18,535	Leighton	Kennedy	Rougvie	Watson	McLeish	Miller*	Strachan	Cooper	McGhee	Hewitt	Weir*	Simpson
16/9	*Cooper*	*Mills*	*McCall*	*Thijssen*	*Osman*	*Butcher*	*Wark*	*Muhren*	*O'Callaghan*/Brazil*	*Gates*	*D'Avray*	

Hewitt 51 — Thijssen 45 — Ref: G Menegali (Italy)

Aberdeen have been paired with the defending UEFA Cup-holders. The English press concur that Aberdeen turn in a superb show. They become only the third team to avoid defeat at Portman Road in 24 European ties. Alex McLeish knocks down Weir's corner to John Hewitt.

Match	1	2	3	4	5	6	7	8	9	10	11	subs used
1:2 — H IPSWICH TOWN 3 W 3-1 H-T 1-1 — 24,000	Leighton	Kennedy	Rougvie	Watson*	McLeish	Miller	Strachan	Cooper*	McGhee	Hewitt	Weir	Bell/Simpson
30/9	*Cooper*	*Mills*	*McCall*	*Thijssen*	*Osman*	*Butcher*	*Wark*	*Muhren*	*Mariner*	*Brazil*	*Gates*	*O'Callaghan*

Strachan 33p, Weir 55, 85 — Wark 33p — Ref: M Vautrot (France) — (Dons win 4-2 on aggregate)

Before the match Bobby Robson said Aberdeen couldn't play better than they had at Ipswich. Then two crackers from Weir, one with each foot. Cooper felled Gates for the first penalty, Strachan's twice-taken, last-minute penalty was saved.

European ties

2:1 H ARGES PITESTI (Romania) — 2 W 3-0
21/10 · 22,000 · Scorers: Strachan 11, Weir 24, Hewitt 44 · Ref: S Thime (Norway)

Aberdeen										
Leighton	Kennedy	Rougvie	Watson	Cooper	Miller	Strachan	McMaster*	McGhee	Hewitt*	Weir
Arichu*	Zamfir	Barbulescu*	Tulpan	Stancu	Cristea	Baluta	Kalo	Radu	Ignat	Turcu

Subs: Angus/McCall · Cristian/Moicieanu

At half-time Aberdeen had every reason for celebration. By the end of the match they left nagging doubts. How could they miss so many chances to kill the tie? Best of the goals was Peter Weir's: he somehow netted as the ball was about to go out of play for a goal-kick.

2:2 A ARGES PITESTI — 2 D 2-2
4/11 · 8,500 · Scorers: Strachan 55p, Hewitt 85; Radu 31, Barbulescu 36 · Ref: J Redfelfs (W Germany)
(Dons win 5-2 on aggregate)

Aberdeen										
Leighton	Kennedy	Rougvie*	Cooper	McLeish	Miller	Strachan	Watson	McGhee	Hewitt*	Weir
Cristian	Barbulescu	Badea	Stancu	Edward	Cirstea	Baluta*	Kalo	Radu	Ignat	Turcu

Subs: Simpson/Hewitt · Nica/Moicieanu

For a while, those missed chances looked to be expensive. Radu's far-post header and Barbulescu's curling free-kick cut the deficit. Romanian hopes died when Weir was tripped in the box. The Dons progress beyond Round 2 of a European competition for the first time.

3:1 H SV HAMBURG (W Germ) — 2 W 3-2
25/11 · 24,000 · Scorers: Black 23, Watson 65, Hewitt 81; Hrubesch 52, 87 · Ref: P Schoeters (Belgium)

Aberdeen										
Leighton	Kennedy	McMaster	Watson	Rougvie*	Miller	Strachan	Black	McGhee*	Simpson	Hewitt
Stein	Kaltz	Memering	Groh	Beckenbauer	Hartwig*	Milewski*	Wehmeyer	Hrubesch	Magath	Bastrup

Subs: Cooper/McCall · Hildien/Hieronymus

36-year-old Franz Beckenbauer is one of countless stars on show. Black soars like a bird. 1-0. He then heads against the bar. Leighton and Kennedy play silly beggars outside the box. 1-1. At 2-1 Stein saves Strachan's penalty. With Rougvie off injured, Hrubesch scores a vital goal.

3:2 A SV HAMBURG — 4\ L 1-3
9/12 · 45,000 · Scorers: McGhee 79; Hrubesch 33, Memering 59, Jakobs 67 · Ref: R Juschka (Russia)
(Dons lose 4-5 on aggregate)

Aberdeen										
Leighton	Kennedy*	McMaster	Watson	McLeish	Miller	Strachan*	Black	Cooper	Simpson	Hewitt
Stein	Wehmeyer	Groh	Jakobs	Beckenbauer	von Heesen	Milewski	Memering	Hrubesch	Magath	Bastrup

Subs: McGhee/Bell

Aberdeen lost this tie at Pittodrie, not in the Volksparkstadion. Once snow had been cleared from the pitch Hamburg taught the Dons a lesson. Aberdeen were chasing a lost cause once Hrubesch's header put Hamburg ahead on away goals. McGhee scored his first goal for months.

League table

	P	W	D	L	F	A	W	D	L	F	A	Pts
		Home					Away					
1 Celtic	36	12	5	1	41	16	12	4	2	38	17	55
2 ABERDEEN	36	12	5	1	36	14	10	5	3	35	14	53
3 Rangers	36	10	5	3	34	16	6	6	6	23	29	43
4 Dundee Utd	36	10	4	4	40	14	6	5	7	21	24	40
5 St Mirren	36	8	4	6	30	23	3	7	8	19	29	37
6 Hibernian	36	8	7	3	23	14	3	7	8	15	26	36
7 Morton	36	9	6	3	20	12	2	0	6	11	42	30
8 Dundee	36	7	2	9	28	34	4	2	12	18	38	26
9 Partick This	36	4	5	9	19	23	2	0	11	16	36	22
10 Airdrie	36	5	4	9	24	36	0	4	14	7	40	18
	360	85	46	49	295	203	46	46	85	203	295	360

	P	W	D	L	F	A	Pts	Cup	W	D	L	F	A
v St Mirren	4	4	0	0	13	3	8	SC	1			1	0
v Dundee	4	3	1	0	10	1	7	LC	1			1	0
v Airdrie	4	3	1	0	9	0	7	SC	1			1	0
v Rangers	4	3	1	0	10	2	7	LC	1			1	0
v Hibernian	4	3	1	0	8	2	7						
v Partick This	4	3	1	0	7	2	7	LC	1			1	0
v Dundee Utd	4	2	1	1	6	7	5						
v Morton	4	1	1	2	4	4	3	SC	1			2	0
v Celtic	4	1	0	3	4	8	2						
	36	23	7	6	71	29	53						

Appearances and Goals

Player	Lge	Sub	LC	Sub	SC	Sub	Eur	Sub	Lge	LC	SC	Eur	Tot
Angus, Ian	11	2							1				3
Bell, Dougie	10	3		2									4
Black, Eric	22	5	8		5		5	1					5
Cooper, Neale		10		1		5							3
Cowan, Steve	1		1		1								
Hamilton, Derek	3	3	3	2	2	1							3
Harrow, Andy	3	3	3	5									
Hewitt, John	22	3	6	2	6	1	5		11	2	2	4	19
Jarvie, Drew	3	7		5					2				2
Kennedy, Stuart	34		9		6		6		1		1		2
Leighton, Jim	36		10		6		6						
McCall, Walker	6	2	2		2				4	1			5
McGhee, Mark	29	2	8		6		4		8	4	3	1	16
McLeish, Alex	32		8		6		5		5	1			6
McMaster, John	21	10	6	2	5	1	4	1	1				2
Miller, Willie	36		10		6		6						2
Mitchell, Brian	1												
Rougvie, Doug	28		5		5		5		6				6
Simpson, Neil	24	5	3		3		6		2	3			6
Strachan, Gordon	30		8		6		6		6	4	6	3	20
Watson, Andy	18	12	4	2	2	2	6	1	6		1		7
Weir, Peter	25		10		3		4		2	2	1	3	8
(own-goals)													2
22 players used	396	64	110	18	66	9	66	11	71	21	14	13	119

Odds & ends

Never lost: (6) St Mirren, Dundee, Airdrie, Rangers, Hibs, Partick.

Never beat: (0).

Won from behind: (3) St Mirren (h), Kilmarnock (SC), Rangers (SC).

Lost from in front: (2) Celtic h, twice.

High-spots: Winning the Scottish Cup from Rangers.

Also taking 7 league points out of 8 from Rangers.

Winning 15 of the last 16 league games.

Reaching semi-final of League Cup and taking first-leg lead.

Only three Premier League teams beat Aberdeen at all.

Reaching Round 3 of a European competition for the first time.

Beating the UEFA Cup holders, Ipswich, in the first round.

Low spots: Losing first two league games for first time since 1959-60.

7 league games without a win from 21 November.

Losing semi-final of League Cup to Dundee Utd at Pittodrie.

Conceding two stupid home goals to Hamburg in the UEFA Cup.

Bogey-team: Celtic.

Ever-presents: (2) Jim Leighton, Willie Miller.

Hat-tricks: (1) John Hewitt.

Leading scorer: (20) Gordon Strachan.

SCOTTISH PREMIER DIVISION

Manager: Alex Ferguson

SEASON 1982-83

No	Date	Att	Pos	Pt	F-A	H-T	Scorers, Times, and Referees	1	2	3	4	5	6	7	8	9	10	11	subs used
1	A DUNDEE UTD 4/9	11,663	-	L	0-2	0-2	Malpas 18, Dodds 40. Ref: A Ferguson. Aberdeen were almost a goal down in the first minute of the new league season. Davie Dodds' header was net-bound until Jim Leighton turned it onto the crossbar. A Dodds goal was not denied, only delayed. Never again will Aberdeen lose by two goals in any match this season.	Leighton	Kennedy	McMaster	Cooper*	McLeish	Miller	Strachan	Simpson	McGhee	Bell*	Black*	Weir*/Hewitt
								McAlpine	Malpas	Stark*	Gough	Hegarty	Narey	Britton	Milne	Kirkwood	Sturrock	Dodds	Bannon
2	H MORTON 11/9	7,500	3	W	4-1	2-1	Strachan 15p, Black 42, Simpson 55, [Hewitt 70]. McNeil 11. Ref: C Sinclair. This result is a tonic against the Dons' bugbear of recent years. Morton took the lead, but their cause was handicapped from the 35th minute, when Jim Duffy was sent off for fouling Eric Black. By then Strachan had equalised from the spot. Morton's 10 men can't match the Dons' 11.	Leighton	Kennedy	McMaster	Cooper*	Rougvie	Miller	Strachan	Black*	McGhee	Simpson	Weir	Bell/Hewitt
			10	2				Baines	Houston	Docherty	Rooney	McLaughlin	Duffy*	Gavigan	McNeil*	Hutchison	Cochrane	McNab*	Jackson/Ritchie
3	A ST MIRREN 18/9	4,800	5	D	1-1	0-0	McGhee 64. Scanlon 75. Ref: B Robertson. St Mirren have yet to register a league win. Aberdeen substitute Mark McGhee scores with his first touch. Former Don, Ian Scanlon, takes the smile off his face with the equaliser. It must have been strange for Scanlon, seeing the Dons and Weir - who replaced him - conquering Europe.	Leighton	Kennedy	McMaster	Cooper	McLeish	Miller	Strachan	Simpson*	Black	Hewitt*	Weir	Rougvie/McGhee
			7	3				Thomson	Wilson	McAveety	Fitzpatrick	McCormack	Copland	McAvennie	Stark	McDougall*	Richardson	Scanlon	Logan
4	H RANGERS 25/9	20,300	5	L	1-2	0-0	Strachan 73p. Johnstone 49, Prytz 62. Ref: B McGinlay. A day for Ibrox to celebrate, as - in this of all seasons - Rangers notch their first ever Premier League victory at Pittodrie. Two headed goals from unmarked Rangers players were enough to fend off Aberdeen's furious riposte. Strachan's penalty sets up a nerve-tingling climax.	Leighton	Kennedy	Rougvie*	Cooper	McLeish	Miller	Strachan	Simpson	McGhee	Bell	Black*	Weir
			2	3				Stewart	McKinnon	Dawson	McClelland	Paterson	Bett	Cooper*	Prytz*	Johnstone	Russell	Redford	McAdam
5	H MOTHERWELL 2/10	9,000	5	W	2-1	0-1	Cowan 66, Miller 89. Edvaldsson 25. Ref: D Ramsay. Motherwell journeyed north with just one point to their name. Johannes Edvaldsson looked like trebling that tally as he collected O'Hara's free-kick. But Dons substitute Steve Cowan nets with his first touch and Willie Miller scores an unforgettable winner with an overhead kick.	Leighton	Kennedy	Rougvie*	McMaster	McLeish	Miller	Strachan	Simpson	McGhee	Hewitt*	Weir	Watson/Cowan
			10	5				Sproat	McLeod	Forsyth	Carson	Edvaldsson	Rafferty	Clinging*	Flavell	McClelland	Conn*	O'Hara	Coyle/McClelland
6	A CELTIC 9/10	29,733	5	W	3-1	0-0	Strachan 54p, Simpson 58, McGhee 86. Nicholas 68. Ref: A Waddell. Parkhead is the place for drama as Celtic tumble to their first league defeat. Reid handles to give Strachan a penalty. With the score at 2-1 McGrain removed Weir's legs and was sent off. When McGhee scored a third, Celtic boss Billy McNeill ran onto the pitch to remonstrate.	Leighton	Cooper	Rougvie	McMaster	McLeish	Miller	Strachan	Simpson	McGhee	Bell*	Watson	
			1	7				Bonner	McGrain*	Reid	Aitken	McAdam	Sinclair	Provan	McStay	McGarvey	MacLeod*	Nicholas	Crainie
7	H DUNDEE 16/10	10,800	4	W	1-0	1-0	Weir 34. Ref: E Pringle. Peter Weir teed-up a thumping 20-yarder to open his account for the season. Leighton preserved both points with a flying save from Fleming. Strange to say, this is Aberdeen's first clean sheet of the league season. Young Stewart McKimmie looks promising in Dundee's defence.	Leighton	Cooper	Rougvie	McMaster	McLeish	Miller	Strachan*	Simpson*	McGhee	Bell	Weir	Black/Watson
			5	9				Kelly	Glennie	McKimmie	Fraser	Smith	McDonald*	Ferguson	Fleming	Bell*	Mackie	Stephen	Scrimgeour/Sinclair
8	A KILMARNOCK 23/10	3,400	4	W	2-0	1-0	Black 2, Hewitt 76. Ref: R Cuthill. Kilmarnock are still seeking their first win, but are rocked on their heels by a flawless Aberdeen goal after just two minutes. Gordon Strachan sends Doug Rougvie away down the left, and the big man's cross is met by Eric Black's flashing header. That's four league wins on the trot.	Leighton	Cooper	Rougvie	McMaster	McLeish	Miller	Strachan*	Simpson*	Black	Bell	Weir	Hewitt
			9	11				McCulloch	Robertson	McLeod	Clark	McDicken	Clarke	McGivern	Fleming	Gallacher	McClure	Bryson	Bourke
9	A HIBERNIAN 30/10	6,400	3	D	1-1	0-0	Weir 90. Murray 67. Ref: H Alexander. Hibernian have won just once. They are seconds from a second victory when Doug Rougvie provides the perfect pass and Peter Weir provides the perfect finish. Bryan Gunn has a useful debut in the Dons' goal. This is the only match that Jim Leighton misses all season.	Gunn	Cooper	Rougvie	McMaster	McLeish	Miller	Strachan	Simpson*	Black	Bell*	Weir	Watson/Hewitt
			8	12				McArthur	Sneddon	Duncan	McNamara	Rae	Turnbull	Callachan*	Conroy	Irvine	Thomson	Murray	Robertson
10	H DUNDEE UTD 6/11	14,000	2	W	5-1	3-1	Cooper 23, Rougvie 29, 41, Black 72, [Strachan 85]. Gough 19. Ref: G Smith. United's first defeat of the season will also stand as the future champions' heaviest. Their defence had previously been pierced just three times in nine games. This five-star blitz had Pittodrie roaring. The only disappointment was that Doug Rougvie failed to gain his hat-trick.	Leighton	Kennedy	Rougvie	Cooper	McLeish	Miller	Strachan	Simpson	McGhee	Black	Weir	Hewitt
			3	14				McAlpine	Malpas	Stark	Gough	Hegarty	Narey	Bannon	Milne	Kirkwood	Holt	Dodds*	Reilly
11	A MORTON 13/11	2,500	3	D	1-1	0-1	Simpson 85. McNab 14. Ref: C White. Morton are five minutes away from their first win in six games. Keeper Roy Baines stands between Aberdeen and their equaliser. But Morton's gallant keeper concedes defeat to Neil Simpson's screamer from a Strachan corner. This is the only point the Dons will drop to Morton.	Leighton	Kennedy	Rougvie	Cooper	McLeish	Miller	Strachan	Simpson	McGhee*	Black	Weir	Bell
			7	15				Baines	Houston	Holmes	Rooney	Hutchison	Docherty	McNeil	McNab	Gavigan	Cochrane	Higgins	

12 | H | **ST MIRREN** 20/11 | 10,300 | 3 W 4-0 | 6 17
Black 39, Strachan 66p, McGhee 79, [Hewitt 90]
Ref: R Valentine
Leighton, Thomson 90[Hewitt 90], Kennedy, Rougvie, Cooper, McLeish, Miller, Strachan*, Simpson*, McGhee, Bell, Black, Hewitt
Wilson, Clarke, Fitzpatrick, Fulton, Copland, Stark, Richardson, Sommer, McAvennie, Abercrombie McDougall*

St Mirren lost 0-5 to Celtic last week, and 0-4 to Aberdeen this. Once the Dons had taken the measure of Saints muscular resolve, they won with ease. Strachan scored with a second-half penalty - but later in the season will crucially fail to beat Billy Thomson from the spot.

13 | A | **RANGERS** 27/11 | 23,000 | 3 W 1-0 | 4 19
Black 69
Ref: A Ferguson
Leighton, Stewart, Kennedy, McKinnon, Rougvie, Dawson*, Cooper*, McClelland, McLeish, McPherson, Miller, Bett, Strachan, Cooper, Simpson, Prytz, McGhee, Johnstone*, Bell, Redford, Weir, McDonald, Black, Mackay/Dalziel

It is true the win in five for Rangers, who have hit a rocky patch. Yet they looked to be claiming the ascendancy in the second half until Peter Weir strolled past McKinnon, and Eric Black - a substitute - finished off with a mighty header. The Dons still trail to Celtic and Dundee Utd.

14 | A | **MOTHERWELL** 4/12 | 4,929 | 3 W 2-0 | 9 21
Strachan 50p, Weir 66
Ref: T Muirhead
Leighton, Sproat, Kennedy, McLeod, Rougvie, Forsyth, Cooper, Edvaldsson, McLeish, Mauchlen, Miller, Gahagan, Strachan, Flavell, Simpson*, McClelland, McGhee, Rafferty, Bell*, O'Hara, Weir, Hewitt/Watson, Black*

Motherwell have picked up lately, and climbed to sixth before this match. The result lifts Aberdeen within two points of Celtic at the top. Gordon Strachan converts yet another penalty, this time after defender Mauchlen dives to make a goalkeeper's save on the goal-line.

15 | H | **CELTIC** 11/12 | 24,000 | 3 L 1-2 | 1 21
McGhee 18
MacLeod 16, Provan 59
Ref: K Hope
Leighton, Bonner, Kennedy*, McGrain, Rougvie*, Sinclair, Cooper, Aitken, McLeish, McAdam, Miller, MacLeod, Strachan, Provan, Simpson, McStay, McGhee, Burns, Bell*, McGarvey, Weir, Nicholas, Black, Hewitt/Black

Since losing to Aberdeen in early October, Celtic have now won eight on the trot. The Dons may have been deflated by two wicked deflections that turned harmless shots into goals. Miller changed the direction of MacLeod's effort; Alex McLeish's chest altered the angle of Provan's winner.

16 | A | **DUNDEE** 18/12 | 6,528 | 3 W 2-0 | 5 23
McGhee 28, 54
Ref: J Duncan
Leighton, Kelly, Kennedy, Glennie*, Rougvie, McKimmie, Cooper, Fraser, McLeish, Smith, Miller, MacDonald, Strachan, Murphy, Simpson, Bell, McGhee, Sinclair, Black, Mackie, Weir, Stephen*, Black, McGlash'n/McGeachie

An orange ball was called upon on the white frosty pitch. Dundee tempers became frosty following Mark McGhee's first goal, when both Neil Simpson and Neale Cooper appeared to be yards offside. Before the season's end Dundee will suffer more misery at Aberdeen hands.

17 | H | **KILMARNOCK** 27/12 | 14,500 | 3 W 2-0 | 10 25
Weir 4, Miller 87
Ref: H Young
Leighton, McCulloch, Kennedy, McLean, Rougvie, Robertson, Cooper, Clark, McLeish, McDicken, Miller, Clarke, Strachan, McGivern, Simpson, McLeod, McGhee, Bourke, Black, Cockburn, Weir, Gallagher*, McCall, Bryson

Kilmarnock have won once all season. Arctic weather affected all - especially poor Jim Leighton, who was allowed to stand idle from first to last. The healthy crowd who paid at the turnstiles did not come to see Kilmarnock, but to acquire vouchers for the Bayern Munich match.

18 | H | **HIBERNIAN** 1/1 | 14,000 | 3 W 2-0 | 7 27
McGhee 1, 24
Ref: T Muirhead
Leighton, Rough, Kennedy, Sneddon, Rougvie, Turnbull*, Bell, Rae, McLeish, Jamieson, Miller, McNamara, Strachan*, Callachan*, Simpson, Conroy, McGhee, Duncan, Black*, Reid, Weir, Murray, Watson/McCall, Thomson/Byrne

Dismal Hibs have now won once in 11 games, though they drew they last outing, against Rangers. 20 seconds into the first match of the New Year Mark McGhee sidefooted the first of his two goals past the stranded Alan Rough. Three 2-0 wins on the trot for Aberdeen.

19 | A | **DUNDEE UTD** 3/1 | 17,851 | 2 W 3-0 | 3 29
Simpson 27, Weir 43, McGhee 89
Ref: B McGinlay
Leighton, McAlpine, Kennedy, Stark, Rougvie, Malpas*, Cooper, Gough, McLeish, Hegarty, Miller, Narey, Strachan*, Bannon, Simpson*, Milne, McGhee, Kirkwood*, Bell, Sturrock, Weir, Dodds, Black/McMaster, Holt/Reilly

United's second defeat of the season, and both have been against Aberdeen, who were the last visiting team to win at Tannadice, back in May 1982. Aberdeen have now scored eight in three matches this season against United, who have let in just six goals in their other 15 games.

20 | H | **MORTON** 8/1 | 12,600 | 2 W 2-0 | 8 31
Simpson 70, McGhee 84
Ref: M Delaney
Leighton, Baines, Kennedy, Houston, Rougvie, Holmes, Cooper*, Rooney, McLeish, McLaughlin, Miller, Duffy, Black*, Payne, Simpson, Gibson, McGhee, Hutchison, Bell, Cochrane, Weir, McNab*, Watson/McMaster, Slavin

Morton have won their last two games, to provide respite from their relegation worries. In this match the goalmouths have to be swept clear of snow before kick-off. 20 minutes from time the ball broke to Simpson, 18 yards out. McGhee added a second when dribbling round the keeper.

21 | A | **ST MIRREN** 15/1 | 4,530 | 2 D 1-1 | 8 32
Black 75
Scanlon 45
Ref: A Waddell
Leighton, Thomson, Kennedy, Wilson, Rougvie, Clarke, Watson*, Walter, McLeish, Fulton, Miller, Abercrombie, Strachan*, Stark, Simpson*, Richardson, McGhee, McDougall, Bell, McAvennie, Weir, Scanlon, Black/McMaster

When Ian Scanlon did the dirty on his former team-mates, scoring on the stroke of half-time, he prevented Aberdeen equalling a Premier League record of six successive shut-outs, and halts the Dons' winning run. After the match the players headed for Spain for a short holiday.

22 | H | **RANGERS** 22/1 | 21,600 | 2 W 2-0 | 4 34
Rougvie 34, McGhee 77
Ref: K Hope
Leighton, McCloy, Kennedy, McKinnon, Rougvie, Redford, Cooper*, Stevens, McLeish, Batt, Miller, McClelland, Black*, Cooper*, Simpson, Prytz*, McGhee, Kennedy, Black, Johnstone, Weir, McMaster/Simpson, McDonald/Black

The players return from Spain fired up for this one. Despite the comparatively close score, this was one of the most one-sided matches with Rangers in recent years. The fists also flew. Near the end Rangers' sub John McDonald butted Dougie Bell and off he went amid ugly scenes.

23 | H | **MOTHERWELL** 8/2 | 13,300 | 2 W 5-1 | 8 36
McLeish 36, McMaster 38, McGhee 52, Rafferty 10 [Black 67, Cooper 71]
Ref: J Renton
Walker, Flavell, Kennedy, Dornan, Rougvie, Carson, McMaster, Edvaldsson, McLeish, Forbes*, Miller, McClair, Black*, Rafferty, Simpson, McClair, McGhee, Harrow, Bell, Mauchlen, Weir, O'Hara, Cooper/Watson, Coyne

Motherwell have won four of their last five, including wins over both the Old Firm. The final scoreline conceals the fact that Motherwell held the lead for 26 minutes, until Alex McLeish did the strikers' job for them. The big centre-half netted with his foot, not his head, a rarity.

SCOTTISH PREMIER DIVISION

Manager: Alex Ferguson — SEASON 1982-83

No	Date	Att	Pos	Pt	F-A	H-T	Scorers, Times, and Referees	1	2	3	4	5	6	7	8	9	10	11	subs used
24	A CELTIC 12/2	42,831	1 W 2	38	3-1	2-1	Black 44, 45, 71 / *Nicholas 34* / Ref: R. Valentine	Leighton / *Bonner*	Kennedy / *McGrain*	Rougvie* / *Reid**	Cooper / *Aitken*	McLeish / *McAdam*	Miller / *Sinclair*	Black / *Provan*	Simpson / *McStay*	McGhee / *McGarvey*	Bell / *MacLeod*	Weir / *Nicholas*	*McCluskey*
25	H DUNDEE 26/2	11,500	1 W 6	40	3-1	0-1	Weir 58, Black 85, Bell 90 / *Stephen 6* / Ref: D Syme	Leighton / *Kelly*	Kennedy / *McGeachie*	Rougvie* / *McKimmie*	McMaster / *Fraser*	McLeish / *Smith*	Miller / *MacDonald*	Black / *Ferguson*	Watson* / *Scrimgeour**	McGhee / *Mackie*	Bell / *Stephen*	Weir /	Cooper/Simpson *Bell/Glennie*
26	A KILMARNOCK 5/3	2,400	1 W 10	42	2-1	2-0	Watson 13, McGhee 26 / *Gallagher 65* / Ref: J Duncan	Leighton / *McCulloch*	Kennedy / *McClug*	Rougvie* / *Cockburn*	Cooper* / *Clark J*	McLeish / *McDicken*	Miller / *Clarke P*	Strachan / *McGivern**	Simpson / *McLeod**	McGhee / *Bourke*	Watson / *Simpson*	Black / *Gallagher*	McMaster *Muir/McLean*
27	H DUNDEE UTD 19/3	22,800	1 L 3	42	1-2	0-2	Strachan 66p / *Milne 26, 30* / Ref: E Pringle	Leighton / *McAlpine*	Cooper / *Stark*	Rougvie / *Malpas*	McMaster / *Gough*	McLeish / *Hegarty*	Miller / *Narey*	Strachan / *Bannon*	McLeish / *Milne*	McGhee / *Kirkwood*	Hewitt / *Philip*	Weir* / *Dodds*	Simpson/Black
28	A MORTON 26/3	2,800	1 W 9	44	2-1	0-1	Watson 83, Black 90 / *Ritchie 30* / Ref: H Alexander	Leighton / *Kyle*	Kennedy / *Houston*	McMaster / *Holmes*	Cooper* / *Rooney*	Rougvie* / *McLaughlin*	Miller / *Docherty*	Strachan / *McNeil*	Simpson / *McNab*	McGhee / *Hutchison*	Black / *Cochrane*	Weir / *Payae*	Watson/McLeish *Payae*
29	H ST MIRREN 2/4	16,400	3 L 5	44	0-1	0-0	— / *McEachran 73* / Ref: R Valentine	Leighton / *Thomson*	Kennedy / *Wilson*	McMaster* / *Clarke*	Cooper* / *McCormack*	McLeish / *Fulton*	Miller / *Copland*	Strachan / *Logan*	Simpson / *Richardson*	McGhee / *Wardrope*	Black / *McAvennie*	Weir / *Abercrombie*	Rougvie/Watson *McDougall/McEachran*
30	A RANGERS 9/4	19,800	3 L 4	44	1-2	0-1	McLeish 15 / *Redford 21, Bett 86* / Ref: A Waddell	Leighton / *McCloy*	Kennedy / *Dawson*	Rougvie* / *McCleland*	Cooper / *McPherson*	McLeish / *Paterson*	Miller / *Bett*	Strachan / *Russell**	Simpson / *McKinnon*	McGhee / *Clark*	Bell / *Redford*	Weir* / *McDonald**	McMaster/Black *Cooper/Dalziel*
31	H CELTIC 23/4	24,000	3 W 2	46	1-0	1-0	McGhee 34 / Ref: A Ferguson	Leighton / *Bonner*	Cooper / *McGrain*	Rougvie* / *Reid**	McMaster / *Aitken*	McLeish / *McAdam*	Miller / *MacLeod*	Strachan / *Provan*	Watson / *McStay*	McGhee / *Nicholas*	Hewitt / *Burns*	Weir* / *McGarvey*	Falconer/Simpson *Moyes*
32	A MOTHERWELL 27/4	6,715	3 W 8	48	3-0	1-0	McGhee 11, Strachan 58, Hewitt 74 / Ref: E Pringle	Leighton / *Walker*	Cooper* / *Dornan*	Rougvie / *McLeod*	McMaster / *Wark*	McLeish / *Edvaldsson*	Miller / *Flarell*	Strachan / *Gahagan*	Simpson / *Rafferty*	McGhee / *Harrow**	Watson / *McClair*	Hewitt / *O'Hara*	Angus/Hamilton *Cormack*
33	A DUNDEE 30/4	10,076	3 W 7	50	2-0	2-0	Hewitt 3, Strachan 40 / Ref: D Downie	Leighton / *Kelly*	Cooper* / *McGeachie**	Rougvie / *McKimmie**	McMaster / *Fraser*	McLeish / *Smith*	Miller / *MacDonald*	Strachan / *Mackie*	Simpson / *Glennie*	McGhee / *Davidson*	Watson* / *Scrimgeour**	Hewitt / *Ferguson*	Angus/Black *Kidd/Stephen*
34	A HIBERNIAN 3/5	8,000	3 D 6	51	0-0	0-0	Ref: B McGinlay	Leighton / *Rough*	Cooper / *McFee*	McMaster / *Sneddon*	Watson / *Brazil*	McLeish / *Welsh*	Miller / *Rice*	Strachan / *Callachan*	Hewitt / *Irvine*	McGhee / *Murray**	Angus* / *Thomson*	Weir / *Duncan*	Rougvie/Cowan *Harvey*

Match reports

24 — Aberdeen leap-frog over Celtic to the top of the league thanks to Eric Black's glorious hat-trick. He is the first player to score three times against Celtic in memory. Two of his goals come in the dying seconds of the first-half, and Bayern Munich's watching spy is much impressed.

25 — For an hour it seemed as though Dundee were going to gain revenge for their Scottish Cup elimination of the previous week. But then the Dons put the forthcoming clash with Bayern out of their minds. Peter Weir's diving header was trumped by Eric Black's sensational overhead kick.

26 — A first-half picnic turned into a second-half struggle against demoralised Kilmarnock, who have just lost heavily to Dundee Utd and Celtic. An uncharacteristic mix-up between Leighton and McLeish allowed Killie back into the match. Everyone else thrashes them except Aberdeen.

27 — In retrospect, the most critical league result of the season. But after the heroics against Bayern the Dons hand the match to United's Ralph Milne. His first goes is off the bar, he sweeps his second past Jim Leighton. In the second-half Milne kicked McLeish and was expelled.

28 — The Dons are wobbling. This was brinkmanship at its best. Andy Ritchie scores from a 30-yard free-kick. Near the end Dons' sub Andy Watson stabs a close-range equaliser. In injury-time Black's left foot seals the second precious point to keep Aberdeen on top of the league.

29 — Injury-wrecked St Mirren spoil the Dons' title hopes in driving snow. With the first half into added time, Strachan' penalty slides wide of a post. Worse was to come when Saints' sub, McEachran, drives a rebound from McLeish wide of Leighton. The Dons tumble from first to third.

30 — Alex McLeish marks his 250th appearance for Aberdeen with a typical thumping header. Redford swept home a curling cross to equalise. With Aberdeen pressing continuously for the winner, Rangers broke away for Jim Bett to snatch a cruel winner. The championship looks all but lost.

31 — Celtic have just lost to Dundee United. Aberdeen have booked places in the finals of the Cup-Winners' Cup and Scottish Cup, and simply have to beat Celtic. Under the watchful eyes of Real manager Alfredo di Stefano, McGhee's priceless header goes in via a post and Aitken's foot.

32 — This was not as easy as the final score suggests. Two Motherwell goals were chalked off for one reason or another, and Jim Leighton saved thrillingly from Brian McClair to prevent an equaliser. The Dons were champs in 1980 with 48 points. It's two matches a week from now on.

33 — Goal-difference might prove decisive in the race for the title. While Aberdeen netted two, Dundee Utd were scoring four and Celtic five. Aberdeen have taken a maximum eight-point haul from Dundee, but Dundee United will achieve the same on the final Saturday of the season.

34 — Hibs are going through the motions as their season meanders to a close. Aberdeen needed to win 9-0 to go top on goal-difference. Gordon Strachan's penalty misses look like costing the team the championship. This time his 23rd minute kick is saved by keeper Alan Rough.

35 H KILMARNOCK 5/5 — 1 W 10 53 — 12,000 — 5-0

Strachan 30, 58, McMaster 39, [Angus 46, 85]McCulloch
Ref: R Valentine

Leighton; Mitchell *Cockburn*; McMaster *Clark R*; Watson* *Clark J*; Miller *Clarke P*; Rougvie *McDicken*; Strachan *McGivern**; Porteous^ *McLeod*; Hewitt *Bryson*; Angus *Simpson*; Weir *Gallacher*; Bell/Black *Muir*

This Thursday match was brought forward two days to give Aberdeen more time to prepare for Gothenburg. This easy win permits the Dons to sit on top of the league till the weekend. Goal-of-the-match was the fourth, the fruit of John McMaster's 60-yard chipped pass to Strachan.

---

36 H HIBERNIAN 14/5 — 3 W 7 55 — 24,000 Away — 5-0

Brazil 9 og, McGhee 30, Strachan 70p, [Cowan 78, Angus 87]Rough
Ref: D Syme

Leighton; Rougvie *Conroy**; McMaster *Sneddon*; Watson *Brazil*; Miller *McNamara*; McLeish* *Welsh**; Strachan *Callachan*; Black* *Rice*; McGhee *Irvine*; Angus *Thomson*; Hewitt *Duncan*; Hamilton/Cowan *McKee/Harvey*

The Hibs' team line up to applaud the Cup-Winners onto the pitch. And well they might: they were then flattened. Yet Aberdeen could only lift the title if Dundee Utd lost to Dundee and Celtic drew with Rangers. They both won. Aberdeen's 55 points is a club record; they finish third.

Average Home 15,534 — Away 11,550

Scottish League Cup - Section 2

1 A MORTON 11/8 — D 1 — 2-2 — 3,500 — 1-1

Strachan 12, McGhee 53
Hutchison 21, Ritchie 85p
Ref: H Alexander

Leighton; Kennedy *Houston**; Rougvie *Holmes*; Cooper *Rooney*; Miller *Duffy*; McLeish *McLaughlin*; Strachan *McNeil*; Black* *Docherty*; McGhee *Hutchison*; Angus *Cochrane*; Weir* *Ritchie*; Simpson/Cowan *Higgins*

After weeks of speculation Willie Miller has just re-signed for the club. He cost Aberdeen a point when he handles from Hutchison inside the penalty box. Andy Ritchie squares the match from the spot. As there are three Premier teams in Section 2, it may prove an expensive point lost.

---

2 H DUNDEE 14/8 — D 2 — 3-3 — 9,000 — 2-1

Black 30, 45, 85
Stephen 43, 80, Ferguson 53p
Ref: B McGinlay

Leighton; Kennedy *McKimmie*; Rougvie *McLelland*; Cooper *Fraser*; Miller *Glennie*; McLeish *MacDonald*; Strachan *Ferguson*; Black *Sinclair**; McGhee *McGeachie*; Angus *Stephen*; Weir* *Davidson*

How strange. Aberdeen applied nearly all the pressure, but until Eric Black completed his hat-trick near the end the Dons might easily have lost to three breakaway Dundee goals. This draw is the best Dundee will achieve from six league and League Cup meetings with Aberdeen.

---

3 H DUMBARTON 21/8 — W 4 — 3-0 — 6,500 — 2-0

McGhee 5, Strachan 13, 70
Ref: D Downie

Leighton; Kennedy *Walker**; Rougvie *McGowan*; Cooper *Clougherty*; Miller *Coyle*; McLeish *Close*; Strachan *Blair**; Black *Brown*; McGhee *Dunlop*; Simpson *Donnelly*; Weir *McGrogan*; Hewitt/Angus *Stevenson/Burnett*

First Division Dumbarton have already lost twice and are out of contention. Their keeper, Tom Carson, stands between Aberdeen and an inflated score. For some reason shoot-on-sight skipper Willie Miller seemed determined to score a goal himself. He failed.

---

4 H MORTON 25/8 — W 6 — 3-0 — 11,000 — 2-0

Rougvie 19, Bell 27, 48
Ref: R Valentine

Leighton; Kennedy *Houston**; Rougvie *Holmes*; Cooper *Rooney*; Miller *Duffy*; McLeish *McLaughlin*; Strachan* *McNeil*; Black *Docherty*; McGhee *Hutchison*; Bell *Cochrane*; Simpson* *Ritchie**; Hewitt/Angus *Gavigan*

It is just as well Aberdeen scored their goals when they did. By the end they were down to nine men; Eric Black and John Hewitt were unable to continue, and both substitutions had already been made. Mind you, the Dons could have been down to six and Morton wouldn't have won.

---

5 A DUNDEE 28/8 — W 8 — 5-1 — 7,000 — 2-0

Strachan 23, 52, 53, 63, McGhee 28
Stephen 65
Ref: D Galloway

Leighton; Geddes R *McKimmie*; Rougvie *McLelland*; Cooper *Fraser*; Miller *Glennie*; Rougvie* *Glennie*; Strachan *Ferguson*; Black* *Geddes A**; McGhee *Sinclair^*; Bell *Stephen*; Simpson *Mackie*; Black^/Angus *Kidd/Davidson*

Gordon Strachan still seems to be living off his World Cup memories. He takes Dundee apart single-handedly. The best of his four goals was a cheeky chip over the head of Bobby Geddes from all of 35 yards. This win all but confirms Aberdeen's place in the quarter-finals.

---

6 A DUMBARTON 8/9 — W 10 — 2-1 — 750 — 0-0

Bell 76, Hewitt 85
Donnelly 89p
Ref: J Timmons

Leighton; Mitchell *Carson*; McMaster *Brown*; Cooper *Clougherty*; Miller *Coyle*; McLeish* *McNeil**; Black *Craig*; Watson* *McGowan P Close*; Hewitt *Dunlop*; Simpson* *Donnelly*; Watson *Burnett*; Cowan/Bell *McGowan M/Blair*

Aberdeen needed to lose 0-5 to First Division Dumbarton to let Morton qualify at their expense. That is never likely to happen – especially once Bell scores through a forest of legs to put the Dons belatedly in front. The Dons have also played Sion twice in the Cup-Winners' Cup.

Qual							
ABERDEEN	6	4	2	0	18	7	10
Morton	6	3	2	1	16	11	8
Dundee	6	2	2	2	14	19	6
Dumbarton	6	0	0	6	7	18	0

QF 1 A DUNDEE UTD 22/9 — 5 L 4 — 1-3 — 14,000 — 1-2

McGhee 14
Gough 25, Bannon 31, Kirkwood 80
Ref: H Alexander

Leighton; Rougvie* *Phillip**; McMaster *Stark*; Cooper *Gough*; Miller *Narey*; McLeish *Hegarty*; Strachan *Bannon*; Watson* *Milne*; McGhee *Kirkwood*; Hewitt *Sturrock*; Weir *Dodds*; Kennedy/Black *Malpas*

United's Paul Hegarty hesitates and lets in Mark McGhee. Richard Gough is almost on his haunches when heading the equaliser. Eamonn Bannon fires the next goal off the crossbar. Kirkwood's header into an unguarded net gives Aberdeen an uphill climb in the second leg.

QF 2 H DUNDEE UTD 6/10 — 5 L — 0-1 — 11,700 — 0-0

Sturrock 72p
Ref: G Smith
(Dons lose 1-4 on aggregate)

Leighton; Cooper *Phillip*; Rougvie *Stark*; McMaster *McAlpine*; Miller *Narey*; McLeish *Hegarty*; Strachan *Malpas*; Simpson *Milne*; McGhee^ *Kirkwood*; Hewitt *Sturrock*; Weir *Dodds*; Black

Gordon Strachan and Peter Weir on the flanks meant that United's defence was under almost constant pressure. Aberdeen's chances of making the semi-finals died when Neil Simpson was adjudged to have handled Paul Hegarty's header in the box. United k.o'd the Dons last season too.

SCOTTISH PREMIER (CUP-TIES)

Manager: Alex Ferguson

SEASON 1982-83

Scottish Cup

			F-A	H-T	Scorers, Times, and Referees	1	2	3	4	5	6	7	8	9	10	11	subs used
3	A HIBERNIAN	2 W 4-1		2-0	Weir 33, Simpson 35, Watson 83, [McGhee 84] Rae 65 Ref: A Ferguson	Leighton *Rough*	Kennedy *Sneddon*	Rougvie *Schaedler*	McMaster* *Rice*	McLeish *Rae*	Miller *McNamara*	Black *Callachan* *	Simpson *Conroy* *	McGhee *Duncan*	Bell* *Thomson*	Weir *Murray*	Watson/Cooper Irvine/Welsh
	29/1 14,289 *7*				Aberdeen hit Hibs with the old one-two. Twice. After Rae's 20-yarder threatened to spark a Hibs revival, up popped Andy Watson to run half the length of the rain-sodden pitch to put the game beyond the home team. Both of the Dons' league fixtures at Easter Road will be drawn.												
4	H DUNDEE	1 W 1-0		0-0	Simpson 46 Ref: H Alexander	Leighton *Kelly*	Kennedy *McGeachie*	Rougvie *McKinnie*	Cooper *Fraser*	McLeish *Smith*	Miller *McDonald*	Black *Ferguson*	Simpson *Bell* *	McGhee *Sinclair*	Bell* *Mackie*	Weir *Stephen* ^	Glennie/Murphy
	19/2 19,000 *5*				Dundee may have lost by just one goal, but they were beaten by the breadth of the Tay. Neil Simpson ended their resistance 53 seconds after the turnaround, following up when Eric Black's shot was blocked. Dundee are outclassed by the Dons in all three domestic competitions.												
QF	A PARTICK THISTLE	1 W 2-1		1-0	Cooper 4, Weir 72 McDonald 63 Ref: G Smith	Leighton *McNab*	Kennedy *Doyle G*	Rougvie *Whittaker*	Cooper *Murray*	McLeish *Jackson*	Miller *Watson*	Strachan *Park*	Simpson *McDonald* *	McGhee *Johnston*	Bell* *Doyle J*	Weir *O'Hara*	Black McDowall
	12/3 12,092 *1:3*				Aberdeen prepare for the midweek visit of Bayern Munich with a patchy performance against First Division promotion-chasers Partick. After McDonald blasted Partick level, Peter Weir curled a free-kick - Brazilian style - round the wall and the goalkeeper. Bring on the Germans!												
SF	N CELTIC	3 W 1-0		0-0	Weir 65 Ref: A Ferguson	Leighton *Bonner*	Kennedy *Sinclair*	Rougvie *Reid*	Cooper* *Aitken*	McLeish *McAdam*	Miller *MacLeod*	Strachan *Provan*	Simpson *McStay*	McGhee *Burns*	Bell* *Black* *	Black* *McGarvey*	Weir/Watson Crainie
	16/4 51,152 *1* (at Hampden)				The result is everything. Neither side showed any interest in playing football. There had been little sign of a goal at either end when substitute Weir raced in to head Black's cross just inside a post. The following Saturday Aberdeen beat Celtic in the league as well; four wins out of five.												
F	N RANGERS	3 W 1-0 *(aet)*		0-0	Black 116 Ref: D Syme	Leighton *McCloy*	Rougvie* *Dawson*	McMaster *McClelland*	Cooper* *McPherson*	McLeish *Paterson*	Miller *Bett*	Strachan *Cooper* *	Simpson *McKinnon*	McGhee *Clark*	Black *Russell*	Weir* *McDonald* ^	Watson/Hewitt Davies/Dalziel
	21/5 62,979 *4* (at Hampden)				Aberdeen field the same 11 as beat Real Madrid. Rangers enjoyed the better moments in a lacklustre 90 minutes. Four minutes from the end of extra-time Paterson deflected McGhee's cross into the air, and Eric Black nodded into an open goal. Fergie criticised his team, then apologised.												

European Cup-Winners' Cup

			F-A	H-T	Scorers, Times, and Referees	1	2	3	4	5	6	7	8	9	10	11	subs used
P:1	H SION (Switz'land)	W 7-0		4-0	Black 5, Strachan 21, Hewitt 22, Simpson 34, Balet 56 og, McGhee 62, Kennedy 81 Ref: K Tritachler (W Germany)	Leighton *Pittier*	Kennedy *Valentini J*	McMaster *Valentini P*	Simpson *Balet*	McLeish *Richard*	Miller *Lopez*	Strachan *Bregy*	Black* *Luisier* *	McGhee *Caernicky*	Bell* *Karlen B*	Hewitt *Cina*	Weir/Rougvie Cucinotta
	18/8 13,000				Aberdeen have drawn the short straw and must play a preliminary round with the Swiss cup-holders for right of entry to Round 1. All seven Dons goals are spread around; even a Swiss defender claims one. When was the last time six players from one side scored in one match?												
P:2	A SION	W 4-1		1-1	Hewitt 27, Miller 61, McGhee 65, 72 Bregy 28 Ref: J Glazar (Yugoslavia) (Dons win 11-1 on aggregate)	Leighton *Pittier*	Kennedy *Valentini J*	McMaster *Karlen L*	Simpson *Moulin*	Cooper *Richard*	Miller *Lopez*	Strachan* *Bregy*	Bell* *Luisier* *	McGhee *Caernicky*	Hewitt *Cucinotta*	Weir *Cina* *	Black/McLeish Karlea B/Tachet
	1/9 2,400				Aberdeen take time off from this formality to admire the breathtaking Alpine scenery surrounding the Tourbillon Stadium. The outcome of course, is never in doubt. Four years later the same team will play the same team in the same stadium, and not come off nearly so well.												
1:1	H DINAMO TIRANA (Albania)	W 1-0		1-0	Hewitt 29 Ref: L Delsemme (Belgium)	Leighton *Luarasi*	Kennedy *Kugi*	McMaster* *Bragu*	Cooper* *Targai*	Rougvie *Ruci*	Miller *Xhafa*	Strachan *Gega*	Bell* *Kanai*	McGhee *Zeri*	Hewitt *Fagekugi*	Weir *Demorrail*	Black/Cooper Dauti/Musai
	15/9 15,000				Despite controlling the game from the first minute to the last, Aberdeen take just the slenderest of leads over to Albania. The one goal came when keeper Luarasi failed to hold Dougie Bell's shot. The ball bounced off the keeper's chest and Hewitt found himself with a yawning net.												
1:2	A DINAMO TIRANA	D 0-0		0-0	Ref: J Szaavo (Hungary) (Dons win 1-0 on aggregate)	Leighton *Luarasi*	Kennedy *Kugi*	Rougvie *Dauti* *	Cooper* *Targai*	McLeish *Gega*	Miller *Ruci*	Strachan *Delia*	Simpson *Kanai*	McGhee* *Zeri*	Bell *Marko*	Weir *Demorrail* ^	McMaster/Hewitt Noea/Agalliu
	29/9 20,000				European football at its very worst; professional guarding of a one-goal lead at its very best. This is a far cry from the 11 goals pumped past Sion. Dinamo Tirana never threatened to score, nor Aberdeen to let them. In sweltering conditions that demanded economy of movement,												
2:1	H LECH POZNAN (Poland)	W 2-0		0-0	McGhee 55, Weir 57 Ref: E Mulder (Holland)	Leighton *Plesnierowicz Pawlak*	Cooper *Szewczyk*	McMaster* *Adamiec*	McLeish *Barczak*	Simpson *Kupcewicz* *	Miller *Strugarek* *	Strachan *Oblewski*	Simpson *Malek*	McGhee *Okonski*	Black* *Bak*	Weir *Okonski*	Kennedy/Hewitt Kryz'ski/New'onski
	20/10 17,600				Two goals over to Poland, but it should have been so many more. Eric Black struck the bar twice and Gordon Strachan a post. Mark McGhee converted the Dons' ninth corner of the match. Two minutes later Peter Weir turned in Strachan's cross. Two goals should be enough.												
2:2	A LECH POZNAN	W 1-0		0-0	Bell 59 Ref: T Tokat (Turkey) (Dons win 3-0 on aggregate)	Leighton *Plesnierowicz Pawlak*	Kennedy *Szewczyk* *	Rougvie *Adamiec*	McMaster* *Barczak*	McLeish *Malek*	Miller *Niewiadlonski Oblewski* *	Strachan *Barczak*	Simpson* *Kupcewicz*	McGhee* *Okonski*	Bell *Bak*	Weir *Okonski*	Cooper/Watson Kryz'owski/Stroinski
	3/11 30,000				Aberdeen reach the quarter-finals of a European tournament for the first time after 15 years of trying. Leighton's goal was under no particular threat before Bell bundled in McGhee's back-header from Weir's corner. From that moment Lech Poznan needed four goals to go through.												

European campaign

							Att
QF 1	2/3	A	BAYERN MUNICH (W Germ)	1	D	0-0 (0-0)	35,000

Leighton, Kennedy, McLeish, Miller, Cooper, Rougvie, Simpson, Black*, McGhee, Weir, Bell — *Strachan*
Müller, Dremmler, Augenthaler, Kraus, Grobe, Horsmann, Breitner, Nachtweih, Hoeness, Rummenigge, Del Haye

Ref: E Guruceta (Spain)

Aberdeen's 45th European match, played in Munich's Olympic Stadium, produced a well-earned draw against a team brimming with internationals. Bayern's long-range efforts were thrillingly foiled by Leighton. McGhee and Weir both threatened to score a breakaway goal.

							Att
QF 2	16/3	H	BAYERN MUNICH	1	W	3-2 (1-1)	24,000

Simpson 38, McLeish 76, Hewitt 77
Augenthaler 10, Pflügler 61
Ref: M Vautrot (France)
(Dons win 3-2 on aggregate)

Leighton, Kennedy*, McLeish, Miller, Cooper, Rougvie, Simpson*, Strachan, McGhee, Black*, Weir — *McMaster/Hewitt*
Müller, Dremmler, Augenthaler, Kraus, Grobe, Horsmann, Pflügler, Breitner, Hoeness, Del Haye, Rummenigge, Mathy

The best night in Pittodrie's history. Augenthaler scored from 30 yards; Leighton touched it but could not save. Simpson forced the ball over the line. Pflügler's fine volley seemed decisive. McLeish headed in Strachan's free-kick. Sub Hewitt squeezed the ball through Müller's legs.

							Att
SF 1	6/4	H	WATERSCHEI (Belgium)	3	W	5-1 (2-0)	24,000

Black 2, Simpson 4, McGhee 67, 84, Gudmundsson 74 [Weir 69]
Ref: P Bergamo (Italy)

Leighton, Kennedy, McLeish, Miller, Cooper, Rougvie, Bell*, Strachan, McGhee, Simpson, Weir — *Cooper/Hewitt*
Pudatko, Martos, Van Kraay*, Coenen, Bialousz, David, Voordeckers, Gudmundsson, Jansen R — *Connini/Plessers*

The Dons blitz the unknown Belgians - who put out Paris St Germain - in the quarter-finals. Bell's slalom set up a goal for Black. Simpson bulldozed through to score off the keeper. At 4-0 Gudmundsson headed in off the bar. McGhee replied with No 5 after a goalmouth melee.

							Att
SF 2	19/4	A	WATERSCHEI	3	L	0-1 (0-0)	15,000

Voordeckers 73
Ref: A Prokop (E Germany)
(Dons win 5-2 on aggregate)

Leighton, Kennedy, McLeish, Miller, Cooper, Rougvie, Hewitt, McMaster, Strachan, Simpson, Weir — *Angus/Falconer*
Pudatko, Martos, Van Kraay, Plessers / Jansen P, David, Voordeckers, Gudmundts'n*, Jansen R, Massignani

Before this match in Genk both teams were presented with strawberries. Unless they lose 0-4 the Dons are through. They suffer two setbacks - losing their first tie, after Miller and McLeish failed to halt Voordeckers - and losing Stuart Kennedy to the injury that will end his career.

							Att
F	11/5	N	REAL MADRID (Spain) (in Gothenburg)	3	W	2-1 (1-1) (aet)	17,800

Black 7, Hewitt 112
Juanito 14p
Ref: G Menajali (Italy)

Leighton, Kennedy, McLeish, Miller, Cooper, Rougvie, McMaster, Strachan, Simpson, Black*, Weir — *Hewitt*
Augustin, Juan Jose, Camacho*, Metgod, Bonet, Gallego, Juanito, Angel, Santillana, Stielike* — *San Jose/Salguero*

Real Madrid have won the European Cup a record six times. Black volleys against the bar, then screws the first goal past Augustin. McLeish's back-pass sticks in the mud and Leighton brings down Santillana. In extra-time McGhee on the left chips into the middle for Hewitt to head in.

Scottish Premier Division

		P	W	D	L	F	A	W	D	L	F	A	Pts
1	Dundee Utd	36	13	4	1	57	18	11	4	3	33	17	56
2	Celtic	36	12	3	3	44	18	13	2	3	46	18	55
3	ABERDEEN	36	14	0	4	46	12	11	5	2	30	12	55
4	Rangers	36	9	6	3	32	16	4	6	8	20	25	38
5	St Mirren	36	8	5	5	30	18	3	7	8	17	33	34
6	Dundee	36	8	3	7	29	28	1	8	9	13	25	29
7	Hibernian	36	3	11	4	21	17	4	4	10	14	34	29
8	Motherwell	36	9	3	6	28	27	2	2	14	11	46	27
9	Morton	36	4	4	10	14	26	2	4	12	16	48	20
10	Kilmarnock	36	3	7	8	17	31	0	4	14	11	60	17
		360	83	46	51	318	211	51	46	83	211	318	360

Record against each club

		P	W	D	L	F	A	Pts	Cup
v	Motherwell	4	4	0	0	12	2	8	LC
v	Kilmarnock	4	4	0	0	11	1	8	SC
v	Dundee	4	4	0	0	8	1	8	LC SC
v	Morton	4	3	1	0	9	3	7	
v	Hibernian	4	2	2	0	8	1	6	SC
v	Celtic	4	3	0	1	8	4	6	SC
v	Dundee Utd	4	2	0	2	9	5	4	LC
v	St Mirren	4	1	2	1	6	3	4	SC
v	Rangers	4	2	0	2	5	4	4	SC
		36	25	5	6	76	24	55	

Odds & ends

Never lost to: (5) Motherwell, Kilmarnock, Dundee, Morton, Hibs.
Never beat: (0).

Won from behind: (8) Morton (h), Motherwell (h twice), Dundee U (h).
Celtic (a), Dundee (h), Morton (a), Bayern Munich (h).
Lost from in front: (2) Rangers (a), Dundee Utd (LC).

High spots: Winning European Cup-Winners' Cup.
Winning Scottish Cup.
Dropping 1 point in 11 league games from 18 December.
Breaking Aberdeen's Premier Division points record with 55 points.

Low spots: Taking just 3 points from first 4 games.
Losing 3 out of 4 league matches from 19 March.
Failing to be Scottish champions by just 1 point.

Only one outfield player - Kennedy - who started more than one league game failed to score a league goal.

Bogey-team: Dundee Utd, who beat Aberdeen 4 times in all.
Ever-presents: (1) Willie Miller.
Hat-tricks: (3) Eric Black 2, Gordon Strachan 1.
Leading scorer: (27) Mark McGhee.

Appearances and Goals

	Appearances								Goals					
	Lge	Sub	LC	Sub	SC	Sub	Eur	Sub	Lge	Sub	LC	SC	Eur	Tot
Angus, Ian	3	2	2		2				1					3
Bell, Dougie	20	3	2		3		1		2			3		5
Black, Eric	22	9	5		4		8		12		3	1	3	19
Cooper, Neale	29	2	7		4		6		2			1		3
Cowan, Steve	3	3					1		2					2
Falconer, Willie	1													
Gunn, Bryan														
Hamilton, Derek	1		2		1									
Hewitt, John	9	7	4	1	4	3	9	1	5	1	1		5	11
Kennedy, Stuart	25	4	8		4		9	1						1
Leighton, Jim	35		8		5		11							
McCall, Walker	2													
McGhee, Mark	31	1	7		5		11		16	1	2	2	6	27
McLeish, Alex	33		6		5		11		2				1	3
McMaster, John	19	6	6	1	2		7	2	2					2
Miller, Willie	36		8		5		11		2			1		3
Mitchell, Brian	1		1											
Porteous, Ian														
Rougvie, Doug	32	3	6		5		8		3	1		1		4
Simpson, Neil	29	4	6	1	5		11		5	1	1	1	3	10
Strachan, Gordon	32		7		3		9		12	7	1		1	20
Watson, Andy	9	10	2		4		1		1	1		1	1	3
Weir, Peter	29	2	5		4		10		6	1		3	2	11
(own-goals)												2		2
23 players used	396	58	88	15	55	7	121	20	76		19	9	25	129

SCOTTISH PREMIER DIVISION

Manager: Alex Ferguson

SEASON 1983-84

No	Date	Att	Pos	Pt	F-A	H-T	Scorers, Times, and Referees	1	2	3	4	5	6	7	8	9	10	11	subs used
1	H DUNDEE			W	3-0	1-0	Strachan 40p, Hewitt 49, McGeachie 83 og	Leighton	Rougvie	McMaster	Cooper	McLeish	Miller	Strachan*	Stark	Black	Hewitt^	Weir	Bell/Simpson
	20/8	14,304		2				*Kelly*	*McGeachie*	*McKinlay*	*Fraser*	*Smith*	*Glennie*	*Mackie*	*Geddes**	*Stephen*	*McKimmie*	*Kidd*	*Sinclair*
							Ref: A Waddell	It is now 7½ years since Dundee won a league game at Pittodrie. They fell behind after Gordon Strachan was upended by Glennie in the box, and took the resultant penalty himself. Dundee's young full-back, Stewart McKimmie, was booked for protesting against the decision.											
2	H ST JOHNSTONE		1	W	5-0	2-0	Miller 7, Black 11, 68, McGhee 67,	Leighton	Rougvie	McMaster	Cooper	McLeish	Miller	Stark	Bell	Black	Hewitt*	Weir^	McGhee/Simpson
	3/9	12,400	*10*	4			[Stark 77]	*McDonald*	*Kilgour*	*McVicar*	*Beedie**	*Caldwell*	*Rutherford*	*Gibson*	*Brogan*	*Blair*	*Morton*	*Addison*	*Branigan*
							Ref: H Young	In five league and League Cup games, Aberdeen have now found the net 24 times. Promoted St Johnstone appear to have been promoted out of their depth. They will lose their first seven league games and will be beaten six times out of six by Aberdeen come the end of the season.											
3	A MOTHERWELL		4	D	1-1	1-0	McGhee 33	Leighton	Rougvie	McMaster	Cooper	McLeish	Miller	Stark*	Black^	McGhee	Bell	Weir	Mitchell/Hewitt
	10/9	*6,217*	*6*	5			*Gahagan 80*	*Walker*	*Dornan*	*Wark*	*Carson*	*Edvaldsson*	*Mauchlen*	*Gahagan*	*Rafferty*	*Gillespie**	*Ritchie*	*Forbes^*	*Harrow/Cormack*
							Ref: D Galloway	Andy Ritchie was a thorn in Aberdeen's side when he was at Morton. He now glides past two defenders and lays his cross on to Gahagan's head. Near the end Leighton booted the ball into the crowd and was booked for time-wasting. Well won't win any of their first eight games.											
4	A RANGERS		4	W	2-0	0-0	McGhee 70, 80	Leighton	Rougvie	McMaster	Cooper	McLeish	Miller	Cowan*	Simpson	McGhee	Bell	Weir	Hewitt
	17/9	*27,500*	*8*	7				*McCloy*	*Dawson*	*McClelland*	*McPherson**	*Pateson*	*McKinnon*	*Prytz^*	*McCoist*	*Clark*	*Russell*	*Cooper*	*Redford/McDonald*
							Ref: J Duncan	Crisis time at Ibrox. Rangers have taken only one point all season. Mark McGhee scored both Aberdeen goals, but veteran keeper McCloy should have stopped them both. Rangers get their act together in their next match, smashing six goals past porous St Johnstone.											
5	H DUNDEE UTD		4	L	1-2	0-1	Strachan 78p	Leighton	Rougvie	McMaster	Cooper	McLeish	Miller	Cowan*	Simpson	McGhee	Bell^	Weir	Hewitt/Strachan
	24/9	21,100	*1*	7			*Bannon 36, Kirkwood 52*	*McAlpine*	*Kirkwood*	*Stark*	*Gough*	*Hegarty*	*Narey*	*Bannon*	*Milne*	*Malpas*	*Holt*	*Dodds*	
							Ref: H Alexander	Three clubs still have 100% records - Dundee Utd, Celtic, and Hearts - and all three win again. Bannon volleyed United ahead. John McMaster hit a penalty over the bar. Ralph Milne was booked for celebrating Kirkwood's goal with United fans. Narey then conceded his second penalty.											
6	A HEARTS		4	W	2-0	1-0	Weir 28, 73	Leighton	Rougvie	McMaster	Cooper	McLeish	Miller	Strachan	Simpson	McGhee	Stark*	Weir	Falconer
	1/10	*18,200*	*3*	9				*Smith*	*Kidd*	*Cowie*	*Jardine*	*MacDonald R*	*McLaren*	*Bowman*	*Robertson*	*Bone*	*MacDonald A*	*Clark*	
							Ref: W McLeish	A rough-house match, which was turned Aberdeen's way by Strachan's delicious pass which set McGhee clear on the right. When the cross came over Stark missed it, but Weir did not. This result ruins Hearts' perfect start to the season. They won't win any of their next three either.											
7	H ST MIRREN		2	W	5-0	1-0	Stark 30, 47, McGhee 56, Falconer 60,	Leighton	McIntyre	McMaster	Cooper	McLeish	Miller	Stark	Simpson	McGhee	Falconer	Weir	
	8/10	13,300	*8*	11			[Miller 76]	*Thomson*	*Clarke!*	*Cousar*	*McCormack*	*Fulton*	*Abercrombie*	*McAvennie*	*Fitzpatrick*	*McDougall**	*Alexander^*	*Scanlon*	*Sinclair/Cameron*
							Ref: B McGinlay	It is eight games without a win now for St Mirren, who have a new manager, Alex Miller. He watched his team's demolition through closed fingers. The best goal was the last, Willie Miller's thunderous shot from outside the box. Saints' full-back Clarke was sent off for fouling Weir.											
8	A HIBERNIAN		4	L	1-2	1-0	Rougvie 13	Leighton	Rougvie	McMaster	Cooper	McLeish	Miller	Stark	Simpson	McGhee	Falconer*	Weir	Hewitt
	15/10	*7,000*	*5*	11			*Irvine 69, 88*	*Rough*	*Sneddon*	*Schaedler*	*Blackley*	*Jamieson*	*McNamara*	*Brazil*	*Turnbull*	*Irvine*	*Thomson*	*Duncan*	
							Ref: A Ferguson	Hibs' prolific Willie Irvine went into the referee's book three times. First for his diving headed equaliser. Then for his dramatic late winner. Finally he was cautioned for time-wasting. It is not often Aberdeen lose having been ahead, and it is a bad way to forfeit their unbeaten record.											
9	H CELTIC		2	W	3-1	1-0	Hewitt 43, McLeish 55, Strachan 74p	Leighton	McIntyre	Rougvie	Cooper	McLeish	Miller	Strachan*	Hewitt	McGhee	Bell	Weir	Simpson
	22/10	22,800	*3*	13			*Aitken 88*	*Bonner*	*McGrain*	*Sinclair*	*Aitken*	*McAdam*	*MacLeod**	*Provan*	*McStay*	*McGarvey*	*Burns*	*McClair*	*Reid*
							Ref: H Alexander	Another unpleasant, violent confrontation. What football there was earned Aberdeen headed goals by Hewitt and McLeish. There followed two Dons penalties in two minutes, conceded by McAdam and McStay. Bonner saved the first; not the second. Celtic haven't won in four games.											
10	A DUNDEE		1	W	3-1	2-1	Strachan 37p, Weir 44, Bell 73	Leighton	Rougvie	Angus	Simpson*	McLeish	Miller	Strachan	Hewitt	McGhee	Bell	Weir	Porteous
	29/10	*7,849*	7	15			*Glennie 27*	*Geddes R*	*McKimmie*	*McKinlay*	*Fraser*	*Smith*	*Glennie**	*Mackie*	*Stephen*	*Ferguson*	*Richardson*	*Geddes A^*	*McGeachie/Kidd*
							Ref: T Muirhead	Aberdeen go top for the first time, while the granite city is rocked by the bombshell that Rangers want Alex Ferguson as manager. Dons' fans chant 'Fergie must stay'. The team cancelled out Bobby Glennie's 35-yard opener with a mysterious penalty award, which Strachan accepted.											
11	A ST JOHNSTONE		1	W	5-0	3-0	Weir 26, Hewitt 32, 33, 64, Strachan 82p	Leighton	McIntyre	Rougvie*	Simpson	McLeish	Miller	Strachan	Hewitt	McGhee^	Bell	Weir	Angus/Black
	5/11	*6,074*	*10*	17				*McDonald*	*Kilgour**	*Caldwell^*	*Lyons*	*Kennedy*	*Rutherford*	*Gibson*	*Brogan*	*Blair*	*Morton*	*Beedie*	*McKay/Day*
							Ref: H Williamson	It is early November but already Aberdeen have beaten St Johnstone four times, including two 5-0 thrashings in the league. John Hewitt's hat-trick was special: two headers either side of a marauding run. A great way to celebrate Fergie's announcement that he is staying at Pittodrie.											

12 · H · RANGERS · 12/11 — Pos 1 · W 3-0 · Att 22,800 · 8 · 19

Aberdeen	Leighton	Cooper	Rougvie	Simpson	Miller	Strachan	Hewitt*	McGhee	Bell	Weir*	Angus/Porteous
Rangers	*McCloy*	*McKinnon*	*Dawson*	*McClelland*	*McPherson*	*McCoist*	*Nichol*	*Mitchel**	*Redford*	*Cooper**	*Kennedy/Russell*

Simpson 5, Hewitt 9, Porteous 68
Ref: A Waddell

Rangers didn't get Fergie, nor Jim McLean. Instead they turned to former manager Jock Wallace. He steps onto the pitch to acknowledge the Gers fans. Neil Simpson's screamer was topped by Ian Porteous's 25-yard belter, which condemns Rangers to their fifth consecutive defeat.

---

13 · H · HEARTS · 19/11 — Pos 1 · W 2-0 · Att 19,800 · 4 · 21

Aberdeen	Leighton	Rougvie	Simpson	McLeish	Miller	Strachan	Hewitt*	McGhee	Bell	Weir*	Porteous
Hearts	*Smith*	*Kidd*	*Cowie*	*Jardine*	*MacDonald R*	*McLaren**	*Park*	*Bone*	*MacDon'ld A.**	*Robertson*	*Johnston/O'Connor*

Rougvie 33, Simpson 89
Ref: M Delaney

Last week Aberdeen had been voted the best team in Europe. SFA officials make a pre-match presentation to the Dons in recognition of their double cup trophies. Hearts have won just one of their last eight games and lose this one from the moment Doug Rougvie scores with his chest.

---

14 · A · DUNDEE UTD · 26/11 — Pos 1 · W 2-0 · Att 16,902 · 3 · 23

Aberdeen	Leighton	Cooper	Rougvie	Simpson	McLeish	Strachan	Hewitt	McGhee	Bell	Weir	
Dundee Utd	*McAlpine*	*Malpas*	*Murray**	*Gough*	*Hegarty*	*Bannon*	*Milne*	*McGinnis**	*Holt*	*Dodds*	*Coyne/Sturrock*

Bell 8, Strachan 74
Ref: G Smith

United have just lost 0-4 at St Mirren. This is a vital win for Aberdeen, highlighted by Strachan's clinching goal. He received the ball from McGhee, rounded Narey and McAlpine, and netted from an acute angle. Real Madrid, Hamburg, and others, say they want to sign Strachan.

---

15 · H · MOTHERWELL · 3/12 — Pos 1 · W 3-1 · Att 17,700 · 9 · 25

Aberdeen	Leighton	Rougvie	McIntyre	Simpson	Miller	Strachan	Falconer	McGhee	Bell*	Weir*	Porteous
Motherwell	*Walker*	*Dornan*	*Wark*	*McLeod*	*Carson*	*Mauchlen*	*Gahagan*	*Alexander**	*Forbes*	*McFadden*	*Cormack*

McGhee 31, Strachan 69p, Falconer 77 · Gahagan 46
Ref: R Cuthill

Motherwell have won just once so far. Gahagan stunned the Dons with an out-of-the-blue equaliser. But McFadden foolishly pulled down Gordon Strachan, who picked himself up to score from the spot. Falconer claimed the third goal, registered in some records as an own-goal.

---

16 · A · CELTIC · 10/12 — Pos 1 · D 0-0 · Att 25,867 · 2 · 26

Aberdeen	Cooper*	McIntyre	Rougvie	Simpson	Miller	Strachan*	Hewitt*	McGhee	Bell	Weir*	Angus/Falconer
Celtic	*Bonner*	*McGrain*	*Reid*	*Aitken*	*McAdam*	*McClair*	*McStay P*	*McGarvey*	*Burns*	*Melrose!*	

0-0
Ref: A Ferguson

No goals, but another no-holds-barred encounter between these arch rivals. In the 71st minute Celtic's Melrose elbowed Doug Rougvie in the face and was sent off. This result keeps the Dons three points clear of Celtic at the top. They will never close that gap.

---

17 · H · HIBERNIAN · 17/12 — Pos 1 · W 2-1 · Att 14,000 · 4 · 28

Aberdeen	McKimmie	Angus	Simpson	McLeish	Rougvie	Strachan*	Hewitt*	McGhee	Bell	Weir*	Falconer/Black
Hibs	*Rough*	*Sneddon*	*Brazil*	*Turnbull*	*Jamieson*	*Blackley*	*Callachan*	*Harvey*	*Irvine*	*Thomson*	*Duncan*

McGhee 1, Blackley 55 og · Irvine 81
Ref: I Cathcart

Stewart McKimmie makes his debut in the first minute. Jamieson missed Bell's cross, which fell to McGhee. Then Blackley went one better, ramming Strachan's cross into his own goal. Stunned Hibs won't win in the next eight.

---

18 · A · ST MIRREN · 24/12 — Pos 1 · W 3-0 · Att 6,654 · 7 · 30

Aberdeen	Leighton	McKimmie	Rougvie	Simpson	Miller	Strachan	Black*	McGhee	Bell	Weir*	Hewitt
St Mirren	*Thomson*	*Winnie!*	*Cooper*	*Fulton*	*Abercrombie*	*Fitzpatrick*	*McAvennie*	*McDougall*	*McCormack*	*Scanlon*	

Bell 4, McLeish 26, McGhee 86
Ref: W McLeish

St Mirren have hit four goals past both Celtic and Dundee Utd, and were unbeaten in seven until losing to bottom-placed St Johnstone. The Dons stayed in fourth gear throughout this match. Strachan was booed every time he saw the ball. Saints' Winnie was sent off after half-time.

---

19 · H · DUNDEE · 31/12 — Pos 1 · W 5-2 · Att 18,250 · 8 · 32

Aberdeen	Leighton	McKimmie	Rougvie	McMaster	Miller*	Strachan	Hewitt	Black	Bell	Weir*	McIntyre/Porteous
Dundee	*Geddes R*	*Glennie*	*McKinlay*	*Fraser*	*McDonald*	*Mackie*	*Richardson**	*Ferguson*	*McCall*	*Geddes A **	*Kidd/Paterson*

McKinlay 4 og, Strachan 22, 80p, Mackie 85, Ferguson 88 [Hewitt 68]
Ref: T Muirhead

Poor Dundee have now taken just one point from six matches. For 85 minutes Aberdeen were as irresistible as gravity. For the last few they became sloppy - which might eventually wreck their attempt to establish a new defensive record. Fergie must have exploded afterwards.

---

20 · A · RANGERS · 7/1 — Pos 1 · D 1-1 · Att 37,500 · 5 · 33

Aberdeen	Leighton	McKimmie	Rougvie	Simpson*	Miller	Strachan	Hewitt	Black	Bell	Weir*	Cooper/Hewitt
Rangers	*Walker*	*Dawson*	*McCleland*	*McKinlay*	*McDonald*	*Redford*	*Russell*	*Williamson*	*Clark**	*McPherson**	*Cooper*	*McDonald/Prytz*

Hewitt 68 · Cooper 48p
Ref: A Huett

After half an hour Ally Dawson and Eric Black flared up and were sent off. Rangers were unbeaten in eight, since Eric Wallace's baptism at Pittodrie, and scored from the spot after Leighton impeded Williamson. McGhee hit a post before Weir's electrifying run set up John Hewitt.

---

21 · H · CELTIC · 4/2 — Pos 1 · W 1-0 · Att 23,000 · 2 · 35

Aberdeen	Leighton	McKimmie	Cooper	Simpson*	Miller	Strachan	Simpson*	McGhee	Hewitt*	Weir*	Falconer/Bell
Celtic	*Bonner*	*McGrain**	*Reid*	*Aitken*	*McAdam*	*Sinclair*	*McClair*	*McStay P*	*McGarvey*	*MacLeod*	*Burns*

Hewitt 19
Ref: L Thow

A month has been lost to the weather. A Celtic win would bring them within two points. They point leaders... A fierce low cross was touched away by Bonner, but landed at the feet of Hewitt. Leighton blocked McClair's would-be equaliser with his legs.

---

22 · A · MOTHERWELL · 11/2 — Pos 1 · W 4-0 · Att 6,051 · 10 · 37

Aberdeen	Leighton	McKimmie	Rougvie	McMaster	Miller	Strachan	Bell*	McGhee	Hewitt	Weir*	Black/Mitchell
Motherwell	*Sproat*	*Dornan*	*McLeod*	*McAllister*	*Mauchlen**	*Kennedy*	*Rafferty*	*Harrow*	*Black*	*McFadden**	*Dobbin/Boyd*

Strachan 37, 51, Black 69, Hewitt 76
Ref: A Waddell

Poor Motherwell. This is their 14th game without a win. Aside from the four goals the game produced six bookings and some unsavoury crowd scenes. During the preceding week Willie Garner was appointed assistant manager. Motherwell will win their next game, against St Johnstone.

---

23 · A · HIBERNIAN · 25/2 — Pos 1 · W 2-0 · Att 8,500 · 7 · 39

Aberdeen	Leighton	McKimmie	Rougvie	Cooper*	Mitchell	Strachan	Black	McGhee	Angus	Hewitt*	McMaster/Porteous
Hibs	*Rae R*	*McKee*	*Schaedler*	*Rae G*	*Jamieson*	*Rice*	*Callachan*	*Kane*	*Turnbull*	*Harvey*	*McGeachie*

Black 28, McGhee 85
Ref: H Williamson

Eric Black's fierce free-kick meant the Dons were forced onto the defensive for the rest of the match. They had much defending to do before Black headed on to McGhee for the second, decisive goal. It is eight without a win for Hibs now, but they will beat Dundee next time out.

SCOTTISH PREMIER DIVISION

Manager: Alex Ferguson

SEASON 1983-84

---

24 · 3/3 (H) ST MIRREN — W 2-0 (HT 1-0) · Att 14,500 · Pos 1 · Pt 41 · Scorers: Strachan 32p, Hewitt 89 · Ref: C Sinclair

Team	1	2	3	4	5	6	7	8	9	10	11	subs used
Aberdeen	Leighton	McKimmie	Rougvie	Cooper	McLeish	Miller	Strachan*	Black	McGhee	Angus	Bell	Hewitt
St Mirren (6)	*Thomson*	*Hamilton*	*Clarke*	*Cooper*	*Fulton*	*McCormack*	*Fitzpatrick**	*McAvennie*	*McDougall**	*Abercrombie*	*Scanlon*	*Cameron/Alexander*

St Mirren are the most inconsistent team in the division, beating and losing to everyone - but always losing to the Dons. When Mark Fulton toppled Neale Cooper without ceremony it gave Gordon Strachan the chance from the penalty spot to score his 100th goal for Aberdeen.

---

25 · 31/3 (A) CELTIC — L 0-1 (HT 0-1) · Att 19,193 · Pos 1 · Pt 41 · Scorers: Melrose 35 · Ref: D Downie

Team	1	2	3	4	5	6	7	8	9	10	11	subs used
Aberdeen	Leighton	McKimmie	Rougvie	Cooper	McLeish	Miller	Strachan	Black*	McGhee	Angus*	Hewitt	Mitchell/Porteous
Celtic (2)	*Bonner*	*McGrain*	*Reid*	*Aitken*	*McAdam*	*McStay W*	*McClair*	*McStay P**	*Melrose*	*MacLeod*	*Burns*	*Provan*

Celtic began this match six points behind, having also played two games more. The result is vital to them, but hardly fatal to Aberdeen. Melrose scored the only goal with a 5 m.p.h. shot that somehow went in. Aberdeen pressed unavailingly throughout the second half.

---

26 · 2/4 (H) HEARTS — D 1-1 (HT 0-0) · Att 16,240 · Pos 1 · Pt 42 · Scorers: Porteous 46, Robertson 62 · Ref: R Valentine

Team	1	2	3	4	5	6	7	8	9	10	11	subs used
Aberdeen	Leighton	McKimmie	Rougvie	Cooper	McLeish	Miller	Porteous	Simpson	McGhee	Angus	Hewitt*	Wright
Hearts (5)	*Smith*	*Kidd*	*Cowie*	*Jardine*	*MacDonald R.Levein**	*Bowman*	*Mackay*	*Bone*	*MacDonald A.*Robertson*			*Park/Johnston*

Aberdeen drop their third point inside three days. They dominated everything but the knack of taking chances. Ian Porteous scored following a one-two with McGhee, but the goal was cancelled out when Hearts' John Robertson took on Neale Cooper before unleashing a low shot.

---

27 · 7/4 (H) MOTHERWELL — W 2-1 (HT 2-0) · Att 15,500 · Pos 1 · Pt 44 · Scorers: McGhee 12, Strachan 37, Rafferty 84 · Ref: A Roy

Team	1	2	3	4	5	6	7	8	9	10	11	subs used
Aberdeen	Leighton	Mitchell	Rougvie	Cooper	McLeish	Miller	Strachan	Black	McGhee	McKimmie*	Angus*	Porteous/Hewitt
Motherwell (10)	*Maxwell*	*McLeod*	*Black*	*Forbes*	*Kennedy*	*Lyall*	*McFadden**	*Rafferty*	*Boyd*	*McAllister*	*Harrow**	*Gahagan/Alexander*

Motherwell know their fate is to be relegated. Up in the stand officials from FC Cologne assess the performance of Gordon Strachan, with a view to signing him. He was brilliant, coolly slotting the ball past Motherwell's debutant keeper Maxwell to put the Dons two up.

---

28 · 18/4 (H) DUNDEE UTD — W 5-1 (HT 3-1) · Att 19,562 · Pos 1 · Pt 46 · Scorers: Rougvie 10, 67, McGhee 27, 37, Black 63, Reilly 34 · Ref: H Young

Team	1	2	3	4	5	6	7	8	9	10	11	subs used
Aberdeen	Leighton	Mitchell	Rougvie	Simpson	McLeish	Miller	Strachan	Black	McGhee*	Bell	Angus*	Stark/Weir
Dundee Utd (3)	*McAlpine*	*Stark*	*Malpas*	*Gough**	*Hegarty*	*Narey*	*Bannon*	*Kirkwood*	*Reilly*	*Coyne*	*Dodds*	*Holt/Clark*

The defending champs are about to be unthroned. No wonder Alex Ferguson purrs with pleasure after this demolition. Eric Black ends his personal goal-famine with a thunderous header. Billy Stark and Peter Weir come of the bench after lengthy injuries. But Weir goes off again.

---

29 · 21/4 (A) ST JOHNSTONE — W 2-0 (HT 0-0) · Att 6,197 · Pos 1 · Pt 48 · Scorers: Stark 75, McGhee 78 · Ref: K Hope

Team	1	2	3	4	5	6	7	8	9	10	11	subs used
Aberdeen	Leighton	Mitchell	Rougvie	Simpson	McLeish	Miller	Stark	Black*	Porteous*	Bell	Hewitt	McGhee/McIntyre
St Johnstone (9)	*Baines*	*Kilgour*	*Morton*	*Beedie*	*Barron*	*Rutherford*	*Gibson*	*Brogan*	*Scott*	*Blair*	*Lyons**	*Reid*

Four recent wins have given St Johnstone the scent of survival. Celtic's 0-1 defeat at Ibrox means the championship is virtually secure for Aberdeen, but it took the arrival of substitute Mark McGhee to spark the Dons into life and complete their fifth win over the Saints this season.

---

30 · 28/4 (A) DUNDEE — W 1-0 (HT 0-0) · Att 6,663 · Pos 1 · Pt 50 · Scorers: Black 67 · Ref: H Young

Team	1	2	3	4	5	6	7	8	9	10	11	subs used
Aberdeen	Leighton	McKimmie	Rougvie	Simpson*	McLeish	Miller	Strachan	Black	McGhee	Stark	Hewitt	Bell
Dundee (8)	*Geddes*	*McInally*	*McKinlay*	*Shannon*	*Smith*	*Glennie*	*Hendry**	*Richardson**	*McCall*	*McGeachie*	*Ferguson*	*Harris/Kidd*

Dundee are peering anxiously over their shoulder at St Johnstone's rise from the ashes. Dundee supporters did not appreciate McKinlay's terrible back-pass which landed at the feet of Eric Black. Dundee have now sacrificed eight league points upon the Aberdeen altar.

---

31 · 30/4 (H) ST JOHNSTONE — W 1-0 (HT 0-0) · Att 11,500 · Pos 1 · Pt 52 · Scorers: Hewitt 80 · Ref: B McGinlay

Team	1	2	3	4	5	6	7	8	9	10	11	subs used
Aberdeen	Leighton	Mitchell*	Rougvie	McKimmie	McLeish	Miller	Strachan	Bell	McGhee	Hewitt	Weir*	Stark/Porteous
St Johnstone (9)	*Baines*	*Beedie*	*Morton*	*Addison*	*Woods*	*Berron*	*Gibson*	*Brogan*	*Scott*	*Blair*	*Reid*	

This game was abandoned in January. St Johnstone are staging a stirring rally in the attempt to avoid the drop. They scarcely deserved to lose to Hewitt's well-timed finishing touch to McGhee's cross. Only freak results can now deprive Aberdeen of the title. St Johnstone look doomed.

---

32 · 2/5 (A) HEARTS — W 1-0 (HT 0-0) · Att 14,000 · Pos 1 · Pt 54 · Scorers: McKimmie 61 · Ref: R Valentine

Team	1	2	3	4	5	6	7	8	9	10	11	subs used
Aberdeen	Leighton	McKimmie	Rougvie	Cooper	McLeish	Miller	Strachan	Simpson	McGhee	Hewitt*	Weir*	Black/Johnston
Hearts (5)	*Smith*	*Kidd*	*Cowie*	*Jardine*	*MacDonald R.Levein*	*Bowman*	*Mackay*	*Bone*	*Robertson*	*Park**		

Willie Miller celebrates his 29th birthday today, and learns that he has been voted Scotland's player of the year. Stewart McKimmie's first goal for Aberdeen officially seals the championship. As in 1980, it was slightly disappointing not to have won it before their own fans at Pittodrie.

---

33 · 5/5 (H) HIBERNIAN — D 2-2 (HT 0-2) · Att 17,000 · Pos 1 · Pt 55 · Scorers: Stark 61, Porteous 90, McGeachie 23, Rice 26 · Ref: A Ferguson

Team	1	2	3	4	5	6	7	8	9	10	11	subs used
Aberdeen	Leighton	Mitchell	McKimmie*	Cooper	Rougvie	Miller	Porteous	Black*	McGhee	Stark	Weir	McIntyre/Hewitt
Hibernian (7)	*Rough*	*McKee*	*Schaedler*	*Sneddon*	*Rae*	*Blackley*	*Callachan*	*Jamieson*	*Irvine*	*Rice*	*McGeachie*	

This was supposed to be Aberdeen's championship party. But Hibs gate-crashed it and would have won except for a possible refereeing error. In injury-time both Billy Stark and Mark McGhee appeared to foul keeper Alan Rough, and the ball broke loose to Ian Porteous.

---

34 · 7/5 (A) DUNDEE UTD — D 0-0 (HT 0-0) · Att 7,990 · Pos 1 · Pt 56 · Ref: D Syme

Team	1	2	3	4	5	6	7	8	9	10	11	subs used
Aberdeen	Leighton	McIntyre*	Rougvie	Cooper	McLeish	Miller	Strachan	McKimmie	Cowan	Hewitt*	Weir	Stark/Falconer
Dundee Utd (3)	*McAlpine*	*Malpas*	*Munro*	*Gough*	*Hegarty*	*Narey*	*Bannon*	*Holt*	*Coyne*	*Sturrock*	*Taylor*	

Not for the first time in recent seasons this fixture ends in deadlock. The point gained by the Dons equals the Premier Division record of 56, and means a 60-point target is still attainable. United's crown slips away with no wins in their last five games, denying them runners-up spot.

Scottish League / Cup Record

#		Date	Opponent	Att		Res	Score	Scorers
35	H	9/5	RANGERS	16,200	1 D 4 57	0-0		Ref: R Valentine
36	A	12/5	ST MIRREN	3,450	1 L 6 57	2-3	Money 23 og, Stark 87p	McDougal 18, Abercromb'47, Alexander 83 · Ref: M Delaney

Average Home 17,220 Away 12,880

35 (Rangers): Leighton, McIntyre, Rougvie, Cooper, McLeish, Miller, Porteous*, Stark, McGhee, McKimmie, Cowan, sub Hewitt
McCloy, Fraser, McClelland, McPherson, Paterson, Redford, Russell, Williamson, Clark, McCoist, Cooper, Ferguson*

Under Jock Wallace Rangers have now lost only once in 21 games. This was not a match to remember, except that it took Aberdeen's points total to 57, a Premier record. Before the match Gordon Strachan signs for Manchester United, but is free to compete in the Scottish Cup Final.

36 (St Mirren): Leighton, Robertson I, McMaster, Cooper, Rougvie, McIntyre, Porteous*, Falconer, Cowan, Stark, Hewitt*, subs McKimmie/McGhee
Money, Clarke, Winnie, Cooper, Fulton, McCormack, Jarvie, McAvennie, McDougall, Abercrombie Cameron, Alexander, Falconer Alexander*

Alex Ferguson sends out a team of babes and reserves, mothballing his best 11 for the Scottish Cup final. No Miller, no McLeish, no Strachan. The Dons concede three goals for the only time this season. They therefore equal, but do not beat, the Premier League's best defensive record.

Scottish League Cup

#		Date	Opponent	Att		Res	Score	Scorers
2:1	H	24/8	RAITH ROVERS	9,650	W	9-0	Stark 19, 62, 78, Porteous 28, Hewitt 59	[Black 44, 51p, 65, 69]Graham · Ref: H Alexander
2:2	A	27/8	RAITH ROVERS	3,000	W	3-0	Hewitt 35, 69, Stark 86	Ref: R Valentine (Dons win 12-0)
1	H	31/8	MEADOWBANK (Section 3)	10,000	W	4-0	McGhee 19, 90, Stark 32, Black 55	Ref: G Smith
2	A	7/9	ST JOHNSTONE	5,100 10	W	1-0	Miller 23	Ref: D Downie
3	H	5/10	DUNDEE	13,200 8	D	0-0		Ref: D Syme
4	H	26/10	ST JOHNSTONE	12,700 10	W	1-0	Simpson 12	Ref: A Roy
5	A	9/11	MEADOWBANK	2,700 1:12	W	3-1	Porteous 55, Stewart 61 og, Hewitt 67, Sprott 72p	Ref: B McGinlay
6	A	30/11	DUNDEE	11,019 7	W	2-1	McGhee 18, Bell 46, Fraser 62	Ref: H Young

2:1 (Raith H): Leighton, Rougvie, McMaster, Bell, McLeish, Miller, Porteous*, Stark, Black, Hewitt, Weir, subs Simpson/Porteous
A new format for the League Cup, delaying the section stage till later. Raith will finish low in Division 2. Aberdeen hit the wood three times.

2:2 (Raith A): Leighton, Rougvie, McMaster, Bell, McLeish, Miller, Porteous*, Stark, Black, Hewitt, Weir, subs Stark/Hewitt
One wonders what was the point of this match. Were Raith looking to score 10? The crowd is the largest Starks Park will see this season.

1 (Meadowbank H): Leighton, Cooper, McMaster, Bell, McLeish, Miller, Black*, Stark, McGhee, Hewitt*, Weir, subs Simpson/Stalker
Three Premier sides, plus Meadowbank Thistle, comprise Section 3 of this new-look League Cup. The Dons have all the ball and all the play.

2 (St Johnstone A): Leighton, Rougvie, McMaster, Cooper, McLeish, Miller, Simpson*, Bell, Black*, McGhee, Weir, subs Stark/Blair
Four days earlier Aberdeen whacked five past St Johnstone in the league. This time they settle for Miller's bundled goal from Weir's corner.

3 (Dundee H): Leighton, Geddes R, McMaster, Cooper, McLeish, Miller, Strachan*, Simpson, McGhee, Falconer*, Weir, subs Stark/Hewitt
Dundee's objective is to keep a clean sheet to share top spot. This is the only joy they will know from seven matches with the Dons this season.

4 (St Johnstone H): Leighton, McIntyre*, Rougvie, Cooper, McLeish, Miller, Strachan, Simpson, McCall, Fraser, McKinlay, subs Angus/Blair-Brogan
After Neil Simpson capitalised on a one-two with John Hewitt, Aberdeen found themselves in a rut. St Johnstone even lose to Meadowbank.

5 (Meadowbank A): Leighton, McIntyre*, Rougvie, Cooper, McLeish, Miller, Strachan, Hewitt, Bell*, Simpson, Bell*, subs Angus/Porteous Tomassi/Smith
Dons substitute Ian Porteous collected Strachan's knock-down to score, but before then Aberdeen had rarely looked like breaking through.

6 (Dundee A): Leighton, Geddes R, Cooper, McMaster, McLeish, Miller, Strachan*, Simpson, McGhee, Hewitt*, Weir, subs Falconer/McMaster McGlashan/Kidd
Dundee must win to qualify. That looked tough until when McGhee scored his 100th Dons goal with a cross-shot which Geddes might have saved.

Qualifying — Section Table

	P	W	D	L	F	A	Pts
ABERDEEN	6	5	1	0	11	2	11
Dundee	6	3	2	1	8	4	8
Meadowbank	6	1	2	3	4	10	4
St Johnstone	6	0	1	5	2	9	1

#		Date	Opponent	Att		Res	Score	Scorers
SF 1	H	22/2	CELTIC	20,074 2	D	0-0		Ref: B McGinlay
SF 2	A	10/3	CELTIC	41,169 2	L	0-1	Raid 54p	Ref: R Valentine (Dons lose 0-1 on aggregate)

SF 1 (Celtic H): Leighton, Rougvie, McMaster*, Cooper, McLeish, Miller, Strachan, Black, McGhee, Angus, Weir*, subs Mitchell/Hewitt
It was Aberdeen who wished to have a first-leg lead, but Celtic who would have deserved it. The nearest Aberdeen came was with a Strachan volley — with spies watching him — from 25 yards which crashed off the bar in the opening minutes. Thereafter the better chances fell to Celtic.

SF 2 (Celtic A): Leighton, Cooper, McGrain, Rougvie, McLeish, Miller, Strachan, Bell, Black, Angus, Hewitt, subs Falconer/Provan
Six more bookings, ugly crowd violence, and a penalty against Aberdeen when Bell and Angus supposedly sandwiched Tommy Burns. Now they are left chasing three. This is the only change Celtic will get from Aberdeen this season.

SCOTTISH PREMIER (CUP-TIES) Manager: Alex Ferguson SEASON 1983-84

Scottish Cup

Column headings: 1 · 2 · 3 · 4 · 5 · 6 · 7 · 8 · 9 · 10 · 11 · subs used

3 H KILMARNOCK 1 D 1-1 H-T 0-0 — 15,000 1:4 — Weir 83 / Gallacher 90 — Ref: J Renton — 13/2

	1	2	3	4	5	6	7	8	9	10	11	subs used
Dons	Leighton	McCulloch	McKimmie	McMaster*	McLeish	Miller	Strachan	Black	McGhee	Hewitt*	Weir	Porteous/Cooper
Killie	McLean	Robertson	McDicken	Clarke P	Clark R	McGivern	MacLeod	Gallacher	Simpson	Bryson*		McKinna/Cockburn

The Dons bang their heads against Killie's wall. McGhee, Porteous, and Strachan set up Weir. Gallacher outpaced Alex McLeish at the death.

3R A KILMARNOCK 1 W 3-1 H-T 2-0 — 9,460 1:4 — Strachan 30, Miller 35, Weir 84 / McKinna 63 — Ref: J Renton — 15/2

	1	2	3	4	5	6	7	8	9	10	11	subs used
Dons	Leighton	McCulloch	McKimmie	McMaster*	McLeish	Miller	Strachan*	Black	McGhee	Angus	Weir	Hewitt/Porteous
Killie	McLean	Robertson	Cochrane	Clarke P	Clark R	McGivern	MacLeod	Gallacher	Simpson	McKinna		

Strachan plays one-twos with Miller, Black, and McGhee to score a classic goal. At 0-2 Killie rally, climaxed with McKinna's back-header.

4 A CLYDE 1 W 2-0 H-T 1-0 — 5,800 1:7 — Angus 15, Cooper 56 — Ref: A Huett — 18/2

	1	2	3	4	5	6	7	8	9	10	11	subs used
Dons	Leighton	McKimmie*	Rougvie	Cooper	McLeish	Miller	Strachan	Black	McGhee*	Angus	Weir	McMaster/Hewitt
Clyde	Atkins	McFarlane	McQueen	Ahern	Flexney	Evans	Reilly	McVeigh	Masterton	O'Neill*	Frye	Doherty

More Division 1 opponents. Clyde did their best on a beautiful spring-like afternoon, but were a beaten side following Angus's deflected drive.

QF H DUNDEE UTD 1 D 0-0 H-T 0-0 — 22,000 3 — Ref: B McGinlay — 17/3

	1	2	3	4	5	6	7	8	9	10	11	subs used
Dons	Leighton	McKimmie*	Rougvie	Cooper	McLeish	Miller	Strachan*	Black	McGhee	Simpson	Angus	Hewitt
Utd	McAlpine	Stark	Malpas	Gough	Holt	Narey	Bannon*	Kirkwood	Coyne	Milne*	Dodds	Page/Clark

Without the injured Sturrock and Hegarty, Dundee Utd look to be content to earn a replay. Even that modest objective would have been beyond them had the woodwork not rescued Hamish McAlpine on two occasions. Still, United won at Pittodrie on their last visit, in October.

QFR A DUNDEE UTD 1 W 1-0 H-T 1-0 — 16,094 3 — McGhee 2 — Ref: B McGinlay — 28/3

	1	2	3	4	5	6	7	8	9	10	11	subs used
Dons	Leighton	McKimmie	Rougvie*	Cooper	McLeish	Miller	Strachan	Simpson	McGhee	Black	Angus	Mitchell
Utd	McAlpine	Stark*	Malpas	McGinnis*	Hegarty	Narey	Holt	Kirkwood	Milne	Sturrock	Dodds	Clark/Taylor

McAlpine's weak goal-kick is chested down by Cooper and switched forward to McGhee, racing in from the left. And that's that. United were without the unfit Gough and Bannon, and missed them badly. This marks Aberdeen's first cup win over United since Ferguson took charge.

SF N DUNDEE 1 W 2-0 H-T 1-0 — 17,654 8 (at Tynecastle) — Porteous 28, Strachan 89 — Ref: B McGinlay — 14/4

	1	2	3	4	5	6	7	8	9	10	11	subs used
Dons	Leighton	Mitchell	Rougvie	Simpson	McLeish	Miller	Strachan	Black	Porteous*	Angus	Hewitt*	Bell/Cowan
Dundee	Geddes	Glennie	McKinlay	Fraser	Smith	MacDonald	Mackie	Richardson*	Harris	McGeachie	Kidd	McSlachan/Stephen

An untidy semi-final that saw six bookings. Dundee had much of the first-half play. Harris jumped higher than Jim Leighton to head home, but the referee decided he had fouled the keeper. Ian Porteous broke the ice when John Hewitt's corner was missed by the entire Dundee defence.

F N CELTIC 1 W 2-1 (aet) H-T 1-0 — 58,900 2 (at Hampden) — Black 23, McGhee 98 / McStay 86 — Ref: R Valentine — 19/5

	1	2	3	4	5	6	7	8	9	10	11	subs used
Dons	Leighton	McKimmie*	Rougvie*	Cooper	McLeish	Miller	Strachan	Simpson	McGhee	Black	Weir*	Stark/Bell
Celtic	Bonner	McGrain	Reid*	Aitken!	McStay W	MacLeod	Provan	McStay P	McGarvey	Burns	McClair*	Melrose/Sinclair

The 99th Scottish Cup final. Black volleys shoulder-high past Bonner. After 40 minutes Aitken races across to send McGhee spinning. Aitken becomes the first player sent off in the Final since 1929. McStay levels for the 10 men. In extra-time Bell hits the post and McGhee scores.

European Cup-Winners' Cup

1:1 A AKRANES (Iceland) 1 W 2-1 H-T 1-1 — 5,500 — McGhee 29, 88 / Halldorsson 28 — Ref: R Daly (Rep Ireland) — 14/9

	1	2	3	4	5	6	7	8	9	10	11	subs used
Dons	Leighton	Mitchell	Rougvie	Cooper*	McLeish	Miller	Stark*	Simpson	McGhee	Bell	Hewitt	McMaster/Cowan
Akranes	Sigurdsson	Pordarson	Askelson	Larusson	Halldorsson	Johansson*	Hakonarsson Jonsson	Omarsson	Tryggvason Sveinsson			Ingolsson

Halldorsson heads in a corner, but then errs for McGhee's instant lob. Leighton parries Sveinsson's penalty. McGhee heads in Hewitt's corner.

1:2 H AKRANES 4 D 1-1 H-T 0-0 — 12,500 — Strachan 89p / Askelson 89p — Ref: R Nyhus (Norway) (2-1 on agg) — 28/9

	1	2	3	4	5	6	7	8	9	10	11	subs used
Dons	Leighton	Cooper	McMaster	Simpson	McLeish	Miller	Strachan*	Black*	McGhee	Hewitt	Weir	Porteous/Bell
Akranes	Sigurdsson	Pardarson	Askelson	Larusson	Halldorsson	Johanesson*	Hakonarsson Jonsson	Omarsson	Tryggvason Sveinsson			Ingolsson

Two penalties. McGhee was felled by Halldorsson for the Dons'. In the final minute Tryggvason was barged off the ball by Neale Cooper.

2:1 A BEVEREN (Belgium) 4 D 0-0 H-T 0-0 — 21,000 — Ref: J Krchnak (Czechoslovakia) — 19/10

	1	2	3	4	5	6	7	8	9	10	11	subs used
Dons	Leighton	Rougvie	McMaster	Cooper	McLeish	Miller	Hewitt	Simpson	McGhee	Bell*	Weir	Strachan
Beveren	de Wilde	Jaspers	Pfaff	Lambrichts	Baecke	Stalmans*	Schonberger Albert	Theunis	Martens	Creve	Gortz	

Beveren are unbeaten on top of the Belgian league. The Dons' tactics are to stifle home attacks well out form Leighton's goal. They work well.

2:2 H BEVEREN 1 W 4-1 H-T 2-0 — 22,500 — Strachan 37p, 60, Simpson 45, Weir 69 / Theunis 83 — Ref: T Sorensen (Den) (4-1 on agg) — 2/11

	1	2	3	4	5	6	7	8	9	10	11	subs used
Dons	Leighton	Cooper	Rougvie	Simpson*	McLeish	Miller	Strachan*	Hewitt	McGhee	Bell	Weir*	Angus/Black
Beveren	de Wilde	Jaspers	Garot	Lambrichts	Baecke	Pfeff*	Schonberger Albert	Theunis	Martens	Kusto*		Creve/Stalmans

Before kick-off Alex Ferguson announces he was not joining Rangers. Keeper de Wilde crashed into Hewitt for the penalty. Weir was magic.

QF1 A UJPEST DOZSA (Hungary) 1 L 0-2 H-T 0-0 — 29,000 — Kiszmyer 50, Heredi 82 — Ref: T Tokat (Turkey) — 7/3

	1	2	3	4	5	6	7	8	9	10	11	subs used
Dons	Leighton	McKimmie	Rougvie	Cooper	McLeish	Miller	Strachan*	Black*	McGhee	Bell	Hewitt	Simpson/Hewitt
Ujpest	Szendrei	Kovacs B	Kovacs J	Kardos	Toth	Steidl	Heredi	Kiszmyer	Kiss	Toriczik	Fekete	Ingoldson

The Megyeri Stadium witnesses Aberdeen's first defeat in 28 matches. The Dons trailed to a free-kick, then wasted many chances. Strachan rounded the keeper but hit the post. Szendrei dropped the ball to McGhee, who missed from two feet. Heredi outpaced Miller for the second.

QF2 H UJPEST DOZSA 1 W 3-0 (aet) H-T 1-0 — 22,800 — McGhee 37, 88, 93 — Ref: A Ponnet (Belgium) — 21/3

	1	2	3	4	5	6	7	8	9	10	11	subs used
Dons	Leighton	Cooper	McKimmie	Rougvie	McLeish	Miller	Strachan*	Black*	McGhee	Bell*	Hewitt*	Angus/Falconer
Ujpest	Szendreil	Kovacs B	Kovacs J	Toth	Kiszmyer	Kardos	Heredi	Steidl	Tarocsik	Fekete*	Heredi	Bogdan?/Szebegynski

A fantastic night. The Hungarian goal endured siege conditions. McGhee headed in Strachan's cross. Two minutes from time McGhee side-...

European Cup-Winners' Cup — Semi-finals

SF 1 — PORTO A 11/4 (Portugal) 65,000 — 1 L 0-1 0-1

Leighton, McKimmie, Rougvie*, Cooper, McLeish, Miller, Strachan, Black, McGhee, Simpson, Bell*
Ze Beto, Joao Pinto, Inacio, Lima Pereira, Ed Luis, Magalhaes J, Frasco*, Sousa, Gomes, Pacheco J, Costa*
Mitchell/Hewitt — Walsh/Vermelinho

Games 14
Ref: J Igna (Romania)

When the semi-final draw was made before Christmas Fergie said he fancied Porto. Silly man. Fernando Gomes' header - after a corner was back-headed to him - was all Porto had to show for their first-half control. In an atmosphere of seething passion, Aberdeen then shut the door.

SF 2 — PORTO H 25/4 23,000 — 1 L 0-1 0-0

Leighton, McKimmie, Rougvie*, Simpson, McLeish, Miller, Strachan, Black, McGhee, Bell, Hewitt*
Ze Beto, Joao Pinto, Ed Luis, Lima Pereira, Eurico, Magalhaes J*, Frasco*, Sousa, Gomes, Pacheco J, Vermelinho, Costa/Quinito
Cooper/Weir

Vermelinho 75
Ref: J Krchnak (Czechoslovakia)
(Dons lose 0-2 on aggregate)

Magnificent Porto end dreams of a second Cup-Winners Cup final. In a misty stadium, McGhee jinked his way round two defenders in the box, but most of the magic came from the Portuguese. A semi-fit Weir came on as sub. Two minutes later Vermelinho broke away to chip Leighton.

European Super Cup

F-1 — SV HAMBURG A 22/11 (W Germ) 15,000 — 1 D 0-0 0-0

Leighton, Cooper, Rougvie, Simpson, McLeish, Miller, Strachan, Hewitt, McGhee, Bell, Weir
Stein, Schroder, Wehmeyer, Jakobs, Hieronymous, Hartwig*, Roff, Groh, Schatzsch'ler/Magath, Von Heesen, Wuttke

Ref: A Christov (Czechoslovakia)

Two years earlier Hamburg k.o'd Aberdeen from the UEFA Cup. This time the Dons tactics are early defence, playing in their opponents' half. They have limited success. It is the back four who do all the defending, though McGhee waltzed round two defenders to shoot tamely at Stein.

F-2 — SV HAMBURG H 20/12 22,500 — 1 W 2-0 0-0

Simpson 47, McGhee 64

Leighton, McKimmie, McMaster, Simpson, McLeish, Miller, Strachan, Hewitt*, McGhee, Bell, Weir
Stein, Kaltz*, Wehmeyer, Jakobs, Hieronymous, Hartwig, Schroder, Groh, Schatzsch'r*/Magath, Hanson/Wuttke
Black

Ref: H Brummeier (Austria)
(Dons win 2-0 on aggregate)

A subdued first half, played in depressing drizzle. Hamburg wore red, Aberdeen white with black shorts to add to the confusion. Simpson's goal, following a 60-yard Weir dash down the touchline, was slightly against the run of play. But from then on Hamburg were overwhelmed.

Appearances and Goals

Player	Lge	Sub	LC	Sub	SC	Sub	Eur	Sub	Goals Lge	LC	SC	Eur	Tot
Angus, Ian	9	3	2	2	5					1			4
Bell, Dougie	21	3	8		9	1	3	1	3		1		4
Black, Eric	14	4	6		7		4	2	6	5	1		12
Cooper, Neale	25	1	8		5		7	1		1			1
Cowan, Steve	5												
Falconer, Willie	4	5		2	3		1		1		1		2
Hewitt, John	22	10	7	3	8	2	8	2	12		4		16
Leighton, Jim	36		10		7		10						
McGhee, Mark	30	3	6		6		10		13	3	2	6	24
McIntyre, Tommy	7	3	3										1
McKimmie, Stewart	17	1	6		7		5		1				2
McLeish, Alex	32		10		7		10		2	1			
McMaster, John	11	1	6	1	9		7		3	1			
Miller, Willie	34		9		7		10		2	1		1	4
Mitchell, Brian	6	3		1	3	1	1		1				
Porteous, Ian	5	9	2	2	2	1	2		3	2	1		6
Robertson, Ian	1												
Rougvie, Doug	35		8		7		7		4				4
Simpson, Neil	21	3	6	1	7		9	1	2	1		2	5
Stark, Billy	11	3	3	2	4		2	1	6	5			11
Strachan, Gordon	24		7		6		8		13	2		3	18
Weir, Peter	26	1	8		4		5	1	5	2		1	8
Wright, Paul	1												
(own-goals)									4		1		5
23 players used	**396**	**55**	**110**	**15**	**77**	**12**	**110**	**16**	**78**	**23**	**11**	**12**	**124**

Odds & ends

Never lost to: (5) St Johnstone, Dundee, Motherwell, Hearts, Rangers.
Never beat: (0).
Won from behind: (3) Dundee (a), Akranes (CWC), Ujpest Dozsa (CWC).
Lost in front: (1) Hibs (a).
High spots: Winning Scottish championship with record 57 points. 7 consecutive league wins from 22 October.
Winning Scottish Cup for second successive year.
Winning European Super Cup.
Reaching semi-finals of European competition for only second time.
Low spots: Finishing league with 4 games without a win.
Conceding 3 goals in final league match, so failing to establish new defensive record.
Semi-final defeat by Celtic in League Cup.
Semi-final defeat by Porto in Cup-Winners' Cup.
Mark McGhee scored in all five competitions.
Aberdeen played a record 63 competitive fixtures.
Bogey-team: Celtic - the only team to beat Aberdeen twice in all.
Ever-presents: (1) Jim Leighton.
Hat-tricks: (4) John Hewitt, Billy Stark, Eric Black, McGhee (1 each).
Leading scorer: (24) Mark McGhee.

Scottish Premier Division

	P	Home W	D	L	F	A	Away W	D	L	F	A	Pts
1 ABERDEEN	36	14	3	1	46	12	11	4	3	32	9	57
2 Celtic	36	13	5	0	46	15	8	3	7	34	26	50
3 Dundee Utd	36	11	3	4	38	14	7	8	3	29	25	47
4 Rangers	36	7	8	3	26	18	8	4	6	27	23	42
5 Hearts	36	5	6	4	23	23	5	8	9	21	24	36
6 St Mirren	36	8	6	4	34	23	3	5	10	24	34	36
7 Hibernian	36	7	4	7	21	21	5	3	10	24	34	32
8 Dundee	36	6	1	11	28	42	5	4	9	22	32	27
9 St Johnstone	36	6	1	11	19	33	4	2	12	17	48	23
10 Motherwell	36	2	5	11	15	36	2	2	14	16	39	15
	360	79	45	56	296	237	56	45	79	237	296	360

Head-to-head

	P	W	D	L	F	A	Pts
v St Johnstone	4	4	0	0	13	0	8
v Dundee	4	4	0	0	12	3	8
v Motherwell	4	3	1	0	10	3	7
v Hearts	4	3	1	0	6	1	7
v St Mirren	4	3	0	1	12	6	6
v Rangers	4	2	2	0	6	1	6
v Dundee Utd	4	2	1	1	8	3	5
v Hibernian	4	2	1	1	7	5	5
v Celtic	4	2	1	1	4	2	5
	36	25	7	4	78	21	57

SCOTTISH PREMIER DIVISION

Manager: Alex Ferguson — SEASON 1984-85

No	Venue	Team	Date	Att	Pos	Pt	F-A	H-T	Scorers, Times, and Referees
1	H	DUNDEE	11/8	14,700		2	W 3-2	1-2	Stark 12, Black 56, 82 / Stephen 29, Rafferty 30
2	A	ST MIRREN	18/8	5,445	1	4	W 2-0	2-0	Stark 5, Falconer 20 — Ref: W Crombie
3	A	DUNDEE UTD	25/8	13,033	5	6	W 2-0	1-0	Black 13p, 89 — Ref: G Smith
4	H	HIBERNIAN	1/9	14,500	8	8	W 4-1	2-0	McKimmie 39, Simpson 42, Black 57, / Jamieson 70 [McDougall 68] — Ref: B McGinlay
5	A	MORTON	8/9	5,000	6	10	W 3-0	2-0	Stark 11, Falconer 15, Black 86p — Ref: D Hope
6	H	RANGERS	15/9	23,000	2	11	D 0-0	0-0	Ref: H Young
7	A	DUMBARTON	22/9	4,500	7	13	W 2-0	0-0	Miller 77, Falconer 85 — Ref: T Muirhead
8	H	HEARTS	29/9	16,344	7	15	W 4-0	0-0	McDougall 46, 84, Falconer 48, Angus 74 — Ref: D Syme
9	A	CELTIC	6/10	31,418	9	15	L 1-2	0-1	McDougall 47 / McGarvey 29, Provan 80 — Ref: R Valentine
10	A	DUNDEE	13/10	10,990	7	17	W 2-1	2-1	McDougall 24, Stark 27 / Connor 45 — Ref: A Roy

Line-ups (1–11) and subs used

1. H Dundee — Aberdeen: Leighton, Mitchell, McQueen, Bell, McLeish, Miller, Stark*, Simpson, Hewitt, Black, Falconer^; subs: Porteous/Cowan.
Dundee: Geddes, McGeachie, McKinlay, Rafferty, McCormack, Glennie, Kidd*, Stephen^, McCall, Connor, Harris; subs: McWilliams/Smith.
What a shock for the defending champions as Dundee's Stephen scores off a post and within seconds Rafferty fires in another from a short free-kick. The aerial ability of Eric Black saves the day in the second half to bring about Aberdeen's 11th successive league win over Dundee.

2. A St Mirren — Aberdeen: Leighton, McKimmie, McQueen, Stark, McLeish, Miller, Porteous, Simpson, McDougall*, Bell, Falconer; subs: Angus.
St Mirren: Money, Wilson, Hamilton, Rooney, Fulton, Clarke, Fitzpatrick, McAvennie, Gallagher, Abercrombie, Scanlon*; subs: Mackie.
Set pieces brought about both Aberdeen goals - both headers. St Mirren had more attempts at goal than Aberdeen, but could not find the net. That is the name of the game. Frank McDougall plays his first full league game for the Dons, against his former team-mates.

3. A Dundee Utd — Aberdeen: Leighton, McKimmie, McQueen, Stark, McLeish, Miller, Black, Simpson*, McDougall, Bell, Falconer.
Dundee Utd: Thomson, Kirkwood, Malpas, Gough, Hegarty, Narey, Bannon, Milne*, Beedie^, Sturrock, Dodds; subs: Coyne/Holt.
Aberdeen enjoy playing at Tannadice. This was their 19th Premier League visit, and they have still lost only four times. Ex-St Mirren keeper Thomson brought down ex-St Mirren striker McDougall for Aberdeen's penalty. United are making a poor start to their league season.

4. H Hibernian — Aberdeen: Leighton, McKimmie, McQueen, Stark, McLeish, Black, Black, Simpson*, McDougall, Bell, Falconer^; subs: Angus/Hewitt.
Hibernian: Rough, McKee, Schaedler, Sneddon, Rae, McNamara, Harvey^, Brazil, Kane, Rice, Thomson*; subs: Jamieson/McGeachie.
Frank McDougall adds the finishing touch to his home debut, bagging Aberdeen's fourth goal. Hibs' manager Pat Stanton was 'sent off' after saying naughty words to a linesman. This result carries on Aberdeen's impressive start, but adds to Hibs' woes. Theirs will be a hard season.

5. A Morton — Aberdeen: Leighton, McKimmie, McQueen, Stark, McLeish, Black, Black, Simpson, McDougall*, Bell, Falconer; subs: Hewitt/Angus.
Morton: McDermott, McClurg, Holmes*, Wilson, Dunlop, Deffy, Robertson, McNab, O'Hara, Docherty, McNeil^; subs: Turner/Clinging.
Aberdeen try to lay their Cappielow bogey, having recorded just three wins on that ground in their previous 10 visits. Eric Black was involved in all three Dons' goals. Morton won their first two games, but are now plummeting like a stone, picking up just eight more points all season.

6. H Rangers — Aberdeen: Leighton, McKimmie, McQueen, Stark, McLeish, Miller, Hewitt*, Simpson*, McDougall, Cooper, Falconer; subs: Porteous/Angus.
Rangers: Walker, McKinnon, Dawson, McClelland, Paterson, Redford, Russell^, Fraser, Ferguson^, Cooper, McCoist; subs: McPhers'n/McDon'ld.
Unbeaten Rangers put a stop to Aberdeen's winning ways. The Gers have gone back to basics, shoring up their defence before bothering to breach their opponents'. Ibrox will see just 21 Rangers goals all season. Frank McDougall drew keeper Walker off his line but then shot wide.

7. A Dumbarton — Aberdeen: Leighton, McKimmie, McQueen, Cooper, McLeish, Miller, Black, Simpson, McDougall*, Bell, Angus^; subs: Porteous/Falconer.
Dumbarton: Arthur, Kay, McGowan, Coyle T, McNeil, Clougherty, Ashwood, Craig, McGowan P, Crawley, Coyle J.
Promoted Dumbarton are making a fist of it. Their physical play is ruffling some feathers. Miller ruffles theirs with a thunderbolt left-footed shot, with time running out, to teach his forwards how to do it. Dumbarton had looked like emulating their recent home draw with Celtic.

8. H Hearts — Aberdeen: Leighton, McKimmie, McQueen, Cooper, McLeish, Miller, Black, Simpson, McDougall*, Bell, Angus*; subs: Stark/McDougall.
Hearts: Smith, Kidd, Cowie, Jardine*, McNeil, MacDonald, R Levein, Park^, Robertson, Bone, MacDonald A; subs: O'Connor/Whittaker.
Hearts' keeper Henry Smith stopped an Eric Black penalty in the first half. Frank McDougall came on as sub in the second and swept home Falconer's cross within 17 seconds of coming on. Then the floodgates opened. Hearts' fourth defeat on the trot leaves them perilously placed.

9. A Celtic — Aberdeen: Leighton, McKimmie, McQueen, Cooper, McLeish, Miller, Black, Simpson, McDougall, Angus*, Stark*; subs: Hewitt/Porteous.
Celtic: Bonner, McGrain, Reid, Aitken, McAdam, Grant, Colquhoun*, McStay P, McGarvey, MacLeod, ...; subs: Provan.
After Aberdeen's sad penalty failures in Berlin they come up with another at Parkhead. Shortly after McDougall had volleyed Aberdeen level, Billy Stark became the latest sinner from the spot. To add insult Provan's 25-yard free-kick deserved to win any match. Celtic stay unbeaten.

10. A Dundee — Aberdeen: Leighton, McKimmie, McQueen, Cooper, McLeish, Miller, Black, Simpson, McDougall*, Angus, Stark*; subs: Porteous/Falconer.
Dundee: Carson, McGeachie, McKinlay, Rafferty, McCormack, Glennie, Forsyth^, Brown, McCall, Connor, Stephen^; subs: McWilliams/Kidd.
Seven players were booked as these two teams set about one another. Robert Connor's goal for Dundee on the stroke of half-time transformed the match. How Aberdeen held out in the second half they will never know. After two painful defeats, it is good to get back to winning.

11 · H · ST MIRREN · 20/10

14,100 | 1 W 4-0 | 4 | 19 | (2-0)

McDougall 13, 69p, Porteous 39, Stark 86

Ref: D McVicar

Leighton	McKimmie	McQueen	Stark	McLeish	Miller	Porteous*	Simpson	McDougall	Black	Angus	Falconer
Stewart Wilson	Winnie	Rooney!	Cooper	Clarke	Fitzpatrick	McAvennie McDowell	McDowell	Abercromb'*Mackie	Mackie	Cameron	

St Mirren's task was difficult enough even before Jim Rooney was sent off just before half-time for a fierce challenge on Ian Angus. Rooney had already been booked. After the misses of recent games, responsibility for taking Aberdeen's penalties has now passed to Frank McDougall.

12 · A · HIBERNIAN · 6/11

8,000 | 1 W 3-0 | 6 | 21 | (1-0)

McDougall 41, Black 53, Stark 89

Ref: W McLeish

Leighton	McKimmie	McQueen	Stark	McLeish	Miller	Porteous*	Simpson	McDougall	Black	Angus	Weir
Rough Sneddon	McKee	Craig	Jamieson	McNamara	Callachan	Durie*	Irvine	Rice	Kane*	Brazil/Thomson	Weir

A tale of two goalkeepers. Jim Leighton comfortably saved Durie's penalty to keep the score at 1-0. Then Alan Rough fumbled Eric Black's header into the net. Hibs won't win for anther 10 games, till mid-January. Celtic have unaccountably lost to Morton, to extend the Dons' lead.

13 · H · MORTON · 10/11

14,500 | 1 W 3-1 | 10 | 23 | (2-1)

McDougall 32, Miller 42, Simpson 73

Clinging 8

Ref: H Williamson

Leighton	McKimmie	McQueen*	Stark*	McLeish	Miller	Black*	Simpson	McDougall	Angus	Weir	Porteous/Mitchell
McDermott Wilson	Holmes	O'Hara	Mackin	Duffy	Robertson Docherty	Gillespie	Pettigrew* Clinging	McNeil			

Morton prop up the table, but last week they inflicted the first league defeat on Celtic. Peter Weir is welcomed back for his first game of the season. Clinging's raging goal for Morton, capitalising on McQueen's feeble clearance, put Aberdeen to the test. They passed comfortably.

14 · A · RANGERS · 17/11

44,000 | 1 W 2-1 | 3 | 25 | (1-1)

Stark 19, McDougall 61

Mitchell 7

Ref: H Alexander

Leighton	McKimmie	Angus	Stark	McLeish	Miller	Black*	Simpson	McDougall	Cooper	Weir	
McCloy	McKinnon Dawson	McPherson Paterson	Redford	Prytz*	Fraser	Mitchell	Ferguson* Cooper	Russell/McMinn	Cowan		

Rangers suffer their first home defeat of the season, despite the deflected goal scored for them by Dave Mitchell - later to play for Australia against Scotland in the World Cup. Frank McDougall won the game for Aberdeen with his 10th league goal of the season. He has settled fast.

15 · H · DUMBARTON · 24/11

13,200 | 1 W 1-0 | 9 | 27 | (1-0)

McDougall 1

Ref: D Galloway

Leighton	McKimmie	Angus*	Stark	McLeish	Black	Black	Simpson	McDougall	Cooper*	Craig	Cowan/McQueen
Arthur	Kay	McGowan McCoyle T	Jardine	Levein	Cahill	Simpson	Robertson Bourke*	Craig	McGowan P* McCaig/Coyle J		

Dumbarton have now won just one of their last 10. The worst thing to happen in this match was for McDougall to score within 30 seconds, and to find his name on the scoresheet for the eighth successive game. Thereafter everything went flat. The Dons still lead Celtic by three points.

16 · A · HEARTS · 1/12

10,037 | 1 W 2-1 | 6 | 29 | (1-1)

Cowan 30, Stark 52

MacDonald 43

Ref: A Ferguson

Leighton	McKimmie	McQueen	Stark	McLeish	Miller	Cowan	Simpson	McDougall*	Angus*	Hewitt/Mitchell	
Smith	Kidd	Whittaker	Jardine	Levein	Black	Bowman	Robertson	Clark	MacDonald* Park*	Bone/Johnston	

Steve Cowan's cracking volley nearly broke Henry Smith's fingers. Miller and Leighton uncharacteristically made a present of a goal to Alex MacDonald. Billy Stark's header would not take 'no' for an answer. Hearts lost recently 1-5 to Celtic, to shatter their promising winning run.

17 · H · CELTIC · 8/12

23,000 | 1 W 4-2 | 2 | 31 | (2-0)

Black 33, 61, McKimmie 44, McDougall 85

Johnston 57p, McGarvey 84

Ref: H Young

Leighton	McKimmie	McQueen	Stark*	McLeish	Miller	Black	Simpson	McDougall*	Cooper*	Angus*	Mitchell/Hewitt
Bonner	McGrain	MacLeod	Aitken	McAdam*	McClair	Provan	McStay P	Johnston	Burns	McGarvey	W'Colquh'n

The match of the season - or any other season. A soaring header by Black and a deflected 30-yarder by McKimmie gave Aberdeen a commanding interval lead. Celtic fought back to score twice after the resumption, but on both occasions Aberdeen hit back within minutes.

18 · H · DUNDEE · 15/12

14,000 | 1 D 0-0 | 8 | 32 | (0-0)

Ref: J Duncan

Leighton	McKimmie	McQueen*	Stark	McLeish*	Miller	Black	Simpson	McDougall	Angus	Cowan/Cooper	
Carson	McGeachie McKinlay	Smith	McCormack	Glennie	Stephen	Brown	McCall*	Connor	Hewitt	Rafferty Richardson	

Archie Knox has been in charge of Dundee for one year since leaving the assistant manager's post at Pittodrie. McDougall's header against a post almost deprived lively Dundee of a point they fully deserved. They had lost their last 12 league fixtures against Aberdeen.

19 · H · DUNDEE UTD · 22/12

16,354 | 1 L 0-1 | 4 | 32 | (0-0)

Gough 48

Ref: K Hope

Leighton	McKimmie	McQueen	Stark	Cooper	Miller W	Falconer*	Simpson	McDougall	Angus*	Miller J/Mitchell	
McAlpine	Malpas	Holt	Gough	Hegarty	Narey	Bannon	Taylor	Coyne*	Beedie	Clark	

Improving United have now gone eight without defeat, and were worth a much larger margin of victory in this match. They were also the last team to win at Pittodrie, 15 months ago. Frank McDougall is the latest Dons penalty-waster, after he had been toppled by Richard Gough.

20 · A · ST MIRREN · 29/12

6,287 | 1 D 2-2 | 5 | 33 | (1-2)

McDougall 12, 82

Gallagher 18, McAvennie 33

Ref: W Crombie

Leighton	McKimmie	McQueen	Stark*	McLeish	Miller	Black	Bell*	McDougall	Mitchell	Weir	Falconer/Angus
Money	Wilson	Hamilton	Rooney	Clark	Fulton	Fitzpatrick	McAvennie	Gallagher	Abercrombie Speirs		

A splendid match to see out the year. Aberdeen must have feared they'd lost it when Frank McAvennie cut inside to beat Leighton. But Frank McDougall latched on to a long through-ball to spare Aberdeen's blushes. Last month St Mirren lost 1-7 at Celtic, but have clearly improved.

21 · A · DUNDEE UTD · 2/1

21,944 | 1 L 1-2 | 4 | 33 | (1-1)

McQueen 24p

Dodds 29, Gough 77

Ref: D Downie

Leighton	McKimmie*	Mitchell	Stark*	McLeish	Miller	Falconer*	Simpson	McDougall	Bell	Weir	Stark/Cowan
McAlpine	Malpas	Holt	Gough	Hegarty	Narey	Bannon	Taylor*	Sturrock*	Beedie	Dodds	Clark/Beaumont

Two points from four games has let other teams have a sniff of the championship. United were always the better team, and won this match - as they had at Pittodrie 11 days earlier - with an unchallenged Gough header. This is 10 without loss, for United; they will now lose to St Mirren.

SCOTTISH PREMIER DIVISION — Manager: Alex Ferguson — SEASON 1984-85

No	Date	Att	Pos	Pt	F-A	H-T	Scorers, Times, and Referees	1	2	3	4	5	6	7	8	9	10	11	subs used
22	H HIBERNIAN 5/1	13,700	1 W 9	35	2-0	1-0	Weir 26, McKimmie 76 Ref: M Delaney	Gunn	Mitchell	McQueen	McKimmie	Cooper	Miller	Falconer*	Simpson	McDougall	Bell*	Weir	Hewitt/Angus
								Rough	*Sneddon*	*Schaedler*	*Brazil*	*Rae*	*McNamara*	*Weir*	*Kane*	*Harris*	*Jamieson*	*Rice**	*Craig*
23	H MORTON 12/1	11,000	1 W 10	37	5-0	1-0	Weir 27, Cooper 58, McDougall 60, [Mitchell 80, Cowan 88] McDermott 80 Ref: H Young	Leighton	McKimmie	McQueen	Stark*	Cooper	Hewitt	Simpson	McDougall*	Bell*	Weir	Mitchell/Cowan
								McDermott	*Docherty*	*Holmes*	*Fleeting**	*Welsh*	*Duffy*	*Robertson*	*Sullivan*	*O'Hara*	*Doak*	*Clinging**	*Turner/Wilson*
24	H RANGERS 19/1	23,000	1 W 3	39	5-1	2-0	McDougall 11, 14, 72, Black 58, Prytz 75 [McQueen 81p] Ref: D Syme	Leighton	McKimmie	McQueen	Stark*	Cooper	Miller	Black	Simpson	McDougall	Bell*	Weir	Mitchell/Hewitt
								Walker	*McKinnon*	*Dawson!*	*McPherson*	*Paterson*	*Prytz*	*McCoist*	*Ferguson D**	*Johnstone*	*McDonald**	*Cooper*	*Redford/McMinn*
25	A DUMBARTON 2/2	3,500	1 W 8	41	2-0	1-0	Stark 36, Black 66 Ref: A ?	Leighton	McKimmie	McQueen	Cooper	McLeish	Miller	Black	Simpson	McDougall	Stark	Weir	Hewitt/Angus
								Arthur	*Kay*	*McGowan M/McCahill*	*McNeill*	*Clougherty*	*McGowan P* Craig*	*Asthwood**	*Coyle T*	*Crawley*	*Coyle J/Bourke*		
26	H HEARTS 9/2	14,700	1 D 6	42	2-2	2-0	Simpson 21, Weir 34 Watson 65, Robertson 71 Ref: T Muirhead	Leighton	McKimmie	McQueen	Cooper	McLeish	Miller	Black	Simpson	McDougall*	Stark	Weir	Hewitt/Angus
								Smith	*Kidd*	*Whittaker*	*Jardine*	*MacDonald*	*Levein*	*Watson*	*Mackay*	*Clark*	*Robertson*	*Black*	
27	A CELTIC 23/2	48,834	1 L 2	42	0-2	0-0	Johnston 66, McStay P 90p Ref: B McGinlay	Leighton	McKimmie	McQueen	Cooper	McLeish	Miller	Black	Simpson*	Cowan*	Angus	Weir	Bell/Hewitt
								Bonner	*McStay W*	*McGrain*	*Aitken*	*McAdam*	*O'Leary*	*Grant**	*McStay P*	*Johnston*	*MacLeod*	*McGarvey*	*Provan*
28	H ST MIRREN 2/3	12,000	1 W 6	44	3-0	1-0	Stark 27, Black 67, Cowan 90 Ref: H Alexander	Leighton	McKimmie	McQueen	Stark	McLeish	Mitchell	Black	Simpson	Porteous	Angus	Weir*	Cowan
								Money	*Wilson*	*Winnie**	*Rooney*	*Godfrey*	*Clarke*	*Fitzpatrick*	*McAvennie*	*Gallagher*	*Abercrombie Mackie*	*McDowall*	
29	A DUNDEE 16/3	9,161	1 W 7	46	4-0	2-0	Black 42, Stark 43, 48, Simpson 66 Ref: D Hope	Leighton	McKimmie	McQueen	Stark*	McLeish	Miller	Black	Simpson	Hewitt*	Angus	Cowan	Bell/Mitchell
								Geddes	*McGeachie*	*McKinlay*	*Rafferty*	*Smith*	*McCormack* Stephen*	*Brown*	*Harvey*	*Connor*	*McWilliams Richardson/McCall*		
30	A HIBERNIAN 23/3	9,000	1 W 9	48	5-0	1-0	Black 13,70,89, McQueen 49p, Hewitt 71 Ref: A Ferguson	Leighton	McKimmie	McQueen	Stark	McLeish	Miller	Black	Simpson	Hewitt	Angus*	Cowan	Bell
								Rough	*Sneddon*	*Schaedler*	*McKee**	*Rae*	*Brazil*	*Callachan*	*Kane*	*Irvine*	*Rice*	*McBride*	*Harris*
31	H DUNDEE UTD 30/3	15,600	1 W 3	50	4-2	2-0	Hewitt 35, 43, Stark 70, Cowan 71 Bannon 49p, Reilly 74 Ref: J Duncan	Leighton	McKimmie	McQueen*	Stark	McLeish	Miller	Black	Bell	Hewitt	Angus	Cowan*	Cooper/Falconer
								Thomson	*Malpas*	*Kirkwood*	*Gough*	*Hegarty*	*Beaumont*	*Bannon*	*Taylor*	*Beedie*	*Sturrock*	*Dodds*	*Reilly*

A sixth successive defeat, and 11 without a win for Hibs, as Aberdeen get back to winning ways. That is the only good thing to come out of this result, as the Dons continue to flounder. Tommy Craig, once of Aberdeen many years ago, came on as a Hibs substitute.

Morton are suffering nothing but defeat after demoralising defeat. The sand on the frozen Pittodrie pitch was presumably to help Aberdeen prepare for their coming mid-winter break to Egypt. Goal-of-the-match was Steve Cowan's chip over keeper McDermott's head.

This result did not do Rangers boss Jock Wallace's hernia any good at all. Derek Johnstone returned to the Ibrox fold and stood back as Frank McDougall bagged his first Dons hat-trick. The game's only black spot was the sending off of McKimmie and Ally Dawson in the first half.

Dumbarton defended stubbornly and made life difficult for Aberdeen, but their resistance was finally overcome by two fine headers. Billy Stark suffered a fractured skull for his pains. The lead over Celtic is now eight points, though Celtic have three games in hand.

Never in Alex Ferguson's seven-year reign at Pittodrie has his team lost a game after being two goals in front. But Hearts came close. McQueen of Aberdeen and Kidd of Hearts both gifted goals to their opponents with daft back-passes. It had all seemed so easy at half-time.

Another thoroughly unpleasant match between these two sides, turned Celtic's way by Mo Johnston's hooked goal, after Roy Aitken had nodded on a Provan corner. The result keeps the championship open. Celtic have closed the gap to five points, and have played two games less.

Magical Aberdeen. This was exhibition stuff for 90 minutes; St Mirren could barely escape from their own half and the only mystery is how the Dons failed to score six. Ian Porteous has a fine game, and Billy Stark will surely never play better. Five without a win for St Mirren.

Dundee have won their last four, including a victory over Celtic. The pitch is cleared of overnight snow. Two crushing goals before the interval sank Dundee's spirits. Thereafter Aberdeen turned on the style. At the final whistle the Dons heard that rivals Celtic had lost at home to Hibs.

Seven days after beating Celtic, Hibs are turned over by Aberdeen. The Edinburgh players are left in no doubt who are the rightful champions. Hibs' relegation cloud hovers lower. After Aberdeen's third goal missiles were thrown onto the pitch. The SFA will take its revenge.

United had lost one of their last 18 games, including two wins over the Dons. Now they take a back seat as Aberdeen sprint to the finishing line with 16 goals in four games. Best of these four goals was John Hewitt's second, an unstoppable shot that left Billy Thomson motionless.

32	A	RANGERS	23,437	1 W 2-1	2-0	Cowan 26, Black 42					
		6/4		4 52		Prytz 63					
						Ref: A Waddell					

	Leighton	McKimmie	Cooper	Stark	McLeish	Miller	Black*	Bell	Hewitt	Angus^	Cowan	Falconer/McQueen
	Walker	Dawson	Munro	McPherson	Johnstone	Redford*	Prytz	Fraser	Ferguson	McCoist^	Cooper	Russell/Fleck

Nicky Walker, the Rangers' keeper, could only palm out McKimmie's cross, and Cowan lashed it back past him. Eric Black's tap-in was Aberdeen's 79th league goal - a Dons record in the Premier League. When Robert Prytz drove in a fine goal, Aberdeen simply shut up shop.

33	H	DUMBARTON	12,500	1 W 4-0	2-0	McLeish 24, Angus 35, Kay 50 og,					
		20/4		9 54		[Stark 65]Arthur					
						Ref: J Renton					

	Leighton	McKimmie	McQueen	Stark	McLeish	Miller	Black	Simpson*	Hewitt	Bell	Angus	Cowan
	Arthur	Kay	Sinclair	Coyle T	McCahill	Montgomerie	Ashwood	Robertson	McIver	Crawley*	Coyle J	Moore

Dumbarton will lose their last nine games without scoring a goal. Alex McLeish's rocket - his first goal of the season - made Willie Miller jealous. Miller spent the rest of the match desperately trying to score one himself. The Dons can now clinch the championship against Celtic.

34	H	CELTIC	23,000	1 D 1-1	0-1	Miller 61					
		27/4		2 55		Aitken 40p					
						Ref: G Smith					

	Leighton	McKimmie	McQueen	Stark	McLeish	Miller	Porteous	Simpson	McDougall*	Bell^	Hewitt*	Cowan/Cooper
	Bonner	McStay W	McGrain	Aitken	McAdam	MacLeod	Grant*	McStay P	Johnston^	Burns	McGarvey	Provan/McClair

Only mathematically are Celtic's hopes still alive. They were gifted a penalty when Stark nudged Johnston. Miller launched himself at Porteous' free-kick to head the equaliser off a post. A second Celtic 'goal' was annulled for a dubious push on Leighton. Hewitt missed a sitter.

35	A	HEARTS	8,251	1 W 3-0	3-0	McDougall 21, 32, 34					
		4/5		7 57							
						Ref: B McGinlay					

	Leighton	Mitchell	McQueen	Stark	McLeish	McKimmie	Porteous	Simpson	McDougall	Bell*	Hewitt^	McMaster/Cowan
	Smith	Kidd	Murray	Jardine	Cowie*	Levein	Sandison	Robertson	Clark	Mackay^	Black	Watson/McNaught'n

Frank McDougall's second hat-trick of the season puts the seal of approval on his first year with the Dons. His third goal was a delicious volley. Aberdeen are now certain champions, while Hearts limp across the finishing line by losing their last five games.

36	A	MORTON	3,600	1 W 2-1	0-1	Stark 59, McDougall 61					
		11/5		10 59		Thomson 40					
						Ref: B McGinlay					

	Gunn	McKimmie	McQueen	Stark	McLeish*	Miller	Simpson	Alexander	Angus	Porteous^	Bell/Hewitt
	McDermott	Docherty	Holmes	Sullivan*	Boag	O'Hara	Turner	Gillespie	Thomson^	Clinging	McNab/Welsh

The day of the Bradford fire. Aberdeen got for two records. One point will break the Premier record which they broke 12 months earlier. Three goals will equal the record of 90 shared by Celtic and Dundee United in 1982-83. The Dons achieve the first milestone, but not the second.

Average Home 16,050 / Away 14,670

Skol League Cup

2	A	AIRDRIE	5,000	L 1-3	1-2	Stark 11					
		22/8				McCabe 3, Flood 33, Yule 55					
						Ref: A Waddell					

	Leighton	McKimmie	Stark	McLeish	Miller	Porteous*	Simpson	Cowan	Bell	Falconer^	Grant/Wright
	Martin	Steven	Black	Lawrie	Gillies	Yule*	McCabe	Fairlie	Flood	Paterson^	Millar

Ally MacLeod - once of Aberdeen and then of Scotland - is now manager of Division 1 Airdrie. His team are part-timers, but they crush the complacent Dons. Billy Stark's equaliser appeared to have settled the team, but it flattered to deceive. MacLeod goes monkeys afterwards.

Scottish Cup

3	H	ALLOA	13,500	1 W 5-0	1-0	Hewitt 29, Stark 58, 69, 83, Simpson 68					
		30/1		2:1							
						Ref: W Crombie					

	Leighton	Mitchell	McQueen	Stark	Cooper	Miller	Black	Simpson	Hewitt	Bell*	Weir	McLeish
	Lowrie	Thompson*	Haggart	Thomson	Dall	Martin	Mackie	Kelly	Sorbie*	Barr	Lloyd	Harris/Murray

Alloa are the pace-setters of Division 2. Only in the last half-hour did Aberdeen make their superiority plain. Nearly all the goals were close-in, messy affairs, but Billy Stark can be proud of his hat-trick.

4	A	RAITH	10,000	1 W 2-1	2-1	McDougall 30, 43p					
		16/2		2:9		Smith 39p					
						Ref: B McGinlay					

	Leighton	Mitchell	McQueen	Cooper	McLeish	Miller	Black	Simpson	McDougall*	Bell*	Weir	Hewitt
	Blair	Candlish	Sweeney	Urquhart	More	Phillip	Smith	Elvin	Marshall	Robertson	Wright

Raith are in the bottom half of Division 2. Frank McDougall puts the Dons in front with a flying overhead kick. Willie Miller then handles on the goal-line to concede a penalty. Peter Weir is then upended by Urquhart for McDougall to restore the lead from the spot.

QF	A	HEARTS	23,900	1 D 1-1	0-0	Black 78					
		9/3		5		Clark 51					
						Ref: B McGinlay					

	Leighton	McKimmie	McQueen*	Stark	McLeish	Miller	Black	Simpson	McDougall*	Angus	Stark	Bell/Porteous
	Smith	Kidd	Whittaker	Cooper*	Jardine	MacDonald R	Berry	Watson*	Mackay	Clark	Robertson^	Black	MacDonald A

Until today all Eric Black's goals in the Scottish Cup had been reserved for finals. This match was all huff and puff. Leighton touched a cross out to Sandy Clark, who gratefully netted from eight yards. Up soared Black to equalise and drown Hearts' premature congratulations.

QF R	H	HEARTS	23,000	1 W 1-0	1-0	Stark 25					
		13/3		5							
						Ref: B McGinlay					

	Leighton	Mitchell*	McKimmie	Stark	McLeish	Miller	Black	Simpson	Porteous*	Angus	Hewitt	Bell/Cowan
	Smith	Kidd	Whittaker	Jardine	MacDon'ld R	Levein	MacDon'ld R	Berry*	Mackay	Clark	Robertson^	Black	Watson/McLaughton

After just 15 minutes Hearts' Roddy MacDonald was sent off for leaving his elbow in Eric Black's face. When Billy Stark, lurking at the far post, headed in John Hewitt's free-kick Hearts were left with a mountain to climb - one which they never looked like scaling.

SCOTTISH PREMIER (CUP-TIES)   Manager: Alex Ferguson   SEASON 1984-85

Scottish Cup

			F-A	H-T	Scorers, Times, and Referees	1	2	3	4	5	6	7	8	9	10	11	subs used
SF	N	DUNDEE UTD 1	D 0-0	0-0		Leighton	McKimmie	Cooper	Stark	McLeish	Miller	Black	Simpson	Hewitt*	Bell	Cowan	Angus
		13/4 18,485 3			*McAlpine*	*McAlpine*	*Malpas*	*Holt*	*Gough*	*Hegarty* *	*Narey*	*Bannon*	*Taylor¯*	*Kirkwood*	*Sturrock*	*Dodds*	*Beedie/Clark*
		(at Tynecastle)			Ref: H Alexander												

Aberdeen had most of the play and most of the chances. Hewitt missed a gaping goal by inches, and Stark's header flew off a post into McAlpine's arms. Miller and Billy Kirkwood became entangled after a frightful collision, whereupon Kirkwood kissed Miller on the forehead.

			F-A	H-T	Scorers, Times, and Referees	1	2	3	4	5	6	7	8	9	10	11	subs used
SF	R	DUNDEE UTD 1	L 1-2	0-1	Angus 86	Leighton	McKimmie	Cooper!	Stark	McLeish	Miller	Black	Simpson	Hewitt*	Bell*	Cowan	McQueen/Angus
		17/4 10,771 3			*Sturrock 5, Beedie 59*	*McAlpine*	*Malpas*	*Holt*	*Gough*	*Beedie*	*Narey*	*Bannon*	*Milne* *	*Kirkwood*	*Sturrock*	*Dodds!*	*Beaumont*
		(at Tynecastle)			Ref: H Alexander												

The Dons' four-year run of 18 unbeaten ties in the Scottish Cup ends in controversy. Sturrock scored with a close-range header. Cooper was sent off for fouling Milne. Beedie's volley flew past Leighton. Dodds molested Miller on the touchline and went off. Angus hooked a late goal.

European Champions' Cup

			F-A	H-T	Scorers, Times, and Referees	1	2	3	4	5	6	7	8	9	10	11	subs used
1:1	H	DYNAMO BERLIN 1	W 2-1	1-0	Black 33, 67	Leighton	McKimmie	McQueen	Stark	McLeish	Miller	Bell*	Hewitt*	Black	Cooper	Angus	Simpson/Falconer
		19/9 (E Germ) 20,000			*Schulz 82*	*Rudwaleit*	*Ksienzyk*	*Trieloff*	*Backs*	*Rohde*	*Troppa*	*Schulz*	*Maeck*	*Pastor* *	*Ernst* *	*Thom*	*Grether/Terletzki*
					Ref: M Van Langenhove (Belgium)												

McDougall was ineligible, banned when with St Mirren for fighting in a tie with Feyenoord. Two Eric Black headers got the better of a 6' 6" keeper. The Germans finished strongly, and Schulz was left unattended at a corner to score the game's third headed goal, and the most vital.

			F-A	H-T	Scorers, Times, and Referees	1	2	3	4	5	6	7	8	9	10	11	subs used
1:2	A	DYNAMO BERLIN 1	L 1-2	0-0	Angus 67	Leighton	McKimmie	McQueen	Cooper	McLeish	Miller	Stark	Simpson	Black*	Angus*	Falconer¯	Porteous/Hewitt
		3/10 20,000		(aet)	*Thom 49, Ernst 84*	*Rudwaleit*	*Ksienzyk*	*Trieloff*	*Backs* *	*Rohde*	*Troppa*	*Schulz*	*Maeck*	*Pastor¯*	*Ernst*	*Thom*	*Grether/Terletzki*
					Ref: L Angolin (Italy)												
					(Dons lose on 4-5 on penalties)												

Thom's flicked goal puts the Germans ahead. Angus' searing drive. 1-1. Ernst forces the ball in. Miller hits the bar in extra-time. Porteous, McQueen, Hewitt and Stark score with penalties. Schulz hits No 3 against the bar. Rudwaleit saves from Miller and Black. Trie;off wins it.

Home / Away record

Pos	Team	P	Home W	D	L	F	A	Away W	D	L	F	A	Pts
1	ABERDEEN	36	13	4	1	49	13	14	1	3	40	13	59
2	Celtic	36	12	3	3	43	12	10	5	3	34	18	52
3	Dundee Utd	36	13	5	0	47	18	7	7	4	20	15	47
4	Rangers	36	7	6	5	21	14	6	6	6	26	24	38
5	St Mirren	36	10	2	6	29	24	7	2	9	22	32	38
6	Dundee	36	9	3	6	25	19	6	4	8	23	31	37
7	Hearts	36	6	3	9	21	26	6	2	9	26	31	31
8	Hibernian	36	5	4	9	23	30	5	3	10	15	31	27
9	Dumbarton	36	4	4	10	17	29	2	3	13	12	35	19
10	Morton	36	3	1	14	18	44	2	1	15	11	56	12
		360	82	32	66	293	229	66	32	82	229	293	360

Results against each club

Opponent	P	W	D	L	F	A	Pts	Cup	W	D	L	F	A
v Hibernian	4	4	0	0	14	1	8						
v Morton	4	4	0	0	13	2	8						
v Dumbarton	4	4	0	0	9	0	8						
v St Mirren	4	3	1	0	11	2	7	SC			1	1	0
v Hearts	4	3	1	0	11	3	7						
v Dundee	4	3	1	0	9	3	7						
v Rangers	4	3	1	0	9	3	7						
v Dundee Utd	4	2	0	2	7	5	4	SC			0	1	1
v Celtic	4	1	1	2	6	7	3						
	36	27	5	4	89	26	59						

Appearances and Goals

Player	App Lge	Sub	LC	Sub	SC	Sub	Eur	Sub	Goals Lge	Sub	LC	SC	Eur	Tot
Angus, Ian	21	7			3	2			2			1	1	4
Bell, Dougie	18	4	1		3	2								
Black, Eric	27				6	2			17			1	2	20
Cooper, Neale	17	3			5	2			1					1
Cowan, Steve	6	10	1		2	1			5					5
Falconer, Willie	10	6			2		1		4	1				4
Grant, Brian						1								
Gunn, Bryan	2													
Hewitt, John	11	10			4	1	1		3			1	1	4
Leighton, Jim	34		1		6		2							
McDougall, Frank	27	1			2				22			2		24
McKimmie, Stewart	34		1		5		2		3					3
McLeish, Alex	30		1		5	1	2		1					1
McMaster, John		1				1								
McQueen, Tommy	33	2	1		2		2		3					3
Miller, Joe		1												
Miller, Willie	34		1		6		2		3					3
Mitchell, Brian	7	7			3				1					1
Porteous, Ian	7	6			1	1			1					1
Simpson, Neil	33		1		6		1		4	1		1		5
Stark, Billy	30	2	1		5		2		15	1		4		20
Weir, Peter	15	1			2				3					3
Wright, Paul						1			1					1
(own-goals)											1			
23 players used	396	61	11	2	66	9	22	4	89		1	10	3	103

Odds & ends

Never lost to: (7) Hibs, Morton, Dumbarton, St Mirren, Hearts, Dundee, Rangers.

Never beat: (0).

Won from behind: (4) Dundee (h), Morton (h & a), Rangers (a).

Lost from in front: (2) Dundee Utd (a), Dynamo Berlin.

High spots: New Premier championship total of 59 points.

8 consecutive league wins from 13 October.

Taking 7 or 8 league points off seven different teams.

Low spots: Defeat by First Division Airdrie in Skol Cup.

Failing the reach the Scottish Cup final for first time in 4 years.

Losing to Dynamo Berlin in First Round of European Cup.

Taking just 2 points from 4 league games over Christmas and New Year.

Bogey teams: Celtic and Dundee Utd.

Ever-presents: (0).

Hat-tricks: (4) Frank McDougall 2, Eric Black 1, Billy Stark 1.

Leading scorer: (24) Frank McDougall.

FINE FARE SCOTTISH PREMIER

Manager: Alex Ferguson

SEASON 1985-86

No	Date	Team	Att	Pos	Pt	F-A	H-T	Scorers, Times, and Referee	1	2	3	4	5	6	7	8	9	10	11	subs used
1	10/8	H HIBERNIAN	14,846	W	2	3-0	0-0	Bett 68, McDougall 79, 89 / Ref: K Hope	Leighton	McKimmie	McQueen	Stark	McLeish	Miller W	Black*	Simpson	McDougall	Bett	Weir	Hewitt
								(opponents)	Rough	Sneddon	Munro	Kane	Rae	Hunter	Weir	Collins	Irvine*	Cowan	McBride	Durie

The Premier League championship flag was unfurled over Pittodrie, whereupon Hibs took it upon themselves to ruin the occasion. They looked the more capable side until Dons' debut-boy Jim Bett rifled in a superb goal. Aberdeen will inflict more misery on Hibs in the months ahead.

No	Date	Team	Att	Pos	Pt	F-A	H-T	Scorers, Times, and Referee	1	2	3	4	5	6	7	8	9	10	11	subs used
2	17/8	A DUNDEE UTD	14,339	D	3	1-1	1-1	McKimmie 36, Sturrock 41 / Ref: D Downie	Gunn	McKimmie	Cooper	Stark	McLeish	Miller W	Black*	Simpson	McDougall	Bett	Weir	Hewitt
								(opponents)	McAlpine	Beaumont	Malpas	Gough	Hegarty	Narey	Bannon	Beedie	Redford*	Sturrock	Dodds	Milne

United lost their opening game at Rangers. Manchester United's chief scout takes in this match at Tannadice, but it is not known who he was watching. High-quality goals at either end would have impressed him, scored by Stewart McKimmie's power and Paul Sturrock's guile.

No	Date	Team	Att	Pos	Pt	F-A	H-T	Scorers, Times, and Referee	1	2	3	4	5	6	7	8	9	10	11	subs used
3	24/8	H MOTHERWELL	14,059	D	4	1-1	1-1	McKimmie 19, Blair 32 / Ref: B McGinlay	Gunn	McKimmie	McQueen*	Stark*	McLeish	Miller W	Black	Simpson	McDougall*	Bett	Weir	Cooper/Black
								(opponents)	Gardiner	McLeod	Murray	Kennedy	Forbes	Boyd	Clark	Doman	Harrow	McStay	Blair	

Another spectacular goal from Stewart McKimmie crowns Aberdeen's bright opening. But Willie Miller's mistimed tackle let in Blair and the Dons struggled thereafter against a team yet to record their first win. Results like this suggest Aberdeen are not quite the power they were.

No	Date	Team	Att	Pos	Pt	F-A	H-T	Scorers, Times, and Referee	1	2	3	4	5	6	7	8	9	10	11	subs used
4	31/8	A DUNDEE	7,592	W	6	3-1	0-0	Simpson 48, Stark 62, 80 / Black 88 / Ref: W Crombie	Leighton	McKimmie	Mitchell	Stark*	McLeish	Miller W	Black	Simpson	McDougall*	Bett	Weir*	McIntyre/Hewitt, McWilliams/Waddell
								(opponents)	Geddes	Shannon	Glennie	McCormack Smith	Duffy	Stephen*	Brown	Black	Connor	Jack*		

Dundee's league record against Aberdeen is lamentable, not having beaten the Dons for 33 games, since March 1976. Dundee held their own in the first half. But then Jim Bett's drive was deflected out to Neil Simpson, and thereafter frustration ruined the home team's chances.

No	Date	Team	Att	Pos	Pt	F-A	H-T	Scorers, Times, and Referee	1	2	3	4	5	6	7	8	9	10	11	subs used
5	7/9	H HEARTS	12,300	W	8	3-0	1-0	Stark 32, Wright 75, Black 90 / Ref: M Delaney	Leighton	McKimmie	Mitchell	Stark*	McLeish	Miller W	Black*	Simpson	McDougall*	Bett	Hewitt	Wright/Cooper, Mackay/Sandison
								(opponents)	Smith	Cowie	Whittaker	Jardine	MacDonald	Levein	Colquhoun* Watson	McNaughton Cherry	Black*			

No sign here of the imminent Hearts revival which will turn this season upside down. Aberdeen's 18-year-old substitute Paul Wright peels off his tracksuit and within minutes fires a 25-yard bullet past Henry Smith. Only Rangers are keeping the Dons off top spot for the moment.

No	Date	Team	Att	Pos	Pt	F-A	H-T	Scorers, Times, and Referee	1	2	3	4	5	6	7	8	9	10	11	subs used
6	14/9	A CELTIC	39,450	L	8	1-2	0-1	McDougall 85 / McClair 32, 88 / Ref: D Syme	Leighton	McKimmie	Mitchell	Stark*	McLeish	Miller W	Black	Simpson	McDougall	Bett	Hewitt*	Cooper/Weir
								(opponents)	Bonner	McGrain	Burns	Aitken	McGugan	Grant	Provan	McStay	Johnston	MacLeod	McClair	

A big crowd pay their respects to Jock Stein with a minute's silence before kick-off. Several Dons fans lay a wreath behind Pat Bonner's goal. A mix-up in the Celtic defence allows Aberdeen a late equaliser they scarcely deserve. Brian McClair then heads in Provan's corner-kick.

No	Date	Team	Att	Pos	Pt	F-A	H-T	Scorers, Times, and Referee	1	2	3	4	5	6	7	8	9	10	11	subs used
7	21/9	H ST MIRREN	12,585	D	9	1-1	0-0	McQueen 46p / Speirs 61p / Ref: J Duncan	Leighton	McKimmie	McQueen*	Stark	McLeish	Miller W	Black	Cooper	Hewitt*	Bett	Gray	McDougall/Porteous, McDowell/Mackie
								(opponents)	Money	Wilson	Hamilton	Rooney	Godfrey	Clarke	Fitzpatrick Cooper*	McGarvey	Gallagher	Speirs*		

St Mirren are as inconsistent as ever. Two unconvincing penalty awards, one to either side, punctuate this match. Campbell Money got a hand to McQueen's kick. Leighton dived the wrong way for Speirs' - but made up for that with a leaping save in the final minute to secure a point.

No	Date	Team	Att	Pos	Pt	F-A	H-T	Scorers, Times, and Referee	1	2	3	4	5	6	7	8	9	10	11	subs used
8	28/9	A RANGERS	37,599	W	11	3-0	1-0	McLeish 30, Stark 38, Hewitt 84 / Ref: G Smith	Leighton	McKimmie	Mitchell	Stark*	McLeish	Miller W	Black	Simpson	McDougall*	Bett	Hewitt	Gray/Falconer, McMinn/McKimmon
								(opponents)	Walker	Burns!	Munro	McPherson Paterson!	Durrant*	McCoist	McCoist	Russell	Williamson* Bell	Cooper		

Gers' Hugh Burns and Craig Paterson are sent off amid violent scenes. While Burns was walking McLeish headed in the ensuing free-kick. Then it was Paterson's turn to go after body-checking Cooper. The second half saw a pitch invasion. This result knocks Rangers off the top.

No	Date	Team	Att	Pos	Pt	F-A	H-T	Scorers, Times, and Referee	1	2	3	4	5	6	7	8	9	10	11	subs used
9	5/10	H CLYDEBANK	11,399	W	13	3-1	2-1	Black 1, McDougall 9, McKimmie 86 / Conroy 7 / Ref: D Downie	Leighton	McKimmie	Mitchell	Stark*	McLeish	Miller W	Black*	Simpson	McDougall	Bett	Hewitt	Angus/Falconer, Smith/Gibson
								(opponents)	Gallacher	Dickson	Given	Treanor	Auld*	Maher	Hughes	Shanks	Larnach	Conroy	Moore*	

Clydebank have won three matches and are holding their own for the moment. Keeper Gallacher's feeble touch out to Eric Black in the first minute was a prelude to scoring. But as the match wore on, the players of both sides went to sleep in the autumn sunshine.

No	Date	Team	Att	Pos	Pt	F-A	H-T	Scorers, Times, and Referee	1	2	3	4	5	6	7	8	9	10	11	subs used
10	12/10	A HIBERNIAN	10,377	D	14	1-1	0-1	Gray 82 / Cowan 26 / Ref: H Williamson	Leighton	McKimmie	Mitchell*	Stark	McLeish	Miller W	Angus	Simpson*	McDougall	Cooper	Hewitt	Gray/Wright
								(opponents)	Rough	Sneddon	Munro	Brazil	Rae	Hunter	Kane	Chisholm	Cowan	Durie	McBride	

Schizophrenic Hibs have lost their first six, but won't lose for the next 10. These two sides will meet again in the Skol Cup final in two week's time, so Aberdeen are grateful for Steve Gray's face-saving late equaliser which takes them to the top of the table for the first time this season.

11 H DUNDEE UTD 19/10 — W 3-2 — 15,148 — 7 16
Hewitt 5, 24, McDougall 17
Sturrock 2, Redford 51
Ref: G Smith

Leighton McKimmie Mitchell Stark McLeish Miller W Gray* Simpson* McDougall Cooper Hewitt
Thomson McGinnis Malpas Gough Hegarty Narey Bannon Milne Kirkwood Sturrock* Redford* Black/McIntyre Holt/Clark*

If Paul Sturrock's 2nd minute goal, wheeling onto the ball from 15 yards, was a cracker, then John Hewitt's answer - a breathtaking volley - was candidate for goal-of-the-season. Alex Ferguson was impressed, both as the manager of Aberdeen and of Scotland following Stein's death.

---

12 A HEARTS 30/10 — L 0-1 — 12,866 — 6 16
Levein 15
Ref: L Thow

Leighton McKimmie Angus* Gray McLeish Miller W Gray Simpson McDougall* Cooper Hewitt
Smith Kidd Whittaker Jardine A Berry Levein Colquhoun Jardine I Clark Robertson Mackay Bett/Wright Black*

This was Hearts' first league victory over Aberdeen at Tynecastle for seven years, as the new Skol Cup-holders are brought down to earth. Craig Levein outjumped Jim Leighton to meet Colquhoun's corner-kick. At the death Henry Smith saved splendidly from Neil Simpson.

---

13 H CELTIC 2/11 — W 4-1 — 23,000 — 2 18
McDougall 27,48, 55, 64
Provan 43
Ref: B McGinlay

Leighton McKimmie Mitchell Stark* McLeish Miller W Black Simpson McDougall* Cooper Hewitt*
Bonner McStay W McGrain Aitken McAdam Grant Provan McStay P McClair Burns McInally McGugan/Chalmers*

Of late Celtic having been shipping goals like a sieve. Frank McDougall enters the record books as the first Aberdeen player in memory to score four goals against Celtic. Eight players were booked - six in green and white hoops. Celtic will lose their next match 0-3 at Rangers.

---

14 H DUNDEE 9/11 — W 4-1 — 12,600 — 8 20
McLeish 21, McDougall 67, Stark 83, 87
Stephen 6
Ref: I Cathcart

Leighton McKimmie Mitchell Stark McLeish Miller W Gray Bett McDougall Angus* Weir
Geddes Shannon Glennie McCormack Smith Duffy McWilliams Brown Stephen Connor McKinlay Harvey Falconer*

A pre-match flu bug cut down Neale Cooper, Neil Simpson and John Hewitt. Then, after taking the lead, Dundee were cut down by the Dons. Three headers and a McDougall half-volley was more than enough to condemn Dundee to their umpteenth league defeat by Aberdeen.

---

15 A MOTHERWELL 16/11 — D 1-1 — 4,960 — 10 21
McDougall 57p
Wright 21p
Ref: D Downie

Leighton McKimmie Mitchell* Stark McLeish Miller W Gray* Simpson McDougall* Bett Weir
Gardiner Wishart Murray Dornan Forbes McCart Gahagan MacLeod Harrow* Wright Blair Angus/Hewitt McStay/Reilly*

A game disfigured by penalties. McLeish punched away the ball for the first. Then Hewitt fell over and was astonished to find he'd won a spot kick. When McLeish almost severed Reilly's legs, the referee ignored it. Motherwell lose to everyone else but have drawn twice with the Dons.

---

16 A ST MIRREN 23/11 — L 0-1 — 5,930 — 7 21
Rooney 45
Ref: D Syme

Leighton McKimmie Mitchell* Stark* McLeish Miller W Hewitt* Simpson McDougall Cooper Weir
Money Wilson Winnie Rooney Godfrey Clarke Fitzpatrick Cooper McGarvey Gallagher Speirs McQueen/Angus

Just before half-time Neale Cooper left the field temporarily for treatment to a facial injury. In his absence Jim Rooney leapt to head Speirs' cross past Jim Leighton. Try as they might Aberdeen could not recover. These are bleak months for the Dons, and Fergie is hopping mad.

---

17 A CLYDEBANK 10/12 — L 1-2 — 2,095 — 9 21
Black 60
Larnach 8, Dickson 53
Ref: W Knowles

Leighton McKimmie Mitchell* Stark McLeish Miller W Black Simpson Cooper Cooper Weir/McDougall
Gallacher Dickson Given Maher Auld Treanor Shanks Hughes Larnach Conroy McCabe Moore/Ronald*

Clydebank's first win in 11 games produces this incredible result. The crowd at Kilbowie Park cannot believe their eyes. Larnach heads in after Hughes' mighty free-kick crashed off the bar. Dickson then stabs in McCabe's drilled cross. The Bankies resist Aberdeen's furious riposte.

---

18 H HIBERNIAN 14/12 — W 4-0 — 11,819 — 7 23
Angus 18, Weir 78, Miller J 87, [McLeish 89]

Gunn McKimmie Mitchell Stark* McLeish Cooper Black Simpson Angus McDougall* Miller J
Rough Sneddon Milne Rae Fulton Hunter Kane Chisholm Gallacher Cowan Duriel Weir/McQueen

Hibs' Durie was sent packing in the second half after Neale Cooper took a ride on his knee. The whole Hibs team was then sent packing as the Dons goal. Aberdeen opened the vaults. Jim Leighton is surprisingly 'rested' for this match, enabling Bryan Gunn a rare opportunity in the Dons goal.

---

19 A DUNDEE UTD 21/12 — L 1-2 — 10,085 — 3 23
Stark 28
Bannon 9p, Sturrock 40
Ref: A Ferguson

Leighton McKimmie Mitchell Stark* McLeish Miller W Black Simpson McDougall* Cooper* Miller J
Thomson Malpas Holt Gough Hegarty Narey Bannon Gallacher Sturrock Redford Dodds Weir/McQueen Page*

Leighton is restored to the team, and promptly whips Hegarty's legs from under him. Billy Stark crashes in an equaliser from outside the box. Then Dodds sends Sturrock away for the winner. In the second half Alex Ferguson was 'sent off' from the dug-out to the jeers of home fans.

---

20 A DUNDEE 1/1 — D 0-0 — 9,096 — 6 24
Ref: J Renton

Leighton McKimmie McQueen Stark McLeish Miller W Black Gray* Falconer* Cooper Miller J
Geddes Glennie McKinlay Kidd Smith Duffy Shannon Brown Stephen Connor Harvey Angus/Wright Rafferty/Hendry*

Aberdeen had won their previous 12 league games at Dens Park, so it is unlucky 13th for them. How Aberdeen's defence survived a tortuous first half is a question Dundee manager Archie Knox cannot explain. Knocked off the top by Hearts last week, the Dons lose more ground.

---

21 H ST MIRREN 4/1 — W 2-0 — 11,500 — 7 26
Black 2, 19, Weir 58
Gallagher 55
Ref: T Muirhead

Leighton Cooper McQueen Stark McLeish Miller W Black Gray* Bett Miller J Weir
Money Wilson Abercrombie Rooney Godfrey Cooper Fitzpatrick Mackie McGarvey Gallagher Winnie Falconer Speirs*

Eric Black's goal-poaching skills restore Aberdeen's winning ways. His first goal arrived after Joe Miller's effort had been blocked; the second when Black snapped up Wilson's foolish back-pass. This result is a mirage, flattering that all is well in the Pittodrie garden.

FINE FARE SCOTTISH PREMIER

Manager: Alex Ferguson   SEASON 1985-86

No	Date	Team	Att	Pos	Pt	F-A	H-T	Scorers, Times, and Referees	1	2	3	4	5	6	7	8	9	10	11	subs used
22	A 11/1	CELTIC	31,305	2 / 5	D / 27	1-1	1-1	Miller J 14; Grant 19 — Ref: J Duncan	Leighton	McKimmie	McQueen	Cooper	McLeish	Miller W	Black	Simpson	Miller J*	Bett	Weir*	McDougall/Stark
		Celtic							*Latchford*	*McStay W*	*McGrain*	*Aitken*	*O'Leary*	*Grant*	*McClair*	*McStay P*	*McGhee**	*MacLeod**	*Johnston*	*McInally/Arch'd'con*
23	H 18/1	HEARTS	21,500	4 / 1	L / 27	0-1	0-0	Colquhoun 83 — Ref: J McCluskey	Leighton	McKimmie	McQueen*	Stark	McLeish	Miller W	Black	Simpson	McDougall*	Bett	Weir	Mitchell/Miller J
		Hearts							*Smith*	*Kidd*	*Black*	*Jardine A*	*Berry*	*Levein*	*Colquhoun*	*Jardine I*	*Clark*	*Mackay*	*Robertson**	*Mc.Adam*
24	A 1/2	RANGERS	29,887	4 / 5	D / 28	1-1	1-0	Miller J 3; Burns 52 — Ref: R Valentine	Leighton	McKimmie	McQueen	Stark*	McLeish	Miller W	Black	Simpson	Miller J	Bett	Weir	Mitchell
		Rangers							*Walker*	*Burns*	*Dawson*	*Johnstone*	*Beattie*	*Bell*	*McMinn*	*McCoist*	*Williamson**	*McPherson*	*Cooper*	*Ferguson I*
25	H 8/2	CLYDEBANK	11,000	4 / 9	W / 30	4-1	3-0	Bett 15p, Black 29, 34, 53; Conroy 88 — Ref: K Hope	Leighton	McKimmie	Angus	Stark*	McLeish	Miller W	Black	Simpson*	McDougall	Bett	Miller J	Porteous/Mitchell
		Clydebank							*Gallacher*	*Dickson*	*Given*	*Fallon*	*Auld*	*McGhie*	*Moore*	*Davies*	*Gibson*	*Lloyd**	*McCabe*	*Conroy*
26	H 19/2	RANGERS	18,700	—	W / 32	1-0	0-0	Angus 67 — Ref: J Duncan	Leighton	McKimmie	Burns	Cooper	McLeish	Miller W	Black	Simpson	McDougall*	Bett!	Miller J	Angus/Wright
		Rangers							*Walker*	*Burns*	*Dawson*	*Johnstone**	*Paterson*	*Bell!*	*McMinn*	*McCoist*	*Williamson*	*McPherson*	*Durrant**	*Cooper/Fraser*
27	A 22/2	HIBERNIAN	9,500	2 / 8	W / 34	1-0	1-0	Wright 13 — Ref: J Renton	Leighton	McKimmie	Angus	Stark*	McLeish	Miller W	Black	Simpson	Wright	Cooper	Miller J*	Mitchell/Hewitt
		Hibernian							*Rough*	*Brazil*	*Munro*	*Rae*	*Fulton*	*Hunter*	*Kane**	*May*	*Cowan*	*Durie*	*Tortolano*	*Harris*
28	A 15/3	ST MIRREN	4,448	3 / 8	D / 35	1-1	1-1	Miller W 33; Clarke 20 — Ref: D McVicar	Leighton	McKimmie	Angus	Cooper	McLeish	Miller W	Miller J*	Black	Wright	Bett	Hewitt	Stark/Porteous
		St Mirren							*Money*	*Wilson**	*Abercrombie*	*Cooper*	*Godfrey*	*Clarke*	*Hamilton*	*Winnie*	*McGarvey*	*Gallagher*	*Speirs*	*Rooney*
29	H 22/3	DUNDEE	13,013	3 / 6	D / 36	0-0	0-0	Ref: T Muirhead	Leighton	McKimmie	Angus	Cooper	McLeish	Miller W	Miller J	Stark	Wright*	Bett	Hewitt*	McCann/Falconer
		Dundee							*Geddes*	*Shannan*	*McKinlay*	*Rafferty*	*Smith**	*Duffy*	*Brown**	*Mennie*	*Harvey*	*Connor*	*Stephen*	*McCann W/Campbell*
30	A 29/3	MOTHERWELL	4,597	3 / 9	W / 38	1-0	1-0	Hewitt 7 — Ref: A Huett	Gunn	McKimmie	McQueen	Stark	McLeish	Miller W	Miller J*	Angus	Hewitt	Bett	McMaster	Gray
		Motherwell							*Gardiner*	*Wishart*	*Murray*	*Doyle**	*Forbes*	*Boyd*	*Baptie*	*MacLeod*	*Reilly*	*Wright**	*Walker*	*Dornan*
31	H 9/4	MOTHERWELL	10,300	3 / 9	W / 40	3-2	2-1	Bett 2, McDougall 35, Weir 81; Reilly 38, Kennedy 76 — Ref: A Ferguson	Gunn	McKimmie	McQueen	McMaster*	McLeish	Miller W	Miller J*	Gray	McDougall*	Bett	Weir	McIntyre/Miller J
		Motherwell							*Gardiner*	*Wishart*	*Murray*	*MacLeod**	*Forbes*	*Boyd*	*Dornan**	*Kennedy*	*Reilly*	*Wright*	*Walker*	*Baptie/Gahagan*

Match reports

22. Hailstones the size of marbles littered the pitch before kick-off. They had melted by the time Joe Miller squeezed the ball past Latchford, at the second attempt. Five minutes later Peter Grant began and ended the move which brought Celtic level. It is three years since a win at Parkhead.

23. Hearts' unbeaten run is now 17 games; they inflict Aberdeen's first home defeat in 13 months. Twice near half-time Hearts were inches from scoring. Leighton pushed Ian Jardine's volley onto a post and Sandy Clark made the miss of the century. Colquhoun raced away near the end.

24. Rangers have won their last three games. With this result Aberdeen complete an unwanted sequence of visiting every Premier League ground without winning once. That sequence might have been broken but for Tommy McQueen's terrible back-pass, intercepted by Burns.

25. Clydebank won when these teams last met. That was two of just two wins for Bankies in 19 games. But this was Eric Black's match, as he ploughed through the snow to claim his hat-trick. Two textbook headers, with a cracking shot thrown in for good measure.

26. Super match, played on a treacherous white pitch, highlighted by substitute Ian Angus's lethal strike which produced the only goal. Sadly there were seven bookings, and Jim Bett and ex-Don Dougie Bell were sent off near the end of the first half after clashing in midfield.

27. Hibs have now won only one of their last 10. This game provides Aberdeen with their first away win in the league for five months, since 28 September. Paul Wright took advantage of Rae's stumble for the vital goal. Hibs had their moments in the second half, but failed to capitalise.

28. Six games without a win now for St Mirren. But following Willie Miller's swerving equaliser St Mirren hit the woodwork three times in the space of a few seconds. Reprieved, Aberdeen missed chance after chance to snatch both points. They are still in with a shout of the league title.

29. Dundee have won their last three in the league, the last of which was over Rangers. But having suffered their cruel Cup elimination at Pittodrie in midweek Dundee are in no mood to assist Aberdeen's late title surge. Just six points off Dundee this season, the lowest tally since 1975-76.

30. Gothenburg have ended Aberdeen's European Cup dreams, and Motherwell do their best to make sure the Dons don't compete in the Champions' Cup next season.

31. What a start for Jim Bett, who almost burst the ball, never mind the net, from McMaster's pass. McDougall's miscued header made it 2-0 before Motherwell began to assert themselves. Aberdeen were finally rescued when Peter Weir latched onto Black's back-header. In the last minute Dornan's header flew back off Aberdeen's post. And that would have been a crucial point lost.

32 H CELTIC 12/4 22,000 4 L 3 40 0-1 0-0

Johnston 49
Ref: W Crombie

Gunn McKimmie McQueen* Stark McLeish Miller W Black Mitchell Miller J Bett Hewitt* McMaster/Falconer
Bonner McGrain Whyte Aitken O'Leary* Grant McClair McStay Johnston MacLeod Burns Archdeacon

A match that both sides desperately needed to win. A scrappy affair was turned Celtic's way by a fine individual goal by Maurice Johnston, who wriggled past several defenders before producing a deadly finish. Celtic will win their final eight games to snatch the title on the last day.

33 H DUNDEE UTD 16/4 8,500 4 L 2 40 0-1 0-1

Gough 26
Ref: D Syme

Gunn McKimmie Mitchell Robertson I McLeish Miller W Black* Angus* Miller J Bett Weir McMaster/Porteous
Thomson Malpas Holt Gough Hegarty Narey Clark* Gallacher* Beedie Sturrock Redford Kirkwood/Bannon

United have just lost 0-3 at home to rivals Hearts, and the title looks beyond them. Filthy weather over Pittodrie, and a filthy result for the Dons as they finally concede defeat in their championship quest. Richard Gough pulls down Paul Sturrock's cross to fire past Bryan Gunn.

34 A HEARTS 20/4 19,047 4 D 1 41 1-1 0-0

Weir 72p
Colquhoun 87
Ref: R Valentine

Gunn McKimmie McQueen McMaster McLeish Miller W Hewitt* Mitchell* Miller J Bett Weir Black/Robertson I
Smith Cowie Whittaker Jardine A Berry Levein Colquhoun Black K Clark Mackay* Robertson McAdam

Scottish TV's first ever live league game, and on Sunday too. With Aberdeen having dropped out of contention, the occasion has lost much of its bite. Aberdeen were awarded a mysterious penalty to threaten Hearts' seven-month unbeaten run. McQueen then fluffed a late clearance.

35 H RANGERS 26/4 17,000 4 D 5 42 1-1 0-0

Hewitt 57
McMinn 50
Ref: J McCluskey

Gunn Mitchell* McIntyre* McMaster McLeish Miller W Gray Robertson I Miller J Hewitt Weir Porteous/Wright
McCloy Burns Munro McKinnon McPherson Dawson Ferguson D Durant McCoist McMinn Cooper

A strange-looking Dons side contest a match best remembered for Ted McMinn's bewildering goal. The lanky Ranger meandered half the length of the pitch before applying the perfect finish. It looked like three consecutive Aberdeen defeats until Hewitt's equaliser from 15 yards.

36 A CLYDEBANK 3/5 2,382 10 44 6-0 5-0

Stark 9, McMaster 10, Weir 16, [Hewitt 29, McDougall 38, 66]
Gibson
Ref: G Dunbar

Gunn McKimmie McQueen Stark Irvine McIntyre Gray* Hewitt Robertson I McDougall Weir Porteous/Robertson I
Gallacher Dickson Given Fallon Auld McGhie Moore Hughes Bain* Conroy McCabe Gibson

A few more performances like this earlier in the season and the Dons would still be champions. Pick of the bunch was Weir's effort, ghosting past three defenders before finishing with aplomb. Elsewhere, Hearts forfeit the title at Dundee in the last seven minutes of the season.

Average Home 14,515
Away 14,200

Skol League Cup

2 H AYR 21/8 12,400 W 5-0 2-0

Stark 3, 55, McQueen 39p, [McDougall 84, 86]Purdie
Ref: R Valentine

Gunn McKimmie* McQueen* Stark McLeish Miller W Hewitt Simpson* Bett Weir Cooper/Black
McCann Buchanan Anderson McAllister Collins March McNiven McDougall* Irons Murphy Adams

Ayr are a poor Division 2 side. And it showed. The Dons displayed a welcome ruthlessness, fighting for the ball even when victory was in their pocket. The Dons appear determined not to follow the example of last season, when they unaccountably lost to Airdrie at this stage.

3 A ST JOHNSTONE 28/8 5,100 2:8 W 2-0 1-0

Hewitt 27, McDougall 86
Ref: A Ferguson

Gunn McKimmie McQueen* Gray McLeish Miller W Hewitt Simpson McDougall Bett Weir Stark
Balavage Miller McGonigle Barron Winter Morton Gibson McGurn Ward* Reid Williamson* Johnston/McDaid

St Johnstone, like Ayr, hail from the Division 2 basement. They put up stiffer resistance. Frank McDougall is developing a taste for late goals, once the opposition is on its way to the mortuary. For too long the Dons had to be thankful to John Hewitt's first-half effort.

QF H HEARTS 4/9 13,100 7 W 1-0 1-0

Black 24
Ref: M Delaney

Leighton McKimmie Mitchell Stark McLeish Miller W Black Simpson McDougall Bett Weir
Smith Kidd Whittaker Jardine A MacDonald Levein Watson Mackay* Clark Robertson* Black Cherry/Colquhoun

Jock Stein popped in to check on his Pittodrie internationals, prior to the World Cup showdown with Wales. He watched as Henry Smith and Roddy MacDonald gifted a goal to Black. Hearts never looked like equalising. It was Stein's last visit to Pittodrie: six days later he was dead.

SF1 A DUNDEE UTD 25/9 12,837 4 W 3-0 1-0

Black 63
Ref: M Delaney

Leighton McKimmie Mitchell Stark McLeish Miller W Black Simpson* McDougall* Cooper Hewitt Weir Gray/Falconer
McAlpine Malpas Holt Gough Hegarty Narey Bannon Beaumont* Beedie Sturrock Dodds Redford/Kirkwood

The Skol Cup retains two-legged semi-finals. This tie has too many fouls and free-kicks to allow free-flowing soccer. Soon after Black headed in Hewitt's cross, Richard Gough was sent off for fouling Hewitt. In 1982-83 the Dons won at Tannadice in the first leg but lost the second.

SF2 H DUNDEE UTD 9/10 20,000 6 W 1-0 0-0

McDougall 68
Ref: R Valentine

Leighton McKimmie Mitchell Stark* McLeish Miller W Angus Simpson McDougall Cooper Hewitt Gray
McAlpine* McGinnis* Holt Gough Hegarty Narey Bannon Milne Malpas Sturrock Dodds Kirkwood/Redford

Three times in recent seasons United have knocked Aberdeen out of the League Cup. This was a stirring cup-tie. Chances fell at both ends - most of them to the Dons - before Hewitt's low cross was converted by McDougall. United keeper Hamish McAlpine had earlier been injured.

FINE FARE PREMIER (CUP-TIES) Manager: Alex Ferguson SEASON 1985-86

Skol League Cup

	Venue	Opponent	Date	F-A	H-T	Scorers, Times, and Referees	Attendance
F	N	HIBERNIAN	27/10 (at Hampden)	1 W 3-0	2-0	Black 9, 62, Stark 12 — Ref: R Valentine	40,061 8

Pos	1	2	3	4	5	6	7	8	9	10	11	subs used
Aberdeen	Leighton	McKimmie	Mitchell	Stark*	McLeish	Miller W	Black*	Simpson	McDougall	Cooper	Hewitt	Gray
Hibernian	*Rough*	*Sneddon*	*Munro*	*Brazil**	*Fulton*	*Hunter*	*Kane*	*Chisholm*	*Cowan*	*Durie*	*McBride^*	*Harris/Collins*

Aberdeen have never won the League Cup under Alex Ferguson. This is known as the 12-minute final, the time it took for Hibs' challenge to be cast asunder. Man-of-the match Hewitt centred for Black, then sets up Stark. Aberdeen have not conceded a goal in the competition.

Scottish Cup

	Rnd	Venue	Opponent	Date	F-A	H-T	Scorers, Times, and Referees	Attendance
3		H	MONTROSE	5/2	4 W 4-1	1-0	Stark 27, Miller 47, McDougall 74, Brown 56p [McLeish 81] — Ref: R Valentine	9,000 1:8

Pos	1	2	3	4	5	6	7	8	9	10	11	subs used
Aberdeen	Leighton	McKimmie	McQueen	Stark	McLeish	Miller W	Black	Simpson	McDougall	Bett	Weir*	Porteous
Montrose	*Charles*	*Barr*	*McLelland*	*Brown*	*Sheran*	*Forbes*	*Allan*	*Bennett*	*Sommer*	*Wright**	*McManus^*	*Duffy/Millar*

A blizzard raged throughout. The Montrose team craftily played in all-white, so they were totally invisible to their opponents - especially McQueen, who obviously failed to see Barr as he brought him down for a second-half penalty that briefly injected life into the contest.

| 4 | | A | ARBROATH | 15/2 | 4 W 1-0 | 0-0 | Miller J 47 — Ref: W Crombie | 6,017 2:6 |

Pos	1	2	3	4	5	6	7	8	9	10	11	subs used
Aberdeen	Leighton	Cooper	McQueen	Bett	McLeish	Miller W	Black	Simpson	McDougall	Angus	Miller J	
Arbroath	*Jackson*	*Lynch*	*Hill*	*Curran*	*Taylor*	*Jack^*	*Fotheringh'mMackie*	*Torrance*	*McWalker*	*Branngian*	*Kirkcaldy*	

It was a bitterly cold and blustery day at bleak and exposed Gayfield Park. Aberdeen's only moment to cheer was Joe Miller's composure in controlling Neale Cooper's cross before beating keeper Jackson. To their credit, the Division 2 side never gave up.

| QF | | A | DUNDEE | 8/3 | 2 D 2-2 | 1-1 | Hewitt 23, 74, Harvey 26, Brown 67 — Ref: B McGinlay | 13,188 6 |

Pos	1	2	3	4	5	6	7	8	9	10	11	subs used
Aberdeen	Leighton	McKimmie	Angus	Cooper	McLeish	Miller W	Black	Simpson*	Hewitt	Bett	Weir*	Stark/Wright
Dundee	*Geddes*	*Forsyth*	*McKinlay*	*Shannon*	*Smith*	*Duffy*	*Hendry^*	*Brown*	*Harvey*	*Connor*	*Mennie*	*Rafferty*

A cup-tie to warm the blood. Nothing to separate the teams. But Aberdeen could be grateful to Dundee keeper Bobby Geddes for the dreadful blunder - letting Simpson poach the ball off his toes - which preceded John Hewitt's second headed goal. The Dons never seem to lose at Dens.

| QF R | | H | DUNDEE | 12/3 | 2 W 2-1 (aet) | 1-1 | Black 37, Weir 101, Stephen 19 — Ref: B McGinlay | 21,000 6 |

Pos	1	2	3	4	5	6	7	8	9	10	11	subs used
Aberdeen	Leighton	Cooper	McKimmie	Stark*	McLeish	Miller W	Black*	Simpson	Hewitt	Bett	Weir	Angus/Wright
Dundee	*Geddes*	*Forsyth**	*McKinlay*	*Shannon*	*Smith*	*Duffy*	*Stephen^*	*Brown*	*Harvey*	*Connor*	*Mennie*	*Glennie/Hendry*

Poor Dundee. They hardly deserved to lose this replay. They grabbed the game by the scruff of the neck in the second half but could not force the winner. They could only stand and admire the genius of Peter Weir, who floated the ball over Bobby Geddes' head and in at the far post.

| SF | | N | HIBERNIAN | 5/4 (at Dens Park) | 3 W 3-0 | 2-0 | Stark 20, Black 35, Miller J 81 — Ref: K Hope | 19,165 7 |

Pos	1	2	3	4	5	6	7	8	9	10	11	subs used
Aberdeen	Gunn	McKimmie	Angus	Stark*	McLeish	Miller W	Black	Cooper*	McDougall	Bett	Hewitt	McMaster/Miller J
Hibernian	*Rough*	*Sneddon*	*Munro*	*May*	*Fulton*	*Rae*	*Tortolano**	*Chisholm*	*Cowan*	*Durie^*	*Collins*	*McBride/Harris*

Aberdeen's seventh Scottish Cup semi-final in eight seasons under Ferguson. Gunn pushed Collins' deflected shot against the bar. Two Dons crosses produced two headed goals by Stark and Black - who had destroyed Hibs in the Skol Cup final. Hewitt centred for Joe Miller's header.

| F | | N | HEARTS | 10/5 (at Hampden) | 4 W 3-0 | 1-0 | Hewitt 5, 48, Stark 75 — Ref: H Alexander | 62,841 2 |

Pos	1	2	3	4	5	6	7	8	9	10	11	subs used
Aberdeen	Leighton	McKimmie	McQueen	Stark*	McLeish*	Miller W	Hewitt*	Cooper*	McDougall	Bett	Weir	Stark/Miller J
Hearts	*Smith*	*Kidd!*	*Whittaker*	*Jardine*	*Berry*	*Levein*	*Colquhoun*	*Black*	*Clark*	*Mackay*	*Robertson*	

Eric Black is dropped after he intends to sign for Metz. Hearts are rocked by Hewitt's breakaway goal. McDougall dummies Weir's cross to set up Hewitt for No 2. Berry hits Leighton's crossbar. Stark heads a third. Hearts skipper Walter Kidd throws the ball at Neale Cooper and is off.

European Champions' Cup

	Rnd	Venue	Opponent	Date	F-A	H-T	Scorers, Times, and Referees	Attendance
1:1		A	AKRANES	18/9 (Iceland)	3 W 3-1	0-1	Black 56, Hewitt 62, Stark 64; Ingolfsson 36p — Ref: T Ass (Norway)	7,000

Pos	1	2	3	4	5	6	7	8	9	10	11	subs used
Aberdeen	Leighton	McKimmie	McQueen	Stark*	McLeish	Miller W	Black*	Cooper	Hewitt	Bett	Gray	Mitchell/Wright
Akranes	*Kristiansson*	*Thord'son*	*G Gudmund's'n*	*Larusson*	*Askelsson*	*Johannes'n*	*Hakonars'n*	*Ingolfsson*	*Thordars'n*	*K Thordars'n*	*O Sveinsson*	

Aberdeen would be happy with a repeat of the 2-1 win in this same stadium two years earlier in the Cup-Winners' Cup. In the event they go one better. But problems loomed when Akranes were given a soft penalty. Black hit a post before levelling, while Billy Stark twice hit the bar.

| 1:2 | | H | AKRANES | 2/10 | 2 W 4-1 | 1-1 | Simpson 5, Hewitt 63, Gray 65, [Falconer 67] Johanesson 32 — Ref: J Kinsella (Rep Ireland) (Dons win 7-2 on aggregate) | 14,700 |

Pos	1	2	3	4	5	6	7	8	9	10	11	subs used
Aberdeen	Leighton	McKimmie	Mitchell*	Gray	McLeish	Miller W	Black	Simpson	Wright*	Cooper	Hewitt	Angus/Falconer
Akranes	*Kristiansson*	*Thord'son*	*G Gudmund's'n*	*Larusson*	*Askelsson*	*Johannes'n*	*Hakonars'n*	*Ingolfsson*	*Thordars'n*	*K Thordars'n*	*O Sveinsson*	*Bardason/Rafnsson*

Three goals in a four-minute spell in the second half gave the Dons supporters something to shout about. Until then Akranes were heading for an honourable draw on the night. In 1983-84 Aberdeen scraped home 3-2 on aggregate. The margin is much more comfortable this time.

European Ties

2:1 A SERVETTE 1 D 0-0 0-0
23/10 (Switz'land) 8,000
McDougall 23
Ref: M Petrovic (Yugoslavia)

| Aberdeen | Leighton | McKimmie | Mitchell | Stark* | McLeish | Miller W | Weir* | Simpson | McDougall | Cooper | Hewitt | Angus/Gray |
| Servette | de Choudens | Schnyder | Bianchi | Hasler | Renquin | Fredericks'n | Geiger | Lei Ravello | Magnusson | Jaccard* | Besnard | Opoku/Christiansen |

Aberdeen went about their task in Geneva against the Swiss champions quietly and unspectacularly, and managed to bore the small crowd to death. The Dons might have won when McLeish headed a Mitchell free-kick against the bar. Servette's Geiger faced England in Euro '96.

2:2 H SERVETTE 1 W 1-0 1-0
6/11 19,000
McDougall 23
Ref: A Castillo (Spain)
(Dons win 1-0 on aggregate)

| Aberdeen | Leighton | McKimmie | Weir | Stark* | McLeish | Miller W | Bett | Simpson | McDougall | Cooper | Hewitt* | Mitchell/Gray |
| Servette | de Choudens | Schnyder | Bianchi | Hasler | Renquin | Decastel | Geiger | Lei Ravello | Magnusson | Castella | Kok | |

Lucky Aberdeen. Once Frank McDougall had dived to head in Weir's cross, the Swiss team turned on the heat. Alex Ferguson described their second-half performance as 'the finest I have seen from a team visiting Pittodrie for a European tie.' Twice Servette struck the woodwork.

QF H IFK GOTHENBURG 2 D 2-2 1-1
1 5/3 (Sweden) 22,000
Miller W 16, Hewitt 79
Tord Holmgren 42, Ekstrom 89
Ref: D Pauly (W Germany)

| Aberdeen | Gunn | Cooper | Angus | Stark | McLeish | Miller W | Black | Simpson* | Miller J* | Bett | Weir | McKimmie/Hewitt |
| Gothenburg | Wernersson | Svensson* | Hysen | Larsson | Fredericks'n Nilsson R | Petterson | T'd Holmg'n | Tm Holmg'n | Ekstrom | Nilsson T | Kullberg/Carlsson |

Gothenburg won the UEFA Cup in 1982. They are just emerging from their winter shut-down. Pittodrie observes a minute's silence for Sweden's assassinated prime minister. Miller's 50th European tie is marked by a raging left-footer. Gunn saves the Dons until the last minute.

QF A IFK GOTHENBURG 3 D 0-0 0-0
2 19/3 44,400
Ref: Woehrer (Austria)
(Dons lose on away-goals rule)

| Aberdeen | Leighton | McKimmie | Mitchell* | Cooper | McLeish | Miller W | Black* | Angus | Bett | Hewitt | Weir | Stark/McDougall |
| Gothenburg | Wernersson | Svensson* | Hysen | Larsson | Fredericks'n Nilsson R | Petterson | T'd Holmg'n | Tm Holmg'n | Ekstrom | Nilsson T | Kullberg/Johansson |

Gothenburg rest on the goals they scored at Pittodrie. Neither side creates a scoring chance worthy of the name. Aberdeen bow out of the European Cup unbeaten. Worse, their gorgeous memories of the Ullevi Stadium - scene of their greatest triumph - are dimmed with sadness.

League Table

			Home					Away					Pts
	P	W	D	L	F	A	W	D	L	F	A		Pts
1 Celtic	36	10	6	2	27	15	10	4	4	40	23		50
2 Hearts	36	13	5	0	38	10	7	5	6	21	23		50
3 Dundee Utd	36	10	6	2	38	15	8	5	5	21	16		47
4 ABERDEEN	36	11	4	3	38	15	5	8	5	24	16		44
5 Rangers	36	10	4	4	34	18	3	10	5	19	27		35
6 Dundee	36	11	2	5	32	20	3	5	10	13	31		35
7 St Mirren	36	9	4	5	26	24	4	3	11	16	39		31
8 Hibernian	36	6	4	8	27	25	5	2	11	22	38		28
9 Motherwell	36	7	3	8	23	23	0	3	15	10	43		20
10 Clydebank	36	4	6	8	18	32	2	2	14	11	45		20
	360	91	42	47	301	197	47	42	91	197	301		360

	P	W	D	L	F	A	Cup	W	D	L	F	A	Pts
v Hibernian	4	3	1	0	9	1	LC	1	0	0			7
							SC	1	0	0			
v Clydebank	4	3	0	1	14	4							6
v Dundee	4	2	2	0	7	2	SC	1			1		6
v Rangers	4	2	2	0	6	2							6
v Motherwell	4	2	2	0	6	4							6
v St Mirren	4	1	2	1	5	4							4
v Celtic	4	1	1	2	6	5	LC	1			1	0	3
v Hearts	4	1	1	2	4	3	SC	1			1	0	3
v Dundee Utd*	4	1	1	2	5	6	LC	2			2	0	3
	36	16	12	8	62	31		44					

Odds & ends

Never lost to: (4) Hibs, Dundee, Rangers, Motherwell.
Never beat: (0).
Won from behind: (4) Dundee U (h), Dundee (h & SC), Akranes.
Lost from in front: (0).
High spots: Winning both domestic cups in one season for the first time.
1 defeat in first 11 league games.
Top of the table from 12 October to 21 December.
Reaching quarter-final of the European Cup.
Low spots: Lowest points tally (44) since 1978-79.
Only 2 league wins in 10 games from 16 November.
Losing late goal to Gothenburg at Pittodrie in European Cup.
No own-goals for Aberdeen all season.
Bogey-team: Celtic.
Ever-presents: (0).
Hat-tricks: (2) Frank McDougall (1), Eric Black (1).
Leading scorer: (20) Frank McDougall.

Appearances / Goals

	Appearances								Goals				
	Lge	Sub	LC	Sub	SC	Sub	Eur	Sub	Lge	LC	SC	Eur	Tot
Angus, Ian	12	5	3				1	2	2				2
Black, Eric	23	3	3	1	5		4		8	4	2	1	15
Bett, Jim	22	2	3		6		4		3				3
Cooper, Neale	20	3	3	1	5	1	6						
Falconer, Willie	2	6		1		1		1	1				1
Gray, Steve	10	3		3			2	1					
Gunn, Bryan	10		2		1		1						
Hewitt, John	18	5	5		4		5		6	1	4	3	14
Irvine, Brian	1												
Leighton, Jim	26		4		5		2						
McDougall, Frank	22	3	6		4		2	1	14	4	1	1	20
McIntyre, Tommy	2	3											
McKimmie, Stewart	34		6		5		6	1	3				3
McLeish, Alex	34		6		6		6		3		1		4
McMaster, John	5	2	1			1	1		1				1
McQueen, Tommy	15	2	3		2			1					2
Miller, Joe	17	2	1	2	2	1	3		3		2		5
Miller, Willie	33		6		6		6		1	1		1	3
Mitchell, Brian	18	5	4		3	2							
Porteous, Ian		6											
Robertson, Ian	2	2											
Simpson, Neil	22		6		4		4		1			1	2
Stark, Billy	28	2	5	1	3	2	4	1	8	3	3	1	15
Weir, Peter	17	4	4		3		4		5			1	6
Wright, Paul	3	7		2		1		2	2				2
25 players used	396	65	66	7	66	9	66	12	62	13	15	10	100

FINE FARE SCOTTISH PREMIER — Manager: Ferguson → Ian Porterfield — SEASON 1986-87

No		Opponent	Date	Att	Pos	Pt	F-A	H-T	Scorers, Times, and Referees
1	A	DUNDEE UTD	9/8	10,910	L	–	1-2	0-1	Stark 87 / Gough 33, Redford 73 — Ref: G Smith
2	H	HIBERNIAN	13/8	12,983	W	2	4-0	1-0	Miller J 21, Angus 51, Gray 68, Stark 77 — Ref: R Valentine
3	H	HAMILTON	16/8	10,316	4 W	4	2-0	2-0	Stark 15, 43 — Ref: C Sinclair
4	A	CELTIC	23/8	46,073	4 D	5	1-1	1-0	Miller J 23 / MacLeod 58 — Ref: A Waddell
5	H	DUNDEE	30/8	12,486	2 W	7	2-0	0-0	Hewitt 54, Miller J 64 — Ref: D Syme
6	A	ST MIRREN	6/9	4,435	4 D	8	1-1	1-1	Stark 40 / Lambert 41 — Ref: D Hope
7	H	HEARTS	13/9	15,625	5 L	8	0-1	0-1	Clark 34 — Ref: M Delaney
8	A	CLYDEBANK	20/9	2,766	4 W	10	3-1	2-0	Hewitt 14, 67, Weir 28 / Conroy 54 — Ref: G Evans
9	A	RANGERS	27/9	40,155	5 L	10	0-2	0-0	Souness 50, McCoist 81 — Ref: J Duncan
10	H	MOTHERWELL	4/10	8,751	6 D	11	2-2	1-1	Dodds 20, Miller W 47 / Kennedy 14, Walker 74p — Ref: A Ferguson
11	A	FALKIRK	8/10	4,800	6 D	12	3-3	1-2	Stark 44, McLeish 61, Bett 90p / Hetherston 16, 22p, Eadie 68 — Ref: J McGilvray

Line-ups (Aberdeen in roman, opponents in italic)

1. Dundee Utd (A)
Aberdeen: Leighton, McKimmie, Mitchell, Stark, Irvine, Gray, Simpson*, Hewitt*, Angus, Weir — subs: Falconer/Miller J
Dundee Utd: Thomson, Malpas, Holt, Gough, Hegarty, Narey, Bowman, Milne, Bannon, Sturrock, Redford — sub: Clark*
Neil Simpson missed the end of last season through injury and damages an ankle after just four minutes of this opener. United's unsettled Richard Gough heads in Narey's free-kick, but will sign for Spurs in a few days. Sub Joe Miller provides the cross for Billy Stark's late effort.

2. Hibernian (H)
Aberdeen: Leighton, McKimmie, Mitchell, Stark, Irvine, Gray*, Miller J*, Weir, Angus — subs: Falconer/McDougall
Hibernian: Rough, Sneddon, Tortolano, Kirkwood, Fulton, Chisholm, Beedie, Weir, Cowan, Irvine, May — sub: Kane*
Hibs beat Rangers on Saturday. Aberdeen are wrecked by injury. Mitchell plays at right-back, and McKimmie - who's signed a new four-year contract - in midfield. Ferguson is keen to sign Bradford City's Stuart McCall. This is the Dons' 15th win in 21 Premier matches with Hibs.

3. Hamilton (H)
Aberdeen: Leighton, McKimmie, Mitchell*, Stark, Irvine, Miller J*, Bett, Connor — subs: Gray/Robertson D
Hamilton: McKellar, McVeigh, Hamill, Collins, Brazil, Mitchell, Taylor, Barr, Jamieson, O'Neill, Craig* — subs: Clarke/Brogan*
Hamilton's first Premier League visit to Pittodrie. Leighton suffers a bad head injury. Brian Irvine deputises in goal, and Bryan Gunn's transfer is delayed. Jim Bett makes his comeback, and Robert Connor makes a solid debut for his new club. A 20-yarder and a diving header for Stark.

4. Celtic (A)
Aberdeen: Gunn, McKimmie, Irvine, Stark, McLeish, Miller J, Gray*, Hewitt*, Connor, Weir — subs: Mitchell/Falconer
Celtic: Bonner, McStay W, Whyte, Aitken, McGugan, Grant, McClair, McStay, Johnston, MacLeod, Burns — sub: Archdeacon*
Aberdeen played without a left-back until Celtic began to exploit the space in the second half. Weir's corner was knocked back by McLeish for Joe Miller to head the opener. Tommy Burns played for a foul by Willie Miller. MacLeod levelled from the free-kick, enraging Alex Ferguson.

5. Dundee (H)
Aberdeen: Gunn, McKimmie, Irvine*, Stark, McLeish, Miller J*, Bett, Connor — subs: Mitchell/Wright
Dundee: Geddes, McGeachie, McKinlay, Shannon, Smith, Duffy, Jack, Brown*, Harvey, Angus, Stephen — subs: Hendry/Mennie*
Dundee have been whipping boys for Aberdeen for so long it is a wonder they have any heart left. They hold out for nearly an hour, but goals by Hewitt and Joe Miller condemn them to another dispiriting defeat. They had won their last three Premier matches too. Aberdeen go second.

6. St Mirren (A)
Aberdeen: Leighton, Mitchell, McQueen, Stark, Irvine, Gray, McMaster*, Connor — subs: McIntyre/Falconer
St Mirren: Money, Clarke, Hamilton D, Bell, Godfrey, Cooper, Lambert, Hamilton B, McGarvey, Abercrombie, Chalmers* — subs: Wilson/Gallagher*
Seven Dons first-teamers are out injured. There is little atmosphere at Love St, where Aberdeen enjoy most of the play, St Mirren most of the chances. Both goals are down to goalkeeping errors - Stark capitalises on Money's fumble, and Lambert's header was down to Jim Leighton.

7. Hearts (H)
Aberdeen: Leighton, McKimmie, Mitchell, Stark, McLeish, Miller J, Bett, Connor, Irvine I*, Weir — subs: McIntyre/Gray
Hearts: Smith, Kidd, Whittaker, Jardine A, Black, Levein, Colquhoun, Jardine I, Clark, Mackay*, Foster — subs: Watson/Robertson*
Leighton, Strachan, and Miller played for Scotland against Bulgaria in midweek. Now McLeish returns for his 450th first team game, starting the match in midfield. The only goal was a ricochet off Sandy Clark's legs. 'We must learn to fight as well as play good football,' says Fergie.

8. Clydebank (A)
Aberdeen: Leighton, McKimmie, Mitchell, Stark*, McLeish, Miller J, Hewitt*, Bett, Wright, Robertson D, Weir* — subs: McIntyre/Porteous
Clydebank: Gallacher, Dickson, Given, Treanor, Auld, Maher, Shanks, Irons, Grant, Conroy, McCabe — subs: Coyle/Sirrel*
Davie Dodds is about to sign from Xamax Neuchatel for £215,000 - having gone to Switzerland in the summer. He watches the game from the stand. Jim Bett plays despite the effects of flu. Johns Hewitt's first goal was scored from 18 yards out, his second from one.

9. Rangers (A)
Aberdeen: Leighton, McKimmie, Mitchell, Stark*, McLeish, Miller W, Hewitt*, Bett, Fraser, Connor, Weir — subs: Robertson D/Wright
Rangers: Woods, Nicholl, Munro, Souness, McPherson, Butcher, Fraser, McMinn, McCoist, Durrant, Cooper — subs: Dawson/Fleck*
Graham Souness is revolutionising Rangers and Scottish football. He wants to prove Ferguson wrong for dropping him from Scotland's World Cup 86 team. McLeish and Leighton are booked disputing McCoist's 'offside' goal. This is the Dons' first Ibrox defeat for three years.

10. Motherwell (H)
Aberdeen: Leighton, McKimmie, Robertson D*, Stark, McLeish, Miller W, Wright, Bett, Dodds, Connor, Weir — subs: Irvine/Porteous
Motherwell: Gardiner, Wishart, Murray, Phillben, Kennedy, Boyd, Farningham, Kirk, Walker, Wright, Smith — subs: Reilly/Baptie
The sad Dons are out of Europe, beaten by Sion. 0-1 when Bett clears off the line but Alex Kennedy follows up; 1-1 thanks to Dodds' header - his first goal for the Dons. 2-1 when Willie Miller exploits a corner that was not cleared; 2-2 when David Robertson trips Reilly from behind.

11. Falkirk (A)
Aberdeen: Leighton, McKimmie, Mitchell, Stark, McLeish, Miller W, Porteous*, Bett, Robertson I*, Connor, Dodds — subs: Wright/Weir
Falkirk: Watson, Martin, Dempsey, Purdie, Nicol, Kemp, Hetherston, McGuire, Eadie, McCormack, Ashwood — subs: Hughes/Irvine*
Falkirk are denied their first home win because of a contentious late penalty awarded when Weir collided with Watson. The Dons left the pitch to the chants of 'cheats' from the terraces. Mitchell had brought down McGuire for Hetherston's penalty. McLeish's 30-yarder was deflected.

12 — H DUNDEE UTD — 11/10 — 14,922 — 5 2 14 — W 2-0

Scorers: Hewitt 22, 70
Ref: A Huett

Aberdeen	Dundee Utd
Leighton	Thomson
McKimmie	Malpas
Mitchell	McInally
Stark	Beaumont
McLeish*	Hegarty*
Miller W	Narey
Hewitt	Coyne
Bett	Gallacher
Dodds	Bannon
Robertson D	Sturrock*
Weir	Bowman
Gray	Milne/Redford

United are without injured leading scorer Ian Ferguson, and their first league defeat sees them overtaken by Celtic at the top. Davie Dodds set up both goals - against his former Scottish club - for the recalled John Hewitt. McLeish had to be subbed in the first half with a hand injury.

13 — A HIBERNIAN — 18/10 — 9,127 — 5 8 15 — D 1-1

Scorers: Connor 23, Chisholm 67
Ref: D Hope

Aberdeen	Hibernian
Leighton	Rough
McKimmie	Hunter
Mitchell	Tortolano
Stark	Kirkwood
Irvine	Rae
Robertson D	Chisholm
Bett	Kane
Connor	May
Dodds	Irvine
Hewitt	McCluskey
Weir	McBride
Wright*	McIntyre

Miller and McLeish both failed late fitness tests. Irvine and McKimmie take their places at the heart of the Dons defence. Bett assumes the captaincy. Connor, back from suspension, scores after Alan Rough blocks Dodds' effort. But the Dons are hanging on grimly at the end.

14 — A HAMILTON — 25/10 — 3,001 — 5 12 17 — W 1-0

Scorers: Bett 52
Ref: G Smith

Aberdeen	Hamilton
Leighton	McKeller
McKimmie	Barr
Mitchell	Sprott
Robertson D	McVeigh
McLeish	Collins
Miller W	Mitchell
Porteous	Walker
Bett	Reilly*
Dodds	Liddle*
Connor*	Craig
Weir*	McCabe
Wright/Stark	Brogan/Brazil

Accies have now taken just one point from 14 games. An untidy match played in a blustery wind which assisted Hamilton in the first half. Miller and McLeish return to the side. Jim Bett runs into the box and takes the ball round McKeller. Ian Porteous is man of the match.

15 — A DUNDEE — 1/11 — 8,200 — 5 6 19 — W 2-0

Scorers: Dodds 13, Porteous 64
Ref: J Renton

Aberdeen	Dundee
Leighton	Geddes
McKimmie	Shannon
Mitchell*	McFinlay
Robertson D	McGeachie
McLeish	Smith
Miller W	Duffy
Porteous	Mennie*
Bett	Kidd*
Hewitt*	Harvey
Connor	Angus
Dodds	Stephen
Stark/Miller J	Hendry/Rafferty

It is more than 10 years since Dundee last beat Aberdeen at Dens. Dodds headed in Hewitt's corner, and Porteous snapped up Geddes' save from Stark, to give the Dons the points and take them above Dundee in the table. This is Alex Ferguson's last match in charge before leaving.

16 — H ST MIRREN — 8/11 — 11,366 — 5 7 20 — D 0-0

Ref: D McVicar

Aberdeen	St Mirren
Leighton	Money
McKimmie	Clarke
Mitchell	Hamilton D
Robertson D*	Fitzpatrick
McLeish	Godfrey
Miller W	Cooper
Miller J*	Gallagher
Bett	Ferguson
Dodds	McGarvey
Connor	Speirs
Weir	Cameron
Wright/Stark	

Fergie has gone to Old Trafford! He left on Thursday, leaving Archie Knox to supervise the Dons until a replacement is found. Yet the main stand rises to boo Knox. The biggest cheer of the afternoon came at half-time when it was announced that Oxford were beating Manchester U.

17 — A HEARTS — 15/11 — 17,108 — 6 3 20 — L 1-2

Scorers: Hewitt 15. Colquhoun 62, Robertson 82
Ref: K O'Donnell

Aberdeen	Hearts
Leighton	Smith
McKimmie	Kidd
Robertson D	Whittaker
Stark*	Jardine W
McLeish	Berry
Miller W	MacDonald
Hewitt	Colquhoun
Bett	Mackay
Dodds	Clark
Connor	Black
Weir	Foster*
Miller J	Robertson

Managerless Dons fall victim to Hearts, who become the first team to beat Aberdeen twice this season. Alex McLeish stumbles to permit John Colquhoun's equaliser. Hearts' winner is scored by substitute John Robertson, returning to the side after missing Hearts' last five games.

18 — H CLYDEBANK — 19/11 — 7,301 — 5 11 22 — W 5-0

Scorers: Stark 13, 47, Hewitt 39, Connor 54, 73
Ref: D Yeats

Aberdeen	Clydebank
Leighton	Gallacher
McKimmie	Treanor
McMaster	Given
Stark	Fourna
McLeish D*	Auld
Miller W	Maher
Miller J*	Shanks
Bett	Fairlie*
Dodds	Grant
Connor	Rodger
Hewitt	Irons
Weir/Wright	Conroy

Ian Porterfield is appointed manager hours before kick-off, though he does not officially take charge till afterwards. Archie Knox oversees the team for the last time. The ref dismissed three good Dons penalty appeals, and one hopes Porterfield did not think it would always be so easy.

19 — H RANGERS — 22/11 — 21,733 — 5 4 24 — W 1-0

Scorers: Dodds 19
Ref: T Muirhead

Aberdeen	Rangers
Leighton	Woods
McKimmie	Nichol
Robertson D	Munro
Stark	Ferguson D
McLeish	McPherson*
Miller W	Butcher
Miller J	Fraser
Bett	Bel*
Dodds	McCoist
Connor	Durrant
Hewitt	Cooper
	Fleck

Pittodrie stands to acclaim Ian Porterfield. Rangers' only Premier League win at Pittodrie was four years ago. Cammy Fraser's backpass was intercepted by Hewitt. Woods saved, but Dodds poached the rebound. Just before half-time Dave McPherson was sent off for elbowing Dodds.

20 — H CELTIC — 26/11 — 22,040 — 5 1 25 — D 1-1

Scorers: McLeish 49, McClair 81p
Ref: G Cumming

Aberdeen	Celtic
Leighton	Bonner
McKimmie	Grant
Robertson D	Whyte
Stark	Aitken
McLeish	O'Leary
Miller W	McClair
Miller J*	McStay
Bett	Johnston
Dodds	McGhee*
Connor	McInally
Hewitt*	McGrain/Archdeacon
Weir/Wright	

A game of three penalties, two in a minute. McClair's was saved by Bonner after Derek Whyte handled. McLeish's diving header made it 1-0. The same player then bundled over McInally. McClair's penalty hit the bar, Johnston headed against the post and McKimmie allegedly handled.

21 — A MOTHERWELL — 29/11 — 4,479 — 5 9 27 — W 1-0

Scorers: Weir 21
Ref: W Crombie

Aberdeen	Motherwell
Leighton	Maxwell
McKimmie	Wishart
Robertson D	Murray*
Stark*	Kennedy
McLeish	McAdam
Miller W	Philliben
Hewitt	Farningham
Bett	Walker
Dodds	Smith
Connor	Wright*
Weir	Baptie/Mair

Peter Weir has been sub for the past three games. He plays from the start against Motherwell. After Kennedy fouled Davie Dodds, Weir sent a 20-yard free-kick dipping over the wall into the top corner. Just two points now separate the four teams behind Celtic at the top.

22 — H FALKIRK — 3/12 — 9,253 — 5 8 29 — W 1-0

Scorers: Stark 16
Ref: C Sinclair

Aberdeen	Falkirk
Leighton	Watson
McKimmie	Martin
Robertson D	Kerr
Stark*	Purdie
McLeish	Dempsey
Miller W	McCormack
Weir	Stewart*
Bett	Kemp
Dodds*	McGuire
Connor	MacLeod
Hewitt	McGivern*
Hetherston/Hughes	Weir J/Wright

Falkirk's first visit to Pittodrie in 12 years. The rub of the green favoured the Dons, who took the lead through Stark's neat header. But twice in the second half Falkirk had good shouts for a penalty turned down. Behind the scenes, Frank McDougall has been allowed to resume training.

FINE FARE SCOTTISH PREMIER — Manager: Ferguson → Ian Porterfield — SEASON 1986-87

Results

No	Date	V	Opponent	Att	Pos	Pt	F-A	H-T	Scorers, Times	Ref
23	6/12	A	DUNDEE UTD	10,242	5 / 2	30	D 0-0	0-0	—	Ref: W Crombie
24	13/12	H	HIBERNIAN	11,003	5 / 10	32	W 1-0	0-0	Stark 81	Ref: K Hope
25	20/12	A	CELTIC	32,624	4 / 1	33	D 1-1	1-1	Miller J 42 / *McInally 3*	Ref: J Duncan
26	27/12	H	HAMILTON	10,500	5 / 12	34	D 0-0	0-0	—	Ref: K O'Donnell
27	1/1	H	DUNDEE	11,000	/ 11	36	W 2-1	0-0	Wright 70, Grant 80 / *Jack 62*	Ref: D Yeats
28	21/1	H	HEARTS	15,030		38	W 2-1	1-0	Grant 25, Miller W 52 / *Watson 67*	Ref: H Williamson
29	24/1	A	RANGERS	44,000	5 / 2	39	D 0-0	0-0	—	Ref: J McCluskey
30	27/1	A	CLYDEBANK	2,007	/ 11	41	W 5-0	3-0	Connor 11, Dodds 14, Wright 15, 48, [Hewitt 72]	Ref: J McGilvray
31	7/2	H	MOTHERWELL	10,000	4 / 8	43	W 1-0	0-0	Wright 84	Ref: A Ferguson
32	21/2	A	FALKIRK	5,000	4 / 10	45	W 3-0	1-0	Stark 20, 80, McLeish 54	Ref: J McCluskey
33	25/2	A	ST MIRREN	3,553	5 / 7	45	L 0-1	0-0	*Ferguson 62*	Ref: G Evans

Line-ups (Aberdeen in roman; opponents in *italic*)

No	1	2	3	4	5	6	7	8	9	10	11	subs used
23	Leighton	McKimmie	Robertson D	Grant	McLeish	Miller W	Weir	Bett	Dodds	Connor	Hewitt	McGinnis/Coyne
	Thomson	*Beaumont*	*Holt*	*McNally*	*Clark**	*Narey*	*Ferguson^*	*Page*	*Milne*	*Gallacher*	*Redford*	*Tortolano*
24	Leighton	McKimmie	Robertson D	Stark	McLeish	Miller W	Miller J	Bett	Dodds	Connor*	Weir	Hewitt
	Rough	*Sneddon*	*Smith**	*Kirkwood*	*Rae*	*Hunter*	*Kane*	*May*	*McCluskey*	*Collins*	*McBride*	*Tortolano*
25	Leighton	McKimmie	Robertson D	Stark	McLeish	Miller W	Miller J	Bett	Dodds	Connor	Weir*	Hewitt
	Bonner	*Aitken*	*Whyte*	*MacLeod*	*McGugan*	*O'Leary**	*McClair*	*McStay*	*Johnston*	*McInally*	*McGhee**	*Shepherd/Archdeacon*
26	Leighton	McKimmie	Robertson D	Stark	McLeish	Miller W	Miller J*	Bett	Wright	Connor	Weir	Hewitt
	McKellar	*McKee*	*Sprott*	*Brazil*	*Speirs*	*Collins*	*Barr*	*Brogan*	*Phillips*	*Craig*	*Pelosi*	
27	Leighton	McKimmie	Robertson D	Stark*	McLeish	Miller W	Miller J	Bett	Wright	Connor	Weir	Grant
	Geddes	*Glennie*	*Shannon*	*Rafferty*	*Smith*	*Duffy*	*Coyne*	*Brown*	*Harvey*	*Angus*	*Wright**	*Jack*
28	Leighton	Mitchell	Robertson D	Grant	Irvine*	Miller W	Miller J	Bett	Dodds	Wright	Weir*	Stark/Connor
	Smith	*Kidd*	*Black*	*Sandison*	*Whittaker*	*MacDonald^*	*Colquhoun*	*Watson*	*Clark**	*Mackay*	*Robertson*	*Foster/Jardine I*
29	Leighton	McKimmie	Robertson D	Grant	Mitchell	Miller W	Miller J	Bett	Dodds	Wright*	Connor	Hewitt
	Woods	*Nicholl*	*Munro*	*Souness*	*McPherson*	*Butcher*	*Ferguson D*	*Fleck*	*McCoist**	*Dawson*	*Cooper*	*Woods N*
30	Leighton	McKimmie	Robertson D	Grant	Mitchell	Miller W*	Hewitt	Bett	Dodds*	Wright	Connor	Stark/Porteous
	72)Gallacher	*Dickson*	*Given*	*Maher*	*Auld*	*Conn**	*Fairlie*	*Shanks*	*Fulton*	*Conroy*	*Davies**	*McGhie/Gordon*
31	Leighton	McKimmie	Robertson D	Grant	McLeish	Miller W	Hewitt	Bett	Dodds*	Stark	Weir	Wright
	Gardiner	*Wishart*	*Philliben*	*Paterson*	*McAdam*	*Boyd*	*Farningham*	*Kirk*	*Walker**	*Wright*	*Reilly*	*Smith/Gahagan*
32	Leighton	McKimmie	Robertson D	Stark	McLeish	Miller W	Grant	Connor	Dodds	Wright*	Weir	Miller J
	Walker	*Martin*	*McCormack*	*Nicol*	*Manley*	*MacLeod*	*Kidd*	*Gilmour*	*Eadie*	*Ashwood^*	*Kerr*	*Hetherston/Purdie*
33	Leighton	McKimmie	Robertson D	Stark	McLeish	Miller W	Miller J*	Bett	Dodds	Grant*	Weir	Wright/Connor
	Money	*Peebles*	*Hamilton*	*Ferguson I*	*Godfrey*	*Cooper*	*McGarvey*	*Lambert*	*McDowall*	*Abercrombie*	*Chalmers*	

Match notes

23 Brian Grant makes his debut two years after signing from Stirling Albion for £50,000. Neil Simpson is back on the bench, having been out since the first match of the season. The nearest to a goal was Dodds' back-header onto a post. Celtic extend their lead over United to six points.

24 A testing time for two new managers - Alex Miller has taken charge of Hibs. Scottish international keeper Alan Rough had a good game in goal until he weakly palmed out Peter Weir's cross and Billy Stark sidefooted a simple goal. Hibs have now won just one of their last 13 games.

25 Aberdeen began and ended the match seven points behind Celtic. Roy Aitken switched to right back to try to counter Weir. McNally scores with a low volley; Joe Miller's penalty is saved after Whyte flattened McKimmie; but Joe Miller atones with a header before half-time.

26 With only one win all season, and adrift at the bottom, Accies set out to stifle this match. Yet Barr still managed to head against the foot of Leighton's post after seven minutes. The Dons did not come that close. Joe Miller's back injury meant he did not reappear for the second half.

27 Dundee's last league win at Pittodrie was secured in March 1976. Willie Miller is the sole Dons survivor from that occasion. Miller fouls Coyne for a penalty which John Brown hits high and wide at 0-0. Peter Weir, in his 250th game for Aberdeen, manufactures both goals.

28 Three weeks without a game owing to the weather. The Dons lost Peter Weir after 10 minutes with a head injury. Nine minutes later Hearts' Roddy MacDonald was expelled after a clash with Dodds. Andy Watson scored against his former club. Aberdeen are now level with Hearts.

29 Rangers' goalkeeper Chris Woods equals the British record of 12 straight shut-outs, which is held by Aberdeen. Jim Leighton's super save from Ally McCoist after just 45 minutes helps preserve Ian Porterfield's unbeaten run as Dons manager, which now stands at 11 games.

30 Consecutive 5-0 wins for Aberdeen over Clydebank, who have already conceded 69 league goals. This match had the air of a training exercise. Jim Bett hit a post after just two minutes. Midway through the first half - with the Dons 3-0 up - Willie Miller limped off with a thigh strain.

31 Representatives of Liverpool and Manchester U came to eye up Joe Miller, only to find that he was 'rested', and Billy Stark recalled. Substitute Paul Wright, brought on at 54 minutes, headed the only goal from Willie Miller's cross. Ian Porterfield's unbeaten run now stands at 16 games.

32 This is the only Premier fixture of the day, and the win enables Aberdeen to cut Celtic's lead to five points. Falkirk's new manager Dave Clarke can find little to enthuse over. 1-0, Stark's volley, 2-0, McLeish from Dodds' knock-down; 3-0 Stark from sub Joe Miller's back-heel.

33 Porterfield's first league defeat is inflicted by a cracking goal from Saints Under-21 international Ian Ferguson, whose drive flew in off the crossbar. Too many Dons seemed to be going through the motions, too few showed any will to win. Joe Miller was often caught in possession.

34. H DUNDEE UTD — 28/2 — 14,000 — 4 · L · 0-1 · 45 — HT 0-0

Aberdeen: Leighton, McKimmie, Robertson D*, Stark, McLeish, Miller W, Grant, Bett, Hewitt, Connor, Weir — sub Porteous
Dundee Utd: Thomson, Holt, Malpas, McInally, Clark, Narey, Ferguson, Gallacher, Bannon, Sturrock, Radford

Bannon 55
Ref: M Delaney

Another defeat, the third in league and cup, condemns the Dons to also-ran status this season. In contrast, things look bright for United, as they prepare to take on Barcelona. Davie Dodds was dropped for the first time, with Porterfield preferring the new partnership of Hewitt and Grant.

---

35. A HIBERNIAN — 7/3 — 6,000 — 4 · D · 1-1 · 46 — HT 1-0

Aberdeen: Leighton, McKimmie, Robertson D, Stark, McLeish, Miller W, Grant*, Bett, Wright*, Simpson, Weir — sub Dodds
Hibernian: Rough, Hunter, McBride, Bell, Rae, McIntyre, Weir, McCluskey*, Cowan*, Collins, McBride — sub Tortolano

Bett 13, McCluskey 76
Ref: R Valentine

Neil Simpson plays his first full 90 minutes since his comeback. In a match played amid snow flurries Jim Bett's 25-yard drive was cancelled out by McCluskey's equaliser, set up by John Collins' through pass. Hibs kicked with a strong wind behind them in the second half.

---

36. H CELTIC — 14/3 — 20,000 — 4 · W · 1-0 · 48 — HT 0-0

Aberdeen: Leighton, Irvine, Robertson D, Stark, McLeish, Miller W, Grant, Bett, Wright*, Simpson, Weir — sub Porteous
Celtic: Bonner, McGrain, Rogan, Aitken, McGugan, Whyte, McClair, McStay, Johnston, Burns*, Shepherd* — sub MacLeod/Archibald

Irvine 63
Ref: W Crombie

This result benefits Rangers, who go clear at the top from Celtic. Paul Wright had a header disallowed for offside after 30 seconds. Brian Irvine's first goal of the season was a towering header from Willie Miller's free-kick. Tommy Burns escaped dismissal for a lunge at Irvine.

---

37. A HAMILTON — 21/3 — 3,594 — 3 · W · 2-0 · 50 — HT 1-0

Aberdeen: Leighton, Irvine, Robertson D, Stark*, McLeish, Miller J, Wright*, Bett, Connor, Taylor, Hewitt — sub Porteous/Falconer
Hamilton: McKellar, McLee, Sprott, Brazil, Collins, Fulton, McCabe*, Clarke, Jamieson, Brogan, Mailer — sub McWhirter

Bett 33, Porteous 90
Ref: H Adamson

Hamilton will use a grand total of 40 players this season. They take the field with two players wearing No 8. Manager John Lambie later gave Taylor No 10. Jim Bett's goal out of nothing might have been cancelled when Taylor drove the ball against Willie Miller's hand. No penalty.

---

38. H ST MIRREN — 28/3 — 7,000 — 4 · L · 0-1 · 50 — HT 0-0

Aberdeen: Leighton, Irvine, Robertson I, Stark, McLeish, Miller WI, Wright*, Bett, Falconer, Connor, Weir — sub Hewitt
St Mirren: Money, Wilson, Hamilton D, Hamilton B, Winnie*, Cooper, McGarvey, McDowall, Abercrombie, Lambert — sub McWhirter

Wilson 47
Ref: A Huett

Robertson is out with chicken pox. Falconer plays his first game of the season. Willie Miller is sent off for a crude tackle on Ian Ferguson, having been booked two minutes earlier. It is his Miller's third expulsion and his first at Pittodrie. Tommy Wilson scored a wind-assisted goal.

---

39. A DUNDEE — 4/4 — 4,346 — 3 · D · 1-1 · 51 — HT 0-1

Aberdeen: Leighton, Robertson I, Robertson D, Gray, McLeish, Irvine, Grant, Simpson, Hewitt, Connor, Weir
Dundee: Geddes, Forsyth, McKinlay, McGeachie, Smith, Duffy, Rafferty, Brown, Jack, Coyne, Wright

Weir 53, Brown 44
Ref: G Cumming

Dismissals in consecutive matches for the Dons. This time it is the turn of Peter Weir. He had scored direct from a disputed corner - cancelling out John Brown's fine header - and then crossed for Irvine the head a disallowed winner. Weir was sent off for protesting the ref's decision.

---

40. H CLYDEBANK — 11/4 — 6,000 — 3 · D · 1-1 · 52 — HT 0-0

Aberdeen: Leighton, McKimmie, Robertson D, Simpson, McLeish, Irvine, Grant*, Bett, Hewitt, Grant, Weir — sub Gray/Wright
Clydebank: Gallacher, Treanor, Rodger, Maher, Irons, Fairlie*, Shanks, Grant, Conroy, Gordon* — sub Dickson/Given

Irvine 76, Conroy 65
Ref: T Muirhead

Pittodrie's lowest gate of the season sees Clydebank escape with an unlikely point. The Bankies had lost their last two against the Dons 5-0. The Dons might have lost. Conroy ran from the halfway line to put Clydebank in front. Wright's overhead kick came back off a post for Irvine.

---

41. A HEARTS — 18/4 — 12,539 — 3 · D · 1-1 · 53 — HT 0-0

Aberdeen: Leighton, McKimmie, Robertson I, Gray, McLeish, Irvine, Dodds*, Bett, Hewitt, Simpson, Weir — sub Grant
Hearts: Smith, Mackay, Cowie, Jardine A, Whittaker, Black, Colquhoun, Watson, Clark, Robertson*, Foster — sub Moore

Hewitt 66, Foster 60
Ref: D Hope

Davie Dodds is recalled and John Hewitt - who is demanding a transfer - scores when intercepting a misplaced back-pass. Foster had put Hearts in front when he was given an age to control the ball from a corner. Both teams have their sights set on a UEFA Cup place.

---

42. A MOTHERWELL — 25/4 — 2,886 — 3 · W · 2-0 · 55 — HT 2-0

Aberdeen: Leighton, McKimmie, Robertson D, Gray, McLeish, Irvine, Walker, Bett, Hewitt, Simpson, Weir — sub Fraser/McBride
Motherwell: McKeown, Wishart, Philliben, Paterson, McAdam*, Boyd, Walker, Kirk, Smith*, Wright, Mair

Hewitt 17p, Miller J 27
Ref: G Smith

A sparse, sun-drenched crowd sees Aberdeen win their first Premier League match in five attempts. John Hewitt's penalty was the result of Kirk handling Gray's cross. Joe Miller's electric performance was capped by a goal. David Robertson's pass set it up.

---

43. H RANGERS — 2/5 — 23,500 — 4 · D · 1-1 · 56 — HT 1-1

Aberdeen: Leighton, McKimmie, Robertson D*, Irvine, McLeish, Miller W, Gray, Bett, Hewitt, Simpson, Weir — sub Grant
Rangers: Woods, Roberts, Munro, Souness!, McPherson, Butcher, Nicholl, Fleck*, McCoist, Durrant, Cooper — sub Phillips/West

Irvine 45, Butcher 40
Ref: J Duncan

4 mins, Souness is booked. 30 mins, he is sent off, the 13th Ranger to be expelled against Aberdeen in 44 league and cup matches since 1978. Terry Butcher heads 10-man Rangers in front. Irvine sweeps the equaliser. Rangers need one point for the title, and they defend desperately.

---

44. H FALKIRK — 9/5 — 6,500 — 4 · W · 3-1 · 58 — HT 3-0

Aberdeen: Leighton, McKimmie, Robertson D, Irvine, McLeish, Miller W, Gray, Bett, Hewitt, Simpson, Weir — sub Grant
Falkirk: Marshall, MacLeod, Kerr, Baptie*, Dempsey, Manley, Gilmour, Nicol, Eadie, Hetherston, McGivern* — sub Kidd/McGuire

Miller J 8, Grant 23, Hewitt 28p, McGivern 60
Ref: R Valentine

Weir is so angry at being left out against Rangers that he has demanded a transfer. Aberdeen's third goal against Falkirk was their 800th in the Premier League, though Hewitt's penalty only went in after striking both posts. Ian Porterfield says the cup defeat by Celtic ruined the season.

Average Home 12,790
Away 12,730

FINE FARE PREMIER (CUP-TIES) Manager: Ferguson → Ian Porterfield SEASON 1986-87

	1	2	3	4	5	6	7	8	9	10	11	subs used

Skol League Cup

2 · H · ALLOA · 20/8 · 7,000 2:3 · 4 W 4-0 (2-0) — Hewitt 10, 42, Connor 60, Miller J 65 · Ref: J Renton

Aberdeen	Gunn	McKimmie	Robertson D	Irvine	McLeish	Miller W	Gray	Miller J*	Hewitt	Connor	Weir*	Mitchell/Falconer
Alloa	*Lowrie*	*Thomson*	*Haggart*	*Donaldson*	*Dall*	*Sullivan**	*Smith*	*Wilkie**	*Murray*	*Sorbie*	*Jamieson*	*Flaherty/Cole*

Last night Ferguson was appointed to the Aberdeen board, as a 'hands off' to other clubs. Alloa keeper Ronnie Lawrie dropped Joe Miller's 10th minute cross for the first goal. Aberdeen's second went in off a defender. Best of the four goals was Bobby Connor's bullet volley.

3 · H · CLYDE · 27/8 · 8,081 1:11 · 4 W 3-1 (0-1) — Miller J 47p, Stark 52, 82 / Murphy 18p · Ref: T Muirhead

Aberdeen	Gunn	McKimmie	Mitchell	Stark	McLeish	Irvine	Gray	Miller J*	Hewitt	Connor	Robertson D*	Bett/Wright
Clyde	*Atkins*	*McFarlane*	*Dickson*	*Ferguson*	*Flexney*	*Coyle*	*Reilly*	*Logan^*	*Watters*	*Evans*	*Murphy**	*Lloyd/Willock*

Scotland manager Andy Roxburgh sees 17-year-old David Robertson make a hash of a back-pass, as a result of which Watters scores. Paul Flexney fouled McLeish for Aberdeen's penalty. Only after Jim Bett came on after 55 minutes did Aberdeen really take charge.

QF · H · CELTIC · 3/9 · 23,500 · D 1-1 (aet) (1-0) — Connor 14 / Johnston 67 · Ref: R Valentine · (Dons lost 2-4 on penalties)

Aberdeen	Leighton	McKimmie*	Mitchell	Stark	McLeish	Miller W	Gray*	Bett	Miller J	Connor	Weir	Robertson D/Hewitt
Celtic	*Bonner*	*McStay W*	*Whyte**	*Aitken*	*McGugan^*	*Grant*	*McClair*	*McStay P*	*Johnston*	*MacLeod*	*McInally*	*Archibald/Shepherd*

Two hours of electrifying football failed to produce a winner, even though Celtic were reduced to 10 men after 71 minutes when sub Shepherd was sent off. In the shoot-out Aberdeen drew first blood when Leighton saved from Aitken. Bonner then saved from Hewitt and Willie Miller.

Scottish Cup

3 · H · CELTIC · 1/2 · 23,000 1 · 5 D 2-2 (0-2) — Bett 68p, Hewitt 73 / McInally 14, McClair 37p · Ref: G Smith

Aberdeen	Leighton	McKimmie	Robertson D	Grant*	McLeish	Miller J	Miller W	Bett	Dodds	Wright	Connor	Hewitt
Celtic	*Bonner*	*McGrain*	*Rogan*	*Aitken*	*Whyte*	*Grant*	*McClair*	*McStay P*	*Johnston*	*MacLeod*	*McInally*	

Live Sunday TV on an unplayable skating-rink pitch. Leighton slips and McInally heads the opener off the bar. David Robertson fouls McStay for the penalty. McGrain bundles over Wright and Bett pulls one back. Hewitt rounds Bonner to make it 2-2. Aberdeen so nearly win after that.

3R · A · CELTIC · 4/2 · 55,405 1 · 5 D 0-0 (aet) (0-0) — · Ref: G Smith

Aberdeen	Leighton	McKimmie	Robertson D	Grant*	McLeish	Miller J*	Miller W	Bett	Dodds	Wright	Connor	Hewitt/Stark
Celtic	*Bonner*	*McGrain**	*Rogan*	*Aitken*	*Whyte*	*Grant*	*McClair*	*McStay P*	*Johnston*	*MacLeod*	*McInally**	*Shepherd/McGhee*

The kick-off was delayed seven minutes to let in the huge crowd. The replay was as anticlimactic as the original was frenetic; both sides feared the consequences of elimination. Afterwards, neither side agreed to toss a coin to decide the next venue, so it will be played on neutral ground.

RR · N · CELTIC · 9/2 · 21,255 1 (at Dens Park) · 4 L 0-1 (0-0) — McClair 17 · Ref: G Smith

Aberdeen	Leighton	McKimmie	Robertson D	Grant*	McLeish	Miller J*	Miller W	Bett	Dodds*	Wright	Connor*	Weir/Hewitt
Celtic	*Bonner*	*McGrain*	*Rogan*	*Aitken*	*Whyte*	*Grant*	*McClair*	*McStay P*	*Johnston*	*MacLeod*	*McInally**	*McGhee*

Hours of ceaseless rain turned Dens Park into a quagmire. For the third time both sides keep an unchanged line-up. Brian McClair's goal ends Ian Porterfield's 17-game unbeaten run. John Hewitt has made a written transfer request, while Brian Mitchell is set to sign for Bradford City.

European Cup-Winners' Cup

1:1 · H · SION (Switz) · 17/9 · 12,312 · 5 W 2-1 (0-1) — Bett 73p, Wright 80 / Debonnaire 40 · Ref: E Halle (Norway)

Aberdeen	Leighton	McKimmie	Mitchell	Stark	McLeish	Miller W	Hewitt	Bett	Wright*	Robertson D	Connor	Falconer
Sion	*Pittier*	*Rey O**	*Fojevic*	*Balet*	*Sauthier*	*Lopez Alaro*	*Debonnaire*	*Bregy*	*Brigger*	*Weir*	*Bonvin^*	*Rey F/Cina*

Four years earlier Aberdeen swamped Sion 7-0 in the same competition. Alex McLeish's misdirected header lets in Debonnaire for a priceless away goal. Sauthier upended Peter Weir for Jim Bett's penalty, whereupon Paul Wright drove in Weir's well-practised free-kick from 25 yards.

1:2 · A · SION · 1/10 · 11,800 · 5 L 0-3 (0-2) — Leighton 4 og, Bouderbala 29, Brigger 88 · Ref: A Thomas (Holland) · (Dons lose 2-4 on aggregate)

Aberdeen	Leighton	McKimmie	Mitchell*	Stark	McLeish	Miller W	Irvine	Bett!	Hewitt	Connor	Weir*	Robertson D/Wright
Sion	*Pittier*	*Sauthier*	*Balet*	*Rey F*	*Fojevic*	*Lopez Alaro*	*Bregy*	*Debonnaire*	*Brigger*	*Bonvin*	*Fournier*	

The hammer blow fell after just four minutes, when McKimmie errs at Bregy's corner and the ball flies in off Leighton's shoulder. Moroccan international Bouderbala put Sion in front, whereupon Jim Bett was sent off for earning his second caution. Sion did a lap of honour at the end.

League Table

	P	W	D	L	F	A	W	D	L	F	A	Pts
1 Rangers	44	18	2	2	45	6	13	5	4	40	17	69
2 Celtic	44	16	5	1	57	17	11	4	7	33	24	63
3 Dundee Utd	44	15	5	2	38	15	9	7	6	28	21	60
4 ABERDEEN	44	13	6	3	32	11	8	10	4	31	18	58
5 Hearts	44	13	7	2	42	19	8	7	7	22	24	56
6 Dundee	44	11	6	5	49	31	7	6	9	25	26	48
7 St Mirren	44	9	5	8	23	20	3	7	12	13	31	36
8 Motherwell	44	7	5	10	24	28	4	7	11	19	36	34
9 Hibernian	44	6	8	8	24	30	4	5	13	20	40	33
10 Falkirk	44	4	9	9	17	28	4	1	17	14	42	26
11 Clydebank	44	3	7	12	19	40	3	5	14	16	53	24
12 Hamilton	44	2	4	16	15	40	4	5	13	24	53	21
	528	117	69	78	385	285	78	69	117	285	385	528

Cup Record

	P	W	D	L	F	A	Pts	Cup	W	D	L
v Clydebank	4	3	1	0	14	2	7				
v Falkirk	4	3	1	0	10	4	7				
v Dundee	4	3	1	0	7	2	7				
v Hamilton	4	3	1	0	5	0	7				
v Motherwell	4	3	1	0	6	2	7				
v Hibernian	4	2	2	0	7	2	6				
v Celtic	4	1	3	0	4	3	5	LC	0	0	0	1*
								SC	0	0	2	1
v Rangers	4	1	2	1	2	3	4				
v Dundee Utd	4	1	1	2	3	3	3				
v Hearts	4	1	1	2	4	5	3				
v St Mirren	4	0	2	2	1	3	2				
	44	21	16	7	63	29	58				

*penalties

Odds & ends

Never lost to: (7) Clydebank, Falkirk, Dundee, Hamilton, Motherwell, Hibs, Celtic (in the league).

Never beat: (1) St Mirren.

Won from behind: (2) Dundee (h) Sion (CWC).

Lost from in front: (1) Hearts (a).

High spots: 15 unbeaten league games from 19 November.

Only 29 league goals conceded in 44 matches.

Low spots: Knocked out of all cup competitions early.

Allowing Sion sweet revenge in European Cup-Winners' Cup.

Losing Alex Ferguson as manager.

Scoring just 32 home league goals, which was exceeded by 5 other clubs.

Only 2 wins from 9 league games from 25 February.

Aberdeen faced Celtic 8 times in total in league and cup competition, never losing in the league, never winning in the cups.

Bogey teams : St Mirren (league); Celtic (cups).

Ever-presents: (0).

Hat-tricks: (0).

Leading scorers: (14) Billy Stark, John Hewitt.

Appearances and Goals

	Lge	Sub	LC	Sub	SC	Sub	Eur	Sub	Lge	Sub	LC	SC	Eur	Tot
Angus, Ian	2													
Bett, Jim	38	2	1	1	3		2		4		1	1		6
Connor, Robert	30	2	3		3		1		4			2		6
Dodds, Davie	24	1			3			1	4					4
Falconer, Willie	1	5	1	1					1					1
Grant, Brian	12	3			3				4					4
Gray, Steve	9	4							1					1
Gunn, Bryan	2		2											
Hewitt, John	28	5	2	1	3		2		11		2	1		14
Irvine, Brian	19	1	2		1		1		3					3
Leighton, Jim	42		1		3		2							
McDougall, Frank		1		1										
McIntyre, Tommy	4													
McKimmie, Stewart	37		3		3		2	2	3					3
McLeish, Alex	40		3		3		2							
McMaster, John	2													
McQueen, Tommy	1													
Miller, Joe	23	5	3		3				6			2		8
Miller, Willie	36		3		3		2	1	2					2
Mitchell, Brian	15	2	2	1	2		2							
Porteous, Ian	3	6												
Robertson, David	32	2	2	1	3		1	1	2	1				2
Robertson, Ian	4													
Simpson, Neil	8													
Stark, Billy	31	5	2	1	1	1	2		12			2		14
Weir, Peter	32	3	2	1	1		1		2					2
Wright, Paul	13	12	3				1	1	4		1			5
27 players used	484	61	33	6	33	5	22	3	63		8	2	2	75

FINE FARE SCOTTISH PREMIER

Manager: Ian Porterfield   SEASON 1987-88

No	Date	Match	Att	Pos	Pt	F-A	H-T	1	2	3	4	5	6	7	8	9	10	11	subs used
1	8/8	A DUNDEE	10,223	D	1	1-1	0-0	Leighton	McKimmie	Robertson	Simpson	McLeish	Miller W	Hackett*	Grant*	Miller J	Nicholas P	Hewitt	Connor/Dodds
								Geddes	Forsyth	McKinlay	Shannon	Glennie	Duffy	Mennie	Brown	Wright	Coyne	Angus	Lawrence
2	12/8	H MORTON	8,000	W	3	3-1	2-1	Leighton	McKimmie	Robertson	Simpson	McLeish	Miller W	Dodds	Bett	Miller J*	Nicholas P	Hewitt	Grant/Hackett
								Wylie	Clinging	Holmes	McNamara	Doak	McMaster	Turner	Clinging	Alexander	McNeil*	Robertson J*	Robertson J/Robertson D/Boag Jnr
3	15/8	H RANGERS	22,500	W	5	2-0	1-0	Leighton	McKimmie	Robertson	Simpson	McLeish*	Miller W	Dodds*	Bett	Miller J	Nicholas P	Hewitt	Irvine/Hackett
				3				Woods	Nicholl	Munro	Roberts	McGregor	Butcher	Kirkwood*	Souness	McCoist	Durrant	Phillips	Falco/Fleck
4	22/8	A MOTHERWELL	4,858	W	7	1-0	0-0	Leighton	McKimmie	Robertson	Simpson	Irvine	Miller W	Dodds	Bett	Miller J	Nicholas P	Hewitt	Wright/Kennedy
				1				Duncan	Wishart	Murray*	Paterson	McAdam	Boyd	Fairlie	Kirk*	Smith	Russell*	Mair	
5	29/8	H DUNDEE UTD	16,000	D	8	1-1	1-0	Leighton	McKimmie	Robertson	Simpson*	Irvine	Miller W	Dodds*	Bett	Miller J	Nicholas P	Hackett	Grant/Falconer
				2				Thomson	Holt	Malpas	McPhee*	Hegarty	Narey	Ferguson	Bannon	Irvine*	Sturrock	Redford	Kirkwood/Gallacher
6	5/9	A FALKIRK	5,327	D	9	2-2	0-2	Leighton	McKimmie	Robertson	Connor*	Irvine	Miller W	Hewitt	Bett	Miller J*	Nicholas P	Hackett*	Grant/Falconer
				3				Marshall	MacLeod*	Conn	Hill	Burgess	Dempsey	Gilmour	Baptie	Eadie	Nicol	McWilliams	Manley/Rae
7	12/9	H ST MIRREN	11,000	W	11	2-0	2-0	Leighton	McKimmie	Robertson	Connor*	McLeish	Miller W	Hewitt*	Bett	Miller J	Nicholas P	Falconer	Hackett
				3				Money	Dawson	Wilson*	Abercrombie	Winnie	Cooper	McGarvey	Walker	Gallagher	McDowall*	McWhirter	Chalmers/Butler
8	19/9	A CELTIC	38,944	D	12	2-2	0-1	Leighton	McKimmie	Robertson*	Connor	McLeish	Miller W	Hewitt	Bett	Miller J	Nicholas P	Irvine*	Falconer/Hackett
				2				McKnight	Morris	Rogan	Aitken	Whyte	Grant	Stark	McStay	McGhee*	Walker	Burns	Shephard
9	26/9	A HIBERNIAN	10,500	W	14	2-0	0-0	Leighton	McKimmie	Robertson	Connor	McLeish	Miller W	Hewitt*	Bett	Miller J*	Nicholas P	Falconer	Porteous/Hackett
				3				Rough	McIntyre	Grant	May*	Rae	Irvine	Kane	Orr	McCluskey*	Collins	Watson	Bell/Tortolano
10	3/10	H DUNFERMLINE	11,313	W	16	3-0	0-0	Leighton	McKimmie	Robertson	Connor	McLeish	Miller W	Hewitt	Bett	Miller J	Nicholas P	Grant*	Edwards
								Westwater	Robertson R	Holt	McCathie	Riddell*	Robertson C	Morrison*	Merrilees	Kirkwood	Smith T	Smith R	Ferguson/Wardell
11	7/10	A HEARTS	17,741	L	16	1-2	1-2	Leighton	McKimmie	Irvine*	Connor	McLeish	Miller W	Hewitt	Bett	Miller J	Nicholas P	Falconer	Edwards
								Smith	Burns	Whittaker	Levein	Berry	McPherson	Foster	Black	Colquhoun*	Mackay	Robertson	Clark

Scorers, Times, and Referees

1. Dodds 84 / Angus 34. Ref: T Muirhead. Dons' debuts for Peter Nicholas, a Welsh international, and Gary Hackett. A late equaliser by substitute Dodds denied Dundee their first home win over Aberdeen since the opening match of 1975-76. Former Don Ian Angus had earlier pounced when Leighton parried Wright's header.

2. Miller J 20, Simpson 30, Dodds 50 / McMaster 15. Ref: J Renton. Celtic have had a £300,000 bid for John Hewitt rejected. Morton lost their opening match of the season 0-4. Against Aberdeen, five Morton players were booked in a few minutes in the second half. Among them was ex-Don John McMaster, who had put Morton in the lead.

3. Dodds 28, Nicholas P 68. Ref: W Crombie. Rangers adopted unusual tactics of playing Ally McCoist alone up front. His 12th minute 25-yard 'goal' was disallowed because Phillips was offside. Dodds' brave header, followed by a first goal from £350,000 Peter Nicholas, settled a match that began with a welter of early fouls.

4. Dodds 65. Ref: J Evans. Davie Dodds' header from Hewitt's corner was enough to take Aberdeen to the top of the league. The win was easier than the score suggests, because Nicholas hit the bar and Joe Miller a post. After the match Ian Porterfield left for Dublin to spy on UEFA Cup opponents Bohemians.

5. Bett 27p / Redford 73p. Ref: A Waddell. United parade Alan Irvine, signed from Liverpool for £100,000. Both goals resulted from soft penalties. Aberdeen went in front when John Holt was accused of handling; United levelled when Willie Miller committed the same offence. Celtic overtake the Dons on goal-difference.

6. Falconer 68, Miller J 70 / McWilliams 23, Burgess 36. Ref: A Ferguson. Aberdeen have rejected a £500,000 bid from FA Cup-holders Coventry for David Robertson. McWilliams, on loan from Dundee, netted with a 15-yard volley and Burgess doubled Falkirk's lead with a header. Bairns' Sammy Conn was sent off in the second half for fouling Joe Miller.

7. Miller J 8, Falconer 38. Ref: A Huett. Bohemians' long-serving manager Billy Young watches this comfortable win. Aberdeen failed to beat St Mirren at all last season. Alex McLeish returns after a six-match absence. Joe Miller scores the first after a spate of corners; Willie Falconer adds a lovely header.

8. Nicholas P 61, Miller J 90 / Burns 38, Stark 48. Ref: R Valentine. Billy Stark was the Dons' leading scorer last season. He has signed for Celtic for £75,000 and scores their second goal. Peter Nicholas halves the deficit with a neat chip. In injury time Gary Hackett cut in from the wing to set up Joe Miller's equaliser. That goal keeps Celtic off the top.

9. Grant 57, Falconer 89. Ref: K O'Donnell. Willie Miller and David Robertson were ruled out. Ex-Don Dougie Bell comes on as a second-half sub for Hibs, and within minutes Brian Grant is presented with a gift goal. The result - Aberdeen's 14th without loss - takes them to within one point of Hearts at the top.

10. Nicholas P 58, Falconer 66, Edwards 78. Ref: G Cumming. Keith Edwards has signed from Leeds for £65,000, comes off the bench and scores from Bett's pass. Early in the second half Tommy Smith was expelled for dragging down Hewitt, having been booked minutes earlier. Peter Nicholas had broken the deadlock with a 25-yard drive.

11. Bett 7p / Robertson 13, McPherson 15. Ref: R Valentine. Having overtaken them to go top on Saturday, Hearts promptly halt the Dons' 22-game unbeaten run that dated from March 1987. On a quagmire pitch Smith felled Bett for an early penalty. This was overtaken by Robertson's angled shot and Mackay's backheel to McPherson.

12 · H DUNDEE · 10/10 · 12,500 · 3 D 6 17 · 0-0 0-0 · Ref: G Smith

| Leighton | McKimmie | Falconer | Connor | McLeish | Miller W | Hewitt | Bett | Edwards* | Nicholas P | Hackett* | Miller J/Jones |
| Geddes | Forsyth | Angus | Glennie | Smith | Frail | Shannon | Brown | Wright | Coyne | Lawrence | |

Dundee did nothing but defend against a new Dons' front line of Hewitt and Edwards. Substitute Tom Jones, on his debut, forced a fine save from Geddes. Willie Falconer played left-back, and earned his corn with a thrilling block to stop Tommy Coyne during a rare Dundee sortie.

13 · A DUNDEE UTD · 17/10 · 11,281 · 3 D 8 18 · 0-0 0-0 · Ref: J McGilvray

| Leighton | McKimmie | Falconer | Grant | McLeish | Miller J | Hewitt | Bett | Edwards | Nicholas P | Hewitt | |
| Thomson | Bowman | Malpas | McInally | Hegarty | Narey | Ferguson | Bannon | McGinnis | Kinnaird | French* | Irvine/Clark |

United have drawn more than half their games, so this is no surprise. Hamish French returns for United after breaking his leg. John Hewitt's cross hit the base of Thomson's post. Clark did the same at the other end after Leighton was penalised for carrying the ball outside the box.

14 · A ST MIRREN · 28/10 · 4,707 · 3 W 5 20 · 2-0 3-1 · Bett 29, 81p, Falconer 35; Cooper 62 · Ref: J Duncan

| Leighton | McKimmie | Connor | Simpson | McLeish | Miller W | Hewitt | Bett | Falconer* | Nicholas P | Weir | |
| Money | Wilson | Dawson | Fitzpatrick | Godfrey | Cooper | Davies | Ferguson | Chalmers* | Hamilton | Cameron | Shaw |

The Dons are shattered by their Skol Cup final penalty shoot-out defeat by Rangers. Ex-Dons Neil Cooper scores for St Mirren, then felled Hewitt for the penalty. Love St has been a bogey ground of late, so Bett's 12-yarder and Willie Falconer's volley lifted spirits considerably.

15 · H CELTIC · 31/10 · 21,000 · 3 L 2 20 · 0-1 0-1 · McAvennie 72 · Ref: A Ferguson

| Leighton | McKimmie | Connor | Simpson | McLeish | Miller W | Hewitt* | Bett | Falconer* | Nicholas P | Weir | |
| Bonner | Morris | Whyte | Aitken | McCarthy | Grant | Stark | McStay | McAvennie | Walker | McGhee | Edwards/Miller J |

Frank McAvennie, signed from West Ham for £850,000, scores a gift goal to inflict a first home defeat on Aberdeen. Celtic's Mark McGhee also overran the ball with just Leighton to beat. Crowd trouble among Celtic fans in the Beach End flared briefly in the second half.

16 · A MORTON · 7/11 · 3,000 · 4 D 11 21 · 0-0 0-0 · Ref: K O'Donnell

| Leighton | McKimmie | Connor | Porteous* | McLeish | Miller W | Hewitt | Bett* | Edwards | Nicholas P | Falconer | |
| Wylie | O'Hara | Holmes | Hunter | Boag John | McMaster* | Boag Jim | Collins | Alexander | Clinging | Robertson J McNeil | Jones/Hackett |

Morton boast the worst defence in the Premier League. Aberdeen show a much-changed side since the defeat by Feyenoord. The Dons might even have lost: on the stroke of half-time Jim Boag went round Leighton but shot into the side netting. Jim Bett limped off after 78 minutes.

17 · H HEARTS · 14/11 · 20,000 · 4 D 1 22 · 0-0 0-0 · Ref: A Huett

| Leighton | McKimmie | Falconer | Simpson | McLeish | Miller W | Dodds* | Bett | Hewitt | Nicholas P | Connor | |
| Smith | Burns | Whittaker | Levein | Berry* | McPherson | Foster | Black | Colquhoun | Mackay | Robertson* | Kidd/Clark |

Joe Miller has transferred to Celtic for £650,000. Davie Dodds returns to the side after three months out. Hearts' Mackay is injured in a collision with TV cameras behind the goal. Simpson's foul on Kidd provoked a second-half brouhaha. Sub Tom Jones's shot hit Hearts' post.

18 · A RANGERS · 17/11 · 41,371 · W 1-0 24 · 1-0 · Miller W 31 · Ref: K Hope

| Leighton | McKimmie | Falconer | Connor | McLeish | Miller W | Dodds | Bett | Hewitt | Nicholas P* | Jones | |
| Woods | McGregor | Gough | Roberts | Ferguson | Butcher* | Francis | Fleck | McCoist | Durrant | Cooper | Simpson Munro/Falco |

Aberdeen's first goal in five games smashes Rangers' 24-game unbeaten home record. Terry Butcher, back from suspension, broke his leg in a ninth-minute clash with McLeish. Willie Miller headed in at the far post from Robert Connor's cross. The Dons' debt to Leighton is immense.

19 · H MOTHERWELL · 21/11 · 9,700 · 3 W 10 26 · 1-0 1-0 · Dodds 25 · Ref: D Syme

| Leighton | McKimmie | Falconer | Connor | McLeish | Miller W | Dodds | Bett | Edwards | Jones | Hewitt* | |
| Duncan | Wishart | Murray | Paterson | Philliben | Boyd | Kirk | Russell | Cowan* | Fraser | Candlish | Hackett Gahagan/Caughey |

Aberdeen boast the best defensive record in the league, but have scored the fewest goals of any of the top 5 sides. Davie Dodds' bullet header from Tom Jones' corner marks his first goal since his return, and leaves Aberdeen five points behind Hearts with one game in hand.

20 · H HIBERNIAN · 24/11 · 9,000 · 3 D 8 27 · 1-1 1-1 · Edwards 33; Kane 14 · Ref: J Renton

| Leighton | McKimmie | Falconer | Connor | McLeish | Miller W | Dodds | Bett | Edwards* | Jones | Weir* | |
| Goram | Sneddon | Mitchell | May* | Rae | Orr | Bell | Watson | Kane | Collins | Tortolano | Hewitt/Hackett McCluskey |

Paul Kane's awkward hook crept over the line. Dodds has two close-range efforts blocked before Edwards forces in the equaliser. Goram's professional foul on Edwards inflicts a severe knee injury on the Dons' striker. Willie Miller hit the bar after 80 minutes with Hibs hanging on.

21 · A DUNFERMLINE · 28/11 · 7,500 · 3 W 10 29 · 0-0 3-0 · Jones 55, Wright 58, 82 · Ref: W Crombie

| Leighton | McKimmie | Falconer | Connor | McLeish | Miller W | Dodds | Bett | Wright* | Jones | Weir | |
| Westwater | Robertson R Smith R | McCathie | Holt | Beedie | Smith M | Kirkwood | Watson | Robertson C* Andersen | Smith T | Hewitt | |

Chunky Paul Wright's first game of the season brings him two super goals - under the eyes of Scotland's assistant manager Craig Brown. Aberdeen's first - a close-range header - was also the first Dons' goal for English player Tom Jones. Davie Dodds set up Wright's opener.

22 · A DUNDEE · 5/12 · 8,799 · 3 W 5 31 · 2-0 2-1 · Dodds 15, Wright 25; Forsyth 90 · Ref: G Hope

| Leighton | McKimmie | Falconer | Connor | McLeish | Miller W | Dodds | Bett | Wright | Nicholas P | Weir* | |
| Geddes | Forsyth | McGeachie* Shannon | Smith | Chisholm | Mennie | Rafferty | Angus | Coyne | Wright | Harvey/Lawrence | Jones/Hewitt |

Dundee manager Jocky Scott played for the Dons the last time they lost at Dundee in the league, back in 1975. Peter Weir's corner is nodded in by Dodds; Falconer's long pass allows Paul Wright to drive in from the edge of the box. Forsyth's late riposte flattered the home side.

No	Date		Att	Pos/Pt	F-A	H-T	Scorers, Times, and Referees
23	9/12	H FALKIRK	8,000	3 W 11 33	3-1	2-0	Dodds 2, Bett 21, Wright 60 / Burgess 74 / Ref: M McGinley
24	12/12	H MORTON	8,000	3 W 12 35	4-0	2-0	Bett 4p, 76p, Dodds 10, Connor 70 / Ref: I Cathcart
25	16/12	H ST MIRREN	6,500	3 W 7 37	2-1	1-0	Bett 34p, Miller W 76 / Cameron 52p / Ref: T Muirhead
26	19/12	A CELTIC	37,721	3 D 1 38	0-0	0-0	Ref: R Valentine
27	26/12	A FALKIRK	5,000	2 W 11 40	2-0	0-0	McLeish 77, Hewitt 88 / Ref: D Miller
28	2/1	H DUNDEE UTD	21,500	2 D 6 41	0-0	0-0	Ref: K Hope
29	9/1	A HIBERNIAN	16,000	3 D 7 42	0-0	0-0	Ref: J McCluskey
30	16/1	H DUNFERMLINE	20,000	2 W 11 44	1-0	1-0	Falconer 39 / Ref: D McVicar
31	23/1	A MOTHERWELL	6,584	3 L 9 44	1-2	0-2	Nicholas C 60 / Paterson 14, Farningham 41 / Ref: M McGinley
32	6/2	H RANGERS	22,500	4 L 2 44	1-2	0-2	Bett 46p / McCoist 21, Gough 33 / Ref: J McCluskey
33	13/2	A HEARTS	18,817	4 D 3 45	2-2	1-1	Bett 6, Jones 88p / Clark 43, Robertson 56p / Ref: A Ferguson

Line-ups (Aberdeen top, opponents in italics)

No	1	2	3	4	5	6	7	8	9	10	11	subs used
23	Leighton	McKimmie	Robertson	Connor	McLeish	Miller W	Dodds*	Bett	Wright	Nicholas P	Falconer	Jones
	Marshall	*MacLeod**	*Dempsey*	*Baptie*	*Burgess*	*Manley*	*Romaines**	*Nicol*	*Grant*	*McWilliams*	*Conn*	*Hill/Stewart*
24	Leighton	McKimmie	Robertson	Connor	McLeish	Miller W	Dodds*	Bett	Wright*	Nicholas P	Falconer	Hewitt/Jones
	Wylie	*O'Hara*	*Holmes*	*Hunter*	*MacDonald*	*Boag John*	*McGeachy**	*McMaster*	*Boag Jim*	*Collins*	*Turner*	*Arthur*
25	Leighton	McKimmie	Robertson	Connor	McLeish	Miller W	Dodds	Bett	Wright	Nicholas P	Jones*	Hewitt
	Money	*Wilson*	*Hamilton**	*Davies*	*Godfrey*	*McWhirter*	*Lambert*	*Hamilton*	*Conroy**	*Chalmers*	*Cameron*	*Dawson/McGarvey*
26	Leighton	McKimmie	Robertson	Connor	McLeish	Miller W	Dodds	Bett	Wright*	Nicholas P	Falconer*	Hewitt/Jones
	Bonner	*Morris*	*Rogan*	*Aitken*	*Whyte*	*Grant*	*Miller J*	*McStay*	*McVennie*	*Walker**	*Stark*	*McGhee*
27	Leighton	McKimmie	Robertson	Connor	McLeish	Miller W	Dodds	Bett	Wright*	Nicholas P	Falconer*	Hewitt/Gray
	Marshall	*MacLeod*	*McWilliams*	*Romaines*	*Burgess*	*Manley*	*McGivern**	*Nicol*	*Grant*	*Conn*	*Stewart*	*Rae*
28	Leighton	McKimmie	Robertson	Connor	McLeish*	Miller W	Dodds*	Bett	Wright	Nicholas P	Hewitt	Gray/Jones
	Thomson	*Bowman*	*Malpas*	*McInally*	*Clark*	*Narey*	*French*	*Gallacher*	*Hegarty*	*Paatelainen*	*Ferguson*	
29	Leighton	McKimmie	Robertson	Connor	McLeish*	Miller W	Nicholas C	Gray	Falconer	Hewitt*	Watson*	Jones
	Goram	*Sneddon*	*Mitchell*	*May*	*Rae*	*Hunter*	*Kane*	*Orr*	*McCluskey*	*Collins*	*Watson*	*McBride*
30	Leighton	McKimmie	Robertson	Connor	Irvine	Miller W	Nicholas C	Gray	Falconer	Nicholas P	Hewitt*	Jones
	Westwater	*Holt*	*Smith R**	*McCathie*	*Riddell*	*Smith T**	*Jack*	*Andersen*	*Robertson C**	*Kirkwood*	*Watson**	*Watson/Morrison*
31	Leighton	McKimmie	Robertson*	Connor	Irvine	Miller W	Nicholas C	Bett	Falconer	Nicholas P	Hackett	Hewitt
	Duncan	*Wishart*	*Phillihen*	*Paterson*	*Paterson*	*McAdam*	*Smith*	*Farningham*	*Cowan*	*Kirk*	*Mai**	*Russell/Gahagan*
32	Leighton	McKimmie	Irvine*	Connor	McLeish	Miller W	Nicholas C	Bett	Falconer	Nicholas P	Hackett*	Hewitt/Jones
	Woods	*Gough*	*Bartram*	*Roberts*	*Wilkins*	*Brown*	*Ferguson**	*McGregor**	*McCoist*	*Durrant*	*Walters*	*Souness/Cooper*
33	Leighton	McKimmie	Robertson	Connor	McLeish	Miller W	Dodds*	Bett	Nicholas C	Nicholas P	Falconer	Hackett/Jones
	Smith	*Berry*	*Whittaker*	*Black*	*Galloway*	*Mackay*	*McPherson*	*Jardine**	*Robertson*	*Colquhoun*	*Clark*	

23. Most of the managers of Scotland's top teams take in this fixture. They see Davie Dodds swoop after the ball comes back off the crossbar, and later commit the miss of the match from six yards before withdrawing, suffering from of laryngitis. Bett's goal was a swerving free-kick.

24. Morton have taken only nine points all season. Bett nets with two penalties. MacDonald climbed all over Falconer's back for the first penalty. Wylie later upended Bett as the midfielder went round him.

25. The Dons did not claim it, and ex-Don John McMaster was booked for protesting. Much speculation attends the future of Saints' Ian Ferguson, who is left out. Bett's penalty came when Bryan Hamilton needlessly handled; Cameron's was the consequence of Willie Miller bringing down Chalmers. Miller made amends with the winner when Chalmers miskicked.

26. The Dons five-year jinx at Parkhead continues. Joe Miller lines up against his former team-mates, and Mark McGhee too, when he comes off the bench. Fists and legs fly in the rain-sodden Dons goalmouth in the last minute. Celtic, Hearts and Aberdeen are all locked on 38 points.

27. The Dons deny making a club record bid of £700,000 for Norwich striker Kevin Drinkell. In driving wind and rain Aberdeen provoke raised tempers by repeatedly passing back to Leighton from the halfway line. There are first goals of the season for both McLeish and Hewitt.

28. Hundreds are locked out of Pittodrie after rumours that the Dons are about to sign Charlie Nicholas from Arsenal. Aberdeen have rejected a £600,000 bid for McLeish by Fergie's Manchester United. Both teams hit a post. After the match Davie Dodds has a cartilage operation.

29. After five years at Highbury Charlie Nicholas returns to Scottish football. He becomes Aberdeen's record signing and runs out to a rapturous reception. Though short of match fitness he twice hits the Hibs crossbar. Hibernian had not scored at all in their previous five home games.

30. Charlie fever. Only 12,500 turned up for the Pars last visit, but this time Charlie Nicholas is playing. The Dons have returned from a week's break in Spain and win thanks to Falconer's header from Connor's free-kick. Charlie has no chances to score. Dunfermline field three Smiths.

31. On a heavily sanded pitch Charlie Nicholas taps in his first goal for the Dons, but cannot prevent their first defeat in 16 outings. Charlie was roughly marked by ex-Ranger Craig Paterson, who headed Motherwell in front. Jim Bett returned for the Dons after a two-game suspension.

32. Explosion for Richard Gough after 54 minutes. He trips Willie Falconer having previously been booked. Rangers player-manager Souness comes off the bench early on and is quickly into the fray. Aberdeen's penalty is the result of John Brown needlessly handling Bett's free-kick.

33. A game of three penalties. Dodds was brought down by Henry Smith for the first. The keeper saved from Bett, who reacted quickest to the rebound. David Robertson felled Colquhoun for Hearts' spot-kick. Aberdeen's second penalty was a softie, after Jardine appeared to handle.

Match-by-match record (matches 34–44)

No	H/A	Date	Opponent	Att	Pos	W/D/L	FT	HT	Pts	Scorers	Ref
34	H	27/2	DUNDEE	13,500	4	W	1-0	0-0	6 / 47	Dodds 76	T Muirhead
35	A	5/3	ST MIRREN	4,858	3	D	0-0	0-0	8 / 48	—	D McVicar
36	A	19/3	DUNDEE UTD	10,403	4	W	2-0	1-0	6 / 50	Nicholas C 7, Jones 59	J McCluskey
37	H	26/3	FALKIRK	9,410	4	W	2-0	1-0	10 / 52	Falconer 33, Miller W 71	W Crombie
38	H	30/3	CELTIC	22,700	4	L	0-1	0-0	1 / 52	Walker 60	A Ferguson
39	A	2/4	DUNFERMLINE	7,132	4	D	1-1	0-0	11 / 53	Falconer 61, Robertson 54	G Evans
40	A	16/4	MORTON	3,200	4	W	2-0	1-0	12 / 55	Nicholas C 20, Porteous 78	J McGilvray
41	H	23/4	HEARTS	10,500	4	D	0-0	0-0	2 / 56	—	D Syme
42	A	30/4	RANGERS	36,010	4	W	1-0	0-0	3 / 58	Irvine 80	D Hope
43	H	4/5	HIBERNIAN	7,000	4	L	0-2	— / 58		Kane 5, Tortolano 89	D Miller
44	H	7/5	MOTHERWELL	5,500	4	D	0-0	0-0	8 / 59	—	J Duncan

Average Home 13,460 — Away 14,090

Line-ups and reports

34. DUNDEE
Aberdeen: Leighton, McKimmie, Robertson, Connor*, Irvine, Miller W, Dodds, Jones, Nicholas C, Nicholas P, Gray — Hewitt
Dundee: *Geddes, Forsyth, McKinlay, Kirkwood, Smith, Mennie, Lawrence*, Rafferty, Wright, Coyne, Angus — Harvey*
Dodds, back from his cartilage operation, sinks Dundee with another late goal, though Dundee claimed he was offside from Miller's long pass. Dundee paraded their overnight signing, Billy Kirkwood, from Dunfermline. Dodds was booked in the last minute and now faces suspension.

35. ST MIRREN
Aberdeen: Leighton, McKimmie, Robertson, Connor*, Irvine, Miller W, Edwards, Bett, Nicholas C, Nicholas P, Gray* — Falconer/Jones
St Mirren: *Money, Martin, Wilson*, McWhirter, Godfrey, Walker, McGarvey, Fitzpatrick, Chalmers, Hamilton, Cameron — Lambert*
Keith Edwards scored a hat-trick in the Aberdeenshire Cup and is recalled to the first team after a gap of four months. St Mirren, managed by Alex Smith, lost this season's first three matches to the Dons but hold out in the fourth. This result leaves Aberdeen nine points behind Celtic.

36. DUNDEE UTD
Aberdeen: Leighton, McKimmie, Falconer, Simpson, McLeish, Miller W, Dodds, Bett, Nicholas C, Nicholas P, Jones
United: *Main, Bowman, McGinnis*, McInally, Hegarty, Narey, Bannon, Gallacher, Malpas, French*, Redford — Paatelainen/Ferguson*
Ian Porterfield celebrates his first victory over United, who were previously unbeaten in 12. Charlie Nicholas nets with a close-in header, and Tom Jones adds an angled second. United will get their revenge in the Scottish Cup. Leighton, Miller and Bett threaten to quit the Dons.

37. FALKIRK
Aberdeen: Leighton, McKimmie, Falconer, Simpson, McLeish, Miller W, Dodds, Bett, Nicholas C, Nicholas P, Jones*
Falkirk: *Marshall, McNair*, McWilliams, McVeigh, Burgess, Manley, Romaines, Nicol, McIntyre, Conn*, Stewart — Hill/Dempsey*
An unchanged Dons team. Davie Dodds knocked down Miller's cross to set up Willie Falconer's volley from 10 yards. Miller then notches his third goal of the season, being set up by Tom Jones. Celtic are almost home and dry, leaving Aberdeen to battle for second place.

38. CELTIC
Aberdeen: Leighton, McKimmie, Falconer, Simpson, McLeish, Miller W, Dodds, Bett, Nicholas C, Nicholas P, Jones*
Celtic: *Bonner, Morris, Rogan, Aitken, Baillie, Whyte, Grant, McStay, McAvennie, Walker, Miller J — Hewitt*
Aberdeen are determined not to hand Celtic the championship on a plate. Celtic have set a new Premier League record of 28 league and cup games without defeat. Aberdeen are almost overrun in the second half. Charlie Nicholas has still to score his first Dons' goal at Pittodrie.

39. DUNFERMLINE
Aberdeen: Leighton, McKimmie, Falconer, Simpson*, McLeish, Miller W, Dodds, Bett, Nicholas C*, Nicholas P*, Hewitt
Dunfermline: *Westwater, Robertson R* Andersen, Holt, Riddell, Irons, McCathie, Morrison, Callaghan*, Robertson C, Beedie — Jones/Gray, Watson/Smith R*
Dunfermline look odds-on to go down, but they played well in the early stages. Aberdeen levelled from a goalmouth scramble after Morrison had earlier crossed for Robertson to blast past Jim Leighton. Peter Nicholas plays one of his least effective games for Aberdeen.

40. MORTON
Aberdeen: Leighton, McKimmie, Robertson, Simpson*, Irvine, Falconer, Gardner, Wright, Nicholas C*, Connor, Hewitt*
Morton: *Wylie, Collins, Rogers, Doak, Boag, John Bateman* Turner, Clinging, Alexander, McGeachy, O'Hara — McArthur/Porteous, Verlaque*
Porterfield rests six players following the Scottish Cup draw with Dundee United. Lee Gardner makes his debut in midfield, and Michael McArthur plays his first game when coming off the bench. Charlie Nicholas breaks the deadlock, firing a free-kick through the Morton wall.

41. HEARTS
Aberdeen: Leighton, McKimmie, Robertson, Jones, Irvine, McArthur, Connor, Nicholas C*, Falconer, Hewitt*, Irvine
Hearts: *Smith, Murray, Whittaker, Black, Galloway, McPherson, Colquhoun, Sandison, Foster*, Berry, Gavin* — Clark/Burns*
The Dons are out of the Scottish Cup. A nothing match with little entertainment. European representatives are said to be up there somewhere keeping tabs on Robert Connor. A head wound kept McLeish in the dressing room at half-time. The match petered out long before the end.

42. RANGERS
Aberdeen: Leighton, Irvine, Robertson, Simpson, McLeish, Miller W, Jones, Bett, Nicholas C, Hewitt, Falconer
Rangers: *Woods, Nicholl, Munro, Roberts, Wilkins, Gough, Ferguson, Walters, McCoist, Brown*, Cooper — Nisbet*
Aberdeen become the only side to beat the deposed champions twice at Ibrox. After eight minutes McCoist blasted against the bar. Long back passes to Leighton infuriate the Ibrox hordes. A Dons free-kick is not properly cleared and Irvine appears unattended to score the only goal.

43. HIBERNIAN
Aberdeen: Leighton, Irvine, Harvie, Jones*, McLeish, Miller W, Hewitt*, Orr, Nicholas C, Kane, Falconer
Hibs: *Goram, Sneddon, Mitchell, May, Rae, McIntyre, Weir*, Collins, Kane, McCluskey* Evans/Tortolano*
Andy Roxburgh is in the crowd to observe this shapeless, dreary match. Hibs have not lost this season when Paul Kane scores. After the final whistle Dons supporters demonstrated outside the stadium. Sacked St Mirren boss Alex Smith has been offered a coaching post at Pittodrie.

44. MOTHERWELL
Aberdeen: Leighton, McKimmie, Connor, Simpson, McLeish, Miller W, Hewitt, Bett, Nicholas C, Nicholas P, Falconer
Motherwell: *Duncan, Boyd, Philliben, Paterson, McAdam, Shanks, Farningham, Russell, Cowan*, Kirk, Kinnaird* — Smith/McCart*
Cut-price admission cannot prevent the lowest gate of the season. Jim Leighton plays his last match for Aberdeen, though as yet his new club is not known. He establishes a new record of 35 clean sheets from 59 first-team matches, and waves to the crowd as he departs the stage.

FINE FARE PREMIER (CUP-TIES) Manager: Ian Porterfield SEASON 1987-88

Skol League Cup

			F-A	H-T	Scorers, Times, and Referees	1	2	3	4	5	6	7	8	9	10	11	subs used
2	H	BRECHIN 18/8 9,000	W 5-1	1-0	Miller J 2, 75, 85, Hewitt 50, Irvine 54 / Candlish 87p / Ref: J Duncan	Leighton	McKimmie	Robertson	Simpson*	Irvine	Miller W	Dodds	Bett	Miller J	Nicholas P	Hewitt*	Grant/Hackett
						Lawrie	*Watt*	*Candlish*	*Inglis*	*Stevens*	*Taylor*	*Gallacher*	*Adam**	*Lees*	*Scott*	*Lyall**	*Brown/Bourke*
3	H	ST JOHNSTONE 26/8 10,800	W 3-0	1-0	Dodds 11, 80, Bett 78	Leighton	McKimmie	Robertson	Simpson	Irvine	Miller W	Hewitt	Bett	Miller J	Nicholas P*	Hewitt	Grant/Hackett
						Balavage	*Wilson*	*McVicar*	*Barron*	*McKillop*	*McGurn**	*Coyle*	*Johnstone**	*Brown*			*Smith/Lloyd*
QF	H	CELTIC 1/9 24,000	W 1-0	0-0	Bett 60 / Ref: J McCluskey	Leighton	McKimmie	Robertson	Connor	Irvine	Miller W	Hewitt	Bett	Miller J	Nicholas P	Hackett	
						McKnight	*Morris*	*Rogan*	*Aitken*	*Whyte*	*Grant*	*Stark*	*McStay*	*McGhee*	*Walker*	*Burns*	
SF	N	DUNDEE 23/9 22,034 (at Tannadice)	W 2-0	2-0	Connor 1, Irvine 37 / Ref: D Syme	Leighton	McKimmie	Robertson	Connor	McLeish	Miller W	Hewitt	Bett	Miller J	Falconer	Irvine	Jack
						Geddes	*McGeachie*	*McKinlay*	*Mennie**	*Smith*	*Glennie*	*Harvey*	*Brown*	*Wright*	*Coyne*	*Angus*	
F	N	RANGERS 25/10 71,961 (at Hampden)	L 3-3 (aet)	1-2	Bett 9p, Hewitt 72, Falconer 81 / Cooper 22, Durrant 40, Fleck 86 / Ref: B Valentine / (Dons lose 3-5 on penalties)	Leighton	Walker	Connor	Simpson*	McLeish	Miller W	Hewitt	Bett	Miller J	Nicholas P	Falconer*	Weir
						Nicholl	*Munro*	*Roberts*	*Ferguson**	*Gough*	*McGregor**	*Fleck*	*McCoist*	*Durrant*	*Cooper*		*Francis/Cohen*

Brechin: John Inglis plays for Brechin. Ex-Pittodrie keeper Dave Lawrie performed creditably in the Brechin goal, and his outfield colleagues tried to play football at all times. Joe Miller's hat-trick earned him the man-of-the-match award. All five Dons' goals were scored from close-in.

St Johnstone: Jim Bett plays his 100th first-team game for Aberdeen; Stewart McKimmie his 200th. St Johnstone had put out St Mirren in the previous round and had to be treated with respect. Davie Dodds was man-of-the-match. Liverpool manager Kenny Dalglish took in the match from the stand.

Celtic: Celtic are on a high after beating Rangers at the weekend. Davie Dodds misses this game and is expected to be out for three months. An excellent match was settled by an excellent goal, scored by Bett, but made by Robert Connor. Willie Miller was made man-of-the-match.

Dundee: Peter Nicholas is suspended. Aberdeen have signed £65,000 striker Keith Edwards, though he does not play. Both goals were prompted by Jim Bett, who earned his man-of-the-match award. After just 40 seconds Joe Miller and then Hewitt dummied for Connor to fire in a rocket.

Rangers: A final that began and ended with penalties. Leading 1-0 and 3-2 Aberdeen needed to hold out just four more minutes when Fleck scrambled a late equaliser. Aberdeen had never won a penalty shoot-out, and when Peter Nicholas misses the Dons' second kick, the curse continues.

Scottish Cup

			F-A	H-T	Scorers, Times, and Referees	1	2	3	4	5	6	7	8	9	10	11	subs used
3	A	ST JOHNSTONE 30/1 10,000 2:2	W 1-0	0-0	Connor 83 / Ref: A Waddell	Leighton	McKimmie	Falconer	Connor	McLeish	Miller W	Nicholas C	Bett	Hewitt*	Nicholas P	Hackett	Jones
						Balavage	*Thomson K*	*McVicar*	*Barron*	*McKillop*	*Johnston*	*Thomson G*	*Coyle*	*Maskrey*	*Watters**	*Heddle**	*Powell/McGurn*
4	A	HAMILTON 20/2 7,270 1:1	W 2-0	0-0	Nicholas C 46, Dodds 48 / Ref: K Williamson	Leighton	McKimmie	Robertson*	Connor	McLeish	Miller W	Dodds	Hackett*	Nicholas C	Nicholas P	Falconer	Hewitt/Jones
						Ferguson	*McKee*	*Kerr**	*Martin*	*Jamieson*	*Collins*	*Fairlie*	*Taylor*	*Scott†*	*Sprott*	*Thomson**	*McCabe/McDonald*
QF	H	CLYDE 12/3 12,000 1:7	W 5-0	2-0	Dodds 18, 32, 72, Falconer 62, Edwards 88 / Ref: J Duncan	Leighton	Grant	Falconer	Simpson*	Irvine	Miller W	Dodds	Bett	Nicholas C	Nicholas P	Jones*	Connor/Edwards
						Atkins	*McFarlane*	*Napier*	*Donnelly*	*Flexney**	*Clark*	*Willock*	*Millar*	*McGlashan*	*Walker*	*Tait**	*McEataggart/Murphy*
SF	N	DUNDEE UTD 9/4 20,488 (at Dens Park)	D 0-0	0-0	Ref: W Crombie	Leighton	McKimmie	Robertson	Simpson	McLeish	Miller W	Dodds	Bett	Nicholas C	Nicholas P	Hewitt	Ferguson/Clark
						Thomson	*Bowman*	*Malpas*	*McInally*	*Hegarty*	*Narey*	*Bannon*	*Gallacher*	*French**	*McLeod J**	*Redford**	
SF R	N	DUNDEE UTD 13/4 17,288 (at Dens Park)	D 1-1 (aet)	0-0	Nicholas C 46 / Paatelainen 69 / Ref: W Crombie	Leighton	McKimmie	Clark	Simpson	McLeish	Miller W	Dodds	Bett*	Nicholas C	Nicholas P	Hewitt	Gray /Falconer
						Thomson	*Clark*	*Malpas*	*McInally*	*Hegarty†*	*Narey*	*Bannon*	*Gallacher*	*Paatelainen*	*McLeod J**	*Redford*	*Ferguson/McGinnis*
SF RR	N	DUNDEE UTD 20/4 19,048 (at Dens Park)	L 0-1	0-0	Ferguson 76 / Ref: W Crombie	Leighton	McKimmie	Robertson	Simpson	McLeish	Miller W	Dodds*	Bett	Nicholas C	Nicholas P	Hewitt	Falconer
						Thomson	*Bowman*	*Malpas*	*McInally*	*Hegarty*	*Narey*	*Bannon*	*Gallacher*	*Paatelainen*	*Ferguson*	*Redford*	*Clark*

St Johnstone: Muddy Muirton. St Johnstone put up a better show than in the Skol Cup earlier in the season. They have gone 11 games without loss in Division 2 and are full of confidence. Connor settles the match after Charlie Nicholas ran the ball off the post. Crowd trouble mars the win.

Hamilton: Last season Hamilton knocked out Rangers. Double quick headers from close range immediately after the turnaround put paid to the Division 1 pacemakers. Eight minutes before half-time Hamilton's Gordon Scott was sent off after an off-the-ball incident with Willie Miller.

Clyde: Davie Dodds claims his first hat-trick for Aberdeen. Neil Simpson plays his first game for four months. Brian Grant, out for 27 games, takes the place of McKimmie, leaving Miller as the only regular member of the back four. Clyde can do little to prevent Aberdeen's onward march.

Dundee Utd (SF): An awful match between two sides too scared of losing to play with any enterprise. David Robertson is surprisingly recalled, having slagged off the club in an English paper. Porterfield and his assistant Jimmy Mullen are ordered to the stand following a confrontation with a linesman.

Dundee Utd (R): In 41 minutes Hegarty is ordered off for felling Charlie Nicholas. Jim McLean rushes down the track at half-time and squares up to Willie Miller for his involvement. McLean is fined and banned. Man-of-the-match Charlie nets from Hewitt's pass, but McGinnis sets up Paatelainen.

Dundee Utd (RR): Muddy Dens. Man of the match Kevin Gallacher sweeps the ball across for Ian Ferguson who takes advantage of Alex McLeish's stumble to head down past Leighton. Try as they might the Dons cannot get back on terms, and their last hope of silverware vanishes in the mire.

UEFA Cup

1:1 A **BOHEMIANS** 0-0 D 0-0 0-0
15/9 (Rep Ireland)*10,000*

Ref: Den Wijngaert (Belgium)

Leighton	McKinnie	Robertson	Connor	McLeish	Miller W	Hewitt	Simpson*	Nicholas P	Miller J*	Hewitt	Falconer	Weir/Hackett
O'Neill	Kinsella	Duffy	Murphy B	Murphy R	O'Brien	Lawless	Murray*	Jameson	Jameson	McGee	Byrne

The Dublin part-timers resorted to the offside-trap, and it succeeded in stifling the Dons' creativity. Goalscoring chances were few and far between for both sides. The second half was played in heavy rain. Ian Porterfield afterwards described himself as disappointed with his team.

1:2 H **BOHEMIANS** 1-0 W 1-0 1-0 Bett 2p
30/9 10,000

Ref: E Norwig (Norway)
(Dons win 1-0 on aggregate)

Leighton	McKinnie	Robertson*	Connor	McLeish	Miller W	Hewitt*	Bett	Nicholas P	Miller J	Falconer	Grant/Hackett
O'Neill	Kinsella	Duffy	Murphy B	Murphy R	O'Brien	Murray	Byrne	Lawless	Jameson	McGee

Bohemians rarely ventured out of their cocoon, despite Bett's early penalty, awarded when Ronnie Murphy fouled Falconer and Connor in quick succession. An away goal in the 88 minutes that followed would have taken Bohs through, but keeper O'Neill was kept busy throughout.

2:1 H **FEYENOORD** 1-1 W 2-1 1-1 Falconer 34, Miller J 68
21/10 (Holland) 16,000 Estrup 21p

Ref: E Frederiksson (Sweden)

Leighton	McKinnie	Falconer	Connor	McLeish	Miller W	Hewitt	Bett	Nicholas P	Miller J	Weir	Hewitt
Hiele	Proost	Van Herpen	Wijnstekers/	Molenaar	Hofman	Estrup	Mitchell*	Been	Hoekstra	Blinker	Barendse '/Monkou

Ex-Ranger and Aussie international Dave Mitchell is brought down by Leighton. Falconer's header levels. On 48 minutes Feyenoord skipper Wijnstekers is sent off for a foul on Weir, who is starting his first match of the season. Norwich boss Ken Brown watches Weir and Connor.

2:2 A **FEYENOORD** 0-0 L 0-1 0-0
4/11 26,390 Hoekstra 74

Ref: M Vautrot (France)
(Dons lose on away-goals rule)

Leighton	Irvine	Simpson	McLeish	Miller W*	Bett	Falconer	Weir	Blinker
Hiele	Monkou	Van Herpen	Hoekstra	Molenaar	Hofman	Estrup	Been

Irvine plays as stand-in right-back. It is his error which permits the cross for Hoekstra to head into the corner. It is Feyenoord's only scoring chance - which is one more than Aberdeen created. Their unashamedly safety-first tactics win few friends. Aberdeen's challenge fizzled out.

Home / Away league table

		P	W	D	L	F	A		W	D	L	F	A	Pts
				Home							Away			
1	Celtic	44	16	5	1	42	11		15	5	2	37	12	72
2	Hearts	44	13	8	1	37	17		10	8	4	37	15	62
3	Rangers	44	14	4	4	49	17		12	4	6	36	17	60
4	ABERDEEN	44	11	7	4	27	11		10	10	2	29	14	59
5	Dundee Utd	44	8	7	7	29	24		8	6	8	25	23	47
6	Hibernian	44	8	8	6	18	17		4	11	7	21	25	43
7	Dundee	44	9	5	8	31	25		8	2	12	39	39	41
8	Motherwell	44	10	2	10	25	31		3	8	11	12	25	36
9	St Mirren	44	5	11	6	22	28		5	3	13	19	36	35
10	Falkirk	44	8	4	10	26	35		2	7	13	15	40	31
11	Dunfermline	44	6	6	10	23	35		2	4	16	18	49	26
12	Morton	44	3	7	12	19	47		0	3	19	8	53	16
		528	111	74	79	348	298		79	74	111	298	348	528

		P	W	D	L	F	A	Pts						
v	Morton	4	3	1	0	9	1	7						
v	Dunfermline	4	3	1	0	8	1	7						
v	Falkirk	4	3	1	0	9	3	7						
v	St Mirren	4	3	1	0	7	2	7						
v	Rangers	4	3	0	1	5	2	6						
v	Dundee	4	2	2	0	4	2	6						
v	Dundee Utd	4	1	3	0	3	1	5						
v	Motherwell	4	2	1	1	3	2	5						
v	Hibernian	4	1	2	1	3	3	4						
v	Hearts	4	0	3	1	3	4	3						
v	Celtic	4	0	2	2	2	4	2						
		44	21	17	6	56	25	59						

Cup results:
	W	D	L					
Cup								
LC	0	0	1					
LC	1	0	0					
SC	0	2	1					
LC	1	0	0					

Odds & ends

Never lost to: (6) Morton, Dunfermline, Falkirk, St Mirren, Dundee, Dundee Utd (league only).

Never beat: (2) Hearts, Celtic (league only).

Won from behind: (2) Morton (h), Feyenoord (UC).

Lost from in front: (1) Hearts (a).

High spots: Unbeaten in first 10 games, and top of the league. Unbeaten in 15 league games from 7 November.

Beating Rangers twice at Ibrox.

Reaching Skol Cup final.

Low spots: Back-to-back league defeats in late January and early February to effectively end title hopes.

Losing Scottish Cup semi-final after two replays.

Losing Skol Cup final to Rangers after penalty shoot-out.

Bogey-team: Hearts.

Ever-presents: (1) Jim Leighton.

Hat-tricks: (2) Davie Dodds (1), Joe Miller (1).

Leading scorer: (15) Davie Dodds.

Appearances / Goals

	Appearances							Goals						
	Lge	Sub	LC	Sub	SC	Sub	Eur	Sub	Lge	LC	SC	Eur	Tot	
Bett, Jim	38		5		5		3		10	3		1	14	
Connor, Robert	32	2	1		2	1	4		1	1	1		3	
Dodds, Davie	22	1	2		5				9	2	4		15	
Edwards, Keith	6	3		1		1			2	1			3	
Falconer, Willie	32	4	2		3	2	4		8	1	1	1	11	
Gardner, Lee	1													
Grant, Brian	4	3			2	1			1				1	
Gray, Steve	4	3			3									
Hackett, Gary	6	9	1		1		2		1				1	
Harvie, Scott	1													
Hewitt, John	26	11	5		4	1	3	1	1	2			3	
Irvine, Brian	14	2	4		1		1	1	1	2			3	
Jones, Tom	14	14			1	2			3				3	
Leighton, Jim	44		5		6		4							
McArthur, Michael	1	2												
McKimmie, Stewart	42		5		5		3		1				1	
McLeish, Alex	36		2		5		4		4	3		1	8	
Miller, Joe	12	2	5		6		4		4			1	5	
Miller, Willie	42		5		6		4		3				3	
Nicholas, Charlie	16		2		6		3	2	3		2		5	
Nicholas, Peter	39		4		6		4		3				3	
Porteous, Ian	1	2												
Robertson, David	23		4		4		2		1				1	
Simpson, Neil	14	1	3		4	1	2			1			1	
Weir, Peter	5						2							
Wright, Paul	9								4				4	
26 players used	484	59	55	5	66	8	44	5	56	14	9	3	82	

B & Q SCOTTISH PREMIER

Manager: Alex Smith & Jocky Scott — SEASON 1988-89

No	Date	Att	Pos	Pt	F-A	H-T	Scorers, Times, and Referees	1	2	3	4	5	6	7	8	9	10	11	subs used
1	A DUNDEE 13/8	12,222		1	D 1-1	0-0	Dodds 63 / *Chisholm 57* / Ref D Syme	Snelders / *Geddes*	McKimmie / *Forsyth*	Robertson D / *McKinlay*	Simpson / *Chisholm*	McLeish / *Smith*	Miller / *Saunders**	Gray / *Lawrence*	Bett / *Angus**	Nicholas* / *Wright*	Connor* / *Harvey*	Hewitt / *Campbell*	Dodds/Irvine / *Rafferty/Mennie*
2	H ST MIRREN 20/8	12,046	5 / *9*	2	D 1-1	0-0	Connor 48 / *Godfrey 75* / Ref G Smith	Snelders / *Fridge*	McKimmie / *Wilson*	Robertson D / *Winnie*	Simpson / *Hamilton!*	McLeish / *Godfrey*	Miller / *Cooper*	/ *Cameron*	Bett / *Martin*	Wright / *McGarvey*	Connor / *McWalter**	Hewitt / *Chalmers*	Grant / *Lambert*
3	A DUNDEE UTD 27/8	14,735	4 / *2*	3	D 2-2	0-1	Bett 49p, Hewitt 82 / *Meade 26, Clark 80* / Ref J Duncan	Snelders / *Thomson*	McKimmie / *Bowman*	Robertson D / *Malpas*	Simpson / *Beaumont*	McLeish / *Clark*	Miller / *Narey*	Wright / *Meade**	Bett / *McKinlay*	Dodds / *Paatelainen*	Connor / *Gallacher*	Hewitt / *Redford*	Nicholas / *Cleland*
4	H HIBERNIAN 3/9	13,583	4 / *3*	4	D 0-0	0-0	Ref D Yeats	Snelders / *Goram*	McKimmie / *Hunter*	Robertson D / *Sneddon*	Simpson / *Orr*	McLeish / *Rae*	Miller / *Milne*	MacLeod* / *Tortolano*	Grant / *Archibald**	Dodds / *Kane*	Connor / *Collins*	Hewitt / *Evans**	Nicholas, May/McCluskey
5	A CELTIC 17/9	37,769	3 / *7*	6	W 3-1	2-1	Grant 28, Bett 33p, Dodds 60 / *Miller J 44p* / Ref J McCluskey	Snelders / *Andrews*	McKimmie / *Morris*	Robertson D / *Rogan*	Grant / *Aitken*	McLeish / *McCarthy*	Miller / *Whyte**	Nicholas / *Miller J*	Bett / *McStay*	Dodds / *McAvennie*	Connor / *Walker**	Hewitt* / *Burns*	Mason / *Stark/Archdeacon*
6	H HEARTS 24/9	14,000	3 / *9*	8	W 1-0	1-0	Nicholas 11 / Ref I Cathcart	Snelders / *Smith*	McKimmie / *Kidd*	Robertson D / *Berry*	Grant / *Whittaker*	McLeish / *Galloway*	Miller / *Murray*	Nicholas / *Colquhoun**	Bett / *Mackay*	Dodds* / *Foster*	Connor / *Black**	Hewitt / *Bannon*	Mason / *Ferguson/Jardine*
7	A HAMILTON 27/9	3,634	3 / *10*	10	W 1-0	0-0	Connor 79 / Ref R Morrison	Snelders / *Ferguson*	McKimmie! / *McKee*	Irvine / *Kerr*	Simpson* / *Weir*	McLeish / *Jamieson*	Miller / *Collins*	Nicholas / *Fairlie!*	Bett / *McCabe**	Grant / *Harris*	Connor / *Scott*	Hewitt / *McDonald**	Mason / *Chernley/Roseburgh*
8	A MOTHERWELL 1/10	4,225	4 / *10*	11	D 1-1	1-1	Miller 15 / *Farningham 17* / Ref W Crombie	Snelders / *Duncan*	Mason* / *Wishart*	Robertson D / *Phillben*	Grant / *Paterson*	McLeish / *McCart*	Miller / *Boyd*	Nicholas / *Farningham*	Bett / *Russell**	Dodds* / *McCabe*	Connor / *Kirk*	Hewitt / *Kinnaird*	Irvine/Wright / *Gahagan/Arnott*
9	H RANGERS 8/10	22,370	3 / *1*	13	W 2-1	0-1	Bett 55p, Nicholas 85 / *Cooper N 38* / Ref L Thow	Snelders / *Woods*	McKimmie / *Stevens*	Robertson D / *Brown*	Simpson* / *Gough*	McLeish / *Cooper N*	Miller / *Butcher*	Nicholas / *Drinkell*	Bett / *Ferguson I*	Dodds / *McCoist*	Connor / *Durrant**	Hewitt / *Walters**	Irvine / *Munro/Cooper D*
10	A ST MIRREN 12/10	4,284	3 / *14*	14	D 1-1	1-0	Dodds 4 / *Martin 90* / Ref A Waddell	Snelders / *Money*	McKimmie / *Wilson*	Robertson D / *Winnie*	Simpson / *Hamilton*	McLeish / *Godfrey*	Miller / *Cooper*	Nicholas* / *Cameron*	Bett / *Martin*	Dodds / *McGarvey**	Connor / *Davies*	Hewitt / *Chalmers*	Irvine / *McDowall*

1 — DUNDEE: New manager Alex Smith has overseen £2 million worth of close-season transfers. Leighton, Falconer and Peter Nicholas have all gone to England. Dundee's new manager, Dave Smith, addresses the crowd before kick-off. Dons sub Davie Dodds equalised with his first touch.

2 — ST MIRREN: The Buddies' Peter Godfrey gave away a first-half penalty when handling the ball, but Bett's penalty-kick was saved. After 55 minutes Bryan Hamilton was ordered off for trampling on David Robertson. Godfrey's header levelled the scores, with McKimmie desperately trying to clear.

3 — DUNDEE UTD: A minute's silence to mark the death of United chairman George Grant. United's £400,000 signing from Sporting Lisbon, Raphael Meade, makes his debut. Meade scored, then fouled Bett for the penalty. Clark then seemed to knock Paatelainen's cross from Snelders' hands.

4 — HIBERNIAN: These teams meet again, four days after Hibs were sent tumbling from the Skol Cup. This dull match is notable only for a swirling wind and a Dons' debut for Andy MacLeod. Charlie Nicholas was relegated to the bench. Things got so bad the crowd chanted 'Charlie, Charlie'.

5 — CELTIC: Celtic's 3,000th league game brings Aberdeen their first win at Parkhead in five years. The 'jungle' abused Charlie Nicholas throughout. Both sides scored from penalties, the Dons when Rogan tumbled Bett, and Celtic when Snelders felled McAvennie. Dodds' header clinched the win.

6 — HEARTS: Charlie Nicholas' first Pittodrie goal for the Dons earns him huge acclaim. Poor Hearts are having a wretched time of it, and Henry Smith endured a nightmare Skol Cup semi-final against Rangers in midweek. After six matches four teams are still unbeaten in the Premier League.

7 — HAMILTON: Referee Ray Morrison takes charge of his first Premier League fixture and does not earn high marks. Torrential pre-match rain turned the pitch into a skid-pan, which partly accounted for the 42nd minute touchline flare-up between McKimmie and Jamie Fairlie. Both were sent off.

8 — MOTHERWELL: Motherwell earn their second point of the season, and but for Theo Snelders' excellence would have earned another. Farningham brought them quickly level when Kinnaird skipped past Mason to lay on the chance. At half-time police went into the crowd to investigate a bomb threat.

9 — RANGERS: Neil Simpson goes over the top against Durrant to unleash a media witch-hunt. Simpson was only booked. In the first minute Nicholas hooks against the post. Neale Cooper fires a cracker on his Rangers' debut. Ferguson trips Hewitt for Bett's penalty. Nicholas' header wins it.

10 — ST MIRREN: Miserable weather, miserable match. Simpson was booed throughout, on account of the Durrant business. On Saturday St Mirren lost 1-7 to Celtic. When Money fumbled Hewitt's cross to Dodds, a repeat looked likely. In stoppage time McWalter hit the post and Martin swooped.

League fixtures 11–21

11. A HEARTS — 29/10 · 3 · D 1-1 · Att 12,644 · pos 8 · pts 15
- **Aberdeen:** Snelders, McKimmie, Robertson D, Mason*, Bett, Nicholas, Irvine, McLeish, Connor, Dodds, Grant, Hewitt
- **Hearts:** *Smith, Kidd, Whittaker, Berry*, Mackay, Moore, McPherson, Galloway, Ferguson~, Black, Bannon, Jardine/Colquhoun*
- Whittaker 45 og, Jardine 78 — Ref: H Williamson

Aberdeen are now the only unbeaten team in Scotland - if one overlooks the Skol Cup final. Hearts' substitute, Ian Jardine, is unmarked to head the equaliser. On half-time Davie Dodds goes in for Connor's cross but Whittaker gets the fatal touch.

12. H CELTIC — 2/11 · 3 · D 2-2 · Att 22,000 · pos 5 · pts 16
- **Aberdeen:** Snelders, McKimmie, Robertson D, Grant, Bett, Nicholas, Irvine, McLeish, Connor, Dodds*, Hewitt*, Mason/Wright
- **Celtic:** *Bonner, Morris, Rogan, Aitken, McStay, Stark, Whyte, McCarthy, McGhee, McAvennie, Burns*
- Dodds 15, Nicholas 16 / Stark 40, 64 — Ref: R Valentine

A thrill-a-minute match that Aberdeen looked to have sewn up with two goals inside a minute. Dodds hooks the first after Bonner had blocked from Hewitt. Celtic's equaliser was a Billy Stark 30-yard special that flew in off a post. Late in the game Robert Connor spurned a gift header.

13. A HIBERNIAN — 5/11 · 2 · W 2-1 · Att 11,500 · pos 4 · pts 18
- **Aberdeen:** Snelders, McKimmie, Robertson D, Grant, Bett, Nicholas, Irvine, McLeish, Connor, Dodds, Mason, May
- **Hibernian:** *Goram, Hunter, Sneddon*, McIntyre, Rae, Milne, Orr, Archibald, Kane, Collins, Evans*
- Nicholas 52, 80 / Archibald 1 — Ref: D Hope

Former Don Steve Archibald nets close in within 30 seconds. Four minutes after Nicholas equalised, Irvine pulled down Milne but Archibald fired high and wide from the penalty spot. McLeish was involved in both Aberdeen goals. The Dons remain four points behind Rangers.

14. H DUNDEE UTD — 12/11 · 2 · D 1-1 · Att 15,184 · pos 3 · pts 19
- **Aberdeen:** Snelders, McKimmie, Robertson D, Grant, Bett, Nicholas*, Irvine, Miller, Connor, Dodds, Mason, Hewitt
- **Dundee Utd:** *Thomson, Beaumont, Malpas, McNally*, Hegarty, Narey, Meade^, Preston, Krivokapic, Paatelainen, Bowman/French*
- Mason 41 / Preston 70 — Ref: A Huett

Willie Miller returns after his groin injury. Paul Mason scores his first goal - a header - since signing from Groningen. United are downcast after being dumped from Europe in their midweek trip to Romania but bounce back to level through Alan Preston's shot from Bowman's cross.

15. H DUNDEE — 16/11 · 2 · W 1-0 · Att 11,181 · pos 7 · pts 21
- **Aberdeen:** Snelders, McKimmie, Robertson D, Grant*, Bett, Hewitt, Miller, McLeish, Connor, Dodds, Mason, Wright
- **Dundee:** *Geddes, Shannon, McKinlay, Frail, Forsyth, Saunders, Lawrence*, Rafferty, Wright, Coyne, Campbell^, Kirkwood/Harvey*
- Wright 83 — Ref: J McGilvray

An evening of frustration ends satisfactorily, thanks to substitute Paul Wright, a 58th minute replacement for Brian Grant. Nicholas was ruled out by injury. Dundee were denied two fine saves from Snelders and by a kind referee, who ignored Bett's handling offence in the box.

16. H MOTHERWELL — 19/11 · 2 · W 2-1 · Att 10,028 · pos 9 · pts 23
- **Aberdeen:** Snelders, McKimmie, Robertson D, Mason, Bett, Nicholas*, Miller, McLeish, Connor, Dodds, Hewitt*, Wright
- **Motherwell:** *Duncan, Wishart, Philliben, Paterson*, McAdam, O'Neill, Farningham, Russell, Cowan, Shanks^, McCabe, Boyd/Gahagan*
- Hewitt 40, Nicholas 44 / Russell 84 — Ref: G Smith

Motherwell are the only side in Britain still searching for their first win. They lose this match in the crucial period before half-time, when Hewitt's shot was deflected in by Wishart, and by Nicholas' 20-yarder, set up by Dodds' back-heel. Leaders Rangers dropped a point at Dens.

17. A RANGERS — 26/11 · 2 · L 0-1 · Att 42,239 · pos 1 · pts 23
- **Aberdeen:** Snelders, McKimmie, Robertson D, Irvine*, Bett, Nicholas, Miller, McLeish, Connor, Dodds, Hewitt*, Grant/Wright
- **Rangers:** *Walker, Stevens, Brown, Gough, Wilkins, Butcher, Drinkell, Ferguson I, Cooper D, Cooper N, Walters*, MacDonald*
- Gough 42 — Ref: K Hope

Had Aberdeen won they would have drawn level with Rangers. Instead they suffer their first league defeat. A dour encounter was settled by Gough after a free-kick flew around the Dons' penalty box. Rangers brought on Kevin MacDonald, their overnight signing from Liverpool.

18. H HAMILTON — 3/12 · 2 · D 1-1 · Att 8,324 · pos 10 · pts 24
- **Aberdeen:** Snelders, McKimmie, Robertson D, Irvine*, Bett, Nicholas, Miller, McLeish, Connor, Dodds*, Mason, Hewitt*
- **Hamilton:** *Ferguson, McKee, Napier, Jamieson, Martin, Rosebaugh, Harris, Weir^, Gallagher, Gordon*, Charnley, Fraser/Nelson*
- Nicholas 78 / Gallagher 49 — Ref: J Renton

Bottom-placed Accies have the worst defence in the league. They defend in depth. Snelders is idle throughout the first half, then fails to gather Harris's effort and Eddie Gallagher pounces. Nicholas levelled from a free-kick awarded for a foul on himself, shooting low from 20 yards.

19. A CELTIC — 10/12 · 3 · D 0-0 · Att 42,437 · pos 4 · pts 25
- **Aberdeen:** Snelders, McKimmie, Robertson D, Simpson*, Mason, Hewitt, Irvine, McLeish, Connor, Gray*, Mason, Grant
- **Celtic:** *Bonner, Morris, Rogan, Aitken, Whyte, Baillie, Whyte, Stark, McStay, McAvennie, McGhee*
- Ref: A Waddell

A frantic match despite the lack of goals. In the 67th minute Chris Morris's free-kick rebounded off both Snelders' posts, and McAvennie's follow-up hit the bar. John Hewitt had his turn, rattling Bonner's upright. Snelders also saved well from former Don Mark McGhee.

20. H ST MIRREN — 17/12 · 3 · W 3-1 · Att 8,500 · pos 6 · pts 27
- **Aberdeen:** Snelders, McKimmie, Robertson D, Grant, Bett, Gray, Irvine, McLeish, Connor, Robertson C / Wright*, Mason, Hewitt
- **St Mirren:** *Money*, Wilson, Winnie, Hamilton, Godfrey, Cooper, McGarvey, Martin, Chalmers, Weir, Cameron/Shaw*
- Robertson C 19, Irvine 48, Hewitt 77 / McWalter 89 — Ref: J McCluskey

New recruit Craig Robertson, a goalscoring midfielder signed from Dunfermline for £200,000, scores with a header. Keeper Campbell Money, attempting to save, was carried off with a knee injury. Irvine's header after half-time settled a match in which Peter Weir lined up for Saints.

21. A DUNDEE — 31/12 · 3 · L 0-2 · Att 9,828 · pos 7 · pts 27
- **Aberdeen:** Snelders, McKimmie, Robertson D, Simpson*, Mason, Gray^, Irvine, Grant, Connor, Dodds, Rafferty, Wright/Robertson C
- **Dundee:** *Geddes, Shannon, Holt, Chisholm, Forsyth, Saunders, Frail, Rafferty, Wright, Coyne, McBride, Mason/Dodds*
- Coyne 10, 64 — Ref: R Orr

Dundee's first league win over Aberdeen in 35 attempts. The injury-wrecked Dons are without Miller, McLeish, Bett and Nicholas. McKimmie assumes the captaincy and plays sweeper. A one-two between Tommy Coyne and Keith Wright - wanted by the Dons - brought the first goal.

B & Q SCOTTISH PREMIER   Manager: Alex Smith & Jocky Scott   SEASON 1988-89

No	Date	Att	Pos	Pt	F-A	H-T	Scorers, Times, and Referees	1	2	3	4	5	6	7	8	9	10	11	subs used
22	A DUNDEE UTD 3/1	17,952	3 D 2	28	1-1	1-1	Nicholas 42 / French 15 — Ref: H Williamson	Snelders	McKimmie	Robertson I	Simpson	McLeish	Irvine	Nicholas*	Bett	Wright*	Connor	Mason	Grant/Dodds
								Thomson	*Bowman**	*McInally*	*Malpas*	*Krivokapic*	*Narey*	*French*	*Beaumont*	*Gallacher*	*McKinlay*	*Paatelainen*	*McGinnis*
	This result benefited no one but leaders Rangers. Snelders half-saved Hamish French's effort. Aberdeen levelled when Nicholas ran through to latch on to a headed pass from Paul Wright. The deadlocked match withered away as both teams realised a winner was beyond either of them.																		
23	H HIBERNIAN 7/1	13,500	3 W 5	30	2-0	0-0	Nicholas 62, 82 — Ref: D Syme	Snelders	McKimmie	Robertson I	Simpson	McLeish	Irvine	Nicholas*	Bett	Wright	Connor	Mason*	Hewitt
								Goram	*Hunter*	*McIntyre*	*May**	*Rae*	*Mitchell*	*Orr*	*Archibald*	*Kane*	*Collins*	*Evans**	*Tortolano/Weir*
	Charlie Nicholas celebrates the first anniversary of his arrival from Highbury with two breathtaking goals. He weaves through the Hibs defence for the first, and trapped the ball on his chest for the second. Neil Simpson struck Goram's post from 20 yards. Rangers lose at Motherwell.																		
24	H RANGERS 14/1	22,000	4 L 1	30	1-2	1-2	Nicholas 38 / Ferguson D 12, Munro 24 — Ref: D Hope	Snelders	McKimmie	Robertson I*	Simpson	McLeish	Irvine	Nicholas*	Bett	Wright	Connor	Mason	Dodds, Cooper N
								Walker	*Stevens*	*Munro*	*Gough*	*Wilkins**	*Butcher*	*Drinkell*	*Ferguson I*	*Ferguson D*	*Brown*	*Walters*	
	This is only the third occasion Rangers have recorded a Premier League victory at Pittodrie. It brings about Aberdeen's first home defeat of the season, watched by Dutch manager Thys Libregts, keeping an eye on the uncapped Snelders. Nicholas can't stop scoring at the moment.																		
25	A MOTHERWELL 21/1	5,906	4 W 9	32	2-0	2-0	van der Ark 26, Connor 36 — Ref: T Cathcart	Snelders	Maxwell	Wishart	Boyd	Paterson	Irvine	Nicholas	Bett	Dodds*	Connor	van der Ark*	Mason/Wright
									McAdam			*McCart*		*Mair*	*O'Neill*	*McCabe*	*Kirk*	*McBride*	
	The Dutch invasion continues. Following the arrival of Theo Snelders, gangling 6ft 5in Willem van der Ark arrives for £350,000. He stretches out a long leg to poke in Nicholas' pass. Ark was later fouled 25 yards out, inviting Robert Connor to drive the free-kick into the top corner.																		
26	A HAMILTON 14/2	2,016	10 W	34	2-0	1-0	Connor 40, Wright 59 — Ref: J McGilvray	Snelders	McKimmie	Robertson I	Simpson	McLeish	Irvine	Nicholas	Bett	Wright	Connor	Hewitt	Watson/Dodds
								Ferguson	*McKee*	*Napier*	*Weir*	*Jamieson*	*Archer*	*Fraser*	*Miller*	*Gordon*	*Roseburgh*	*McDonald*	
	This match was postponed from the Saturday, but conditions are arguably worse. In driving wind and rain Charlie Nicholas manufactures both Dons goals, with a cross and flick-on respectively. Hamilton are then awarded a soft penalty, but Stuart Gordon blazed wide from the spot.																		
27	H HEARTS 25/2	15,000	3 W 7	36	3-0	3-0	Irvine 24, McPherson 31 og, Wright 37 — Ref: J McCluskey	Snelders	McKimmie	Roberts'n D*	Robertson C	McLeish	Irvine	Mason	Grant	Wright	Connor	Hewitt*	Sandison/Ferguson
								Smith	*McLaren*	*McKinlay*	*McPherson*	*Berry*	*Levein*	*Galloway*	*Robertson**	*Colquhoun**	*Black*	*Bannon*	
	Aberdeen's biggest win of the season does little for Hearts' confidence on the eve of their UEFA Cup-tie with Bayern Munich. Brian Irvine headed in Paul Mason's free-kick. Wright then walked the ball round Henry Smith and Dave McPherson somehow put through his own goal.																		
28	H DUNDEE 11/3	11,800	2 W 9	38	2-0	1-0	Nicholas 36, Wright 64 — Ref: B McGinlay	Snelders	McKimmie	Robertson I	Grant	McLeish	Miller	Nicholas	Bett	Wright	Connor	Hewitt	Rafferty/McBride
								Geddes	*Forsyth*	*Holt*	*Chisholm*	*Craib*	*Saunders*	*Frail*	*McGeachie*	*Lawrence**	*Wright*	*Campbell**	
	Miller returns after a 14-match absence and plays with his right knee heavily strapped. Dundee's new manager is Gordon Wallace. Connor's cross and Hewitt's corner brought the goals. McLeish had captained Scotland in his 60th international v France in the World Cup in midweek.																		
29	A ST MIRREN 25/3	7,541	2 W 6	40	3-1	1-1	Wright 10, Nicholas 48, Mason 53 / Chalmers 44 — Ref: A Huett	Snelders	McKimmie*	Robertson I	Grant	McLeish	Miller	Nicholas	Bett	Wright*	Connor	Mason	Irvine/van der Ark
								Fridge	*Dawson*	*Winnie*	*Walker*	*Martin*	*Cooper*	*Shaw*	*Lambert**	*McGarvey**	*Chalmers*	*Cameron*	*McWalter/Kinnaird*
	Connor heads against the crossbar in the build-up to the first goal. Chalmers equalises from two yards from Lambert's cross. Paul Wright is fouled, enabling Nicholas to strike the free-kick past Les Fridge. Mason wrapped it up when Fridge and Martin dithered about challenging him.																		
30	H DUNDEE UTD 1/4	16,700	2 W 4	42	1-0	0-0	Nicholas 67 — Ref: J Duncan	Snelders	McKimmie	Robertson I	Grant	McLeish	Miller	Nicholas	Bett	van der Ark*	Connor	Hewitt*	Irvine/Dodds
								Thomson	*Cleland*	*Malpas*	*McInally*	*Hegarty*	*Narey*	*Irvine*	*McKinlay*	*Bowman**	*Sturrock*	*Gallacher*	*McGinnis/Adam*
	Paul Wright misses the game with a heavy cold and is replaced by van der Ark. Aberdeen's sixth league win in a row, and their first over United this season, is earned by Nicholas taking Bett's cross on the drop. United brought on £30,000 signing Charlie Adam from Brechin.																		
31	A HIBERNIAN 8/4	11,000	2 W 5	44	2-1	1-1	Mason 16, Bett 57p / Houchen 43 — Ref: H Williamson	Snelders	McKimmie	Irvine	Grant	McLeish	Miller	Nicholas*	Bett*	Wright	Connor	Mason	Robertson C/Hewitt
								Goram	*McIntyre*	*Sneddon**	*Orr*	*Rae*	*Mitchell*	*Houchen*	*Archibald*	*Kane*	*Collins*	*Evans*	*Tortolano*
	Hibs give a home debut to Keith Houchen, a £300,000 buy from Coventry. Nicholas has scored five times against Hibs already this season, but this time he leaves the glory to others. He supplies the killer pass for Mason's opener. Andy Goram clipped Wright's heels for Bett's penalty.																		

32 H HAMILTON 15/4 — 2 W 10 46 — 9,712 — **3-0** (1-0)

Mason 17, Nicholas 52, 75
Ref: W Crombie

| Snelders | McKimmie | Irvine | Grant* | McLeish | Miller | Nicholas | Bett | Wright | Connor | Mason | van der Ark |
| Ferguson | McKee | Napier | Weir | Martin | Miller | Harris* | Morrison | Gordon | Prentice* | McDonald | Archer/Andrews |

This is the day of the Hillsborough disaster in Sheffield. Hamilton ended a run of 11 league defeats by beating Celtic last week. Aberdeen's eighth successive league win brings them within two points of Rangers. Charlie Nicholas' two goals make him Scotland's leading scorer.

---

33 A HEARTS 22/4 — 2 L 6 46 — 13,367 — **0-1** (0-1)

Galloway 14
Ref: M McGinley

| Snelders | McKimmie* | Irvine | Grant | McLeish | Miller | Nicholas | Bett | Wright | Connor | Mason* | Hewitt/van der Ark |
| Smith | McLaren | McKinlay | McPherson | Berry | Sandison | Galloway | Ferguson* | Colquhoun | Black | Bannon* | Robertson/Jardine |

Aberdeen's slim hopes of the title are killed off by Mike Galloway's superb header, which saw him climb high above McKimmie. The Dons switched to 4-2-4 in the second half. The nearest they came was when Paul Wright's overhead kick hit a post and flew into Smith's arms.

---

34 H CELTIC 29/4 — 2 D 4 47 — 21,500 — **0-0** (0-0)

Ref: A Waddell

| Snelders | McKimmie | Robertson D | Grant | McLeish | Irvine | Nicholas | Bett | Wright* | Connor* | Mason | Watson/van der Ark |
| Bonner | Grant | Rogan | Aitken | McCarthy | Burns | Stark | McStay | Walter* | McGhee | Miller J | Elliott |

Theo Snelders suffered a jittery international debut for Holland in midweek, but recovers his confidence against Celtic. David Robertson returns after a lengthy knee injury. The half-time news that Rangers were leading Hearts 2-0 extinguished Aberdeen's last championship hopes.

---

35 H MOTHERWELL 6/5 — 2 D 9 48 — 6,500 — **0-0** (0-0)

Ref: K Hope

| Snelders | McKimmie | Roberts'n D* | Grant | McLeish | Irvine | Nicholas | Bett | van der Ark | Connor | Jess* | Watson/Mason |
| Maxwell | Wishart | Boyd* | Paterson | McAdam | McCart | Russell | O'Neill | Arnott | Kirk | Gahagan | Dolan |

Pittodrie's lowest gate of the season witnesses Aberdeen's third match without a goal. Eoin Jess enjoys a promising debut, though he was tightly marked by Wishart. Kirk scored four goals v St Mirren last week. Five minutes from time O'Neill shoots against Snelders' crossbar.

---

36 A RANGERS 13/5 — 2 W 1 50 — 42,480 — **3-0** (1-0)

Wright 43, Bett 51, van der Ark 72
Ref: R Valentine

| Snelders | McKimmie | Robertson D | Grant | McLeish | Irvine | van der Ark | Bett | Wright* | Connor | Mason* | Jess/Watson |
| Woods | Sterland | Munro | Gough | Roberts'n A* | Butcher | Drinkell | Ferguson | McCoist* | Brown | Walters | Cooper D/Gray |

The Dons spoil Rangers title celebrations, ending their 19-game unbeaten run with their heaviest defeat. Rangers' Sandy Robertson starts his first Premier game. Gers also have next week's Scottish Cup final to look forward to. Pick of Aberdeen's goals was Bett's 30-yard free-kick.

Average Home 14,107 Away 16,432

Skol League Cup

2 H ARBROATH 17/8 — W 4-0 — 9,139 — **2-0**

Bett 5, Hewitt 7, Miller 87, 89
Ref: R Valentine

| Snelders | McKimmie | Roberts'n D* | Simpson | McLeish | Miller | Gray* | Bett | Dodds! | Connor | Hewitt | Mason/Irvine |
| McAlpine | Mitchell | Jack | McEwan | Anderson P/Todd | Forrest* | Stewart | Brand | Fotheringm*Richardson | Tindal/McKenna |

The outcome was settled within seven minutes, with two quick Aberdeen goals. It therefore seems odd that the match would explode after 33 minutes with the sending off of Dodds and Arbroath's Paul Anderson for fisticuffs. Willie Miller's two late goals made him man of the match.

---

3 A MORTON 23/8 — W 2-1 — 3,131 — **1-1**

Bett 13, 47
Alexander 4
Ref: W Crombie

| Snelders | McKimmie | Robertson D | Simpson | McLeish | Miller | Irvine | Bett | Dodds | Connor | Hewitt* | Wright |
| Wylie | Collins | Hunter | Boag John | MacDonald Clinging | Ronald | McInnes | Alexander | Turner* | Fowler/Robertson D |

Brian Irvine wears No 7 but plays right-back. Rowan Alexander shocks the Dons when his header after four minutes. McLeish's head flick set up Bett's leveller. The Dons' winner came when Jim Bett burst through the middle. Not surprisingly, Bett was named man of the match.

QF A HIBERNIAN 31/8 — 4 W 2-1 (aet) — 13,500 — **1-1**

Nicholas 10, Grant 115
Kane 35
Ref: D Syme

| Snelders | McKimmie | Robertson D | Simpson | McLeish | Miller | Nicholas* | Bett | Dodds | Connor | Hewitt | Grant |
| Goram | Hunter | Sneddon | Orr | Rae | Milne | Tortolano* | Archibald | Kane | Collins | Evans* | McCluskey/Fellinger |

Six players were booked in this tense cup-tie, including both goalkeepers. Charlie Nicholas' near-post header gave the Dons an early advantage, cancelled out by Kane's angled drive. Seven minutes into extra time Grant replaced Nicholas and scored from Dodds' head flick.

SF N DUNDEE UTD 20/9 — 3 W 2-0 — 18,491 — **1-0** (at Dens Park)

Hewitt 2, Dodds 80
Ref: D Hope

| Snelders | McKimmie | Roberts'n D* | Simpson | McLeish | Miller | Nicholas | Bett | Dodds | Connor | Hewitt* | Mason/Grant |
| Thomson | Bowman | Malpas | McInally* | Hegarty | Narey | Paatelainen | McKinlay | Cleland | Gallacher | Meade* | Krivokapic/French |

Aberdeen have twice lost to Dundee United in this competition - in 1979-80 and again last season. The Dons enjoyed the luxury of a quick-fire goal, netted by John Hewitt and originating from Jim Bett's corner. Willie Miller was named man of the match.

F N RANGERS 23/10 — 3 L 2-3 — 72,122 — **1-1** (at Hampden)

Dodds 20, 63
McCoist 14p, 86, Ferguson 56
Ref: G Smith

| Snelders | McKimmie | Robertson D | Simpson* | McLeish | Miller | Nicholas | Bett | Dodds | Connor | Hewitt | Irvine |
| Woods | Stevens | Brown | Gough | Wilkins | Butcher | Drinkell | Ferguson I | McCoist | Cooper N | Walters |

Last season revisited. Kevin Drinkell intercepted David Robertson's throw to Snelders and was brought down for Ally McCoist's penalty. Two fine headers earn Dodds the man of the match award. The ball bobbed about before McCoist's winner. Bett and Dodds had late efforts blocked.

B & Q PREMIER (CUP-TIES)

Manager: Alex Smith & Jocky Scott

SEASON 1988-89

Scottish Cup

	1	2	3	4	5	6	7	8	9	10	11	subs used
3 A DUNFERMLINE 4 D 0-0 0-0 — 28/1, 16,656 1:1	Snelders	McKimmie	Robertson I	Simpson	McLeish	Irvine	Nicholas	Bett	Dodds	Connor	Mason*	Grant
(Dunfermline)	*Westwater*	*Robertson R*	*Smith R*	*Riddell*	*Tierney*	*Beedie*	*Burns*	*Smith P*	*Jack*	*Watson*	*Irons*	

Ref: D Syme

Aberdeen are indebted to wonder saves from Snelders to keep the Dons alive against the Division 1 pace-setters. Best of all was Snelders left-handed stop from Jack. East End Park's biggest crowd of the season enjoys end-to-end action. Willie Miller misses the game with knee trouble.

	1	2	3	4	5	6	7	8	9	10	11	subs used
3R H DUNFERMLINE 4 W 3-1 1-0 — 1/2, 21,500 1:1	Snelders	McKimmie	Robertson I	Simpson*	McLeish	Irvine	Nicholas	Bett	Dodds	Connor	Wright	Robertson C *Smith T/Smith M*
(Dunfermline)	*Westwater*	*Robertson G*	*Smith R*	*Riddell*	*Tierney*	*Beedie*	*Burns*	*Smith P*	*Jack*	*Watson**	*Irons**	

Scorers: Wright 3, 59, Nicholas 74, Smith T 84. Ref: D Syme

This cup-tie had a sting in the tail. At 2-0 Irvine handled a deflected ball, unseen by the referee. Irvine later fouled Trevor Smith in the box. Snelders saved Jack's penalty, but not Smith's follow-up. Four minutes from time Grant Tierney was stretchered off after a clash with Bett.

	1	2	3	4	5	6	7	8	9	10	11	subs used
4 H DUNDEE UTD 4 D 1-1 1-0 — 18/2, 23,000 2	Snelders	McKimmie	Robertson I	Simpson	McLeish	Irvine	Nicholas	Bett	Wright	Connor	van der Ark*	Hewitt
(Dundee Utd)	*Thomson*	*Clark*	*Malpas*	*McInally*	*Hegarty*	*Narey*	*French**	*Krivokapic*	*Gallacher*	*Bowman*	*Paatelainen Meade*	

Scorers: Connor 26, Paatelainen 46p. Ref: R Valentine

It took three ties to separate these sides in the Scottish Cup last season, and they have drawn three times this season. Connor netted from a pass by Nicholas lying on his back. Ian Robertson then tripped Gallacher, who was going nowhere. United later hit both posts within seconds.

	1	2	3	4	5	6	7	8	9	10	11	subs used
4R A DUNDEE UTD 4 D 1-1 0-0 (aet) — 22/2, 18,756	Snelders	McKimmie	Robertson I*	Simpson	McLeish	Irvine	Nicholas	Bett	Wright	Connor*	Hewitt	Dodds/Grant
(Dundee Utd)	*Thomson*	*Clark*	*Malpas*	*McInally*	*Hegarty*	*Narey*	*Meade**	*McGinnis*	*Gallacher*	*McKinlay**	*Paatelainen Sturrock/Krivokapic*	

Scorers: Grant 111, Paatelainen 93p. Ref: R Valentine

This is the 10th draw from the last 13 meetings between these sides. It is also the fifth draw this season. On each occasion the away team has come from behind to level. Alex McLeish handled for Paatelainen's extra-time penalty. Brian Grant then headed in Connor's corner-kick.

	1	2	3	4	5	6	7	8	9	10	11	subs used
4 RR A DUNDEE UTD 4 L 0-1 0-0 — 27/2, 21,095	Snelders	McKimmie	Robertson I	Simpson*	McLeish	Irvine	Nicholas	Bett	Wright	Connor	Grant	Dodds
(Dundee Utd)	*Thomson*	*Clark*	*Malpas*	*Meade**	*Hegarty*	*Narey*	*Krivokapic*	*McKinlay*	*Sturrock*	*Paatelainen McLeod*		

Scorers: Paatelainen 82. Ref: R Valentine

A tossed coin determined that United would have home advantage. United are without the injured Kevin Gallacher. Alex Smith said afterwards that if the match were settled on points, Aberdeen would have won. Paatelainen's 20-yarder settled the issue. He has scored in all three games.

UEFA Cup

	1	2	3	4	5	6	7	8	9	10	11	subs used
1:1 H DYNAMO DRESDEN (E Germ) D 0-0 0-0 — 7/9, 14,500	Snelders	McKimmie	Robertson D	Simpson	McLeish	Miller	Nicholas	Bett	Dodds	Connor	Hewitt*	Mason
(Dynamo Dresden)	*Teuber*	*Trautmann*	*Lieberman*	*Diebitz*	*Dotschner*	*Sammer*	*Stubner*	*Pilz*	*Kirsten*	*Hauptman*	*Kirschner*	

Ref: P Mikkelsen (Denmark)

Aberdeen's 18th European campaign, and their 8th in this competition. Among Dresden's four East German internationals is Matthias Sammer, a vital cog in Germany's Euro 96 winning side. Dresden retreated behind a five-man defence. Aberdeen played quite well but created little.

	1	2	3	4	5	6	7	8	9	10	11	subs used
1:2 A DYNAMO DRESDEN L 0-2 0-1 — 5/10, 36,000	Snelders	McKimmie	Robertson D	Simpson	McLeish	Miller	Mason*	Bett	Grant	Connor	Dodds	Wright
(Dynamo Dresden)	*Teuber*	*Trautmann*	*Lieberman*	*Diebitz*	*Dotschner*	*Sammer*	*Stubner*	*Pilz*	*Kirsten*	*Kirschner*	*Gutschow*	

Scorers: Gutschow 4, Kirsten 66. Ref: B Galler (Switzerland). (Dons lose 0-2 on aggregate)

On a good night for other Scottish teams in Europe Aberdeen fall victim to a catalogue of disasters. Nicholas and Hewitt failed fitness tests. Kirsten's speed made a quick goal for Gutschow and in 39 minutes it brought about David Robertson's expulsion. Bett's free-kick hit the post.

Appearances / Goals and League Tables — Aberdeen

League Table

	P	Home W	D	L	F	A	Away W	D	L	F	A	Pts
1 Rangers	36	15	1	2	39	11	11	3	4	23	15	56
2 ABERDEEN	36	10	7	1	26	10	8	7	3	25	15	50
3 Celtic	36	13	1	4	35	18	8	3	7	31	26	46
4 Dundee Utd	36	6	8	4	20	16	10	4	4	24	20	44
5 Hibernian	36	8	4	6	20	16	5	5	8	17	20	35
6 Hearts	36	7	6	5	22	17	2	7	9	13	25	31
7 St Mirren	36	5	6	7	17	19	6	1	11	22	36	29
8 Dundee	36	8	4	6	22	21	1	6	11	12	27	28
9 Motherwell	36	5	7	6	21	21	2	6	10	14	23	27
10 Hamilton	36	5	0	13	9	42	1	2	15	10	34	14
	360	82	44	54	231	191	54	44	82	191	231	360

Cup Records

	P	W	D	L	F	A	Pts	Cup	W	D	L	F	A	Pts	L
v Hamilton	4	3	1	0	7	1	7	Cup							
v Hibernian	4	3	1	0	6	2	7	LC	1	0	0	1	0	0	
v St Mirren	4	2	2	0	8	4	6								
v Motherwell	4	2	2	0	6	2	6								
v Hearts	4	2	1	1	5	2	5								
v Celtic	4	1	3	0	5	3	5	LC / SC	1 / 0	0 / 0	0 / 2	1 / 0	0 / 2	0 / 1	
v Dundee Utd	4	1	3	0	5	4	5								
v Dundee	4	2	1	1	4	3	5	LC	0	0	1	0	0	1	L
v Rangers	4	2	0	2	6	6	4								
	36	18	14	4	51	25	50								

Odds & ends

Never lost to: (5) Hamilton, Hibs, St Mirren, Motherwell, Celtic,
Dundee Utd (league only).
Never beat: (0).

Won from behind: (3) Rangers (h), Hibs (a), Morton (a).
Lost from in front: (0).

High spots: 16 unbeaten league games at the start of the season.
8 successive league wins from 21 January.
Reaching the Skol Cup final for the second successive year.

Low spots: Never scored more than 3 goals in any league match.
Only one player scored more than 6 league goals.
As in 1987-88, losing a Scottish Cup semi-final after two replays.
Losing the Skol Cup final to Rangers for the second successive year.

Aberdeen lost two fewer matches than champions Rangers.

Bogey-team: Rangers.
Ever-presents: (2) Theo Snelders, Robert Connor.
Hat-tricks: (0).
Leading scorer: (18) Charlie Nicholas.

Appearances / Goals

	Lge	Sub	LC	Sub	SC	Sub	Eur	Sub	Lge	LC	SC	Eur	Tot
Bett, Jim	31		5		5	2	2		5		3		8
Connor, Robert	36	6	5		5		2		4	1			5
Dodds, Davie	17	4	5		2	2	2		4		3		7
Grant, Brian	22			2	1	2	1		1	1	1		3
Gray, Steve	4		1										
Hewitt, John	21	6	5		1	1	1		3		2		5
Irvine, Brian	21	6	1	2	5				2				2
Jess, Eoin	1	1											
McKimmie, Stewart	35		5		5		2						
MacLeod, Andrew	1												
McLeish, Alex	34		5		5		2		4				4
Mason, Paul	21	7		2	1		2	1	1		2		3
Miller, Willie	21		5		5								
Nicholas, Charlie	28	1	3		5		1		16		1	1	18
Robertson, Craig	2	2											
Robertson, David	23		5			1	2						
Robertson, Ian	7												
Simpson, Neil	16		5		5		2						
Snelders, Theo	36		5		5		2						
van der Ark, Willem	4	4			1					2			2
Watson, Gregg		4											
Wright, Paul	15	8		1	4			1	6	2			8
(own-goals)									2				2
22 players used	396	49	55	7	55	6	22	2	51	12	5	0	68

B & Q SCOTTISH PREMIER

Manager: Alex Smith & Jocky Scott — SEASON 1989-90

No	Date	Att	Pos	Pt	F-A	H-T	Scorers, Times, and Referees	1	2	3	4	5	6	7	8	9	10	11	subs used
1	H 12/8 HIBERNIAN W 1-0	16,000	2		1-0	0-0	Mason 86 / Ref: J Renton	Snelders	McKimmie	Robertson D	Grant	Irvine	Miller	Nicholas	Bett	van der Ark*	Connor	Mason	Dodds
	(Hibernian)							*Goram*	*Kane*	*Sneddon*	*Cooper*	*Mitchell*	*Hunter*	*Weir**	*Orr*	*Evans*	*Hamilton*	*Findlay*	*Tortolano*

Paul Wright has gone to QPR and Aberdeen have signed no one. With four minutes left it seemed the Dons would fail to win their opening match for the fourth year running. Then Mason exchanged passes with Bett to net. After the match John Hewitt signed for Celtic for £250,000.

No	Date	Att	Pos	Pt	F-A	H-T	Scorers, Times, and Referees	1	2	3	4	5	6	7	8	9	10	11	subs used
2	A 19/8 MOTHERWELL D 0-0	6,491	2	3	0-0	0-0	Ref: McGinlay	Snelders	McKimmie	Robertson D	Simpson	Irvine	Miller	Nicholas	Bett	van der Ark*	Connor	Cameron	Mason
	(Motherwell)							*Maxwell*	*Burley*	*Boyd*	*Dolan*	*Philliben*	*McCart*	*Russell*	*O'Neill*	*Cusack**	*Kirk^*	*Mair*	*Arnott/McLean*

Motherwell's former Ranger Davie Cooper was ruled unfit. Aberdeen make their second trip to Fir Park in four days, having defeated Albion Rovers in the Skol Cup in midweek. This dour, dreary draw is put into perspective by Rangers, who have lost their first two and are bottom.

No	Date	Att	Pos	Pt	F-A	H-T	Scorers, Times, and Referees	1	2	3	4	5	6	7	8	9	10	11	subs used
3	H 26/8 DUNDEE W 1-0	12,500	2	5	1-0	0-0	Jess 56 / Ref: W Crombie	Snelders	McKimmie	Robertson D	Grant*	McLeish	Miller	Nicholas	Bett	Mason	Connor	Jess*	Cameron/Simpson
	(Dundee)							*Geddes*	*Shannon*	*Albiston*	*Craig**	*Chisholm*	*Forsyth*	*McGeachie*	*Beedie*	*Wright*	*Campbell A**	*McBride*	*McLeod/Harvey*

A congested midfield leaves the Dons with little option but to play the ball over the top. On the stroke of half-time the ball hits a Dundee arm and Aberdeen get a harsh penalty. Bett's spot-kick was saved. All ends well, however, as Eoin Jess scores his first goal for the Dons.

No	Date	Att	Pos	Pt	F-A	H-T	Scorers, Times, and Referees	1	2	3	4	5	6	7	8	9	10	11	subs used
4	A 9/9 RANGERS L 0-1	40,283	3	5	0-1	0-0	Johnston 53 / Ref: J McCuskey	Snelders	McKimmie	Robertson D	Grant	McLeish	Miller	Nicholas	Bett	Mason	Connor	van der Ark*	Robertson C
	(Rangers)							*Woods*	*Stevens*	*Munro*	*Brown**	*Wilkins*	*Butcher*	*Steven*	*Ferguson*	*Drinkell*	*Johnston^*	*Walters*	*Nisbet/McCoist*

Rangers begin and end this match bottom of the league. Mo Johnston, Rangers' £1.5 million Catholic signing from Nantes, scores with a close-in header from Trevor Steven's cross. Hans Krankl, manager of Aberdeen's UEFA Cup opponents Rapid Vienna, sees the Dons' first defeat.

No	Date	Att	Pos	Pt	F-A	H-T	Scorers, Times, and Referees	1	2	3	4	5	6	7	8	9	10	11	subs used
5	H 16/9 DUNFERMLINE W 2-1	13,000	2	7	2-1	1-0	Mason 15, Robertson C 65 / Jack 80p / Ref: R Orr	Snelders	McKimmie	Robertson D	Robertson C	McLeish	Miller	Nicholas	Bett	Mason	Connor	Jess*	van der Ark
	(Dunfermline)							*Westwater*	*Robertson*	*Rougvie*	*McCathie*	*Tierney*	*Abercrombie*	*Farningham*	*Kozma*	*Jack^*	*O'Boyle*	*Irons*	*van der Ark*

Paul Mason's dipping 20-yarder takes his tally to five. Craig Robertson adds a second, against his former club, after Westwater parried Connor's effort. David Robertson brought down Ross Jack for the penalty. The latest Dons old boy to line up against them is Doug Rougvie.

No	Date	Att	Pos	Pt	F-A	H-T	Scorers, Times, and Referees	1	2	3	4	5	6	7	8	9	10	11	subs used
6	A 23/9 ST MIRREN W 2-0	5,872	1	9	2-0	1-0	Mason 12, Grant 76 / Ref: D Hope	Snelders	McKimmie	Robertson D	Grant	McLeish	Miller	Nicholas	Bett	Mason	Connor	Cameron*	van der Ark
	(St Mirren)							*Fridge*	*Wilson*	*Black*	*Walker**	*Manley*	*Winnie*	*Shaw*	*Martin*	*Torfason**	*McWalter*	*Kinnaird*	*Chalmers/Davies*

Not as comfortable as the score suggests, for Snelders made super saves from Winnie, McWalter and Chalmers. Mason's sixth goal of the season was followed by Grant's tap in after Nicholas had done all the work. This win keeps Aberdeen top and St Mirren bottom.

No	Date	Att	Pos	Pt	F-A	H-T	Scorers, Times, and Referees	1	2	3	4	5	6	7	8	9	10	11	subs used
7	H 30/9 CELTIC D 1-1	21,374	1	10	1-1	0-0	McLeish 47 / Miller 62 / Ref: A Waddell	Snelders	McKimmie	Robertson C	Grant*	McLeish	Miller	Nicholas	Bett	Mason	Connor	Cameron*	Irvine/van der Ark
	(Celtic)							*Bonner*	*Morris*	*Rogan*	*Aitken*	*Elliott*	*Whyte*	*Galloway*	*McStay*	*Dziek`owski**	*Walker**	*Miller*	*Coyne*

Having dumped Celtic from the Skol Cup, Aberdeen move two points clear at the top, despite dropping a point. Paul Mason's cross had found Alex McLeish's head for the opener, but Joe Miller capitalised for Celtic when Mike Galloway's cross was deflected out by Willie Miller.

No	Date	Att	Pos	Pt	F-A	H-T	Scorers, Times, and Referees	1	2	3	4	5	6	7	8	9	10	11	subs used
8	A 4/10 DUNDEE UTD L 0-2	11,879	1	10	0-2	0-1	McInally 44, Malpas 54 / Ref: A Huett	Snelders	McKimmie	Robert's'n C*	Grant	McLeish	Miller	Nicholas	Bett	Mason*	Connor	van der Ark	Irvine/Cameron
	(Dundee Utd)							*Thomson*	*Cleland*	*Malpas*	*McInally*	*Clark*	*Narey*	*Jackson**	*Bowman*	*Gallacher*	*O'Neill^*	*Krivokapic*	*McGinnis/McLeod*

Aberdeen play Charlie Nicholas alone up front, leaving the Dons like a paper tiger in attack. Jim McInally rounded Willie Miller to put United one up. Malpas added a second when his shot rebounded back to him on the run. This will be United's only win over the Dons in five matches.

No	Date	Att	Pos	Pt	F-A	H-T	Scorers, Times, and Referees	1	2	3	4	5	6	7	8	9	10	11	subs used
9	H 14/10 HEARTS L 1-3	15,000	5	10	1-3	0-1	van der Ark 90 / McKinlay 20, Crabbe 58, 71 / Ref: D Syme	Snelders	McKimmie	Robertson D	Robertson C*	McLeish	Miller	Nicholas*	Bett	Mason	Connor	Cameron*	Grant/van der Ark
	(Hearts)							*Smith*	*McLaren*	*McKinlay*	*Levein*	*McCreery*	*McPherson*	*Colquhoun*	*Mackay*	*Foster**	*Crabbe*	*Bannon*	*Robertson*

Aberdeen tumble down to fifth and lose their unbeaten home record. On a rain-sodden pitch McKinlay finds the top corner with a 25-yard volley, and Scott Crabbe adds insult to injury with two close-range efforts. Now the Dons must pick themselves up for the Skol Cup final.

No	Date	Att	Pos	Pt	F-A	H-T	Scorers, Times, and Referees	1	2	3	4	5	6	7	8	9	10	11	subs used
10	A 25/10 HIBERNIAN W 3-0	12,000	4	12	3-0	1-0	Robertson C 4, Mason 46, van der Ark 59 / Ref: M McGinley	Snelders	McKimmie	Robertson D	Robertson C*	McLeish	Miller	Nicholas*	Bett	Mason	Connor	Jess*	Harvie/Nicholas
	(Hibernian)							*Goram*	*Kane*	*Hamilton*	*Cooper*	*Mitchell**	*Hunter*	*Weir**	*Orr*	*Houchen*	*Collins*	*Evans*	*McGinlay/Archibald*

The Dons are on Cloud Nine after winning their first trophy in four seasons. They inflict Hibs' first home defeat on a wet and windy night. The key player is undoubtedly Paul Mason, who in addition to rounding Pane Kane for his goal, supplies the crosses for two scoring headers.

11 | H **MOTHERWELL** 28/10 — 13,500 — 2 W 1-0 — 6 14
1-0 Bett 34p
Ref: G Smith

Snelders McKimmie Robertson D* Robertson C McLeish Miller Nicholas Bett Mason Connor van der Ark Irvine
Maxwell Burley Boyd Paterson McAdam McCart Russell Reilly^ Arnott* Kirk Cooper Cusack/Dolan

Willie Miller shows off the Skol Cup before kick-off. Aberdeen enjoy a lucky break early on, when Arnott heads against Theo Snelders' crossbar. Paul Mason, sprinting into the box, is then upended by McAdam, and Jim Bett sends Maxwell the wrong way from the spot.

---

12 | A **DUNDEE** 4/11 — 7,041 — 2 D 1-1 — 10 15
1-0 Connor 13
Dodds 90
Ref: J McGilvray

Snelders McKimmie Irvine Roberts'n C* McLeish Miller van der Ark Bett Mason Connor Jess Grant
Carson Forsyth Shannon Beedie Chisholm Saunders Frail^ McLeod^ Wright Dodds McBride Albiston/Campbell A

Four minutes of injury time have elapsed when Billy Dodds fires goalwards from 15 yards and sees the ball fly in off Stewart McKimmie. It was a cruel counter to Robert Connor's 40-yard run and shot, and enables Rangers to overtake the Dons at the top on goal-difference.

---

13 | A **DUNFERMLINE** 18/11 — 11,882 — 2 W 3-0 — 4 17
2-0 Gillhaus 12, 14, Robertson D 75
Ref: J Herald

Snelders McKimmie Robertson D Grant McLeish Irvine Nicholas Bett* Mason Connor Gillhaus^ Robertson C/van Ark
Westwater Robertson Rougvie McCathie Tierney* Sharp Smith Rafferty Jack O'Boyle Kozma^ Wilson/Farningham

Willie Miller was crocked against Norway in midweek. Hearts, Rangers and Aberdeen are tied on 17 points. Dunfermline were unbeaten in eight games, but are overturned by stylish Aberdeen. Hans Gillhaus enjoys a sensational debut, scoring with an overhead kick and a header.

---

14 | H **RANGERS** 22/11 — 23,000 — W 1-0 — 19
1-0 Gillhaus 25
Ref: D Syme

Snelders McKimmie Robertson D Grant McLeish Irvine Nicholas* Bett Mason Connor Gillhaus van der Ark
Woods Stevens Munro Brown Wilkins Butcher Steven Ferguson McCoist Johnston Walters

Record singing Hans Gillhaus is an instant hit at Pittodrie. Charlie Nicholas lays the ball off to him and Gillhaus takes aim for the far corner from 20 yards. Ally McCoist ends the match still trying to equal Frank McGarvey's Premier League scoring record of 127 goals.

---

15 | H **ST MIRREN** 25/11 — 13,500 — 1 W 5-0 — 9 21
3-0 Nicholas 6, 22, 33, McLeish 70, [Mason 80]Money
Ref: G Evans

Snelders McKimmie Roberts'n D* Grant McLeish Irvine Nicholas Bett Mason^ Connor Gillhaus Robertson C/van Ark
Carson Wishart Black Lambert Godfrey* Manley Kinnaird Martin Torfason McDowall^ McWhirter Davies/McWalter

A noisy group of Dutchmen descend on Pittodrie to cheer on Aberdeen's three Dutch imports. Charlie Nicholas's first goal of the season is set up by Gillhaus, who does not score but hits the woodwork. Gillhaus was also felled in the penalty box, but Jim Bett's penalty was saved.

---

16 | A **CELTIC** 2/12 — 38,300 — 1 L 0-1 — 3 21
0-0 Walker 65p
Ref: W Crombie

Snelders McKimmie Robertson D Grant* McLeish Irvine Nicholas* Bett Mason Connor Gillhaus Robertson C/van Ark
Bonner Morris Wdowczyk Aitken Elliott Whyte Grant McStay Dziek'owski Walker* Hewitt Galloway

A game of two penalties. David Robertson needlessly sticks out a hand to interrupt ex-Don John Hewitt's shot. Nine minutes from time Gillhaus was hacked down from behind by Paul Elliott, who luckily escaped dismissal. Bonner guessed right and saved Gillhaus's spot-kick.

---

17 | H **DUNDEE UTD** 9/12 — 15,500 — 1 W 2-0 — 5 23
0-0 Nicholas 50, Mason 75
Ref: P Yeats

Snelders McKimmie Robertson D Grant McLeish Irvine Nicholas Bett Mason Connor* Gillhaus van der Ark
Main van d'Hoorn Malpas McInally McGinnis Narey McKinlay Bowman O'Neill Paatelainen^Gallacher Cleland/Hinds

Van der Ark is the player to lose his place, following the arrival of Gillhaus, who heads in McKimmie's cross after three minutes but is given offside. United keeper Alan Main got his hand to Nicholas's 20-yarder but could not keep it out. Mason's goal from a tight angle is his 11th.

---

18 | A **HEARTS** 20/12 — 11,370 — 4 D 1-1 — 24
0-1 Grant 59
Robertson 20
Ref: D Syme

Snelders McKimmie Robertson D Grant McLeish Irvine Nicholas Bett Mason Connor Gillhaus
Smith McLaren McKinlay Levein McCreery^ McPherson Colquhoun Mackay Robertson Crabbe* Bannon Kidd/Sandison

An incident-packed match. As early as the fourth minute a Gary Mackay free-kick rebounded off Snelders' upright. John Robertson diverted Levein's header to give Hearts a merited lead. Aberdeen salvaged a point with Brian Grant's near-post header from Charlie Nicholas's cross.

---

19 | H **HIBERNIAN** 26/12 — 16,500 — L 1-2 — 24
0-1 Grant 47
Archibald 29, Kane 56
Ref: D Hope

Watt McKimmie Robertson D Grant* McLeish Irvine Nicholas Bett Mason Connor* Gillhaus^ Robertson C/van Ark
Goram Kane Sneddon Cooper Mitchell Hunter Orr Archibald^ Evans Collins Hamilton Houchen

In terms of the title chase this is a dreadful result for Aberdeen. Ex-Don Neil Cooper's savage tackle took Gillhaus from the pitch after 18 minutes. The deciding goal came from Irvine upending Archibald. Paul Kane's 22-yard free-kick was deflected past debutant Michael Watt.

---

20 | A **MOTHERWELL** 30/12 — 7,267 — 2 D 2-2 — 8 25
1-0 van der Ark 33, 54
Cooper 74p, 76
Ref: G Evans

Watt McKimmie Cameron Grant McLeish Irvine Nicholas Simpson Mason Connor van der Ark* Robertson C
Maxwell Burley Boyd Paterson Philliben McCart* Arnott O'Neill Cusack! Kirk Cooper^ Russell/Gahagan

Gillhaus's injury allows van der Ark to return. He becomes hero and villain. Two goals - both with his feet - are followed by a senseless foul on O'Neill, which results in a booking for Ark and a penalty for Davie Cooper. At 0-0 Nick Cusack had lunged at Irvine and been expelled.

---

21 | H **DUNDEE** 2/1 — 16,054 — 10 W 5-2 — 27
4-2 Grant 13, Ark 36, 45, Bett 37, Nicholas 75, Wright 11, Campbell D 23
Ref: H Williamson

Watt McKimmie Watson G Grant McLeish Irvine Nicholas Bett Mason Connor* van der Ark Simpson/Jess
Carson Dinnie Shannon Chisholm Forsyth Craib Campbell D Beedie* Wright Dodds McLeod Craig

The Dons trail twice to the bottom team. Keith Wright did most of the damage, and Aberdeen must regret not signing him. The Dons were lucky when Irvine lashed Campbell's cross into Watt's side-netting. Pick of Aberdeen's five-goals was Ark's 30-yarder after 45 minutes.

B & Q SCOTTISH PREMIER

Manager: Alex Smith & Jocky Scott

SEASON 1989-90

No	Date	Att	Pos	Pt	F-A	H-T	Scorers, Times, and Referees	1	2	3	4	5	6	7	8	9	10	11	Subs used
22	A RANGERS 6/1	41,351	1	L 27	0-2	0-0	Walters 77, McCoist 88 — Ref: B McGinlay	Watt	McKimmie	Gillhaus*	Grant	McLeish	Irvine	Nicholas*	Bett	Mason	Connor	van der Ark*	Simpson/Robertson C
								Woods	Stevens	Munro	Gough	Spackman	Butcher	Steven	Walters*	McCoist	Johnston		Vanicombe, Brown
23	H DUNFERMLINE 13/1	14,000	2	W 29	4-1	4-1	Grant 15, Mason 38, Nicholas 39, Irons 16, [Bett 40] — Ref: J McGilvray	Watt	McKimmie	Robertson D	Grant*	McLeish	Irvine	Nicholas	Bett	Mason	Connor	van der Ark*	Simpson/Jess
								Westwater	Nicholl*	Rougvie	McCathie	Bonnyman	Manley	Martin	Rafferty	Gallagher	O'Boyle	Irons*	Smith/Jack
24	A ST MIRREN 27/1	7,855	3	L 29	0-1	0-1	McDowall 6 — Ref: K Hope	Watt	McKimmie	Robertson I*	Grant	McLeish	Irvine	Nicholas*	Simpson	Mason	Connor	van der Ark	Robertson C/Gillhaus
								Money	Wishart	Black	Davies	Godfrey	Manley	Martin	Lambert	McWalter	McDowall		Kinnaird
25	H HEARTS 3/2	15,000	3	D 30	2-2	2-1	Nicholas 19p, 45, Sandison 17, Ferguson 86 — Ref: J McCluskey	Snelders	McKimmie	Robertson I	Grant	McLeish	Irvine	Nicholas	Watson Gg	Gillhaus	Connor	van der Ark	
								Smith	Kidd	McKinlay*	Levein	McCreery*	McPherson	Colquhoun	Sandison	Robertson	Crabbe	Bannon	Mackay/Ferguson
26	A DUNDEE UTD 10/2	10,533	2	D 31	1-1	1-0	Mason 10, McInally 56 — Ref: A Waddell	Watt	McKimmie	Robertson I	Grant	McLeish	Irvine	Nicholas	van der Ark	Mason	Connor	Gillhaus*	Cameron
								Main	van d'Hoom	Malpas	McInally	Krivokapic	Narey	Preston	McKinnon	Jackson	Connolly*	Paatelainen	Clark
27	H CELTIC 17/2	22,100	2	D 32	1-1	1-0	Nicholas 11, McStay 59 — Ref: D Syme	Mimms	McKimmie	Robertson I*	Grant	McLeish	Irvine	Nicholas	Bett*	Mason	Connor	Gillhaus	Roberts'n C/Cameron
								Bonner	Morris	Wdowczyk	Galloway	Elliott	Whyte	Grant	McStay	Dziek'owski	Coyne	Fulton*	Miller
28	A DUNFERMLINE 3/3	8,228	2	W 34	4-2	1-0	Mason 34, Nicholas 53, Gillhaus 75, 79, Tierney 69, Gallagher 71 — Ref: D McVicar	Mimms	McKimmie	Robertson I*	Grant	McLeish	Irvine	Nicholas	Bett*	Mason	Connor	Gillhaus	
								Westwater	Nicholl	Wilson	McCathie	Tierney	Sharp	Smith	Rafferty	Jack	Gallagher	Kozma	
29	A HIBERNIAN 10/3	9,550	7	L 34	2-3	0-1	van der Ark 84, Hunter 86 og, Orr 40, McGinlay 71, Wright 89 — Ref: L Thow	Mimms	McKimmie	Irvine	Grant*	McLeish	Miller	Nicholas	Bett	Mason	Connor	Gillhaus	Robertson C/van Ark
								Goram	Kane	Sneddon	Miller	Mitchell	Hunter	Orr*	Hamilton	Houchen	Collins	McGinlay	Wright
30	H MOTHERWELL 24/3	10,000	2	W 36	2-0	1-0	Gillhaus 5, 74 — Ref: J Duncan	Mimms	McKimmie	Harvie	Robertson C	McLeish	Irvine	Nicholas	Bett*	Mason	van der Ark*	Gillhaus	Grant/Jess
								Maxwell	Burley	Gardner	Dolan	McNair	McCart	Arnott	Russell	Cusack	Kirk	Mair*	Gahagan
31	A DUNDEE 31/3	8,071	2	D 37	1-1	1-1	Gillhaus 34, Wright 14 — Ref: L Mottram	Mimms	McKimmie	Connor	Grant	McLeish	Irvine	Nicholas	Bett	Mason	van der Ark*	Gillhaus	Robertson C
								Mathers	Forsyth	Shannon	Chisholm	Jamieson	Duffy	Campbell*	Dinnie	Wright	Dodds	McLeod	Campbell

22 — Aberdeen play second fiddle throughout, failing to win a corner until the second half, and not having their first shot until the 67th minute. Mark Walters wrong-foots McLeish for Rangers' opener, and Vinnicombe crosses for McCoist to add a second and open a four-point lead at the top.

23 — This match was marked by two goals in one minute, followed by three Dons goals in two minutes. Irons' downward header cancelled out Nicholas's pull-back to Brian Grant. Then comes the blitz: Paul Mason's 20-yarder, Nicholas's overhead kick, Jim Bett's long-range volley.

24 — Kenny McDowall's early header, which stemmed from Stewart McKimmie's foul on Kinnaird, proved to be the goal which sent the Dons down to third, six points behind Rangers. Charlie Nicholas was so ineffectual he was pulled off to make way for the fit-again Gillhaus.

25 — Another precious point slips away, this time through a penalty four minutes from time, when Snelders indulged in some argy-bargy at a Hearts corner. Snelders kept out John Robertson's spot-kick, but not Ferguson's follow-up. Aberdeen's penalty was given when Kidd felled Gillhaus.

26 — Van der Ark becomes the first Don sent off this season. Having been booked just after the hour, he then protested too loudly when Connor does not win a penalty. Paul Mason began and ended the move which put Aberdeen in front. Connor might have cleared before McInally levelled.

27 — For the umpteenth time this season Aberdeen score first but fail to win. A long clearance by on-loan keeper Bobby Mimms lit the fuse for Nicholas's goal. Joe Miller's 50-yard raid down the touchline set up McStay's equaliser. Celtic are unbeaten at Pittodrie for three years.

28 — Willie Miller returns after three and a half months. Four goals in 10 minutes leave the spectators breathless. Nicholas scores his first away goal of the season. Tierney's header and Gallagher's hook pull the Pars level. Bett is fouled and Gillhaus fires in a 20-yard free kick to make it 3-2.

29 — A game of two Willie Millers, one on each side. Former Don Paul Wright, who arrived at Hibs via QPR, netted from the edge of the box in the last minute to inflict Aberdeen's first defeat at Easter Road for 6½ years. Minutes earlier Hunter had deflected Bett's shot past Andy Goram.

30 — Motherwell have a UEFA Cup place in their sights. Robert Connor's calf-strain enabled Scott Harvie to make a rare appearance. Hans Gillhaus intercepted Dolan's attempted headed back-pass to Maxwell, and later added a second when heading in from Paul Mason's corner-kick.

31 — This has been a poor, low scoring season in the Premier League. Dundee are bottom, with 37 goals, which is only two fewer than Rangers, who are top. Aberdeen have scored the most, 50. Dundee's Chisholm cut the ball back to Keith Wright. Nicholas then laid a goal in for Gillhaus.

No		Date	Opponent	Att		Result	HT	Scorers	Ref
32	H	8/4	RANGERS	23,000	2 D 1 38	0-0	0-0		Ref: D Syme
33	H	18/4	DUNDEE UTD	10,000	2 W 40	1-0	0-0	Grant 82	Ref: W Crombie
34	A	21/4	HEARTS	11,616	3 L 2 40	0-1	0-0	Mackay 78	Ref: M McGinley
35	H	28/4	ST MIRREN	7,977	3 W 9 42	2-0	0-0	Irvine 75, Nicholas 86	Ref: J Renton
36	A	2/5	CELTIC	20,154	W 44	3-1	0-1	Jess 56, 57, Watson Graham 70 (Walker 3)	Ref: D Hope

Average Home 15,400 — Away 14,983

Match 32 — v Rangers
Mimms, McKimmie, Connor, Grant, McLeish, Irvine, Nicholas, Bett, Mason, Simpson*, Cameron
Woods, Stevens^, Munro, Gough, Spackman, Butcher, Steven, Ferguson^*, McCoist, Johnston, Walters, Dodds/Brown
This Sunday match saw nae goals and nae fitba. Martial arts outweighed footballing arts, yet Gillhaus and John Brown were the only players booked. Neither keeper was tested until the 65th minute when Woods parried point-blank from Grant. Rangers stay six points out in front.

Match 33 — v Dundee Utd
Snelders, Watson Gg*, Robertson D, Grant, McLeish, Irvine, Nicholas, Bett, Mason*, Connor, Gillhaus
Main, Clark, Welsh, McInally, Krivokapic, Narey, O'Neil, French, Jackson^, McKinnon^, Preston, Cleland/Paatelainen
Having beaten United 4-0 in the Scottish Cup on Saturday, this was something of an anti-climax. Jim McLean reshuffled his team but could not prevent another Dons win. Bett's cross was deflected into the path of Brian Grant. Gregg Watson started the match in place of McKimmie.

Match 34 — v Hearts
Snelders, Watson Gra, Robertson D, Grant, McLeish, Irvine, Jess, Bett*, Mason, Connor, Gillhaus
Smith, McLaren, McKinlay, Levein, Berry, McPherson, Colquhoun^, Mackay, Robertson, Foster, Bannon, Crabbe/Kirkwood*
Minds are on Hampden, which explains this toothless end-of-season affair. Charlie Nicholas is unhappy at Aberdeen. He wants away and is dropped. The winning goal came when Scott Crabbe shot, McLeish blocked, and Gary Mackay fired in. Hearts overtake the Dons by one point.

Match 35 — v St Mirren
Snelders, Robertson C, Watson Gra*, Grant, Irvine, Miller, Nicholas*, Jess, Mason, Connor, Gillhaus
Money, Wishart^, Black, Lambert, McWhirter, Manley, Shaw, Martin, Stickroth, Torfason, Kinnaird, McGill/McIntosh*
End of season tedium. Stephen Wright and Scott Booth make their debuts. Willie Miller also returns to the fray, but his right knee pains him. Will he or won't he make it for the Scottish Cup final? Nicholas's corner led to the first goal, his header from Booth's cross added a second.

Match 36 — v Celtic
Snelders, McKimmie, Robertson D, Watson Gra*, Irvine, Miller, Nicholas C, Simpson C, Booth, Jess, Cameron, Watson Gg
Bonner, Galloway, Wdowczyk, Grant, Rogan, Whyte, Stark^, Simpson, McStay, Dziekan'owski/Walker, Fulton^, Miller/Creaney
These teams meet again at Hampden in 10 days. Several Dons in this match know they will not be called upon in the final. Jess's two goals in a minute wipe out Walker's early strike, when Snelders could only parry Dziekanowski's hook. This win allows the Dons to finish above Hearts.

Skol League Cup

No		Date	Opponent	Att		Result	HT	Scorers	Ref
2	A	16/8	ALBION ROVERS (at Fir Park)	2,384	W	2-0	1-0	Robertson D41, van der Ark 88	Ref: J Duncan
3	H	23/8	AIRDRIE	10,000	W	4-0	2-0	Mason 34, 86, Cameron 38, Bett 81	Ref: J Duncan
QF	H	30/8	ST MIRREN	11,500	W	3-1	1-0	Mason 8, Bett 46p, Winnie 68 og, Shaw 65	Ref: D Syme
SF	N	20/9	CELTIC (at Hampden)	45,367	W	1-0	0-0	Cameron 76	Ref: B McGinlay
F	N	22/10	RANGERS (at Hampden)	61,190	W	2-1	1-1 (aet)	Mason 20, 102, Walters 34p	Ref: G Smith

Skol 2 — v Albion Rovers
Snelders, McKimmie, McCulloch, Robertson D, Grant, Irvine, Miller, Nicholas, Bett, Dodds*, Connor, Mason*
McCulloch, McDonald, McGowan, McKenzie, Oliver, Watson^, Clark, Cadden, Graham, Chapman, Granger^, Teevan/McAnenay
With half-time approaching David Robertson heads in Robert Connor's corner. Dons' new £250,000 signing from St Mirren, Ian Cameron, comes off the bench to provide the cross for van der Ark's header. Albion Rovers' Jim Chapman was declared man of the match.

Skol 3 — v Airdrie
Snelders, McKimmie, Robertson D, Irvine, McLeish, Miller, Nicholas, Bett, Mason, Connor, Cameron*
Martin, Boyle, Jack, McKeown, Grant, McPhee, Lawrence, Butler, Balfour, Conn, MacDon'ld, MacDonald K*
Paul Mason's two goals made him man of the match. Ian Cameron bags his first goal for the club – a header. Bett's goal was deflected. Though Airdrie got little change from Aberdeen's three-man central defence of Miller, McLeish, and Brian Irvine, they did hit the post at 2-0.

Skol QF — v St Mirren
Snelders, McKimmie, Robertson D, Grant, McLeish, Miller, Nicholas, Bett, Mason, Connor, Jess*
Money, Wilson, Black, Walker, Martin, Winnie, Shaw, Kinnaird, Torfason, Davies^, Weir, Godfrey/Lambert*
Davie Dodds has signed for Rangers for £125,000. On a foul evening, Saints were up against it from the moment Mason's shot squeezed under Money. Bett's penalty was punishment for Black 'saving' McLeish's header. Shaw scored the first goal conceded by Aberdeen this season.

Skol SF — v Celtic
Snelders, McKimmie, Robertson D, Roberts'n C*, McLeish, Miller, Nicholas, Bett, Mason, Connor, Cameron^
Bonner, Rogan, Aitken^, McCahill, Burns, Galloway, McStay, Dziekan'ski, Coyne, Fulton, Miller^, Walker*
Celtic's best chances came early, and they missed them all. Ian Cameron set up a place in the final with a crisp shot from 22 yards, earning him the man of the match award. Celtic's Roy Aitken was booked in the first half for fouling Cameron and sent in injury time for toppling Bett.

Skol F — v Rangers
Snelders, McKimmie, Robertson D, Grant, McLeish, Miller, Nicholas, Bett, Mason, Connor, Jess*
Woods, Stevens, Munro, Gough, Wilkins, Butcher, Steven, Ferguson, McCoist, Johnston, Walters, McCall*
The bookies offer Rangers '15-8 on' to win. Rangers are going for their fourth Skol Cup, having won their previous 19 ties. Mason outjumps Munro – 1-0. McCoist backs into Miller yet wins a farcical penalty – 1-1. In extra-time Mason fires through a ruck of players to win the Cup.

B & Q PREMIER (CUP-TIES)

Manager: Alex Smith & Jocky Scott

SEASON 1989-90

Scottish Cup

		F-A	H-T	Scorers, Times, and Referees
3 A PARTICK THISTLE 2	W	6:2	2:2	Ark 18, 47, 89, Grant 43, Kerr 65 og, Watt
20/1 11,875 1:3				Campbell 3, Charnley 36p [Mason 72]Duncan
				Ref: D Hope
4 H MORTON 2	W	2:1	0:1	Gillhaus 56, Nicholas 76
24/2 14,500 1:8				Turner 3
				Ref: W Crombie
QF H HEARTS 2	W	4:1	1:1	Bett 7, Gillhaus 55, Irvine 59,
17/3 22,500 3				Colquhoun 38 [Nicholas 84]
				Ref: D Syme
SF N DUNDEE UTD 2	W	4:0	2:0	Irvine 11, Paatelainen 36 og,
14/4 16,581 4				van der Hoorn 58 og, Gillhaus 85
(at Tannadice)				Ref: D Hope
F N CELTIC 2	W	0:0	0:0	
12/5 60,493 5		(aet)		
(at Hampden)				Ref: G Smith
				(Dons win 9-8 on penalties)

Team line-ups

	1	2	3	4	5	6	7	8	9	10	11	subs used
3 A PARTICK THISTLE	Watt	McKimmie	Robertson I	Grant	McLeish	Irvine	Nicholas*	Simpson	Mason	Connor	van der Ark^	Jass/Robertson C
(Partick Thistle)	Duncan	Kennedy*	Law	Kerr	Collins	Flood	Corrie	Jardine	Campbell	Gallagher	Charnley	Mitchell/Craig
4 H MORTON	Mimms	McKimmie	Robertson I	Grant	McLeish	Irvine	Nicholas	Bett	Mason	Connor	Gillhaus	McInnes/Boag John
(Morton)	Wylie	Collins	Pickering	Reid	O'Hara	Hunter	Turner	McDonald*	Alexander	Fowler	McNeil^	
QF H HEARTS	Mimms	McKimmie	Connor	Grant*	McLeish	Irvine	Nicholas	Bett	Mason	van der Ark^	Gillhaus	Roberts'n C/Cameron
(Hearts)	Smith	Kidd	McKinlay	Levein	McCreery	McPherson	Colquhoun	Berry	Robertson	Crabbe*	Bannon^	Foster/Mackay
SF N DUNDEE UTD	Snelders	McKimmie	Robertson D	Grant*	McLeish	Irvine	Nicholas*	Bett	Mason	Connor	Gillhaus	Watson Gra/van Ark
(Dundee Utd)	Main	van d'Hoorn	Clark	McInally	Krivokapic	Narey	McKinlay	Bowman	Jackson	Connolly^	Paatelainen	French
F N CELTIC	Snelders	McKimmie	Robertson D	Grant	McLeish	Irvine	Nicholas	Bett	Mason*	Connor	Gillhaus	Watson Gra
(Celtic)	Bonner	Wdowczyk	Rogan	Grant	Elliott	Whyte	Stark*	McStay	Dziek'owski	Walker*	Miller	Galloway/Coyne

Notes:

Partick Thistle — Aberdeen score six without the injured Gillhaus. Thistle twice take the lead, first when Watt parries Flood's effort, and second when Irvine fouled Calum Campbell in the box. Gillhaus's replacement, van der Ark, helps himself to a hat-trick as Thistle wilt in the second half.

Morton — Morton, like Partick in the previous round, take a third-minute lead. Turner heads past Mimms from a tight angle. Fowler's floater then hit the Dons crossbar. Gillhaus's header after the break calmed the nerves. Nicholas lashed the winner after the ball flew around the penalty box.

Hearts — This time an early goal for the Dons as Bett fires in from 20 yards. Hearts level from a disputed corner. Bobby Mimms saves from Crabbe but Colquhoun follows up. Aberdeen go on the rampage in the second half, yet still allow keeper Henry Smith to make several fine saves.

Dundee Utd — United have beaten Aberdeen in protracted cup-ties twice in previous seasons. David Robertson returns after cracking a bone in his foot in December. Aberdeen play in all white. Two own goals for the Dons. One of them was vainly claimed by Brian Irvine, the man of the match..

Celtic — Not the best of finals, which goes to a penalty shoot-out for the first time. Celtic are underdogs, and must win or miss out on Europe for the first time in 12 seasons. It is Charlie Nicholas' last match for the Dons. At 8-8 on penalties Snelders saves from Rogan. Irvine kicks the winner.

UEFA Cup

		F-A	H-T	Scorers, Times, and Referees
1:1 H RAPID VIENNA 3	W	2:1	0:1	Robertson C 76, Grant 88
13/9 (Austria) 16,800				Kranjcar 7
				Ref: E Negreira (Spain)
1:2 A RAPID VIENNA 1	L	0:1	0:1	Fjortoft 17
27/9 19,000				Ref: D Pauly (W Germany)
				(Dons lose on away-goals rule)

	1	2	3	4	5	6	7	8	9	10	11	subs used
1:1 H RAPID VIENNA	Snelders	McKimmie	Roberts'n C*	Simpson	McLeish	Miller	Nicholas	Bett	Mason*	Connor	Jess^	Grant/van der Ark
(Rapid Vienna)	Konsel	Reisinger	Blizenec	Pecl	Schottel	Kienast	Keglevits	Pfeif'berger	Kranjcar*	Herzog	Fjortoft^	Weber/Polger
1:2 A RAPID VIENNA	Snelders	McKimmie	Roberts'n C*	Irvine	McLeish	Miller	Nicholas	Bett	Mason	Connor	Cameron^	Grant/van der Ark
(Rapid Vienna)	Konsel	Reisinger	Blizenec	Brauneder	Schottel	Kienast	Keglevits	Pfeif'berger	Kranjcar*	Herzog	Fjortoft^	Weber/Polger

Notes:

Rapid Vienna (home) — Rapid manager Hans Krankle captained his side in infamous matches against Celtic and Man U in 1984. Miller fells Herzog and Kranjcar curls in the free-kick. On the hour Robert Pecl is sent off for fouling Nicholas. Craig Robertson's volley paves the way for Grant's late header.

Rapid Vienna (away) — In the hate-filled, rain-swept Hanappi Stadium Rapid's offside tactics stifle the Dons. Willie Miller deflects a shot into the path of Jan Fjortoft, later to play for a host of English clubs. Keeper Konsel is rarely troubled after that, and Aberdeen make a sad early exit from Europe yet again.

League Table

	P	W	D	L	F	A	W	D	L	F	A	Pts
			Home						**Away**			
1 Rangers	36	14	2	2	32	7	6	9	3	16	12	51
2 ABERDEEN	36	12	4	2	33	13	5	6	7	23	20	44
3 Hearts	36	8	6	4	28	17	8	6	4	26	18	44
4 Dundee Utd	36	8	8	2	21	12	3	5	10	15	27	35
5 Celtic	36	6	6	6	21	20	4	8	6	16	17	34
6 Motherwell	36	6	7	5	23	21	4	7	7	20	26	34
7 Hibernian	36	8	5	5	25	23	4	5	9	9	18	34
8 Dunfermline	36	6	5	7	17	23	3	7	8	20	27	30
9 St Mirren	36	6	6	6	14	15	4	4	10	14	33	30
10 Dundee	36	4	8	6	23	26	4	0	14	18	39	24
	360	78	57	45	237	177	45	57	78	177	237	360

Record v each club

	P	W	D	L	F	A	Pts	Cup	W	D	L
v Dunfermline	4	4	0	0	13	4	8	LC	1	0	0
v St Mirren	4	3	0	1	9	1	6				
v Dundee	4	2	2	0	8	3	6				
v Motherwell	4	2	2	0	5	3	6	SC	1	0	0
v Dundee Utd	4	2	1	1	4	3	5				
v Hibernian	4	2	0	2	7	5	4	LC	1	0	0
								SC	*1	0	0
v Celtic	4	1	2	1	5	4	4	LC	1	0	0
								SC	1	0	0
v Rangers	4	1	1	2	1	3	3	LC	1	0	0
v Hearts	4	0	2	2	4	7	2	SC	1	0	0
	36	17	10	9	56	33	44				

* penalties

Odds & ends

Never lost to: (3) Dunfermline, Dundee, Motherwell.
Never beat: (1) Hearts (in the league).

Won from behind: (4) Dundee (h), Celtic (a), Partick (a), Morton (h).
Rapid Vienna (UC).
Lost from in front: (0).

High spots: Winning both domestic cup finals, as in 1985-86.
Topping the league table in late September and early December.

Low spots: Never winning more than three successive matches.
Back-to-back league defeats in early October.
44 league points was the lowest since 1985-86.
Elimination from Europe in the first round.

Bogey-team: Hearts.
Ever-presents: (0).
Hat-tricks: (2) Charlie Nicholas (1), van der Ark (1).
Leading scorer: (15) Paul Mason.

Appearances and Goals

			Appearances						Goals				
	Lge	Sub	LC	Sub	SC	Sub	Eur	Sub	Lge	LC	SC	Eur	Tot
Bett, Jim	30		5		4		2		3		2	1	6
Booth, Scott	1	5											
Cameron, Ian	6	5	2	2			1	1		2			2
Connor, Robert	33		5		5		2		1				1
Dodds, Davie	19	1	1		4		1						
Gillhaus, Hans	28		3		4		2		8		3		11
Grant, Brian	28	3	3	2	5		2		6	1	1		8
Harvie, Scott	1	1											
Irvine, Brian	28	3	2	1	5		1		1		2		3
Jess, Eoin	7	4	2	1		1	1	1		3			3
McKimmie, Stewart	33		5		5		2						
McLeish, Alex	32		4		5		2			2			2
Mason, Paul	33	1	5		5		2		9		5	1	15
Miller, Willie	15		5		2		2						
Mimms, Bobby	6				2								
Nicholas, Charlie	32	1	5		5		2		11	2			13
Robertson, Craig	10	12	1			2	2		2	1			3
Robertson, David	20		5		2		2		1	1			2
Robertson, Ian	5	4		1									
Simpson, Neil	5		1		1		1						
Snelders, Theo	23		5		5		2						
van der Ark, Willem	16	11	3		2	1	2		7		3	1	11
Watson, Graham	3	1				2			1				1
Watson, Gregg	3	1											
Watt, Michael	7				1								
Wright, Stephen		1											
(own-goals)													5
26 players used	396	51	55	10	55	7	22	4	56	12	16	2	86

B & Q SCOTTISH PREMIER

Manager: Alex Smith & Jocky Scott — SEASON 1990-91

No	Date	Venue / Opponent	Att	Pos	Pt	H-T	F-A	Scorers, Times, and Referees	1	2	3	4	5	6	7	8	9	10	11	subs used
1	25/8	H HIBERNIAN	15,500	W	2	1-0	2-0	Gillhaus 40, Connor 55 — Ref: H Williamson	Snelders	McKimmie	Robertson D	Grant	McLeish	Irvine	van de Ven	Bett*	Mason	Connor	Gillhaus	Watson
		Hibernian							*Goram*	*Miller*	*Mitchell*	*Kane*	*Cooper*	*Farrell**	*Evans**	*McGinlay*	*Findlay*	*Houchen*	*Tortolano*	*McGraw/Fallenger*
2	1/9	A CELTIC	45,222	1	4	0-0	3-0	Mason 53, Connor 65, Gillhaus 80 — Ref: J McCluskey	Snelders	McKimmie*	Robertson D	Grant	McLeish	Irvine	van de Ven	Bett	Mason	Connor	Gillhaus	Watson
		Celtic							*Bonner*	*Morris*	*McLaughlin*	*Grant*	*Elliott*	*Whyte\`*	*Hayes*	*McStay*	*Dziekowski*	*Nicholas**	*Collins*	*Walker/Miller*
3	8/9	A DUNFERMLINE	10,200	2	5	1-1	1-1	Robertson D 22 / Moyes 18 — Ref: D McVicar	Snelders	McKimmie	Robertson D	Grant	McLeish	Irvine	van de Ven	Bett	Mason	Connor	Gillhaus	
		Dunfermline							*Rhodes*	*Wilson*	*Sharp*	*McCathie*	*Moyes*	*Nicholl*	*Smith*	*Rafferty*	*Jack*	*McCall\`*	*Kozma\`*	*Irons/Leitch*
4	15/9	H DUNDEE UTD	15,500	4	6	0-0	1-1	Bett 83p / McKinnon 53 — Ref: D Hope	Snelders	McKimmie	Robertson D	Grant	McLeish	Irvine	van de Ven*	Bett	Mason	Connor	Gillhaus	Watson/Booth
		Dundee Utd							*Thomson*	*Cleland*	*Malpas*	*McInally*	*Paatelainen*	*Welsh*	*van d'Hoorn*	*McKinlay*	*Daily**	*Jackson*	*McKinnon*	*Bowman*
5	22/9	H ST MIRREN	12,500	2	8	2-1	2-1	Irvine 4, Bett 34p / Kinnaird 10 — Ref: D Miller	Snelders	Watson	Robertson D	Grant	McLeish	Irvine	van de Ven*	Bett	Mason	Jess	Gillhaus	Shaw
		St Mirren							*Money*	*Wishart*	*Black*	*Lambert*	*Dawson*	*Manley*	*McDowall*	*Martin*	*Stickroth*	*McWalter**	*Kinnaird*	*Shaw*
6	29/9	A ST JOHNSTONE	8,711	3	8	0-3	0-5	[Maskrey 80] Grant 12, 55, Treanor 34, 42p — Ref: L Thow	Snelders	Watson	Robertson D	Grant	McLeish	Irvine	van de Ven*	Bett	Mason	Connor	Gillhaus*	Robertson C/Jess
		St Johnstone							*Hamilton*	*Treanor*	*Baltacha*	*Cherry*	*Inglis*	*McGinnis*	*Moore*	*Turner**	*Maskrey*	*Grant*	*Curran**	*Lee/Deas*
7	6/10	H RANGERS	24,000	3	9	0-0	0-0	Ref: L Mottram	Snelders*	Watson	Robertson D	Grant	McLeish	van de Ven	Jess*	Bett	Mason	Connor	Gillhaus*	Watson/Robertson C
		Rangers							*Woods*	*Stevens*	*Munro*	*Gough*	*Spackman*	*Brown*	*Steven*	*Hurlock*	*McCoist*	*Johnston*	*Walters**	*Hateley*
8	13/10	A MOTHERWELL	6,602	3	10	0-0	0-0	Ref: A Huett	Dibble	McKimmie	Robertson D	Grant	McLeish	Irvine	van de Ven*	Bett	Mason	Connor	Gillhaus	Paterson/McLeod
		Motherwell							*Maxwell*	*Burley*	*Boyd*	*O'Neill*	*Nijholt*	*McCart**	*Arnott\`*	*Angus*	*Cusack*	*Kirk*	*Cooper*	*Paterson/McLeod*
9	20/10	H HEARTS	14,800	3	12	1-0	3-0	Bett 44, Grant 54, Gillhaus 73 — Ref: J Renton	Dibble	McKimmie	Robertson D	Grant	McLeish	Irvine	van de Ven	Bett	Mason	Connor	Gillhaus*	Jess/Robertson C
		Hearts							*Smith*	*McLaren*	*McKinlay*	*Levein*	*Kirkwood*	*McPherson*	*Colquhoun*	*Berry*	*Robertson**	*Ferguson*	*Bannon*	*Foster*
10	27/10	A HIBERNIAN	10,500	2	13	0-1	1-1	Gillhaus 77 / Wright 38 — Ref: J Herald	Dibble	McKimmie	Robertson D	Grant	McLeish	Irvine	van de Ven*	Bett	Mason	Connor	Gillhaus	Robertson C/Jess
		Hibernian							*Goram*	*Miller*	*Milne*	*Kane*	*Hamilton*	*Hunter*	*Findlay**	*Wright*	*MacLeod*	*Houchen*	*McGinlay*	*Mitchell*

Match notes

1. Stewart McKimmie asked for a transfer in June but has signed a new four-year contract. Willie Miller will never play again, and Brian Irvine lays claim to the No 6 shirt. Newcomer Peter van de Ven almost made a dramatic introduction. Mason headed his early cross against the post.

2. Charlie Nicholas takes the field to a tumultuous Parkhead reception. Aberdeen soak up fierce Celtic pressure, then hit them three times on the break to go top and send Celtic to the bottom goalless. Celtic claimed Paul Mason was offside when racing onto McLeish's long pass for No 1.

3. Pars' Tom Wilson crosses from the right and centre-half Moyes is permitted an unchallenged header. Aberdeen's equaliser was unexpected on two counts: first, it was scored by full-back David Robertson; second, he hit it with his right foot. The point lost helps Dundee United go top.

4. On 17 minutes Stewart McKimmie is sent off for elbowing Mixu Paatelainen, who fell clutching his face. Van de Ven moved to full-back. Cleland pulled the ball back for McKinnon to score. Aberdeen's equaliser came from the penalty spot after he struck McInally's arm.

5. McKimmie is out, suspended, and Connor has pulled a hamstring. Aberdeen go in front from their first corner-kick. The Buddies level when Irvine blocks Kinnaird's first effort but not his second. When full-back Wishart handles needlessly, Jim Bett puts the Dons ahead once more.

6. This astonishing score - on the first visit to Perth's new stadium - records Aberdeen's heaviest league thumping since losing to Celtic 1-7 in 1965, and comes three days after the Dons surrendered the Skol Cup. After 31 minutes David Robertson was sent off for violent conduct.

7. Atrocious conditions required three pitch inspections. These are partly responsible for the flash-point on the hour, when Snelders and McCoist compete to claim Hateley's knock-down. The collision results in the unconscious goalkeeper being stretchered off with a fractured cheekbone.

8. This was better than most goalless draws. The match was preceded by a minute's silence in honour of Dons director Bobby Morrison. In view of Snelders' dreadful injury Aberdeen have borrowed Manchester City's goalkeeper Andy Dibble. Aberdeen are three points behind Dundee U.

9. Jim Bett scores Aberdeen's first goal in four games. His cross-sum-shot, which went in over Henry Smith's head, earned derisory applause. Andy Dibble has little to do on his home debut. Metz's former Don, Eric Black, announces his retirement from football owing to back trouble.

10. Hibs' muster hardly any attacks worthy of the name, but looked likely to take both points after ex-Don Paul Wright got the final touch from Findlay's corner-kick. Relentless Aberdeen pressure was finally rewarded when Eoin Jess cut the ball back to Gillhaus from the by-line.

No		Opponent	Date	Att	Pos			Result		HT	Scorers	Referee
11	H	CELTIC	3/11	21,500	2	W	3-0	5	15	2-0	Jess 22, 59, Gillhaus 37	Ref: G Smith
12	A	ST MIRREN	10/11	7,638	2	W	4-0	10	17	2-0	Grant 10, Robertson C 12, Jess 65, [Gillhaus 76]Fridge	Ref: J Timmons
13	H	ST JOHNSTONE	17/11	16,000	2	D	0-0	5	18	0-0		Ref: J Duncan
14	A	DUNDEE UTD	24/11	12,344	1	W	3-2	2	20	2-2	Jess 10, 16, 47, McKimmie 7 og, Malpas 38g	Ref: L Mottram
15	H	DUNFERMLINE	1/12	12,000	2	W	3-2	9	22	1-1	Irvine 16, Gillhaus 49, Mason 55, O'Boyle 15, Irons 67	Ref: J McGilvray
16	A	HEARTS	8/12	9,811	2	L	0-1	6	22	0-1	Colquhoun 33	Ref: B McGinlay
17	H	MOTHERWELL	15/12	9,500	2	D	1-1	6	23	1-1	Jess 27, Arnott 26	Ref: D Syme
18	A	RANGERS	22/12	37,998	2	D	2-2	1	24	0-0	Bett 74p, 89, McCoist 62, 72	Ref: W Crombie
19	H	ST MIRREN	26/12	8,755	2	W	1-0		26	0-0	Jess 89	Ref: M Clark
20	H	DUNDEE UTD	2/1	19,000	2	L	0-1	3	26	0-1	Dailly 23	Ref: H Williamson
21	A	DUNFERMLINE	5/1	7,422	2	W	4-1	7	28	2-1	Jess 36, 45, 76, 77, Irons 6	Ref: J MacKinnon

11. CELTIC
Aberdeen: Dibble, McKimmie, Robertson D, Grant, Robertson, McLeish, Irvine, van de Ven, Bett, Jess, Connor*, Gillhaus, Cameron
Celtic: Bonner, Grant, Wdowczyk, Fulton^, Elliott, Rogan, Galloway, McStay, DziekowskI, Creaney, Collins, Hayes/Miller
It is only November, but Aberdeen have already beaten Celtic twice by this handsome score. A scuffle among the crowd at the Beach End preceded the first goal, which went in off a post. The Dons' second was achieved despite a linesman flagging against Robert Connor.

12. ST MIRREN
Aberdeen: Dibble, McKimmie, Robertson D, Grant*, Black*, Lambert, Robertson C, Irvine, Bett, van de Ven, Connor, Jess, Gillhaus, Robertson I/Cameron
St Mirren: Fridge, Dawson, Black*, Lambert, Godfrey, McWhirter, Martin, Archibald, Stickroth, Torfason, Kinnaird^, McDowall/Shaw
Aberdeen were dumped by Legia in midweek. St Mirren are now led by Steve Archibald, but they provide Aberdeen's biggest away win since January 1987. The rout began when van de Ven sidestepped two Saints and slid the ball through to Grant. Gillhaus ran 30 yards for his goal.

13. ST JOHNSTONE
Aberdeen: Watt, McKimmie, Robertson D, Robertson C, McLeish, Irvine, van de Ven, Jess, Bett, Connor, Gillhaus, Cameron
St Johnstone: Hamilton, Treanor^, Baltacha, Cherry, Inglis, McGinnis, Moore, Curran, Maskrey, Grant*, McVicar, Davies/Barron
The Dons are still smarting from the 5-0 debacle. The match sponsors offer £5,000 if Aberdeen can avenge that drubbing but their money is safe. A second-half siege fails to break through. Near the end Saints bring on John Davies, their £165,000 record signing from Clydebank.

14. DUNDEE UTD
Aberdeen: Watt, McKimmie, Robertson D, Jess*, McLeish, Irvine, Mackay, van de Ven, Bett, Mason, Connor, Gillhaus, Cameron
Dundee Utd: Main, Cleland^, Malpas, McInally, Krivokapic, Welsh, van d'Hoom, McKinlay, Dailly, McKinnon, Ferguson, Steinmann
Aberdeen switch places with United at the top following this thrilling win, in which Eoin Jess notched his first hat-trick. Stewart McKimmie headed an own-goal from a corner and Connor fouled McInally for the penalty, which the referee awarded only after consulting his linesman.

15. DUNFERMLINE
Aberdeen: Watt, McKimmie, Robertson D, Jess*, McLeish, Irvine, van de Ven, Bett, Mason, Connor, Gillhaus, Cameron
Dunfermline: Rhodes, Wilson, Sharp^, McCathie, Moyes, Irons, Rafferty, Davies, O'Boyle*, McCall, Kosma, Jack/Haro
Dunfermline have never beaten the Dons in 10 Premier League matches, but they ran them close on this occasion. Stocky Irishman O'Boyle even gave them the lead, and at 1-1 Sharp hit the base of Watt's upright. Irons' looping header set up an anxious closing period for the Dons.

16. HEARTS
Aberdeen: Watt, Wright, Robertson D, Jess*, McLeish, Irvine, Mackay, van de Ven, Berry, Mason, Connor, Gillhaus, Cameron
Hearts: Smith, Sandison, McKinlay, Levein, Mackay, McPherson, Colquhoun, Berry, Foster*, Ferguson, Robertson, Crabbe
Tynecastle has become an unhappy hunting ground for the Dons of late. In icy conditions and driving snow Colquhoun outjumps David Robertson to head the only goal. Aberdeen had most of the play but none of the joy. Snelders may soon be fit enough to reclaim his place.

17. MOTHERWELL
Aberdeen: Snelders, McKimmie, Robertson D, Jess*, McLeish, Jess, van de Ven, Bett, Mason*, Connor, Gillhaus^, Wright/Booth
Motherwell: Maxwell, Burley, Boyd, O'Neill, Paterson, McCart, Arnott^, Griffin, Cusack, Russell*, Cooper, Dolan/McLeod
Pittodrie is misty and half-empty. Arnott's angled right-footer comes out of the blue, but seconds later Paul Mason's header comes off the bar and Eoin Jess pounced to equalise. In the second half Alex McLeish appeared to bundle Arnott off the ball, but the referee waved play on.

18. RANGERS
Aberdeen: Snelders, McKimmie, Robertson D, Jess, McLeish, Irvine, van de Ven, Booth, Gillhaus, Huistra/McCoist
Rangers: Woods, Stevens, Munro, Gough, Robertson*, Brown, Steven^, Hurlock, Hateley, Johnston, Walters, Huistra/McCoist
Rain-soaked Ibrox endures a miserable first half but a gripping second. Without Jess and Connor Aberdeen trail by two goals when John Brown, on the deck, handles Grant's pass. In the final minute Grant swings over a corner and Bett fires the equaliser through a heap of bodies.

19. ST MIRREN
Aberdeen: Snelders, McKimmie*, Robertson D, Grant, McLeish, Irvine, van de Ven*, Mason, Booth, Gillhaus*, Booth/Robertson C
St Mirren: Fridge, Godfrey, Black, Lambert*, Victor, Martin!, Wishart, Shaw, McWalter*, Stickroth, Manley, McDowall/Broddle
St Mirren have Spanish international Victor in their ranks. They had two players sent off against Hibs on Saturday and another today. On 55 minutes John Martin tripped Mason and was expelled. Keeper Les Fridge defied the Dons until the final minute, when Booth headed on to Jess.

20. DUNDEE UTD
Aberdeen: Snelders, McKimmie*, Robertson D, Grant, McLeish, Clark, French, van de Ven*, Bett, Jess, Gillhaus*, Cameron/Booth
Dundee Utd: Main, Steinmann*, Malpas, McInally, Clark, French, van d'Hoom, McKinlay, Dailly, Jackson^, Paatelainen, Cleland/O'Neil
Aberdeen went through 1990 unbeaten at home in 24 games, but lose their first match of 1991. Theo Snelders palmed away Darren Jackson's effort, but 17-year-old Christian Dailly reacted fastest to the rebound. Aberdeen managed just two shots on target throughout the 90 minutes.

21. DUNFERMLINE
Aberdeen: Snelders, Wright, Robertson D, Grant, McLeish, Moyes, Irvine, Cameron, Bett, Mason, Jess, Gillhaus, Gallagher/Hero
Dunfermline: Rhodes, Wilson, Sharp, McCathie, Moyes, Irons, Rafferty*, Davies, Smith, Jack, Kosma, Gallagher/Hero
Windy, rainy, cold, and Dunfermline take an early lead when David Irons squeezed past Stephen Wright to head in. It all sounds pretty wretched, but Eoin Jess responded with all four goals of Aberdeen's riposte. For his fourth he skipped past Wilson and Rhodes for a loose ball.

B & Q SCOTTISH PREMIER Manager: Alex Smith & Jocky Scott SEASON 1990-91

No	Date	Team	Att	Pos	Pt	F-A	H-T	Scorers, Times, and Referees	1	2	3	4	5	6	7	8	9	10	11	subs used
22	12/1	H HIBERNIAN	13,500	2	W 30	2-0	1-0	Cameron 24, Booth 76 — Ref: M McGinley	Snelders	Wright	Robertson	DGrant	McLeish	Irvine	Cameron	Bett	Mason	Jess*	Gillhaus	Booth
		(Hibernian)	*10*						*Goram*	*Miller*	*Milne*	*Kane*	*Hamilton*	*MacLeod*	*Cooper*	*Wright*	*Tortolano*	*Mitchell*	*McGinlay*	*McGinlay*
23	19/1	A CELTIC	18,187	2	L 30	0-1	0-0	*Coyne 89* — Ref: D Hope	Snelders	Wright	Robertson	DGrant	McLeish	Irvine	van de Ven*	Bett	Mason	Cameron	Gillhaus	Jess
		(Celtic)	*5*						*Bonner*	*Morris*	*Rogan*	*McNally*	*Elliott*	*Whyte*	*Miller*	*McStay*	*Coyne*	*Creaney^*	*Collins*	*Fulton/Walker*
24	2/2	H HEARTS	9,500	2	W 32	5-0	3-0	Connor 1, Booth 9, 18, Mason 82, [Gillhaus 86] — Ref: J McCluskey	Snelders	Wright	Robertson	DGrant	McLeish	Irvine	Jess	Bett*	Booth^	Connor	Gillhaus*	van de Ven/Mason
		(Hearts)	*6*						*Smith*	*Sandison*	*McKinlay*	*Levein*	*Mackay*	*McPherson*	*Colquhoun*	*Berry*	*Ferguson*	*Robertson*	*McCreery*	
25	13/2	A ST JOHNSTONE	7,046	2	W 34	1-0	0-0	Booth 87 — Ref: R Orr	Snelders	Wright	Robertson	DGrant	McLeish	Irvine	Booth	Bett	Mason	Connor	Gillhaus*	Watson
		(St Johnstone)	*4*						*Hamilton*	*Treanor*	*Baltacha*	*Cherry*	*Inglis*	*Davies*	*Moore*	*Turner*	*Maskrey*	*Grant*	*Curran*	
26	2/3	H RANGERS	22,500	2	W 36	1-0	0-0	Gillhaus 89 — Ref: D Syme	Snelders	Wright	Robertson	DGrant*	McLeish	Irvine	Booth	Bett	Mason*	Connor	Gillhaus*	van de Ven/van Ark
		(Rangers)	*1*						*Woods*	*Stevens*	*Nisbet*	*Spackman*	*Brown*	*Gough*	*Steven*	*Hurlock*	*Hateley*	*Johnston*	*Walters*	*Huistra*
27	5/3	A MOTHERWELL	5,567	2	W 38	2-0	1-0	Wright 1, Bett 68p — Ref: J Duncan	Snelders	Wright	Robertson	DGrant*	McLeish	Irvine	Booth*	Bett	Mason*	Connor	Gillhaus	van de Ven/van Ark
		(Motherwell)	*9*						*Maxwell*	*Nijholt*	*Boyd*	*O'Neill*	*Paterson*	*McCart*	*McLeod^*	*Griffin*	*Cusack*	*Angus^*	*Cooper*	*Russell/Kirk*
28	13/3	H DUNFERMLINE	10,400	2	D 39	0-0	0-0	Ref: K Hope	Snelders	Wright	Robertson	DGrant	McLeish	Irvine*	Booth	Bett	Mason*	Connor	Gillhaus	Jess/van der Ark
		(Dunfermline)	*7*						*Rhodes*	*Farningham*	*Cunningham*	*McCathie*	*Moyes*	*Irons*	*Davies*	*Smith*	*Jack^*	*McCall*	*Kosma*	*Williams'n/Gallagher*
29	23/3	A DUNDEE UTD	10,643	2	W 41	2-1	1-1	van der Ark 30, Gillhaus 82 / *McInally 8* — Ref: D McVicar	Snelders	Wright	Robertson	DGrant	McLeish	Irvine	Jess*	Bett	van der Ark*	Connor	Gillhaus	van de Ven/Booth
		(Dundee Utd)	*3*						*Main*	*Clark*	*Malpas*	*McInally*	*Krivokapic*	*Bowman*	*van d'Hoom*	*O'Neil*	*McKinnon^*	*Ferguson^*	*French*	*McKinlay/Paatel'en*
30	30/3	A HIBERNIAN	7,400	2	W 43	4-2	3-1	Gillhaus 5, 14, 45, Booth 16 / *Evans 11, Hamilton 47* — Ref: M McCluskey	Snelders*	Wright	Robertson	DGrant	McLeish*	McKimmie	Booth	Bett	Mason*	Connor	Gillhaus	van de Ven/Jess
		(Hibernian)	*9*						*Goram*	*Miller*	*Milne*	*Hunter*	*Nicholls*	*MacLeod*	*Weir*	*Wright*	*McGinlay*	*Hamilton^*	*Evans*	*McGraw/Findlay*
31	6/4	H CELTIC	22,500	2	W 45	1-0	1-0	Jess 20 — Ref: W Crombie	Watt	Wright	Robertson	DGrant	McLeish	McKimmie	van de Ven*	Bett	Jess*	Connor	Gillhaus	van der Ark/Booth
		(Celtic)	*4*						*Bonner*	*Morris*	*Rogan*	*Wdowczyk*	*Elliott*	*Whyte*	*Miller*	*McStay*	*Coyne^*	*Creaney*	*Collins*	*McNally/Walker*

22 — Hibs are bottom. They have scored just 11 goals all season, and not surprisingly kick-off with a five-man defence. Ian Cameron plays a one-two with Paul Mason and scores past Andy Goram off a post. Goram then parries Bett's 25-yarder and sub Scott Booth is first to the rebound.

23 — Eoin Jess is the Premier League's leading scorer, but he starts this crucial match on the substitutes' bench. Kick-off was delayed by a supporter waving a newspaper who ran to the centre circle. Snelders parried Elliott's header, but the ball fell to Tommy Coyne. Aberdeen create little.

24 — Recent defeats and live TV coverage explain the small crowd. Van de Ven and Mason are dropped. It takes just 54 seconds for Stephen Wright's cross to be nodded in by Connor. Oddest goal was the third. Sandison belted Wright's shot off the line, straight into Booth's body.

25 — It is 0-5 and 0-0 to St Johnstone so far. They might have won this latest encounter, too, but for some controversial refereeing. After 65 minutes Snelders handles outside the box to prevent Maskrey scoring. Snelders was shown yellow, not red. McLeish headed on to Booth for the goal.

26 — Van de Ark is on the bench, having been out for 11 months. Mo Johnston clipped Snelders' post after half an hour. Another late winner: Gillhaus beats Woods at the near post from Robertson's cross. Rangers' lead was eight points. It is now six, and the Dons have a game in hand.

27 — Aberdeen's first win over Motherwell in league or cup sees the gap behind Rangers close to four points. After 51 seconds Wright's cross from the by-line eludes keeper Maxwell at the near post. The Dons had created little else by the time Griffin pulled down Robert Connor in the box.

28 — Despite mounting Dons pressure, Dunfermline goalkeeper Rhodes is not overworked in this disappointing match. The moment that Aberdeen players and supporters would rue came two minutes into injury time, when substitute van der Ark headed against the foot of the post.

29 — Aberdeen return to their happy habit of poaching late winners. United defender van der Hoom was at fault, trying to shepherd the ball back to Alan Main despite the close attention of Scott Booth. The ball broke off the keeper for Hans Gillhaus to snatch an unlikely winner.

30 — Unsettled Paul Mason is dropped. McKimmie returns after a three-month lay-off. Alex McLeish is injured in a collision with ex-Don Paul Wright, and Snelders goes off after 34 minutes after injuring his shoulder. Van de Ven takes over in goal. Snelders' injury will prove critical.

31 — Van de Ven starts his first game in eight. Aberdeen score from their second corner. Gillhaus heads over Bonner and Jess prods the ball over the line. Bett missed a penalty 10 minutes later, hitting the post after Whyte had pulled down Gillhaus. Elliott's 'equaliser' is ruled out for offside.

32 A HEARTS 13/4 — 2 W 5 47 — **4-1** / **2-1**
Gillhaus 18, McKimmie 37, McKimmie 2 og [Connor 64, 80]
Ref: D Hope   16,771

Watt	Wright*	Robertson DGrant	Irvine	McKimmie	Jess	Bett	van der Ark	Connor	Gillhaus*	van de Ven/Booth
Walker	Sandison* McKinlay* Levain		Wright	McPherson Colquhoun Bannon				Crabbe	Robertson/ Mackay/McLaren	

Stewart McKimmie and John Robertson had most reason to remember this match. McKimmie, because he scored at both ends – his goal for the Dons was his first for five years and flew in off the bar from 30 yards. Robertson, because he flung the ball into Irvine's face and was sent off.

---

33 H MOTHERWELL 20/4 — 2 W 7 49 — **3-0** / **1-0**
van der Ark 23, 54, Connor 67
Ref: G Smith   14,500

Watt	Wright	Robertson DGrant	McLeish*	McKimmie	Jess	Bett	van der Ark	Connor	Gillhaus	van de Ven/Booth
Maxwell	Nijholt Angus Paterson	Philliben*		Griffin	Arnott	McCart	McLeod	O'Donnell	Cooper*	Ferguson/Kirk

Two mysteries here. Why isn't Gillhaus playing? And why are there so many empty seats for this crunch match? Motherwell will soon create a sensational climax by beating Rangers 3-0. Rangers' Ian Durrant has just returned after 2½ years and has announced he is to sue Neil Simpson.

---

34 A ST MIRREN 27/4 — 2 W 10 51 — **1-0** / **0-0**
Bett 76
Ref: G Evans   8,513

Watt	Wright	Robertson DGrant	McLeish	McKimmie	Jess*	Bett	van der Ark*	Connor	Gillhaus	van de Ven/Booth
Fridge	Dawson Black McWhirter	McGowne	Martin	Shaw*		McIntyre	Stickroth	Irvine	Lambert	McWalter

St Mirren are adrift at the bottom. A large Dons travelling support watch through their fingers as Watt collides with McLeish without any St Mirren player to punish them. Aberdeen score shortly after they throw on both subs. McLeish's free-kick is flicked on by van de Ven to Bett.

---

35 H ST JOHNSTONE 4/5 — 1 W 7 53 — **2-1** / **2-1**
van der Ark 15, Booth 37 — Maskrey 12
Ref: D Brooks   18,000

Watt	Wright	Robertson DGrant	McLeish	McKimmie	Bett	van der Ark*	Connor	Gillhaus	Booth*	van de Ven/Jess
Hamilton	Nicholson Baltacha* Sweeney	Inglis	McGinnis	Bingham	Davies	Maskrey	Grant	Curran		Barron

Topsy-turvy emotions. Van der Ark's poor clearance instigates Maskrey's hooked goal. Gillhaus combines with Ark for the equaliser. Booth's header puts the Dons in front. A huge roar greets news that Motherwell have scored against Rangers. Motherwell then score two more goals.

---

36 A RANGERS 11/5 — 2 L 1 53 — **0-2** / **0-1**
Hateley 40, 55
Ref: B McGinlay   37,652

Watt	Wright	Robertson DGrant	McLeish	McKimmie	van der Ven*Bett	Bett	Jess*	Connor	Gillhaus	van der Ark/Booth
Woods	Stevens Cowan* Nisbet	Spackman	Brown*	Hurlock	Ferguson	Hateley	Johnston	Walters		Durrant/McCoist

Snelders is unfit. 20-year-old Michael Watt keeps goal and is immediately clattered by Mark Hateley. The Dons create chances, noticeably van de Ven's weak chip into Woods' arms. But Rangers are undeniably superior on the day. Aberdeen have no answer to Hateley's aerial power.

Average Home 15,550   Away 15,457

Skol League Cup

2 A QUEEN'S PARK 21/8 — W 2-1 / 1-1
Jess 15, Bett 68 — Hendry 18
Ref: W Crombie   2,201

Snelders	McKimmie	Robertson DGrant	Irvine	Miller	Jess*	Bett*	Mason	Connor	Gillhaus	van de Ven/Booth
Monaghan	Callan Ogg Jack	McNamee	McEntegart Caven	O'Brien*		Crooks	Mackenzie* Hendry	Morris/Greig		

With hindsight this match is memorable only for being Willie Miller's last competitive game in an Aberdeen shirt. Van der Ark's playing future, too, is threatened by a groin injury. Queen's Mike Hendry had the cheek to unleash a cracker when the Dons defence backed off him.

---

3 H STRANRAER 29/8 — W 4-0 / 2-0
Mason 4, 17, Irvine 47, van de Ven 52
Ref: D Yeats   10,000

Snelders	McKimmie*	Robertson DGrant	McLeish	Irvine	van de Ven	Bett*	Mason*	Connor	Gillhaus	van de Ven 52 — Watson/Cameron
Duffy	Corrie Lindsay* McIlwin	Duncan	McCutcheon George	McMillan	Jess	Grant*	Spittal	Henderson	Harkness/Cook	

The fourth Dutchman arrives, Peter van de Ven, and he gets on the scoresheet in his first match. Mason set things rolling by side-footing the opener. Stranraer got off lightly. Three minutes from time David Robertson was pushed in the penalty area but Gillhaus missed from the spot.

QF H HEARTS 5/9 — 1 W 8 — 3-0 / 2-0
van de Ven 7, Mason 12, Bett 73p
Ref: G Smith   15,500

Snelders	McKimmie	Robertson DGrant	McLeish	Irvine	van de Ven	Bett	Mason	Connor	Gillhaus*	van de Ven/Booth
Smith	Berry McKinlay Levein	McCreery*	McPherson Colquhoun Mackay	Robertson	Foster	Bannon	Kidd			

A match played in depressing drizzle. Man of the match Jim Bett looks a class apart. He kills off Hearts with a furiously argued penalty after Gillhaus went down in the box after tussling with Levein and Kidd. Van de Ven scored an early goal when Smith punched out Mason's cross.

SF N RANGERS 26/9 (at Hampden) — L 0-1
Steven T 30
Ref: B McGinlay   40,855

Snelders	McKimmie	Robertson DGrant	McLeish	Irvine	van de Ven	Bett	Mason	Connor	Jess*	Robertson C
Woods	Stevens G Munro Gough	Spackman Brown	Steven T	Hurlock	McCoist	Johnston	Walters			

These clubs meet in this competition for the fourth successive year, though this time not in the final. A live TV audience watched Rangers dominate midfield, with the best player on view scoring the goal, handling while bursting through the middle and finding himself in the clear.

B & Q PREMIER (CUP-TIES) Manager: Alex Smith & Jocky Scott SEASON 1990-91

Scottish Cup

		F-A	H-T	Scorers, Times, and Referees	1	2	3	4	5	6	7	8	9	10	11	subs used
3	H MOTHERWELL 26/1 15,000	L	0-1	0-0	Snelders	Wright	Robertson D	Jess	McLeish	Irvine	van de Ven	Bett	Mason*	Connor	Gillhaus^	Cameron/Booth
				Kirk 78	Maxwell	Philliben	Boyd	O'Neill	Paterson	McCart	Arnott	Dolan	Ferguson*	Angus	Cooper	Kirk
				Ref: A Huett												

Van de Ven fouls Boyd. Before the free-kick is taken Steve Kirk comes on as sub. Davie Cooper taps the ball sideways and Kirk blasts it past Snelders. The goal sent Motherwell players and supporters into raptures, and earned Kirk a booking for excessive celebrations behind the goal.

European Cup-Winners' Cup

			F-A	H-T	Scorers, Times, and Referees	1	2	3	4	5	6	7	8	9	10	11	subs used
1:1	A SALAMINA 19/9 (Cyprus) 7,000	2 W	2-0	0-0	Mason 61, Gillhaus 81	Snelders	McKimmie	Robertson D	Grant	McLeish	Irvine	van de Ven	Bett	Mason*	Booth^	Gillhaus	Jess/Watson
					Ref: I Streng (Romania)	Christofi	Andreou A	Tsikelis	Yiannaki	Nicolaou	Dyer	Andreou G	David	McNeill	Elia	Adamou	
1:2	H SALAMINA 3/10 7,000	3 W	3-0	2-0	Robertson C 13, Andreou A 33 og. [Jess 67]	Snelders	McKimmie	Robertson D	Robertson C	McLeish*	Irvine	Jess	Bett	Mason*	Connor	Gillhaus	van de Ven/Gardner
					Ref: A Ritchie (N Ireland) (Dons win 5-0 on aggregate)	Joannou	Andreou A	Tsikelis	Yiannaki	Nicolaou*	Dyer	Adamou	Mavrou	McNeill*	Elia	Georgiou	David/Andreou C
2:1	H LEGIA WARSAW 24/10 (Poland) 16,000	D	0-0	0-0	Ref: C Silva (Portugal)	Watt	McKimmie	Robertson D	Grant	McLeish	Irvine	van de Ven*	Bett	Mason	Connor	Gillhaus	Robertson C
						Szczesny	Kubicki	Gmur	Wiak	Budka	Czykier	Pisz*	Iwanicki	Latka	Kosecki	Cyzio	Modzelewski
2:2	A LEGIA WARSAW 7/11 5,665	L	0-1	0-0	Iwanicki 84	Watt	McKimmie	Robertson D	Grant	McLeish	Irvine	van de Ven	Bett	Mason*	Connor	Gillhaus	Jess
					Ref: L Sundell (Sweden) (Dons lose 0-1 on aggregate)	Szczesny	Kubicki	Gmur	Wiak	Budka	Czykier	Bak	Iwanicki	Modzel'ski	Kosecki	Cyzio	

Salamina Famagusta play in a bumpy ground in Limassol. At 0-0 Snelders pulled off two sharp saves to deny English player Nigel McNeill. Mason's turn and shot settled the nerves. Van de Ven lashed a second from substitute Watson's cross. Ven also scored in his first Skol Cup-tie.

Aberdeen have just lost 0-5 at St Johnstone. Alex Smith rings the changes and brings back McLeish, Jess, and Craig Robertson. Any lingering doubts over the tie were settled by half-time - by Craig Robertson's header and Andreou's own-goal, after the defender went up with Gillhaus.

On loan Andy Dibble is ineligible, so Michael Watt keeps goal. Celtic pair Dziekanowski and Wdowczyk both used to play for Legia, who come nearest to a goal when Watt touches a free-kick given against McLeish onto the bar. Bett forces the save of the match from Szczesny.

All four Scottish representatives are bundled from Europe. Aberdeen did not contrive a single worthwhile chance throughout the 90 minutes. The best they could hope for was extra-time, but that was denied them when McKimmie headed out to Iwanicki, who chipped over Watt.

Season review — League table (Scottish Premier Division)

	P	W	D	L	F	A	W	D	L	F	A	Pts
			Home						**Away**			
1 Rangers	36	14	3	1	40	8	10	4	4	22	15	55
2 ABERDEEN	36	12	5	1	30	7	10	4	4	32	20	53
3 Celtic	36	10	4	4	30	14	7	3	8	22	24	41
4 Dundee Utd	36	11	3	4	28	16	6	4	8	13	13	41
5 Hearts	36	10	3	5	28	22	4	4	10	20	33	35
6 Motherwell	36	9	5	4	28	18	3	4	11	23	32	33
7 St Johnstone	36	6	4	8	23	25	5	5	8	18	29	31
8 Dunfermline	36	5	7	6	23	26	3	4	11	15	35	27
9 Hibernian	36	6	5	7	17	25	0	8	10	7	26	25
10 St Mirren	36	4	5	9	14	25	1	4	13	14	34	19
	360	87	44	49	261	186	49	44	87	186	261	360

Aberdeen — head-to-head and overall record

	P	W	D	L	F	A	Pts	Cup	W	D	L
v St Mirren	4	4	0	0	8	1	8				
v Hibernian	4	3	1	0	9	3	7				
v Hearts	4	3	0	1	12	2	6	LC	1	0	0
v Celtic	4	3	0	1	7	1	6				
v Motherwell	4	2	2	0	6	1	6	LC		1	0
v Dunfermline	4	2	2	0	8	4	6				
v Dundee Utd	4	2	1	1	6	5	5	SC	0	0	1
v St Johnstone	4	2	1	1	6	5	5				
v Rangers	4	1	2	1	3	4	4	LC	0	0	1
v Rangers	36	22	9	5	62	27	53				

Appearances and Goals

		Appearances							Goals				
	Lge	Sub	LC	Sub	SC	Sub	Eur	Sub	Lge	LC	SC	Eur	Tot
Bett, Jim	36		3		1		4		7		2		9
Booth, Scott	8	11		1		1		1	6				6
Cameron, Ian	3	7	1		1		1		1				1
Connor, Robert	29		4				3		6				6
Dibble, Andy	5												
Gardner, Lee								1					
Gillhaus, Hans	35				1		4		14		1		15
Grant, Brian	32		3				3		2				2
Irvine, Brian	29		4				4		2		1		3
Jess, Eoin	20	7	3	1			1	2	13		1	1	15
McKimmie, Stewart	25		4				4		1				1
McLeish, Alex	33		3				4		3		3	1	7
Mason, Paul	25	1	4				4		3				3
Miller, Willie	1												
Robertson, Craig	2	6	1			1		1	1	1			2
Robertson, David	35		4				4		1				1
Robertson, Ian		1											
Snelders, Theo	21		4		2		2						
van de Ven, Peter	23	9	3	1	1		3	1					
van der Ark, Willem	6	5							4				4
Watson, Gregg	2	5			1								
Watt, Michael	10						2						
Wright, Stephen	17	1							1				1
(own-goals)												1	1
23 players used	396	53	44	6	11	2	44	6	62		9	5	76

Odds & ends

Never lost to: (4) St Mirren, Hibs, Dunfermline, Motherwell (in league).
Never beat: (0).

Won from behind: (6) Dundee U (a, a), Dunfermline (h & a), Hearts (a), St Johnstone (h).
Lost from in front: (0).

High spots: Topping the league in late November. Then taking 23 points from 12 games from 2 February to lead the table with one match left.

Low spots: Losing to Rangers in Ibrox title-decider. Being humiliated 0-5 at St Johnstone. Surrendering the Scottish Cup at the first hurdle. Falling tamely to Legia Warsaw in Cup-Winners' Cup.

11 first-team players played 21 league games or more.

Bogey-team: Rangers.
Ever-presents: (1) Jim Bett (league only).
Hat-tricks: (3) Eoin Jess (2), Hans Gillhaus (1).
Leading scorer: (15) Hans Gillhaus and Eoin Jess

B & Q SCOTTISH PREMIER

Manager: Alex Smith → Willie Miller — SEASON 1991-92

No	Date		Att	Pos	Pt	F-A	H-T	Scorers, Times, and Referees	1	2	3	4	5	6	7	8	9	10	11	subs used
1	A AIRDRIE 10/8	W	6,337		2	2-1	0-1	Irvine 53, Gillhaus 89 / *Lawrence 25* / Ref: W Crombie	Snelders	Wright	Connor	Grant	Irvine	McKimmie	van de Ven	Bett	Jess*	Ten Caat*	Gillhaus	Winnie/Booth
									McKnight	*Kidd*	*Jack*	*Sandison*	*Honor*	*Conn*	*Lawrence*	*Balfour*	*Stewart*	*Coyle*	*Kirkwood*	
2	A FALKIRK 14/8	W	8,462		4	1-0	0-0	Booth 58, Ref: A Waddell	Snelders	Wright	Winnie	Grant	Irvine	McKimmie	van de Ven*	Bett	Booth*	Connor	Gillhaus	Watson Gg/Jess
									Westwater	*Duffy*	*McQueen*	*Hughes*	*Godfrey*	*Rice*	*McGivern**	*Taylor*	*McAllister**	*Stainrod*	*Smith*	May/Baptie
3	H DUNFERMLINE 17/8	W	13,849	2	6	3-0	1-0	Bett 13, Grant 89, Jess 90, Ref: J McCluskey	Snelders	Wright	Winnie	Grant	Irvine	McKimmie	van de Ven	Bett	Booth*	Connor	Gillhaus	van de Ven/Jess
									Rhodes	*Farningham*	*Cunnington*	*McCathie*	*Moyes*	*Haro*	*Davies**	*McParland*	*O'Boyle**	*McCall*	*Kosma*	Leitch/McWilliams
4	H CELTIC 24/8	W	20,503	1	8	1-0	1-0	Gillhaus 26, Ref: D Syme	Snelders	Wright	Winnie	Grant	Irvine	McKimmie	van de Ven	Bett	van der Ark*	Cameron*	Gillhaus	Watson Gg/Booth
									Bonner	*Morris*	*Rogan*	*Grant*	*Whyte*	*Gillespie*	*Fulton*	*Coyne*	*Creaney*	*Nicholas**	*Collins*	Galloway/Wdowczyk
5	A DUNDEE UTD 31/8	D	11,961	7	9	0-0	0-0	Ref: J Timmons	Snelders	Wright	Winnie	Grant*	Irvine	McKimmie	van de Ven	Bett	Jess*	Connor	Gillhaus	van de Ven/Booth
									Main	*Clark*	*Malpas*	*Bowman*	*van d' Hoorn*	*Cleland**	*McLaren**	*McKinlay*	*French*	*Paatelainen*	*Bollan*	Muller/O'Neill
6	H ST JOHNSTONE 7/9	L	12,071	9	9	1-2	1-0	van der Ven 29 / *Curran 48, Redford 58* / Ref: G Smith	Snelders	Wright*	Winnie	van de Ven	Irvine	McKimmie	Mason*	Bett	Booth	Connor	Gillhaus	Ten Caat/van Ark
									Hamilton	*Treanor*	*Baltacha*	*McGinnis*	*Inglis*	*Davies**	*Maskray**	*Turner*	*Wright**	*Redford*	*Curran*	Barron/Ward
7	A MOTHERWELL 14/9	W	6,452	7	11	1-0	1-0	Gillhaus 29, Ref: R Orr	Snelders	Thomson	Connor	Grant*	Irvine	McKimmie	Mason*	Bett	van der Ark*	Ten Caat*	Gillhaus	van de Ven/Booth
									Maxwell	*Griffin*	*Nijholt*	*Simpson**	*Philliben*	*McCart*	*McGrillen*	*O'Donnell*	*Cusack*	*Angus*	*Cooper**	Kirk/Verheel
8	H HIBERNIAN 21/9	D	11,850	3	12	1-1	1-0	Grant 28 / *Weir 49* / Ref: G Evans	Snelders	Wright	Connor	Grant	Irvine	McKimmie	van de Ven	Bett	Mason	Ten Caat*	Gillhaus	van der Ark/Booth
									Burridge	*Orr*	*Mitchell*	*Hunter*	*McIntyre*	*MacLeod*	*Weir**	*Hamilton*	*Wright*	*McGraw**	*McGinlay*	Evans/Miller
9	A RANGERS 28/9	W	36,330	3	14	2-0	0-0	Jess 72, Grant 86, Ref: B McGinlay	Snelders	Connor	Robertson D	Grant	Irvine	McKimmie	van de Ven*	Bett	Booth*	Ten Caat	Gillhaus	van Ark/Watson Gra
									Goram	*Stevens*	*Brown*	*Spackman*	*Nisbet*	*McCall*	*Robertson A*	*Hateley**	*Johnston*	*Mik'chenk**	*Spencer/Huistra*	Mik'chenk*/Spencer/Huistra
10	H ST MIRREN 5/10	W	10,154	11	16	4-1	2-0	Ten Caat 13, Grant 29, Irvine 67, Irvine 76, Mason 76 / *Charnley 54* / Ref: D Miller	Snelders	Mason	Connor	Grant	Irvine*	McKimmie	van de Ven	Bett	Booth*	Ten Caat	Jess	van Ark/Watson Gra
									Fridge	*McGowne**	*Reid*	*Aitken*	*Martin*	*Manley*	*Lambert*	*Torfason*	*Irvine*	*Charnley*	*Broddle*	McDowall/McGill
11	A HEARTS 9/10	L	15,569	16	16	0-1	0-1	*Crabbe 10* / Ref: D Hope	Snelders	Smith	Connor	Grant	Irvine	McKimmie	van de Ven*	Bett	Ferguson D	Ten Caat	Jess	van Ark/Watson Gra
									Smith	*McLaren*	*McKinlay*	*Levein*	*Mackay*	*McPherson*	*Crabbe*	*Baird**	*Baird**	*Millar*	*Robertson*	Ferguson I

Match notes:

1. Theo Ten Caat and David Winnie are in, Alex McLeish is out, chipping an ankle-bone. The Dons lost on penalties to Manchester United in pre-season warm-up. Promoted Airdrie take the lead but lose to two headers. Gillhaus's late far-post winner came from Scott Booth's cross.

2. The score flattered the Dons, for apart from Robert Connor's cross which was touched in by Scott Booth, Falkirk's keeper was largely untroubled. Theo Snelders, on the other hand, had a jittery game. After five minutes he fumbled Simon Stainrod's 20-yarder against a post.

3. Bett scores direct from a free-kick, but three minutes later misses from the penalty spot - Rhodes turning the ball onto a post after Moyes handled. The miss meant Aberdeen took their slender lead into the final minute, when Grant pounced after Rhodes saved from van de Ven.

4. Charlie Nicholas makes his first competitive return to Pittodrie since his transfer to Celtic. He accomplished little, and was subbed after 54 minutes. Ian Cameron makes his first start of the season for Aberdeen. Hans Gillhaus chipped Pat Bonner, having been set up by van der Ark.

5. Aberdeen's 100% start to the season ends at misty Tannadice. Paul Mason returns to the side, having been left out since the end of 1990-91. The game's best chance came after 52 minutes. Connor's header was touched by Main to Gillhaus, who struck the bar from five yards out.

6. Following Airdrie in the Skol Cup a home defeat by 10-man St Johnstone. Three minutes after van de Ven puts Aberdeen in front Davies is booked for shoving a hand in his face. Four minutes later Davies speaks out of turn and is expelled. Two second-half headers sink the Dons.

7. Motherwell field two former Dons - Ian Angus, and Neil Simpson, recently signed from Newcastle. Gillhaus headed the only goal, and for his pains required treatment for injuries sustained. Gillhaus later missed badly from close in, when the ball bounced off him.

8. John Burridge will later stand in for the Dons; now he stands in for Hibs, who are the only unbeaten team in Scotland. Winnie is stretchered off with a twisted knee. Grant's header was cancelled out controversially when Mickey Weir appeared to handle as he ran from the halfway line.

9. Jocky Scott has been sacrificed in the wake of Aberdeen's three wretched home defeats. He becomes manager of Dunfermline, leaving Alex Smith in sole charge. This wonderful win lifts spirits. Ten Caat finds the unmarked Jess; then van der Ark skins former Don David Robertson.

10. Pittodrie's smallest crowd so far sees this handsome demolition. Ten Caat scores his first Aberdeen goal, after being set up by van de Ven and Booth. At 2-0 Snelders spills Charnley's hopeful 30-yarder over the line. Brian Irvine made it 3-1 when Bett's free-kick was cleared to him.

11. Aberdeen dominated but lost to Joe Jordan's Hearts. The vital goal was the result of a free-kick given for Connor's foul on Crabbe. Later in the first half Irvine clashed with Levein and afterwards sported a black eye. The referee took no action. Booth and Grant missed good chances.

Aberdeen F.C. 1991–92 — match-by-match (games 12–22)

12 · H AIRDRIE · 12/10
8,998 | 3 W 11 18 | 3-1 | 1-0
Ten Caat 8, Jess 60, 82 / *Gray 70*
Ref: M Clark
Aberdeen: Snelders, Mason, Connor, Grant*, Irvine, McKimmie, van de Ven, Bett, Booth*, Ten Caat, Jess; subs van der Ark, Gray
Airdrie: *Martin, Kidd, Stewart, Sandison, Honor, Kirkwood, Boyle, Balfour*, Smith, Coyle, Black; Gibson, Watson*
Ten Caat scores after Jess rounds the keeper and has his shot cleared off the line. Coyle heads against Snelders' bar and is shortly involved in an off-the-ball tussle with van de Ven, who is sent off on advice from the linesman. Scott Booth was booked for handling the ball into the net.

13 · A DUNFERMLINE · 19/10
5,157 | 3 D 12 19 | 0-0 | 0-0
Ref: A Huett
Aberdeen: Snelders, Watson Gra, Connor, Grant*, Winnie, McKimmie, Mason, Bett, Booth*, Ten Caat, Jess; subs van der Ark, Gillhaus
Dunfermline: *Rhodes, Wilson, Sharp, McCathie, Moyes, Robertson, McWilliams, Leitch, Kozma, Cunnington, Sinclair*
A forgettable game. Irvine is a late call-off, Winnie deputising in a match played in an icy wind. Dunfermline's Hungarian international, Kozma, races clear but is superbly tackled inside the box by acting skipper Bett. Gillhaus reappears as a substitute after his long lay off.

14 · A ST JOHNSTONE · 26/10
5,682 | 3 W 9 21 | 3-1 | 1-1
van de Ven 12, Jess 85, Mason 90 / *Curran 43*
Ref: W Morrison
Aberdeen: Snelders, van de Ven, Winnie, Jess, Irvine, McKimmie, Mason, Bett, Booth*, Ten Caat, Gillhaus*; subs Watson, Grant
St Johnstone: *Hamilton, Treanor, McVicar, McGinnis, Inglis, Davies, Maskrey*, Turner, Wright, Curran, Redford*
St Johnstone have caused the Dons endless headaches of late, and Curran's equaliser at the second attempt - Snelders having pushed his effort against a post - looked likely to continue the sequence. Jess's 85th minute effort required a deflection off Turner to beat Hamilton in goal.

15 · H MOTHERWELL · 30/10
9,092 | 1 W 23 | 3-1 | 0-0
Winnie 46, Mason 86, Gillhaus 88 / *Arnott 51*
Ref: D Yeats
Aberdeen: Snelders, van de Ven, Winnie, Jess*, Irvine, McKimmie, Mason, Bett, Booth*, Ten Caat, Gillhaus*; subs Watson, Gardner
Motherwell: *Thomson, Dolan, Griffin, Simpson, Philliben, McCart, Arnott, O'Donnell*, Cusack, Kirk, Cooper*
A replica of the previous match. Aberdeen score twice in the closing seconds, having squandered the advantage. Neil Simpson cleared off the line from Irvine before Winnie dived to head his first goal for Aberdeen. The tiny Arnott headed Motherwell's goal before Paul Mason struck.

16 · H DUNDEE UTD · 2/11
13,728 | 3 L 6 23 | 0-1 | 0-1
McInally 18
Ref: L Mottram
Aberdeen: Snelders, van de Ven, Winnie, Watson Gg, Irvine, McKimmie, Mason*, Bett, Jess, Ten Caat, Gillhaus*; subs Booth
Dundee Utd: *van der Kamp, Clark, Malpas, Bowman, van d'Hoorn, Narey, McKinlay, Ferguson, McKinnon*, Paatelainen; Roddie*
Hearts overtake Aberdeen at the top of the table as a result of Jim McInally dispossessing Theo Ten Caat inside the Aberdeen half and racing upfield to score off the base of a post. The Dons' powder-puff front line threatened van de Kamp only twice in the whole game.

17 · A CELTIC · 9/11
36,837 | 4 L 3 23 | 1-2 | 1-1
Jess 11 / *Nicholas 13, Creaney 64*
Ref: G Smith
Aberdeen: Snelders, Watson Gra, Winnie*, Jess*, Irvine, McKimmie, Watson Gg, Bett, Booth, Ten Caat, Gillhaus; subs Roddie
Celtic: *Bonner, McNally, Morris*, Galloway, Mowbray, Gillespie, O'Neil, McStay, Coyne, Nicholas*, Collins; Creaney/Cascarino*
Celtic were knocked out of Europe in midweek. Their much-changed side includes £1 million centre-half Tony Mowbray from Middlesbrough. Jess's far-post goal was against the run of play, and was instantly cancelled out when Collins dispossessed Bett and freed Charlie Nicholas.

18 · A ST MIRREN · 16/11
3,634 | 3 W 11 25 | 1-0 | 0-0
McIntyre 51 og
Ref: W Innes
Aberdeen: Snelders, Watson Gra, Winnie, Jess, Irvine, McKimmie, van de Ven, Bett, van der Ark*, Ten Caat*, Gillhaus; subs Booth/Watson Gra, McGill
St Mirren: *Money, McGowne, Broddie, Aitken, Baillie*, Manley, Lambert, McKinlay, Irvine, McDowall, Elliott*
Love St is cold and empty. For the first time Aberdeen field all five of their Dutch players from the start. The only goal was a mess. Ten Caat's free-kick reached Jess, who failed to control it. Buddies' Paul McIntyre, attempting to clear, charged the ball into the far corner from 18 yards.

19 · H HEARTS · 20/11
15,338 | 5 L 25 | 0-2 | 0-1
Baird 9, Robertson 83
Ref: J Renton
Aberdeen: Snelders, Smith!, Winnie, Jess, Irvine, McKimmie, van de Ven*, Bett, van der Ark*, Ten Caat, Gillhaus; subs Watson Gra
Hearts: *Smith, McLaren, McKinlay, Levein, Mackay, McPherson, Crabbe, Wright, Baird*, Miller, Robertson*; Ferguson l/Hogg*
Gary Smith, a £175,000 summer signing from Falkirk, makes his debut, and is sent off eight minutes from time for his first foul - on George Wright. From the resulting free-kick John Robertson scores Hearts' second. Aberdeen commit only 12 fouls in total, but earn three bookings.

20 · A HIBERNIAN · 23/11
8,942 | 4 L 5 25 | 0-1 | 0-0
Lennon 90
Ref: D Syme
Aberdeen: Snelders, Watson Gra, Winnie, Kane*, Irvine, McKimmie, van de Ven, Bett, Booth, Ten Caat, Gillhaus; subs Cameron
Hibernian: *Burridge, Miller, Tortolano, Beaumont, McIntyre^, Hunter, Bailey^, Hamilton, Wright, Nicholls, McGinlay; Lennon/Sneddon*
Paul Kane - £300,000 from Oldham - makes his debut. Wright goes down in the box. Before the penalty is taken Snelders hits him and is sent off. Irvine saves McGinlay's spot-kick. Then Sneddon fouls Jess. Bett shoots over from the spot. In injury-time Lennon fires in Miller's cross.

21 · H FALKIRK · 30/11
10,614 | 5 D 8 26 | 1-1 | 0-1
Gillhaus 83p / *Duffy 38*
Ref: D Syme
Aberdeen: Watt, Smith, Winnie, Kane*, McLeish, Irvine, McLeish, Bett, Booth, Jess, Gillhaus; subs Roddie/Cameron
Falkirk: *Westwater, Duffy, Oliver, Hughes, Baptie, Rice, McAllister, Taylor^, May, Sloan; Lennon/Mooney*
Gillhaus's penalty earns the Dons their first home point since late October. Skipper McLeish plays his first full game of the season. McKimmie has a knee injury and Snelders is suspended. Duffy's goal at the far post was cancelled out when Roddie was fouled chasing Rice's back-pass.

22 · H RANGERS · 4/12
20,081 | 5 L 3 26 | 2-3 | 1-2
Ten Caat 7, Irvine 66 / *Hateley 3, 36, McCoist 62*
Ref: L Mottram
Aberdeen: Snelders, Winnie, Cameron, Kane, McLeish, Irvine, McLeish, Bett, van de Ven*, Ten Caat*, Gillhaus; subs van der Ark/Roddie, Jess/Booth
Rangers: *Goram, Robertson D, Gough, Stevens, Spackman, Kuznetsov, Gordon, McCall, McCoist, Hateley, Mik'chenko^, Brown*
A first return to Pittodrie for David Robertson. McLeish's poor back-pass sets up Rangers' third goal, giving them their first win at Pittodrie for three years. After Hateley put Rangers 1-0 up, Stevens fouled Gillhaus in the box. Gillhaus' penalty kick rebounded off a post to Ten Caat.

B & Q SCOTTISH PREMIER

Manager: Alex Smith → Willie Miller — SEASON 1991-92

Opponent line-ups are shown in the second (italic) row of each match. Metadata: the leading column is Aberdeen's position + result; the italic "Pos" column is the opponents' league position.

No	Date			Att	Pos	Pt	F-A	H-T	Scorers, Times, and Referees	1	2	3	4	5	6	7	8	9	10	11	subs used
23	A AIRDRIE 7/12	6	L	3,071	10	26	0-2	0-1	Coyle 31, 62 Ref: J McCluskey	Snelders	Smith	Winnie	Grant	McLeish	Irvine	van de Ven	Bett	van der Ark	Cameron*	Gillhaus*	Kane/Jess
										Martin	*Kidd*	*Stewart*	*Sandison*	*Conn*	*Black*	*Boyle*	*Balfour*	*Smith*	*Kirkwood*	*Coyle*	
24	H ST JOHNSTONE 14/12	5	W	9,292	8	28	4-1	1-1	Jess 21, Grant 72, Booth 75, Roddie 85 Stewart 3p Ref: D McVicar	Snelders	Smith	Watson Gra	Grant*	Irvine	Kane	van de Ven	Bett	Booth*	Ten Caat	Jess	Ferguson/Roddie
										Hamilton	*Stewart*	*Redford*	*McGinnis*	*Inglis**	*Dunne*	*Davies**	*Turner*	*Wright*	*Arkins*	*Curran*	*Baltacha/Moore*
25	H CELTIC 28/12	5	D	20,442	3	29	2-2	2-0	Ten Caat 14, Jess 21 Mowbray 52, Cascarino 68 Ref: W Crombie	Snelders	McKimmie	Smith	Grant	McLeish	Irvine	Jess	Bett	Booth*	Ten Caat	Kane*	Roddie/Watson Gra
										Marshall	*Morris*	*McNally*	*Grant*	*Mowbray*	*Whyte*	*O'Neil**	*McStay*	*Coyne*	*Nicholas**	*Collins*	*Cascarino/Fulton*
26	A DUNDEE UTD 1/1		L	7,777		29	0-4	0-0	Ferguson E2, Paatelainen 54, [Jackson 80, 81] Ref: H Williamson	Snelders	Smith	Watson Gra*	Grant	McLeish	McKimmie	van der Hoorn	Mason	Booth*	Ten Caat*	Jess	Kane/Gillhaus
										van de Kamp	*Clark*	*Malpas*	*Bowman*	*van der Hoorn*	*McInally*	*McLaren**	*Cleland*	*Jackson*	*Ferguson*	*Paatelainen*	*McKinnon*
27	H ST MIRREN 4/1	6	D	8,774	11	30	0-0	0-0	Ref: D Hope	Snelders	McKimmie	Smith	Grant	McLeish	Irvine	Mason	Kane	Ten Caat	Jess	Gillhaus	Roddie
										Money	*McGowne*	*Beattie*	*Baillie*	*Charnley**	*Manley*	*Lambert*	*Elliott*	*Stickroth*	*Broddie*	*Reid*	*McDowall/Irvine*
28	A HEARTS 11/1	6	W	16,291	2	32	4-0	1-0	Jess 39, 70, Booth 51, Mason 65 Ref: B McGinlay	Snelders	McKimmie	Winnie	Grant*	McLeish*	Irvine	Mason	Kane	Booth*	Jess	Gillhaus	Smith/Roddie
										Smith	*McLaren*	*McKinlay*	*Levein*	*Mackay*	*McPherson*	*Crabb*	*Ferguson D*	*Baird*	*Millar*	*Robertson*	
29	A MOTHERWELL 14/1	6	D	5,221	7	33	3-3	1-2	Kane 22, Jess 53, Roddie 81 Kirk 4, Nijholt 29p, O'Donnell 69 Ref: M Clark	Snelders	Nijholt	Winnie	Kane	McLeish*	Wright	Mason*	Bett	Booth*	Jess	Gillhaus	Ferguson/Roddie Shepherd
										Thomson	*McKinnon*	*McKinlay*	*Dolan*	*Philliben*	*Martin*	*Arnott*	*Angus*	*Kirk*	*O'Donnell*	*Cooper*	
30	A FALKIRK 18/1	5	D	5,122	9	34	2-2	0-2	Mason 64, Booth 78 Grant 13 og, Cadette 38 Ref: W Morrison	Snelders	Oliver	Winnie	Kane	Wright	Irvine	Mason*	Bett	Cameron	Jess	Gillhaus*	Gillhaus/Booth Taggart
										Westwater	*McQueen*	*Duffy*	*Hughes*	*Baptie*		*McAllister*	*Taylor**	*Cadette*	*Sloan*	*May*	
31	H DUNFERMLINE 1/2	5	D	7,549	12	35	1-1	0-0	Jess 73 McParland 81 Ref: D Smye	Snelders	McKimmie	Smith	Grant	Irvine	Wright	Booth*	Bett	Roddie*	Jess	Gillhaus	Booth/Ferguson Kozma
										Rhodes	*Bowes*	*Cunnington*	*McCathie*	*Moyes*	*Cooper*	*Davies*	*Shannon*	*French*	*Leitch**	*Kozma*	*McParland*
32	H HIBERNIAN 8/2	5	L	9,568	4	35	0-1	0-0	Weir 88 Ref: J Timmons	Snelders	McKimmie	Smith	Grant	Irvine	Wright	Booth*	Bett	Cameron	Ten Caat*	Jess	Gillhaus Lennon
										Burridge	*Orr*	*Mitchell*	*Hunter*	*McIntyre*	*MacLeod**	*Weir*	*Hamilton*	*Tortolano*	*McGinlay*	*Lennon*	
33	A RANGERS 25/2		D	38,513		36	0-0	0-0	Ref: G Smith	Snelders	McKimmie	Smith	Grant	Irvine	Wright	Booth*	Bett	Cameron	Ten Caat	Jess	Durrant
										Goram	*Stevens*	*Robertson D*	*Gough*	*Spackman*	*Brown*	*Gordon**	*Ferguson*	*McCoist*	*Hateley*	*Huistra*	

Match notes:

23 — The kick-off was delayed because Broomfield's turnstile operators went on strike. Ex-Peterhead striker Andy Smith leads Airdrie's attack. Both goals came from Black crosses. Two minutes after Ark Gillhaus's penalty was saved and he was subbed.

24 — Only six of the team beaten by Airdrie have kept their places. Three of the young replacements scored. Aberdeen had the worst possible start when Irvine charged Arkins in the back. At 1-1 van de Ven flattened ex-Don Paul Wright and was sent off for the second time this season.

25 — Last Saturday's game with Motherwell was postponed. McLeish and McKimmie return to the side. The Dons go two up when Ten Caat's shot is turned on to the post and Booth's follow-up comes back off the bar. Cascarino completes Celtic's fight-back by heading in O'Neil's cross.

26 — Dundee United's biggest ever New Firm win sends shock-waves through the Dons. Transitional United are having a bad run, but they run riot in the second half against a full-strength Dons team. Duncan Ferguson begins the rout, sprinting away from Gary Smith from the halfway line.

27 — This dreary match provokes yet another demonstration against Alex Smith. St Mirren had lost their last four and had not scored a goal for 11 hours. At the end Snelders saves with his finger-tips from Broddie. Jim Bett misses his first game of the season. Pittodrie is not a happy place.

28 — Aberdeen's biggest ever win at Tynecastle knocks Hearts - who were unbeaten in 16 games - off the top. The Dons' three-man attack brought a first-half goal for Jess, who silences Tynecastle by controlling Gary Smith's long pass, sidestepping McLaren, and scoring from 20 yards.

29 — Three times the Dons come from behind. Sub Roddie's late goal preserves Aberdeen's four-year unbeaten record against Motherwell. At 3-3 Jess hit the bar. Kirk had scored Motherwell's first goal when the ball bouced off the referee. Winnie pulled down Arnott for the penalty.

30 — Richard Cadette makes his Falkirk home debut after signing from Brentford, and puts the Bairns two up after controlling the ball on his chest and shooting on the turn. Earlier, Brian Grant turns ex-Don Tommy McQueen's corner past his own keeper. Jim Bett sets up Booth's leveller.

31 — Pittodrie's smallest crowd so far watches the worst match so far. Bottom-club Dunfermline - who include Neale Cooper - would have won but for super saves by stand-in skipper Snelders. Jess's mis-hit gave the Dons the lead. McParland headed in at the near post from Kozma's cross.

32 — One of the worst games ever seen at Pittodrie is settled at the death by Weir's close-in header from Tortolano's cross. Aberdeen have now won just three of their last 18 games. Demonstrations against Alex Smith help bring about his dismissal, which is announced on Monday morning.

33 — Willie Miller's managerial baptism is rewarded by this backs-to-the-wall, televised draw. Hans Gillhaus is missing from the team. When asked if Gillhaus is injured or has been dropped, Miller replies: 'He is not injured.' Snelders saved well from Hateley, newly returned from injury.

34 A ST MIRREN 29/2 2-0 Mason 2, Smith 27 Ref: L Thow
3,853 11 38 | 5 W 2-0

Watt · McKimmie · Smith · Grant · Irvine · Wright · Mason* · Bett · Kane · Ten Caat · Jess · Watson Gg
Money · Dawson · Beattie · Aitken · McIntyre · McGowne · Elliott* · Lambert · Torfason · Hewitt · Bradlie · Stickroth/Kinsey*

Gary Smith's first goal for Aberdeen confirms Willie Miller's first win. Theo Snelders is injured and Hans Gillhaus dropped. Paul Mason gave the Dons an early lead when playing a one-two with Eoin Jess outside the box. Smith's goal came from a corner-kick that was not cleared.

---

35 A CELTIC 14/3 0-0 Collins 74 Ref: H Williamson
29,380 3 38 | 6 L 0-1

Snelders · McKimmie · Smith · Grant · Irvine · Wright · Mason · Bett · Kane · Ten Caat* · Jess · Gibson
Marshall · Morris · Boyd · Fulton · Mowbray · Gillespie · Miller · McNally · Coyne · Creaney · Collins · O'Neil*

This bruising match was settled by a Creaney cross that saw Coyne challenge Snelders hard in the air. The ball broke free to Collins. Collins had hit the post in the first half, but in the second it was Aberdeen who showed the better ideas. Willie Miller's first defeat was a bit harsh.

---

36 H HEARTS 18/3 1-0 Ten Caat 36, Mason 81 Ref: L Mottram
10,581 40 | W 2-0

Snelders · McKimmie · Smith · Grant · Irvine · Wright · Mason · Bett · Kane* · Ten Caat · Jess · Gillhaus
Smith · McLaren · McKinlay · Levein · Mackay · McPherson · Crabbe · Ferguson D · Millar! · Ferguson I · Robertson` · Snodin/Wright

Hearts have never recovered from that 0-4 thrashing last month. John Millar becomes the ninth Heart to be sent off this season when he elbows Bett. The game was still simmering from Kane's tackle on Crabbe which Hearts were convinced was a penalty. Crabbe was booked for diving.

---

37 H DUNDEE UTD 21/3 0-1 Ferguson 45, McNally 83 Ref: B McGinlay
10,350 4 40 | 5 L 0-2

Snelders · McKimmie · Smith · Grant · Irvine · Wright · Mason · Bett · Jess* · Ten Caat · Gillhaus* · Kane/Ferguson
Main · Cleland · Malpas · McInally · van d'Hoorn Welsh · Ferreya · Johnston · Ferguson · Jackson · Paatelainen · O'Neil*

On the stroke of half-time Snelders allows Ferguson's half-hit shot to trundle into the net. Aberdeen substitute Graeme Ferguson was then dispossessed by Jim McInally for the second goal. Willie Miller included Hans Gillhaus for the first time, but still suffers his first home defeat.

---

38 H AIRDRIE 28/3 0-0 Irvine 62 Ref: D Yeats
6,805 42 | 5 W 1-0

Snelders · McKimmie · Smith · Grant · Irvine · Winnie · Mason · Bett · Kane · Ten Caat · Jess
Martin · Jack · Stewart · Sandison · Caesar · Black · Boyle · Balfour · Smith* · Coyle · Kirkwood · Reid/Abercrombie*

Mixu Paatelainen played against Aberdeen last week. Now he becomes Miller's first signing. He was signed too late to play but is paraded before kick-off. Stephen Wright missed the game through injury picked up in an Under-21 game v Germany. The Dons hit the wood twice.

---

39 A DUNFERMLINE 4/4 0-0 Ref: R Tait
3,033 12 43 | 5 D 0-0

Snelders · McKimmie · Humphries · Grant · Irvine · Winnie · Mason* · Bett · Kane · Ten Caat · Jess · Paatelainen Ten Caat
Rhodes · Bowes · Sharp · McCathie · Moyes · Robertson · Kelly · Davies · French · McWilliams · Cunnington

Torrential pre-match rain results in a pitch that is heavily sanded. Brian Irvine's suspension and Gary Smith's knee injury allow a debut for Mark Humphries. First-half controversy when Mason is body-checked by keeper Rhodes outside the box. No red card, no foul, but a goal-kick.

---

40 A ST JOHNSTONE 8/4 0-0 Ref: J Timmons
4,524 8 44 | 5 D 0-0

Snelders · McKimmie · Humphries · Grant · Irvine · Wright · Mason · Bett · Winnie · Jess* · Kane · Paatelainen Gillhaus
Hamilton · Treanor · Baltacha · Cherry · Inglis · Redford · Turner · Davies · Grant · Curran* · Wright · Arkins/Maskrey*

Had Aberdeen won they would have climbed above Dundee United on goal-difference. Paatelainen twice spurned chances to score his first goal. St Johnstone came nearest to scoring when Curran's header crashed against Snelders' bar. John Inglis was booked for persistent fouling.

---

41 A MOTHERWELL 11/4 2-0 Grant 14, Kane 33 Ref: W Crombie
6,902 7 46 | 4 W 2-0

Snelders · McKimmie · Humphries · Grant · Irvine · Wright · Mason · Jess* · Kane · Winnie · Gillhaus* · Paatelainen Mason/Gibson
Thomson · Nijholt · McKinnon · Martin · Jones · McCart · McLeod · Dolan` · Gardner` · Davies · Cooper · Kirk/Bryce

Miller plays Gillhaus, Jess, and Paatelainen in a three-man attack. Gillhaus set up Grant for the first goal, and Bett's corner led to the second. Aberdeen have a lucky escape when McKimmie's headed clearance bounced on top of Snelders' crossbar. Bett was the best player on view.

---

42 A HIBERNIAN 18/4 0-0 Paatelainen 74, Donald 85 Ref: B McGinlay
6,777 6 47 | 4 D 1-1

Snelders · McKimmie · Winnie · Grant · Irvine · Wright · Mason · Bett · Kane* · Jess* · Gillhaus* · Paatelainen Jess/Roddie
Burridge · Miller · Mitchell · Orr · McIntyre · Hunter · Weir · Hamilton · Findlay · Evans* · McGinlay · Donald/Farrell*

Andy Gibson starts his first match for Aberdeen. Gillhaus is not even on the bench. Jess comes on as sub and sends McKimmie away down the right, and Paatelainen heads in the cross. Graeme Donald heads Hibs' equaliser, having earlier helped Hibs' youth team win the BP Youth Cup.

---

43 H FALKIRK 25/4 0-1 Booth 58 McQueen 36p Ref: G Smith
6,461 7 48 | 5 D 1-1

Snelders · McKimmie · Winnie · Grant · Irvine · Wright · Gibson* · Bett · Kane · Ten Caat* · Paatelainen Mason/Booth
McDougall · Oliver · McQueen · Duffy · Hughes · Lennox · McAllister · McGvern · May · Baptie · Smith · Johnston*

A group of Brentford fans have come up to cheer Falkirk and Richard Cadette, but he does not play. McKimmie fouled Lennox for the penalty. McKimmie was booked for protesting. A hamstring has kept Booth out since February, but he scores seven minutes after coming off the bench.

---

44 H RANGERS 2/5 0-1 McCoist 37, 55 Ref: A Waddell
16,580 1 48 | 6 L 0-2

Snelders · McKimmie · Winnie · Grant · Irvine · Wright · Mason* · Bett · Kane · Booth · Ten Caat · Paatelainen Jess/Roddie
Goram · Stevens · Robertson · Gough · Rideout · Durrant · Gordon · McCall · McCoist · Hateley · Mik'chenko

Two McCoist goals keeps him in the hunt for Europe's Golden Boot award. Rangers have now scored over 100 goals. At 0-0 Gough trips Mixu, but Goram saves his penalty. Ian Durrant makes his first return to Pittodrie since the Simpson affair. The Beach End is now demolished.

Average Home 11,798
Away 12,224

B & Q PREMIER (CUP-TIES)

Manager: Alex Smith → Willie Miller   SEASON 1991-92

Skol League Cup

		F-A	H-T	Scorers, Times, and Referees	1	2	3	4	5	6	7	8	9	10	11	subs used
2 A CLYDE 21/8 2,107	W	4-0	1-0	Grant 19, van de Ven 73, Winnie 86, [Booth 89]Stevenson Ref: D McVicar	Snelders *Stevenson*	Wright *Knox*	Winnie *Tennant*	Grant *Morrison**	Irvine	McKimmie *McVie*	van de Ven *Thompson*	Bett* *Wilson*	van der Ark	Jess* *Scott**	Gillhaus *Wylde*	Watson Gra/Booth McCoy/McAuley
3 H AIRDRIE 28/8 13,000	L	0-1	0-0	Watson 78 Ref: L Mottram	Snelders *Martin*	Wright *Kidd**	Winnie *Stewart*	Grant *Sandison*	Irvine *Watson**	McKimmie *Honor*	van de Ven *Lawrence*	Bett *Balfour*	van der Ark* *Coyle*	Cameron* *Conn*	Gillhaus *Jack*	Jess/Booth *Kirkwood/Boyle*

It may have looked comfortable by the end, but until van de Ven's header from Gillhaus's cross produced a second goal after 73 minutes an upset was always on the cards. Brian Grant had opened the scoring from 25 yards, and his overall performance made him man of the match.

Promoted Airdrie gain revenge for their opening day defeat by the Dons. Some observers felt Airdrie did not play as well this time. They were under the cosh for much of the time, but stunned Pittodrie when Coyle laid the ball back to Watson. Keeper John Martin was man of the match.

Tennents Scottish Cup

		F-A	H-T	Scorers, Times, and Referees	1	2	3	4	5	6	7	8	9	10	11	subs used
3 H RANGERS 22/1 23,000	L	0-1	0-1	McCoist 20 Ref: J Timmons	Snelders *Goram*	McKimmie *Stevens*	Winnie* *Robertson D Gough*	Grant *Spackman*	Irvine *Brown*	Wright *Gordon*	Mason	Bett *McCall*	Booth* *McCoist*	Jess *Ferguson**	Gillhaus *Mik'chenko**	Roddie/Kane *Huistra*

McCoist is Scotland's leading scorer with 25 already. A scrappy goal, begun by Mikhailichenko's short corner, decides a surprisingly scrappy cup-tie. Only when Irvine powered forward at the end did Aberdeen threaten. The demands of TV meant this match was played in midweek.

UEFA Cup

		F-A	H-T	Scorers, Times, and Referees	1	2	3	4	5	6	7	8	9	10	11	subs used
1:1 H BK1903 COPEN' 18/9 (Denmark) 13,000	L	0-1	0-0	Kaus 86 Ref: V Christov (Czechoslovakia)	Snelders *Petersen*	Wright* *Wegner*	Irvine *Nielsen I*	McKimmie *Piechnik*	Connor *Tur*	Grant *Larsen*	Bett *Juul*	Ten Caat *Uldbjerg*	Jess *Manniche*	van der Ark* *Johans'n Mr**	Gillhaus *Nielsen L*	Watson Gra/Booth Kaus
1:2 A BK1903 COPEN' 2/10 5,237	L	0-2	0-0	Johansen Martin 57, Jensen 87 Ref: F Keupe (Austria) (Dons lose 0-3 on aggregate)	Snelders *Petersen*	Watson Gra* *Wegner*	Irvine *Nielsen I*	McKimmie *Piechnik*	Connor *Tur*	van de Ven *Larsen*	Bett *Jensen*	Ten Caat *Uldbjerg*	Booth* *Nielsen K*	Grant *Johansen Mar/Johansen Mic*	Jess	van der Ark/Cameron

Successive home defeats by Airdrie, St Johnstone, and BK1903 provoke supporter unrest never previously witnessed at Pittodrie. Chants of 'Smith must go' followed substitute Kaus's goal. Team spirit seems to be crumbling, with McKimmie arguing with team-mates and supporters.

Aberdeen have no answer to the combative, well-drilled Danes in the Gentofte Stadium. Brian Irvine's wayward thrown-in enabled the Johansen twins to work a goal between them. Torben Fiechnik, later to sign for Liverpool, heads on to Jensen for the Danes' second goal.

League Table

	P	Home W	D	L	F	A	Away W	D	L	F	A	Pts
1 Rangers	44	14	5	3	50	14	19	1	2	51	17	72
2 Hearts	44	12	7	3	26	15	15	2	5	34	22	63
3 Celtic	44	15	3	4	47	20	11	7	4	41	22	62
4 Dundee Utd	44	10	7	5	37	25	9	6	7	29	20	51
5 Hibernian	44	7	8	7	28	25	9	9	4	25	20	49
6 ABERDEEN	44	9	6	7	32	23	8	8	6	23	19	48
7 Airdrie	44	7	5	10	25	33	6	5	11	25	37	36
8 St Johnstone	44	5	7	10	21	32	8	3	11	31	41	36
9 Falkirk	44	7	2	13	29	41	5	9	8	25	37	35
10 Motherwell	44	5	6	11	25	29	5	8	9	18	32	34
11 St Mirren	44	2	5	15	18	36	4	7	11	15	37	24
12 Dunfermline	44	2	7	13	11	35	2	3	17	11	45	18
	528	95	68	101	349	328	101	68	95	328	349	528

Aberdeen's record against each club

	P	W	D	L	F	A	Pts	Cup	W	D	L
v St Mirren	4	3	1	0	7	1	7				
v Motherwell	4	3	1	0	9	4	7				
v Airdrie	4	3	0	1	6	4	6	LC	0	0	1
v St Johnstone	4	2	1	1	8	4	5				
v Dunfermline	4	1	3	0	4	1	5				
v Falkirk	4	1	3	0	5	4	5				
v Hearts	4	2	0	2	6	3	4				
v Celtic	4	1	1	2	3	5	3				
v Rangers	4	1	1	2	4	5	3	SC	0	0	1
v Hibernian	4	0	2	2	2	4	2				
v Dundee Utd	4	0	1	3	2	7	1				
	44	17	14	13	55	42	48				

Odds & ends

Never lost to: (4) St Mirren, Motherwell, Dunfermline, Falkirk.

Never beat: Hibs, Dundee Utd.

Won from behind: (2) Airdrie (a), St Johnstone (h).

Lost from in front: (2) St Johnstone (h), Celtic (a).

High spots: Good start. Winning first 4 league games to head the table.

Still third in the league by the end of October.

Low spots: 1 point from 5 games from 20 November, down to sixth.

Lowest league position for 15 seasons, since 1976-77.

Failing to beat, or even to score against local rivals Dundee Utd.

Only one player scored more than 7 goals.

Early exits from all domestic and European cup competitions.

Bogey-team: Dundee Utd.

Ever-presents: (0).

Hat-tricks: (0).

Leading scorer: (12) Eoin Jess.

Appearances and Goals

	App Lge	Sub	LC	Sub	SC	Sub	Eur	Sub	Goals Lge	Sub	LC	SC	Eur	Tot
Bett, Jim	38		2		1		2		1					1
Booth, Scott	21	12		2		1	1	1	5	1				6
Cameron, Ian	4	2	2		1									
Connor, Robert	11						2							
Ferguson, Graeme		4												
Gibson, Andrew	2	3												
Gillhaus, Hans	24	5	2		1		1		5					5
Grant, Brian	33		2		1		2		6			1		7
Humphries, Mark	2													
Irvine, Brian	41		2		1		2		4					4
Jess, Eoin	33	6	1	1	1		2	2	12					12
Kane, Paul	22	3	1			1	2		2					2
McKimmie, Stewart	39		2		1		2							
McLeish, Alex	7													
Mason, Paul	28	3	2		1		1		7					7
Paatelainen, Mixu	6								1					1
Roddie, Andrew	1	9				1			2					2
Smith, Gary	15	1							1					1
Snelders, Theo	42		2		1		2							
Ten Caat, Theo	28	2	2		1		2		5					5
van de Ven, Peter	20	3	1				1		2			1		3
van der Ark, Willem	7	11		1			1	1	1	1				
Watson, Graham	5	6												
Watson, Gregg	3	5												
Watt, Michael	2													
Winnie, David	27	1	2		1		1		1			1		2
Wright, Stephen	23		2		1				1					1
(own-goals)														1
27 players used	484	76	22	4	11	2	22	4	55	4		2		59

SCOTTISH PREMIER DIVISION — Manager: Willie Miller — SEASON 1992-93

For each fixture the upper (roman) line is Aberdeen, the lower (italic) line is the opposition.

No	Date	Venue / Opponent	Att	Pos	Pt	Res	F-A	H-T	1	2	3	4	5	6	7	8	9	10	11	subs used
1	1/8	H HIBERNIAN	12,503		2	W	3-0	0-0	Snelders	Wright	Winnie	Aitken	Irvine	Smith	Mason	Bett	Booth	Shearer*	Paatelainen	Jess
		Hibernian							*Reid*	*Orr*	*Mitchell*	*Beaumont*	*McIntyre*	*MacLeod*	*Weir*	*Hamilton*	*Wright*	*Jackson D**	*McGinlay*	*Evans*
2	5/8	H CELTIC	14,618		3	D	1-1	1-1	Snelders	Wright	Winnie	Aitken	Irvine	Smith	Mason	Bett	Booth*	Shearer	Paatelainen	Jess
		Celtic							*Marshall*	*Morris*	*Boyd*	*Wdowczyk*	*Mowbray*	*Gillespie**	*O'Neil*	*McStay*	*Creaney*	*Nicholas**	*Collins*	*Coyne/Whyte*
3	8/8	A FALKIRK	5,925	1	5	W	1-0	0-0	Snelders	McKimmie	Winnie	Aitken	Irvine	Smith	Mason*	Bett	Jess	Shearer	Paatelainen	Wright
		Falkirk							*Westwater*	*Oliver*	*McQueen*	*Duffy*	*Hughes*	*Rice**	*McAllister*	*May*	*Drinkell*	*Sloan*	*Smith*	*McCall*
4	15/8	A MOTHERWELL	5,561	2	5	L	1-2	1-1	Snelders	McKimmie	Winnie*	Aitken	Irvine	Smith	Mason	Wright	Jess	Shearer*	Paatelainen	Roddie/Ferguson
		Motherwell							*Thomson*	*Snedden*	*McKinnon*	*Simpson*	*Krambeer*	*Martin*	*Ferguson*	*Kirk*	*Arnott**	*Angus*	*Cooper*	*Shepherd*
5	22/8	H DUNDEE	11,604	1	7	W	2-1	2-1	Snelders	McKimmie	Wright	Aitken	Irvine	Smith	Kane*	Bett*	Jess	Shearer	Paatelainen	Winnie/Thomson
		Dundee							*Leighton*	*Dinnie*	*Beedie*	*McKeown*	*McGowan*	*Ratcliffe*	*den Bieman**	*Vrto*	*Paterson**	*Dodds*	*Rix*	*Campbell/Stainrod*
6	29/8	A RANGERS	41,636	5	7	L	1-3	1-0	Snelders	McKimmie	Wright	Aitken	Irvine	Smith	Mason*	Kane*	Jess	Shearer!	Paatelainen	Thomson/Winnie
		Rangers							*Goram*	*Spackman*	*Robertson*	*Gough*	*McPherson*	*Brown*	*Durrant*	*Ferguson I*	*McCoist*	*Mik'chenko*	*Huistra*	
7	2/9	H AIRDRIE	9,021		8	D	0-0	0-0	Snelders	McKimmie	Wright*	Aitken	Irvine	Smith	Mason	Grant	Jess	Winnie	Paatelainen	Roddie
		Airdrie							*Martin*	*Kidd*	*Stewart*	*Sandison*	*Caesar*	*Black*	*Boyle*	*Balfour*	*Lawrence**	*Coyle*	*Honor*	*Kirkwood/Smith*
8	12/9	A HEARTS	10,630	6	8	L	0-1	0-1	Snelders	McKimmie	Winnie	Aitken	Irvine	Smith	Grant	Bett*	Jess	Shearer	Paatelainen*	Mason/Wright
		Hearts							*Smith*	*Hogg*	*McKinlay*	*Levein*	*Mackay*	*van de Ven*	*Robertson*	*Ferguson D**	*Baird**	*Mauchlen*	*Foster*	*Crabbe/Snodin*
9	19/9	H PARTICK THISTLE	9,755	5	10	W	2-0	0-0	Snelders	McKimmie	Winnie	Grant	McLeish	Smith	Mason	Ten Caat*	Jess	Shearer	Paatelainen	Richardson
		Partick Thistle							*Nelson*	*Law*	*McVicar*	*Peebles*	*Jamieson*	*Chisholm**	*Shaw*	*Farningham*	*Britton*	*Irons*	*Cameron**	*McGlashan/Johnston*
10	26/9	A ST JOHNSTONE	7,320	2	12	W	3-0	0-0	Watt	McKimmie	Winnie	Grant	McLeish*	Smith	Mason°	Richardson	Jess	Shearer	Paatelainen*	Mason°/Ten Caat
		St Johnstone							*Rhodes*	*McGinnis*	*McAuley*	*Redford**	*Inglis*	*McCleland*	*Maskrey*	*Turner*	*Wright*	*Ardins*	*Curran*	*Treanor/Davies*
11	3/10	H DUNDEE UTD	12,936	5	12	L	0-1	0-0	Snelders	Wright	Winnie	Grant	McLeish	Smith	Ten Caat	Richardson*	Jess	Shearer	Paatelainen*	Mason/Kane
		Dundee Utd							*Main*	*Clark*	*Malpas*	*McInally*	*van d'Hoorn*	*Cleland*	*McKinlay*	*Bowman*	*Crabbe**	*Ferguson D*	*O'Neil*	*Connolly*

Scorers, Times, and Referees

1. Shearer 49, 51, Booth 77 — Ref: D McVicar
2. Shearer 20 / Creaney 16 — Ref: J McGilvray
3. Aitken 87 — Ref: J Renton
4. Jess 7 / Arnott 42, Angus 69 — Ref: J McCluskey
5. Shearer 23, Paatelainen 44 / Paterson 7 — Ref: D McVicar
6. Aitken 30 / Durrant 53, McCoist 61, Mik'chenko 88 — Ref: B McGinlay
7. — Ref: A Huett
8. Robertson 40 — Ref: L Mottram
9. Grant 58, Paatelainen 70 — Ref: W Morrison
10. Shearer 48, 52, Paatelainen 50 — Ref: C Ross
11. Ferguson 90 — Ref: W Crombie

Match notes

1. Much-travelled Duncan Shearer makes his debut alongside assistant manager Roy Aitken, who sets up Shearer's first goal. He is substituted after his second and earns a huge ovation. Both goals were scored with his feet. Skipper McLeish misses the game through hamstring trouble.

2. Two home matches to open the season. That is an oddity in itself. Shearer's spectacular shot cancelled out Creaney's goal, but in the second half Celtic are indisputably in control. Twice Creaney hit the woodwork, and near the end he tries to chip Snelders, who holds on to the ball.

3. Stewart McKimmie returns after suspension. Five players are booked in this hurly-burly match and Aberdeen are denied two strong penalty claims. Roy Aitken ends the frustration with his first goal for the Dons, a sweet header after Paatelainen won the ball on the left and crossed.

4. Davie Cooper, despite his years, shines for Motherwell, who include ex-Dons Ian Angus and Neil Simpson. Aberdeen miss the guile of the absent Jim Bett. Simpson is at fault for Aberdeen's goal, misjudging the bounce as he attempts to clear. Ian Ferguson sets up Angus's winner.

5. Jim Leighton makes his first appearance at Pittodrie in 4½ years. Dundee's 6ft 5in new signing, Gary Paterson, heads the opening goal. Against the run of play Bett plays a one-two with Jess to set up Shearer's equaliser. Mixu Paatelainen's winner was manufactured by Shearer.

6. A foul-tempered match which saw Rangers' assistant manager Archie Knox ordered into the stand and Shearer sent off for fouling Durrant. It was Shearer's second yellow card. Durrant was at the heart of everything, equalising Aitken's sweet volley and making a goal for McCoist.

7. Shearer is suspended and misses another match full of aggro. Bett is injured and Brian Grant plays his first game of the season. Kidd is sent off after 77 minutes, but still Aberdeen can find no way through. Afterwards Willie Miller complains Airdrie only came looking for a point.

8. Aberdeen tried to sign Hearts' John Robertson in the summer, and lose to his close-range volley from Foster's cross. Jim Bett failed to come out for the second half. Paatelainen wasted Aberdeen's best chance, missing from six yards. McKimmie had to miss Scotland's midweek game.

9. Lee Richardson, a £150,000 signing for Blackburn, makes his debut as a second-half substitute. McLeish and Ten Caat both play their first game of the season. Richardson sets up Grant's 25-yarder. Three minutes from time Jamieson is sent off for pulling down Duncan Shearer.

10. Snelders is out injured and McLeish hobbles off after 26 minutes. Richardson plays instead of the injured Aitken. Winnie nods across the box for Shearer to score. Ten Caat beat two St Johnstone players before crossing for Paatelainen to head No 2. Shearer fired No 3 from 16 yards.

11. Aberdeen are thwarted by man-of-the-match keeper Alan Main. Shearer was floored by van der Hoorn only to be booked for diving. In the last seconds, Bowman's corner was headed goalwards by Duncan Ferguson, but the ball flew into the net off Gary Smith. Ferguson claims the goal

12 A HIBERNIAN 7/10 — 8,824 — W 3-1 (14) — HT 0-1
Shearer 61, Jess 63, 84 — Wright 4
Ref: G Evans

Snelders/Burridge · Wright/Miller · Winnie/Mitchell · Grant/Orr · Irvine/Beaumont · Smith/Milne* · Mason/Weir · Richardson/Hamilton · Jess/Wright · Shearer*/Jackson D* · Paatelainen*/Kane/Roddie · McGinlay · Evans/Findlay

Paatelainen has to go off after only eight minutes. One-time Dons target Keith Wright scores with a low shot after Weir collides with Snelders. Paul Mason makes Aberdeen's first and third goals. Jess's first goal went through Burridge's legs; his second was a cheeky back-heel.

13 H FALKIRK 17/10 — 9,016 — W 3-1 (16) — HT 1-1
Jess 11, Paatelainen 56, Booth 79 — Sloan 18
Ref: J Herald

Snelders/Westwater · Wright/Oliver · Winnie/McQueen · Grant*/Duffy* · Irvine/McLeish · Smith/Johnston · Aitken/McAllister · Richardson/Lennox · Jess/May · Shearer*/Sloan · Paatelainen/McCall · Mason/Booth

Aitken returns after a three-game suspension. Falkirk leave out Kevin Drinkell. Jess scores at the second attempt from Wright's cross, but Scott Sloan's super volley levels the scores. Richardson's short corner leads to the second goal, and super-sub Booth converts Paatelainen's header.

14 A AIRDRIE 31/10 — 3,221 — W 2-1 (18) — HT 1-1
Sandison 6 og, Shearer 61 — Balfour 3
Ref: D McVicar

Snelders/Martin · Wright/Kidd · Winnie/Stewart · Grant/Sandison · Irvine/Honor · Smith/Black · Richardson/Boyle · Bett/Balfour · Jess/Lawrence* · Shearer*/Coyle · Paatelainen/Kirkwood · Kane/Smith

Aberdeen have just lost to Rangers in the Skol Cup Final. Shearer fouls Stewart, and from the resulting free-kick Balfour volleys Airdrie in front. Minutes later Airdrie skipper Jimmy Sandison turns Winnie's deep cross into his own goal. Shearer's glancing header wins the game.

15 A DUNDEE 7/11 — 6,902 — W 2-1 (20) — HT 0-0
Shearer 73, Richardson 90 — Dodds 59
Ref: J McGilvray

Snelders/Mathers · Wright/Dinnie* · Winnie/Pittman · Grant*/Duffy* · Irvine/Bain · Smith/Beedie · Richardson/den Bieman · Bett/McGowan · Jess/Gallagher · Shearer/Dodds · Paatelainen/McQuillan · Mason/Christie

Dundee manager Simon Stainrod enjoyed Billy Dodds' goal, after McQuillan had charged down David Winnie's clearance. Duncan Shearer hit the post before helping Brian Irvine's header over the line. Lee Richardson won the game from a close-range header from Paul Mason's cross.

16 H MOTHERWELL 11/11 — 8,725 — W 2-0 (22) — HT 0-0
Shearer 61, Grant 89
Ref: M Clark

Snelders/Dykstra · Wright/Sneddon* · Winnie/McKinnon · Grant/Simpson · Irvine/Philliben · Smith/Kromheer · Richardson/Martin · Bett/Griffin · Jess/Arnott* · Shearer/Angus · Paatelainen/Cooper · Mason/Nijholt/McLeod

Motherwell have won only twice all season, so it would have been a major shock if they had held out. Duncan Shearer's goal, his 15th of the season, was Aberdeen's first effort on goal. Brian Grant seals the win after a goalmouth melee, but the Dons are still six points behind Rangers.

17 A PARTICK THISTLE 24/11 — 3,986 — W 7-0 (24) — HT 1-0
Shearer 32, 51, 85, Jess 47, Mason 68, [Booth 80, Kane 88]
Ref: W Innes

Snelders/Murdoch · Wright/Clark · Winnie/McLaughlin · Grant/Jamieson · Irvine/Tierney · Smith/Irons · Richardson*/Shaw* · Bett*/Johnston · Jess/Britton · Shearer/Kinnaird · Paatelainen/Cameron* · Kane/Booth · McGlashan/English

This fixture was abandoned on Saturday with Aberdeen 2-0 up. Shearer is the first Don to score in five successive games since McDougall. The result betters Aberdeen's previous best Premier away win – 6-0 v Clydebank in 1986.

18 H HEARTS 28/11 — 13,555 — W 6-2 (26) — HT 2-0
Irvine 11, Shearer 45, 72, 74, Mason 66, [Booth 90] — Baird 46, Hogg 58
Ref: J McCluskey

Snelders/Smith · Wright*/McLaren · Winnie/McKinlay! · Grant/Levein · Irvine/Mackay · Smith/Hogg · Richardson/Robertson* · Bett*/Ferguson D · Jess/Baird · Shearer/Millar · Paatelainen/Berry* · Mason/Booth · Ferguson I/Snodin

Aberdeen become the first team since September to score more than one goal against Hearts. Shearer's second hat-trick in five days takes him up to 21 goals. Hearts had pulled back from 0-2 to 2-2. At 5-2 Tosh McKinlay was sent off for his second caution after body-checking Booth.

19 A CELTIC 2/12 — 29,122 — D 2-2 (27) — HT 2-1
Jess 11, Kane 32 — Slater 7, Vata 46
Ref: R Tait

Snelders/Bonner · Wright/McNally · Winnie/Boyd · Grant/Grant* · Irvine/Mowbray · Smith/Wdowczyk* · Mason/O'Neil · Richardson/McStay · Jess*/Slater · Shearer*/Creaney · Paatelainen/Collins · Mason/Roddie · Payton/Vata

Though the winning run comes to an end, Aberdeen stay second, one point ahead of Celtic. Shearer was out, and both Jess and Booth had to be taken off. Stuart Slater scores his first goal for Celtic since signing for West Ham. Paul Kane's flying 20-yarder had put the Dons in front.

20 H ST JOHNSTONE 5/12 — 11,750 — W 3-0 (29) — HT 2-0
Irvine 3, Roddie 40, Mason 77
Ref: R Morrison

Snelders/Rhodes · Wright/McGowne · Winnie/McAuley · Grant/Baltacha · Irvine/Inglis · Smith/Deas · Richardson/Davies · Bett/Cherry* · Jess*/Wright · Booth/Arkins · Roddie/Curran · Mason/Moore

Shearer and Eoin Jess fail late fitness tests. Brian Irvine 'chested' the first goal from Jim Bett's corner-kick. Man-of-the-match Lee Richardson crossed for Andy Roddie's goal. Paul Mason concluded the scoring with a curling shot. This result cuts Rangers' lead to just three points.

21 A DUNDEE UTD 12/12 — 10,394 — D 2-2 (30) — HT 1-0
Jess 20, Irvine 50 — Crabbe 72, McKinlay 77
Ref: D Syme

Snelders/Main · Wright/Krivokapic* · Winnie/Malpas · Grant/McInally · Irvine/van d'Hoorn Welsh · Smith/O'Neil J · Richardson/O'Neil M · Bett*/Crabbe* · Jess/Ferguson D · Booth/Perry · Shearer*/McKinlay/Connolly · Mason/Scott

Tomorrow Eoin Jess celebrates his 22nd birthday. Today he celebrates scoring Aberdeen's first goal, set up by Booth's cut-back. At 0-2 Scott Crabbe fired in a free-kick from 25 yards. McKinlay's equaliser took a dreadful deflection. Out-of-contract Gillhaus has turned down Rangers.

22 H HIBERNIAN 19/12 — 11,018 — W 2-0 (32) — HT 0-0
Richardson 56, Booth 73
Ref: H Dallas

Snelders/Reid · Wright*/Milne · Winnie/Mitchell · Grant/Orr · Irvine/Beaumont* · Smith/MacLeod · Richardson/Evans · Bett/Hamilton · Jess/Wright · Booth*/McGraw* · Paatelainen/Tortolano · Mason/Kane/Winnie · Miller/Fellenger

English hard-man Richardson is the Don in form. He caps his performance with a stunning 22-yard effort, and then helps make a goal for Scott Booth. Hibs' over-aggressive approach to the game wins them few friends. After one awful tackle Stephen Wright was unable to continue.

SCOTTISH PREMIER DIVISION   Manager: Willie Miller   SEASON 1992-93

No	Date	Att	Pos	Pt	F-A	H-T	Scorers, Times, and Referees	1	2	3	4	5	6	7	8	9	10	11	subs used
23	A MOTHERWELL 26/12	7,907 *12*	2 W	34	2-0	0-0	Irvine 69, Jess 82 — Ref: L Mottram	Snelders	Winnie	McLeish	Grant	Irvine	Smith	Richardson*	Bett	Jess	Booth	Mason	Kane
								Dykstra	Nijholt	Martin	Dolan	Philliban	McCart	Arnott	Griffin	Ferguson	O'Donnell*	Cooper	Kirk
24	H DUNDEE 2/1	13,201 *9*	2 D	35	0-0	0-0	Ref: W Crombie	Snelders	Wright	McLeish	Grant	Irvine	Smith	Richardson	Bett	Jess	Booth	Mason	
								Mathers	Dinnie	Pittman	Wieghorst	Duffy	Dow	McQuillan	Vrto	Ritchie*	Dodds	Kiwomya	den Bieman/Peterson
25	H AIRDRIE 16/1	8,805 *11*	2 W	37	7-0	4-0	Paatelainen 2, 37, 42, 78, Jess 17, Booth 53, Irvine 65 — Ref: H Williamson	Snelders	Wright	McLeish	Grant	Irvine	Smith	Richardson*	Mason	Jess	Booth*	Mason*	Aitken/Kane
								Martin	Jack	Boyle	Sanderson	Caesar*	Conn*	Reid	Balfour	Coyle	Kirkwood	Smith/Wilson	
26	A FALKIRK 30/1	6,886 *10*	2 W	39	4-1	2-0	Jess 25, 84, Shearer 33, Booth 72 — McCall 81 — Ref: H Dallas	Snelders	Wright	McLeish	Grant	Irvine	Smith	Richardson*	Booth	Jess	Shearer*	Mason	McCall/Wishart
								Parks	Oliver*	McQueen*	Duffy	Weir	May	McAllister	Cadette	Drinkell	MacKenzie	Sloan	
27	H RANGERS 2/2	15,055 *1*	2 L	39	0-1	0-1	Hateley 59 — Ref: H Williamson	Snelders	Wright	Smith	Grant	Irvine	McLeish	Richardson*	Booth	Jess	Paatelainen	Mason*	Shearer/Kane
								Goram	Stevens	Robertson	Gordon	McPherson	Brown	Steven	McCall	Hateley	Mik'chenko		
28	H CELTIC 13/2	14,673 *3*	2 D	40	1-1	1-0	Paatelainen 39 — Payton 74 — Ref: D Hope	Snelders	Wright	Winnie	Grant	Irvine	McLeish	Aitken	Richardson	Jess	Shearer*	Mason	Paatelainen/Booth
								Bonner	Boyd	Wdowcyk	O'Neil	McNally	Galloway	Slater*	McStay	McAvennie	Coyne	Collins	Payton/Vata
29	A ST JOHNSTONE 20/2	6,176 *8*	2 W	42	2-0	1-0	Jess 33, Booth 90 — Ref: M Clark	Watt	Wright	Smith	Grant	Irvine	McLeish	Richardson	Mason	Jess	Shearer*	Mason*	Paatelainen*/Aitken/Booth
								Rhodes	McGowne	Deas	McCleland	Inglis	Baltacha	Turner	McGinnis	Wright	Atkins*	Curran	Moore/Redford
30	H DUNDEE UTD 24/2	12,603 *5*	2 D	43	0-0	0-0	Ref: W Crombie	Snelders	Wright	Smith	Aitken	Irvine	McLeish	Richardson	Mason	Jess	Shearer*	Mason*	Paatelainen/Booth
								Main	Perry	Malpas	Bowman	Clark	Narey	Crabbe	McKinlay	O'Neill M	Ferguson D	Connolly*	Dailly
31	H PARTICK THISTLE 2/3	8,287 *9*	2 W	45	1-0	0-0	Paatelainen 81 — Ref: R Evans	Snelders	Wright	Smith	Grant	Irvine	McLeish	Richardson	Booth	Jess	Shearer*	Mason*	Paatelainen*/Aitken
								Nelson	Law	McVicar	Craig	Jamieson	Cameron	Palin*	Farningham	Britton	Irons	Broddie	English/McGlashan
32	A HIBERNIAN 9/3	7,029 *6*	2 W	47	2-1	0-1	Kane 81, Paatelainen 88 — McGinlay 45 — Ref: J McCluskey	Snelders	Wright	Smith	Grant	Irvine	McLeish	Richardson*	Aitken	Ten Caat	Shearer*	Paatelainen	Kane/Roddie
								Burridge	Farrell	Mitchell	McIntyre	Tweed	Tortolano	Lennon*	Hamilton	Wright	Jackson D	McGinlay	Evans
33	H FALKIRK 13/3	9,095 *11*	2 D	48	0-0	2-2	Roddie 62, Shearer 75 — Drinkell 53, Johnston 84 — Ref: A Waddell	Snelders	Wright	Winnie*	Grant	Irvine	McLeish	Kane	Aitken	Ten Caat	Shearer	Paatelainen	Roddie
								Westwater	Wishart	McQueen	Oliver	Weir	Duffy	McAllister	Drinkell	Cadette*	McCall	May	Johnston

23. Motherwell are still rooted to the bottom. For three-quarters of the game boredom reigns. McLeish was booked for kicking Arnott in the face, though he had actually kicked the ball. Irvine heads in the important first goal from Jim Bett's corner. Aberdeen are undefeated in 12 games.

24. Jim Leighton has been replaced by Mathers in Dundee's goal. Their offside trap spoils the entertainment, but they are not bothered. Veteran defender Jim Duffy is in control for most of the game. Dundee's captain, Billy Dodds, misfit his team's best chance straight to Theo Snelders.

25. Mixu Paatelainen had not scored since October; now he scores four in one game. He is only the third Aberdeen player in history to do so in the league. The kick-off had to be delayed while a practice ball could be dislodged from the netting. Jim Bett had a stomach operation yesterday.

26. Shearer returns after a month out through injury and scores Aberdeen's second goal. He is so excited by his far-post header, his 22nd goal, that he is booked for excessive celebrations. Falkirk's hopes disappeared when Drinkell headed against the post at 0-2. Booth's lob killed the game.

27. This is a match Aberdeen have to win, but Mark Hateley's header extends Rangers unbeaten run to 33 games and inflicts Aberdeen's first loss in 16 games, dating back four months. Aberdeen had seven shots on target compared to Rangers' four, but Andy Goram in goal was inspired.

28. Roy Aitken plays his first game since the Skol Cup Final, replacing the previously ever-present Gary Smith. Shearer hooked the ball across the face of the goal for Paatelainen to score against the run of play. Substitute Andy Payton was left unmarked to level. Rangers draw with Airdrie.

29. Eoin Jess starred for Scotland in midweek in a World Cup game against Malta. Snelders is out with a back injury. Arkins and Paul Wright missed good chances for Saints before Jess unleashes a screamer from outside the box. Keeper Rhodes fluffed his kick-out for the second goal.

30. A game of five bookings, many missed chances and much controversy. Paatelainen comes closest to scoring in the 73rd minute when heading against the bar. Both sides had strong penalty claims turned down, and for a period in the second half things looked to be getting out of control.

31. Pittodrie's smallest gate so far sees Paatelainen's 13th goal of the season, after keeper Craig Nelson spilled Wright's cross. Partick looked traumatised by the memory of the earlier 7-0 thrashing, and looked only to defend. Sub Mason was carried off eight minutes after coming on.

32. This dramatic escape led Hibs boss Alex Miller to declare: 'Aberdeen got out of jail.' Ten Caat started his first game for four months, and sent over the free-kick which Mixu Paatelainen dives to head the late winner. Hans Gillhaus has signed for Vitesse Arnhem for £300,000.

33. A match Andrew Roddie will never forget. He comes off the bench to score with his first touch - a volley to equalise Kevin Drinkell's header. Aberdeen-born Forbes Johnston levels for Falkirk from McAllister's cross. Roddie then crosses for Shearer to score off keeper Neil Oliver.

Season fixtures 34–44 (Aberdeen FC match log)

No	Date	V	Opponent	Att	Pos	Res	Opp Pos	Pts	HT	FT	Scorers (Aberdeen / Opponents)	Referee
34	20/3	A	DUNDEE	5,783	2	W	9	50	1-0	2-1	Paatelainen 2, Booth 53 / Stainrod 71	R Tait
35	27/3	H	MOTHERWELL	9,155	2	W	10	52	1-0	1-0	Booth 40	J Renton
36	30/3	A	RANGERS	44,570	2	L	1	52	0-0	0-2	Ferguson 65, McCoist 89	J Timmons
37	10/4	A	AIRDRIE	3,005	2	D	12	53	1-0	1-1	Shearer 19 / Fashanu 48	H Williamson
38	17/4	H	HEARTS	9,700	2	W	5	55	2-0	3-2	Shearer 36, Paatelainen 41, Mason 57 / Levein 64, Ferguson I 68	D Syme
39	20/4	A	PARTICK THISTLE	3,445	2	W	8	57	2-0	3-1	Paatelainen 27, 42, Kane 71 / Taylor 70	D Hope
40	1/5	A	CELTIC	20,642	2	L	3	57	0-1	0-1	McAvennie 8	J Timmons
41	5/5	A	HEARTS	6,038	2	W	5	59	1-0	2-1	Shearer 31, Paatelainen 69 / Thomas 66	W Morrison
42	8/5	H	ST JOHNSTONE	7,727	2	D	6	60	1-1	1-1	Booth 44 / Torfason 9	W Young
43	12/5	H	RANGERS	13,079	2	W	1	62	1-0	1-0	Shearer 42	L Mottram
44	15/5	A	DUNDEE UTD	9,078	2	W	4	64	1-1	4-1	Booth 6, 68, Gibson 66, Grant 88 / Dailly 9	J McCluskey

Average Home 11,176 Away 11,698

Line-ups (Aberdeen / Opponent, * = substituted, subs after |)

34 v Dundee: Snelders, Wright, Smith, Grant, Irvine, McKimmie, Kane, Aitken, Booth, Ten Caat*, Paatelainen* | Shearer/Mason
Mathers, McQuillan, Pittman, Wieghorst, Duffy, Bain, Ritchie, Vito*, Stainrod, Dodds, Dow | Paterson

35 v Motherwell: Snelders, Wright, Smith, Grant*, McLeish, McKimmie, Mason, Richardson, Booth, Ten Caat, Paatelainen* | Kane
Dykstra, Nijholt, McKinnon, Martin, Philliben, McCart, Kirk, Angus, Arnott*, O'Donnell, Cooper* | McGrillen/Dolan

36 v Rangers: Snelders, Aitken, Smith, Kane, McLeish, McKimmie, Richardson*, Mason*, Booth, Shearer, Paatelainen | Ten Caat/Roddie
Goram, McCall, Robertson, Gough, McPherson, Brown, Steven, Ferguson, McCoist, Hateley, Huistra* | Mik'chenko/Murray

37 v Airdrie: Snelders, McKimmie, Smith, Kane, Irvine, McLeish, Richardson*, Mason, Booth*, Shearer, Paatelainen | Aitken/Roddie
Martin, Boyle, Stewart, Sandison, Caesar, Black, Jack, Honor, Fashanu, Lawrence*, Coyle | Smith

38 v Hearts: Snelders, McKimmie, Smith, Aitken, Irvine, McLeish, Ten Caat, Mason, Booth*, Shearer, Paatelainen | Roddie
Baird, Hogg, McKinlay*, Levein, Mackay, van de Ven, Ferguson D, Ferguson I, Berry, Bannon, Harrison/Snodin

39 v Partick Thistle: Snelders, McKimmie, Smith, Kane, Irvine, McLeish, Ten Caat*, Mason, Bett, Shearer*, Paatelainen | Connor/Booth
Murdoch, Law, McVicar, McLaughlin, Jamieson, Irons, Taylor, Farningham, Britton, Craig, English

40 v Celtic: Snelders, McKimmie, Connor, Aitken, Irvine, McLeish, Kane, Mason*, Ten Caat*, Shearer, McAvennie* | Booth/Roddie
Marshall, Smith, Boyd, Grant, Vata, Galloway, Fulton, Slater, Payton, Gray, Miller

41 v Hearts: Watt, McKimmie, Connor, Aitken, Irvine, McLeish, Kane, Mason*, Booth, Shearer, McAvennie* | Ten Caat
Smith, Hogg, McKinlay, Harrison, McLaren, van de Ven, Foster*, Fulton, Bairfl, Mackay, Thomas | Robertson/Thomas

42 v St Johnstone: Snelders, Wright, Connor, Kane*, Irvine, Smith, Mason*, Richardson, Booth, Shearer*, Torfason* | Aitken/Ten Caat
Rhodes, Inglis, Deas, Curran, McGowne, Cole, Byrne, McGinnis*, Wright, Davies, McAuley/Buglione

43 v Rangers: Snelders, Wright, Connor, Kane, Irvine, Smith, Mason, Richardson!, Booth, Shearer, Torfason | Ten Caat*
Maxwell, Murray, Kuznetsov!, Reid, McPherson, Brown*, Gordon, Ferguson I, Robertson L, Hagen, Durrant/McSwegan | Mik'chenko

44 v Dundee Utd: Snelders, Wright, Connor, Kane, Irvine, Smith, Grant, Mason*, Booth, Gibson, Ten Caat* | Aitken/Jess
Main, Clark, Cleland, Bowman*, van d'Hoorn Welsh, McPherson, McInally*, McKinlay, Dailly, O'Neill M, Connolly | Crabbe/Perry

Match notes

34. Shearer has again been left on the bench. Ten Caat's corners pave the way for Paatelainen's early header and Booth's shot. Dundee's goal was initially credited to Snelders, who appeared to punch a dropping ball into his own net. Rangers lose at Celtic and now lead by just 7 points.

35. Poor Brian Grant, called into the Scotland squad to play Germany, falls awkwardly in the 57th minute and fractures his arm. Scott Booth had earlier scored his 15th goal of the season, following up when Lee Richardson's shot was blocked. This win sets up Tuesday's crunch match.

36. A marvellous match, even though the result effectively ends Aberdeen's title challenge. Hateley knocks down for Ian Ferguson to score the all-important first goal. Miller pulls off Richardson before the referee could send him off. Rangers extend their unbeaten home run to 26 games.

37. The surprise packet in this match is Airdrie's Justin Fashanu, who leads Brian Irvine a merry dance. In the first minute Fashanu announces his presence by barging Snelders against a post. McKimmie's free-kick set up Aberdeen's goal. Fashanu turned Irvine to lob a superb equaliser.

38. Hearts' keeper Nicky Walter hurts his ankle before kick-off and striker Ian Baird plays in goal. Walker stands behind the pitch to coach him. Shearer's goal makes him the first Don to exceed 24 a season since Joe Harper. Hearts' fight-back leaves the Dons at sixes and sevens.

39. Bett and Connor return after long layoffs - in Connor's case 19 months with Achilles trouble. Partick show few ideas in attack. Shearer and Paatelainen combine for Aberdeen's first two goals. Snelders should have saved from Taylor. The Dons are now off to Majorca on holiday.

40. The worst game between these sides this season, and the goal is in keeping with the scrappy play. McAvennie's early trundler was the signal for both sides to slumber in the sunshine. Perhaps the Dons are still dreaming of Majorca. Rangers wrapped up the championship at Airdrie.

41. Hearts' Ian Baird played in goal last time. Now he sets up Hearts' equaliser for 18-year-old Kevin Thomas and angrily gesticulates towards Dons' fans. The linesman intervenes and Baird is sent off. Shearer had ducked to head the first goal. Mason crossed for Paatelainen's winner.

42. Aberdeen create umpteen chances but take only one. St Johnstone had gone ahead with one of their few attacks, Deas finding Torfason who headed in. Irvine headed down for Booth's equaliser. Somehow Saints hang on to snatch their one and only point off Aberdeen this season.

43. This was no gentle, end-of-season affair. Aberdeen had never yet failed to beat Rangers at least once. One of the goals of the season helps them maintain that record, Shearer beginning and ending a seven-pass move. Richardson was sent off after 48 minutes and Kuznetsov after 83.

44. Jim McLean's farewell match. Brian Grant returns for his 250th Dons' game and scores the fourth goal. Eoin Jess had been out since 6 March, but comes on for the final 20 minutes. Andy Gibson put Aberdeen 2-1 up and then played a one-two to enable Scott Booth to score his second.

SCOTTISH PREMIER (CUP-TIES)

Manager: Willie Miller — SEASON 1992-93

Skol League Cup

	Match	Att.	F-A	H-T	Scorers, Times, and Referees
2	A ARBROATH	4,130	W 4-0	1-0	Paatelainen 29, 65, Shearer 55, Jess 66 — Ref: D Hope
3	H DUNFERMLINE	10,791	W 1-0	0-0 (aet)	Paatelainen 100 — Ref: H Williamson
QF	A FALKIRK	8,022	W 4-1	2-1	Shearer 13, 25, 90, Irvine 64 — McQueen 39p — Ref: J Timmons
SF	N CELTIC (at Hampden)	40,618	W 1-0	1-0	Jess 41 — Ref: B McGinlay
F	N RANGERS (at Hampden)	45,298	L 1-2	0-1 (aet)	Shearer 63 — McCall 15, Smith 114 og — Ref: D Hope

2 — ARBROATH
Aberdeen: 1 Snelders, 2 McKimmie, 3 Winnie*, 4 Aitken, 5 Irvine, 6 Smith, 7 Mason, 8 Bett*, 9 Jess, 10 Shearer, 11 Paatelainen; subs Thomson/Wright
Arbroath: *Balfour, Hamilton*, Martin, Mitchell, Godfrey, Boyd, Farnan, Adam, Macdonald, Tosh^, Sorbie*; subs Holmes/McNaughton

Despite the opponents, despite the score, Arbroath's Paul Tosh is chosen as man of the match for his constant threat to the Aberdeen goal. For almost an hour all that separated the sides was Paatelainen's header from Mason's cross. Jess was instrumental in all three second-half goals.

3 — DUNFERMLINE
Aberdeen: 1 Snelders, 2 McKimmie, 3 Wright, 4 Aitken*, 5 Irvine, 6 Smith, 7 Mason, 8 Bett, 9 Jess, 10 Shearer, 11 Paatelainen; subs Thomson/Kane
Dunfermline: *Hamilton, Shannon*, Sharp, McCathie, Robertson, Cooper, McWilliams, O'Boyle*, Grant!, Leitch, Davies*; subs Laing/Cumington

Dunfermline manager Jocky Scott protests afterwards that his team were unlucky. Keeper Lindsay Hamilton was man of the match, and ex-Don Neale Cooper was also prominent. In extra-time Roddy Grant was sent off for two bookings and from the free-kick Paatelainen headed in.

QF — FALKIRK
Aberdeen: 1 Snelders, 2 McKimmie, 3 Winnie, 4 Aitken, 5 Irvine, 6 Smith, 7 Mason, 8 Bett*, 9 Jess, 10 Shearer, 11 Winnie*; subs Winnie/Smith
Falkirk: *Westwater, Oliver*, McQueen, Duffy, Hughes, Rice, McAllister, May, Drinkell, Baptie, Thomson*; subs Cadette/McCall

Falkirk have in their side Ex-Ranger Kevin Drinkell and ex-Don Tommy McQueen, who scores from the spot after McKimmie had pushed Drinkell. Aberdeen's hero was undoubtedly Duncan Shearer who scored three goals himself and nodded down for Irvine to bag the other.

SF — CELTIC
Aberdeen: 1 Snelders, 2 Wright, 3 Winnie, 4 Grant, 5 McLeish, 6 Smith, 7 Aitken, 8 Jess, 9 Shearer*, 10 —, 11 Paatelainen; subs Richardson
Celtic: *Bonner, Boyd, Wdowczyk*, Grant, Galloway, Gillespie^, Slater, McStay, Payton, Creaney, Collins*; subs McNally/Miller

A fantastic cup-tie which saw Aberdeen soak up waves of Celtic pressure both before and after man-of-the-match Jess's goal. Celtic boss Liam Brady blames the Hampden hoodoo when Creaney hit Snelders' bar in the final minute. Gary Smith was the pick of the Dons' defenders.

F — RANGERS
Aberdeen: 1 Snelders, 2 Wright, 3 Winnie, 4 Grant, 5 McLeish, 6 Smith, 7 Aitken, 8 Bett*, 9 Jess, 10 Shearer, 11 Paatelainen; subs Richardson/Booth
Rangers: *Goram, McCall, Robertson D Gough*, McPherson, Brown, Steven*, Ferguson, McCoist, Hateley, Durrant*; subs Milichenta/Gordon

Agony for Gary Smith, Aberdeen's best player, when deep into extra-time he heads Rangers' winner from Robertson's centre. Earlier, Rangers had gone in front as a consequence of the new back-pass law, which befuddled Snelders. Duncan Shearer swivelled to fire a super equaliser.

Tennents Scottish Cup

	Match	Att.	F-A	H-T	Scorers, Times, and Referees
3	H HAMILTON	10,800	W 4-1	1-1	Booth 11, 70, 85, Irvine 90 — Reid 15 — Ref: H Williamson
4	H DUNDEE UTD	14,500	W 2-0	0-0	Jess 76, 85 — Ref: D Syme
QF	H CLYDEBANK	11,300	D 1-1	1-0	Shearer 2p — McIntosh 82 — Ref: W Crombie
R	A CLYDEBANK	8,000	W 4-3	2-1	Irvine 16, Paatelainen 23, Booth 75, 81 — Eadie 44, Maher 52, Henry 68 — Ref: W Crombie
SF	N HIBERNIAN (at Tynecastle)	21,413	W 1-0	0-0	Booth 55 — Ref: D Syme
F	N RANGERS (at Parkhead)	50,715	L 1-2	0-2	Richardson 77 — Murray 22, Hateley 42 — Ref: J McCluskey

3 — HAMILTON
Aberdeen: 1 Snelders, 2 Wright, 3 Winnie*, 4 Grant, 5 Irvine, 6 McLeish, 7 Richardson, 8 Bett*, 9 Jess, 10 Booth, 11 Paatelainen; subs Smith/Mason
Hamilton: *Ferguson, Hillcoat, Miller, Millen, Weir, Napier*, Ward, Reid, Harris, Clark, McDonald*; subs Cramb

Paatelainen returns after missing eight games through injury. Despite the score Hamilton had their moments. Reid's equaliser stemmed from Snelders' poor punch and went in off Winnie's legs. On the hour, McDonald's volley scraped the bar. Booth made it 2-1 from Mason's corner.

4 — DUNDEE UTD
Aberdeen: 1 Snelders, 2 Wright, 3 Smith, 4 Grant, 5 Irvine, 6 McLeish, 7 Richardson, 8 Mason*, 9 Jess, 10 Shearer*, 11 Booth; subs Booth/Aitken
Dundee Utd: *Main, Clark, Malpas, Bowman, Perry, Narey, McKinlay, Dailly, Johnston*, Crabbe, Bollan*; subs Connolly

Aberdeen dominated this Sunday cup-tie. United left out Duncan Ferguson after a public outburst. Jess scored No 1 with a header and No 2 with a side-foot. 'We have no excuses' said Jim McLean. Duncan Shearer celebrates his international call-up against Malta at the age of 30.

QF — CLYDEBANK
Aberdeen: 1 Snelders, 2 Wright, 3 Smith, 4 Grant, 5 Irvine, 6 McLeish, 7 Richardson, 8 Aitken*, 9 Jess*, 10 Shearer*, 11 Booth; subs Booth/Ten Caat
Clydebank: *Woods, Maher, Hay*, Murdoch, Sweeney, McIntosh, Harvey, Eadie, Flanigan C, Henry*, Jack*; subs Crawford/Lansdowne

Joy and despair for Aberdeen in the first four minutes. Joy when Shearer scores from the spot after Maher pulled back Paatelainen. Despair when Scott Murdoch's tackle fractures Jess's ankle. No penalty-kick. McIntosh levelled from a free-kick following McLeish's foul on Eadie.

R — CLYDEBANK (replay)
Aberdeen: 1 Snelders, 2 Wright, 3 McKimmie, 4 Grant, 5 Irvine, 6 McLeish, 7 Kane, 8 Aitken, 9 Booth, 10 Ten Caat, 11 Paatelainen; subs Paatelainen
Clydebank: *Woods, Maher, Hay, Murdoch, Sweeney, McIntosh, Harvey, Eadie, Henry, Flanigan C, Jack*; subs

Kick-off was delayed 15 minutes because the turnstile operators had no change. McKimmie returns after six months. 2-0 to the Dons becomes 3-2 to Clydebank. Then Ten Caat's free-kick crashes off the bar and Booth scores the equaliser. From Kane's corner Booth heads the winner.

SF — HIBERNIAN
Aberdeen: 1 Snelders, 2 McKimmie, 3 Smith, 4 Grant, 5 Irvine, 6 McLeish, 7 Kane, 8 Booth*, 9 Jess, 10 Ten Caat, 11 Paatelainen; subs Paatelainen/Ten Caat/Shearer
Hibernian: *Burridge, Miller, Mitchell, Hunter, Tweed, MacLeod*, Lennon, Hamilton^, Wright, Jackson, McGinlay*; subs Evans/Orr

Hibs have won at Tynecastle just once in 10 years. Irvine returns after suspension and Shearer is left on the bench. Kane manufactured the Dons' goal, rolling the ball from the by-line to Booth. Hibs' best chance came at the end, but Snelders saved thrillingly from Evans' volley.

F — RANGERS
Aberdeen: 1 Snelders, 2 McKimmie, 3 Wright*, 4 Grant, 5 Irvine, 6 McLeish, 7 Richardson, 8 Mason, 9 Booth, 10 Shearer*, 11 Paatelainen; subs Paatelainen/Smith/Jess
Rangers: *Goram, McCall, Robertson D Gough, McPherson, Brown, Murray, Ferguson, Durrant, Hateley, Huistra*, Pressley*; subs Hateley/Pressley

More despair for Aberdeen as they finish second to Rangers yet again. Murray's goal went in off Irvine, and Richardson's went in off Brown. Aberdeen started the match brightly but lost their way once they fell behind. It is the first time in six finals that Alex McLeish has lost one.

Final League Table

Pos	Team	P	Home W	D	L	F	A	Away W	D	L	F	A	Pts
1	Rangers	44	20	2	0	52	11	13	5	4	45	24	73
2	ABERDEEN	44	13	7	2	41	13	14	3	5	46	23	64
3	Celtic	44	13	5	4	37	18	11	7	4	31	23	60
4	Dundee Utd	44	8	7	7	25	27	11	2	9	31	22	47
5	Hearts	44	12	6	4	26	15	3	8	11	20	36	44
6	St Johnstone	44	8	10	4	29	27	2	10	10	23	39	40
7	Hibernian	44	8	8	6	32	28	4	5	13	22	36	37
8	Partick This	44	5	6	11	26	41	7	6	9	24	30	37
9	Motherwell	44	7	4	11	27	37	4	9	9	19	25	36
10	Dundee	44	7	4	11	25	34	4	8	10	23	34	35
11	Falkirk	44	7	5	10	40	39	2	8	16	20	47	29
12	Airdrie	44	4	9	9	22	27	2	8	12	13	43	29
		528	112	73	79	382	317	79	112	317	382	528	

Aberdeen head-to-head (League)

Opponent	P	W	D	L	F	A	Pts	Cup
v Partick This	4	4	0	0	13	1	8	Cup
v Hibernian	4	4	0	0	10	2	8	SC
v St Johnstone	4	3	1	0	9	1	7	
v Falkirk	4	3	1	0	10	4	7	LC
v Dundee	4	3	1	0	6	3	7	
v Airdrie	4	2	2	0	10	2	6	
v Hearts	4	3	0	1	11	6	6	
v Motherwell	4	3	0	1	6	2	6	SC
v Dundee Utd	4	1	2	1	6	4	4	LC
v Celtic	4	0	3	1	4	5	3	LC
v Rangers	4	1	0	3	2	6	2	SC
	44	27	10	7	87	36	64	

Odds & ends

Never lost to: (6) Partick, Hibs, St Johnstone, Falkirk, Dundee, Airdrie.
Never beat: (1) Celtic (in the league).

Won from behind: (7) Dundee (h & a), Hibs (a, a), Airdrie (a), Dundee (a), Dundee Utd (a), Clydebank (SC).
Lost from in front: (2) Motherwell (a), Rangers (a).

High spots: Reaching two cup finals in one season for the third time in eight years.
15 unbeaten league games, dropping just 3 points, from 7 October.
Scoring 7 goals against two different teams.
Finishing second for the fourth time in five seasons.

Low spots: Finishing second to Rangers in every competition.
Poor start to the season, lying 6th after eight games.
Being beaten by Rangers five times in one season.
Winning just 2 of 11 matches against the Old Firm.

Bogey-team: Rangers (who beat Aberdeen 5 times overall).
Ever-presents: (0).
Hat-tricks: (5), Duncan Shearer (3), Paatelainen (1), Booth (1).
Leading scorer: (28) Duncan Shearer.

Appearances and Goals

Player	Lge	Sub	LC	Sub	SC	Sub	Goals Lge	LC	SC	Tot
Aitken, Roy	18	8	5		3	1	2			2
Bett, Jim	17		4		1					
Booth, Scott	21	8		1	4	2	13		6	19
Connor, Robert	5	1								
Ferguson, Graeme		1								
Gibson, Andrew	1						1			1
Grant, Brian	29		2		5		3			3
Irvine, Brian	39		3		6		5	1	2	8
Jess, Eoin	28	3	5		3		12	2	2	16
Kane, Paul	13	14		1	2		4			4
McKimmie, Stewart	14		3		3					
McLeish, Alex	27		2		6					
Mason, Paul	31	8	4		3	1	4			4
Paatelainen, Mixu	33		4		6		16	3	1	20
Richardson, Lee	28	1		2	5		2	1		3
Roddie, Andrew	1	10					2			2
Shearer, Duncan	32	2	5		3	1	22	5	1	28
Smith, Gary	40		5		3	2				
Snelders, Theo	41		5		6					
Ten Caat, Theo	11	4			1	2				
Thomson, Scott		2		3						
Watt, Michael	3									
Winnie, David	18	3	4		1					
Wright, Stephen	34	2	4	1	5	1	1			1
(own-goals)							1			
24 players used	484	67	55	8	66	10	87	11	13	111

BELL'S SCOTTISH PREMIER
Manager: Willie Miller — SEASON 1993-94

No	Date	Opponent	Att	Pos	Pt	F-A	H-T	Scorers, Times, and Referees	1	2	3	4	5	6	7	8	9	10	11	subs used
1	A 7/8	DUNDEE UTD	13,881	D 1	1	1-1	0-1	Booth 75 / McKinlay 38 / Ref: D Hope	Snelders	McKimmie	Connor	Grant	Irvine	Smith	Richardson	Bett	Booth	Jess*	Paatelainen	Shearer
		Dundee Utd							*Main*	*van d' Hoorn Malpas*	*Cleland*		*Welsh*	*Narey*	*Bowman*	*McKinlay*	*Connolly**	*Dailly*	*Brewster*	*Bollan*
2	H 14/8	KILMARNOCK	13,535	W 4	3	1-0	0-0	Kane 46 / Ref: W Morrison	Snelders	McKimmie	Connor	Kane	McLeish	Smith	Richardson	Bett*	Booth	Shearer	Paatelainen*	Miller/Jess
		Kilmarnock							*Geddes*	*MacPherson Black*	*Montgomery Skilling*		*Millen*	*Mitchell**	*Williamson*	*Reilly*	*McCluskey*	*McSkimming–Crainie/Roberts*		
3	A 21/8	DUNDEE	7,505	D 4	4	1-1	1-0	Shearer 3 / Dodds 54 / Ref: J Kelly	Snelders	McKimmie	Wright	Kane	McLeish	Smith	Richardson	Miller*	Jess	Shearer*	Paatelainen	Aitken/Connor
		Dundee							*Mathers*	*McQuillan Pitman*	*Wieghorst Paterson*		*McGowan*	*Adamczuk**	*Vrto*	*Tosh*	*Dodds*	*McKeown Frail*		
4	H 28/8	ST JOHNSTONE	11,682	D 5	5	0-0	0-0	Ref: J McGilvray	Snelders	McKimmie	Smith	Kane	McLeish	Irvine	Jess*	Richardson*	Booth	Shearer	Ten Caat*	Paatelainen/Miller
		St Johnstone							*Rhodes*	*McGowne* Deas*	*McGinnis Inglis*		*Turner*	*Davies*	*McAuley*	*Wright*	*Ramsey*	*Curran*	*Morgan*
5	A 4/9	CELTIC	34,311	W 3	7	1-0	0-0	Paatelainen 56 / Ref: L Mottram	Snelders	McKimmie	Connor	Kane	McLeish	Irvine	Richardson*	Bett	Booth	Shearer*	Paatelainen/Jess	Payton/Slater
		Celtic							*Bonner*	*Boyd*	*Wdowczyk Grant*		*McNally*	*Galloway*	*Vata*	*McAvennie Nicholas**	*Collins**		
6	A 11/9	HIBERNIAN	8,506	L 6	7	1-2	0-2	Shearer 89 / McAllister 8, Wright 37 / Ref: W Young	Snelders	McKimmie	Connor*	Kane	McLeish	Irvine	Miller	Richardson*	Jess	Shearer	Paatelainen	Winnie/Gibson, Evans/Hamilton
		Hibernian							*Leighton*	*Miller Mitchell*	*Farrell*		*Tweed*	*Hunter*	*McAllister* Findlay**	*Wright*	*Jackson D O'Neill*		
7	H 18/9	RANGERS	19,138	W 3	9	2-0	2-0	Shearer 16, Pressley 34 og / Ref: W Crombie	Maxwell	Stevens	Wright	Kane	McLeish	Irvine	Miller	Richardson	Jess*	Shearer	Connor	Paatelainen/Booth
		Rangers							*Maxwell*	*Robertson McCall*	*McPherson Pressley*		*Steven*	*Ferguson I Miller*	*Hateley*	*Huistra**	*Ferguson D*		
8	H 25/9	RAITH ROVERS	11,472	W 1	11	4-1	1-0	Shearer 32, Jess 56, Richardson 77, 84 / Dennis 88 / Ref: D McVicar	Snelders	McKimmie	Wright*	Kane	McLeish*	Irvine	Miller	Richardson	Jess*	Shearer	Ten Caat*/Paatelainen	Dair, Graham
		Raith Rovers							*Carson*	*McStay*	*Rowbotham Coyle*		*Dennis*	*McBeachie Nicholl*	*Cameron*	*Hetherston Crawford**	*Dair*		
9	A 2/10	MOTHERWELL	8,597	D 1	12	0-0	0-0	Ref: I Taylor	Snelders	McKimmie	Wright	Kane	McLeish	Irvine	Miller	Richardson	Jess*	Shearer	Connor*	Paatelainen/Smith, Cooper/Angus
		Motherwell							*Dykstra*	*Shannon McKinnon*	*Krivokapic*		*Martin McCart*	*Lambert*	*Dolan*	*Arnott**	*Kirk*	*McGrillen**		
10	H 5/10	HEARTS	13,798	D 2	13	0-0	0-0	Ref: H Williamson	Snelders	McKimmie	Wright*	Kane	McLeish	Irvine	Miller	Richardson	Jess	Shearer	Connor	Ten Caat/Paatelainen, Colquhoun
		Hearts							*Walker*	*Locke McKinlay*	*McLaren*		*Hogg*	*Berry*	*Weir*	*Mackay Fashanu*	*Gibson*	*Leitch*	*Ferguson**
11	A 9/10	PARTICK THISTLE	5,600	L 2	13	2-3	0-2	Paatelainen 53, Shearer 55 / Taylor 4, Craig 5, Grant 70 / Ref: J O'Hare	Watt	McKimmie*	Wright	Kane	McLeish	Irvine	Miller	Bett	Jess	Shearer	Paatelainen	Connor/Smith, Tierney/Smith
		Partick Thistle							*Nelson*	*Law Milne*	*Watson*		*Jamieson Taylor*	*Shaw**	*Craig*	*Britton*	*Cameron*	*Grant**	

Match reports

1. A dynasty has ended, now that Jim McLean has relinquished the reins of power at Tannadice. Billy McKinlay's last goal for United was in December; now he scores at the near post following sustained United pressure. Lee Richardson crosses for Booth to side-foot the equaliser.

2. The Richard Donald Stand is due to open next week against Hamburg, but now suffers an embarassing power failure. Kilmarnock's first league match at Pittodrie for 10 years kicked off 12 minutes late. Willie Miller had not yet taken his seat when Kane scored from the edge of the box.

3. Polish international Dariusz Adamczuk makes his Dundee debut, and twice goes close after Duncan Shearer converted Jess's slide-rule pass. Wieghorst's shot is deflected by Gary Smith to Billy Dodds, who levels the scores. The crowd disapprove when Shearer is replaced by Connor.

4. St Johnstone have 15 unfit players and sought vainly to have this match postponed. One might think they shut up shop in this dreary spectacle, but in truth Saints created the more and better chances. Andy Rhodes' only save of note came three minutes from time from McKimmie.

5. Celtic have been a jinx team for Aberdeen in recent seasons, and things looked bad when McAvennie 'scored' after 10 minutes, but was ruled offside. The only goal came from a corner, taken by Connor, which came off the heads of McAvennie and Shearer to the feet of Paatelainen.

6. Hibs might have scored from the kick-off, following Irvine's dreadful back-pass. Ex-Falkirk winger Kevin McAllister then beat Snelders from the edge of the box. When Keith Wright doubled Hibs' lead the Dons looked out of it. McLeish's header hit a post before Shearer's late volley.

7. The Dons strike against the early run of play, when Maxwell spills Jess's hopeful shot to the feet of Shearer. Jess later projected a low cross that was turned into his own net by Steven Pressley. Rangers' £4 million substitute Duncan Ferguson almost scored with an overhead kick.

8. Raith broke their Premier duck at Dundee last week and look the stronger side for half an hour: Dair even hit the underside of the bar. The tide turned when Kane set up Shearer. At 2-0 Raith boss Jimmy Nicholl brought on his new signing from Motherwell, Ally Graham. To no avail.

9. Scotland's match of the day finished goalless. The key factors in this match were Motherwell's desire to avenge Aberdeen's 5-2 win in the Coca-Cola Cup, and the defiance of Theo Snelders who single-handedly prevented them doing so. Had they won Well would have gone top.

10. Hearts have yet to win away, but the draw knocks the Dons off the top. Sandy Clark's team lined up with six men in defence. Their best chance fell to Justin Fashanu, brother of England international John. Aberdeen's best chance fell to Shearer, who headed onto the bar from three yards.

11. Partick avenge last season's 7-0 mauling by the Dons. They go two up in five minutes with a deflected free-kick, followed by a goal by Albert Craig, set up by ex-Don Ian Cameron. The Dons stage a superb fightback and are surging for the winner when Roddy Grant turned McLeish.

Match-by-match record (matches 12–23)

12 · A KILMARNOCK · 16/10 · 3 D 1-1 · 9,108 · 5 · 14 · (0-0)
Scorers: Paatelainen 73 / *Mitchell 76* · Ref: E Martindale
Dons: Snelders, McKimmie, Smith, Kane, McLeish, Irvine, Richardson, Grant, Jess*, Shearer*, Paatelainen, Connor/Booth
Kilmarnock: *Geddes, MacPherson, Black, Montgomerie, Stilling, Millen, Mitchell, Reilly, Williamson*, Brown, McSkimming/McCluskey*
Only the Dons have beaten Kilmarnock so far. Not the best of games, which featured an injured linesman having to be replaced. Kilmarnock had their sights set on a draw, but fell behind when Paatelainen headed in from Kane. Ally Mitchell's 25-yard equaliser flew past Snelders.

13 · H DUNDEE UTD · 23/10 · 2 W 2-0 · 13,566 · 10 · 16 · (2-0)
Scorers: Paatelainen 26, Shearer 36 · Ref: A Huett
Dons: Snelders, McKimmie, Smith, Kane, McLeish, Irvine, Richardson, Grant*, Jess*, Shearer, Paatelainen, Connor/Booth
Dundee Utd: *Main, Clark, Malpas, van d'Hoorn Welsh, Cleland, Johnston, McKinlay, McLaren, O'Neil, Crabbe*
Such is United's liking for Pittodrie that this home win took some by surprise. Accusing eyes were directed at Welsh after he let McKimmie's cross bypass him, and Mixu netted at the far post. Shearer's hooked goal set the seal on a first defeat in seven visits for Ivan Golac's new side.

14 · H DUNDEE · 30/10 · 1 W 1-0 · 11,885 · 12 · 18 · (0-0)
Scorers: Shearer 82 · Ref: K Clark
Dons: Snelders, McKimmie, Smith, Kane, McLeish, Irvine, Richardson, Grant*, Jess, Shearer*, Paatelainen, Connor/Booth
Dundee: *Mathers, Frail, Adamczuk, Farningham, Paterson, Duffy, Ritchie, Vrto, Ristic*, Dodds, Czachowski/McQuillan*
Another disappointing match. Dundee propped up the table, but did not look noticeably inferior to their high-flying hosts. The vital goal was engineered by Jess, whose drilled centre across the goalmouth was turned in by Shearer almost on the line. Aberdeen go to the top again.

15 · A ST JOHNSTONE · 6/11 · 1 D 1-1 · 5,757 · 10 · 19 · (0-1)
Scorers: Booth 90 / *McGinnis 6* · Ref: J Timmons
Dons: Snelders, McKimmie, Connor, Kane, McLeish, Irvine, Richardson*, Grant, Jess, Shearer*, Paatelainen, Wright/Booth
St Johnstone: *Rhodes, McGowne, Deas, Cherry, Inglis, McGinnis, Davies, Curran, Wright*, Torfason, McAuley/Moore*
Torino have just k.o'd the Dons from Europe. Aberdeen were a mite lucky not to lose to St Johnstone, who led for most of the match, thanks to a first Premier League goal - a strong header - from Gary McGinnis. Six minutes into injury time Kane's corner, Irvine's header, Booth's goal.

16 · H CELTIC · 9/11 · 1 D 1-1 · 19,474 · 20 · (0-0)
Scorers: Grant 72 og / *O'Neil 53* · Ref: H Dallas
Dons: Snelders, McKimmie, Connor, Kane, Wright, Irvine, Richardson, Grant*, Booth, Miller*, Paatelainen, Shearer/Winnie
Celtic: *Bonner, Gillespie*, Boyd, Grant, Wdowczyk, McGinlay, Byrne, McStay, O'Neil, Creaney, Collins/Vata/Nicholas*
Willie Miller drops some big names following the dismal effort at Perth. Lou Macari's unbeaten run in front when Snelders dithered over a through ball. Jess created space for the equaliser, which flew in off Peter Grant. Jess claimed it, but officially it stands as an own-goal.

17 · H MOTHERWELL · 13/11 · 1 D 1-1 · 12,494 · 2 · 21 · (1-1)
Scorers: Booth 1 / *Kirk 4* · Ref: J Herald
Dons: Watt, McKimmie, Connor, Kane, Wright, Irvine, Richardson, Grant, Booth, Miller*, Paatelainen, Shearer
Motherwell: *Dykstra, Philliben, McKinnon, Krivokapic, Martin, McCart, Lambert, Kirk, Arnott*, Dolan, O'Donnell*/McGrillen/Shannon*
Not a match to arrive late at. Booth's glancing header was a prelude to kamikaze defending which allowed Steve Kirk to level. Both goals came from corner-kicks. Brian Grant, playing at left-back, later hit the bar, and Watt saved well from Kirk. A bad point for the leaders to drop.

18 · H HIBERNIAN · 27/11 · 1 W 4-0 · 12,334 · 5 · 23 · (1-0)
Scorers: Kane 36, Connor 79, Shearer 84, Grant 89 · Ref: R Tait
Dons: Snelders, Leighton, Wright, Kane, McLeish, Irvine, Miller*, Grant, Jess, Shearer*, Connor, Paatel'en/Richardson
Hibernian: *Miller W, Mitchell, Farrell, Tweed, Hunter, Tortolano, Hamilton, Evans, Jackson D, O'Neill, Donald*
Gareth Evans' shot came back off Snelders' post at 0-0. Following a one-two with Shearer, came against the run of play. Jim Leighton got a touch but couldn't keep it out. Hibs seemed to lose heart after O'Neill limped off after 50 minutes, and fell apart by the end.

19 · A RANGERS · 1/12 · 2 L 0-2 · 45,182 · 1 · 23 · (0-2)
Scorers: *Hateley 28, 32* · Ref: D McVicar
Dons: Watt, McKimmie*, Wright, Kane, McLeish*, Irvine, Miller*, Grant, Jess, Shearer, Connor, Paatelainen/Richardson
Rangers: *Maxwell, McCall, Robertson, Gough*, McPherson Brown, Steven, Ferguson I, Durie, Hateley, Murray, Pressley/Durrant*
Snelders had to pull out when injuring himself before kick-off. Aberdeen fell behind in untidy circumstances, Gough's header eluding Watt and falling to Mark Hateley. Four minutes later Watt dived at Hateley's feet and the ball broke unkindly. Rangers' win takes them to the top.

20 · A HEARTS · 4/12 · 4 D 1-1 · 9,402 · 9 · 24 · (0-1)
Scorers: Shearer 75 / *Colquhoun 5* · Ref: W Innes
Dons: Snelders, Wright, Smith!, Kane, McLeish, Irvine, Miller*, Grant*, Booth, Miller, Connor, Shearer/Richardson
Hearts: *Walker, Weir, McKinlay, Gough*, Berry, Leitch, Colquhoun*, Mackay, Thomas, Johnston M Robertson, Johnston A*
Mo Johnston has joined Hearts from Everton. It is he who sets up John Colquhoun's early goal. A match of 33 fouls never flowed freely. The Dons were handicapped by the expulsion of Gary Smith for his second yellow card, after clashing with Johnston. Jess crafted Shearer's goal.

21 · A RAITH ROVERS · 7/12 · D 1-1 · 4,205 · 25 · (1-1)
Scorers: Miller 31 / *Dalziel 41* · Ref: D Syme
Dons: Snelders, Wright, Connor, Kane, McLeish, Irvine, Miller*, Grant, Booth, Jess, Paatelainen, Richardson*/Jess/Rowbotham
Raith Rovers: *Thomson, McStay, Broddle, Coyle, Dennis, McGeachie, Sinclair, Dalziel, Cameron, Graham, Dair*/Rowbotham*
It is one win in seven now, and the Dons are tumbling down the table. Things looked good following Miller's exquisite 35-yard lob over Scott Thomson. The Dons were pegged back when Dair shot, Snelders parried, and Gordon Dalziel headed in. The Dons seldom threatened again.

22 · H PARTICK THISTLE · 14/12 · 2 W 2-1 · 8,248 · 27 · (0-0)
Scorers: Irvine 56, Shearer 61 / *Craig 80* · Ref: A Huett
Dons: Snelders, Wright, Smith, Kane, McLeish, Irvine, Miller*, Grant*, Jess, Shearer, Connor, Paatelainen/Booth
Partick Thistle: *Nelson, McKee, Milne, Watson, Jamieson, Taylor, Shaw, Craig, English*, Cameron, Clark*/Britton/Charnley*
A bitingly cold night tempted over 8,000 fans from their homes. The match came to life after half-time. Irvine headed in Connor's corner. The Dons twice hit the crossbar before Shearer added a second. Following Albert Craig's 18-yard goal, Connor headed Britton's shot off the line.

23 · H KILMARNOCK · 18/12 · 1 W 3-1 · 10,834 · 7 · 29 · (1-0)
Scorers: Miller 39, Shearer 57, Richardson 58 / *Stilling 84* · Ref: A Waddell
Dons: Snelders, Wright, Smith, Kane, McLeish, Irvine, Richardson, Grant*, Jess, Shearer, Connor*, Paatelainen/Booth
Kilmarnock: *Geddes, MacPherson Black, Montgomerie Stilling, Millen, Brown, Reilly, Williamson, Mitchell, McSkimming*
Bobby Geddes had kept five successive clean sheets before Miller seized on Snelders' downfield punt to lob the Kilmarnock keeper. Miller engineered the other two goals as well, both scored in the space of a minute. This win takes Aberdeen back to the top of the table.

Results summary

No	Date	Venue	Opponent (opp. pos.)	Att	Pos	Res	Pt	F-A	H-T	Scorers, Times	Ref
24	27/12	A	Dundee Utd	12,248	2	W	31	1-0	1-0	Jess 16	H Dallas
25	8/1	H	St Johnstone (10)	12,712	2	D	32	1-1	0-0	Shearer 65; Ferguson 60	D Hope
26	11/1	A	Dundee (12)	5,219	2	W	34	1-0	0-0	Irvine 76	L Mottram
27	19/1	A	Celtic	19,083	2	D	35	2-2	1-1	Irvine 31, Jess 50; Byrne 30, McStay 59	H Williamson
28	22/1	H	Rangers (1)	20,267	2	D	36	0-0	0-0	—	J McGilvray
29	5/2	A	Hibernian (4)	9,556	2	L	36	1-3	1-0	Richardson 16; Wright 60, 72, Lemon 87	G Evans
30	12/2	H	Raith Rovers (11)	10,553	2	W	38	4-0	1-0	Paatelainen 43, 77, Shearer 75, Booth 78	D Syme
31	5/3	H	Hearts (8)	13,059	2	L	38	0-1	0-1	Leitch 31	H Dallas
32	8/3	A	Motherwell	7,018	2	D	39	1-1	1-0	Shearer 38; McLeish 88 og	R Orr
33	19/3	A	Kilmarnock (8)	8,544	3	W	41	3-2	1-0	Miller 23, Shearer 57, Jess 70; Black 64, McCloy 88	D McVicar
34	26/3	H	Dundee Utd (6)	12,574	3	W	43	1-0	1-0	Shearer 15	J McCluskey

Line-ups, substitutes and reports

24. A Dundee Utd
- Aberdeen (1–11): Snelders, McKimmie, Wright, Kane, McLeish, Irvine, Miller, Winnie, Jess*, Shearer*, Connor — subs used: Paatelainen/Booth
- *Dundee Utd: van de Kamp, van d' Hoorn, Malpas, McInally, Petric, Welsh, Bowman, McKinlay, Connolly, Brewster, Dailly* — sub: McLaren*

Fast and frantic. The early breakthrough is in Aberdeen's favour, as Joe Miller threads the ball in and Eoin Jess turns and scores. End to end stuff thereafter, though when the Dons thought they'd done enough and sat back, they almost paid dearly. Connolly blazed over at the death.

25. H St Johnstone
- Aberdeen: Snelders, McKimmie*, Wright, Kane, McLeish, Irvine, Miller, Winnie*, Jess, Shearer, Connor — subs used: Grant/Booth
- *St Johnstone: Rhodes, McGowne, McAuley, Ramsey, Deas, Cherry, Torfason*, Turner, Ferguson, Curran, Davies* — subs: Wright/Scott*

A minute's silence for the death of Dick Donald. The Dons have still to defeat the relegation-threatened Saints in three attempts. A floodlight failure delayed the start of the second half by 15 minutes. This affected the Dons. McLeish's error let in Saints new signing, Ian Ferguson.

26. A Dundee
- Aberdeen: Snelders, McKimmie, Wright, Kane, McLeish, Irvine, Jess*, Grant, Booth, Shearer, Connor* — subs used: Winnie/Roddie
- *Dundee: Mathers, Frail, Pittman, McQuillan, Blake, Duffy*, Shaw, Wieghorst, Britton, Dinnie, McCann — sub: Ritchie*

All change at Dens Park. Billy Dodds and Grant McMartin have gone. Gerry Britton and George Shaw make their debuts. But Jim Duffy's team look little better. Paul Kane's cross found Brian Irvine unmarked to head the only goal. Dundee created little that could save the match.

27. A Celtic
- Aberdeen: Watt, McKimmie, Wright, Grant, McLeish, Irvine, Miller*, Grant, Jess*, Shearer, Richardson — subs used: Winnie/Booth
- *Celtic: Bonner, Gillespie*, Martin, McGinlay, Mowbray, McNally, Byrne, McStay, Biggins*, Nicholas, Collins — subs: Galloway/O'Neil*

Four days previously this fixture was abandoned goalless through fog after half-time. Paul Byrne heads his first goal for Celtic, but Irvine connects with a Joe Miller corner seconds later. Byrne had the last laugh: it was his cross that Charlie Nicholas knocked down for McStay.

28. H Rangers
- Aberdeen: Snelders, McKimmie, Wright, Kane, McLeish, Irvine, Miller*, Grant*, Jess, Shearer, Richardson — subs used: Paatelainen/Booth
- *Rangers: Maxwell, Stevens, Robertson, Gough, Murray, Brown*, Steven, McCall, Durie*, Hateley, Mik'chenko — subs: Durrant/Huistra*

The game is preceded by a minute's silence in memory of Sir Matt Busby. The tension between these top-of-the-table sides squeezes all creativity out of the match. Aberdeen's best moments came near the start, when Duncan Shearer twice powered his way through Gers' defence.

29. A Hibernian
- Aberdeen: Snelders, McKimmie, Wright, Grant, McLeish, Irvine, Jess, Richardson, Booth, Shearer, Connor* — subs used: Paatelainen
- *Hibernian: Leighton, Miller W, Mitchell, Farrell, Tweed, Beaumont, McAllister, Lennon, Wright, Evans, O'Neill*

Not the kind of result associated with the Dons, leading at half-time, then sliding to their heaviest defeat of the season. Willie Miller is not a happy man. To cap it all, Lee Richardson, who had scored with a deflected 25-yarder, was sent off after 77 minutes for a second booking.

30. H Raith Rovers
- Aberdeen: Snelders, McKimmie, Wright, Grant, McLeish, Irvine, Jess, Bett*, Kane, Shearer, Paatelainen — subs used: Booth
- *Raith Rovers: Thomson, McStay, Rowbotham, Coyle, Dennis, Sinclair, Nichol*, Graham, Crawford, Dair*, Cameron — subs: McAnespie/Dalziel*

With Lee Richardson suspended, Jim Bett continues his comeback. The end result against lowly Raith was the biggest win of the season for the Dons and the heaviest defeat for Raith. That Rovers failed to score was down to sub Gordon Dalziel, whose penalty was saved by Snelders.

31. H Hearts
- Aberdeen: Snelders*, McKimmie, Wright, Grant*, McLeish, Irvine, Miller, Richardson, Booth, Shearer, Kane — subs used: Stillie/Paatelainen
- *Hearts: Smith, Weir, McKinlay, Levein, Berry, McLaren, Colquhoun*, Leitch, Foster, Johnston M, Millar — subs: Robertson/Locke*

Aberdeen could find no way through Hearts' defence. Scott Leitch beat Snelders at his near post. Theo hurt his shoulder trying to save. With Michael Watt having broken his leg in midweek, young Derek Stillie made his debut - the Dons' first substitute keeper in a domestic match.

32. A Motherwell
- Aberdeen: Stillie, McKimmie, Wright, Smith, McLeish, Irvine, Jess, Richardson, Booth*, Shearer*, Kane — subs used: Grant/Paatelainen
- *Motherwell: Dykstra, Philliben, McKinnon, Krivokapic, Martin, McCart, Lambert*, Dolan*, Arnott, O'Donnell, Coyne — subs: McBrilleny/Shannon*

Derek Stillie plays his first full 90 minutes. Motherwell are having a fine season, but they cause little threat to Stillie's goal until the closing quarter. Brian Martin hit a post, Stillie made a double save from Coyne and Arnott, but was finally beaten by McLeish's misdirected header.

33. A Kilmarnock
- Aberdeen: Stillie, McKimmie, Wright, Smith, McLeish, Irvine, Jess*, Miller, Booth, Shearer, Kane — subs used: Paatelainen
- *Kilmarnock: Geddes, MacPherson*, Black, Montgomery, Burns, Millen, Napier, Reilly, McCluskey*, McSkimming, — subs: McCloy/Williamson*

Killie have not won since 4 January, 19 games earlier. Both sides seem distracted by looming Scottish Cup semi-finals. At 0-0 McSkimming struck Stillie's crossbar, but that was their only real misfortune. Aberdeen won with something to spare. Both sides hit woodwork near the end.

34. H Dundee Utd
- Aberdeen: Stillie, McKimmie, Wright*, Kane, McLeish, Irvine, Jess, Richardson, Miller, Shearer*, Robertson — subs used: Grant/Paatelainen
- *Dundee Utd: van de Kamp, Cleland, Malpas, McInally, Petric, Narey, Bowman, McKinlay, Dailly*, Brewster, Johnston — sub: McLaren*

United look very ordinary this season. The outcome of this match is identical to that of the last between these sides, settled by an Aberdeen goal on the quarter-hour. Guido van de Kamp was wrong-footed by Duncan Shearer. McInally hit the Dons' woodwork in the second half.

Aberdeen FC — 1993-94 Match Record (continued)

35 H HIBERNIAN 29/3 — L 2-3 · 4 · 43 · Att 10,832
Scorers: Jess 44, Miller 54 / Wright 34, 53, Tweed 80
Ref: D McVicar
Aberdeen: Stillie, McKimmie, Wright, Kane, McLeish*, Jess, Irvine, Richardson, Miller, Shearer, Robertson, Paatelainen
Hibernian: Leighton, Farrell, Mitchell, Jackson C, Tweed, McAllister*, Hunter, Hamilton, Wright, Evans, O'Neill, Jackson D
Hibs' third win over the Dons this season. When Tweed impeded Shearer in the box it resulted in Aberdeen's first penalty since May 1992. Shearer wasted the chance as Leighton saved. Keith Wright struck twice, the Dons levelled twice, then Tweed headed in McAllister's corner.

36 A RANGERS 2/4 — 3 D 1-1 · 1 · 44 · Att 45,888
Scorers: Kane 78 / McCall 13
Ref: H Williamson
Aberdeen: Burridge, McKimmie, Wright, Kane, McLeish, Jess, Irvine, Richardson, McKinnon, Shearer*, Robertson, Paatelainen
Rangers: Goram, Stevens, Murray, Gough, McPherson, McCall, Brown, Ferguson I, McCoist*, Durie, Mikhailichenko, Hateley
Rangers have won all seven matches since they last played Aberdeen, and the Premier title looks decided. Aberdeen's goalkeeping crisis sees a debut for 42-year old keep-fit fanatic John Burridge. McCoist sets up McCall, Paul Kane scores his first for the Dons, and Hateley hits a post.

37 A PARTICK THISTLE 5/4 — D 1-1 · 45 · Att 4,280
Scorers: Tierney 8 og, Grant 40 /
Ref: R Tait
Aberdeen: Burridge, McKimmie, Robertson, Kane, McLeish, Jess, Irvine, Richardson, McKinnon*, Shearer*, Grant, Thomson
Partick Thistle: Nelson, Byrne, Law, Watson, Tierney, Cameron, Jamieson, Craig, Grant, English, Charnley
Strikers Shearer, Booth and Joe Miller are all injured. Help is at hand in the shape of Tierney, who heads an own-goal from Hugh Robertson's corner. After Roddy Grant's equaliser, Burridge saved Charnley's free-kick at the second attempt, and McKimmie's 20-yarder strikes the bar.

38 H MOTHERWELL 16/4 — 3 D 0-0 · 2 · 46 · Att 9,642
Ref: L Mottram
Aberdeen: Snelders, McKimmie, Smith, Kane, McLeish, Jess, Irvine, Richardson, Booth, Shearer*, Wright*, Grant
Motherwell: Dykstra, Shannon, Burley, Krivokapic, Martin, Philliben, Davies, Dolan, Arnott*, O'Donnell, Coyne, McGrillen
McLeish returns from suspension, and Booth and Wright from injury. The Scottish Cup has gone, the league title - barring improbables - likewise, and the season inevitably begins to wind down. The second half becomes tetchy, but the chief beneficiaries of the result were Rangers.

39 H PARTICK THISTLE 23/4 — 3 W 2-0 · 8 · 48 · Att 7,827
Scorers: Jess 85, Grant 89 /
Ref: E Martindale
Aberdeen: Snelders, McKimmie, Smith, McKinnon, McLeish, Jess, Irvine, Grant, Booth*, Shearer, Wright, Grant
Partick Thistle: Nelson, Law, Byrne, Watson, Jamieson, Cameron, Taylor*, Craig, Grant, English, Charnley, Milne
A belated home debut for Ray McKinnon. The unlikely named Isaac English shot wide for Partick with only Snelders to beat. A second successive goalless draw was beckoning when Jess fired Grant's cross past Nelson. The scorer then turned provider, as the roles were reversed.

40 A HEARTS 27/4 — 3 D 1-1 · 7 · 49 · Att 13,811
Scorers: Irvine 34, Robertson 60p /
Ref: R Tait
Aberdeen: Snelders, McKimmie, Wright, McKinnon*, Smith, Irvine, Jess, Grant, Booth*, Shearer, Robertson, Paatelainen/Roddie
Hearts: Smith, Frail, McKinlay, Levein, Berry, McLaren, Colquhoun, Mackay, Robertson, Johnston M, Miller
Irvine's free header from McKinnon's corner was against the flow of play. Losing Booth and McKinnon to injury disrupted the Dons after that, and Snelders celebrated his call up to the Dutch World Cup squad by making save after save. Stephen Wright fouled Robertson for the penalty.

41 H DUNDEE 30/4 — 3 D 1-1 · 12 · 50 · Att 7,568
Scorers: Irvine 56 / Duffy N 57
Ref: J McCluskey
Aberdeen: Snelders, McKimmie, Wright, Grant, Smith, Jess, Irvine, Richardson*, Booth*, Shearer*, Robertson, Paatelainen/Thomson
Dundee: Pageau, McQuillan, Duffy J, Wieghorst*, Blake, Shaw, Duffy N, Vrto, Tosh, McKeown*, McCann, Britton/Teasdale
Dundee are going down, but they played brightly. Aberdeen were still celebrating Brian Irvine's header from Jess's free-kick when Neil Duffy launched himself at Neil McCann's cross to level. Fine saves by Snelders maintained the Dons' 18-year unbeaten home record against Dundee.

42 A RAITH ROVERS 3/5 — W 2-0 · 52 · Att 2,798
Scorers: Roddie 26, Shearer 83 /
Ref: W Morrison
Aberdeen: Snelders, McKimmie, Wright, Grant, Smith, Jess*, Irvine, Richardson, Booth*, Shearer, Robertson, Paatelainen/Thomson
Raith Rovers: Thomson, Rowbotham, Broddie, Coyle, Dennis, Lennon, Nicholl*, Graham, Hetherston, Crawford, Cameron, Dair
Raith might have been two ahead by the time Aberdeen woke themselves up. Andrew Roddie might have finished with two goals, never mind one - his inswinging corner was hacked away by Julian Broddie. Overall Raith scarcely deserved to lose this match; the story of their season.

43 A ST JOHNSTONE 7/5 — 2 W 1-0 · 10 · 54 · Att 6,107
Scorers: Irvine 88 /
Ref: W Young
Aberdeen: Snelders, McKimmie, Wright, Grant, Smith, Jess*, Irvine, Kane, Booth*, Shearer, Roddie, Richardson/Robertson
St Johnstone: Rhodes, McGowne, Miller, Scott, Inglis, Preston*, Davies*, Turner, Ferguson, Dodds, McGinlay, McMartin/Maskrey
Billy Dodds and Ian Ferguson tormented the Dons for long stretches. Aberdeen improved after the break, but a winner seemed a long way off when Tommy Turner obstructed Roddie and from the free-kick Irvine headed the winner. If he had not, St Johnstone would have stayed up.

44 H CELTIC 14/5 — 2 D 1-1 · 4 · 55 · Att 16,417
Scorers: Irvine 37 / Donnelly 3
Ref: D Hope
Aberdeen: Burridge, McKimmie, Wright, Grant, McLeish, Jess, Irvine, Richardson*, Booth*, Shearer, Roddie, Robertson
Celtic: Bonner, Smith, Martin, Wdowczyk, Sweeney, Hay*, Mowbray, Gillespie*, Donnelly, Falconer, Collins, McNally/Byrne
John Burridge deputises for Theo Snelders - off to World Cup '94 - but tries to dribble clear rather than welly Gary Smith's pass-back. Simon Donnelly dispossessed him to score. Burridge's blushes faded when Irvine headed in Kane's corner. The Dons finish runners-up yet again.

Average Home 12,723   Away 13,025

Scottish League Cup

2 H CLYDEBANK 10/8 — W 5-0 · Att 11,394
Scorers: Shearer 4, 69, 73p, McLeish 50, Richardson 66 [Richardson 68] /
Ref: A Waddell
Aberdeen: Snelders, Wright, Connor, Kane, McLeish, Richardson, Bett*, Booth*, Shearer, Paatelainen, Miller/Jess
Clydebank: Woods, Treanor, Hay, Maher, McIntosh*, Harvey, Henry, Eadie, Flannigan, Lansdowne*, Crawford D/Jack
Willie Miller 'rests' McKimmie, Grant, Irvine, and Jess. One of the replacements - Shearer - ensures there is no repeat of last season's close-fought Scottish Cup-tie. McLeish's goal is his first in almost four years, and the first competitive goal scored before the Richard Donald Stand.

BELL'S PREMIER (CUP-TIES)

Manager: Willie Miller

Scottish League Cup

Match / Team	1	2	3	4	5	6	7	8	9	10	11	subs used
3 H 24/8 MOTHERWELL — Aberdeen	Snelders	McKimmie	Smith	Kane	McLeish	Irvine	Jess	Bett*	Booth	Shearer	Ten Caat*	Connor/Miller
Motherwell	*Dykstra*	*Shannon*	*McKinnon*	*Krivokapic*	*Martin*	*McCart*	*Dolan*	*Angus*	*Arnott**	*O'Donnell*	*Burns**	*McGrillen/Cooper*
QF A 1/9 RANGERS — Aberdeen	Snelders	McKimmie	Smith*	Kane	McLeish	Irvine	Richardson	Bett	Booth*	Jess	Paatelainen	Miller/Shearer
Rangers	*Maxwell*	*Stevens*	*Robertson D*	*Gough*	*Pressley*	*Murray**	*Steven*	*Ferguson I*	*Durrant*	*Hateley*	*Huistra**	*Ferguson D/Wishart*

3 H 24/8 MOTHERWELL — W 5-2 (aet), H-T 1-0. 12,996. Scorers: Shearer 15, Miller 79, Booth 98, 120, [Jess 119]; Arnott 52, Shannon 55. Ref: J McCluskey

Tiny Dougie Arnott heads Motherwell level from McKinnon's corner, and worse is to come following Theo Snelders' wayward punch. Joe Miller nets for the first time since his return from Celtic to force extra-time, whereupon Miller crosses for Booth to restore Aberdeen's lead.

QF A 1/9 RANGERS — L 1-2 (aet), H-T 0-1. 44,928. Scorers: Miller 49p; Hateley 1p, Ferguson 92. Ref: D Syme

Within 15 seconds Rangers get a penalty, as Irvine challenges Durrant. Aberdeen's reward for their subsequent pressure was a spot-kick themselves, when Gough drags down Scott Booth. In extra-time Huistra's cross was cleared to Ian Ferguson who beat Snelders from 25 yards.

Tennents Scottish Cup

Match / Team	1	2	3	4	5	6	7	8	9	10	11	subs used
3 A 8/2 EAST STIRLING (at Falkirk) — Aberdeen	Snelders	McKimmie	Wright	Grant	McLeish	Irvine	Jess*	Bett	Winnie	Shearer	Paatelainen	Booth/Miller
East Stirling	*McDougall*	*Russell*	*Lee*	*McAulay**	*Craig*	*Ross*	*Conway*	*Millar*	*McCallum*	*Geraghty*	*Loney*	*Conroy*
4 H 19/2 RAITH ROVERS — Aberdeen	Snelders	Smith	Wright	Kane	McLeish	Irvine	Jess*	Bett*	Kane	Shearer	Paatelainen	Booth/Miller
Raith Rovers	*Thomson*	*McStay*	*Rowbotham*	*Coyle*	*Dennis*	*Sinclair*	*Nicholl*	*Cameron*	*Hetherton*	*Crawford**	*Dair*	*Graham*
QF A 12/3 ST JOHNSTONE — Aberdeen	Stillie	McKimmie	Wright	Smith	McLeish	Irvine	Jess*	Richardson	Booth	Shearer	Kane	Miller
St Johnstone	*Rhodes*	*McGowne*	*Inglis*	*Ramsey*	*Deas*	*Cherry**	*Scott*	*Turner*	*Ferguson*	*Dodds*	*Torfason*	
R 15/3 ST JOHNSTONE — Aberdeen	Stillie	McKimmie	Wright	Smith	McLeish	Irvine	Jess*	Richardson	Booth*	Shearer	Kane	Miller
St Johnstone	*Rhodes*	*McGowne*	*Inglis*	*Ramsey**	*Deas*	*Cherry**	*Scott*	*Turner*	*Ferguson/*	*Dodds*	*Curran**	*McMartin/Torfason*
SF N 9/4 DUNDEE UTD (at Hampden) — Aberdeen	Burridge	McKimmie	Robertson*	Kane	Smith	Irvine	Jess*	Richardson	McKinnon*	Shearer	Grant	Miller/Paatelainen
Dundee Utd	*van de Kamp*	*Cleland*	*Malpas*	*McInally*	*Petric*	*Welsh*	*Bowman*	*McKinlay*	*McLaren*	*Brewster**	*Bollan*	*Dailly*
SF R 12/4 DUNDEE UTD (at Hampden) — Aberdeen	Snelders	McKimmie	Robertson*	Kane	Smith	Irvine	Jess	Bett	McKinnon*	Shearer	Grant	Booth/Miller
Dundee Utd	*van de Kamp*	*Cleland*	*Malpas*	*McInally*	*Petric*	*Welsh*	*Bowman*	*McKinlay*	*McLaren**	*Brewster**	*Bollan*	*Nixon/Dailly*

3 A 8/2 EAST STIRLING (at Falkirk) — W 3-1, H-T 0-0. 3,853:10. Scorers: Craig 57 og, Shearer 64, 72; Geraghty 83. Ref: A Roy

On paper this looked so easy. In reality East Stirling showed most of the early promise, with Aberdeen looking unlikely to score before they did so - David Craig deflecting Stephen Wright's header into his own goal.

4 H 19/2 RAITH ROVERS — W 1-0, H-T 0-0. 13,740 11. Scorers: Miller 81. Ref: K Clark

Last Saturday the Dons beat Raith 4-0 in the league. It is a different story in the Cup. Rovers were nine minutes from a replay when Rowbotham miscues his attempted clearance to Joe Miller. There was time enough before the end for Miller to hit the crossbar from 20 yards.

QF A 12/3 ST JOHNSTONE — W 1-0, H-T 1-0. 8,847 10. Scorers: Booth 30; Dodds 61. Ref: K Clark

The fourth consecutive draw between these sides so far. Aberdeen are anxious about rookie goalkeeper Derek Stillie, but they need not have been. Scott Booth's header was cancelled out by Billy Dodds, newly signed from Dundee.

R 15/3 ST JOHNSTONE — W 2-0, H-T 2-0. 14,325 10. Scorers: Shearer 3, Richardson 14. Ref: H Williamson

Jess was carried off at McDiarmid Park with a thigh injury, but makes a speedy recovery. Saints did not take kindly to the two quick goals that ruined their cup aspirations. Just before half-time Ferguson stamped on Irvine's head and was duly expelled on the linesman's intervention.

SF N 9/4 DUNDEE UTD (at Hampden) — D 1-1, H-T 1-0. 21,397 6. Scorers: Shearer 7; Welsh 88. Ref: J McCluskey

A post rescued the Dons early on, and more good fortune was enjoyed when van de Kamp let Shearer's shot squirm under his body. Ex-United player Ray McKinnon later volleyed straight at Burridge, and was adjudged to have made a pass back. Welsh's late header earned the replay.

SF R 12/4 DUNDEE UTD (at Hampden) — L 0-1, H-T 0-0. 13,936 6. Scorers: McInally 70. Ref: J McCluskey

In the end Aberdeen were two minutes from the final, but that counted for nothing. With McLeish still suspended and extra-time looming, Aberdeen fell to the best move of the match. Brewster crossed, Bowman shot, Snelders parried, and back-pedalling McInally pounced.

European Cup-Winners' Cup

Match / Team	1	2	3	4	5	6	7	8	9	10	11	subs used
1:1 A 14/9 VALUR (Iceland) — Aberdeen	Snelders	McKimmie	Wright	Kane	McLeish	Irvine	Miller*	Bett*	Jess	Shearer	Connor	Aitken/Winnie
Valur	*Sigurdsson*	*Stefansson*	*Helgason*	*Jonsson*	*Davidsson*	*Jonsson E*	*Gylfason*	*Adolfsson*	*Gregory*	*Larusson*	*Magnusson*	*Valsson/Hreidarsson*
1:2 H 29/9 VALUR — Aberdeen	Snelders	McKimmie*	Wright	Kane	Irvine	Smith	Miller*	Bett	Jess	Richardson	Paatelainen	Winnie/Gibson
Valur	*Sigurdsson*	*Gajic*	*Helgason*	*Jonsson J*	*Davidsson**	*Jonsson S*	*Gylfason*	*Adolfsson**	*Gregory*	*Larusson*	*Magnusson*	*Peturs'on/Hreidarsson*

1:1 A 14/9 VALUR (Iceland) — W 3-0, H-T 2-0. 656. Scorers: Shearer 8, Jess 28, 56. Ref: M Piraux (Belgium)

Duncan Shearer's European baptism is crowned with a goal after eight minutes, as Sigurdsson fails to hold Joe Miller's long-range drive. Jess's two goals - a header and a breathtaking individual goal - condemn Valur to early elimination. Now minds turn to Rangers in the league.

1:2 H 29/9 VALUR — W 4-0, H-T 0-0. 10,004. Scorers: Miller 51, Jess 60, 69, Irvine 65. Ref: R Pedersen (Norway). (Dons win 7-0 on aggregate)

A pointless match that failed to enthuse the crowd. Joe Miller extended the aggregate lead when Sigurdsson spilled Kane's cross. By the time the overall lead was 7-0 Willie Miller gave Andy Gibson his first taste of European soccer. By then everyone was going through the motions.

2:1 A TORINO 20/10 (Italy)	30,000	L 2:3	2:1	Paatelainen 9, Jess 24 / Sergio 45, Fortunato 51, Aguilera 88 / Ref: S Krondi (RCS)
2:2 H TORINO 3/11	21,655	L 1:2	1:1	Richardson 12 / Carbone 40, Silenzi 53 / Ref: M Merk (Germany) / (Dons lose 3-5 on aggregate)

Match 1 line-ups / scorers:
Snelders *Galli* | McKimmie *Mussi* | Smith *Sergio* | Kane *Gregucci** | McLeish *Annoni* | Irvine *Fusi* | Richardson *Francescoli* | Grant *Fortunato* | Jess* *Silenzi* | Connor *Carbone^* | Paatelainen^ *Venturin* | Wright/Booth *Osio/Aguilera*

A nightmare. Two up, yet conceding goals in the closing seconds of each half. Mixu's glancing header and Jess's sweeping shot from Mixu's cross had left Torino stunned. The tie turned right on half-time. Aguilera's free-kick was deflected.

Match 2 line-ups / scorers:
Snelders *Galli* | McKimmie *Mussi** | Smith *Sergio* | Kane *Gregucci** | McLeish *Dellicari* | Irvine *Fusi* | Richardson *Shingalia* | Grant* *Fortunato* | Jess *Silenzi* | Connor *Carbone* | Paatelainen *Venturin* | Connor/Miller *Cois/Falcone*

More agony for the Dons. Richardson's blazing shot into the top corner put Aberdeen in front on the away-goals rule. Fusi's slide-rule pass enabled Carbone to turn McKimmie for the equaliser. Silenzi's header meant the Dons needed to score two more goals just to force extra-time.

League table

	P	W	D	L	F	A	W	D	L	F	A	Pts
		Home					*Away*					
1 Rangers	44	12	6	4	43	22	10	8	4	31	19	58
2 ABERDEEN	44	11	9	2	33	12	6	12	4	25	24	55
3 Motherwell	44	11	4	7	31	20	7	6	9	27	23	54
4 Celtic	44	8	11	3	25	17	7	9	6	26	21	50
5 Hibernian	44	11	7	4	29	15	5	8	9	24	33	47
6 Dundee Utd	44	5	11	6	26	25	6	9	7	21	23	42
7 Hearts	44	6	9	7	26	24	5	11	6	15	19	42
8 Kilmarnock	44	6	10	6	18	19	6	6	10	18	26	40
9 Partick This	44	9	8	5	23	17	3	8	11	23	40	40
10 St Johnstone	44	7	7	8	24	26	3	13	6	11	21	40
11 Raith Rovers	44	3	12	7	25	35	3	7	12	21	45	31
12 Dundee	44	6	7	9	26	26	2	6	14	16	31	29
	528	95	104	65	325	258	65	104	95	258	325	528

Aberdeen's record against each club

	P	W	D	L	F	A	Pts	Cup	W	D	L
v Raith Rovers	4	3	1	0	11	2	7	SC	1	0	0
v Kilmarnock	4	3	1	0	8	4	7				
v Dundee Utd	4	3	1	0	5	1	7	SC	0	1	0
v Dundee	4	2	2	0	4	2	6				
v Partick This	4	2	1	1	7	5	5				
v Celtic	4	2	1	1	5	4	5	SC	1	0	0
v St Johnstone	4	1	3	0	3	2	5	SC	1	0	0
v Rangers	4	1	2	1	3	3	4	LC	0	1	0
v Motherwell	4	0	4	0	2	2	4	LC	1	0	0
v Hearts	4	0	3	1	2	3	3				
v Hibernian	4	0	2	2	3	8	2				
	44	17	21	6	58	36	55				

Odds & ends

Never lost to: (7) Raith, Kilmarnock, Dundee, Celtic, St Johnstone, Motherwell, Dundee Utd (in the league).

Never beat: (2) Hearts, Motherwell (in the league).

Won from behind: (1) Motherwell (LC).

Lost from in front: (2) Hibs (a), Torino (CWC).

High spots: Aberdeen finish with the division's best defensive record. The Dons led the table three times - in late September, November, and late December.

Low spots: Never winning more than 3 league games in a row. One win in seven games from 6 November. Losing a two-goal lead in Torino. Being two minutes away from the Scottish Cup final.

Aberdeen finish second to Rangers for the fifth time in six seasons.

Aberdeen used 4 different goalkeepers in one season.

Bogey-team: Hibs.

Ever-presents: (0).

Hat-tricks: (1) Duncan Shearer.

Leading scorer: (26) Duncan Shearer.

Appearances and Goals

	Lge	Sub	LC	Sub	SC	Sub	Eur	Sub	Lge	LC	SC	Eur	Tot
	Appearances								*Goals*				
Aitken, Roy	6	1	3		2		2						
Bett, Jim	14	11	3		2	3	1		4	2		1	7
Booth, Scott	3			1						1			1
Burridge, John	3												
Connor, Robert	21	4	1		2	1			1				1
Gibson, Andrew	1	1			1					1			1
Grant, Andrew	26	4			4		2		2				2
Irvine, Brian	42		2		6		4		7		1		8
Jess, Eoin	38	3	2	1	6		4		6		1	5	12
Kane, Paul	39				5		4		3				3
McKimmie, Stewart	40		2		5		4						
McKinnon, Ray	5				2								
McLeish, Alex	35		3		4		3		1				1
Miller, Joe	24	3		3	6	1	3	2	4	2	1	1	8
Paatelainen, Mixu	14	22		3	2	1	3		6			1	7
Richardson, Lee	31	4	2		4		3		4	1	1	1	7
Robertson, Hugh	6	2			2								
Roddie, Andrew	3	3			2				1				1
Shearer, Duncan	39	4	2	1	6		2		17	4	4	1	26
Smith, Gary	19	2	3		5		3						
Snelders, Theo	33		3		3		4						
Stillie, Derek	4	1			2								
Ten Caat, Theo	1	2	1										
Thomson, Scott	3												
Watt, Michael	4												
Winnie, David	2	4			1		1						
Wright, Stephen	34	2	1		4		2	1	3			1	4
(own-goals)													
27 players used	484	76	33	6	66	10	44	8	58	11	8	10	87

BELL'S SCOTTISH PREMIER

Manager: Willie Miller → Roy Aitken   SEASON 1994-95

No	Date	Att	Pos	Pt	F-A	H-T	Scorers, Times, and Referees	1	2	3	4	5	6	7	8	9	10	11	subs used
1	H HEARTS 13/8	14,238	W *3*	3	3-1	1-0	Robertson 29, Dodds 58, Booth 74 / Colquhoun 53 / Ref: H Dallas	Snelders	McKimmie	Winnie	Grant	Irvine	Wright	Jess*	Shearer*	Kane	Dodds	Robertson	Hetherston/Booth
								Smith	*Frail*	*McKinlay**	*Locke*	*Weir*	*McLaren*	*Colquhoun**	*Mackay*	*Robertson*	*Leitch*	*Millar J*	*Johnston/Thomas*
2	H FALKIRK 20/8	11,143	D *6*	4	2-2	1-1	Robertson 37, Booth 87 / Cadette 29, McDonald 75 / Ref: T Brown	Snelders	McKimmie	Winnie	Grant	Irvine*	Wright	Booth	Shearer*	Kane	Dodds	Robertson	Miller/Jess
								Parks	*Weir*	*McGowan*	*Oliver*	*McLaughlin*	*MacKenzie*	*May*	*Fulton*	*Cadette*	*Rice**	*McDonald*	*McStay*
3	A DUNDEE UTD 27/8	9,332	L *8*	4	1-2	0-0	Grant 61 / Welsh 77, Brewster 85 / Ref: W Crombie	Snelders	McKimmie	Woodth'rpe	Grant	Irvine	Wright	Jess	Shearer*	Kane	Dodds	Miller	McKinnon
								Main	*Cleland*	*McInally*	*Hannah**	*Petric*	*Welsh*	*Bowman*	*McKinlay*	*Ristic**	*Brewster*	*McLaren*	*Dailly/Nixon*
4	A HIBERNIAN 10/9	9,728	D *2*	5	2-2	1-2	Dodds 33, Grant 74 / O'Neill 1, Jackson D 23 / Ref: L Thow	Snelders	McKimmie	Woodthorpe	Grant	Smith	Wright	Jess	McKinnon	Booth	Dodds	Winnie	McGraw/Love
								Leighton	*Farrell*	*Tortolano*	*Findlay**	*Tweed*	*Beaumont*	*McAllister*	*Hamilton*	*Evans**	*Jackson D*	*O'Neill*	
5	H PARTICK THISTLE 17/9	10,425	D *7*	6	1-1	0-0	Dodds 78 / Charnley 74 / Ref: G Simpson	Watt	McKimmie	Woodthorpe	Grant	Irvine	Wright	Jess	Smith	Booth*	Dodds	Winnie	Miller
								Nelson	*Byrne*	*Dinnie*	*Watson**	*Jamieson*	*McWilliams*	*Cameron*	*Craig*	*Grant**	*Gibson*	*Charnley*	*Smith.McKee*
6	H RANGERS 24/9	19,191	D *2*	7	2-2	1-1	Booth 13, Dodds 81p / Hateley 42, Moore 71 / Ref: L Mottram	Watt	McKimmie	Woodthorpe	Grant	Irvine	Wright	Jess	Smith!	Booth	Dodds*	McKinnon*	Hetherston/Miller
								Goram	*Moore*	*Robertson*	*Gough*	*McPherson*	*Boli*	*Murray*	*McCall**	*Durie*	*Hateley*	*Laudrup*	*Durrant*
7	A KILMARNOCK 1/10	7,445	L *9*	7	1-2	1-1	Booth 39 / Winnie 6 og, Brown 85 / Ref: R Tait	Watt	McKimmie	Woodthorpe	Grant	Irvine	Wright	Hetherston*	Winnie	Booth	Dodds	McKinnon	Miller
								Geddes	*Montgomerie*	*Black*	*Connor*	*Whitworth*	*Millen*	*McKee**	*Henry*	*Williamson*	*Brown*	*McSkimm'g**	*Reilly/Maskrey*
8	A CELTIC 8/10	29,454	D *2*	8	0-0	0-0	Ref: A Huett	Watt	McKimmie	Woodthorpe	Grant	Irvine	Wright	Smith	Kane	Booth	Dodds	McKinnon	Nicholas/Falconer
								Marshall	*Galloway**	*Boyd*	*McNally*	*O'Neil**	*O'Donnell*	*McGinlay*	*Donnelly*	*Walker*	*Collins*		
9	H MOTHERWELL 15/10	12,489	L *4*	8	1-3	1-0	Dodds 34p / McKinnon 56, Kirk 75, Coyne 80 / Ref: M Clark	Watt	McKimmie	Woodthorpe	Grant	Irvine*	Wright	Smith	Kane	Booth	Dodds	Hetherston*	Miller
								Woods	*Shannon*	*McKinlay*	*Philliben*	*Martin*	*McCart*	*Lambert*	*Dolan**	*Coyne*	*Arnott**	*Davies*	*Kirk/Roddie*
10	A HEARTS 22/10	10,655	L *5*	8	0-2	0-2	Frail 12, Robertson 41 / Ref: G Evans	Watt	McKimmie	Woodthorpe	Grant	Irvine*	Wright	Smith	Kane	Booth	Dodds	Hetherston*	Winnie/Robertson
								Smith	*Frail*	*McKinlay*	*Levein*	*Berry*	*McLaren*	*Mackay*	*Bett*	*Robertson*	*Millar J**	*Johnston*	*Colquhoun/Leitch*

1. The Dons have drawn 0-0 in Latvia. The new mascot, Angus the Bull, gets a rousing reception at Pittodrie. McKinnon and Woodthorpe are both suspended. Hugh Robertson blasts a goal from 30 yards. Record signing Billy Dodds took advantage of Henry Smith's hesitancy for No 2.

2. Stewart McKimmie is involved in horrendous tangles for both Falkirk goals. The second of which sees McKimmie head back to Snelders, who parries the ball up in the air for McDonald. Hugh Robertson's second rocket in a week is followed by Booth's late header to rescue a point.

3. Dundee United officially open their new East Stand. Scotland manager Craig Brown takes in this match. Aberdeen are still smarting over the Skonto Riga fiasco. Miller makes three changes to that side. Pity the Dons could not hold on to Grant's chip. They lose to two United headers.

4. Knee injuries rule out Shearer and Irvine. Gary Smith starts his first game of the season. Seconds after kick-off Tweed heads Farrell's free-kick across goal for O'Neill. Findlay and Woodthorpe both hit the woodwork. Dodds' goal was the first conceded by Jim Leighton in 578 minutes.

5. Snelders injurted himself in training. Aberdeen recently beat Partick 5-0 in the Cola-Cola Cup. Chic Charnley plays his first game since being sent off in that match, and heads in Craig's cross from close range. Dodds equalises at the far post, heading in Colin Woodthorpe's cross.

6. More trouble between these teams. Seven players booked, Gary Smith sent off, and Laudrup's 'winner' disallowed when the referee blows for time. After the match Hateley was apparently assaulted by Dons fans and Durie apparently red-carded. The result knocks Rangers off the top.

7. Jess is out with a foot injury. Ex-Don Bobby Connor was the architect of Kilmarnock's opener, Winnie diverting Williamson's effort. Billy Dodds twice hit the bar before Irvine deflected Brown's shot.

8. Owing to Parkhead's redevelopment this match is played at Hampden. It is memorable for no other reason than Jimmy Johnstone's half-time rendition of 'You'll Never Walk Alone'. O'Donnell hit the post for Celtic; Marshall pulled off fine saves from Billy Dodds and Scott Booth.

9. Pittodrie gives Alex McLeish a standing ovation. The new offside law denies Dodds a goal. Martin tripped Booth for the penalty, delayed for two minutes because of protests. McKimmie deflected I Well's equaliser. Coyne's lob confirms Motherwell's first Premier win at Pittodrie.

10. The Dons slip one place further, down to ninth, at the hands of revitalised Hearts. Full-back Stephen Frail scored from 16 yards early on, and when John Robertson netted from a rebound off the post Aberdeen were left without hope. They scarcely had a look-in in the second half.

11 H DUNDEE UTD 7 W 3-0
11,744   8 11
Kane 13, 78, Booth 15
Ref: J McCluskey

Snelders McKimmie Woodthorpe Grant* Winnie Wright Smith Kane Booth Dodds McKinnon^ Hetherston/Glass
O'Hanlon Cleland Malpas Hannah* Petric Welsh Bowman McKinlay McLaren Dailly Johnston^ McInally/Nixon

Corners brought the first two goals. The first, from Kane on the left, was helped in by the keeper. The second, from Woodthorpe, was powered in by Booth for his eighth goal of the season. No 3 was a cheeky curler. Substitute Stephen Glass hits the post on his debut. The first win in 10.

---

12 A FALKIRK 8 L 1-2
6,185   4 11
Booth 10
Cramb 27p, McGowan 66
Ref: J Smith

Snelders McKimmie Woodthorpe* Grant Winnie Wright Smith Kane Booth Dodds McKinnon* Shearer/Inglis
Parks* Weir McGowan Oliver McLaughlin MacKenzie May Clark Cramb Henderson McDonald Lamont

Scott Booth's far-post header is just the start Aberdeen wanted. Stephen Wright fouls Nicky Henderson for the equalising penalty. Full-back Jamie McGowan headed the Bairns' second, to earn Falkirk their first league victory over Aberdeen since April 1971. Inglis makes his debut.

---

13 H HIBERNIAN 8 D 0-0
10,882   3 12
Ref: J Rowbotham

Snelders McKimmie Woodthorpe Kane Winnie Smith Thomson Shearer* Booth Dodds McKinnon Winnie
Leighton Miller W Love McGinlay Tweed Hunter McAllister* Hamilton Harper Jackson D O'Neill Evans

This is Hibs' fourth 0-0 away draw in five games, so this result was always on the cards. Winger Scott Thomson plays his first full match in three years since signing from Brechin for £100,000. After seven minutes Shearer collides with Gordon Hunter and aggravates a knee injury.

---

14 A PARTICK THISTLE 8 L 1-2
3,795   10 12
Dodds 24
Craig 53, Gibson 56
Ref: H Williamson

Snelders McKimmie Woodthorpe Kane Inglis Smith Thomson Jess Glass Dodds* McKinnon^ Hetherston/Wright
Nelson McKee Dinnie Watson Jamieson McWilliams McDonald Craig Gibson Cameron Charnley

Booth scored against Russia in midweek but is now unfit. Jess returns after eight games out with a broken foot. Having walloped Partick 5-0 in the Coca-Cola, Aberdeen are humiliated by Albert Craig heading in Charnley's corner and ex-Don Ian Gibson exploiting McKimmie's error.

---

15 A RANGERS L 0-1
45,072   1 12
McCoist 55
Ref: J McGilvray

Snelders McKimmie* Woodthorpe Kane Inglis Wright Smith Grant Thomson Dodds Jess* Hetherston/Glass
Goram Wishart Robertson McCall McLaren Boli Huistra Miller McCoist Hateley^ Laudrup Durie

A Friday night game. Minus Shearer and Booth, Aberdeen look toothless in attack. Their only complaints after this latest defeat were that Ally McCoist may have been offside for the goal, and that Basile Boli was not even penalised when dragging down Billy Dodds, who was clear.

---

16 H KILMARNOCK 10 L 0-1
10,345   7 12
Maskrey 1
Ref: I Taylor

Snelders McKimmie Woodthorpe* Kane Inglis Jess Jess Grant* Miller Dodds Glass Hetherston/Thomson
Lekovik MacPherson Napier Reilly Whitworth Anderson Mitchell Skilling McKee Connor Maskrey^ Williamson/Roberts

This is too awful to contemplate. Even the most blinkered follower of the club now knows something is critically wrong with Aberdeen FC. There can be no excuses after this lamentable display, which saw the Dons try for 89 laborious minutes to retrieve Maskrey's quick-fire goal.

---

17 A MOTHERWELL 9 W 1-0
7,020   2 15
McCart 35 og
Ref: L Mottram

Snelders McKimmie* Woodthorpe* Kane Inglis Wright Smith Jess Grant* Miller Glass Shearer/Jess
Woods Shannon McKinnon Philliben Martin^ McCart Lambert Dolan Coyne Arnott Davies* Kirk/Roddie

Charity from McLeish's team. Aberdeen won just twice in the first half of the season. This unconvincing win suggests they will do little better in the second round of 18 matches. They even needed an own-goal to pick up the three points. Dons' forwards have scored once in five games.

---

18 H CELTIC 9 D 0-0
19,206   5 16
Ref: H Dallas

Snelders McKimmie Wright Kane Inglis Hetherston Smith Grant Miller* Glass Shearer/Jess
Bonner Boyd McKinlay O'Neil Mowbray Grant Hay* McStay McLaughlin Walker Collins Donnelly

Celtic's seventh successive draw is also their 11th league game without a win, an all-time record. Andy Walker shot wide in the second half. Mowbray's header was cleared off the line by Joe Miller, and Aberdeen survived a penalty claim. Aberdeen have scored twice in five games.

---

19 H HEARTS 9 W 3-1
11,392   6 19
Shearer 13, 52, Inglis 28
Thomas 66
Ref: G Simpson

Snelders McKimmie Wright Kane Inglis Hetherston* Shearer Jess Hetherston Smith Grant McKinnon
Nelson Frail Miller C Jamieson^ Berry McPherson Colquhoun Bett Robertson* Mackay Hagen Thomas/Wright

Duncan Shearer returns from knee injury to score twice, first with a brave header, then with a super curler round keeper Craig Nelson. John Inglis scored his first goal for the Dons when capitalising on Wright's cut-back, which Nelson helped into the net. 1994 ends on a high note.

---

20 A DUNDEE UTD D 0-0
10,560   20
Ref: J Timmons

Snelders McKimmie* Wright Kane Inglis Smith Shearer* Grant Miller Dodds McKinnon Aitken/Jess
O'Hanlon Cleland Malpas Hannah Petric Bollan Bowman McKinlay Connolly* Brewster^ Dailly Winters/Nixon

A 0-0 draw that could have ended 3-3. Billy Dodds and Brian Grant squandered the chances that came Aberdeen's way, but Theo Snelders was kept busy throughout. His best save was from Jim McInally. Roy Aitken comes off the bench for his first game since Valur in Iceland in 1993.

---

21 H FALKIRK 7 D 0-0
14,141   5 21
Ref: R Tait

Snelders Glass Wright Kane Inglis Grant Smith Grant Shearer Miller Dodds McKinnon^ Jess
Parks Weir Hughes Oliver McLaughlin* MacKenzie May Clark McDonald Fulton Rice^ McGowan/Paterson

How does one write 50 words about such a forgettable game? Falkirk defended in depth and Aberdeen hadn't the wit to break through. The only two Dons to take credit were Stephen Glass as overlapping full-back and Gary Smith, who wore the captain's armband for the first time.

BELL'S SCOTTISH PREMIER

Manager: Willie Miller → Roy Aitken   SEASON 1994-95

No	Date	Att	Pos	Pt	F-A	H-T	Scorers, Times, and Referees	1	2	3	4	5	6	7	8	9	10	11	subs used
22	H 14/1	9,833	6 W	10 24	3-1	1-0	Dinnie 3 og, Jess 54, Shearer 59, Pittman 86. Ref: J O'Hare	Snelders	Walker	Wright*	Kane	Inglis	Smith	Jess	Shearer*	Miller	Dodds	Grant	Thomson/Glass
	PARTICK THISTLE							Dinnie	Pittman	Watson	Welsh	Turner*	McDonald	Craig	McWilliams	Charnley*	Taylor		Cameron/Gray
23	A 21/1	8,076	8 L	2 24	2-4	1-3	Dodds 27p, 77; McGinlay 7, Jackson 11, 41p, Wright 63. Ref: K Clark	Snelders	McKimmie	Glass	Kane	Inglis	Smith	Jess	Shearer	Miller*	Dodds	Grant	McKinnon
	HIBERNIAN							Leighton	Miller W	Mitchell	McGinlay	Tweed	Farrell	McAllister	Evans^	Wright	Jackson D*	Tortolano	Findlay/Weir
24	A 4/2	9,384	9 L	6 24	1-3	1-2	McKimmie 4; Maskrey 27, Brown 34, Roberts 88. Ref: T Brown	Snelders	McKimmie	Wright	Kane*	Inglis	Smith	Thomson^	Grant	Miller	Dodds	Glass	Aitken/Shearer
	KILMARNOCK							Lekovic	MacPhersonBlack	Reilly	Whitworth	Anderson	Mitchell	Henry	Brown^	Connor	Maskrey		Roberts
25	H 12/2	18,060	7 W	1 27	2-0	0-0	Dodds 57p, Shearer 88. Ref: J McCluskey	Snelders	McKimmie*	Wright	Kane	Inglis	Smith	Jess	Shearer	Miller	Dodds	McKinnon	Glass
	RANGERS							Maxwell	Moore	Robertson	Gough	Bollan^	Cleland	McCall	Miller*	Hateley	Laudrup		Durrant/Durie
26	A 25/2	10,319	9 L	2 27	0-2	0-1	Burns 4, McKinnon 83p. Ref: R Orr (Dons' 3rd sub Watt)	Snelders!	Wright	Glass	Kane	Irvine	Smith	Jess*	Shearer*	Miller*	Dodds	McKinnon^	Hetherston/Thomson
	MOTHERWELL							Woods	May	McKinnon	Krivokapic	Philliben	McCart	Lambert	Dolan	Burns^	Arnott		McSkimmy*/Shannon/Roddie
27	A 5/3	20,261	9 L	4 27	0-2	0-1	van Hooijdonk 40p, 78. Ref: A Waddell	Watt	Bonner	Wright	Grant*	Irvine	Smith	Jess*	Glass	Miller	Dodds	McKinnon^	Shearer/Hetherston
	CELTIC							Boyd	McKinlay	O'Neil	Mowbray	Grant	McLaughlin*	McStay	v Hooijdonk	Falconer	O'Donnell		Collins
28	A 11/3	6,886	9 D	10 28	2-2	2-0	Wright 8, Dodds 43; Pittman 52, Turner 73. Ref: J Rowbotham	Snelders	Walker	Wright	Grant	Irvine	Smith	Jess*	Glass*	Miller	Dodds	McKinnon^	Hetherston/Jess
	PARTICK THISTLE							McKimmie	McKee	Pittman	Watson	Welsh	Turner*	McDonald^	Craig	Foster	Cameron	McWilliams	Smith/Grant
29	H 18/3	10,384	9 D	3 29	0-0	0-0	Ref: J Herald	Snelders*	Leighton	Wright	Kane	Inglis	Smith	Hetherston	Shearer	Miller	Dodds*	Grant	Jess/Thomson/Watt
	HIBERNIAN							Miller W	Mitchell*	McGinlay	Tweed	Hunter	Harper^	Tortolano	Wright	Jackson D	O'Neill		Weir/Farrell
30	H 1/4	14,041	9 L	7 29	0-1	0-0	Skilling 50. Ref: L Mottram	Watt	McKimmie	Wright	Kane	Inglis	Smith	Hetherston	Shearer	Miller	Dodds	Grant*	Jess
	KILMARNOCK							Lekovic	MacPhersonBlack	Reilly*	Whitworth	Anderson	Mitchell	Skilling	Wright^	Brown	Connor		Findlay/Maskrey
31	A 8/4	44,460	10 L	1 29	2-3	2-2	Dodds 32, Shearer 45; Durrant 19, Murray 24, Hateley 52. Ref: H Williamson	Watt	McKimmie	Wright	Kane	Inglis	Smith	Hetherston	Shearer	Miller	Dodds	Grant*	Jess
	RANGERS							Thomson	Cleland	Brown	Gough	McLaren	Boli!	Steven	Miller	Durrant	Hateley	Laudrup^	Murray/Mik'chenko

Match notes:

22 – Just the tonic when the Jags' Alan Dinnie turned Billy Dodds' cross past future Dons keeper Nicky Walker. Eoin Jess's thumping shot was his first goal in 267 days. Duncan Shearer's header from the outstanding Joe Miller's cross settled the outcome. These are three priceless points.

23 – Having conceded just one goal in five games this was an unwelcome return to bad habits. Hibs had five efforts on target in 90 minutes and scored from four of them. Dodds pulled it back to 1-2 from the spot after Tweed dragged him down. Jim Leighton played a blinder for Hibs.

24 – Killie's Maskrey and Brown are two of the smallest strikers around, yet they both score with close-range headers against. And this after McKimmie had given Aberdeen a dream start. Snelders worked hard to stem the Kilmarnock tide. The final score flattered the dismal Dons.

25 – Roy Aitken takes over and masterminds this great win. Shearer was tripped by Maxwell for Dodds' penalty. Dodds also hit the bar before Shearer's late goal sealed the win. Gers were denied two good penalty claims in what was, all things considered, a surprisingly low key game.

26 – Motherwell did not have to play well to beat this shower. When Gary Smith failed to clear Alex Burns gave McLeish the perfect start. Snelders was sent off for a professional foul on Arnott. Watt came on, but the Dons' 'wall' disintegrated as Rob McKinnon's free-kick blazed through it.

27 – A TV Sunday match at Hampden. Celtic fans were jeering their team when Irvine barged into the back of van Hooijdonk for the penalty. Joe Miller headed against the bar and Shearer shot against Bonner's legs before Tosh McKinlay crossed to the far post onto van Hooijdonk's head.

28 – The club pay for supporters' buses to travel to Partick. Wright lobbed Nicky Walker from near the halfway line and Dodds swivelled to make it 2-0. All the more disappointing, then, that two points should disappear. Two free-kicks by Pittman brought the Bairns level. Jess hit a post.

29 – Jim Leighton is 36 but showed all his old agility in keeping Aberdeen at bay. At least the Dons showed spirit. In 34 minutes Snelders injured a foot in a collision with Miller and had to be replaced. This is Hibs' ninth away draw in 14 games, in which they have scored just six goals.

30 – Words cannot describe the impact of this shattering defeat - the fourth against Kilmarnock - despite pounding the Killie goal from first to last. Mark Skilling scored with a thunderbolt from 18 yards. Before and after the goal, Killie's Serbian keeper Lekovic pulled off save after save.

31 – Aberdeen go bottom of the league. At 0-2 they looked down and out, but Shearer sets up a goal for Dodds, then volleys a brilliant equaliser. But after Mark Hateley heads his 15th goal from Cleland's cross the Dons have to start over again. Rangers aren't in the mood to be generous.

32 H CELTIC 15/4 — 16,668 · 10 · W · 6 · 32 — **2-0**
Shearer 30, Irvine 41
Ref: J McCluskey

Watt	McKimmie	Wright	Kane	Irvine	Smith	Hetherston	Shearer	Miller^	Dodds*	Grant	Jess/Glass
Bonner	Boyd	McKinlay^ Vata	O'Neil	Grant	McLaughlin McStay	Falconer	Walker*	Collins			Donnelly/O'Donnell

Celtic have drawn more than half their games and having reached the Scottish Cup Final seemed ill-inclined to roll up their sleeves and scrap. Shearer's soaring header from Stephen Wright's cross lifted spirits. Brian Irvine's first goal of the season was a super volley at the far post.

---

33 A MOTHERWELL 18/4 — 7,155 · 10 · L · 2 · 32 — **1-2**
Dodds 42
McSkimming 38, Arnott 56
Ref: G Clyde

Watt	McKimmie	Wright	Kane	Irvine	Smith^	Hetherston	Shearer	Miller	Dodds	Grant*	Jess/Glass
Woods	May	McKinnon	Krivokapic* Martin	Philliben	Lambert	Dolan	Coyne	Arnott^			McSkimming Burns/Roddie

This defeat looks fatal, and one wonders how Alex McLeish feels at pushing his old club over the edge. Dodds 13th goal of the season - from Shearer's knock-down -equalised McSkimming's shot. Arnott tapped in after Watt pushed out May's cross. Irvine and Glass hit the woodwork.

---

34 H HEARTS 29/4 — 11,466 · 10 · W · 7 · 35 — **2-1**
Dodds 61p, 85
McPherson 64
Ref: T McCurry

Watt	McKimmie	Wright	Grant	Irvine	Smith^	Hetherston	Shearer	Miller^	Dodds*	Jess	McKinnon/Glass
Nelson	Wishart^ Miller C	Levein	Berry	McPherson Hamilton	Bett	Colquhoun* Mackay	Hagen				Robertson/Jamieson

Aberdeen's missed chances in the first half look to be expensive. Hagen pushed Shearer in the back and Dodds sent Nelson the wrong way from the spot. McPherson looked offside when heading the equaliser. Dodds' glancing header means the Dons' fate is back in their own hands.

---

35 H DUNDEE UTD 6/5 — 20,124 · 9 · W · 10 · 38 — **2-1**
Dodds 38, Shearer 68
Winters 85
Ref: H Williamson

Snelders	McKimmie	Wright	Grant	Irvine	Smith	Hetherston	Shearer	Miller	Dodds	Jess*	Glass
O'Hanlon	Perry	Malpas	Dailly	Craig	Johnston	Crabbe*	Mcinally	Gomes	Brewster* Hannah		McLaren/Winters

Make no mistake, Aberdeen were streets ahead of United. Jess's header is parried by O'Hanlon and Dodds swoops from two yards. A mighty shot by Shearer from 18 yards makes it 2-0. Robbie Winters' goal ensures a panic-stricken climax, but the Dons finally climb off the bottom.

---

36 A FALKIRK 13/5 — 12,835 · 9 · W · 5 · 41 — **2-0**
Thomson 14, Glass 50
Ref: J McGilvray

Snelders	McKimmie	Wright	Grant	Irvine	Smith	Thomson^	Shearer	Miller	Dodds*	Jess	Kpedekpo
Parks	Weir	McGowan* Hughes	McLaughlin Clark	Kirk	Rice	Fulton	Johnston	MacKenzie McDonald			

If Aberdeen win and Hearts lose, the Dons will avoid the play-offs. 7,000 travelling fans outnumber and outshout home fans. Scott Thomson heads in Glass's free-kick, then Glass scores from a move begun by Thomson. Hearts beat Motherwell to send Aberdeen into the play-offs.

Average Home 13,424 · Away 14,432

PO 1 H DUNFERMLINE 21/5 — 21,000 · W · 3-1 · 1-0
Glass 39, Shearer 56, 87
Robertson 49
Ref: L Mottram

Snelders	McKimmie	Wright	Grant	Irvine	Smith	Hetherston	Shearer	Miller	Thomson	Glass
van de Kamp McNamara Fleming	McCathie Tod	Smith	den Bieman Robertson	Moore*	Petrie	McCulloch^ Shaw/Hawkins

Stephen Glass's free-kick speeds past van de Kamp into the corner. Ex-Don Craig Robertson is unmarked to head in Paul Smith's corner. The second half belongs to Duncan Shearer. His glancing header was meat and drink; his rampaging run and shot was a thing of beauty.

PO 2 A DUNFERMLINE 25/5 — 16,000 · W · 3-1 · 0-0
Dodds 49, Miller 65, Glass 80
Smith 72
Ref: J McCluskey
(Dons win 6-2 on aggregate)

Snelders	McKimmie	Wright	Grant	Irvine^	Smith	Hetherston	Shearer	Miller^	Dodds	Glass	Inglis/Kane
van de Kamp McNamara Fleming	McCathie Tod	Smith	den Bieman Robertson	Moore	Petrie	McCulloch^ Shaw

Aberdeen deflated the Pars by keeping them at bay until half-time. When Dodds headed in Wright's cross the nightmare was finally over. The party began. Stephen Glass almost scored a sensational goal in the first leg. Now he wraps things up by taking the ball round van de Kamp.

BELL'S PREMIER (CUP-TIES)

Manager: Willie Miller → Roy Aitken — SEASON 1994-95

Coca-Cola League Cup

		F-A	H-T	Scorers, Times, and Referees	1	2	3	4	5	6	7	8	9	10	11	subs used
2 H STRANRAER 17/8 — 8,158	W	1-0	0-0	Shearer 71 — Ref: J Rowbotham	Snelders	McKimmie	Winnie	Grant	Irvine	Wright	Jess*	Shearer*	Kane	Dodds	Robertson	Miller/Booth
					Ross	Treanor	Hughes	McCaffrey*	Brannigan	Millar	McLean	Duncan*	Walker	Cody	Henderson	Ferguson/Brown

Hero of this match is undoubtedly Stranraer's keeper Stevie Ross, who had undergone heart surgery some years earlier. The best of his many saves was to keep out Shearer's fierce free-kick. Shearer had the last laugh, scoring the winner with the assistance of Paul Kane in the build-up.

		F-A	H-T	Scorers, Times, and Referees	1	2	3	4	5	6	7	8	9	10	11	subs used
3 A PARTICK THISTLE 30/8 — 5,046	W	5-0	2-0	Shearer 29,33,62p, Kane 60, Dodds 69 — Ref: L Mottram	Snelders	McKimmie	Woodthorpe	Grant	Irvine*	Wright	Jess	Shearer	Kane	Dodds	McKinnon*	Winnie/Booth
					Nelson	Byrne	Law	Jamieson	Tierney	McWilliams	Taylor	Cameron	Grant*	English	Charnley!	Smith

Shearer has turned 32 and celebrates his first hat-trick in over a year. It earns him a £500 bonus from Cola-Cola. He has also been called up for the midweek international against Finland. Chic Charnley was sent off for retaliating against Shearer. Best of the goals was Paul Kane's bullet.

		F-A	H-T	Scorers, Times, and Referees	1	2	3	4	5	6	7	8	9	10	11	subs used
QF A FALKIRK 21/9 — 9,450	W	4-1	2-1	Booth 6, 20, 63, Rice 83 og; McDonald 23 — Ref: W Young	Watt	McKimmie	Woodthorpe	Grant	Winnie	Wright	Jess	Smith	Booth	Dodds*	McKinnon	Miller
					Parks	McGowan	McQueen	Clark	McLaughlin	McKenzie	May	Henderson*	Cadette	Rice	McDonald	McAvennie

Snelders, Shearer, Irvine and Kane are all out. The kick-off was delayed 10 minutes to accommodate the large number of Dons fans. Miller's controversial 5-3-2 system is working better away than at home. The turning point was Richard Cadette's header, disallowed for offside, at 1-2.

		F-A	H-T	Scorers, Times, and Referees	1	2	3	4	5	6	7	8	9	10	11	subs used
SF N CELTIC 26/10 (at Ibrox) — 44,000	L	0-1	0-0	O'Neil B 99 (aet) — Ref: L Mottram	Snelders	McKimmie	Woodthorpe	Grant	Winnie	Wright	Smith	Kane*	Booth	Dodds	McKinnon*	Robertson/Hetherston
					Marshall	Smith	Boyd	McNally	O'Neil B	Grant	Byrne*	McStay	Donnelly	Walker*	Collins	McGinlay/Nicholas

Snelders returned after missing seven games through injury. A tense semi-final saw so few chances that any mistake was likely to prove critical. In extra-time central defender Brian O'Neil heads in John Collins' cross to send Celtic through to a mouth-watering final with Raith.

Tennents Scottish Cup

		F-A	H-T	Scorers, Times, and Referees	1	2	3	4	5	6	7	8	9	10	11	subs used
3 H STRANRAER 28/1 — 9,183	W	1-0	1-0	Jess 41 — Ref: M Clark	Snelders	Wright	Glass	Kane	Inglis	Smith	Jess	Shearer*	Miller	Dodds	Grant	Thomson
					Ross	McLean	Hughes	Gallagher	Howard	Millar	Sloan	Walker	Duncan	Callaghan*	Reilly	Cody

Stranraer did not want to score and Aberdeen couldn't. That sums up this frustrating cup-tie which Aberdeen won on corners 15-2, but which had only one goal to show for all Aberdeen's effort. Willie Miller was so angry by what he had seen that he kicked the dressing room door.

		F-A	H-T	Scorers, Times, and Referees	1	2	3	4	5	6	7	8	9	10	11	subs used
4 A STENHOUSEMUIR 18/2 — 3,452 2:1	L	0-2	0-0	Steel 60, 85 — Ref: J Rowbotham	Snelders	Wright	Glass	Kane	Inglis*	Smith	Jess	Shearer	Miller*	Dodds	McKinnon	Irvine/Hetherston
					Harkness	Clarke	Donaldson	Armstrong	McGeachie	Christie	Steel	Fisher	Mathieson	Hutchison	Sprott	

Tommy Steel is not an ageing pop-star but a milk farmer. He hits the headlines for the first time in his life for scoring twice against the Dons' team of prima donnas. Muir's part-time team cost just £80,000. Stephen Glass excepted, Aberdeen look awful. Their worst result ever.

UEFA Cup

		F-A	H-T	Scorers, Times, and Referees	1	2	3	4	5	6	7	8	9	10	11	subs used
P:1 A SKONTO RIGA (Latvia) 9/8 — 2,300	D	0-0	0-0	Ref: U Meyers (Switzerland)	Snelders	McKimmie	Woodthorpe	Grant	Irvine	Wright	Robertson	Shearer*	McKinnon	Dodds	Winnie	Booth
					Laizan	Troytsky	Zemlinsky	Mikutsky	Shevlyakov	Monyak	Semenov	Blagonadez*	Stepanov	Babichev	Yeliseyez	

Skonto Riga were denied entry to the Champions' Cup. They are full-time, not part-time, as rumoured, but have nine Latvian internationals in their side. Keeper Laizan has conceded just five goals in two years, he says. Willie Miller tries to put a brave front on the Dons' awful display.

		F-A	H-T	Scorers, Times, and Referees	1	2	3	4	5	6	7	8	9	10	11	subs used
P:2 H SKONTO RIGA 23/8 — 8,500	D	1-1	0-0	Kane 90; Semenov 55 — Ref: T Hauge (Norway) (Dons lose on away-goals rule)	Snelders	McKimmie	Woodthorpe	Kane	Irvine*	Wright	Booth	Hetherston*	McKinnon	Dodds	Winnie	Miller/Shearer
					Laizan	Troytsky	Monyak	Shevlyakov	Mikutsky	Lobanev	Stepanov	Babichev	Blagonadez*	Yeliseyev	Semenov	

Dreadful weather, dreadful performance. Latvian international Alexai Semenov silences Pittodrie with his shock goal, which means Aberdeen must score twice. Afterwards the air is thick with criticism of Willie Miller's management. Radio phone-ins are even suggesting he should go.

League Table

	P	W	D	L	F	A	W	D	L	F	A	Pts
			Home						Away			
1 Rangers	36	11	5	2	31	14	9	4	5	29	21	69
2 Motherwell	36	8	6	4	29	23	6	6	6	21	27	54
3 Hibernian	36	9	7	2	37	19	6	5	12	18	14	53
4 Celtic	36	6	8	4	23	19	5	10	3	16	14	51
5 Falkirk	36	8	3	7	26	24	4	9	5	22	23	48
6 Hearts	36	9	4	5	26	14	3	3	12	18	37	43
7 Kilmarnock	36	8	4	6	22	16	6	9	4	18	32	43
8 Partick This	36	4	9	5	23	23	6	4	8	17	27	43
9 ABERDEEN*	36	7	7	4	24	16	3	4	11	19	30	41
10 Dundee Utd	36	6	6	6	24	20	3	3	12	16	36	36
	360	76	59	45	265	188	45	59	76	188	265	481

* survived after play-off

	P	W	D	L	F	A	Pts	Cup	W	D	L	F	A
v Hearts	4	3	0	1	8	5	9						
v Dundee Utd	4	2	1	1	6	3	7	LC	W	1	0	0	
v Partick This	4	2	1	1	7	6	5	LC	D	1	0	0	
v Falkirk	4	1	2	1	5	4	5	LC	L	0	0	1	
v Celtic	4	1	2	1	2	2	5						
v Rangers	4	1	2	1	6	6	4						
v Hibernian	4	0	3	1	4	6	3						
v Motherwell	4	1	0	3	3	7	3						
v Kilmarnock	4	0	0	4	2	7	0						
	36	10	11	15	43	46	41						

Odds & ends

Never lost to: (0).

Never beat: (2) Kilmarnock, Hibernian.

Won from behind: (0).

Lost from in front: (5). Dundee U (a), Motherwell (h), Falkirk (a), Partick (a), Kilmarnock (a).

High spots: Reaching semi-final of Coca-Cola Cup.

Losing just one of the first six league games, keeping 4th position.

Winning the final five matches (including play-offs) to avoid relegation.

Low spots: Losing to Skonto Riga in UEFA Cup.

Losing to Stenhousemuir in Scottish Cup.

Losing all four league matches to Kilmarnock.

Lowest ever position in Scottish Premier League.

Lowest position in Scottish league since 1968-69.

Bogey-team: Kilmarnock.

Ever-presents: (0).

Hat-tricks: (2) Scott Booth (1), Duncan Shearer (1).

Leading Scorer: (16) Billy Dodds.

Appearances and Goals

	Appearances								Goals					
	Lge*	Sub	LC	Sub	SC	Sub	Eur	Sub	Lge	Sub	LC	SC	Eur	Tot
Aitken, Roy	11		1	2										
Booth, Scott	36	1	4		2	2		1	6	1	3			9
Dodds, Billy	13				2	2			16		1			17
Glass, Stephen	34	8			2	1	1		3					3
Grant, Brian	15		4		1			1	2					2
Hetherston, Peter	16	9			2	1	1							
Inglis, John	19	2	2		2	2			1					1
Irvine, Brian	15				1		2		1					1
Jess, Eoin	15	10	3		2	1	2		1			1		2
Kane, Paul	27	1	3	1	2	1	1		2		1		1	4
Kpedekpo, Malcolm		1												
McKimmie, Stewart	36		4		2	2			1					1
McKinnon, Ray	17	3	3		1	2		1	1					1
Miller, Joe	23	6		2	1		1		1	1				2
Robertson, Hugh	2	1	1	1										
Shearer, Duncan	21	4	2	2	2	2	1	1	9	1	4			13
Smith, Gary	33		2		2	2								
Snelders, Theo	26		3		2	2								
Thomson, Scott	7	4			1		2							
Watt, Michael	12		2		2									
Winnie, David	6	2	3	1					1					1
Woodthorpe, Colin	14		3		2	2								
Wright, Stephen	35	1	4		2	2			2		1			3
(own-goals)														3
23 players used	418	57	44	7	22	3	22	3	49	3	10	1	1	61

BELL'S SCOTTISH PREMIER

SEASON 1995-96

Manager: Roy Aitken

Match summary

No	Date		Att	Pos	Pt	F-A	H-T	Scorers, Times, and Referees
1	A FALKIRK	26/8	6,647		3	W 3-2	2-0	Inglis 30, Dodds 42, Booth 63 / McLaughlin 55, Kirk 68 — Ref: W Crombie
2	H CELTIC	10/9	16,489		3	L 2-3	2-3	Boyd 7 og, Jess 10 / Collins 21, 38, Thom 33 — Ref: A Huett (Celtic's 3rd sub McLaughlin)
3	A HIBERNIAN	16/9	11,161	6	4	D 1-1	0-0	Shearer 72 / Jackson D 74 — Ref: R Tait
4	A KILMARNOCK	23/9	7,198	4	7	W 2-1	2-0	Miller 30, Woodthorpe 42 / Brown 48 — Ref: G Evans
5	H RAITH ROVERS	30/9	13,983	2	10	W 3-0	2-0	Booth 6, 71, Miller 26 — Ref: I Taylor (Raith's 3rd sub Nicholl)
6	A HEARTS	4/10	10,927	2	13	W 2-1	1-1	Dodds 18, Booth 60 / Robertson 24 — Ref: H Dallas
7	H RANGERS	7/10	20,351	1	13	L 0-1	0-0	Moore 78 — Ref: L Mottram
8	A MOTHERWELL	14/10	6,842	3	13	L 1-2	1-1	Booth 24 / Coyne 42, Lambert 56 — Ref: R Orr (Motherwell's 3rd sub Hendry)
9	H PARTICK THISTLE	21/10	12,719	3	16	W 3-0	1-0	Craig 24 og, Jess 54, Bernard 79 — Ref: G Simpson (Partick's 3rd sub Cameron)
10	A CELTIC	28/10	32,275	4	16	L 0-2	0-1	McLaughlin 40, van Hooijdonk 59p — Ref: J Herald

Line-ups (Aberdeen in roman, opponents in *italic*)

No	1	2	3	4	5	6	7	8	9	10	11	subs used
1	Snelders	McKimmie	Woodthorpe	Hetherston	Inglis	Smith	Miller*	Jess	Booth	Dodds	Glass	Thomson
	Parks	*Clark*	*Napier*	*Oliver*	*McLaughlin*Rice*		*McGowan*	*Kirk*	*McDonald*	*Johnston*	*M Elliott*	*McGraw*
2	Snelders	McKimmie	Woodthorpe	Hetherston	Inglis	Smith	Miller*	Jess	Booth	Dodds	Glass	Shearer/McKinnon, Mackay/Walker
	Marshall	*Boyd*	*McKinlay**	*Vata*	*Hughes!*	*Grant*	*O'Donnell*	*Donnelly*	*v Hooijdonk 'Thom'*	*Collins*		
3	Snelders	McKimmie	Woodthorpe	Hetherston	Inglis	Smith	Miller	Jess	Booth*	Dodds	Glass	Shearer
	Leighton	*Millen*	*Love*	*McGinlay*	*Tweed*	*Hunter*	*Evans**	*Jackson C*	*Wright*	*Jackson D*	*O'Neill*	*Harper*
4	Watt	McKimmie	Woodthorpe	Hetherston	Inglis	Smith	Miller*	Jess	Booth	Dodds	Glass	Shearer/Christie
	Lekovic	*MacPherson*Reilly*	*Connor*		*Whitworth*	*Anderson*	*Mitchell*	*Skilling*	*McKee*	*Wright**	*Brown*	*Henry/Roberts*
5	Watt	McKimmie	Woodthorpe	Hetherston	Inglis	Smith	Miller	Jess	Booth	Dodds*	Glass	Bernard/Shearer, Coyle/Raeside
	Thomson	*Kirkwood**	*Broddle*	*McInally*	*Dennis*	*Sinclair*	*Wilson**	*Cameron*	*Crawford*	*Lennon*	*Dair*	
6	Watt	McKimmie	Woodthorpe	Hetherston	Inglis	Smith	Miller*	Jess	Booth*	Dodds	Glass	Bernard/Shearer, Colquhoun
	Nelson	*Wright*	*Winnie*	*Miller C*	*McPherson*	*Hunter*	*Leitch*	*Lawrence**	*Robertson*	*Millar J*	*Hagen*	
7	Watt	McKimmie	Woodthorpe	Hetherston	Inglis	Smith	Miller	Jess	Booth*	Dodds	Glass	Shearer/Bernard, Moore/Murray
	Goram	*Wright*	*Robertson*	*Gough*	*McLaren*	*Petric*	*Cleland*	*Durrant**	*Salenko*	*McCall*	*Durie**	
8	Watt	McKimmie	Woodthorpe*	Hetherston	Inglis	Smith	Miller	Jess	Booth*	Dodds	Glass	Shearer/Bernard, Roddie/Denham
	Howie	*May*	*McKinnon*Philliben*	*Martin*	*Krivokapic*	*Lambert*	*Dolan*	*Coyne*	*Arnott**	*Davies**		
9	Watt	McKimmie*	Glass	Grant	Inglis	Smith	Miller	Shearer	Bernard	Dodds	Jess	Thomson
	Walker	*Dinnie*	*Milne*	*McKee**	*Welsh*	*Watson*	*McDonald R*Craig*	*Docherty*	*MacLeod*	*Smith*		
10	Watt*	McKimmie	Glass*	Grant	Inglis	Smith	Miller*	Bernard	Booth	Dodds	Jess	Shearer/Hether/Snell
	Marshall	*Boyd*	*McKinlay*	*McNamara*	*Hughes*	*Grant*	*Donnelly**	*McStay*	*v Hooijdonk Walker**	*McLaughlin*	*Vata/McQuilken*	*Gibson/McWilliams*

Commentary

1. Brockville was the venue for Aberdeen's last season and their first match of this. John Inglis' flashing header is the highlight of the Dons' impressive first half. For some reason they went to sleep in the second, and had to survive several anxious moments before the end.

2. A live TV Sunday match on a rain-sodden pitch. Aberdeen are two up in 11 minutes but are behind soon after. Snelders misjudges the German Thom's cross-cum-shot, then spilling the same player's shot for Celtic's third. John Hughes was sent off on 72 minutes for deliberate handball.

3. Last season Hibs were almost suffocatingly boring. Theo Snelders saves twice before substitute Shearer, with his second touch, fires a 30-yard volley past Jim Leighton, who is playing his 100th game for Hibs. Darren Jackson's quick equaliser from 18 yards is almost as impressive.

4. Not for the first time this season the Dons are caught napping after taking firm command. Stewart McKimmie was upfield to head over the top of the Killie defence for Joe Miller to slide in. Woodthorpe's 30-yarder should have killed the game but Tom Brown's header kept it alive.

5. Aberdeen's first clean sheet of the season helps lift them to second place. Raith performed UEFA Cup heroics in midweek, and don't look to have their minds on the game. Joe Miller hit the bar early on, and the first goal is way overdue when Scott Booth scored after a mazy build-up.

6. Scotland manager Craig Brown takes in what is possibly Michael Watt's finest game for Aberdeen. Ex-Don David Winnie dishes out some harsh treatment to Scott Booth. It is from one such foul on the striker that Booth heads the winning goal from Stephen Glass's cross.

7. Aberdeen are unchanged, except in goal, for the ninth successive game, and team understanding is paying off. Rangers were on the back foot throughout, protected by a five-man defence. Aberdeen won 14-6 on corners, 8-2 on shots on target, but lost to Craig Moore's diving header.

8. Aberdeen won here in the Coca-Cola Cup, but look a disorganised, ill-motivated lot in the league. They went in front when Watt's punt downfield evaded Krivokapic, allowing Booth to chip Howie. Tommy Coyne levelled from a tight angle, and Davies set up Paul Lambert.

9. Partick have won just once, and it shows as the Dons cruise to victory. Injuries force Aitken to make changes after the Motherwell setback. Albert Craig heads Miller's cross into his own net, Jess fired in from Glass, and Paul Bernard's first goal for the Dons flew into the top corner.

10. Aberdeen beat Rangers in midweek at Hampden, but come quickly back to earth. After three minutes Watt was stretchered off after colliding with Andy Walker. Brian McLaughlin beat sub keeper Snelders from an acute angle. John Inglis fouled Walker in the box for Celtic's penalty.

11 H HIBERNIAN 4/11 — 0-1 / 1-2 — 4 3 16 — 14,774
Glass 53
Wright 23, O'Neill 76
Ref: J McCluskey

Snelders, McKimmie, Glass, Grant, Inglis, Smith, Miller, Bernard, Booth*, Dodds, Jess
Leighton, Dods, Tortolano, McGinlay, Tweed, Hunter, Jackson C, Harper*, Wright, Jackson D, O'Neill — Shearer / McAllister

Hibs have only lost once, and they have Jim Leighton to thank for not losing this one. Keith Wright's near-post header was answered by Stephen Glass's first goal of the season - a dipping 25-yarder. Against the run of play Northern Ireland's Michael O'Neill hit a screamer.

---

12 H FALKIRK 8/11 — W 3-1 — 19 — 11,214
Dodds 3, Miller 24, McGowan 58 og
McGrillen 36
Ref: A Waddell

Snelders, McKimmie, Glass*, Grant, Inglis, Smith, Miller, Shearer, Bernard, Dodds, Jess
Parks, Weir, Munro, Clark, McLaughlin MacKenzie, Johnston F, McGowan, McGrillen, Johnston M, Hagen — Thomson/Hetherston, McDonald

Falkirk look so awful the Dons take little credit for beating them. Billy Dodds' goal came off his stomach, when Parks cleared straight at him. Miller volleyed in the second at the far post. Paul McGrillen made it 1-2 from Weir's cross. McGowan chested Bernard's cross over the line.

---

13 A RANGERS 11/11 — D 1-1 — 4 1 20 — 45,427
Jess 28
Salenko 40
(Rangers' 3rd sub Brown)
Ref: J Rowbotham

Snelders, McKimmie, Glass, Grant, Inglis, Smith, Miller, Bernard, Booth, Dodds*, Jess
Thomson, Cleland, Bollan", Gough, McLaren, Petric, Ferguson, Gascoigne*, Salenko, McCall, Mik'chenko "Durrant/McCoist — Shearer

An tetchy match, largely due to Gascoigne's elbows and head. Eoin Jess's solo run and 25-yard shot will have added to his reputation, and deserved all three points. Rangers' equaliser was questionable. The ball looked out of play before McCall hooked it back for Salenko's header.

---

14 A RAITH ROVERS 18/11 — L 0-1 — 4 5 20 — 5,786
Lennon 16g
Ref: W Young

Watt, McKimmie, Glass, Grant, Inglis, Smith, Miller, Bernard, Booth, Dodds, Jess*
Thomson, McInally, Broddie, Coyle, Dennis, Sinclair, Crawford, Cameron, Graham", Lennon, Dair — Hetherston, Shearer/Robertson, Wilson

Raith's first win in seven comes from the penalty spot after Inglis shoved Alastair Graham. Jess has a virus. The restored Michael Watt did most to keep the score down to one, as the Dons went from bad to worse. The worst possible preparation for the Coca-Cola Cup Final.

---

15 A PARTICK THISTLE 2/12 — 0-0 — 5 20 — 4,286
Smith 63
Ref: M Clark

Watt, McKimmie, Robertson, Grant, Inglis, Smith, Miller*, Bernard, Dodds, Jess*
Cairns, Dinnie, Pittman, Smith, Welsh, Milne, McWilliams, Turner, Gibson, Cameron*, Docherty — Windass/Thomson, MacDonald W

Despite lifting the Coca-Cola Cup the Dons have lost six of the last nine in the league, and this could spell trouble. Aberdeen committed just three fouls in 90 minutes, but one of them saw McKimmie sent off for up-ending Calum Milne. Tom Smith's looping header won the game.

---

16 H MOTHERWELL 9/12 — W 1-0 — 4 23 — 11,299
Shearer 57
Ref: A Huett

Watt, Grant, Glass, Bernard, Irvine, Smith, Miller, Shearer, Windass, Dodds, Jess
Howie, May, McKinnon, Krivokapic, Martin, Denham, Lambert, Dolan", Burns, Arnott", Davies — Hendry/Roddie

Motherwell are in the midst of a run that will bring them just two goals in 14 games. Brian Irvine made his first start of the season, since learning he had multiple sclerosis. Also starting his first game was Dean Windass, and it was his precise pass that set up Shearer's winner.

---

17 A KILMARNOCK 13/12 — W 4-1 — 26 — 14,060
Miller 12, 28, 65, Windass 90
Wright 22
Ref: J McGilvray

Watt, McKimmie, Glass, Bernard, Irvine, Smith, Miller*, Shearer, Windass, Dodds*, Jess
Lekovic, MacPhersonReilly, Henry, Whitworth, Anderson, Mitchell, Connor, Wright, Brown, Holt — Grant/Robertson

This match was abandoned last week at 1-1 after a power failure. Joe Miller now celebrates his first ever Premier League hat-trick, though he had scored three against Brechin in the Skol Cup in 1987. Dean Windass scored his first Aberdeen goal, capitalising on Shearer's cross.

---

18 H HEARTS 16/12 — L 1-2 — 4 6 26 — 12,308
Windass 1
Johnston 81, Colquhoun 84
Ref: R Tait

Watt, Grant, Glass, Bernard, Irvine, Smith, Miller, Shearer, Windass, Dodds*, Jess
Rousset, McManus, Ritchie, Mackay, Pointon, Bruno, Johnston, Estikson", Robertson, Fulton, Millar J — Robertson, Hamilton/Colquhoun

Aberdeen had the chance to pick up nine home points in eight days. They were ahead in 45 seconds through Windass's volley, and then missed chances to tie up the game. Instead they were forced back by Hearts sub John Colquhoun, who set up Allan Johnston, then volleyed the winner.

---

19 A HIBERNIAN 8/1 — W 2-0 — 4 5 29 — 8,191
Miller 11, Dodds 33
Harper 88
Ref: W Young

Watt, McKimmie, Glass, Grant, Inglis, Smith, Miller, Bernard, Windass, Dodds, Jess
Leighton, Millen, Tortolano, McGinlay, Tweed, Hunter, McAllister, Harper, Wright, Jackson D, O'Neill

Not the best game to show live on satellite TV, though it brought Aberdeen's first win at Hibs in three years. Glass drove in a cross, turned in by Miller. Dodds' header from Miller's corner was cleared off the line, but the linesman signalled a goal. Kevin Harper scored off a post.

---

20 H CELTIC 14/1 — L 1-2 — 4 2 29 — 16,760
Dodds 18
Collins 50, van Hooijdonk 55
Ref: T McCurry

Watt, Glass, Glass, Grant, Inglis, Smith, Miller*, Bernard, Dodds*, Jess*
Marshall, Boyd, McKinlay, Grant, O'Donnell, Hughes, Donnelly, McStay, v Hooijdonk Thom", Collins — Shearer, Walker

Another live TV match shows Celtic's third win over Aberdeen so far. Gordon Marshall failed to deal with Miller's corner and Dodds headed his 10th goal of the season. Andreas Thom set up both Celtic goals.

---

21 A FALKIRK 16/1 — D 1-1 — 4 9 30 — 4,003
Windass 66
Clark 30
Ref: G Evans

Watt, McKimmie, Glass*, Grant, Inglis, Smith, Miller, Bernard, Windass, Dodds, Jess*
Parks, Weir, Munro, Clark, James, Gray", Ferguson, McGrillen, Kirk", Elliot — Shearer/Robertson, Hagen/Wright

Aberdeen were inches from victory when Dean Windass hit the underside of the bar in the last minute. John Clark's close-range header was scarcely deserved, but looked to have won the game until Glass drove against the bar from 30 yards and Windass pounced on the loose ball.

BELL'S SCOTTISH PREMIER

SEASON 1995-96 — Manager: Roy Aitken

No	Date		Att	Pos	Pt	F-A	H-T	Scorers, Times, and Referees
22	20/1	.H PARTICK THISTLE	9,149	4 / 8	33	W 1-0	0-0	Dodds 59p — Ref: T Brown
23	23/1	A KILMARNOCK	6,703	3 / 7	34	D 1-1	1-0	Irvine 4 / Wright 82 — Ref: K Clark
24	7/2	H RAITH ROVERS	6,628	3 / 6	37	W 1-0	1-0	Windass 14 — Ref: W Crombie
25	10/2	A HEARTS	14,314	3 / 4	40	W 3-1	2-1	Windass 3, Shearer 20, Glass 69 / Robertson 39 — Ref: K Clark
26	13/2	A MOTHERWELL	5,090	3 / 4	40	L 0-1	0-0	Burns 65 — Ref: G Clyde (Motherwell's 3rd sub Davies)
27	25/2	H RANGERS	19,842	3 / 1	40	L 0-1	0-1	Gascoigne 32p — Ref: H Dallas
28	2/3	H KILMARNOCK	7,177	3 / 7	43	W 3-0	1-0	Booth 34, 51, Miller 72 — Ref: A Waddell
29	16/3	A RAITH ROVERS	4,932	3 / 6	44	D 2-2	1-2	Miller 24, Buchan 84 / Kirk 10, Cameron 34 — Ref: K Clark
30	23/3	H HIBERNIAN	10,924	3 / 5	47	W 2-1	0-1	Dodds 71, Booth 79 / McAllister 35 — Ref: S Dougal
31	1/4	A CELTIC	35,284	3 / 2	47	L 0-5	0-2	Donnelly 2, 67, van Hooijdonk 17, 74, [Cadete 75] — Ref: H Dallas

Line-ups (1–11 and subs used), with commentary

*(Aberdeen listed in roman; opponents listed in italics; * = substituted)*

22 — Partick Thistle (H)
Aberdeen: Watt, McKimmie, Glass, Grant, Inglis*, Smith, Miller, Windass, Bernard, Dodds, Jess — subs: Irvine/Shearer
Partick: Walker, Dinnie, Milne, Smith, Welsh, Watson, Macdonald W, Henderson, Docherty* — subs: Foster, Cameron, McDonald R*
Arctic cold meant only the bravest turned out for this game. Jess might have given the Dons an early lead when hitting the post, but the only goal came from the penalty spot. Ex-Don Gregg Watson interrupted Miller's surging run down the right. Dodds converted for his 11th goal.

23 — Kilmarnock (A)
Aberdeen: Watt, McKimmie, Glass, Grant*, Irvine, Smith, Miller, Windass, Bernard, Shearer, Jess — subs: Christie
Kilmarnock: Lekovic, MacPherson·Black, Reilly, Whitworth, Anderson, Mitchell, Henry, Wright, Maskrey, Holt* — subs: McKee/Brown*
Brian Irvine's first goal of the season lifts Aberdeen to third, but they are 21 points behind second-placed Celtic. Irvine headed in McKimmie's flick from Joe Miller's corner. Ex-Don Paul Wright levelled with a crisp volley, but by then Kilmarnock should have been dead and buried.

24 — Raith Rovers (H)
Aberdeen: Watt, McKimmie, Glass, Grant, Irvine, Smith, Miller, Shearer*, Bernard, Windass, Jess* — subs: Graham/Broddle
Raith: Geddes, Kirkwood, Humphries·Coyle, Dennis, Dair, Cameron, Crawford, Lennon, Rougier* — subs: Graham/Broddle*
This is Raith's final game under Jimmy Nicholl before he takes over at Millwall. Dean Windass has become an instant hit at Pittodrie. He plays a one-two with Bernard to score his fifth goal in nine games. Raith protested that Miller was offside. Pittodrie's lowest gate on a freezing night.

25 — Hearts (A)
Aberdeen: Watt, McKimmie, Glass, Grant, Irvine, Smith, Miller, Shearer, Bernard, Windass, Jess* — subs: Booth
Hearts: Rousset, Locke, Ritchie, McPherson, McManus, Brunol, Johnston, Colquhoun, Robertson, Mackay, Pointon — subs: Miller J*
Over 50 fouls and offsides made this match like treacle. Hearts had won five of their past six. Windass's goal went in off Gilles Rousset's hand and a post. Windass also won and took a penalty. Rousset saved but Shearer swooped. At 1-2 Bruno was sent off for elbowing Windass.

26 — Motherwell (A)
Aberdeen: Watt, McKimmie, Glass, Grant, Irvine, Smith, Miller, Shearer, Bernard, Windass, Jess* — subs: Dodds
Motherwell: Howie, May, McKinnon·van de Gaag·Martin, McCart, Lambert, Brown, McLaren, McMillan·Hendry, Falconer — subs: Dodds*
Aberdeen's first defeat in seven brings Motherwell their second league win in 18. The Dons spent much of the game in defence, but seldom looked like falling behind to goal-shy Well until Lambert's corner was headed goalwards by Falconer. Sub Alex Burns got the final touch.

27 — Rangers (H)
Aberdeen: Watt, McKimmie*, Glass, Grant, Irvine, Smith, Miller, Shearer, Windass, Dodds, Bernard — subs: Booth
Rangers: Goram, Moore, Robertson·Petric, Petric, McLaren, Brown, Miller, Gascoigne·Ferguson, McCall, Laudrup — subs: Van Vassen/Cleland*
Irvine trips Laudrup for the penalty. Gascoigne scores from the spot. He is one of 10 players booked. McKimmie was stretchered off after 20 minutes following a clash with Ian Ferguson. Gascoigne tries to walk in a goal but makes an ass of himself. Jess has transferred to Coventry.

28 — Kilmarnock (H)
Aberdeen: Watt, Grant, Woodthorpe, Bernard, Irvine, Smith, Miller*, Robertson, Booth, Dodds, Glass* — subs: Buchan/Rowson
Kilmarnock: Lekovic, MacPherson·Black, Reilly, McInally, Whitworth, Anderson, Mitchell, Brown, Wright, Connor, McKee — subs: Henry/Montgomerie*
This was all too easy against Aberdeen's bogey team from last season. Glass plants a cross on Booth's head for the first, and Dodds sets up Booth's simple tap in for the second. Irvine is captain for the first time in McKimmie's absence. Two young Dons make their debuts as subs.

29 — Raith Rovers (A)
Aberdeen: Watt, Grant, Woodthorpe, Bernard, Irvine, Smith, Miller, Shearer*, Booth, Windass!, Robertson! — subs: Dodds/Buchan
Raith: Geddes, McCulloch, Kirkwood, McInally, Raeside, Sinclair, Thomson, Cameron, Duffield, Lennon*, Kirk — subs: Crawford/Rougier*
In injury time Dean Windass is sent off for his second caution, diving to try to win a penalty after being tackled by David Sinclair. The decision sparks a touchline row between Roy Aitken and referee Ken Clark. Substitute Jamie Buchan had made it 2-2 with a rising drive.

30 — Hibernian (H)
Aberdeen: Watt, Grant, Woodthorpe, Bernard, Irvine, Smith, Miller, Shearer*, Booth*, Bernard, Robertson — subs: Dodds/Buchan
Hibernian: Leighton, Miller, Mitchell, Millen, McLaughlin·Tweed, McAllister*, Farrell, Evans, Jackson D, Dow — subs: McGinlay/O'Neill*
The ball rebounded off the referee in the build-up to Hibs' goal. Hibs had chances to extend their lead before Aberdeen levelled. Joe Miller's corner, Booth's header, Leighton's parry - but Dodds ran in the loose ball. Booth chipped Gary Smith's long ball over Leighton for the winner.

31 — Celtic (A)
Aberdeen: Watt, Grant, Woodthorpe, Bernard, Irvine, Smith, Miller, Windass, Booth*, Dodds, Glass* — subs: Robertson/Rowson; [Cadete 75]
Celtic: Marshall, Boyd, McKinlay, McNamara·Hughes, Grant, Donnelly, McStay·v Hooijdonk·Thom, Gray — subs: Cadete/O'Neil
Not even the excuse of a looming Scottish Cup semi-final can explain Aberdeen's joint-heaviest ever Premier League defeat. Portuguese striker Jorge Cadete scores Celtic's fifth seconds after coming on for his debut. The Dons' best chance came when Marshall dropped Miller's corner.

32 H MOTHERWELL 13/4 — 3 W 2-1 — 8,943 — 6 — 50

McCart 54 og, Irvine 86 / Falconer 41
Ref: J Rowbotham

Watt	McKimmie	Woodthorpe	Rowson	Irvine	Inglis	Bernard	Shearer*	Windass	Dodds*	Glass*
Howie	*May*	*van der Gaag Martin*			*McCart*	*Lambert*	*Dolan*^	*Arnott*^	*Falconer*	*Davies*

Grant/Booth/K'dekpo — Philliben/Burns

Motherwell are the form team, having taken 19 points from seven games. Stephen Glass was stretchered off early after a collision with Dolan. Willie Falconer held off Irvine to score. When Chris McCart turned in Dodds' low cross it was the first goal conceded by Well in 700 minutes.

33 A PARTICK THISTLE 16/4 — 3 D 1-1 — 4,568 — 9 — 51

Booth 2 / McWilliams 10
Ref: W Crombie

Watt	McKimmie	Woodthorpe	Rowson	Irvine	Inglis	Bernard	Windass	Booth*	Dodds!	Robertson^
Walker	*McKee*^	*Watson*	*McWilliams Slavin*		*Welsh*	*Macdonald W/Foster**	*Henderson Cameron*	*Lyons*	*Shearer/K'pedekpo*	*Gibson/Milne*

This match was abandoned at 0-0 on 10 April, so the Dons offer free transport to supporters. Booth headed through a packed area to put the Dons ahead, but ex-Don Ian Cameron set up McWilliams' fine equaliser. After 42 minutes Dodds was expelled after clashing with Cameron.

34 H HEARTS 20/4 — 3 D 1-1 — 11,303 — 4 — 52

Windass 53p / Locke 63
Ref: A Waddell

Watt	McKimmie	Woodthorpe*	Rowson	Irvine	Inglis	Bernard	Shearer	Booth*	Windass	Glass
Rousset	*Locke*	*Ritchie*^	*McManus*	*McPherson Berry*		*Johnston Cameron*^	*Robertson Fulton*	*Pointon*	*Robertson/K'pedekpo*	*Colquhoun/Mackay*

An undistinguished match. Aberdeen's only incentive is to keep hold of third place. They score against the balance of play when McManus pulled down Booth with the Hearts goal in no danger. Windass scored from the spot. Hearts' skipper Gary Locke angled a freak equaliser.

35 A RANGERS 28/4 — 4 L 1-3 — 47,247 — 1 — 52

Irvine 19 / Gascoigne 21, 81, 86p
Ref: L Mottram (Rangers' 3rd sub Durrant)

Watt	McKimmie	Smith	Rowson	Irvine	Inglis	Bernard*	Windass	Booth	Dodds	Glass
Goram	*Steven*^	*Robertson Gough*	*Brown*	*McLaren*	*Durie*^	*Gascoigne Andersen**	*McCall*	*Laudrup*	*K'pedekpo*	*McCoist/Petric*

Irvine stabs Aberdeen ahead from an uncleared corner, which ignites Gascoigne's hat-trick. His first goals are the result of boring deep into the Dons' nerve centre. His penalty comes after Bernard bundled over Durie. The Dons have failed to beat either of the Old Firm all season.

36 H FALKIRK 4/5 — 3 W 2-1 — 11,831 — 10 — 55

Glass 16, McGowan 46 og / McGrillen 45
Ref: T Brown (Falkirk's 3rd sub Abbott)

Watt	McKimmie	Smith	Buchan	Irvine	Inglis	Bernard*	Windass	Booth*	K'pedekpo	Glass
Parks	*Finnigan*^	*McGowan Lawrie*	*James*	*Gray*	*MacKenzie Craig*	*Graham*^	*McGrillen*	*Elliott**	*Grant/Craig*	*Whiteside/Hamilton*

A win over doomed Falkirk will secure third place. How different from last year, when they needed the points to have a chance of staying up. Aberdeen use five players under 20. Elliott pulls down Windass, and Park's saves from Windass, and Booth's follow-up goes in off McGowan.

Average Home 12,764 — Away 14,493

Coca-Cola League Cup

2 H ST MIRREN 19/8 — W 3-1 — 10,397

Dodds 31, Booth 41, 52 / McLaughlin 23
Ref: J Rowbotham

Snelders	McKimmie	Ireland	McKinnon*	Inglis	Hetherston Miller	Jess	Booth	Dodds	Glass	
Money	*Dawson*	*Baker*	*Taylor*	*McLaughlin Watson*	*Law*	*Fullarton*	*Gillies**	*Bone*	*Boyd*^	*Dick/Lavety*

Verveer

Barry McLaughlin's acrobatic overhead kick is the worst possible start to the new campaign. But Dodds was sent clear by Jess to equalise, and Joe Miller flighted the cross from which Scott Booth headed the second. Campbell Money's disastrous pass out presented a gift goal to Booth.

3 A FALKIRK 30/8 — W 4-1 — 6,387

Clark 6 og, Booth 39, Woodthorpe 59, [Miller 88]
Johnston 24p / Miller 88
Ref: W Young (Falkirk's 3rd sub Henderson)

Snelders	McKimmie	Woodthorpe	Hetherston^	Inglis	McLaughlin McKenzie^	Miller	Jess	Booth*	Dodds	Glass
Parks	*Clark*	*Napier*^	*Oliver*	*McKenzie McGowan Kirk*	*McDonald*^	*Johnston Elliot*	*Inglis/Rice*		*Thomson/McKinnon*	

Aberdeen won here 3-2 four days earlier. The Dons are helped on their way by John Clark heading Glass's free-kick past Tony Parks. Gary Smith flattens Steve Kirk for Mo Johnston's penalty. Parks was then sent off for handling outside the box, whereupon Aberdeen ran riot.

QF A MOTHERWELL 20/9 — W 2-1 (aet) — 9,137

Dodds 58, Inglis 115 / Arnott 5
Ref: K Clark (Motherwell's 3rd sub Burns)

Watt	McKimmie	Woodthorpe^	Inglis	Smith	McCart	Miller	Jess	Booth	Dodds	Glass
Howie	*May*	*McKinnon*^	*Philliben Martin*	*Lambert*	*Dolan*	*Coyne*	*Arnott*^	*Shearer/Christie*	*McSkimming Davies/Roddie*	

Snelders is on paternity leave. McKimmie's miscued clearance allows Doug Arnott to score. Almost an hour had been played before Dodds levelled from Glass's cross. In extra-time John Inglis headed the winner from Joe Miller's corner. Kevin Christie plays the last three minutes.

SF N RANGERS 24/10 — W 2-1 — 26,131 — 1

(at Hampden)

Dodds 51, 69 / Salenko 85
Ref: H Dallas

Watt	McKimmie	Glass	Inglis	Smith	Miller	Bernard	Booth	Dodds	Glass	Jess
Goram	*Wright*	*Brown*	*Moore**	*McLaren*	*Petric*	*Cleland*^	*Gascoigne McCoist*	*Salenko*	*Durie*	*Durrant/Mik'chenko*

Wet and windy Hampden. Salenko loses possession in the Dons' half and man-of-the-match Jess's 60-yard run sets up the first goal for Dodds. Glass's cross was met by Dodds for the second. Salenko's reply ensured a nail biting climax. Dundee and Airdrie's semi-final is tomorrow.

F N DUNDEE 26/11 — W 2-0 — 33,096

(at Hampden)

Dodds 33, Shearer 46
Ref: L Mottram (Dundee's 3rd sub Anderson)

Watt	McKimmie	Glass	Inglis	Smith	Miller^	Bernard	Shearer	Dodds	Dodds	Jess*
Pageaud	*Duffy J*	*McQueen*	*Manley*	*Wieghorst*	*Duffy C*	*Shaw*	*Vrto*^	*Tosh*^	*Hamilton*	*McCann*^

Hetherston/Robertson — Farningham/Britton

Dundee can barely escape from their own half. Aberdeen turn the screw from the first whistle. Jess looks inspired since switching to midfield. Man-of-the-match Stephen Glass laid on the crosses for both goals. Pageaud spilled the ball for the first, Shearer's head bulleted the second.

BELL'S PREMIER (CUP-TIES)

Manager: Roy Aitken

Tennents Scottish Cup

		F-A	H-T	Scorers, Times, and Referees	1	2	3	4	5	6	7	8	9	10	11	subs used
3	A MOTHERWELL 30/1	3 W 6,035	2-0 1-0 10	Windass 37, Shearer 48 Ref: L Mottram	Watt	McKimmie	Glass	Grant	Irvine	Smith	Miller	Shearer*	Bernard	Windass	Jess	Dodds
					Howie	*May*	*McKinnon*	*Philliben*	*Martin*	*Denham*	*Lambert*	*Dolan*	*Arnott*	*Burns*	*McSkimm'g**	*Hendry*
4	A STIRLING ALB 17/2	3 W 3,808	2-0 1-0 2:1	Windass 6, Shearer 70 Ref: R Orr	Watt	McKimmie	Glass	Grant	Irvine	Smith	Miller	Shearer	Windass	Dodds*	Jess	Booth
					McGeown	*Paterson A*	*Deas*	*Mitchell*	*McQuilter*	*Paterson G*	*Bone*	*Tait**	*McCormick*	*Taggart*	*McLeod**	*Gibson/Wood*
QF	H AIRDRIE 9/3	3 W 11,749	2-1 1-1 1:6	Windass 31, Bernard 88 Bonar 18 Ref: J Rowbotham	Watt	Grant	Woodthorpe	Bernard	Irvine	Smith	Miller*	Windass	Booth	Dodds	Glass	Shearer
					Martin	*Stewart*	*Bonar*	*Sandison*	*Sweeney*	*Black**	*Boyle*	*Davies*	*Cooper*	*Harvey*	*McIntyre J*	*Wilson*
SF	N HEARTS 6/4 (at Hampden)	3 L 27,785	1-2 0-0 4	Shearer 87 Robertson 80, Johnston 90 Ref: W Young	Watt	McKimmie	Woodthorpe	Glass	Inglis	Smith	Miller*	Windass	Bernard	Dodds	Robertson*	Grant/Shearer
					Rousset	*Locke*	*Ritchie*	*Mackay*	*McManus*	*Bruno*	*Johnston*	*Colquhoun*	*Lawrence**	*Fulton**	*Pointon*	*Roberts'n/McPherson*

This is Sky TV's live UK match. Aberdeen won at Fir Park in the Coca-Cola Cup, but lose there twice in the league. Alex McLeish's team are bottom of the league, scoring once in their last nine games. Windass scored at the back post, and after Shearer had made it two, the game died.

Stirling's rallying cry is 'Stenhousemuir', but they have no chance of an upset. Windass's early lob took the wind out of Stirling's sails. Mind you, the killer goal was a long time coming. Deas header out was deflected to Shearer. Miller was man of the match. This was Jess's last game.

Wet and windy conditions do nothing for good football. Having fallen behind to Airdrie's left-back, Dean Windass levels following a free-kick. Though Aberdeen pressed hard after half-time, the Diamonds looked like holding out until Dodds and Booth linked up for Paul Bernard.

Aberdeen looked better without looking threatening. Hearts scarcely deserved to go in front from John Robertson's bundled goal, but Shearer's far-post header rescued the Dons. Michael Watt will reproach himself for not stopping Allan Johnston's header, which squirmed under him.

League Table

	P	W	D	L	F	A	W	D	L	F	A	Pts
		Home					**Away**					
1 Rangers	36	13	3	2	47	16	14	3	1	38	9	87
2 Celtic	36	12	5	1	40	12	12	6	0	34	13	83
3 ABERDEEN	36	11	1	6	31	17	5	6	7	21	28	55
4 Hearts	36	10	2	6	33	26	6	5	7	22	27	55
5 Hibernian	36	7	5	6	25	26	4	5	9	18	31	43
6 Raith Rovers	36	7	5	6	23	21	5	2	11	18	36	43
7 Kilmarnock	36	8	4	6	25	21	3	4	11	14	33	41
8 Motherwell	36	6	6	6	15	16	3	6	9	13	23	39
9 Partick This*	36	3	5	10	12	28	5	1	12	17	34	30
10 Falkirk	36	4	4	10	17	26	2	2	14	14	34	24
	360	81	40	59	268	209	59	40	81	209	268	500

* relegated after play-off

Record v Opponents

	P	W	D	L	F	A	Pts
v Kilmarnock	4	3	1	0	10	3	10
v Falkirk	4	3	1	0	9	5	10
v Raith Rovers	4	2	1	1	6	3	7
v Partick This	4	2	1	1	5	2	7
v Hearts	4	2	1	1	7	5	7
v Hibernian	4	2	1	1	6	5	7
v Motherwell	4	2	0	2	4	4	6
v Rangers	4	0	1	3	2	6	1
v Celtic	4	0	0	4	3	12	0
	36	16	7	13	52	45	55

Cup Results

Cup	W	D	L	F	A
LC	1	—	0	1	0
SC	0	0	1	0	1
LC	1	0	0	1	0
SC	1	0	0	1	0
LC	1	0	0	1	0

Odds & ends

Never lost to: (2) Kilmarnock, Falkirk.

Never beat: (2) Celtic, Rangers (in the league).

Won from behind: (5) Hibs (h), Motherwell (h & LC), St Mirren (LC), Airdrie (SC).

Lost from in front: (5) Celtic (h, h), Motherwell (a), Hearts (h), Rangers (a).

High spots: Winning the Coca-Cola Cup.

Finishing third, having so nearly been relegated the previous season.

Winning three league games in a row, climbing to second on 4 October.

Low spots: Losing in the last minute of the Scottish Cup semi-final.

Two wins in nine league games from 7 October, dropping to fifth.

Failing to beat either of the Old Firm in the Premier League for first time.

Winning just 3 games more than they lost, the second worst Dons' performance since 1975-76.

Losing 0-5 to Celtic.

Falkirk scored three own-goals for the Dons.

Bogey-team: Celtic (the only team Aberdeen failed to beat).

Ever-presents: (0).

Hat-tricks: (1) Joe Miller.

Leading scorer: (12) Scott Booth, Billy Dodds.

Appearances and Goals

	Appearances						Goals			
	Lge	Sub	LC	Sub	SC	Sub	Lge	LC	SC	Tot
Bernard, Paul	27	4	2		3			1	1	2
Booth, Scott	20	4	4		1	1	9		3	12
Buchan, Jamie	1	3		1			1			1
Christie, Kevin		2								
Craig, Michael		1								
Dodds, Billy	28	3	5		3	1	7	5		12
Glass, Stephen	32		5		4		3			3
Grant, Brian	22	3	3		3	1				
Hetherston, Peter	9	2	3	2						
Inglis, John	24		5		1		1		1	2
Ireland, Craig			1							
Irvine, Brian	17	1			3		3			3
Jess, Eoin	25		5		2		3			3
Kpedekpo, Malcolm	1	4								
McKimmie, Stewart	29		5		3					
McKinnon, Ray	1	1		1						
Miller, Joe	31	1	5		4		9		1	10
Robertson, Hugh	5	6		1		1				
Rowson, David	7	2								
Shearer, Duncan	15	15	1	1	2	2	3	1	3	7
Smith, Gary	33		4		4					
Snelders, Theo	6	1	2							
Thomson, Scott		4		1						
Verveer, Etienne				1						
Watt, Michael	30									
Windass, Dean	19	1	3		4		6		3	9
Woodthorpe, Colin	15		2		2		1	1		2
(own-goals)							5		1	6
27 players used	396	57	55	8	44	5	52	13	7	72

1. H CELTIC — 10/8 — Att 18,595 — D 2-2 (HT 0-1) — Pt 1
Scorers, Times: Windass 74p, Shearer 80 / van Hooijdonk 24, Thom 90 — Ref: H Dallas

	1	2	3	4	5	6	7	8	9	10	11	subs used
Dons	Watt	Buchan	Woodthorpe	Tzvetanov*	Irvine	Inglis	Miller*	Windass	Bernard	Kiriakov	Glass	Shearer/Rowson
Celtic	*Marshall*	*Boyd*	*McKinlay*	*McNamara*	*Stubbs!*	*Grant*	*O'Donnell*	*McStay*	*v Hooijdonk*	*Thom*	*Cadete**	*O'Neil*

Aberdeen kick off with just one forward - Windass - and for an hour are blown over. Alan Stubbs topples sub Shearer in the box and is sent off. Windass scores off the post. Celtic look finished. In injury time van Hooijdonk heads down, Thom shoots, and Watt might have saved.

2. A MOTHERWELL — 17/8 — Att 6,206 — D 2-2 (HT 1-1) — Pt 2
Scorers, Times: Windass 24, Shearer 72 / McSkimming 40p, 51 — Ref: W Young

	1	2	3	4	5	6	7	8	9	10	11	subs used
Dons	Watt	Buchan	Tzvetanov	Bernard*	Irvine	Inglis	Miller	Dodds	Windass	Kiriakov	Glass	Woodth'pe*/Shearer
Motherwell	*Howie*	*May*	*McMillan*	*van der Gaag*	*Martin*	*McSkimming*	*Wishart*	*Dolan*	*Arnott*	*Falconer**	*Ross*	*Burns*

The man at the hub of this rough match is Motherwell's Shaun McSkimming, who crocks Bernard's ankle on six minutes, scores from the spot when shoved by Buchan, then nets again. Windass's curling free-kick and Shearer's header just three minutes after coming on earn a point.

3. H HEARTS — 25/8 — Att 13,600 — W 4-0 (HT 1-0) — Pos 7, Pt 5
Scorers, Times: Miller 45, Dodds 54, Windass 76, [Glass 84]Rousset — Ref: J Herald (Hearts' 3rd sub McCann)

	1	2	3	4	5	6	7	8	9	10	11	subs used
Dons	Walker	Grant	Tzvetanov*	Young	Irvine	Inglis	Miller	Dodds	Windass	Kiriakov	Glass	Frail/Colquhoun
Hearts	*84]Rousset*	*McManus**	*Ritchie*	*Weir*	*McPherson*	*Mackay**	*Goss*	*Cameron*	*Thomas**	*Fulton*	*Pointon*	

Following the near-disaster against Zalgiris, the Dons hit form in this Sunday fixture. Hearts get off lightly. Gary Mackay fouled Kiriakov in the sixth minute but Dodds' penalty was saved. Dean Windass also headed against a post. Goal of the match was Windass's 30-yard free-kick.

4. A RAITH ROVERS — 7/9 — Att 5,055 — W 4-1 (HT 3-1) — Pos 10, Pt 8
Scorers, Times: Windass 11, Dodds 19p, 26, 84p, Bonar 3 — Ref: T Brown (Raith's 3rd sub McCulloch)

	1	2	3	4	5	6	7	8	9	10	11	subs used
Dons	Walker	Grant	Tzvetanov	Young	Inglis	Kombouare	Miller*	Dodds	Windass	Kiriakov	Glass*	Rowson/Woodth'rpe
Raith	*Thomson*	*McInally*	*Bonar*	*Krivokapic*	*Dennis*	*Browne**	*Thomson*	*Kirkwood**	*Duffield**	*Lennon*	*Rougier*	*Millar/Kirk*

15 goals in three games for rampant Dons, with Billy Dodds scoring successive hat-tricks. Yet the game began well for Raith's new manager, Tommy McLean, Paul Bonar giving them a quick lead from close-in. Krivokapic's push on Dodds, and Bonar's handball, resulted in penalties.

5. H KILMARNOCK — 14/9 — Att 12,000 — W 3-0 (HT 0-0) — Pos 8, Pt 11
Scorers, Times: Kombouare 47, Dodds 66, 75 — Ref: G Mitchell (Dons' 3rd sub Woodthorpe)

	1	2	3	4	5	6	7	8	9	10	11	subs used
Dons	Walker	McKimmie	Tzvetanov	Rowson	Inglis*	Kombouare	Young	Dodds	Windass*	Kiriakov	Glass*	Bernard/Shearer
Kilmarnock	*Lekovic*	*MacPherson Anderson*	*Reilly*	*Whitworth*	*McGowne*	*Mitchell*	*Hendry**	*Wright*	*McIntyre*	*Holt*	*McKee*	

Billy Dodds' second-half double takes him to 11 goals in ten games, the highest tally in Britain. French import Tony Kombouare had marked his home debut by flicking in Kiriakov's near-post corner. Equally important to Aitken is the rare clean sheet. Will Irvine get his place back?

6. H HIBERNIAN — 21/9 — Att 12,500 — L 0-2 (HT 0-1) — Pos 4, Pt 11
Scorers, Times: Jackson 44, Wright 68 — Ref: E Martindale

	1	2	3	4	5	6	7	8	9	10	11	subs used
Dons	Walker	McKimmie*	Tzvetanov*	Young	Irvine	Kombouare	Bernard*	Dodds	Shearer	Kiriakov	Woodthorpe	Kjpedekpo/Rowson
Hibs	*Leighton*	*Miller*	*Dow*	*Millen*	*Dods*	*Welsh*	*Schmugge*	*Wilkins*	*Wright*	*Jackson D**	*McGinlay*	*Jackson C/Harper*

Which team includes Leighton, Willie Miller, Harper and Dods? Why, Hibs, of course. They also have 40-year-old Ray Wilkins in midfield. Against the run of play Darren Jackson scores from a tight angle, and Keith Wright - once a target of Aberdeen - heads his 100th Premier goal.

7. A DUNDEE UTD — 28/9 — Att 10,359 — L 0-1 (HT 0-0) — Pos 8, Pt 11
Scorers, Times: McSwegan 67 — Ref: T Brown (United's 3rd sub Robertson)

	1	2	3	4	5	6	7	8	9	10	11	subs used
Dons	Walker	McKimmie	Tzvetanov	Rowson*	Irvine	Kombouare	Young	Dodds	Windass!	Kiriakov	Woodth'rpe*	Shearer*/Wyness
Dundee Utd	*Maxwell*	*Shannon*	*Malpas*	*Pressley*	*Perry*	*McQuilken*	*Winters**	*Bowman*	*McSwegan*	*Hannah*	*Coyle**	*McLaren*/Benneker*

Injuries to Joe Miller and Stephen Glass mean Aberdeen have no width. McSwegan's shot deflected off Kombouare and spun over Walker. Dean Windass's free-kick hit the post before he was sent off for butting Rab Shannon. Brondby manager Ebbe Skovdahl looks on confidently.

8. H DUNFERMLINE — 12/10 — Att 10,500 — W 3-0 (HT 2-0) — Pos 7, Pt 14
Scorers, Times: Dodds 10, 26, Young 90 — Ref: J Underhill

	1	2	3	4	5	6	7	8	9	10	11	subs used
Dons	Walker	McKimmie	Tzvetanov	Rowson	Inglis	Kombouare	Miller*	Dodds	Shearer	Kiriakov	Young*	Wyness/Craig
Dunfermline	*Lemajic*	*Millar!*	*Fleming*	*den Bieman*	*Tod*	*Clark*	*French*	*Robertson*	*Smith**	*Britton**	*Petrie*	*Moore/McCulloch*

Not content with scoring his 15th and 16th goals of the season, Dodds gets himself carried off. He punished John Clark for No 1 and enjoyed a deflection off Tod for No 2. Marc Millar was sent off on the hour for scything Kiriakov. Young fired a bullet. Will Dodds be fit for Brondby?

9. A RANGERS — 19/10 — Att 50,076 — D 2-2 (HT 1-2) — Pos 1
Scorers, Times: Irvine 40, Dodds 89, Gascoigne 28, Laudrup 37 — Ref: J Rowbotham (Rangers' 3rd sub McInnes)

	1	2	3	4	5	6	7	8	9	10	11	subs used
Dons	Walker	McKimmie*	Tzvetanov*	Young	Irvine	Kombouare	Miller*	Dodds	Booth	Kiriakov	Shearer	Woodth'rpe*Shearer/Wyness
Rangers	*Snelders*	*Sheilds*	*Albertz*	*Gough*	*Moore*	*Bjorklund*	*van Vossen**	*Gascoigne*	*Miller**	*Cleland*	*Laudrup*	*Ferguson*/Durrant*

Despite being sent off in midweek, plus allegations of wife-beating, Gascoigne plays - and scores with a curling free-kick. Laudrup squeezes a second inside the near post. Irvine's volley keeps the game alive. Dodds sweeps in a knock-down. Booth starts his first match of the season.

10. H RAITH ROVERS — 26/10 — Att 11,200 — W 1-0 (HT 0-0) — Pos 10
Scorers, Times: Miller 77 — Ref: I Taylor (Raith's 3rd sub Thomson)

	1	2	3	4	5	6	7	8	9	10	11	subs used
Dons	Walker	McKimmie	Tzvetanov	Rowson	Irvine	Kombouare	Young	Dodds	Windass*	Kiriakov	Young*	Booth/Ingolfsson
Raith	*Scott*	*Taylor**	*Bonar**	*Millar*	*Dennis*	*Mitchell*	*Twaddell*	*Harvey**	*Duffield*	*Lennon*	*Rougier*	*Kirk/Lorimer*

Aberdeen maintain their 100% home league record against Raith since 1962. But that is the only satisfaction taken from this dull match. Raith barely cross the halfway line, and seem on a damage limitation exercise from the start. Miller won the points with a 20-yarder off the bar.

Coca-Cola League Cup

	1	2	3	4	5	6	7	8	9	10	11	subs used
	Watt	McKimmie	Tzvetanov*	Rowson*	Irvine	Inglis	Miller*	Windass	Shearer	Kiriakov	Glass	Craig/Young
	Bruce	*Wilson*	*McGoldrick*	*Maxwell*	*Caven*	*King*	*Kennedy**	*Arbuckle*	*Edgar**	*McLaughlan*Graham*		*Falconer/Cameron*

2 A QUEEN'S PARK 13/8 2,021 — F-A 2-0 — H-T 1-0
Scorers, Times, and Referees: Glass 42, Windass 82
Ref: M Clark
(Queen's 3rd substitute Orr)

Aberdeen's defence of the Coca-Cola Cup begins where they left off, at Hampden. Queen's enjoyed few moments in attack. They were saved early on by the bar, which denied Shearer's header. After Glass's 20 yarder it took 40 minutes for the next on-target effort - Windass's header

	1	2	3	4	5	6	7	8	9	10	11	subs used
	Walker	Grant	Tzvetanov* Young		Inglis	Kombouare Miller*		Dodds	Windass	Kiriakov	Glass	Woodthorpe/Shearer
	Wylie	*Collins*	*Cormack*	*Reid*	*McCahill*	*Lindberg**	*Lilley*	*Mahood*	*Hawke**	*Anderson*	*Rajamaki**	*McArthur/Flannary*

3 A GREENOCK MOR 3/9 6,000 1:1 — F-A 7-3 — H-T 1-0 (aet)
Scorers, Times, and Referees: Dds13,52,89p, Wind 104,109,111,117 Walker
Lilley 77p, 87, Anderson 78
Ref: M McCurry
(Morton's 3rd sub McPherson)

Unbelievable drama. The Dons are coasting at 0-2 when Inglis tackles Flannary and concedes a penalty. Within minutes it is 3-2. At the death Cormack fouls Miller and Dodds completes his hat-trick. Dodds is overshadowed by Windass's four goals in extra-time. Komboare is captain.

	1	2	3	4	5	6	7	8	9	10	11	subs used
	Walker	McKimmie	Tzvetanov	Rowson*	Inglis	Kombouare	Bernard	Dodds	Windass!	Kiriakov	Glass	Shearer
	Thomson	*Smith*	*Rae*	*Bain*	*Raeside*	*Winnie*	*Shaw**	*Charnley*	*Tosh*	*Hamilton*	*Adamczuk**	*Ferguson/Farnigh'm*

QF A DUNDEE 17/9 8,760 1:3 — F-A 1-2 — H-T 0-1
Scorers, Times, and Referees: Dodds 72p
Tosh 35, Hamilton 89
Ref: J Rowbotham

Last year's final repeated. Tosh volleys Dundee into the lead. Keeper Thomson dubiously fouls Dodds, who scores from the spot. Windass was sent off for fouling Charnley. With extra-time looming Hamilton shoots under Walker to bring Dundee's first win over the Dons since 1988.

UEFA Cup

	1	2	3	4	5	6	7	8	9	10	11	subs used
	Watt	McKimmie	Woodthorpe Bernard		Irvine	Inglis	Miller*	Windass*	Kiriakov	Dodds	Glass	Shearer/Rowson
	Spetyla	*Sorokinas*	*Skerla*	*Zvigzt'skas Stonkas*		*Rimkus*	*Razanauskas Mikulenas*	*Puteliavicius Morinas*		*Preiksaipis Morinas*	*Preiksaipis Darincevas*	

P:1 A ZALGIRIS VILNIUS (Lithuania) 1,800 6/8 — W 4-1 — H-T 1-0
Scorers, Times, and Referees: Dodds 4, 43, 81p, Glass 72, Shearer 90
Razanauskas 49
Ref: L Gordosi (Slovakia)

Aberdeen have had a wretched pre-season, losing to all and sundry. So this result brings cheer, especially without the injured Booth. 'Dodsas' - according to the scoreboard -made two and scored two. The first was a volley, the second a penalty after Dodds himself was brought down

	1	2	3	4	5	6	7	8	9	10	11	subs used
	Watt	Buchan*	Woodthorpe Kiriakov		Irvine	Inglis	Miller	Shearer	Windass	Dodds*	Glass	Grant/Kpedekpo
	Merkelis	*Sorokinas*	*Skerta*	*Zvigzt'skas Suliauskas* Novitovas*		*Pukelivicius Morinas*		*Preiksaltis Vencevicius Mikulenas*			*Ratbius*	

P:2 H ZALGIRIS VILNIUS 8,772 20/8 — L 1-3 — H-T 0-0
Scorers, Times, and Referees: Irvine 85
Mikulenas 53, 86, Pukelivicius 76p
Ref: Clarsen (Sweden)
(Dons win 5-4 on aggregate)

Zalgiris arrive at 4 am after a bus ride from London and inflict Aberdeen's heaviest home defeat in 29 years of European football. Mikulenas outpaced Woodthorpe for the first, was felled by Irvine for the second and shot from 25 yards for the third. The Dons held out for four minutes.

	1	2	3	4	5	6	7	8	9	10	11	subs used
	Walker	McKimmie	Tzvetanov Young*		Grant	Inglis	Miller	Dodds	Windass	Kiriakov	Glass	Rowson/Woodth'rpe
	Ovendale	*Johnson*	*Lloyd*	*French*	*York*	*Barnett*	*Loss*	*Bird*	*Jones*	*Pike*	*Ryan*	

1:1 H BARRY TOWN (Wales) 13,400 10/9 — W 3-1 — H-T 1-1
Scorers, Times, and Referees: Windass 7, Glass 57, Young 65
Jones 13
Ref: A Snoddy (N Ireland)
(Dons win 3rd sub Shearer)

A dream draw for both sides. McKimmie returns after knee surgery. Miller's through ball sets up Windass's cheeky chip, his sixth goal in three matches. Richard Jones' 20-yarder makes it 1-1. In the second half Stephen Glass and Darren Young capitalised on poor clearances.

	1	2	3	4	5	6	7	8	9	10	11	subs used
	Walker	McKimmie	Tzvetanov Young		Irvine	Woodthorpe Rowson		Dodds	Windass	Kiriakov*	Grant	Shearer Evans/Huggins
	Ovendale	*Lloyd*	*Johnson*	*French*	*O'Gorman**	*Barnett*	*Jones*	*Ryan**	*Pike/Griffith/Bird*	*York*		

1:2 A BARRY TOWN 6,500 24/9 — D 3-3 — H-T 2-1
Scorers, Times, and Referees: Dodds 15, 25, Rowson 83
O'Gorman 4, Ryan 71p, Bird 82
Ref: M Lubos (Slovakia)
(Dons win 6-4 on aggregate)

Injuries mean Aitken is without six regulars. In teeming rain Walker parries Pike's header and O'Gorman pounces. Kiriakov was instrumental in both Dodds' goals, which left Barry needing four more goals. Rowson fouled Bird for the penalty, and Walker was at fault for Barry's third.

	1	2	3	4	5	6	7	8	9	10	11	subs used
	Walker	McKimmie	Tzvetanov Young*		Irvine	Ingles	Miller	Dodds	Windass	Kiriakov*	Rowson	Booth/Shearer Thogersen/Hansen
	Krogh	*Colding*	*Nielsen Eggen*		*Skarbalius*	*Vilfort*	*Ravn**	*Jensen*	*Daugaard**	*Sand*	*Moller**	

2:1 H BRONDBY (Denmark) 14,159 15/10 — L 0-2 — H-T 0-1
Scorers, Times, and Referees: Sand 44, Hansen 89
Ref: M Beusan (Croatia)
(Brondby's 3rd sub Bjerregaard)

For the third tie in a row, Aberdeen face national champions. Brondby's 28 fouls about the Dons' sixth failure to score in 47 home Euro ties. Never before this season had they lost by more than one goal at home; now it has happened twice.

	1	2	3	4	5	6	7	8	9	10	11	subs used
	Walker	McKimmie	Tzvetanov	Young	Irvine	Booth*	Miller*	Dodds	Windass	Kiriakov	Rowson	Woodthorpe/Craig Risager/Baggor
	Krogh	*Colding*	*Nielsen Eggen*		*Skarbalius*	*Vilfort*	*Ravn**	*Hansen**	*Daugaard*	*Sand [Bjur] Moller*		

2:2 A BRONDBY 12,005 29/10 — D 0-0 — H-T 0-0
Scorers, Times, and Referees: Ref: M Vasily (Ukraine)
(Dons lose 0-2 on aggregate)

Nicky Walker plays his finest game since joining Aberdeen. Brondby contained the Dons with ease. Rowson shot wide early on, but Aberdeen carved out few other chances. Windass got a yellow card for kicking Sand. Brondby thought it should have been red. Irvine was also booked.

POINTS EARNED IN THE SCOTTISH PREMIER DIVISION – TO 1995-96

	The number of seasons Aberdeen finished higher – lower	75-76	76-77	77-78	78-79	79-80	80-81	81-82	82-83	83-84	84-85	85-86	86-87	87-88	88-89	89-90	90-91	91-92	92-93	93-94	94-95	95-96	Total
Rangers	7-14	54	46	55	45	37	44	43	38	42	38	35	69	60	56	51	55	72	73	58	69	87	1127
Celtic	9-12	48	55	36	48	47	56	55	55	50	52	50	63	72	46	34	41	62	60	50	51	83	1114
ABERDEEN		32	43	53	40	48	49	53	55	57	59	44	58	59	50	44	53	48	64	55	41	55	**1060**
Dundee Utd	16-5	32	41	40	44	37	43	40	56	47	47	47	60	47	44	35	41	51	47	42	36		877
Hibernian	18-3	43	34	37	37	18		36	29	31	27	28	33	43	35	34	25	49	37	47	53	43	719
Hearts	16-5	35	27		23		18			36	31	50	56	62	31	44	35	63	44	42	43	55	695
Motherwell	19-2	40	32	33	17				27	15		20	34	36	27	34	33	34	35	54	54	39	564
St Mirren	21-0			30	36	42	44	37	34	32	38	31	30	41	29	30	19	24					497
Dundee	21-0	32				26		26	29	27	37	35	54	35	28	24			34	29			416
Partick Thistle	20-1		35	33	34	36	30	22											36	40	43	30	339
Kilmarnock	20-1		17			33	19		17											40	43	41	210
Falkirk	20-1												26	31				35	29		48	24	193
St Johnstone	21-0	11								23							31	36	40	40			181
Morton	21-0				36	36	28	30	20		12			16									178
Airdrie	21-0						29	18										36	29				112
Dunfermline	21-0													26		30	27	18					101
Ayr	20-1	33	30	24																			87
Raith Rovers	21-0																			31		43	74
Clydebank	21-0			19								20	24										63
Hamilton	21-0												21		14								35
Dumbarton	21-0										19												19
(21 teams)		360	360	360	360	360	360	360	360	360	360	360	528	528	360	360	360	528	528	528	481	500	8661